THE GREEK COMMENTARIES

ON PLATO'S PHAEDO

II DAMASCIUS

EDITED WITH TRANSLATION

BY

L G WESTERINK

The Prometheus Trust

The Prometheus Trust
28 Petticoat Lane
Dilton Marsh, Westbury
Wiltshire, BA13 4DG, UK

A registered charity, number 299648

The Greek Commentaries on Plato's Phaedo - Damascius
A revised second edition

L G Westerink

ISBN 978 1 898910 47 3

(Complete work 978 1 898910 50 3)
© The Estate of L G Westerink

First edition published by
North Holland Publishing in 1977

British Library Cataloguing-in-Publication Data.
A catalogue record for this book is
available from the British Library.

Printed in Great Britain by the MPG Books Group, Bodmin and King's Lynn

THE GREEK COMMENTARIES

ON PLATO'S PHAEDO

II DAMASCIUS

L G Westerink

Platonic Texts and Translations

Volume III

Contents

Introduction 7

I – Life of Damascius 7

II – The Writings 9

III – Lectures on the Phaedo 15

IV – The Tradition 17

Abbreviations 19

Sigla 24

Damascius I 25

Damascius II 287

Marginalia 373

Index I - References 379

Index II – Vocabulary and proper names 384

PREFACE
to the Second Edition

L G Westerink's fine translations of the Commentaries on Plato's Phaedo by Olympiodorus and Damascius were originally published in 1976 and 1977 in two volumes and have been highly regarded ever since. The two authors, living and writing as they did at the end of the era of pagan philosophy, were able to draw on a long and uninterrupted tradition of philosophical thought which stretched back beyond Pythagoras, and which was given impetus by Plato, Aristotle, Plotinus and Proclus amongst many others. These volumes, then, give us a glimpse at least of the insights which were being transmitted from thinker to thinker in late antiquity in the schools of philosophy.

The Prometheus Trust editions of the Commentaries have additions and amendments taken from the marginal notes of Westerink's own copies of the original publications. We would like to thank Joannes Westerink for allowing us to use his father's notes, as well as for permission to publish the resulting editions. Our thanks, too, to all those who have had a hand in the production of our new edition. Most of the amendments comprise added cross-references, occasional corrections to typographical errors, some slight adjustments to the phrasing of the translations, and the very occasional adjustment to a word or two in the text itself.

INTRODUCTION

I. LIFE OF DAMASCIUS

Damascius' *Life of Isidorus*, in its fragmentary condition, is not the best possible foundation for a chronology; it is rarely possible to tell with certainty whether Damascius is continuing his story or digressing, and the order of the events often depends on the way in which one chooses to arrange the fragments and fill the gaps. However, it seems plausible that the excerpts at 258.1 (somebody, probably Isidorus, arrives and stays at Damascius' house) and 258.2-3 (somebody, possibly Isidorus, but more probably another friend, comes to Athens for Proclus' funeral) are closely connected in the context and in the order of the events. This would mean that by 485 Damascius lived at Athens in a house of his own and that consequently his birthdate is 465 at the latest. Kroll,[1] basing his calculation on the assumption that the nine years during which Damascius says he taught rhetoric (274.10-14) were spent at Alexandria prior to this episode, arrives at a date not later than 458. If we decide for that year, Damascius would have begun his teaching career at seventeen, there would be no margin between his settling at Athens and the events described, and even then he would have been seventy-three when he led the Athenian philosophers in the famous exodus to Persia. We can gain a little leeway by supposing, with R. Asmus,[2] that Damascius taught rhetoric at Athens, starting his school a few years before 485; the date of his birth could then be about 462. Once this view is accepted, Damascius' statements about his own education (319.9-21) fit in smoothly: three years of rhetorical studies under Theo at Alexandria in the late seventies; after he had given up his rhetorical career, studies in mathematics with Marinus and in philosophy with Zenodotus, in the early nineties; later, after his return to Alexandria, in astronomy and philosophy with Ammonius.

As a young student in Alexandria, he moved in the circles of the pagan élite, which still set the tone in literature, scholarship and social life. He knew Aedesia, Hermias' widow, and her sons Ammonius and Heliodorus; Isidorus, who was to be his predecessor on the Athenian chair; the philosopher-theurgist Asclepiodotus and his family; Severianus, a distinguished citizen of Damascus, who dabbled in literature and politics and read Isocrates and the poets with Damascius and his brother Julian (Damascius says Callimachus made him so furious that he would spit

---

[1] RE, art. Damaskios (2), 4, 1901, 2039-2042 (2039.66-2040.2).
[2] *Das Leben des Philosophen Isidoros von Damaskios aus Damaskos*, Leipzig 1911, note at 113.37.

in his copy from time to time). Damascius must have belonged to this small closed community by birth and upbringing, for it can hardly have been on the strength of his poetical talents alone that he was invited to recite a *laudatio* in verse at Aedesia's funeral.[3]

His reason for moving to Athens to teach rhetoric can only have been that at Alexandria competition was too heavy for a beginner in that field. There can have been no question, at that stage, of a hope, however vague, of succeeding eventually to the chair of Platonic philosophy. Damascius' preparation was entirely in rhetoric, and he never studied with Proclus, who during the last five years of his life was an invalid.[4] In his subsequent reconversion to the philosophical and religious ideals of his earlier years, though, such considerations may well have played a part. He says that his decision to abandon rhetoric was prompted by a feeling of dissatisfaction with a purely verbal skill which turned a man away from his soul and from the teachings that purify it (274.10–14). This is no doubt true as far as it goes; another point is whether the tensions and conflicts around the ailing Marinus and the obvious lack of a worthy successor for Proclus also influenced him.

If Asmus' precarious reconstruction of that part of the narrative is sound, Damascius was eventually sent to Alexandria as a delegate of the Athenian school (270.4–5), when Marinus' condition aggravated. His mandate may have been to offer the succession to Isidorus; in any case they met again and returned to Athens together by way of Arabia, Syria and Asia Minor (270.6–284.7). At Marinus' deathbed, Isidorus was elected his successor, "titulary rather than actual" (292.3–5); finding that the situation at Athens was beyond mending, he returned to Alexandria the following spring (296.3–4). Damascius followed him (later?), to attend the courses of Ammonius and Heliodorus (101.2–3). Nothing is known as to when and under what circumstances he succeeded to the Athenian chair himself. If the *Life of Isidorus*, which was written between the death of Ammonius (after 517) and that of Theodoric (526), were nothing more than the customary tribute to a predecessor, it would follow that the appointment took place in the early twenties. But it is in fact a larger and more ambitious work, which may have been delayed for a long time by the more urgent task of reorganizing the Academy. As far as the available information goes, any date between ca. 500 and ca. 520 is possible; a later date would leave insufficient margin for Damascius' considerable teaching activity and his no less considerable publication record.

---

[3] *Vit. Isid.* 107.20–22 ἔτι νέος ὢν τότε καὶ κομιδῇ μειράκιον. Asmus, *Leben*, note at 47.27, says that this means below 16, but the current sense is rather about 20.

[4] Marinus, *Vit. Pr.* 26. When Simplicius (*phys.* 795.4–5) calls Proclus the teacher of his professors (i.e. Amm. and Dam.), either "teacher" is used in a looser sense, or "professors" refers to Amm. alone, a not unusual idiom (e.g. Ol., *Alc.* 9.23).

A. Cameron [5] has recently argued on plausible grounds that it was the new flowering of the Academy under Damascius and Simplicius which prompted Justinian's action in 529. He has also shown [6] that Olympiodorus' commentary on the *Alcibiades*, in which the Academy is mentioned as still in possession of part of its endowment (141.2–3), can hardly be earlier than 560. The action was therefore not completely effective. After the short Persian episode (which apparently did not start before late 531, when Chosroes came to the throne, and ended ingloriously before the end of the next year) the philosophers returned to the Roman empire, and scholarly activity in some form must have resumed at Athens. The last we hear of Damascius is six years later, when he wrote the epitaph for the slave-woman Zosime, at Emesa.[7] In view of this it is possible that he never returned to Athens and that it was Simplicius who took his place there.

II. The Writings

The two great works, the DE PRINCIPIIS and the IN PARMENIDEM, have been preserved together in one MS., Marc. gr. 246 (ca. 900 A.D.). Here, as in the tradition of Olympiodorus, the joining of two books into one volume has caused confusion: both editors, Kopp as well as Ruelle, thought that there was actually only one work, with a sizable lacuna in the middle, where f. 210 (partly) and ff. 211–216 have been left blank. Hence Ruelle coined the title "Dubitationes et solutiones de primis principiis in Platonis Parmenidem". Kroll rightly says that all the evidence, external and internal, contradicts this view, but without going into details.[8] I list the essential points.

(1) The scribe used two different exemplars, one for the *De principiis* (ff. 1–210r), in which the end was missing, another for the *In Parmenidem* (ff. 216r–435r), of which the beginning was lost. This is proved by the numbering of the quires: while in the *De principiis* there are no numbers (now), the *In Parmenidem* has a continuous series from $\bar{\beta}$ (f. 216) to $\bar{\varkappa\theta}$ (f. 433), the $\bar{\alpha}$ having obviously been left out because of the missing beginning. As always, a new series of numbers means a new MS.; the first instance of a new series after a lacuna still has to be produced (cf. *infra* n. 24). Finally, the damage to the text of f. 216r, unless a pure coincidence, must be explained by its original having become the first page of the incomplete volume.

(2) There are two distinct titles: Δαμασκίου διαδόχου ἀπορίαι καὶ λύσεις περὶ τῶν πρώτων ἀρχῶν, at the beginning of Part I, and Δαμασκίου διαδόχου

---

[5] *The Last Days of the Academy at Athens*, Proc. Cambridge Philol. Soc., No. 195, 1969, 7–29 (24–25).
[6] *Ibid.* 11–12.
[7] *Anthol. Pal.* 7,553; W. Peek, *Griechische Versinschriften*, I 1714 (stone dated 538).
[8] *Op. cit.* 2041.35–39.

εἰς τὸν Πλάτωνος Παρμενίδην ἀπορίαι καὶ ἐπιλύσεις ἀντιπαρατεινόμεναι τοῖς εἰς αὐτὸν ὑπομνήμασιν τοῦ φιλοσόφου, at the end of Part II. Both, and especially the second, are clearly authentic; even if a later redactor had detected Damascius' dependence on Proclus, he would never have called Proclus "the Philosopher" *simpliciter*.

(3) The contents of the two parts tally exactly with these two titles: Part I deals with the *first* principles (not with the intermediate and lower ones, cf. *Parm.* 212.18–19), partly in the form of deductive argument, partly on the basis of the various theologies, without especially frequent reference to the *Parmenides* (Ruelle lists only 17 cases in 328 pages), while Part II is a critical account of Proclus' commentary on the dialogue, from close to the beginning of the second hypothesis (142b) to the end of the ninth and last (166c). The missing portion that preceded it can have dealt with the One only in terms of the first hypothesis, corresponding to Pr., *Parm.* 1039–1243.

(4) The disposition of the two works is different also: the *De principiis*, while systematic in its main outline (downward progress from the First Principle) is discursive and digressive in execution. In the *In Parmenidem*, Damascius follows a strict schema: for each section of the text (i.e., in the second hypothesis for each conclusion, and in the later ones for each hypothesis) the problems are enumerated first, then solved in the same order.

(5) In my introduction to Dam., *Phil.*, p. XX, I have given a count of the formulas used to cite Proclus, or to introduce Damascius' own opinions; Πρόκλος princ. 4 times, *Parm.* 5 times; οἱ φιλόσοφοι princ. 16 times, *Parm.* once; ὁ ἐξηγητής princ. never, *Parm.* 3 times (and once in plural); αὐτός princ. never, *Parm.* 50 times; φησί princ. never, *Parm.* 68 times; ἄμεινον λέγειν princ. once, *Parm.* 21 times; βέλτιον λέγειν princ. never, *Parm.* 14 times. The ratio between references to Proclus (or alternatives proposed by Damascius) is roughly one in *princ.* to ten in *Parm.*, which proves the different character of the latter (critical observations on Proclus); on the other hand, the deliberate use of "the philosophers" in *princ.*, as against "the commentator" in *Parm.*, points to a different kind of work used as material for discussion, a treatise in the one case (the plural may also mean joint authorship with Syrianus), a commentary in the other.

To these two written works by Damascius himself can now be added a third, the MONOGRAPH ON THE ARGUMENT FROM OPPOSITES IN THE PHAEDO (I §§ 207–252 in the present volume).

The reports of the LECTURES ON THE PHAEDO and ON THE PHILEBUS show that in his courses Damascius followed the same technique as in the *Parmenides* commentary: using Proclus as the starting-point for the discussion he developed his own ideas, critical or supplementary, but seldom affecting the fundamentals of the system. In the written works he assumes that the reader will be using Proclus' basic work and his

own addenda side by side (*Ph.* I § 208), rather a bold assumption, which limited his potential readers' circle to those who had access to the library of the Academy plus, perhaps, the Alexandrian professors and one or two privileged students there. In his courses, on the contrary, he was realistic enough not to count on so much industry or on availability of the texts to all students, and therefore Proclus' interpretation is reported extensively. In fact, in the lectures on the *Phaedo* and the *Philebus* Proclus' contribution considerably outweighs that of Damascius himself.

The same format was followed in the COMMENTARY ON THE ALCIBIADES; at least, in the seven different instances that Olympiodorus cites Damascius,[9] it is always to contrast his opinion with Proclus's, which is more than can be accounted for as accidental. It is not certain whether this was a published commentary, or lectures, of which Olympiodorus may have had a copy, as he had of those on the *Phaedo*.[10] The COMMENTARY ON THE TIMAEUS was almost certainly published by Damascius himself; his frequent references [11] seem to imply that the book could be consulted, and this is confirmed by the present tense at *Ph.* I § 527.3 and II § 36.12. Here, once more, most of Damascius' remarks are directed against Proclus, and it may be safely assumed that it was another commentary on a commentary. There are finally a few isolated references to other lectures or commentaries: ON THE SOPHIST, *Parm.* 197. 4–5; ON THE PHAEDRUS, *princ.* 263.9, *Ph.* I §392.4 and §527.4 (this last in the future tense, hence certainly a course); ON THE LAWS I § 198.2 (Dam. or Plato?) and II § 44.3 (Dam. or Proclus?); ON THE REPUBLIC, I § 114.3 (against Proclus); ON THE CHALDEAN ORACLES, *Parm.* 9.21–22; 11.11–15; 132.9–10 (a course, spoken of as planned).

It seems almost inevitable that Damascius, following the example of his predecessors Plutarch of Athens, Syrianus and Proclus, must have lectured on Aristotle also, but on the whole the evidence is remarkably scanty. Discussing the *skopos* of the *Categories*, Simpl. (*cat.* 13.15–18) mentions the opinions of his "own teachers" (οἱ ἡμέτεροι διδάσκαλοι); though it is not uncommon for the plural to be used loosely, Simplicius always has the singular when he mentions Ammonius,[12] so that it seems Damascius is included here; and an opinion on the *skopos* usually means a commentary. If Simplicius knew a COMMENTARY ON THE CATEGORIES by Damascius, its influence on his work was probably considerable.

A stronger claim exists in the case of the COMMENTARY ON THE DE CAELO, printed under Simplicius' name, but of which the first book is attributed to Dam. by the best MS. authorities (*CAG* VII, Praef. IX). In book I,

---

[9] See index Ol., *Alc.*
[10] Ol., *Ph.* 4 § 10.1; 8 § 9.9.
[11] *Ph.* I § 527.3; § 531.4*; II § 36.12*; § 132.5*; *Parm.* 216.11–17*; 236.13–18; 251.22–23*; 252.7–13*; 269.1–2; 15–17 (in the passages marked with asterisks Dam. differs from Pr.).
[12] Except perhaps at *phys.* 795.4–5, on which see above, note 4.

Damascius is the author according to MSS. A and C and a large independent group containing excerpts; it is attributed to Simplicius in B and William of Morbeka's translation; the other independent witnesses, D and E, have no title. But B derives from the same hyparchetype as A, and since its copy J has no heading, its authority is practically nil. In book II, however, A has Simplicius' name in the title, the others none; in books III and IV there is no attribution. The conclusion can be only that in the archetype book I was probably attributed to Damascius, and this is confirmed indirectly by Psellus, who reckons Damascius among the Aristotelians and natural philosophers, very probably on the ground of this work (see below p. 17); the attribution of book II (and the following?) to Simplicius would explain the different heading in B and Morbeka. Against the evidence of the MSS. stands the hard fact, already pointed out by Diels, that the contents in their present form can only be the work of Simplicius: the manner is his, and most of the commentary on I 1–4 is devoted to his private war against Philoponus, as also is *Phys.* 1129–1169 and 1326–1336. The only hypothesis by which the conflicting evidence can be reconciled is that we have a course by Damascius edited and completed by Simplicius. In itself such a procedure was quite common, and the finished version could bear either the teacher's or the student's name; only, the editing would have been very drastic in this case.

The quotations in Philoponus, *In meteora*, are from a work ON ARISTOTLE'S METEOROLOGY, though not necessarily a commentary. In each of the cases cited by Philoponus, Damascius combats an opinion of Aristotle's. At 44.21–36 (Ar. I 3, 341a17) he says that the Sun does not heat because it is hot; the celestial bodies have powers *sui generis*, which in the earthly bodies are converted into the corresponding passive qualities; thus the constrictive power of Saturn becomes cold, the expansive power of Mars becomes heat. *Ibid.* 97.20–21 (Ar. I 7, 344b8–17): Damascius denies that comets are a phenomenon in the atmosphere and describes their motion as supernatural. *Ibid.* 116.36–117.27 (Ar. I 8, 346a31–b3): in Damascius' view the Galaxy is not a product of exhalation nor part of the sublunary world; as it is unchangeable and shares the motion of the sky, it must be considered a conglomeration of celestial bodies. Damascius also adopts the doctrine of Empedotimus (i.e. of Heraclides Ponticus), that it is the road of souls passing through the celestial Hades, where they are cleansed from their birth in heaven. Yet the small stars which we can see are not vehicles of souls, but divine bodies. Kroll[13] misses the point when he thinks this could have come from the *Paradoxa* (see below) rather than from a commentary on the *Meteorology*: on the contrary, it is a deliberate and consistent attempt to maintain a Platonic cosmology, in which the celestial holds an intermediate position between the terrestrial and the transcendent.

---

[13] *Op. cit.* 2041.65–2042.2.

The treatise ON NUMBER, SPACE AND TIME is known from a detailed report with extensive quotations in Simplicius' digressions on Space (*phys.* 601–645) and Time (*ibid.* 773–800). There is reason to think that Damascius has also contributed some of the information on the opinions of other philosophers, in particular Proclus (on space 611.8–614.7; on time 795.4–26). Nevertheless, this work did not have the character of a revised version of a work of Proclus. It is true that there was a monobiblon by him *On Space*,[14] but no similar treatises on Time and Number are known, nor can they be inferred on the ground of Damascius' work, since the combination is the result of the theory developed by Damascius himself at 625.27–32: the world of generation, which is severed from the indivisible and non-dimensional, can be saved from total disintegration only by unifying measure; in action, this is Time, in substance Number (discrete quantity), Magnitude (continuous quantity) and Space (location). Of the section on Number, nothing is known. It must have included Magnitude, which is omitted elsewhere, too.[15]

The PARADOXA, known only from a short notice in Photius, *Bibl.* 130, contained an imposing amount of paradoxographic knowledge: book I (352 chs.) miraculous actions;[16] book II (52 chs.) stories of the demonic; book III (63 chs.) ghost stories; book IV (105 chs.) miracles of Nature. Asmus[17] has collected all the comparable material from the *Life of Isidorus*, which gives at least an idea of the character of the contents.

The LIFE OF ISIDORUS has been reconstructed in its main outline and in many of its details by Asmus, later by Zintzen, from two reports in Photius (cod. 181, a review of the work as a whole, and cod. 242, which contains over 300 extracts in two separate consecutive series plus a few additional ones) and from some 400 articles and extracts in the *Suda*, partly marked as such, partly identified by the style and the subject (some items inevitably remaining doubtful). The total quantity of extant text, at a rough estimate based on the sixty chapters mentioned by Photius, could be between one half and one quarter of the complete work. The quantity of concrete information on persons and things preserved in the fragments must be proportionately higher, since the compiler of the *Suda* went through the entire book with this purpose in mind. The main difficulty is that owing to the intricate composition the context

---

[14] Beutler, art. Pr. 201.23–32: Pr., *Rep.* II 199.22–23 and schol. *ibid.* 380.29–381.2; *Fihrist* 252.19 "On Primary Space" (this is Flügel's reading, ḥayyiz; variants "Good", ḥayr, as in Dodge's transl., and "Knowledge", ḥubr).

[15] 644.26–645.4.

[16] Περὶ παραδόξων ποιημάτων. A more natural meaning would be "artefacts", if the number of 352 cases, far exceeding those of the three other books together, did not make this unlikely. The sense "deed" is extremely rare; in the two cases in Plato, *Rep.* IV 437b4 and *Soph.* 248d5, it serves as the counterpart of πάθημα, but this may have been the intention in Dam., too.

[17] *Leben*, p. 211.

of the extracts remains too often obscure or questionable, so that all in all we have only a very imperfect picture of what must have been in many ways a fascinating work. Though belonging to the time after Damascius' appointment as *diadochos*, it is the only surviving sample of the ornate manner of his rhetorical period, something very different, in spite of a certain amount of Neoplatonic jargon, from the technical language of the philosophical works.

His occasional POETRY, judging by the extant distich,[18] may have been better than his prose; yet it is not very likely that Greek literature lost much with the encomium on Aedesia in heroic verse. Formally, it was no doubt flawless, in contrast with Isidorus' hymns, which Damascius corrected for him (*Vit.* 90.1-3).

So much for the work, lost or extant. Its abstruse and esoteric character has tended to deter readers, so that discussion has hardly begun;[19] judgments have varied widely. After the scathing contempt of some 19th century critics, here and there such terms as "brilliancy" and even "genius" can now be heard.[20] In this connection it may be not without interest to point out that Simplicius, who was certainly more fully informed than we are, contrasts Damascius' capacity for hard work ($\varphi\iota\lambda o\pi o\nu\iota\alpha$) with the brilliancy ($\check{\alpha}\kappa\rho\alpha\ \varepsilon\dot{\upsilon}\varphi\upsilon\dot{\iota}\alpha$) of his older contemporary Asclepiodotus (*phys.* 795.13-17). It is true that fuller information does not necessarily mean clearer insight, and Simplicius' judgment may have been obscured by the circumstances or by personal relations. However, if Damascius was a genius who came close to shattering the structure, not only of Neoplatonism, but of ancient philosophy generally, his situation was very much that of those "many Platos who dig the soil," of whom Olympiodorus speaks – men who cannot fulfil their destiny because of their condition in life (*Ph.* 7 § 4). Damascius' task was not to create a new system, but to provide the security of the old for those few who still believed in it. And so, after each daring sortie, we see him retreat into the shelter of Proclus' metaphysics.

In the interpretation of Plato,[21] Damascius compares favorably to Proclus by a tendency to prefer commonsense explanations (in other words, the obvious meaning of the text) to the search for intricate metaphysical patterns which was part of the heritage of Iamblichus. In this, he was only pursuing a trend common to the later Neoplatonists, who, as has already been pointed out,[22] saw the importance of reading

---

[18] Above, note 7.
[19] Zeller 901-908; Ueberweg-Praechter, 633-634, 195*; Kroll (above, n. 1); R. Strömberg, *Damascius. His personality and significance*, Eranos 44, 1946, 175-192.
[20] See the exchange between Dörrie and Puech in *Les sources de Plotin* (Entretiens Hardt V), Geneva 1960, 209; 230-231.
[21] Cf. my paper *Damascius, commentateur de Platon*, Le Néoplatonisme, Paris 1971, 253-260.
[22] Introduction vol. I, p. 17.

the dialogues as dialogues rather than as philosophical treatises. However crude and irrelevant some of their comments may appear by our own (not infallible) literary standards, they did mark considerable progress with respect to their predecessors. This may have something to do with their literary studies, for both Syrianus and Damascius taught rhetoric — but then so did Porphyry and Iamblichus.

A few cases of protest against Aristotelian heresies in Platonism can be noticed also,[23] but they are too incidental to be construed as representing a movement. Simplicius (*phys.* 795.15–17) noticed a preference for Iamblichus as against Proclus, of which there is more evidence in the *De principiis* than in the commentaries.

III. The Lectures on the Phaedo

The case for the attribution to Damascius of the anonymous commentaries on the *Phaedo* and the *Philebus* in Marc. gr. 196 ff. 242–337 has been stated in full in the introduction to my edition of the *Lectures on the Philebus* (XV–XX). I shall briefly recapitulate the essential points here.

The Venice MS., though written throughout by the same copyist and corrected and annotated by the same scholar, really consists of two independent parts, derived from different exemplars: a volume containing three commentaries by Ol. (*Gorg.*, *Alc.*, *Ph.*) and another containing commentaries on the *Phaedo* and *Philebus*, anonymous owing to the loss of the beginning in an earlier copy. The different origin of the two parts is proved by the missing beginning of Part II and the damaged condition of the text on its first page, as well as by the separate numbering of the quires.[24]

Though in Part II the numbering of the sections (which is no older than the MS. itself) suggests a subdivision of the *Phaedo* commentary into five separate units (numbered B, C I–III and D by Norvin), the only clear break is at II § 1, which begins at the top of a new folio. We have therefore three commentaries: *Phaedo* I, *Phaedo* II, *Philebus*.

This entire collection is divided into lectures by the astronomical symbol for the Sun (☉), found only here in this function. Its meaning can be inferred from three cases where lectures have been displaced and the correct order has been restored in a marginal note indicating that two lectures (πράξεις) should change places: *Ph.* I §§ 183 and 191, §§ 253 and 262, *Phil.* §§ 41–42. It follows that there can be no question of mere excerpts; what we have is the original lecture notes as written down by one of the students. Only the *reportator* could know what was wrong with the order of the lectures: in the second case the context gives no

---

[23] Ol., *Alc.* 217.23–220.1; *Ph.* 4 § 6.
[24] Cf. D. Harlfinger, *Die Textgeschichte der pseudo-aristotelischen Schrift Περὶ ἀτόμων γραμμῶν*, Amsterdam 1971, 28–29.

clue at all, in the other two no sufficient clue for the definitive correction (as adopted in the present text).

The three courses are all done on the same plan: lectures marked by the same unusual sign; no lemmata, but short independent notes; as regards the substance, the lecturer's practice is to sum up and discuss the commentary of Proclus (mostly called "the commentator" or simply "he"[25]) and provide it with critical observations of his own. In view of this, and of the absence of any indication to the contrary in the headings, the natural assumption is that the lectures were all given by the same person, whose name was lost at the beginning.

That the commentator reported and criticized is Proclus appears from a great many parallels: see e.g. notes at *Ph.* I §§ 3, 83–86, 163, 193–200, 371, 531, II §§ 36 and 145, *Phil.* §§ 53, 70, 133, 235; it is confirmed by the expression "Proclus himself" at *Ph.* I § 100. The critic, sometimes called "our professor", whose comments are introduced by a variety of formulas,[26] is proved to be Damascius by parallels cited at *Ph.* I §§ 31, 163, 531, *Phil.* §§ 62, 104, 108.

Ph. §§ 207–252 are not part of the course, but are announced explicitly as a written essay by "our professor". The treatise replaces the corresponding lectures, in which Damascius examined Syrianus' view of the argument from opposites (summarized in the two preceding lectures, §§ 183–206) and proposed an entirely new solution of his own. We have the complete text of the treatise, not just extracts: at § 208.1 the author announces his intention to write down his ideas in precisely the summary form (ἐπὶ κεφαλαίων) adopted in the treatise.

The insertion of the monograph at this point has created the impression that §§ 1–206 (B) came from a different work; however, the exact correspondence between §§ 193–200 and §§ 243–251, both dealing with Syrianus' problems iii–x (as inadequately answered on Syrianus' own assumptions, § 243) is definitive proof that the author of the monograph is also the lecturer of §§ 1–206. The fact that at §§ 82–86 Proclus' doctrine on the senses of the Star-gods passes unchallenged in spite of Damascius' known dissent, must be due to chance; we have comparable cases in C (I §§ 325, 334, 473, 541) and in D (II § 60).

The two *Phaedo* commentaries are reports of the course as given at different times; on closer examination, I think it now impossible that they should represent two reports of the same lectures. The second reportator (Dam. II) entered the course when it was well on its way, and seems to have added the earlier version to his own incomplete set of notes. The choice of some formulas used indicates that the course on the *Philebus* was also edited by him. Thus Proclus is cited by his name 4 times in *Ph.* I, 10 times in *Ph.* II, 12 times in *Phil.*; he is called "the

---

[25] See index s.v. Proclus.
[26] Index s.v. Damascius.

commentator" (ὁ ἐξηγητής) once in *Ph.* I, 11 times in *Ph.* II, 3 times in *Phil.*; Damascius is "our professor" (ὁ ἡμέτερος καθηγεμών) only in *Ph.* II (twice) and *Phil.* (4 times), apart from the title of the monograph (I § 207), which the second reportator may have added in editing the texts. In introducing Damascius' opinions phrases with ἄμεινον are used 6 times in *Ph.* I, 12 times in *Ph.* II, 11 times in *Phil.*; with βέλτιον twice in *Ph.* I, 10 times in *Ph.* II, 4 times in *Phil.*; with κάλλιον 23 times in *Ph.* I, not in *Ph.* II or *Phil.* The notes correcting the order of the lectures, which occur both in *Ph.* I and in *Phil.* in more or less the same terms, may also be the work of the final redactor.

IV. THE TRADITION

It had been a long time before Damascius succeeded in achieving the status of a major philosopher, on a par with such men as Proclus, Syrianus and Iamblichus. Once he had acquired it, it seemed destined to last. In Athens Simplicius continued his work, in Alexandria he was accepted as the leading authority on Plato,[27] and to the Christian Agathias in Constantinople the story of his Persian adventures had become a saga.

Until the end of the ninth century all was well. A considerable portion of his work survived the "dark ages" of Byzantium: most of the *De principiis*, most of the *In Parmenidem*, also the commentaries on the *Phaedo* and *Philebus* (which had, however, already lost their beginning with the author's name); further the lengthy biography of Isidorus, which was read and excerpted by Photius (9th cent.) and later by the author of the *Suda* (10th cent.), and the four books of the *Paradoxa*. Then suddenly everything seems to have collapsed: the *Life of Isidorus* and the *Paradoxa* perished, the volume with the commentaries on Plato (Ol. and Dam.) disappeared for five centuries [28] and so (simultaneously no doubt) did the volume containing the metaphysical writings of Damascius (*De princ.* and *In Parm.*). Further research may modify the picture, but as far as we can tell at present, the name of Damascius was hardly mentioned again until the end of the Middle Ages. Michael Psellus (11th cent.) ranks him among the Aristotelians, as opposed to the Platonists, Proclus, Syrianus, Plotinus and Iamblichus;[29] this is, I believe, positive evidence that he knew him only as the author

---

[27] Ol., *Alc.* 209.15–19.
[28] Cf. introd. vol. I, pp. 31–32.
[29] Psellus, Λόγος περὶ ψυχῆς, Vat. gr. 2231, ff. 264ʳ–268ʳ (264ᵛ–265ʳ) καὶ τοῦτο πάντες οἱ μετ' αὐτὸν (Aristotle) προσήκαντο φυσικοί, Ἀλέξανδρος καὶ Πορφύριος καὶ Ἀμμώνιος, ἔτι δὲ καὶ Δαμάσκιος καὶ Σιμπλίκιος καὶ Πρισκιανός, καὶ μετ' αὐτοὺς ὁ φιλοπονώτατος Ἰωάννης, πρὸ δὲ τούτων ἁπάντων Θεόφραστος ὁ Ἀριστοτέλους διάδοχος καὶ ὁ λοιπὸς τῶν φυσιολόγων χορός. ... καὶ ἥξουσιν ἡμῖν ἐνταῦθα πάλιν μαρτυρήσοντες ἄλλοι, ὁ φιλόσοφος Πρόκλος καὶ ὁ μέγας Συριανός, Πλωτῖνοί τε καὶ Ἰάμβλιχοι ... καὶ ξύμπαντες οἱ Πλατωνικοί. (Cited as a work of Simplicius by Psellus, *Theol.* 105 (Paris, 1182, f. 25a). See also Theodorus Matochites, p. 96 Kiessling, *Philosophia*.

or co-author of Simpl., *De caelo,* book I. After the reappearance of the Damascius MS. in Bessarion's library (and eventually in the Marciana as Gr. 246), it shared in the interest due to the Renaissance revival of Platonism. Ruelle [30] lists about thirty 15th and 16th century copies, and there are no doubt a few more. A testimony to Damascius' new fame is also that the forger Andrew Darmarios used his name to promote the sales of some anonymous medical texts.[31] There was a new, long decline after the Platonist fashion had blown over: the first printed edition of the *De principiis* appeared in 1826,[32] and it remained the only one until Ruelle's complete publication of the Marcianus in 1889; another half-century passed before the *Phaedo* and *Philebus* commentaries were returned to their rightful owner by Beutler.[33]

---

[30] Dam., *princ.*, pp. III–IV.

[31] Ps.-Damascius=Stephanus, *In Prognosticum*; Ps.-Damascius, *In Aphorismos.* See H. Diels, *Die Handschriften der antiken Ärzte*, II, Berlin 1906 (repr. Leipzig-Amsterdam 1970) 26.

[32] J. Kopp, Frankfurt am Main.

[33] Art. Ol. 211–219.

ABBREVIATIONS

LITERATURE

Beutler, art. Ol.: R. Beutler, *RE* art. Olympiodoros (13), vol. 18,1, 1939, 207–228.
Beutler, art. Pr.: id., *RE* art. Proklos (4), vol. 23, 1957, 186–247.
Dodds: see Pr., *elem.*
Festugière: see Pr., *Tim.*
Finckh: see Ol., *Ph.*
Kern: see *Orphica*.
Krause: H. Krause, *Studia neoplatonica*, Leipzig 1904.
Kroll: see *Chald. Or.*
Lewy: H. Lewy, *Chaldaean Oracles and Theurgy*, Cairo 1956.
LSJ: Liddell-Scott-Jones, *A Greek-English Lexicon*.
Nilsson: M. P. Nilsson, *Geschichte der griechischen Religion*, I, ²Munich 1955.
Norvin: see Ol., *Ph.*
Norvin 1915: W. Norvin, *Olympiodoros fra Alexandria og hans commentar til Platons Phaidon*. Copenhagen 1915.
Pépin: J. Pépin, *Mythe et allégorie*, Paris [1958].
PGL: G. W. H. Lampe, *A Patristic Greek Lexicon*.
RE: Pauly-Wissowa-Kroll, *Realencyclopädie der classischen Altertumswissenschaft*.
Theiler: W. Theiler, *Forschungen zum Neuplatonismus*, Berlin 1966.
Ueberweg-Praechter: F. Ueberweg-K. Praechter, *Die Philosophie des Altertums*, ¹² 1925 (repr. Darmstadt 1960).
Zeller: Ed. Zeller, *Die Philosophie der Griechen in ihrer geschichtlichen Entwicklung*, III 2, 5th ed., Leipzig 1923 (repr. Hildesheim 1963).

TEXTS

Aen. Gaz.: Aeneas Gazaeus, *Theophrastus*, ed. M. E. Colonna, Naples 1958.
Alcin., *did.*: Alcinous, *Didascalicus*, ed. C. F. Hermann, *Platonis Dialogi VI*, Leipzig 1853, 152–187; =Albinos, *Epitomé*, ed. P. Louis, Paris 1945.
Alex., *an. mant.*: Alexander, *De anima mantissa*, ed. Bruns, Suppl. Ar. II 1, Berlin 1887.
Amm., *cat.*: Ammonius, *In categorias*, *CAG* IV 4.
Amm., *int.*: Ammonius, *De interpretatione*, *CAG* IV 5.
Amm., *isag.*: Ammonius, *In Porphyrii Quinque voces*, *CAG* IV 3.
Ar.: Aristotle.
Ascl., *met.*: Asclepius, *In metaphysica*, *CAG* VI 2.
Ascl., *Nicom.*: Asclepius, *Commentary to Nicomachus' Introduction to Arithmetic*, ed. L. Tarán, Philadelphia 1969.
Atticus: *Fragments*, ed. E. des Places (to appear Paris 1976).
CAG: *Commentaria in Aristotelem Graeca*, ed. Acad. litt. reg. Boruss., Berlin 1882–1909.
Chald. Or.: *Oracles chaldaïques*, ed. E. des Places, Paris 1971.
Chald. Or.: W. Kroll, *De oraculis Chaldaicis*, Breslau 1894 (repr. Hildesheim 1962).
Cornutus: *Cornuti theologiae Graecae compendium*, ed. C. Lang, Leipzig 1881.
CPG: *Corpus Paroemiographorum Graecorum*, edd. Leutsch-Schneidewin, 2 vols., Göttingen 1839–51 (repr. Hildesheim 1958).
Dam., *Parm.*: Damascius, *In Parmenidem*, ed. C. A. Ruelle, *Damascii Dubitationes et solutiones*, Paris 1889 (repr. Amsterdam 1966), II 5–322.
Dam., *Ph.*: Damascius, *In Phaedonem*: see Ol., *Ph.*
Dam., *Phil.*: Damascius, *On the Philebus*, ed. Westerink, Amsterdam 1959.

Dam., *princ.*: Damascius, *De principiis*, ed. C. A. Ruelle, *Damascii Dubitationes et solutiones*, I; II 1–4.
Dam., *vit. Isid.*: Damascius, *Vitae Isidori reliquiae*, ed. C. Zintzen, Hildesheim 1967.
Dav.: David, *In isagogen*, *CAG* XVIII 2.
Doxographi: *Doxographi Graeci*, ed. H. Diels, Berlin 1879 ([3] 1958).
El., *cat.*: Elias, *In categorias*, *CAG* XVIII 1, 105–255.
El., *isag.*: Elias, *In isagogen*, *CAG* XVIII 1, 1–104.
Eunap., *vit. soph.*: Eunapius, *Vitae sophistarum*, ed. G. Giangrande, Rome 1956.
Heraclides Ponticus: F. Wehrli, *Die Schule des Aristoteles*, Heft 7, [2] Basel-Stuttgart 1969.
Hermias: *Hermiae Alexandrini in Platonis Phaedrum scholia*, ed. P. Couvreur, Paris 1901.
Hierocl., *carm. aur.*: Hierocles, *In aureum carmen*, ed. F. W. A. Mullach, *Fragm. philos. Gr.* I, Paris 1857, 416–484.
Iambl., *comm. math.*: Iamblichus, *De communi mathematica scientia*, ed. N. Festa, Leipzig 1891.
Iambl., *myst.*: Iamblichus, *Les mystères d'Egypte*, ed. E. des Places, Paris 1966.
Iambl., *protr.*: Iamblichus, *Protrepticus*, ed. H. Pistelli, Leipzig 1888.
Iambl., *frgs.*: Iamblichus, *In Platonicos dialogos commentariorum fragmenta*, ed. J. M. Dillon, Leiden 1973.
Marin., *vit. Pr.*: Marinus, *Vita Procli*, ed. J. F. Boissonade, Leipzig 1814.
Nicom., *harm.*: Nicomachus, *Harmonicum enchiridium*, ed. C. Jan, *Musici scriptores Graeci*, Leipzig 1895 (repr. Hildesheim 1962), pp. 235–265.
Numenius: *Fragments*, ed. E. des Places, Paris 1973.
E. A. Leemans, *Studie over den wijsgeer Numenius van Apamea met uitgave der fragmenten*, Brussels 1937.
Ol., *Alc.*: Olympiodorus, *On the Alcibiades*, ed. Westerink, Amsterdam 1956.
Ol., *cat.*: Olympiodorus, *In categorias*, *CAG* XII 1.
Ol., *Gorg.*: Olympiodorus, *In Gorgiam*, ed. Westerink, Leipzig 1970.
Ol., *mete.*: Olympiodorus, *In meteora*, *CAG* XII 2.
Ol., *Ph.*: Olympiodorus, *In Phaedonem*, vol. I of this ed.
ed. Norvin, Leipzig 1913.
ed. Finckh, Heilbronn 1847.
Orphica: O. Kern, *Orphicorum fragmenta*, Berlin 1922 (repr. 1963).
PG: J. P. Migne, *Patrologiae cursus completus*, Series Graeca.
Philodemus, *de diis*: H. Diels, *Philodemos über die Götter*, Berlin 1916–17 (repr. Leipzig-Amsterdam 1970).
Philop., *aet.*: Philoponus, *De aeternitate mundi*, ed. H. Rabe, Leipzig 1899.
Philop., *an.*: Philoponus, *De anima*, *CAG* XV.
Philop., *an.* III: Philoponus, *Commentaire sur le De anima d'Aristote*, trad. de G. de Moerbeke, ed. G. Verbeke, Louvain 1966.
Philop., *anal. pr.*: Philoponus, *In analytica priora*, *CAG* XIII 2.
Philop., *Nicom.*: Philoponus, *In Nicomachi arithmeticam introductionem*, ed. R. Hoche, Wesel 1864–67.
PL: J. P. Migne, *Patrologiae cursus completus*, Series Latina.
Porph., *abst.*: Porphyry, *De abstinentia*, ed. Nauck (*Porphyrii opuscula selecta*, [2] Leipzig 1886).
Porph., *ad Gaur.*: Porphyry, *Die neuplatonische, fälschlich dem Galen zugeschriebene Schrift Πρὸς Γαῦρον περὶ τοῦ πῶς ἐμψυχοῦται τὰ ἔμβρυα*, ed. K. Kalbfleisch, Berlin 1895.
Porph., *de antro*: Porphyry, *The Cave of the Nymphs*, ed. Seminar Cl. 609, Buffalo 1969.
Porph., *de regressu*: Porphyry, *de regressu animae* (J. Bidez, *Vie de Porphyre*, Gand 1913 [repr. Hildesheim 1964], 25*–44*).

Porph., *Marc.*: Porphyry, *Ad Marcellam*, ed. Pötscher, Leiden 1969.
Porph., *Ptol.*: Porphyry, *Kommentar zur Harmonielehre des Ptolemaios*, ed. I. Düring, Göteborg 1932.
Porph., *sent.*: Porphyry, *Sententiae ad intelligibilia ducentes*, ed. E. Lamberz, Leipzig 1975.
Porph., *vit. Plot.*: Porphyry, *Vita Plotini* (*Plotini opera*, edd. Henry-Schwyzer, I, Paris-Brussels 1951).
Pr., *Alc.*: Proclus, *On the Alcibiades*, ed. Westerink, Amsterdam 1954.
Pr., *Crat.*: Proclus, *In Cratylum*, ed. G. Pasquali, Leipzig 1908.
Pr., *de arte hier.*: Proclus, *De arte hieratica*, ed. J. Bidez (*Catalogue des manuscrits alchimiques grecs* VI, Brussels 1928, 148–151).
Pr., *dec. dub.*: Proclus, *De decem dubitationibus*, ed. H. Boese (*Procli Tria opuscula*, Berlin 1960, 3–108).
Pr., *elem.*: Proclus, *The Elements of Theology*, ed. E. R. Dodds, [2] Oxford 1963.
Pr., *Eucl.*: Proclus, *In Euclidem*, ed. Friedlein, Leipzig 1873.
Pr., *Hes.*: Proclus, in: *Scholia vetera in Hesiodi opera et dies*, ed. A. Pertusi, Milan 1955.
Pr., *hyp.*: Proclus, *Hypotyposis astronomicarum positionum*, ed. Manitius, Leipzig 1909.
Pr., *mal. subs.*: Proclus, *De malorum subsistentia*, ed. Boese (*Tria opuscula* 172–265).
Pr., *Parm.*: Proclus, *In Parmenidem*, ed. V. Cousin, *Procli opera*, Paris 1864 (repr. Hildesheim 1961).
Pr., *prov.*: Proclus, *De providentia et fato*, ed. Boese (*Tria opuscula* 109–171).
Pr., *Rep.*: Proclus, *In Rempublicam*, ed. W. Kroll, 2 vols., Leipzig 1899–1901, (repr. Amsterdam 1965).
Pr., *theol.*: Proclus, *Théologie platonicienne*, Livres I/II, edd. Saffrey-Westerink Paris 1968/74. *In theologiam Platonis*, ed. Portus, Hamburg 1618 (repr. Frankfurt am Main 1960).
Pr., *Tim.*: Proclus, *In Timaeum*, ed. E. Diehl, 3 vols., Leipzig 1903–06 (repr. Amsterdam 1965).
Id., traduction et notes par A. J. Festugière, 5 vols. Paris 1966–69.
Proleg.: *Anonymous Prolegomena to Platonic Philosophy*, ed. Westerink, Amsterdam 1962.
Psell., *omnif. doctr.*: *De omnifaria doctrina*, ed. Westerink, Nijmegen-Utrecht 1948.
Ps.-El.: Pseudo-Elias (Pseudo-David), *On Porphyry's Isagoge*, ed. Westerink, Amsterdam 1967.
Ps.-Tim.: Timaeus Locrus *De natura mundi et animae*, ed. W. Marg, Leiden 1972.
Ptol., *harm.*: *Die Harmonielehre des Klaudios Ptolemaios*, ed. I. Düring, Göteborg 1930.
Schol. Pl.: *Scholia Platonica*, ed. W. C. Greene, Haverford 1938.
Simpl., *cael.*: Simplicius, *De caelo*, *CAG* VII.
Simpl., *cat.*: Simplicius, *In categorias*, *CAG* VIII.
Simpl., *Epict.*: Simplicius, *In Epicteti enchiridion*, ed. F. Dübner (in: *Theophrasti characteres*, etc., Paris 1840).
Simpl., *phys.*: Simplicius, *In physica*, *CAG* IX–X.
Speusippus: P. Lang, *De Speusippi Academici scriptis, accedunt fragmenta*, Bonn 1911.
Steph., *an.*: Stephanus, *De anima* = Philop., *an.*, lib. III, pp. 406–607.
Strato: F. Wehrli, *Die Schule des Aristoteles*, Heft 5, [2] Basel-Stuttgart 1969.
SVF: *Stoicorum veterum fragmenta*, ed. H. von Arnim, 4 vols., Leipzig 1905–24 (repr. Stuttgart 1964).
Syr., *met.*: Syrianus, *In metaphysica*, *CAG* VI 1.
Theo Smyrn.: Theonis Smyrnaei *Expositio rerum mathematicarum ad legendum Platonem utilium*, ed. E. Hiller, Leipzig 1878.

Theodorus of Asine: W. Deuse, *Theodoros von Asine, Sammlung der Testimonien und Kommentar*, Wiesbaden 1973.

Tim. soph.: Timaei sophistae *Lexicon vocum Platonicarum*, edd. Ruhnken-Koch, Leipzig 1828.

Vors.: *Die Fragmente der Vorsokratiker*, edd. Diels-Kranz, 3 vols., [12] Dublin-Zürich 1966.

Xenocrates: R. Heinze, *Xenokrates*, Leipzig 1892 (repr. Hildesheim 1965).

SIGLA

M	Marcianus graecus 196 Z., ca. a. 900
M[1]	scriba in scribendo aut corrigendo
M[c]	corrector, qui et titulos et marginalia adscripsit
M[x]	utrum M[1] an M[c] incertum
M[r]	manus Bessarionis in margine
M[s]	alia manus recens in margine
μ	apographa
Fh	Finckh
Nv	Norvin
Wk	Westerink
⟨ ⟩	addenda
[[ ]]	delenda
[ ]	spatium vacuum in codice
* *	lacuna
≡	rasura unius litterae

DAMASCIUS I

PART ONE: ON DEATH

I. FIRST PROBLEM: SUICIDE

§§ 1-13. The esoteric argument. Dionysus and the Titans. 61c2-62b6

1. [62b2-6] ... opinions and show what is the true interpretation. In the first place, then, the reason must be peculiar to the original problem and not of general application, since it says 'the reason given *for this* in esoteric doctrine.' Secondly it must not be obvious and within easy reach, or it would not be referred to as 'esoteric,' 'deep,' or 'not easy to grasp.' Thirdly, the mystic reason must command greater reverence than the philosophical account, which Socrates feels justified in revealing, because it is exoteric; accordingly, if the philosophical account proceeds from the multitude of the Gods, the other must have a monad as its starting-point. Fourthly, the multitude here must be continuous with the monad there, and the characteristics of . . should not be disparate, for abrupt transition is against scientific method. Fifthly, the .... demonstration results in the particular .... kept in custody .... the reason should be visibly connected with .... because even for the body custody .... it is described as 'a certain' custody, i.e. as it were ...., either there is a possibility .... or because being equipped for knowledge .... In the tenth place, the reason belongs to the initiatory order of things and should be ranked neither higher nor lower.

---

§§ 1-13. The prolegomena to the dialogue and the commentary on the introductory conversation are lost. The commentary on the 'esoteric' argument seems to be nearly complete, though a general discussion of suicide corresponding to Ol. 1 §§ 1-2 and 7-9 may have preceded it. – Both Pr. and Dam. (who expresses disagreement on one particular point in §§ 4 and 11) follow Porphyry and Xenocrates in connecting the φρουρά with Dionysus. The myth of Dionysus according to the Orphic epic is outlined by K. Ziegler, *RE*, art. *Orphische Dichtung*, vol. 18,2, 1354.7-50 (frgs. 205-220, 232, 235 Kern; a few details overlooked by Kern can be added from Dam. I § 14.8, § 170.3-6 and II § 8.2, see notes): Dionysus, son of Zeus and Persephone, is enthroned by Zeus as king of the Gods; Hera plots against him with the Titans. Neglecting Apollo's warnings he rises from his Father's throne to join the Titans, who have disguised themselves as Bacchants, carrying the thyrsus. They hand him a thyrsus instead of his royal sceptre, and some toys, among which a mirror. While he is contemplating his face in the mirror, they attack him, tear him to pieces and devour his flesh. His heart is saved by Athena, Apollo gathers what is left of the limbs. The Titans are burnt by the lightning-bolts of Zeus, out of their ashes man is created. Dionysus is reborn from Semele.

§ 1. The list is from Pr., for the fourth point (referred to in § 3) is contested by Dam. in § 4. Each point is either elicited somehow from the text of the *Ph.* or deduced from general principles, and formulated so as to support Pr.'s interpretation of the 'custody'. – The text is too badly damaged for reconstruction,

PART ONE: ON DEATH

I. FIRST PROBLEM: SUICIDE

§§ 1–13. The esoteric argument. Dionysus and the Titans. 61c2–62b6

α'. – [62b2–6] ... δοξῶν, ἀποδεικτικὰ δὲ τῆς ἀληθοῦς ἐξηγήσεως. πρῶτον 1(84) μὲν οὖν ὅτι ἰδίαν εἶναι χρὴ τοῦ ἐξ ἀρχῆς ζητουμένου τὴν αἰτίαν, ἀλλὰ μὴ κοινήν· εἴρηται γὰρ 'περὶ αὐτῶν ὁ ἐν ἀπορρήτοις λόγος'. δεύτερον δὲ μὴ εὐφώρατον εἶναι καὶ τῇ ἑτέρᾳ ληπτόν· πῶς γὰρ ἔτι 'ἐν ἀπορρήτοις' ἢ 'μέγας' ἢ 'οὐ ῥᾴδιος διιδεῖν'; τρίτον σεμνοτέραν εἶναι τῆς φιλοσόφου τὴν μυστικήν, διόπερ ἐκείνην 5 ἐκφέρει ὡς ῥητήν· ὥστε εἰ αὕτη ἀπὸ τοῦ πλήθους ἀποδίδοται τῶν θεῶν, ἐκείνην χρὴ ἀπό τινος μονάδος ὡρμῆσθαι. τέταρτον ἐφεξῆς εἶναι τὸ πλῆθος ἐκείνῃ τῇ μονάδι καὶ μὴ ἀπηρτῆσθαι τοὺς λόγους .. εων· οὐ γὰρ ἐπιστημονικὸν ἡ ἄμεσος μετάβασις. πέμπτον τὸ τὴν ἀ............ ἡ ἀπόδειξις τῶν μερικῶν εἶναι .... τῶν ἐν φρουρᾷ οὐσῶν .... ὅτι ἐμφαίνει δεῖ τῇ αἰτίᾳ 10 .... καὶ γὰρ τῷ σώματι καὶ φρουρᾶς .... ἡ φρουρὰ 'τίς' ἐστι καὶ οἷον .... τόμος ἢ ὅτι δύναταί τις ἀ............ ἢ ὅτι γνωστικαὶ .... δεῖν. δέκατον ὅτι τῆς τελεστικῆς ἐστιν ἰδιότητος ἡ αἰτία καὶ οὔτε κρείττονος οὔτε καταδεεστέρας.

---

§ 1. 7 ἀπό τινος] accent. mut., -ινο- in ras., M[c] (ἀπὸ τῆς ut vid. M[1]) — 10 τῶν M[c]: spat. vac. M[1]

even the division between points 5–9 is not discernible with certainty. The following is merely by way of an example: καὶ μὴ ἀπηρτῆσθαι τοὺς λόγους [τῶν τάξ]εων· οὐ γὰρ ἐπιστημονικὸν ἡ ἄμεσος μετάβασις. πέμπτον τὸ τὴν ἀ[πόρρητον καθολικωτέραν εἶναι, πέφυκε γάρ] ἡ ἀπόδειξις τῶν μερικῶν εἶναι. [ἕκτον ὅτι περὶ ἀνθρωπίνων ψυχῶν] τῶν ἐν φρουρᾷ οὐσῶν [ὁ λόγος. ἕβδομον] ὅτι ἐμφαίνει⟨ν⟩ δεῖ τῇ αἰτίᾳ [καὶ σωματικόν τι·] καὶ γὰρ τῷ σώματι [[καὶ]] φρουρᾶς [δεῖ. ὄγδοον ὅτι ... ἔνατον ὅτι] ἡ (ἢ M) φρουρὰ 'τίς' ἐστι καὶ οἷον [μερικὴ καὶ ἄ]τομος, ἢ ὅτι δύναταί τις ἀ[ποδιδράσκειν] ἢ ὅτι γνωστικαῖ[ς τῶν καθόλου οὔσαις ταῖς ψυχαῖς οὐ ῥᾴδια ἐστὶ δι]ιδεῖν. "The characteristics of the [orders] should not be disparate, for abrupt transition is against scientific method. Fifthly, the [esoteric reason is more general, since by its nature] logical demonstration results in the particular. [Sixthly, it is with human souls] kept in custody [that the discourse is concerned. Seventhly,] the reason should be visibly connected with [corporeal being,] because even for the body custody [is needed. Eighthly, ... Ninthly,] it is described as a 'certain' custody, i.e. as it were [particular and in]dividual; or this may be because there is a possibility [of escape,] or because, being equipped for knowledge [of the universal, souls cannot easily dis]cern it." Number nine is especially questionable, since Pr. is trying to delimit the character of the 'custody' by means of data from the text, so that a choice of possibilities is out of place. However, without more drastic changes in the extant words, I see no possibility of avoiding this.

3–4. Cf. Ol. 1 § 3.11–12.
4. τῇ ἑτέρᾳ ληπτόν : Pl., Soph. 226a7.

2. Guided by these principles, we shall have no difficulty in proving that the 'custody' is neither the Good, as some think, nor pleasure, as Numenius [frg. 38] says, nor the Creator, as is the opinion of Paterius, but we must hold with Xenocrates [frg. 20] that it is of the Titanic order and culminates in Dionysus. Porphyry has already hinted at this in his commentary.

3. Creation being twofold, either indivisible or divided, the latter, according to the commentator, is ruled by Dionysus, and therefore divided, the former by Zeus; each of the two has his own multitude of subordinates, Zeus of Olympian Gods, Dionysus of Titans; and in both cases we have a monad as well as a triad of Creators.

---

§§ 2–12. Cf. Ol. 1 § 3.6–14.
§§ 2–3. Ol. 1 § 5.11–13.
§ 2. See P. Boyancé, *Note sur la φρουρά platonicienne*, Rev. de philol. 37, 1963, 7–11. – The first, anonymous, view is original in that it takes 'custody' to mean neither 'prison' (the prevailing opinion in antiquity) nor 'guard duty' (as many modern commentators do, following Cicero, *Cato* 20,73), but 'divine protection'. Since it identifies this protective Providence with the transcendent Good, no doubt in order to account for the mystic character of the doctrine, it must be post-Plotinian. – Numenius takes the usual view that 'custody' means imprisonment in the body, and makes pleasure the cause of the soul's downfall, a belief ascribed to the 'Pythagoreans' by Dam., *Phil.* § 229: 'souls fall down into genesis through honey'; cf. Porphyry, *de antro* 16–18, a passage probably depending on Numenius and Cronius. – Paterius, too, interprets the 'custody' as divine care, presumably that of the supreme Demiurge of the *Timaeus*; Pr.'s objection to this is that it is too comprehensive and ignores the reference to an esoteric tradition. – For Porphyry's view, adopted by Pr., we have a parallel text in Macrobius, *somn. Scip.* I 12,12: "ipsum autem Liberum patrem Orphaici νοῦν ὑλικόν suspicantur intelligi, qui ab illo individuo natus in singulos ipse dividitur. ideo in illorum sacris traditur Titanio furore in membra discerptus et frustis sepultis, rursus unus et integer emersisse, quia νοῦς, quem diximus mentem vocari, ex individuo praebendo se dividendum, et rursus ex diviso ad individuum revertendo et mundi implet officia et naturae suae arcana non deserit." Combined with the present text this shows that to Porphyry Dionysus symbolizes the world mind, and the Titans its vestiges in the material world. – Heinze, *Xenokrates* pp. 149–155, trying to decide in how far Xenocrates shared this interpretation, points out two possibly relevant texts: Plutarch, *de esu carn.* 7, 996C καίτοι δοκεῖ παλαιότερος οὗτος ὁ λόγος εἶναι· τὰ γὰρ δὴ περὶ τὸν Διόνυσον μεμυθευμένα πάθη τοῦ διαμελισμοῦ καὶ τὰ Τιτάνων ἐπ' αὐτὸν τολμήματα γευσαμένων τε τοῦ φόνου κολάσεις … καὶ κεραυνώσεις, ᾐνιγμένος (ἀνηγμένος MSS.) ἐστὶ μῦθος εἰς τὴν παλιγγενεσίαν· τὸ γὰρ ἐν ἡμῖν ἄλογον καὶ ἄτακτον καὶ βίαιον, οὐ θεῖον ἀλλὰ δαιμονικόν, οἱ παλαιοὶ Τιτᾶνας ὠνόμασαν, τοῦτ' ἔστι κολαζομένους καὶ δίκην τίνοντας. Dio Chrysost., *or.* 30,10–11 ὅτι τοῦ τῶν Τιτάνων αἵματός ἐσμεν ἡμεῖς ἅπαντες οἱ ἄνθρωποι. ὡς οὖν ἐκείνων ἐχθρῶν ὄντων τοῖς θεοῖς καὶ πολεμησάντων οὐδὲ ἡμεῖς φίλοι ἐσμέν, ἀλλὰ κολαζόμεθά τε ὑπ' αὐτῶν καὶ ἐπὶ τιμωρίᾳ γεγόναμεν, ἐν φρουρᾷ δὴ ὄντες ἐν τῷ βίῳ τοσοῦτον χρόνον ὅσον ἕκαστοι ζῶμεν. … εἶναι δὲ τὸν μὲν τόπον

β'. — Ὅτι τούτοις χρώμενοι τοῖς κανόσι ῥᾳδίως διελέγξομεν ὡς οὔτε 2
τἀγαθόν ἐστιν ἡ φρουρά, ὥς τινες, οὔτε ἡ ἡδονή, | ὡς Νουμήνιος [frg. 38], (85)
οὔτε ὁ δημιουργός, ὡς Πατέριος, ἀλλ', ὡς Ξενοκράτης [frg. 20], Τιτανική
ἐστιν καὶ εἰς Διόνυσον ἀποκορυφοῦται. οὕτω δὲ καὶ Πορφύριος προϋπενόησεν
ἐν τῷ ὑπομνήματι. 5

γ'. — Ὅτι οὔσης διττῆς δημιουργίας, ἢ ἀμερίστου ἢ μεμερισμένης, ταύτης 3
μὲν προεστάναι φησὶ τὸν Διόνυσον, διὸ μερίζεσθαι, ἐκείνης δὲ τὸν Δία, καὶ
πλῆθος ὑποτετάχθαι οἰκεῖον τῷ μὲν Ὀλυμπίων θεῶν, τῷ δὲ τῶν Τιτάνων, εἶναι
δὲ ἑκατέρωθι καὶ μονάδα καὶ τριάδα δημιουργικήν.

§ 2.   2 ἡ² ins. M^c: om. M¹
§ 3.   3 τιτανῶν M

τοῦτον, ὃν κόσμον ὀνομάζομεν, δεσμωτήριον ὑπὸ τῶν θεῶν κατεσκευασμένον χαλεπόν τε καὶ δυσάερον. The ultimate origin of the second text is unknown (Antisthenes has been suggested, cf. Dio § 25), the first may derive from Xenocrates, who has been cited a few lines before (996A). It seems fairly certain that he used the symbols of the prison (the body or the material world), the Titans (guilt and disintegration of the individual soul) and also that of Dionysus (the world mind divided in creation); though he may have done so in direct reference to the *Phaedo*, a commentary in the proper sense is out of the question. Porphyry, who had some material from Xenocrates at his disposal (cf. H. Dörrie, *RE*, art. *Xenokrates*, ser. II, vol. 9, 1518.10-25), took up the suggestion.

4. *προϋπενόησεν*: Porphyry's ideas as vague premonitions of Pr.'s solutions: cf. Pr., *Rep.* II 196.24-25 οἶδα μὲν οὖν ὅτι καὶ ὁ φιλοσοφώτατος Πορφύριος ὑπώπτευσεν ὅσα νυνὶ γράφομεν ἡμεῖς.

§ 3. 1-2. Pr., *Tim.* III 53.6-9 διττῆς τῆς δημιουργίας οὔσης, ὡς πολλάκις ὑπεμνήσαμεν, τῆς μὲν ἀφανοῦς καὶ μιᾶς καὶ ἁπλῆς καὶ ὑπερκοσμίου καὶ ὁλικῆς, τῆς δὲ ἐμφανοῦς καὶ πεπληθυσμένης καὶ πολυειδοῦς καὶ ἐν τῷ κόσμῳ μεριζομένης, ... Ibid. I 446.1-7 τῆς γὰρ δημιουργίας ἡ μέν ἐστιν ὅλη καὶ μία καὶ ἀμέριστος, ἡ δὲ μερικὴ καὶ πεπληθυσμένη καὶ προϊοῦσα κατὰ μερισμόν, ἡ δὲ οὐ μόνον οὖσα μεριστή, ... ἀλλὰ καὶ τῶν γενητῶν ἐφαπτομένη ... καὶ ἔχεις τῶν τριῶν τούτων δημιουργιῶν καὶ παρ' αὐτῷ τὰς μονάδας, τὴν Δίιον, τὴν Διονυσιακήν, τὴν Ἀδωναϊκήν. Ibid. I 173.2-4 μετὰ τὸν τοῦ Διονύσου διασπασμόν, ὃς δηλοῖ τὴν ἐκ τῆς ἀμερίστου δημιουργίας μεριστὴν πρόοδον εἰς τὸ πᾶν.

3-4. *εἶναι δὲ ἑκατέρωθι καὶ μονάδα καὶ τριάδα δημιουργικήν*: the demiurgic triad in relation to Zeus is the triad of the three sons of Kronos, Zeus-Poseidon-Pluto (*infra* II § 131.1-3, note): subordinate to the one transcendent Zeus, the Creator of the *Timaeus*, is the intramundane Zeusian triad of the celestial, the marine and the chthonic Zeus. Although a comparable Dionysian triad is not attested (elsewhere, Dionysus appears on two levels only, cf. II § 8), it can be thought of as its exact replica: a chthonian Dionysus is mentioned by Pr., *Tim.* III 140.24, a 'marine' Dionysus could easily be elicited from Hom., *Il.* 6.135-137 ('marine' representing of course the entire realm of genesis between the heavens and the subterranean world, as at II § 131.3-4), the celestial Dionysus is the God seated on his Father's throne. The triad Helios-Apollo-Dionysus, which might be considered also (cf. § 14), is not identified with Dionysus as a whole.

4. What he says about a monad and a triad is true, but we must maintain that the Titans who plot against Dionysus belong to another divine character, because no manifold opposes or destroys its own monad, otherwise it would destroy itself also. Besides, it is not to the Titans, but to the other Gods that Zeus says [*Orph.* frg. 208]:

'Hearken, ye Gods, this is the King I give you.'

So long, indeed, as Dionysus sits on the throne of Zeus, he is undivided .... to the Titans that he is divided and undergoes a metamorphosis in the way of ...., but in the Titanic way. In fact, even .... when he is divided, he is still made whole .... is more according to his nature. Let us say, therefore .... the forms or of the whole, though only .... his own as Titanic .... because they are dispersed or intermediate and constitute the universe, but not the whole, as belonging to the sphere of Dionysus. Hence he can be said to be at the same time indivisible and divisible, for such is the nature of the universe, which has rather the character of an aggregate and is held together by a totality whose parts are distinct.

5. Why are the Titans said to plot against Dionysus? — Because they initiate a mode of creation that does not remain within the bounds of the multiform continuity of Dionysus.

6. Their punishment consists in the checking of their dividing activities. Such is all chastisement: it aims at restraining and reducing erroneous dispositions and activities.

---

§ 4. Criticism of Pr. §§ 1–3 by Dam.

5. δίδωμι: Pr., *Crat.* 55.9 (and *Tim.* III 310.32) reads τίθημι.

6–12. A tentative restoration of the damaged passage: ἐπεὶ καὶ ὁ Διόνυσος ἐν μὲν τῷ θρόνῳ τοῦ Διὸς ἀμέριστος [μένει, καταβὰς δὲ] εἰς τοὺς Τιτᾶνας μερί[ζεται καὶ ἀπει]ρακῶς μεταμορφοῦται, κ[αὶ τοῦτο οὐ Διονυσιακῶς,] ἀλλὰ Τιτανικῶς. ἀμέλει καὶ [διασπώμενος καὶ] μεριζόμενος ὅμως συμφύεται [ἅτε ὅλος εἶναι] μᾶλλον πεφυκώς. λέγε τοίνυν [ἢ τοῦ παντὸς εἶναι] τὰ εἴδη ἢ τοῦ ὅλου εἶναι (εἰ καὶ M) μόνου ... τὸν ἑαυτοῦ, ὡς Τιτανικὰ [μέντοι] τῷ διεσπασμένα ἢ μέσα εἶναι καὶ τὸ πᾶν συμπληροῦν, ἀλλ' οὐ τὸ ὅλον ὡς Διονυσιακά. "So long, indeed, as Dionysus sits on the throne of Zeus, he is undivided, [and it is only after his descent] amid the Titans that he is divided and undergoes [countless] metamorphoses, [not in the Dionysiac,] but in the Titanic way. In fact, even [when he is torn and] divided, he is still made whole because [integrity] is more in agreement with his nature. Accordingly we can state that forms belong [either to the sum total] or to the whole only ... his own ..., [but then] as Titanic forms, inasmuch as they are dispersed or intermediate (half-united) and constitute the sum total, but not the whole, as Dionysiac forms would." Practically

δ'. – Ὅτι τὰ μὲν περὶ μονάδος καὶ τριάδος ἀληθῶς εἴρηται, Τιτᾶνας δὲ τῷ 4
Διονύσῳ ἐπιβουλεύοντας ἄλλης εἶναι φήσομεν ἰδιότητος· οὐδεὶς γὰρ ἀριθμὸς
ἐναντιοῦται τῇ οἰκείᾳ μονάδι οὐδὲ ἀναιρεῖ αὐτήν, ἢ οὕτω γε καὶ ἑαυτόν. ἀλλὰ καὶ
ὁ Ζεὺς οὐ πρὸς τοὺς Τιτᾶνας λέγει, ἀλλὰ πρὸς τοὺς ἄλλους θεούς [Orph. frg. 208]·
'κλῦτε, θεοί, τόνδ' ὕμμιν ἐγὼ βασιλῆα δίδωμι'. 5
ἐπεὶ καὶ ὁ Διόνυσος ἐν μὲν τῷ θρόνῳ τοῦ Διὸς ἀμέριστος . . . .
εἰς τοὺς Τιτᾶνας μερι . . . . ρακως μεταμορφοῦται, κ . . . .
ἀλλὰ Τιτανικῶς. ἀμέλει καὶ . . . . μεριζόμενος ὅμως συμφύεται
. . . . μᾶλλον πεφυκώς. λέγε τοίνυν . . . . τὰ εἴδη ἢ τοῦ
ὅλου, εἰ καὶ μόνου . . . . τὸν ἑαυτοῦ ὡς Τιτανικὰ 10
τῷ διεσπασμένα ἢ μέσα εἶναι καὶ τὸ πᾶν συμπληροῦν, ἀλλ᾽ οὐ τὸ ὅλον ὡς
Διονυσιακά. διὸ καὶ ἀμέριστος ἅμα καὶ μεριστός· τοιοῦτον γὰρ τὸ πᾶν οἷον
ἀθροίσματι μᾶλλον ἐοικὸς καὶ ὁλότητι διακεκριμένῃ τοῖς μέρεσι συνεχόμενον.
ε'. – Διὰ τί λέγονται οἱ Τιτᾶνες ἐπιβουλεύειν τῷ Διονύσῳ; – Ἢ ὅτι δημιουρ- 5
γίας ἐξάρχουσιν οὐκ ἐμμενούσης τοῖς ὅροις τῆς Διονυσιακῆς πολυειδοῦς
συνεχείας.
ς'. – Ὅτι δίκας τίνουσιν ἐπεχόμενοι τὰς διαιρετικὰς ἐνεργείας. τοιοῦτον γὰρ 6(86)
πᾶσα κόλασις· ἀνακόπτειν βούλεται καὶ συστέλλειν τὰς ἁμαρτωλοὺς ἕξεις τε
καὶ ἐνεργείας.

§ 4. 5 -μιν, 6 ἐν, 11 τῶι δ- in spat. vac. M^c

all the details are open to doubt: the passage Pr., *Tim.* II 297.28–31, which contains some of the key words, does not help; there is no authority for ἀπειρακῶς (for which cf. ἀρτιακῶς and περισσακῶς), but in Kretschmer-Locker, *Rückläufiges Wörterbuch* (²Göttingen 1963), there are no words in -ρακῶς, -ρακός, -ρακος, -ρακής or -ράκης that could serve; I see no possibility of construing the singular τὸν ἑαυτοῦ, which would suppose the mind or Dionysus as the subject and a masculine singular as the direct object. Yet the general purport must be to point out (against Pr.) that the Dionysiac and the Titanic orders are fundamentally different, Dionysiac form being characterized by unity, Titanic form by dispersal.
9–13. Cf. Pr., *Alc.* 217.10–12 πάντα γὰρ τὰ πράγματα τῷ ὅλῳ καὶ παντὶ διῄρηται, τῆς μὲν ἑνώσεως αὐτῶν κατὰ τὸ ὅλον ὑφισταμένης, τῆς δὲ διακρίσεως κατὰ τὸ πᾶν. Dam., *Parm.* 42.23–27 ἔστιν γὰρ ἡ μὲν ὁλότης ἡνωμένη παντότης, ἡ δὲ τελειότης παντότης ἐπανάγουσα τὰ μέρη πρὸς τὴν ὁλότητα· ἁπλῶς δὲ εἰπεῖν ἡ παντότης ὡς μὲν γεννῶσα τὰ μέρη ὁλότης ἐστὶν ἡ ἐν ἐκείνοις ὁριζομένη, ὡς δὲ ἐπιστρέφουσα τὰ μέρη πρὸς τὴν ὁλότητα τελειότης.

7. Tradition knows three kinds of punishments inflicted on the Titans: lightning-bolts, shackles, descents into various lower regions. This last kind is in the nature of a retribution, as it aggravates their leaning towards division and uses their shattered remains for the constitution of individuals, human and otherwise; the second is coercive, checking their powers of division; the first is purificatory and makes them whole, though only by participation. All three should be regarded as imposed upon each, though the myth distributes them, for each possesses higher, intermediate and lower powers.

8. In what sense are men created from the fragments of the Titans? — From the fragments, because their life is reduced to the utmost limit of differentiation; of the Titans, because they are the lowest of Creators and in immediate contact with their creation. For Zeus is the 'Father of men and Gods,' the Titans of men only, not of Gods, and they cannot even be called fathers, but have become men themselves, and not simply themselves, but their dead bodies, and even of these only the fragments, the fragmentary condition of our existence being thus transferred to those who are its causes.

9. The Titanic mode of life is the irrational mode, by which rational life is torn asunder.

It is better to acknowledge its existence everywhere, since in any case at its source there are Gods, the Titans; then also on the plane of rational life, this apparent self-determination, which seems to aim at belonging to itself alone and neither to the superior nor to the inferior, is wrought in us by the Titans; through it we tear asunder the Dionysus in ourselves, breaking up the natural continuity of our being and our partnership, so to speak, with the superior and the inferior. While in this condition, we are Titans; but when we recover that lost unity, we become Dionysus and we attain what can be truly called completeness.

---

§ 7. Cf. *Orphica*, frg. 215.

2. τὸ κοιλότερον : κοῖλος as 'low in the existential or moral scale,' practically always in the comparative, opposite often ὑπέρτερος : Hermias 17.23; 19.8; 152.14; 199.17 (here in the positive); Pr., *Tim.* I 213.4 (v.l.); 354.12; III 103.2; *Rep.* II 183.20 (superlative, opp. ὑψηλότατος); *Alc.* 167.12; *Parm.* 874.18; Dam., *princ.* 244.11; *Parm.* 230.20; *Phil.* § 68.2; *infra* I § 540.9; Ol., *Alc.* 109.19; 110.14. The derivation from 'hollow=empty' (*LSJ*, Diehl index Pr. *Tim.*, Festugière II p. 213, n. 2) fits this special use less well than the topographical sense 'hollow=low'; the opposite is 'high', never 'full'. The starting-point may have been *Ph.* 109b5, 110c7 (cf. Pr., *Crat.* 86.2–3).

5–6. Cf. Ol. 1 § 6.8–10 and note. – Pr., *Tim.* I 112.9–11 (Phaethon) ὑπὸ τοῦ Διὸς κεκεραυνῶσθαι λέγεται· δημιουργίας γὰρ σύμβολον ὁ κεραυνὸς ἀναφῶς διὰ πάντων χωρούσης καὶ πάντα σῳζούσης.

6. εἰ καὶ ὁ μῦθος μερίζει : see note on Ol. 1 § 4.3–11.

ζ'. - Ὅτι τρετταὶ παραδέδονται τῶν Τιτάνων κολάσεις· κεραυνώσεις, 7
δεσμοί, ἄλλων ἀλλαχοῦ πρόοδοι πρὸς τὸ κοιλότερον. αὕτη μὲν οὖν οἷον τιμωρίας
ἐπέχει τάξιν, ἐπιτρίβουσα αὐτῶν τὸ διαιρετικὸν καὶ ἀποχρωμένη τῷ κερματισμῷ
αὐτῶν εἰς σύστασιν τῶν ἀτόμων ἄλλων τε καὶ ἀνθρώπων· ἡ δὲ μέση κολαστική,
τὰς διαιρετικὰς ἐπέχουσα δυνάμεις· ἡ δὲ πρώτη καθαρτική, ὁλίζουσα αὐτοὺς κατὰ 5
μέθεξιν. δεῖ δὲ περὶ ἕκαστον τὰς τρεῖς θεωρεῖν, εἰ καὶ ὁ μῦθος μερίζει· ἐν ἑκάστῳ
γάρ εἰσι πρῶται καὶ μέσαι καὶ τελευταῖαι δυνάμεις.

η'. - Πῶς ἐκ Τιτανικῶν θρυμμάτων οἱ ἄνθρωποι γίνονται; — Ἡ ἐκ μὲν 8
τῶν θρυμμάτων, ὡς ἀπεστενωμένοι τὴν ζωὴν εἰς ἔσχατον μερισμόν· ἐκ δὲ
τῶν Τιτανικῶν, ὡς ἐσχάτων δημιουργῶν καὶ τοῖς δημιουργήμασι προσεχεστάτων.
ὁ μὲν γὰρ Ζεὺς ʽπατὴρ ἀνδρῶν καὶ θεῶν', οἱ δὲ ἀνθρώπων μόνων ἀλλ' οὐχὶ καὶ
θεῶν, καὶ οὐκέτι πατέρες ἀλλὰ αὐτοί, οὐδὲ αὐτοὶ ἁπλῶς ἀλλὰ τεθνεῶτες, καὶ 5
οὐδὲ τοῦτο μόνον ἀλλὰ καὶ συντεθρυμμένοι· ὁ γὰρ τοιοῦτος τρόπος τῆς ὑποστά-
σεως εἰς τοὺς αἰτίους ἀναπέμπεται.

θ'. - Ὅτι ἡ Τιτανικὴ ζωὴ ἄλογός ἐστιν, ὑφ' ἧς ἡ λογικὴ σπαράττεται. 9
Κάλλιον δὲ πανταχοῦ ποιεῖν αὐτήν, ἀπὸ θεῶν γε ἀρχομένην τῶν Τιτάνων·
καὶ τοίνυν τῆς λογικῆς τὸ δοκοῦν αὐτεξούσιον καὶ οἷον ἑαυτοῦ βουλόμενον
εἶναι μόνον, οὔτε δὲ τῶν κρειττόνων οὔτε τῶν χειρόνων, τοῦτο ἡμῖν οἱ Τιτάνες |
ἐμποιοῦσιν, καθ' ὃ καὶ τὸν ἐν ἡμῖν Διόνυσον διασπῶμεν, παραθραύοντες ἡμῶν 5 (87)
τὸ ὁμοφυὲς εἶδος καὶ οἷον κοινωνικὸν πρὸς τὰ κρείττω καὶ ἥττω. οὕτω δὲ
ἔχοντες Τιτάνες ἐσμέν· ὅταν δὲ εἰς ἐκεῖνο συμβῶμεν, Διόνυσοι γινόμεθα τετε-
λειωμένοι ἀτεχνῶς.

---

§ 8. 4 οἱ Fh: ὁ M | μόνων M¹: μόνον ὧν Mᶜ
§ 9. 1 Τιτανικὴ] τι- s.l. M¹ | post ἐστιν] ∼ in ras. Mˣ | σπαράτ-∽τεται, ∽ in ras. 2 litt. Mᶜ — 2 γε revera M | ἀρχομένην Fh: -ων M

---

§ 8. Orphica, frg. 220.
2. ἀπεστενωμένοι τὴν ζωήν : the term occurs Hermias 71.4; Pr., Rep. I 53.2; II 347.3; 8; infra § 23.3; 166.3; 171.5.
ibid. εἰς ἔσχατον μερισμόν : the phrase (also found § 128.5) is from Plato, Laws X 903b7-9 (whatever happens to the part is for the preservation and the well-being of the whole) τούτοις δ' εἰσὶν ἄρχοντες προστεταγμένοι ἑκάστοις ἐπὶ τὸ σμικρότατον ἀεὶ πάθης καὶ πράξεως, εἰς μερισμὸν τὸν ἔσχατον τέλος ἀπειργασμένοι. The ἄρχοντες are here identified with the Titans.
4. Hom., Il. 1.544, and often.
6-7. See note on Ol. 1 § 5.14.
§ 9. Ol. 1 § 5.12-13. Cf. also Dam., princ. 57.20-23, cited in note on Ol.
5. παραθραύοντες : see Dam., Phil., index s.v. παράθραυσις.
7. On becoming Dionysus infra § 166.5-6.

10. What is the 'kind of custody' [62b3–4]? — Viewed as the guarding power, it is Dionysus himself, who loosens the shackle for whom he will, since he is also the cause of individual life. Viewed as the object of the custody, on the other hand, it is the experience itself of being bound in the body, which has befallen us of necessity as an act of justice; for by actualizing her own separate existence the soul has been locked up in a body which, though her own, has also many wants, to make her feel her dependence on the common form and teach her what it is to be an individual.

11. Dionysus is the cause of deliverance only; therefore this God is also named Lyseus, and Orpheus says [frg. 232]:

'And men shall bring to thee rich hecatombs,
yearly, in season, and celebrate thy rites,
seeking deliverance from their forebears' sins;
and thou, their Lord, shalt free whomever thou wilt
from weary toil and agony unrelieved.'

The guarding power, however, in the most comprehensive sense, is Zeus, or, more immediately, the Young Gods, or, most directly, the generative Gods, who have also the power to destroy.

It should be observed that Dionysus, too, is a God in charge of creation, because of his connection with rebirth.

12. [62b4–5] It is the Gods who appoint the term of the imprisonment, as long as it is better for embodied souls to be under restraint, in view of the final goal, which is deliverance by Dionysus. This measure and this appointed term we can never know; therefore, if we free ourselves, such a way of gaining our freedom is not release, but flight, because we still need to be kept in custody.

13. [62b4] Socrates qualifies suicide now as 'unlawful' [61c10], then as 'impious' [62a6], then again as 'undue' [62b4]. The first term measures it by the standard imposed by the Gods, the second by the standard of what we owe to the Gods, while the notion of what is 'due' seems to include both.

§§ 14–25. The exoteric argument. 62b6–c8

14. In the mystic account the ruling principle is the monad of the Young God, in the philosophical demonstration, inasmuch as this latter

---

§§ 10–11. The obvious relation between the two sections is that § 10 presents the view of Pr. as reported by Ol. 1 § 6 (Dionysus the Lord of death and life), whereas in § 11 Dam., insisting on the fundamental difference between Dionysus and the Titans (§ 4), opposes this and makes Dionysus the Deliverer only, while the creating Gods and esp. the Titans are responsible for the incarceration which is incarnation.

§ 10. 4. ἐνεδέθη (Finckh) rather than προσεδέθη (Norvin) is Pl.'s word (*Ph.* 81e2; 92a1; *Tim.* 43a5; it is true that he construes it with εἰς or ἐν, not with the dative, but cf. *infra* I § 352.5 and Ol. 8 § 7.6).

ι'. – Τίς ἡ ʿτὶς φρουρά' [62b3–4]; – ʿΩς μὲν τὸ φρουροῦν, αὐτὸς ὁ Διόνυσος· 10
οὗτος γάρ ἐστιν ὁ λύων τὸν δεσμὸν ὧν ἂν ἐθέλῃ, ἅτε καὶ αἴτιος ὢν τῆς μερικῆς
ζωῆς. ὡς δὲ τὸ φρουρούμενον, αὐτὸ τὸ πάθος τοῦ ἐν σώματι δεσμοῦ, ὅπερ
κατὰ δίκην ἐπεγένετο ἀναγκαίως· προβαλομένη γὰρ τὸ ἴδιον ἡ ψυχὴ [ἐνε]δέθη
σώματι ἰδίῳ, ἀλλὰ καὶ πολυδεεῖ, ἵνα τοῦ κοινοῦ εἴδους ἐν χρείᾳ γένηται καὶ 5
μάθῃ οἷόν ἐστι τὸ ἴδιον.

ια'. – Ὅτι ὁ Διόνυσος λύσεώς ἐστιν αἴτιος· διὸ καὶ Λυσεὺς ὁ θεός, καὶ ὁ 11
Ὀρφεύς φησιν [frg. 232]·
  ʿἄνθρωποι δὲ τεληέσσας ἑκατόμβας
  πέμψουσιν πάσῃσιν ἐν ὥραις ἀμφιέτῃσιν
  ὄργιά τ' ἐκτελέσουσι λύσιν προγόνων ἀθεμίστων 5
  μαιόμενοι· σὺ δὲ τοῖσιν ἔχων κράτος, οὕς κε θέλῃσθα
  λύσεις ἔκ τε πόνων χαλεπῶν καὶ ἀπείρονος οἴστρου'.
τὸ δὲ φρουροῦν ὁ Ζεύς ἐστι κατὰ περιοχήν, προσεχέστερον δὲ οἱ νέοι θεοί,
καὶ προσεχέστατα οἱ γενεσιουργοὶ οἱ καὶ τὴν φθορὰν ἐπάγειν κύριοι.
Ἦ καὶ ὁ Διόνυσος γενεσιουργός ἐστιν ἔφορος κατὰ τὴν παλιγγενεσίαν. 10

ιβ'. – [62b4–5] Ὅτι ⟨θεοί⟩ εἰσιν οἱ τὸν ὅρον τῆς φρουρᾶς ὁρίζοντες, μέχρις 12
ὅσου φρουρεῖσθαι ἄμεινον ταῖς ἐν σώματι ψυχαῖς, ἀποβλέποντες εἰς τὸ τέλος
τῆς Διονυσιακῆς λύσεως. τοῦτο δὲ τὸ μέτρον καὶ τοῦτο τὸ χρέος οὐκ ἂν ἡμεῖς
εἰδείημεν· τοιγαροῦν εἰ ἐξάγοιμεν, οὐκ ἄφεσίς ἐστιν, ἀλλὰ ἀπόδρασις ἡ ἐξαγωγή·
δεόμεθα γὰρ τῆς ἔτι φρουρᾶς. 5

ιγ'. – [62b4] Ὅτι ποτὲ μὲν ʿἀθέμιτον' [61c10] λέγει τὸ ἐξάγειν, ποτὲ 13(88)
δὲ ʿοὐχ ὅσιον' [62a6], ποτὲ δὲ ʿοὐ δέον' [62b4]· ἔστι δὲ τὸ μὲν πρῶτον παρὰ
τὸ θεόθεν ἧκον μέτρον, τὸ δὲ δεύτερον παρὰ τὸ μέτρον ἡμῶν τὸ θεοῖς ὀφειλό-
μενον, τὸ μέντοι γε ʿδέον' ἔοικεν εἶναι συναμφότερον.

§§ 14–25. The exoteric argument. 62b6–c8

ιδ'. – Ὅτι τοῦ μὲν μυστικοῦ λόγου μονὰς ἡγεῖται ἡ τοῦ νέου θεοῦ· τῆς δὲ 14
φιλοσόφου ἀποδείξεως, ἅτε ἀνελιττούσης τὸν ἀπόρρητον λόγον, τὸ πλῆθος τῶν
θεῶν, οὓς ἀντιστρόφως ὁ Πλάτων ʿνέους' καλεῖ [Tim. 42d6], τὸν δὲ βασιλέα

---

§ 10. 4 [ἐνε]δέθη Fh: spat. vac. 4 litt. et δεηθη M
§ 12. 1 θεοί Wk: om. M – 4 ᾐδείημεν M
§ 14. 3 οὓς Nv: ὅτι, -ι in ras. M^x | τὸν M^c: τὸ M^1

---

§ 11. 10. This sentence may be either an objection by the redactor (we have a clear example of this in § 210) or an afterthought of Dam. himself, in which case possibly εἰ καί should be read instead of ἦ καί. On Dionysus as the monad of the new Gods and cause of παλιγγενεσία, i.e. the renewal of creation, cf. Pr., Tim. III 241.5–18 and 29–30; infra II § 8.1–2 and note.

§§ 14–15. In § 14.1–5 Pr. makes two points: (1) the exoteric argument is a development of the esoteric one, analogous to the Titanic manifold, which is the development of the Dionysiac monad; (2) the relation Dionysus-Titans is analogous to that of Helios-Young Gods, since Dionysus and Helios meet in the triad Helios-Apollo-Dionysus. – Dam. § 14.6–8, instead of the latter, proposes a different triadic

develops the esoteric reason, it is the multitude of the Gods to whom Plato [*Tim*. 42d6] gives the corresponding name of the 'Young Gods'; their king he makes the Sun [*Rep*. VI 509d2–3], who, according to Orpheus [frg. 172, 212] is closely connected with Dionysus through the intermediary of Apollo.

Rather, we should make the Sun King of the Gods in so far as he is identical with Zeus, while in his quality of Dionysus he is divided over the world, and as Apollo he holds an intermediate position, gathering the dividedness of Dionysus and standing by the side of Zeus.

15. If the exoteric account is a development of the esoteric reason, just as the manifold is of its own monad, how can the occult reason still be so? A monad heading an exoteric manifold cannot be occult itself, because multitude and monad belong to the same kind. Therefore the truth seems to be rather that in each of the two cases the monad as well as the manifold are both exoteric and occult; but in the one case Plato discusses in philosophical terms the unlawfulness of suicide and the reason for which it is forbidden, in the other he informs us of the symbol by which the commandment was expressed, without explaining its nature (since he was not allowed to do so), only stating that it was given in a mystic form. One who considers this contrary to reason does not know the nature of symbolical utterance; therefore it is described as 'deep' and 'not easy to grasp': 'not easy to grasp' for the profane and among the profane, 'deep,' because it is not a cause, but the source of all causality.

16. The Young Gods imprison souls in bodies, when they have modeled living organisms fit to receive a soul, 'borrowing parts' from the elements [*Tim*. 42e6–43a6]; when, on the other hand, returning what they have borrowed, they decompose the organisms, at that moment they free the souls from their shackles.

17. [62b7] 'Care' is the direct providence that bestows on each, according to circumstances and set limits, what is best for him.

---

arrangement: Helios-Zeus, Helios-Apollo, Helios-Dionysus. In § 15, following up his distinction between the Dionysiac and the Titanic series (§ 11), he detaches also the two arguments from each other.

§ 14. 4–5. Pr., *theol*. VI 12, 376.21–29 (=*Orphica*, frg. 172) πρῶτον δὴ τοῦτο κατανοήσωμεν, ὅπως καὶ αὐτός, ὥσπερ 'Ορφεύς, τὸν ῞Ηλιον εἰς ταὐτόν πως ἄγει τῷ 'Απόλλωνι καὶ ὡς τὴν κοινωνίαν πρεσβεύει τούτων τῶν θεῶν. ἐκεῖνος μὲν γὰρ διαρρήδην λέγει καὶ διὰ πάσης ὡς εἰπεῖν ⟨τῆς⟩ ποιήσεως, ὁ δὲ 'Αθηναῖος ξένος ἐνδείκνυται διὰ τῆς ἑνώσεως αὐτῶν, κοινόν τινα νεὼν 'Απόλλωνι καὶ 'Ηλίῳ κατασκευάζων (*Laws* XII 945e6). Apollo is identified with Helios *Orphica*, frg. 62, cf. also 297a10; the "connection" with Dionysus in the Orphic epic is of course no identity, but simply Apollo's role in the myth.

6–8. Cf. Julian, *or*. 11 [4], 144b–c: (impossible to discuss all the manifold powers of the Sun) ἀπόχρη ⟨δὲ⟩ τῆς μὲν χωριστῆς καὶ πρὸ τῶν σωμάτων ἐπ' αὐτῶν οἶμαι τῶν αἰτιῶν αἳ κεχωρισμέναι τῆς φανερᾶς προϋπάρχουσι δημιουργίας, ἴσην 'Ηλίῳ καὶ Διὶ τὴν δυναστείαν καὶ μίαν ὑπάρχουσαν τεθεωρηκέναι, τὴν δὲ ἁπλότητα τῶν νοήσεων μετὰ τοῦ διαιωνίου καὶ κατὰ ταὐτὰ μονίμου ξὺν 'Απόλλωνι τεθεαμένοις, τὸ δὲ μεριστὸν τῆς δημιουργίας μετὰ τοῦ τὴν μεριστὴν ἐπιτροπεύοντος οὐσίαν Διονύσου, τὸ δὲ τῆς

αὐτῶν ποιεῖ τὸν Ἥλιον [Rep. VI 509d2–3], ὃς πολλὴν ἔχει πρὸς τὸν Διόνυσον κοινωνίαν διὰ μέσου τοῦ Ἀπόλλωνος κατ' Ὀρφέα [frg. 172, 212].

Κάλλιον δὲ τὸν Ἥλιον ὡς μὲν Δία βασιλέα ποιεῖν, ὡς δὲ Διόνυσον περὶ τὸν κόσμον διῃρημένον, ὡς δὲ Ἀπόλλωνα μέσον, συνάγοντα μὲν τὴν Διονυσιακὴν διαίρεσιν, τῷ δὲ Διὶ παριστάμενον.

ιε'. – Εἰ ἀνέλιξίς ἐστι τοῦ ἀπορρήτου λόγου ὁ ῥητός, ὡς τὸ πλῆθος τῆς οἰκείας μονάδος, πῶς ἄρρητος ἐκεῖνος; οὐδὲ γὰρ ἄρρητος ἡ μονὰς ἡ ῥητοῦ πλήθους ἡγουμένη· ὁμοειδὴς γὰρ ὁ ἀριθμὸς τῇ μονάδι. μήποτε οὖν ἡ μὲν μονὰς καὶ ὁ ἀριθμὸς ἑκατέρως καὶ ῥητὸς καὶ ἀπόρρητος· ἀλλ' ὅπου μὲν φιλοσοφεῖ τῆς ἐξαγωγῆς τὸ ἀθέμιτον, κατὰ τίνα λόγον ἀπηγόρευται, ὅπου δὲ τὸ σύμβολον ἱστορεῖ τοῦ παραγγέλματος, οὐ φράζων οἷον (οὐ γὰρ ἦν θέμις), ἀλλ' ὅτι παρήγγελται μυστικῶς. ὁ δὲ τούτου λόγον ἀπαξιῶν οὐκ οἶδεν ὅστις ὁ τρόπος τῆς συμβολικῆς ἀποδόσεως· διὸ 'μέγας' καὶ 'οὐ ῥᾴδιος διδεῖν', τοῦτο μὲν [ἐν] βεβήλῳ τε καὶ ἐν βεβήλοις, 'μέγας' δέ, ὅτι οὐκ αἰτία, πηγὴ δὲ πάσης αἰτίας.

ις'. – Ὅτι οἱ νέοι θεοὶ δεσμεύουσι μὲν τὰς ψυχὰς ἐν τοῖς σώμασιν, ὅταν τὰ ζῷα συνυφήνωσιν ἐπιτήδεια πρὸς ψύχωσιν, 'δανειζόμενοι μόρια' ἀπὸ τῶν στοιχείων [Tim. 42e6–43a6]· ὅταν δὲ ἀποδιδόντες τὰ δανείσματα διαλύσωσι τὰ ζῷα, τότε λύουσι τὰς ψυχὰς ἀπὸ τῶν δεσμῶν.

ιζ'. – [62b7] Ὅτι ἡ 'ἐπιμέλεια' πρόνοιά ἐστι προσεχὴς καὶ κατὰ καιρούς τε καὶ ὅρους ἀποδιδοῦσα ἑκάστοις τὰ πρόσφορα.

---

§ 15. 1 ἀνέλιξις] -ελι- in ras. 4 litt. M^c — 6 ἀλλ' ὅτι M¹ ante corr.: ἄλλό τι M¹ post corr. — 8 ἐν ins. M^c: om. M¹

καλλίστης συμμετρίας καὶ νοερᾶς κράσεως περὶ τὴν τοῦ Μουσηγέτου δύναμιν τεθεωρηκόσι, τὸ συμπληροῦν δὲ τὴν εὐταξίαν τῆς ὅλης ζωῆς ξὺν Ἀσκληπιῷ νοοῦσι. Both Julian and Dam. seem to depend on Iamblichus. Some speculations on the pluriformity of Helios (from a different angle) Dam., Parm. 203.26–204.15. Pr., too (theol. VI 12, 375.40–47), finds a prototype of Helios in Zeus, the first Demiurge.

7–8. On Apollo gathering the remains of Dionysus cf. Orphica, frgs. 209 and 210. Apollo standing by the side of Zeus may refer to another, otherwise unknown scene in the epic; or it may be a simplified expression for Apollo standing by the throne of Zeus, on the occasion when he tries in vain to dissuade Dionysus from leaving his Father's throne and joining the Titans (frg. 211).

§ 15. 7. ὁ δὲ τούτου λόγον ἀπαξιῶν : the normal construction would be τοῦτο λόγον, and even this sounds a little awkward. Another possibility is "one who demands a reason for this", with ἀπαξιῶν as the result of a confusion between ἀξιῶν and ἀπαιτῶν, for which, however, there is no example in the dictionaries.

§ 16. From Pr.: cf. § 14.2–3 and note on §§ 10–11.

§ 17. Pr., Tim. I 158.32–159.2 (on Tim. 24b8) ἐπιμέλειαν δὲ [scil. φήσομεν] τὴν πρόνοιαν τὴν μέχρι τῶν μερικῶν ἀπὸ τῶν ὅλων πεφοιτηκυῖαν.

18. [62b7-8] Socrates combines the two notions, that 'the Gods take care of us' and that 'we are their possessions,' not only in imitation of the processes of emanation and reversion, but also to establish the major of his hypothetical syllogism all the more securely. For if we were their possessions and they did not take care of us, or conversely, escape would not be punishable; it follows that, both being true, we are liable to punishment.

19. [62c1-4] How can Socrates draw inferences with regard to the Gods on the analogy of the human situation, though they are obviously not subject to our emotions? — The inference is based on rational behavior in the fields of social life and household administration, since it is evident that all regulating care has its prototype in the Gods. Anger and punishment, however, should be given a different meaning, when applied to them, anger being a withholding of their own light, punishment a secondary, coercive form of providence towards the erring soul.

20. If suicides are punished, their souls must exist somewhere, or no punishment would be possible; so that the doctrine of the separability of the soul is already stated here.

21. If we can leave this body against the will of the Gods, our soul must be self-moved, for the impulse is our own; if they punish us, we must be subject to motion from without, for chastisement is only for those who can be compelled by others.

22. [62c7-8] A man who takes his own life under compulsion is none the less a suicide, but he is granted forgiveness because he acted with God's will. By 'compulsion' we must understand only that kind which affects the wise man.

Or possibly any kind.

23. The more completely human free-will submits itself to the Gods, the wider the range of its sovereignty becomes; the farther it withdraws from the Gods into itself, the more it is restricted and passes into the bondage of being really dependent on external impulses, because it recedes from the truly autonomous and approaches the truly heteronomous.

24. How can one speak of 'necessity,' when escape is possible? — Because the strongest necessity is the compelling force of the good; Socrates could not do wrong to anyone, let alone his native city, and he would have wronged it by upsetting its order, which he knew to be suitable and profitable to the city.

25. Necessity is fourfold: it is intrinsic or extrinsic, and in each of the two cases it can be either good or evil. Examples of intrinsic necessity, if

---

§ 18. Ol. 1 § 7.
§ 22. 2. τοῦ σπουδαίου : as defined in § 24 and § 25.2–3.

ιη'. — [62b7–8] Ὅτι τὰ δύο συνέπλεξεν, καὶ ὅτι 'ἐπιμελοῦνται ἡμῶν οἱ θεοὶ' 18
καὶ ὅτι 'ἡμεῖς ἐκείνων κτήματα,' οὐ μόνον τὴν πρόοδον καὶ ἐπιστροφὴν
μιμούμενος, ἀλλὰ καὶ τὸ συνημμένον βεβαιότερον ποιῶν. εἴτε γὰρ κτήματα
ἦμεν, ἐκεῖνοι δὲ οὐκ ἐπεμελοῦντο, εἴτε ἀνάπαλιν, οὐκ ἂν ἦμεν ὑπεύθυνοι
ἀποδιδράσκοντες· εἰ ἄρα τὸ συναμφότερον, ὑπεύθυνοι. 5

ιθ'. — [62c1–4] Πῶς ἐκ τῶν ἀνθρωπίνων τὰ περὶ τοὺς θεοὺς εἰκάζει ἔχειν 19
ὁμοίως; οὐ γὰρ δὴ καὶ ἐκεῖνοι ἐμπαθεῖς. — Ἡ ἀπὸ τῶν κατὰ λόγον εἰκάζει
πολιτικῶς τε καὶ οἰκονομικῶς· δῆλον γὰρ ὅτι πάσης κοσμητικῆς ἐπιμελείας
τὰ παραδείγματα ἐν θεοῖς προείληπται. ἡ δὲ ἀγανάκτησις ἐπ' αὐτῶν καὶ ἡ
τιμωρία ἀλλοῖον νοείσθω τρόπον, ἡ μὲν ἀναστολὴ οὖσα τοῦ οἰκείου φωτός, 5
ἡ δὲ τιμωρία δευτέρα πρόνοια περὶ τὴν ἀποφοιτήσασαν ψυχὴν κολαστική τις.

κ'. — Ὅτι εἰ τιμωροῦνται οἱ ἐξάγοντες, ἀναγκαῖον εἶναί που αὐτῶν τὰς 20
ψυχάς, ἵνα καὶ τιμωρῶνται· ὥστε προαποπέφανται καὶ διὰ τούτου χωριστὴ
ἡ ψυχή.

κα'. — Ὅτι εἰ παρὰ γνώμην θεῶν ἐξάγομεν, αὐτοκίνητός ἐστιν ἡμῶν ἡ 21
ψυχή, οἰκεία γὰρ ἡ ὁρμή· καὶ εἰ τιμωροῦνται ἡμᾶς, ἑτεροκίνητοί ἐσμεν, ἑτέρωθεν
γὰρ ἀναγκαζομένων ἐστὶν ἡ ἐπιτίμησις.

κβ'. — [62c7–8] Ὅτι ἐξάγει μὲν καὶ ὁ σὺν ἀνάγκῃ, συγγνώμης δὲ ἀξιοῦται, 22
ὅτι μετὰ τοῦ θεοῦ. ἀνάγκην δὲ μόνον ἀκουστέον τὴν τοῦ σπουδαίου.
Μήποτε δὲ καὶ πᾶσαν.

κγ'. — Ὅτι τὸ αὐτεξούσιον ἡμῶν ὅσῳ μᾶλλον δουλεύει τοῖς θεοῖς, τοσούτῳ 23
μᾶλλον ἐνεξουσιάζει πλείοσιν· ὅσῳ δὲ ἐκείνων ἀφίσταται πρὸς ἑαυτό, τοσούτῳ
μειζόνως ἀποστενοῦται πρὸς | τὴν ὄντως ἑτεροκίνητον δουλείαν, ἅτε τοῦ μὲν (90)
κυρίως αὐτεξουσίου ἀφιστάμενον, τῷ δὲ κυρίως ὑπεξουσίῳ πλησιάζον.

κδ'. — Πῶς ἀνάγκη, ἣν δυνατὸν φυγεῖν; — Ἡ μεγίστη ἀνάγκη ἡ τοῦ 24
ἀγαθοῦ· πῶς γὰρ ἦν δυνατὸν ἀδικῆσαι Σωκράτη, ἄλλως τε καὶ τὴν οἰκείαν
πατρίδα; ἠδίκει δὲ συγχέων αὐτῆς τὸν κόσμον, ὃν ᾔδει σύμμετρον ὄντα αὐτῇ
καὶ ὠφέλιμον.

κε'. — Ὅτι τετραχῇ ἡ ἀνάγκη· ἡ μὲν γὰρ ἔνδοθεν, ἡ δὲ ἔξωθεν, καὶ ἑκατέρα 25
διττή, ἡ μὲν ἀγαθή, ἡ δὲ κακή. παραδείγματα τῆς μὲν ἔνδον ἀγαθῆς ἡ τοῦ
θεοῦ βούλησις καὶ ἡ τοῦ δικαίου ἀνδρός, τῆς δὲ κακῆς ἡ τοῦ πονηροῦ προαίρεσις·

---

§ 18. 2 καὶ²] in ras. M^c
§ 19. 1 εἰκάζει] εἰ- et -ει in ras. M^c
§ 20. 1 ἐξάγοντες] -τες M^c: spat. vac. M¹
§ 21. 1 ἐξάγομεν] -ο- ex -ω- M^x — 2 ἑτεροκίνητοι Wk: αὐτοκίνητοι M
§ 23. 3 ἀποστενοῦται Nv: ἀ et spat. vac. 12 litt. M¹, ἀποιτισουται mg. M^c —
4 πλησιάζον] -ησι- in ras. 3 litt. M^c
§ 24. 1 ἦν Wk: ἦν M — 2 σωκράτη M^x: -την M¹ — 3 ᾔδει M^c: ᾔδ≡ M¹ | αὐτῇ]
-ντῆι in ras. M^c
§ 25. 1 ἔνδοθεν] -θεν in ras. M^c (ἔνδον M¹?) | καὶ ins. M^c

---

§ 23. Ol. 2 § 9 and note.
§ 25. On necessity see passages cited at Dam., Phil. § 17 (esp. Simpl.,

good, are the will of God and of the just man, if evil, the choice of the wicked man; of extrinsic beneficent necessity, the force of fate as it bestows on us things that are primarily good, and of the harmful kind, its gifts of the violent, the abnormal and the destructive.

II. SECOND PROBLEM: THE WILL TO DIE

§§ 26–35. Questions raised by Cebes and Simmias. 62c9–63a9

26. [62c9–e7] Cebes expresses his difficulty in the form of a syllogism from contradictory premises: 'The philosopher wants to run away from the Gods, a man who wants to run away from the Gods is not a philosopher, therefore the philosopher is not a philosopher.'

27. The flaws in Cebes' argument are, first that he fails to define what kind of death the philosopher is willing to die; secondly that he forgets that in Hades, too, there are Gods who are good masters to us, and who either are superior to those here or exert superior powers.

28. [62d2; 6] Cebes speaks both of 'God' and 'Gods,' imitating the two arguments of Socrates, the exoteric and the esoteric.

Or rather, he is trying to improve the exoteric argument, which also has a monad as its starting-point, as we remarked before [§ 15]; for his objection evidently concerns the second argument.

29. [62d5–6] It is in the nature of *all* that exists to take care of their inferiors, but the Gods have this function primarily and by their very subsistence. The reason is that every God is goodness, and providence is an activity of goodness bringing about the good for that which is already good by its own being. Therefore the Gods are called 'the best rulers of all things that are'; if they are rulers of all things that are, they themselves must transcend being.

30. [62d4] God's 'care' of man consists in making him better than he was, man's 'care' of God in allowing himself to be made better by him.

Unless we should say that man perfects the God that is within him, *and* the transcendent God is so far as he calls forth his providential (i.e. secondary) activity for the benefit of himself and others.

Epict. 11.21–37); add Iambl., *myst.* 44.11–45.4; Hierocl., *carm. aur.* 429–430; Ascl., *met.* 308.33–309.26; Ol., *Gorg.* 10.12–16; El., *isag.* 43.13–31; Dav. 100.20–101.6; Ps.-El. 28,35–42.

§ 26. Ol. 2 § 1.12–16.

§ 28. Ol. 2 § 3.5–7. Pr. has lost sight of the text and is rightly corrected by Dam.

§ 29. Cf. Pr., *elem.* 120 πᾶς θεὸς ἐν τῇ ἑαυτοῦ ὑπάρξει τὸ προνοεῖν τῶν ὅλων κέκτηται· καὶ τὸ πρώτως προνοεῖν ἐν τοῖς θεοῖς. τὰ μὲν γὰρ ἄλλα πάντα μετὰ θεοὺς ὄντα διὰ τὴν ἐκείνων μετουσίαν προνοεῖ, τοῖς δὲ θεοῖς ἡ πρόνοια συμφυής ἐστιν. . . . οἱ δὲ θεοὶ πάντες ἀγαθότητές εἰσιν . . . ἐν θεοῖς οὖν ἡ πρόνοια πρώτως. καὶ ποῦ γὰρ ἡ πρὸ νοῦ ἐνέργεια ἢ ἐν τοῖς ὑπερουσίοις; *Tim.* I 415.10 οὐδὲν ἄλλο ἐστὶ πρόνοια ἢ κατὰ τὸ ἀγαθὸν ἐνέργεια.

3. τῶν κατ' οὐσίαν ἀγαθῶν ἀγαθοποιός: the addition serves to distinguish

τῆς δὲ ἔξω ἀγαθῆς ἡ τῆς εἱμαρμένης τῆς τὰ προηγούμενα παρεχομένης ἀγαθά, τῆς δὲ κακῆς ἡ τῶν βιαίων καὶ παρὰ φύσιν καὶ φθοροποιῶν δόσις.

II. SECOND PROBLEM: THE WILL TO DIE

§§ 26–35. Questions raised by Cebes and Simmias. 62c9–63a9

κϛ΄. – [62c9–e7] Ὅτι τὸν ἐξ ἀντικειμένων πλέκει συλλογισμὸν ὁ Κέβης ἀπορῶν· 'φεύγειν θεοὺς θέλει ὁ φιλόσοφος· ὁ φεύγων θεοὺς οὐ φιλόσοφος· ὁ φιλόσοφος ἄρα οὐ φιλόσοφος'. 26

κζ΄. – Ὅτι διαπταίει ὁ Κέβης, ἓν μὲν οὐ διοριζόμενος ποῖον θάνατον ἐθέλει ἀποθνήσκειν ὁ φιλόσοφος, δεύτερον δὲ οὐκ ἐννοήσας ὅτι καὶ ἐν Ἅιδου θεοὺς ἔχομεν δεσπότας ἀγαθοὺς καὶ ἢ ἄρα κρείττους τῶν τῇδε ἢ κρείττοσι δυνάμεσι χρωμένους. 27

κη΄. – [62d2;6] Ὅτι καὶ 'θεὸν' ἔφη καὶ 'θεοὺς' ὁ Κέβης, μιμούμενος τὸν διττὸν τοῦ Σωκράτους λόγον, τόν τε ῥητὸν καὶ τὸν ἀπόρρητον. 28

Κάλλιον δὲ τὸν ῥητὸν τελειῶν, ὡς καὶ αὐτὸν ἀπὸ μονάδος ἐξηρτημένον, ὡς εἴρηται [§ 15]· ἐπεὶ τῷ β΄ λόγῳ ἐπαπορεῖ σαφέστατα.

κθ΄. – [62d5–6] Ὅτι πάντα μὲν προνοεῖ τῶν δευτέρων κατὰ φύσιν, ἀλλ' οἱ θεοὶ πρὸ πάντων καὶ καθ' ὕπαρξιν. ἀγαθότης γὰρ ἕκαστος, ἡ δὲ πρόνοια τῆς ἀγαθότητός ἐστιν ἐνέργεια τῶν κατ' οὐσίαν ἀγαθῶν ἀγαθοποιός. διόπερ εἴρηνται 'ἄριστοι τῶν ὄντων ἐπιστάται'· εἰ δὲ τῶν ὄντων, αὐτοὶ ὑπερούσιοι. 29(91)

λ΄. – [62d4] Ὅτι 'θεραπεύει' θεὸς μὲν ἄνθρωπον βελτίω ποιῶν ἐκ χείρονος, ἄνθρωπος δὲ θεὸν βελτίων αὐτὸς ὑπ' ἐκείνου γιγνόμενος. 30

Εἰ μὴ ἄρα τὸν ἐν ἑαυτῷ θεὸν τελειοῖ καὶ τὸν χωριστόν, καθόσον εἰς ἑαυτὸν προκαλεῖται καὶ εἰς ἄλλους δευτέραν τὴν προνοητικὴν ἐνέργειαν.

---

§ 27. 1 post οὐ] ÷ in ras. M˟
§ 28. 3 τελειῶν Fh: -οῦν M — 4 ἐπεὶ Wk: ἐπὶ M

Providence from Fate, which is an activity of Providence extending itself to all things below the level of rational soul (Pr., *prov.* 3–4; 13–14).

§ 30. 3. τὸν ἐν ἑαυτῷ θεόν : in the system of Pr. and Dam. there is nothing in the human soul that could be called a God in the strict sense, i.e. a divine henad; only divine souls (those of the world and the spheres) are Gods, intellective souls (angels, spirits, heroes) are 'perpetually attendant upon Gods', particular (human) souls are 'at certain times attendant upon Gods' (Pr., *elem.* 185; cf. Beutler, art. *Proklos*, 234.10–34). The 'one of the soul' is not a divine henad, but a 'one-like' faculty which enables us to know the divine (Beutler 238.5–17). The human soul shares in the divine only through the God to whose 'retinue' it belongs, and only in this restricted sense can Dam. speak of the 'Dionysus' in ourselves (§ 9.5).

31. [62d8] In the same way as in the universe the Intelligence comes first after God and reverts to him, so our own intelligence aspires upward to God, while 'unreason' turns away from the divine.

By intelligence we should understand not only its cognitive aspect, but the appetitive as well, both in the universe and in ourselves, for the Intelligence is both, being the first living being. Thus we shall no longer be troubled by the problem as to which is superior, appetitive or cognitive perfection, in other words, virtue or knowledge, since neither can be perfect without the other.

32. [62e1] In what sense can the Gods be called our 'masters'? A master does not seek the good of his servant, but his own (this is where he differs from a ruler), and what good can God receive through man? — The explanation may be that in the case of the Gods the two functions run parallel. Besides, even an earthly master looks after his slave, but for his own sake, as the Stoics say [SVF II 1118], and this holds true of the Gods also: they do everything primarily for their own sake. It is rather in this meaning that we should take the word 'masters': the higher their transcendence, the greater their superiority; when, on the other hand, they are said to 'rule' us, this implies a kind of coordination with us. Indeed, the servants of the Gods participate more completely in their gifts than mere subjects, since they become entirely theirs and add nothing of their own.

33. [62e8–63a3] The good teacher is characterized by the critical insight that enables him to distinguish between the more superficial and the more pertinent questions, and by his delight in the latter; the learner's qualifications are twofold: a critical insight to decide what deserves belief and what does not, and eagerness to go more deeply into the truth.

34. Questions ought to arise from the facts themselves, not from the opinion we happen to have about them; and from the heart of the matter, which is hidden from laymen, not from its obvious aspects; and they should be such as to please the expert, not the vulgar masses.

---

§ 31. 4–7. This is an observation by Dam., with whom the notion of appetition as a function of *all* (including the transcendental) intelligence is a favorite theme: *princ.* 185.17–20 ἢ ῥητέον ὡς τὸ μὲν γνωστὸν ὀρεκτὸν εἶναί τι βούλεται, τὸ δὲ γνωστικὸν ὀρεκτ⟨ικ⟩όν, ἐν διακρίσει δὲ καὶ ὁπωσοῦν καὶ ταῦτα πρὸς ἄλληλα, καθάπερ νοῦς τε καὶ οὐσία· καὶ ἡ μὲν οὐσία τὸ ὀρεκτόν, κρείττων γάρ, ὁ δὲ νοῦς τὸ ὀρεκτικόν. Cf. *infra* § 77, note; § 142; § 257, note; § 412.4–7. Proclus usually contradistinguishes appetition from cognition; *prov.* 58.5–6 (discussing election) "omnis autem rationalis potentia aut cognitiva est aut appetitiva, sicut et omnis irrationalis." On the other hand *Parm.* 1188.37–38 ὁ δὲ νοῦς [scil. ἔχει] τὴν τοῦ νοητοῦ ὄρεξιν, ἣν οὐκ εἶχε τὸ ὄν.

§ 32. The characterization of the ruler as pursuing the good for his subjects is from Pl., *Rep.* I 341c4–345e2; Pl. does not discuss the master-slave relation, though it is necessarily included under ἄρχων-ἀρχόμενος, as shepherd-sheep is. The

λα'. - [62d8] Ὅτι ὡς ἐν τῷ ὅλῳ μετὰ θεὸν νοῦς ὢν πρῶτος ἐπιστρέφεται πρὸς αὐτόν, οὕτω καὶ ἐν ἡμῖν ὁ νοῦς ἀνατείνεται πρὸς θεόν, ἡ δὲ 'ἄνοια' ἀποστρέφεται τὸ θεῖον.

Νοῦν δὲ ἀκουστέον οὐ τὸν γνωστικὸν μόνον, ἀλλὰ καὶ τὸν ὀρεκτικόν, ἕν τε τῷ ὅλῳ καὶ ἐν ἡμῖν· καὶ γὰρ τὸ συναμφότερον ὁ νοῦς, ζῷον γὰρ τὸ πρῶτον. καὶ οὐκέτι ἐνοχλήσει ἡ ἀπορία, ποτέρα κρείττων, ἡ ὀρεκτικὴ τελειότης ἢ ἡ γνωστική, ἀρετὴ λέγω ἢ ἐπιστήμη· οὐδὲ γὰρ τελεία ἡ ἑτέρα ἄνευ τῆς ἑτέρας.

λβ'. - [62e1] Πῶς 'δεσπόται' ἡμῶν οἱ θεοί, εἴπερ ὁ δεσπότης οὐ τὸ τοῦ δούλου σκοπεῖ ἀγαθόν, ἀλλὰ τὸ ἑαυτοῦ; ταύτῃ γὰρ διαφέρει τοῦ ἄρχοντος· τί δὲ ἂν γένοιτο θεῷ ἀγαθὸν διὰ ἀνθρώπου; — Ἡ ἐκείνοις ἑκάτερον τῷ ἑτέρῳ σύνδρομον. φροντίζει δὲ καὶ ὁ τῇδε δεσπότης τοῦ δούλου, ἀλλὰ δι' ἑαυτόν, φασὶν οἱ Στωικοί [SVF II 1118], ὥστε οὕτω γε καὶ οἱ θεοί· πάντα γὰρ ποιοῦσι δι' ἑαυτοὺς προηγουμένως. καὶ ταύτῃ μᾶλλον ἐκδεκτέον τοὺς 'δεσπότας'· ὅσῳ γὰρ μᾶλλον ἐξῄρηνται, τοσούτῳ κρείττους· 'ἄρχουσι' δὲ κατά τινα σύνταξιν τὴν πρὸς ἡμᾶς. καὶ μᾶλλον οἱ δουλεύοντες ἢ οἱ ἀρχόμενοι μετέχουσι τῶν θεῶν, ἅτε ὅλοι ἐκείνων γιγνόμενοι καὶ τὸ οἰκεῖον οὐ προστιθέντες.

λγ'. - [62e8-63a3] Ὅτι τοῦ μὲν διδασκάλου ἀρετὴ ἥ τε κριτικὴ φρόνησις τῶν ἐπιπολαιότερον καὶ τῶν πραγματειωδέστερον ἀπορουμένων καὶ ἡ ἐπὶ τούτοις εὐφροσύνη, τοῦ δὲ μαθητοῦ β', ἥ τε κριτικὴ φρόνησις τῶν ἀξίων ἢ ἀναξίων πίστεως καὶ ἡ εἰς τὸ βαθύτερον τοῦ ὄντος ἐθέλουσα παριέναι σπουδή.

λδ'. - Ὅτι δεῖ τὰς ἀπορίας ἀπ' αὐτῶν ἐγείρεσθαι τῶν πραγμάτων, ἀλλ' οὐκ ἀπὸ τῶν περὶ αὐτὰ δοκούντων· καὶ ἀπὸ τοῦ βάθους αὐτῶν καὶ τοῦ ἀφανοῦς τοῖς πολλοῖς, ἀλλ' οὐκ ἀπὸ τῶν προχείρων· καὶ εὐφραινούσας τὸν ἐπιστήμονα, ἀλλ' οὐ τὸν πολὺν ὄχλον καὶ ἀγελαῖον.

---

§ 31. 1 θεὸν Nv: θεοὺς M (-ὺς νοῦς ὢν M^c: spat. vac. M¹) — 6 ποτέρα M¹: πότερα M^x — 7 ἢ Fh: καὶ M

§ 32. 2 διαφέρει Fh: -ειν M — 6 ἐκδεκτέον] -δ- in ras. M^c (fort. ἐκλεκτέον M¹) — 9 καὶ in spat. vac. M^c

---

distinction made here is apparently inspired by the Stoic position, which Pr. knows and approves: Tim. II 118.14-17 ὁ μὲν γὰρ δεσπότης πρὸς τὸ οἰκεῖον ἀγαθὸν ἀεὶ τὰ τῶν διοικουμένων ἀναφέρει, ὁ δὲ ἄρχων τὸ τῶν ὑπηκόων ἀγαθὸν ὁρᾷ καὶ πρὸς ἐκεῖνο συντάττει πάντα.

9. ὅλοι ἐκείνων γιγνόμενοι: cf. Hermias 233.23-24 τὸν δὲ Ἔρωτα δεσπότην εἶπεν, ἐπειδὴ ὁ ἐνθουσιῶν ὅλον ἑαυτὸν ὡς δεσπότῃ ἐπιδίδωσι τῷ θεῷ.

§ 33. The subject of the qualifications required for student and teacher is discussed frequently, see note on Pr., theol. I 2 (p. 132); here, of course, it is directly linked with the text of Pl.

§ 34. The three points are drawn from the text: (1) τῇ τοῦ Κέβητος πραγματείᾳ (as in Ol. 2 § 11.2, πραγματεία=πραγματειώδης ἀπορία), (2) ἀεί τοι Κέβης λόγους τινὰς ἐρευνᾷ, (3) ὁ Σωκράτης ἡσθῆναί μοι ἔδοξε.

35. [63a4–9] Each of the two avoids a part of the argument, Cebes expressing the awkward point in a general form, Simmias applying the other one's reasoning to the particular instance.

§§ 36–45. Socrates' answer. 63b1–c7

36. [63b1–2] Socrates says that he can justly be expected to plead for himself 'as in a court of justice,' because when the soul chooses justice as its position, i.e. when it concerns itself with its own affairs, it becomes conscious of its separate life and even of its own immortality; for these are gifts the soul owes to itself.

37. [63b4–5] His defense will carry more conviction with his disciples than with the judges, because with the latter he will be able to use instruction to convince them, while with the former he had to rely on persuasion.

38. [63b5–c4] Dealing with the points raised by Cebes and Simmias, Socrates answers the first question, which was general in purport and used only the argument of the Gods, by assuring that he hopes to come 'to wise and good Gods'; to the personal argument, which brings in the friends too, he replies that the men he will meet there are also 'better than those in this world.'

39. Socrates says correctly and in accordance with the principles of religious practice that he will go to the Gods; for it is right that the changeable should go to the changeless and the inferior to the superior, and this is why he will *come* also to better men.

40. [63b7] Union is brought about by similarity; therefore the wise and good man, that is the philosopher, ennobled by virtue and knowledge, is united to the goodness and wisdom of the Gods. Goodness in the Gods is the activity by which they provide for all things, wisdom that by which they know all things.

41. Why did Plato add beauty in the *Phaedrus* [246d8–e1] where he said: 'The Divine is beautiful, wise and good'? — Because the subject of the dialogue was love; there, the way leading up to the Good was beauty, here it is wisdom.

But if so, why, in the first place, did he add wisdom in the *Phaedrus*? Secondly, why should the upward path in the present dialogue be especially that of wisdom? Rather, it deals with *all* the principles by which the soul is elevated, though in each case from the point of view of purification: it is

---

§ 35. Ol. 2 § 2.4–8. The intention is made clear by Ol.: out of consideration for Socrates, Cebes avoids mentioning Socrates' name when pointing out that running away from a good master is foolish; Simmias, while mentioning Socrates, does not speak of foolishness. For ἐπὶ μέρους ... ἀπαγγείλας, Ol. has τῆς μείζονος προτάσεως οὐκ ἐμνημόνευσε, though this is not quite correct.

§ 36. Ol. 2 § 14.

λε'. - [63a4-9] Ὅτι ἑκάτερος ἐφυλάξατό τι τοῦ λόγου, ὁ μὲν καθόλου 35
τὸ ἄτοπον εἰπών, ὁ δὲ ἐπὶ μέρους τὰ ⟨τοῦ⟩ ἑτέρου ἀπαγγείλας.

§§ 36-45. Socrates' answer. 63b1-c7

λς'. - [63b1-2] Ὅτι 'ὡς ἐν δικαστηρίῳ' δίκαιος εἶναί φησιν ἀπολογήσασθαι, 36
ἐπειδὴ στᾶσα ἡ ψυχὴ κατὰ τὴν δικαιοσύνην καὶ τὰ οἰκεῖα πράξασα συναισθάνεται τῆς χωριστῆς ζωῆς καὶ αὐτῆς γε τῆς ἀθανασίας· ἔχει γὰρ ταῦτα καὶ ἀφ' ἑαυτῆς.

λζ'. - [63b4-5] Ὅτι 'πιθανώτερον ἀπολογήσεται' πρὸς μαθητὰς ἢ τοὺς 37
δικαστάς, ἐπειδὴ τῇ διδασκαλικῇ πειθοῖ χρήσεται πρὸς τούτους, πρὸς δὲ ἐκείνους ἐχρῆτο τῇ πιστευτικῇ.

λη'. - [63b5-c4] Ὅτι οἷς οἱ περὶ Κέβητα λόγοις ἐχρῶντο, λύει τούτους, 38
τὸν μὲν καθόλου ὄντα καὶ ἀπὸ θεῶν μόνων ὡρμημένον λέγων ἀφίξεσθαι 'παρὰ θεοὺς σοφούς τε καὶ ἀγαθούς', τὸν δὲ μερικὸν ἀπὸ τῶν φίλων προσεπιχειρήσαντα εἰπὼν ἥξειν καὶ παρὰ ἄνδρας 'ἀμείνους τῶν τῇδε'.

λθ'. - Ὅτι καλῶς τε καὶ ἱερατικῶς αὐτὸς ἔφη πρὸς θεοὺς ἀφίξεσθαι· τὸ 39
γὰρ μεταβαλλόμενον πρὸς τὸ ἀμετάβλητον καὶ τὸ χεῖρον πρὸς τὸ κρεῖττον ἰέναι θέμις· διὸ καὶ πρὸς ἄνδρας ἥξει.

μ'. - [63b7] Ὅτι δι' ὁμοιότητος ἡ συναφή· διὸ ὁ σοφός τε καὶ ἀγαθός, ὅ 40 (93)
ἐστιν ὁ φιλόσοφος, ἀρετῇ καὶ ἐπιστήμῃ κεκοσμημένος, τῇ ἀγαθότητι καὶ τῇ σοφίᾳ συνάπτεται τῶν θεῶν. ἔστι δὲ ἀγαθότης μὲν αὐτῶν ⟨ἡ⟩ προνοητικὴ τῶν πάντων ἐνέργεια, σοφία δὲ ἡ πάντων γνωστική.

μα'. - Διὰ τί ἐν Φαίδρῳ [246d8-e1] τὸ καλὸν προσετίθει λέγων 'τὸ δὲ 41
θεῖον καλόν, σοφόν, ἀγαθόν'; - Ἢ ὅτι ἐρωτικὸς ἦν ὁ διάλογος· ἐκεῖ μὲν γὰρ διὰ τοῦ καλοῦ πρὸς τὸ ἀγαθὸν ἡ ἄνοδος, ἐνταῦθα δὲ διὰ τοῦ σοφοῦ.
Ἀλλὰ πρῶτον μὲν διὰ τί ἐκεῖ τὸ σοφὸν προσετίθει; δεύτερον δὲ διὰ τί ἐνταῦθα ἀνάγεται διὰ τοῦ σοφοῦ ἐξαιρέτως; πᾶσι γὰρ τοῖς ἀναγωγοῖς στοιχείοις, ἀλλὰ 5
καθαρτικῶς· καὶ γὰρ διὰ τοῦ ἀγαθοῦ καὶ τοῦ σοφοῦ εἰς τὸν καθαρὸν νοῦν ἡ

---

§ 35. 2 τοῦ Wk: om. M
§ 36. 3 γε Wk: τε M
§ 38. 4 τῇδε] ≡≡≡ δε (i.e. τῇιδε) M¹: ἐνθά- in ras. 3 litt., τῇι sscr., Mᶜ (ἐνθάδε Pl.)
§ 39. 2 χεῖρον] -ον in ras., ˉ ex ', Mˣ
§ 40. 3 ἡ Wk: om. M
§ 41. 1; 4 προσετίθει M¹ (ut vid.): προ∼ετίθει, ∼ in ras. Mᶜ — 2 καλόν, σοφόν Nv (M¹ ut vid., Pl.): σοφόν, καλόν, σοφ- et καλ- in ras., Mᶜ

---

2. κατὰ τὴν δικαιοσύνην: κατά c. accus. to denote the dominating principle or function, esp. in ἑστάναι, ὑφεστάναι, ἱδρῦσθαι κατά, is current in Neoplatonic literature; e.g. Dam., Phil. § 8.1-5; 107.4-5; 134.8; 151.3.
ibid. τὰ οἰκεῖα πράξασα: Pl., Rep. IV 443c9-444a2.
§ 37. Ol. 2 § 16.1-4.
2-3. Pl., Gorg. 454e3-455a7.
§ 38. Ol. 2 § 3.4-7.

through goodness as well as through wisdom that we are lifted up to pure intelligence. It is better to say that Socrates is discussing the Providence that watches over us in Hades, and that this is his reason for referring to the omniscience and the all-embracing care of the Gods. If there is to be a question of omission at all, we should wonder why he does not mention the power of the Gods in connection with their Providence, an aspect added in the *Laws* [X 902e7–903a1]. The answer to this is that a detailed discussion of Providence is outside the scope of the present argument, or that the notion of goodness includes everything that is good, for if it were powerless to do good it would no longer be goodness. Actually, in what follows [63c3], goodness is made to imply wisdom as well.

42. [63b8] How does Socrates know that men in the hereafter are 'better'? — It is an inference from his own way of life. This should be understood in the precise sense that those who are nearer to the higher Gods are themselves superior. It would be even better to put it this way: if they are strictly 'yonder,' they do not incline towards the created world; if they do incline to creation, they are not yet 'yonder'; and what Socrates says refers to those who are really there.

43. [63b5–c4] There are two arguments ⟨and two⟩ hypothetical propositions, one of which begins with Gods and ends with men [b5–9], the second the other way [b9–c3]; the one imitates procession, the other reversion.

44. The whole reasoning of Socrates proceeds by taking four points for granted: two of these relate to the Gods, viz. that the Gods take care of men, and that there are two kinds of deities, those in charge of generation and those in charge of ungenerated life; the other two concern man, viz. the belief that souls continue to exist when separated from their bodies and that this possibility of a separate existence is part of their nature, and secondly that Socrates hopes to be able to join them himself.

45. [63b9–c4] Why is Socrates so positive that he will come to good Gods, but less sure where men are concerned? — Because the condition for the latter is an exemplary life, and whether he has achieved this, he will learn only, he says, upon his arrival yonder. For the standards by which human nature measures are too indulgent, and 'we must be careful,' as he says later [95b5–6], 'that no malign influence bring our words to naught,' and besides we need many others to protect us when aspiring to a higher plane of life; but in whatever state we are, worse or better, we are certainly under all circumstances in the care of the Gods.

---

§ 42. 1–2. More about this in § 45.

2. *κεκρατημένως* : besides the examples in *LSJ* cf. Pr., *Tim.* III 8.23, where, as in Sext. Emp., *adv. dogm.* 11.42 and in the present passage, the meaning seems to be 'clearly understood,' 'well-defined' (from *κρατεῖν* 'grasp'). Cf. Pr., *Crat.* 80.15 *ἀσφαλῶς δεῖ ἀκούειν*.

§ 43. Cf. Ol. 2 §§ 4–5. On Pr.'s rather artificial analysis of the argument see

ἀναγωγή. κάλλιον οὖν εἰπεῖν ὅτι περὶ προνοίας τοῦ λόγου ὄντος τῆς ἐν Ἅιδου τοὺς πάντα εἰδότας καὶ πάντων κηδομένους παράγει θεούς. εἴπερ δὲ ἔδει ζητεῖν τὸ παραλελειμμένον, ἐκεῖνο ζητητέον, πῶς οὐχὶ ὡς δυνατοὺς ἔφη τοὺς θεοὺς προνοεῖν, ὡς ἔν γε τοῖς Νόμοις [X 902e7–903a1] καὶ τοῦτο πρόσκειται. καὶ 10 ῥητέον ἢ ὅτι οὐ πρόκειται νῦν ἀκριβολογεῖσθαι περὶ προνοίας, ἢ ὅτι συνείληφεν ἡ ἀγαθότης πᾶν ἀγαθόν· εἰ γὰρ μὴ δύναιτο ὠφελεῖν, οὐδ' ἂν ἀγαθότης εἴη. τοιγαροῦν προϊὼν [63c3] καὶ τὸ σοφὸν συναιρεῖ.

μβ'. – [63b8] Πόθεν οἶδεν ὅτι 'ἀμείνους' οἱ ἐκεῖ; — Ἢ ἀπὸ τῆς οἰκείας 42 ζωῆς τεκμαίρεται. νόησον δὲ αὐτὸ κεκρατημένως, ὅτι τοῖς ὑπερτέροις θεοῖς οἱ πλησιάζοντες ὑπέρτεροί εἰσιν. ἔτι δὲ μᾶλλον, εἰ ἐκεῖ εἰσι κυρίως, οὐ νεύουσι πρὸς γένεσιν· εἰ δὲ νεύουσιν, οὔπω εἰσὶν ἐκεῖ· περὶ δὲ τῶν ἐκεῖ εἴρηται.

μγ'. – [63b5–c4] Ὅτι δύο λόγων ὄντων ** συνημμένων τὸ μὲν πρῶτον 43 ἀπὸ θεῶν ἄρχεται καὶ κάτεισιν ἐπὶ ἄνδρας [b5–9], τὸ δὲ δεύτερον ἀνάπαλιν [b9–c3]· τὸ μὲν γὰρ μιμεῖται πρόοδον, τὸ δὲ ἐπιστροφήν.

μδ'. – Ὅτι ἐκ τεσσάρων ὁμολογημάτων πρόεισιν αὐτῷ ὁ πᾶς λόγος, δύο 44 (94) μὲν θείων, ὅτι προνοητικοὶ τῶν ἀνθρώπων οἱ θεοί, καὶ ὅτι διττοί, οἱ μὲν γενέσεως προστάται, οἱ δὲ τῆς ἀγενήτου ζωῆς, δύο δὲ ἀνθρωπίνων, ὅτι τέ εἰσιν αἱ ψυχαὶ χωρισθεῖσαι σωμάτων καὶ πεφύκασι χωρισταὶ εἶναι, καὶ ὅτι καὶ αὐτὸς ἐλπίζει πρὸς αὐτὰς ἀπιέναι δύνασθαι. 5

με'. – [63b9–c4] Διὰ τί παρὰ μὲν θεοὺς ἀπιέναι ἀγαθοὺς διατείνεται, παρὰ 45 δὲ ἄνδρας οὐ πάνυ; — Ἢ τοῦτο μὲν ἐδεῖτο ζωῆς ἀρίστης, ἣν εἰ ἐξήνυσεν ἐκεῖσε ἐλθών φησι μαθήσεσθαι. καὶ γὰρ τὰ μέτρα τῆς ἀνθρωπίνης φύσεως ἀσθενέστερα, καὶ 'μή τις ἡμῶν βασκανία περιτρέψῃ τὸν λόγον· ἐρεῖ [95b5–6], πολλῶν δὲ καὶ ἄλλων σωτήρων δεόμεθα ἀνάγεσθαι σπεύδοντες· ὅπως δὲ ἂν ἔχωμεν, χειρόνως 5 ἢ κρειττόνως, ὑπὸ θεοῖς ἐσμεν πάντῃ πάντως.

---

§ 43. 1 lac. indic. Wk
§ 45. 4 βασκανία Fh (Pl.): -ίαι M

---

note on Ol. The text as presented by M cannot be construed; the easiest solution would be to delete λόγων as interpolated by a scribe who took συνημμένων in the participial sense of 'connected', but it is too well protected by the parallel text Ol. 2 § 5.1–2 δύο δὲ ὄντων λόγων τί δή ποτε ἐν μὲν τῷ πρώτῳ ... The remaining alternative is a small lacuna after ὄντων, e.g. ⟨καὶ δύο⟩.

§ 45. Ol. 2 § 6.7–11.

§§ 46–47. Interruption by the jailer. 63d3–e8

46. [63d5–e2] Every form strives to assimilate to itself what is capable of being so assimilated and impose on it a form similar to its own. This is the reason why matter-bound demons endeavor to keep souls in their grip; and the man who is going to administer the poison and who now interrupts the discussion plays a part comparable to theirs.

47. [63e3–5] Socrates teaches us what our attitude towards these demons ought to be: in the first place, not to pay attention to them; secondly, not to struggle violently against them, but let them be; thirdly, not to oppose their actions when directed on something that merely belongs to us, or to abandon to them something else instead, on which their menace can spend itself.

§§ 48–54. Socrates on the philosopher's will to die. 63e8–64c2

48. [64a1] There are three kinds of hope: that of the crowd, of the philosopher, of the theurgist.

49. [64a4–9] If our aim is to detach the soul from the body and to achieve complete detachment (the latter being the final goal, the former a way to the goal and a pursuit), and if achieving one's end always causes joy, is it not ridiculous to think that the philosopher alone should grieve when he attains his own goal? The major premise is self-evident, the minor is substantiated at greater length.

50. [64a5] Vice is ignorant both of itself and of virtue, while virtue knows both itself and vice. Therefore 'most people do not realize' the condition of philosophers, but they themselves are well aware of it, so that they will meet death gladly when it comes.

51. [64a6] Why 'to die and be dead'? — Because purification is twofold: it may mean either 'to become pure' or 'to be pure.'

Or the phrase may have been chosen to mark off the end as distinct from the action and the action as incomplete and directed towards the end. It is not, indeed, with every action that we aim at having completed it; e.g. in the case of intellection, we want to exercise this faculty always, not to *have* exercised it, because in this case there is no other goal; similarly with prayer, which has its own perfection, if *euchesthai* ('pray') means *tou eu echesthai* ('cling to the Good').

---

§§ 46–47. Ol. 2 § 8.5–10 and note.

§ 48. Cf. Ol. 7 § 1 and § 6.1–10. The philosopher's hope is hope based on knowledge, as expressed here by Socrates, the theurgist's is the ἐλπὶς πυρίοχος of the Chaldean Oracles (frg. 47).

§ 49. Ol. 3 § 2.1–6.

3. πᾶσα δὲ τεῦξις τοῦ τέλους εὐφροσύνην παρέχεται : an adaptation of Aristotle's definition of pleasure as ἐνέργεια ἀνεμπόδιστος τῆς κατὰ φύσιν ἕξεως (*eth. Nic.* VII 13, 1153a12–15; Dam., *Phil.* § 87.2–3; 136.6–8).

§§ 46-47. Interruption by the jailer. 63d3-e8

μϛ'. - [63d5-e2] Ὅτι πᾶν εἶδος ἐξομοιοῦν ἑαυτῷ βούλεται τὰ δυνάμενα 46
καὶ εἰδοποιεῖν ἑαυτῷ παραπλησίως. διὰ τοῦτο καὶ οἱ ἔνυλοι δαίμονες παρ' ἑαυτοῖς
κατέχειν τὰς ψυχὰς ἐπιχειροῦσιν· οἷς ἀναλογεῖ ὁ τὸ φάρμακον δώσων καὶ τὸν
διάλογον ἐμποδίζων.

μζ'. - [63e3-5] Ὅτι διδάσκει ἡμᾶς ὁ Σωκράτης πῶς δεῖ ἔχειν πρὸς τούτους 47
τοὺς δαίμονας. πρῶτον μὲν μὴ ἐπιστρέφεσθαι· δεύτερον δὲ μὴ ἀγριαίνειν τῇ
μάχῃ, ἀλλὰ ἀφιέναι· τρίτον μὴ κωλύειν τὰς ἐνεργείας εἴς τι τῶν ἡμετέρων
φερομένας, ἢ προβλητέον τι αὐτοῖς ἀντὶ τούτων, περὶ ὃ τὴν ἑαυτῶν ἀμυδρώ-
σουσιν ἀπειλήν. 5

§§ 48-54. Socrates on the philosopher's will to die. 63e8-64c2

μη'. - [64a1] Ὅτι τριττὴ κατὰ γένος ἡ ἐλπίς· ἡ μὲν πάνδημος, ἡ δὲ φιλόσο- 48
φος, ἡ δὲ ἱερατική.

μθ'. - [64a4-9] Ὅτι εἰ ὁ σκοπὸς τὸ χωρίζειν ἀπὸ τοῦ σώματος τὴν ψυχὴν 49
καὶ κεχωρικέναι τελέως, τοῦτο μὲν ὡς τέλος, ἐκεῖνο δὲ ὡς πρὸς τέλος ὁδός
τε καὶ ἐπιτήδευσις, πᾶσα δὲ τεῦξις τοῦ τέλους εὐφροσύνην παρέχεται, πῶς οὐ
γελοῖον μόνον τὸν φιλόσοφον ἀγανακτεῖν τυγχάνοντα τοῦ οἰκείου τέλους; τὸ
μὲν δὴ συνημμένον ἐναργές, ἡ δὲ πρόσληψις διὰ πλειόνων κατασκευάζεται. 5

ν'. - [64a5] Ὅτι ἡ μὲν κακία καὶ ἑαυτὴν ἀγνοεῖ καὶ τὴν ἀρετήν, ἡ δὲ ἀρετὴ 50(95)
γιγνώσκει ἑαυτήν τε καὶ ἐκείνην. διὸ 'λελήθασι τοὺς πολλοὺς' οἱ φιλόσοφοι,
ἀλλ' οὔ τί γε ἑαυτούς, ὥστε αὐτοὶ ἄσμενοι δέξονται τὸν θάνατον ἐπιόντα.

να'. - [64a6] Διὰ τί 'ἀποθνῄσκειν τε καὶ τεθνάναι' ἔφη; — Ἢ ὅτι διττὴ 51
ἡ κάθαρσις, ἡ μὲν ἐν τῷ καθαίρεσθαι, ἡ δὲ ἐν τῷ κεκαθάρθαι.
Ἢ ἵνα καὶ τὸ τέλος ἀφορίσῃ ἄλλο ὂν παρὰ τὴν ἐνέργειαν καὶ τὴν ἐνέργειαν
ἀτελῆ καὶ πρὸς τέλος ὁρῶσαν. οὐ γὰρ ἐπὶ πάσης ἐνηργηκέναι βουλόμεθα, οἷον
ἐπὶ τοῦ νοεῖν, ἀλλ' ἀεὶ νοεῖν, οὐ μέντοι νενοηκέναι, ἐπὶ ταύτης γὰρ οὐκ ἄλλο 5
τὸ τέλος· τοιοῦτον δὲ καὶ τὸ εὔχεσθαι, εἴπερ τέλειον ἤδη τὸ ἔχεσθαι τοῦ εὖ.

---

§ 46. 3 οἷς] -ι- in ras., ʳ ex ⁿ Mᶜ (i.e. οὓς M¹)
§ 49. 5 δὴ] in ras. Mᶜ
§ 50. 3 ἄσμενοι M
§ 51. 6 ἔχεσθαι] ἒ≡χεσθαι Mᶜ (εὔχεσθαι ut vid. M¹)

---

5. This proof of the minor is analyzed *infra* §§ 56-59.
§ 51. Ol. 3 § 2.6-§ 3.6.
3-6. A different interpretation of the perfect tense as applied to the intelligence:
Hermias 143.21-22; Pr., *Parm.* 1158.8-12; Dam., *Phil.* § 136.8-9.
6. Cf. Hierocl., *carm. aur.* 466b2-4 ἡ δὲ εὐχὴ μεθόριον εἶναι τῆς τε παρ' ἡμῶν
ζητήσεως καὶ τῆς παρὰ τοῦ θεοῦ δόσεως, εὖ ἐχομένη τῆς αἰτίας ἡμῶν. *Ibid.* 467a11-12
μετὰ τοῦ εὖ ἔχεσθαι τῆς πρώτης αἰτίας τῶν ἀγαθῶν. In both cases εὖ is an adverb.
Essentially different is *Etym. Magn.* 400.14 ἢ ἡ τοῦ εὖ ἔχειν αἴτησις.

52. [64b8–9] There is correspondence between possession and privation. The philosopher's life is outside the body, the ordinary man's is mixed up with it; accordingly to the ordinary man 'loss of life' means death, to the philosopher, however, it means the life determined by the body.

53. Outsiders fail to see that (1) the subject of the death for which the philosopher prepares himself is the soul, not the living organism; (2) its character is life pure and unalloyed, not bodily death; (3) its cause is the pursuit of wisdom, not suicide. This last fact is expressed in the words 'how they long for death'; the first by '*in what respect* they deserve death,' that is, with regard to the soul; while the words '*what kind* of death' indicate the character of this death, that it is life without admixture.

54. [64c1–2] Socrates defines the character of a discussion whose aim is purification by excluding the crowd from it and reserving it for the worthy; even these are not admitted unrestrictedly, but they are required to turn into themselves; and this is not all, but they are told to turn to reason from the irrational way of life. Such is the meaning of the sentence 'Let us talk among ourselves and not bother about the crowd.'

§§ 55–62. The syllogism. Definition of death. 64c2–8

55. [64c2] The first assumption does not pertain to the question if death exists (this was evident), but whether it is *something* and has a certain definite quality or whether it is a kind of privation and lack of definite form.

56. [64c4–8] The philosopher ⌣⌣⌣ detaches himself from the body ⌣⌣⌣ longs to die.

57. The minor premise of the hypothetical syllogism [§ 49] is proved by means of a categorical syllogism, the middle term of which is a definition of death; this, indeed, is his reason for introducing it.

58. In deductive proof a definition can be used, sometimes of the subject, as in the *Phaedrus* [245c5] of the soul, sometimes of the predicate, as in the *Philebus* [20d1–11] of the Good, in order to demonstrate that pleasure is not the Good; the definition of death given here is another instance.

---

§ 52. The contrast hinges on ἀζωΐα, 'absence of life', therefore ἀζωΐαν is the joint predicative adjunct to τὸν θάνατον (=physical death) and τὴν σωματοειδῆ ζωήν. This is borne out by the use of the article.
§ 53. Ol. 3 § 11.
§ 55. Ol. 3 § 12.
§ 56. Diagrams of this kind are not scholia, but belong to the lecture. The rectilinear type serves to analyze syllogisms of the first figure, with the middle term in the middle place (I §§ 184, 406, II § 34, *Phil.* §§ 179, 196; in the same way for composite syllogisms I §§ 131, 155, 264, 329, 405, 426, II § 77, *Phil.* § 214). For the second figure a triangle is used, with the middle term at the top (I §§ 361, 367, 379, II §§ 45, 50, *Phil.* §§ 26, 196). The two figures combined I § 370.

νβ'. - [64b8-9] Ότι ὡς ἡ ἕξις, οὕτω καὶ ἡ στέρησις. ἡ μὲν γὰρ τῶν φιλοσόφων ζωὴ ἔξω τοῦ σώματος, ἡ δὲ τῶν πολλῶν τῷ σώματι συμπεφυρμένη· διόπερ οὗτοι μὲν ἀζωίαν καλοῦσι τὸν θάνατον, ἐκεῖνοι δὲ τὴν σωματοειδῆ ζωήν.

νγ'. - Ότι λέληθε τοὺς πολλοὺς καὶ τὸ ὑποκείμενον τοῦ θανάτου ὃν οἱ φιλόσοφοι μελετῶσιν, ὅτι ψυχῆς ἐστιν, ἀλλ' οὐχὶ τοῦ ζῴου· καὶ τὸ εἶδος, ὅτι ζωὴ καθαρά, ἀλλ' οὐ νέκρωσις· καὶ τὸ αἴτιον, ὅτι φιλοσοφία, ἀλλ' οὐκ ἐξαγωγή. τούτου μὲν δηλωτικὸν τὸ 'ᾗ τε θανατῶσι'· τοῦ δὲ πρώτου τὸ 'ᾗ ἄξιοί εἰσι θανάτου', τῇ γὰρ ψυχῇ· τὸ δὲ 'οἷον θανάτου' ἐνδεικτικὸν τοῦ εἴδους, ὅτι ζωῆς καθαρᾶς.

νδ'. - [64c1-2] Ότι τὸν καθαρτικὸν ἀφορίζεται τρόπον τῶν λόγων, χωρίζων αὐτοὺς ἀπὸ τῶν πολλῶν καὶ εἰς τοὺς ἐπιτηδείους μόνους περιάγων· καὶ οὐδὲ τούτους ἁπλῶς, ἀλλὰ πρὸς ἑαυτοὺς ἐπιστρέφει· ἀλλ' οὐδὲ τοῦτο ἁπλῶς, ἀλλ' εἰς τὸν λόγον ἀπὸ τῆς | ἀλογίας. τοιοῦτον γὰρ τὸ 'εἴπωμεν γὰρ πρὸς ἡμᾶς (96) αὐτούς, χαίρειν εἰπόντες τοῖς πολλοῖς'.

§§ 55–62. The syllogism. Definition of death. 64c2–8

νε'. - [64c2] Ότι ἡ πρώτη ὑπόθεσις οὐ τὸ εἰ ἔστιν ὑποτίθεται (δῆλον γὰρ ἦν), ἀλλὰ εἴ τί ἐστιν καί τινα ἰδιότητα ἔχον ὁριστὴν ἢ οἷον στέρησίς ἐστι καὶ ἀοριστία.

—. - [64c4-8] ὁ φιλόσοφος χωρίζει ἑαυτὸν τοῦ σώματος θανατᾷ.

νϛ'. - Ότι ἡ πρόσληψις [§ 49] διὰ κατηγορικοῦ συλλογισμοῦ δείκνυται· ὁ τοίνυν μέσος ὅρος ἐστὶ τοῦ θανάτου· διὸ τοῦτον προσέλαβεν.

νζ'. - Ότι ὅρος ἐν ταῖς ἀποδείξεσι προσλαμβάνεται ποτὲ μὲν τοῦ ὑποκειμένου, ὡς ἐν Φαίδρῳ [245c5] τῆς ψυχῆς, ποτὲ δὲ τοῦ κατηγορουμένου, ὡς ἐν Φιλήβῳ [20d1-11] τοῦ ἀγαθοῦ, ἵνα δειχθῇ οὐκ οὖσα ἡδονὴ τὸ ἀγαθόν· ὥσπερ καὶ νῦν ὁ τοῦ θανάτου.

---

§ 53. 1-2 οἱ φιλόσοφοι] -ι[1] s.l., -ι[3] in ras. M[x] (i.e. ὁ φιλόσοφος M[1])
§ 54. 3 ἁπλῶς[1]] -ῶς in ras. M[x] — 4 εἴπωμεν Fh: -ο- M
§ 55. 2 καί τινα μ: καὶ τίνα M
§ 58. 1 ὅρος Wk: ὁ μέσος M

---

§§ 57–58. Ol. 3 § 3.7–15.
§ 57. 1. The minor of the hypothetical syllogism of § 49 is demonstrated by the categorical syllogism in § 56.
2. ὁ τοίνυν μέσος [scil. ὅρος, 'term'] ὅρος [i.e. ὁρισμός, 'definition'] ἐστὶ τοῦ θανάτου. There is no doubt as to the meaning (the middle term, τὸ χωρίζειν ἑαυτὸν τοῦ σώματος, is a definition of death); the double use of ὅρος, however, is confusing, and perhaps we should write ὁ τοίνυν μέσος ὅρος ⟨ὁρισμός⟩ ἐστι. Aristotle, anal. pr. I 4, 25b33, does use τὸν μέσον [scil. ὅρον], but there the word ὅρος occurs in the preceding line. For 'definition', Dam. consistently uses ὅρος in § 59.

§ 58. See note on Ol. The reading ὁ μέσος (for ὅρος) may have been suggested by § 57.2; but perhaps we should correct ὁρισμός, which is closer.

59. The definition has all the points a definition should have: (i) it is evident, for if life is admittedly a union of soul and body, death must be the reverse; (ii) it is brief, being expressed in the necessary minimum of words; (iii) it is also exact, because (1) it deals with death as a state, not as a process; (2) the death it describes is total death, which detaches the soul from the body as well as the body from the soul; (3) with regard to the soul it speaks of 'being,' with regard to the body of 'having become'; (iv) finally the definition is scientific because, death being twofold, it covers the whole kind, which comprises both the aspects.

60. Death as defined here is not the death of a form of life attached to a substrate, since it cannot free itself from the body and lead a separate existence; nor does it apply to ever perfect souls, those of Gods and genii, whose bodies cannot exist by themselves separated from their souls; it belongs to the intermediate form, in which each can exist without the other.

61. Death is twofold also under another point of view: on the one hand it is a striving upwards to the superior, on the other a tending downwards to the inferior. In connection with human souls Plato mentions both, in the *Gorgias* [493a1–3] the death that brings us down to the body as a tomb, and in the present passage the death that is a deliverance and a resurrection from the body.

62. From the point where differentiation among the Gods begins there is a descending scale of death as the principle that bestows the life of the prior upon the secondary, so that even after procession the product is in its cause through reversion, the reverting entity being as it were stripped of its own life; in sleep we have reversion while the subject survives, and such is death for all everlasting beings. The lowest form of death is that of individual animals, as commonly understood, the death of the earthly body. There would be also an intermediate form, the death of pneumatic animals, among them the so-called 'Longeval Ones.'

§§ 63–67. The discourse on detachment. 64d2–66a10

63. The object of this passage is to arrive at a clear understanding of the soul's life separate from the body. This tends to make us aware of the immortal life; Socrates in the *Republic* [X 611b9–d8], too, insists that we should not regard the soul as mortal because of the crust of 'seaweed' that covers it.

---

§ 59. 5–6. Ol. 3 § 13.2–3. Cf. *ibid.* § 3.13–15.

§ 60. Restricts § 59.5–6, and may therefore be an addition by Dam.

§ 62. The metaphysics of death, according to Pr.'s standard formula (*elem.* 140) πᾶσαι τῶν θεῶν αἱ δυνάμεις ἄνωθεν ἀρχόμεναι καὶ διὰ τῶν οἰκείων προϊοῦσαι μεσοτήτων μέχρι τῶν ἐσχάτων καθήκουσι καὶ τῶν περὶ γῆν τόπων. In this case, the series is truncated at the top and at the bottom, because neither on the highest plane nor on the lowest is separation possible.

2–3. προελθόντα ... παράγουσι : Finckh's plausible correction for παρελθόντα ...

νη'. – Ὅτι πάντα ἔχει τὰ τῶν ὅρων πλεονεκτήματα ὁ ὅρος. καὶ γὰρ σαφής· 59
εἰ γὰρ τὸ ζῆν σύνοδος ψυχῆς καὶ σώματός ἐστιν ὁμολογουμένως, πῶς ὁ θάνατος
οὐκ ἀνάπαλιν; καὶ ἔτι σύντομος· διὰ γὰρ τῶν ἀναγκαιοτάτων προῆκται ὀνομάτων. ἀλλὰ καὶ ἀκριβής· πρῶτον μὲν γὰρ τὸν ἐν τέλει θάνατον, ἀλλ' οὐ τὸν
ἐν ὁδῷ παρέλαβεν· δεύτερον δὲ τὸν παντελῆ, οὗτος δὲ καὶ τὴν ψυχὴν ἀφίστησι 5
τοῦ σώματος καὶ τὸ σῶμα τῆς ψυχῆς· τρίτον ἐπὶ μὲν ψυχῆς τὸ 'εἶναι' λέγει,
ἐπὶ δὲ τοῦ σώματος τὸ 'γεγονέναι'. ἔτι δὲ ἐπιστημονικὸς ὁ ὅρος· διττὸς μὲν γὰρ
ἦν ὁ θάνατος, ὁ δὲ τὸ ὅλον εἶδος ὡρίσατο, ἐν ᾧ καὶ ὁ διττός.

νθ'. – Ὅτι ὁρίζεται τὸν θάνατον οὔτε τὸν τῆς ἐν ὑποκειμένῳ ζωῆς (οὐ γάρ 60
ἐστι ταύτην ἀπαλλαγεῖσαν χωρὶς εἶναι τοῦ σώματος)· ἀλλ' οὐδὲ τὸν ἐπὶ τῶν
ἀεὶ τελείων ψυχῶν, οἷον θείων καὶ δαιμονίων (οὐ γάρ ἐστι τούτων τὸ σῶμα
χωρὶς γεγονέναι τῆς ψυχῆς ἀπαλλαγέν)· ἀλλὰ περὶ τοῦ μέσου, ἐν ᾧ ἑκάτερόν ἐστι
τοῦ ἑτέρου χωρὶς εἶναι. 5

ξ'. – Ὅτι ὁ θάνατος ἄλλον τρόπον διττός, ὁ μὲν εἰς τὸ κρεῖττον ἀνάτασις, 61(97)
ὁ δὲ εἰς τὸ χεῖρον κατάτασις. καὶ ἐπὶ τῶν ἡμετέρων ψυχῶν ἑκάτερος λέγεται
παρὰ Πλάτωνι, ἐν μὲν Γοργίᾳ [493a1–3] ὁ εἰς τὸ σῶμα ὡς σῆμα κατάγων,
ἐνταῦθα δὲ ὁ ἀπολύων καὶ ἀναβιώσκων ἀπὸ τοῦ σώματος.

ξα'. – Ὅτι διακρίσεως ἐν θεοῖς γενομένης ὁ θάνατος πρόεισιν τὴν τῶν 62
προτέρων ζωὴν τοῖς δευτέροις παρεχόμενος, ὡς καὶ τὰ προελθόντα ἐν τοῖς
παράγουσι γίγνεσθαι κατὰ ἐπιστροφήν, οἷον τῆς οἰκείας ζωῆς ἀποτριβομένης
τῷ ἐπιστρεφομένῳ· ὁ γὰρ ὕπνος σῳζομένων ποιεῖται τὴν ἐπιστροφήν, τοιοῦτος
δὲ πᾶς θάνατος τῶν ἀϊδίων. ἔσχατος δὲ θάνατος ὁ τῶν μερικῶν ζῴων ὁ συνεγνωσ- 5
μένος τῶν ὀστρεΐνων. εἴη δὲ ἂν καὶ μέσος ὁ τῶν πνευματικῶν ζῴων, ἐν ᾧ καὶ
ὁ τῶν μακραιώνων λεγομένων.

§§ 63–67. The discourse on detachment. 64d2–66a10

ξβ'. – Ὅτι πρόκειται τὴν χωριστὴν τοῦ σώματος ἀνακαθήρασθαι ζωὴν 63
τῆς ψυχῆς. τοῦτο δὲ εἰς αἴσθησιν τείνει τῆς ἀθανάτου ζωῆς· καὶ ὁ ἐν Πολιτείᾳ
Σωκράτης [X 611b9–d8] ἀξιοῖ μὴ θεωρεῖν ὡς θνητὴν τὴν ψυχὴν διὰ τὴν τῶν
φυκίων περιβολήν.

---

§ 59. 4 post ὀνομάτων] ∴ ∴ ∴ ∴ ∴ M¹
§ 61. 1 ἀνάτασις Mˣ: ἀνάστασις M¹
§ 62. 2 προελθόντα... 3 παράγουσι Fh: παρελθόντα... προάγουσι M — 3 ἀποτριβομένης Nv: ἀποβομένης M

προάγουσι (M), since παριέναι in the sense corresponding to παράγειν 'create' is apparently not found in Neoplatonic texts; προάγουσι in itself needs no correction, but the assumption is that the prefixes changed places.
3. ἀποτριβομένης: Norvin's emendation is supported by I § 348.4 (where the middle is used).
4–5. Cf. Pr., Rep. I 135.17–136.14 on the sleep of Zeus, which symbolizes τὴν χωριστὴν ἁπάντων τῶν καταδεεστέρων ζωήν.
6. τῶν πνευματικῶν ζῴων: souls united with pneumatic bodies. See § 168.8–9, note.
7. μακραιώνων: see infra § 528 (and note).

64. Soul must necessarily be either body or incorporeal, in which latter case there are two possibilities: either it has an incorporeal existence of its own, or it exists in a material substrate. It is not body, since it is capable of scorning the body; nor is it in the body, since it is capable of opposing it; therefore it has complete and independent incorporeality. This is what the present discourse proves.

65. Socrates demonstrates the minor of the categorical syllogism [§ 56], i.e. the proposition that the philosopher detaches himself from the body. To this end he uses three lines of argument: (i) the argument from the inferior: the soul can rise above all bodily affects [64d2–65a8]; (ii) the argument derived from soul itself: when staying by itself it attains perfection and contemplates both itself and reality [65a9–d3]; (iii) the argument from the superior, i.e. the intelligible forms: if the soul can enter into contact with transcendent entities, it must have an activity transcending the body, and if so, the same is true *a fortiori* of its essence, for contact through a body is unthinkable [65d4–66a10].

66. Of the proofs of immortality, the argument from opposites [69e6–72e2] corresponds to the first point of the discourse on detachment [64d2–65a8], the argument from recollection [72e3–77a5] to the second [65a9–d3], and the argument from similarity to things intelligible [78b4–80c1] to the third [65d4–66a10].

67. Correspondingly, the life of purification has three degrees: (i) discarding all the confusion of genesis, which has attached itself to our true being; (ii) meeting one's own pure self; (iii) being united with one's own cause by returning to that which is purest in oneself.

§§ 68–73. The first point: the philosopher despises physical pleasure. 64d2–65a8

68. [64d2–3] In what way can 'indifference towards pleasures' be said to be peculiar to man in the stage of purification? Surely he shares it with those who have achieved the civic or the moral virtues? — The answer is that the others, though they do not seek pleasure as an end in itself (for each of them pursues his own end), will sometimes seek it as a means to an end, and even this cannot be said of those on the way to purification.

69. [64d2–65a8] Because purification is its theme, the discourse starts with the lowest functions and proceeds to the highest: nutrition is common to all living beings, copulation goes with the irrational appetites, the

---

§§ 65–67. Ol. 4 §§ 2–3; 5 § 1.
§ 67. 1–2. Pl., *Tim.* 42c5–d1 τὸν πολὺν ὄχλον καὶ ὕστερον προσφύντα ἐκ πυρὸς καὶ ὕδατος καὶ ἀέρος καὶ γῆς.
    3. ἑαυτῆς: the notion of ἡ ψυχή has substituted itself for the impersonal masculine.
§ 68. 2. τοῦ πεπαιδευμένου: not in the sense of the perfect philosopher, as in

ξγ'. — Ότι ανάγκη είναι την ψυχήν ή σώμα ή ασώματον, και τούτο διττόν, **64**
ή καθ' αυτό ή εν σώματι ασώματον. αλλ' ούτε σώμα, καταφρονεί γαρ του σώματος·
ούτε εν σώματι, εναντιούται γαρ αυτώ· πάντη άρα και καθ' αυτήν ασώματος.
ταύτα ούν δείκνυται δια των προκειμένων λόγων.

ξδ'. — Ότι την ελάττω πρότασιν του κατηγορικού συλλογισμού [§ 56] **65**
αποδείκνυσιν, το χωρίζειν τον φιλόσοφον. αποδείκνυσι δε τρισίν εφόδοις· από
των μεθ' εαυτήν, εί γε υπερορά των σωματικών πάντων παθών [64d2–65a8]·
και αφ' εαυτής, εί γε εφ' εαυτής μένουσα τελεία γίγνεται και θεωρεί και εαυτήν
και τα όντα [65a9–d3]· και από των προ εαυτής, των νοητών ειδών, ει γαρ 5
άπτεται των χωριστών, χωριστήν αν έχοι ενέργειαν, και ει ενέργειαν, πολλώ
μάλλον ουσίαν· πώς γαρ άψεται δια σώματος; [65d4–66a10].

ξε'. — Ότι και των περί αθανασίας λόγων ο μεν από των εναντίων [69e6–72e2] **66**(98)
αναλογεί τω πρώτω των καθαρτικών [64d2–65a8], ο δε από των αναμνήσεων
[72e3–77a5] τω δευτέρω [65a9–d3], ο δε από της προς τα νοητά ομοιότητος
[78b4–80c1] τω τρίτω [65d4–66a10].

ξς'. — Ότι και οι της καθαρτικής ζωής βαθμοί τρεις εισιν· αποθέσθαι τον **67**
πολύν προσφύντα όχλον της γενέσεως, και εαυτώ συγγενέσθαι καθαρώ καθαρώς,
και έτι μέντοι τη εαυτής αιτία συγγενέσθαι προς το καθαρώτατον εαυτής
αναδραμούσαν.

§§ 68–73. The first point: the philosopher despises physical pleasure. 64d2–65a8

ξζ'. — [64d2–3] Πώς εξαίρετον του καθαρτικού το μη 'εσπουδακέναι περί **68**
τας ηδονάς'; και γαρ του πολιτικού τούτο και του πεπαιδευμένου. — Ή ούτοι
μεν ουχ ως τελικάς (έπονται γαρ τοις τέλεσιν), ως δε προς τέλη και σπουδάσουσιν
ενίοτε· ο δε καθαρτικός ⟨ουδέ⟩ ούτως.

ξη'. — [64d2–65a8] Ότι ως καθαρτικός ο λόγος από των εσχάτων άρχεται **69**
και εις τα πρώτα επάνεισιν. η μεν γαρ τροφή πάσιν εμψύχοις εστίν, ο δε

---

§ 66. 2 αναλογεί] -εί ex corr. M^c
§ 68. 4 ουδέ Wk (ουχ Nv): om. M

Ar., eth. Nic. I 1, 1094b23; 1095a1; Aristo, SVF I frg. 396; Epict., man. 5. Since he is different from the πολιτικός (as the plural ούτοι proves) and is lower in the scale than the καθαρτικός, the level must be that of the ηθικαί αρεταί (infra § 139).

§ 69. Ol. 3 § 5.3–11 and note. Exceptionally, the first paragraph is Dam. (with the phrase εν ταις λογικαίς αλογιστίαις cf. Phil. § 84 on irrational behavior of the rational faculty), the second is Pr., who follows Epicurus.

wearing of ornaments is a form of irrationality found only in rational creatures. One could also start with the most necessary pleasures and ascend to the least necessary.

The commentator's own division, however, is based on the objects of the appetites: they may be necessary and natural (food) or neither (ornaments) or natural but not necessary (sex) or necessary but not natural (indispensable clothing and shelter).

70. But supposing the philosopher is a ruler, will he not affect the apparel that befits a king? If he becomes a priest, will he not wear the sacerdotal garments? — This is answered by the addition 'except in so far as absolutely inevitable.'

Or rather, there is no question at all here of men in these functions, but only of the man in search of purification; if he should need sacred robes for this purpose, he will wear them as symbols, not as garments.

71. Why does Socrates not declare the philosopher inaccessible to greed or ambition as yet? — Because his object was to prove the soul detachable from the body; that it exists independently of things extraneous to the body, is evident to anyone. Or perhaps the denial of these is implied in the denial of care of the body and in what he calls the 'directing of the soul towards itself' [64e6].

It seems plausible that these arguments also prove the soul immune against the influences of sense-perception and imagination.

72. [64e8–65a2] Plato, too, makes separate activity the proof of separate existence, before Aristotle had used this argument. This is the purport of his conclusion: 'it is evident that the philosopher detaches his soul from the body.'

73. [64e5; 65a2] Why 'as far as possible' and 'more than other people'? — Because the soul can be detached only in the measure in which human nature permits this; genii and Gods detach themselves from the body in a different way.

§§ 74–77. The three points and the progress of the soul. 64d2–66a10

74. Soul has a threefold activity, the object being both the soul itself and what exists on either side, the lower and the higher; hence the three levels of life. In each of these the soul can choose three different ways, as we have said already [§§ 65; 67]: in social life that of ruling the lower, or of finding within itself the principles of its actions, or of looking up towards

---

§ 71. 1. τά γε νῦν : the point is raised later, 68c1–3.

3–5. Pl.'s argument, which relates to love of pleasure only, is extended to cover, first, greed and ambition, then everything below the level of rational soul (τὰ μεθ' ἑαυτήν, § 65.3, cf. § 67.1–2). It is difficult to decide whether the first step (lines 3–4) is still Pr., or already Dam.

§ 72. 1–2. Ar., an. I 1, 403a10–11 εἰ μὲν οὖν ἐστί τι τῶν τῆς ψυχῆς ἔργων ἢ

ἀφροδισιασμὸς ταῖς ἀλόγοις ὀρέξεσιν, ὁ δὲ καλλωπισμὸς ταῖς λογικαῖς ἀλογιστίαις. δύναιο δὲ ἂν καὶ ἀπὸ τῶν ἀναγκαιοτάτων ἀρξάμενος ἀναβαίνειν ἐπὶ τὰς ἥκιστα ἀναγκαίας.

Αὐτὸς δὲ ἀπὸ τῶν ὀρεκτῶν διαιρεῖ· ἢ γὰρ ἀναγκαῖα καὶ φυσικά, ὡς ἡ τροφή, ἢ οὐδέτερα, ὡς ὁ καλλωπισμός, ἢ φυσικὰ μέν, οὐκ ἀναγκαῖα δέ, ὡς τὰ ἀφροδίσια, ἢ ἀναγκαῖα μέν, οὐ φυσικὰ δέ, ὡς τὰ ἀναγκαῖα τῶν ἱματίων καὶ αἱ οἰκήσεις.

ξθ′. – Τί δέ; εἰ ἄρχοι ὁ φιλόσοφος, οὐκ ἀντιποιήσεται βασιλεῖ πρεπούσης 70 (99) περιβολῆς; τί δέ; εἰ γένοιτο ἱερεύς, οὐ σταλήσεται τὸν ἱερατικὸν τρόπον; – ῍Η πρόσκειται ῾ὅσον μὴ πᾶσα ἀνάγκη᾿.

Μᾶλλον δὲ οὐδὲ περὶ τούτων ὁ λόγος, ἀλλὰ περὶ τοῦ καθαρτικοῦ· εἰ δὲ δέοιτο πρὸς τὴν κάθαρσιν ἱερῶν, ὡς συμβόλοις χρήσεται καὶ οὐχ ὡς περιβλήμασιν.

ο′. – Πῶς οὐ χωρίζει αὐτὸν φιλοχρηματίας ἢ φιλοτιμίας τά γε νῦν; – 71 ῍Η ὅτι [οὐ] προὔκειτο δεῖξαι τὴν ψυχὴν χωριστὴν οὖσαν τοῦ σώματος, τῶν δὲ τοῦ σώματος ἔξω παντὶ δῆλον ὅτι κεχώρισται. ἴσως δὲ καὶ ταῦτα ἀναιρεῖ ἐν τῇ κοινῇ ἀναιρέσει τῆς περὶ τὸ σῶμα θεραπείας καὶ ἐν τῇ πρὸς ἑαυτὴν λεγομένῃ τροπῇ.

Μήποτε δὲ ἐν τούτοις καὶ αἰσθήσεων καὶ φαντασιῶν αὐτὴν ἀφίστησιν.

οα′. – [64e8–65a2] ῞Οτι καὶ ὁ Πλάτων τεκμήριον ποιεῖται τὴν χωριστὴν 72 ἐνέργειαν τῆς χωριστῆς οὐσίας πρὸ τοῦ Ἀριστοτέλους. διόπερ ἐπάγει ῾δῆλός ἐστιν ὁ φιλόσοφος ἀπολύων τὴν ψυχὴν ἀπὸ τοῦ σώματος᾿.

οβ′. – [64e5; 65a2] Διὰ τί ῾καθόσον δύναται᾿ καὶ ἔτι ῾διαφερόντως τῶν 73 ἄλλων ἀνθρώπων᾿; – ῍Η ὅτι χωρίζεται κατὰ τὰ μέτρα τῆς ἀνθρώπου φύσεως· ἄλλως γὰρ οἱ δαίμονες χωριστοὶ καὶ οἱ θεοί.

§§ 74–77. The three points and the progress of the soul. 64d2–66a10

ογ′. – ῞Οτι ἡ ψυχὴ τριχῶς ἐνεργεῖ, πρός τε ἑαυτὴν καὶ πρὸς τὰ ἐφ᾽ ἑκάτερα, 74 ἢ τὰ μεθ᾽ ἑαυτὴν ἢ τὰ πρὸ ἑαυτῆς· διὸ τρεῖς | οἱ βίοι. καὶ ἕκαστον δὲ μέτεισι (100) τριχῶς, ὡς εἴρηται· καὶ γὰρ τὸν πολιτικὸν ἢ κοσμοῦσα τὰ δεύτερα ἢ ἐν ἑαυτῇ ζητοῦσα τὰς ἀρχὰς τῶν πράξεων ἢ εἰς τὰ πρὸ αὐτῆς αἴτια ἀνατεινομένη· καὶ

---

§ 71. 2 οὐ M: del. Wk
§ 74. 4 ἢ Fh: καὶ M

παθημάτων ἴδιον, ἐνδέχοιτ᾽ ἂν αὐτὴν χωρίζεσθαι. III 5, 430a17 καὶ οὗτος ὁ νοῦς χωριστὸς καὶ ἀπαθὴς καὶ ἀμιγὴς τῇ οὐσίᾳ ὢν ἐνεργείᾳ. Cf. Pr., prov. 15.1–5.

§ 73. 3. On the 'death' of the Gods cf. above § 62.

§ 74. Ol. 4 §§ 2–3; 5 § 1. This elaborate triple triad construction, which claims to discover each of the ways of detachment in each of the three ways of life, is characteristic of Pr.; see note on Ol. and introduction to Ol., p. 19.

causes higher than soul; in the life of purification there are the ways of drawing back from the lower, of developing its own essential type, or of seeking the principles from which it has sprung; and the same obviously holds of the contemplative life, in which the soul considers the superior entities either as exerting providence over the lower degrees of being, or as remaining within themselves, or as connected with what is beyond.

75. We must take it that the disciplining of young people which precedes the imparting of knowledge shows the same three aspects: it trains them either to be moderate in their emotions, or to avoid them, or even to be completely ignorant of them, as far as possible. This last kind occurs in the *Theaetetus* [173c6–174a2], here in the *Phaedo* we have the training that aims at purification, and in the *Laws* [VII 788a1–VIII 842a3] and the *Republic* [IV 434d2–445b4] and often elsewhere we have civic education.

76. In the first argument [64d2–65a8] Socrates seems to disengage the philosopher in the stage of purification from the emotional commitments of public life, in the second [65a9–d3] to direct his thoughts upon himself, in the third [65d4–66a10] upon intelligence, in accordance with the three degrees of purification.

77. The first pertains to purification of appetites, the second of knowledge, the third of both.

§§ 78–92. The second point: sense-perception an obstacle to true knowledge. 65a9–d3

78. Of the body, ignorance is the natural characteristic, for knowledge unites, while the body is utterly divided; intelligence, on the other hand, is absolute knowledge, because it is indivisible by its very essence. As for the intermediate levels, sense-perception is the dimmest kind of knowledge, because it cannot dispense with the body, which is naturally ignorant; rational soul is brighter and knows itself, being closer to the indivisible; imagination is somehow between them, and it is therefore described as passive and divisible intelligence.

---

6. πάντως δὲ ὅτι : see Dam., *Phil.*, index.

§ 75. Moral virtue, the result of training and habituation, can prepare for any of the three higher degrees of perfection: for social virtue by moderating emotions, for purificatory virtue by avoiding them, for contemplative virtue by ignoring them.

3–5. Cf. I §§ 140–142, where the same references in Pl. are given for civic, purificatory and contemplative virtues, only the *Laws* are said to deal more especially with moral virtue (§ 139).

§ 76. The distinctions of § 74.4–6 related to the text of Pl.

§ 77. The three points being (1) pleasure, (2) attainment of knowledge, (3) perception of ideal forms, it is easy to see why the first is made to correspond

τὸν καθαρτικὸν ἢ φεύγουσα τὰ μεθ' ἑαυτὴν ἢ τὸ οἰκεῖον εἶδος ἐξελίττουσα ἢ 5
τὰς ἑαυτῆς ἀρχὰς ἐπιζητοῦσα· πάντως δὲ ὅτι καὶ τὸν θεωρητικὸν ὁμοίως, ἢ
γὰρ ὡς προνοητικὰ τῶν δευτέρων θεωρεῖ τὰ πρὸ ἑαυτῆς ἢ ὡς ἐν ἑαυτοῖς μένοντα
ἢ ὡς ἐχόμενα τῶν πρὸ αὐτῶν.

οδ'. – Ὅτι οἴεσθαι δεῖ καὶ τὴν ἐθίζουσαν ἀγωγὴν τοὺς νέους τριττὴν εἶναι πρὸ 75
τῆς ἐπιστήμης· ἢ γὰρ ὡς κεχρῆσθαι μετρίως τοῖς πάθεσιν ἢ ὡς φεύγειν αὐτὰ
ἢ ὡς ἀγνοεῖν καὶ αὐτὰ τελέως εἰς δύναμιν. τοῦτο μὲν οὖν ἔχομεν τὸ εἶδος ἐν
Θεαιτήτῳ [173c6–174a2], ἐνταῦθα δὲ τὸ καθαρτικόν, ἐν δὲ Νόμοις [VII 788a1–
VIII 842a3] καὶ Πολιτείᾳ [IV 434d2–445b4] καὶ πολλαχοῦ τὸ πολιτικόν. 5

οε'. – Ὅτι ἔοικεν ἐν μὲν τῷ πρώτῳ ἐπιχειρήματι [64d2–65a8] χωρίζειν 76
τὸν καθαρτικὸν ἀπὸ τῆς πολιτικῆς περὶ τὰ πάθη σπουδῆς, ἐν δὲ τῷ δευτέρῳ
[65a9–d3] εἰς ἑαυτὸν περιάγειν, ἐν δὲ τῷ τρίτῳ [65d4–66a10] εἰς νοῦν κατὰ
τοὺς τρεῖς βαθμοὺς τῆς καθάρσεως.

ος'. – Ὅτι τὸ μὲν πρῶτον ὀρεκτικῶς ἀποκαθαίρει, τὸ δὲ δεύτερον γνωστικῶς, 77
τὸ δὲ τρίτον κατὰ τὸ συναμφότερον.

§§ 78–92. The second point: sense-perception an obstacle to true knowledge. 65a9–d3

οζ'. – Ὅτι τὸ μὲν σῶμα ἀγνοίᾳ συνουσίωται (συναγωγὸς γὰρ ἡ γνῶσις, 78
τὸ δὲ πάντῃ μεμέρισται)· ὁ δὲ νοῦς αὐτογνῶσις, ὅτι κατ' οὐσίαν ἀμέριστος.
τῶν δὲ ἐν μέσῳ ἡ μὲν αἴσθησις σκοτεινοτάτη γνῶσις, ἐπειδὴ οὐκ ἄνευ τοῦ φύσει
ἀγνοοῦντος· ἡ δὲ ψυχὴ ἡ λογικὴ φανοτέρα καὶ ἑαυτῆς γνωστική, ὅτι μᾶλλον |
ἀμέριστος· ἡ δὲ φαντασία μέση πως, διὸ καὶ νοῦς ἐστι παθητὸς καὶ μεριστός. 5(101)

---

to appetition, the second to knowledge, but it is less clear why the third should represent the two jointly. This may be another instance of Dam.'s emphasis on the double function of intelligence (cf. note on § 31), supported by Pl.'s chance use of the word θηρεύειν.

§ 78. Ol. 4 § 7.5–12. On Ar.'s νοῦς παθητικός identified with imagination see II § 130.3–5, note. The form παθητός may be an error for the usual παθητικός. Since, however, the two are practically synonymous, owing to the passive meaning of the verb itself, and both Pr. and Dam. use παθητός not infrequently in other contexts, there is no compelling reason for correction.

79. Aristotle [*an.* III 4, 429a31] says that sense-perception is subject to fatigue when turning from larger to smaller objects; that science, on the contrary, derives its knowledge of the smaller from the larger. He ascribes this to the fact that the one works through the body, the other without.

80. Some hold that the senses are reliable and lead to truth, others despise them as untrustworthy. To the latter group belong Parmenides, Empedocles and Anaxagoras, to the former Protagoras and Epicurus. Plato, however, seems to say both; the reason is that he believes in a great number of degrees of truth, in the objects of cognition as well as in cognition itself, according to the division of the line in the *Republic* [VI 509d6–511e5].

81. In what sense does Plato [*Theaet.* 186c9] say that sense-perception fails to attain truth? — In so far as it involves a passive process, which is not knowledge, knowledge being rather an activity.

82. If sense-perception is not exact, how can it become the principle of demonstration? — Sense-perception stirs the memory, but the soul produces the principles from itself. Nothing indeed can derive its perfection (any more than its existence) from what is inferior to it; take, for example, the lower forms of science, which cannot provide the principles for the higher ones.

83. [65b1–8] Some of the senses have been given us with a view to existence, others to higher perfection.

It is better to make it clear that the difference is one of degree only.

84. Some of the senses are predominantly passive, others active, viz. sight and hearing.

85. The corresponding elements will show the difference in character between the senses, which are assigned to the several elements in the *Timaeus* [61c3–68d7].

---

§ 79. Ol. 4 § 7.12–13. Ar., *an.* III 4, 429a29–b5 ὅτι δ' οὐχ ὁμοία ἡ ἀπάθεια τοῦ αἰσθητικοῦ καὶ τοῦ νοητικοῦ, φανερὸν ἐπὶ τῶν αἰσθητηρίων καὶ τῆς αἰσθήσεως. ἡ μὲν γὰρ αἴσθησις οὐ δύναται αἰσθάνεσθαι ἐκ τοῦ σφόδρα αἰσθητοῦ, οἷον ψόφου ἐκ τῶν μεγάλων ψόφων, οὐδ' ἐκ τῶν ἰσχυρῶν χρωμάτων καὶ ὀσμῶν οὔτε ὁρᾶν οὔτε ὀσμᾶσθαι· ἀλλ' ὁ νοῦς ὅταν τι νοήσῃ σφόδρα νοητόν, οὐχ ἧττον νοεῖ τὰ ὑποδεέστερα, ἀλλὰ καὶ μᾶλλον· τὸ μὲν γὰρ αἰσθητικὸν οὐκ ἄνευ σώματος, ὁ δὲ χωριστός.

§§ 80–82. Ol. 4 § 7 gives a fuller report of Pr.'s discussion of the problem; see note.

§ 80. 2–3. Parmenides, Empedocles and Anaxagoras are included in the list of sceptics, *Doxographi* 396.11 and Cicero, *Acad.* II 5,14. For Protagoras as a believer in the senses the authority is of course Pl., *Theaet.* 151e1–152a9; for Epicurus cf. frgs. [2] 38 and [5] 146–147 Arrighetti.

§ 81. 1. Ol. 4 § 6.5–6.

§§ 83–86. Ol. 4 §§ 9–10 and note. Pr., elaborating the theme of the two senses mentioned by Pl., sight and hearing (65b2), maintained that these were the only ones to be ascribed to the visible Gods (Ol.), to human souls during their abode in the spheres, presumably with pneumatic or astral bodies (§ 86; cf. Pr., *Rep.* II

οη'. – Ὅτι τὴν αἴσθησίν φησιν Ἀριστοτέλης [an. III 4, 429a31] ἀποκάμνειν 79
πρὸς τὰ ἐλάττω τῶν αἰσθητῶν ἀπὸ τῶν μειζόνων μεταστραφεῖσαν, τὴν δὲ
ἐπιστήμην τοὐναντίον καὶ τὰ ἐλάττω γιγνώσκειν ἀπὸ τῶν μειζόνων. αἰτιᾶται
δὲ τοῦ μὲν τὸ διὰ σώματος ἐνεργεῖν, τοῦ δὲ τὸ ἄνευ σώματος.

οθ'. – Ὅτι οἱ μὲν τὰς αἰσθήσεις ἀκριβεῖς εἶναί φασι πρὸς ἀλήθειαν, οἱ δὲ 80
ἀτιμάζουσιν ὡς οὐκ ἀληθεῖς. οὗτοι μὲν Παρμενίδης, Ἐμπεδοκλῆς, Ἀναξαγόρας,
ἐκεῖνοι δὲ Πρωταγόρας, Ἐπίκουρος. ὁ δὲ Πλάτων ἀμφότερα δοκεῖ λέγειν·
αἴτιον δὲ ὅτι πολλοὺς εἶναι τίθεται βαθμοὺς τῆς ἀληθείας ἑκατέρας, καὶ τῆς
τῶν γνωστῶν καὶ τῆς τῶν γνώσεων, κατὰ τὴν ἐν Πολιτείᾳ γραμμὴν διῃρημένην 5
[VI 509d6–511e5].

π'. – Πῶς 'ἀτυχῆ' τὴν αἴσθησιν 'ἀληθείας' φησὶν ὁ Πλάτων [Theaet. 186c9]; 81
– Ἢ ὡς μετὰ πάθους ἐνεργοῦσαν· τὸ γὰρ πάθος οὐ γνῶσις· ἐνέργεια γὰρ
ἡ γνῶσις.

πα'. – Εἰ μὴ ἀκριβὴς ἡ αἴσθησις, πῶς ἀρχὴ γίνεται τῆς ἀποδείξεως; – 82
Ἢ ἀναμιμνήσκει μὲν ἡ αἴσθησις, ἡ ψυχὴ δὲ προβάλλεται τὰς ἀρχάς. οὐδενὶ
γὰρ ἀπὸ τοῦ χείρονος ἡ τελέωσις, ὥσπερ οὐδὲ ἡ ὑπόστασις· ἀμέλει οὐδὲ τῶν
ἐπιστημῶν αἱ χείρους ταῖς κρείττοσι παρέχονται τὰς ἀρχάς.

πβ'. – [65b1–8] Ὅτι τῶν αἰσθήσεων αἱ μὲν πρὸς τὸ εἶναι, αἱ δὲ πρὸς τὸ 83
εὖ εἶναι δέδονται.

Βέλτιον δὲ προστιθέναι τὸ μᾶλλον.

πγ'. – Ὅτι τῶν αἰσθήσεων αἱ μὲν παθητικαὶ μᾶλλον, αἱ δὲ ἐνεργητικαί, ὡς 84 (102)
ὄψις καὶ ἀκοή.

πδ'. – Ὅτι καὶ ἀπὸ τῶν στοιχείων αἱ αἰσθήσεις δῆλαί εἰσιν ὅπως ἔχουσι 85
διαφορᾶς· διανέμονται γὰρ τοῖς στοιχείοις ἐν τῷ Τιμαίῳ [61c3–68d7].

---

§ 83. 3 προστιθέναι M^c: προστίθενται M^1

154.23–27) and also to the 'dwellers on the heights of the earth' (§ 531). Dam., as stated by Ol. 4 § 10 (Dam., Phil. § 209), gave them all the five senses, and it is puzzling to find only Pr.'s arguments summed up here: these two senses do not merely help to maintain life, but contribute to a more perfect life (§ 83); they are active, the others passive (§ 84); they are related to the higher elements, fire and air (§ 85) and (therefore) souls in heaven have these only, while the others are acquired during their descent to earth (§ 86). Dam.'s criticism must have been omitted accidentally (§ 86 ends the lecture); his qualifications at § 83.3 and § 84.1 (μᾶλλον) may have been intended to lead up to it. See Introduction p. 16.

§ 83. 1–2. Ar., an. III 12, 434b22–25 αὗται μὲν οὖν ἀναγκαῖαι τῷ ζῴῳ, καὶ φανερὸν ὅτι οὐχ οἷόν τε ἄνευ ἁφῆς εἶναι ζῷον, αἱ δὲ ἄλλαι τοῦ τε εὖ ἕνεκα καὶ γένει ζῴων ἤδη οὐ τῷ τυχόντι.

§ 85. The senses are explained in reference to the elements by Pl., Tim. 61c3–68d7, cf. 45b2–d6. The obvious simplification is found in Apuleius, de Plat. I 14: sight/fire, hearing/air, taste/water, touch/earth, smell/air-water. Cf. also Tim. 31b4–5 with Pr.'s commentary (II 6.1–13.14).

86. Some senses exist already in heaven, others are acquired by the soul as it descends.

87. [65c2-9] 'Thought' is discursive intelligence, and in so far inferior to intelligence, but *qua* intelligence it is superior to sense-perception and imagination; it is an activity of the rational soul. Therefore when it lifts itself up to intelligence, it is illuminated by the light of intellective truth, but when it stoops down to irrational knowledge, it is dimmed by the darkness of the falsehood that is inherent in the senses.

88. [65b9] Intellection is sometimes described as sight because it is an impassive activity, sometimes as touch because it is united with its objects so as to become all but identical with them. In all forms of knowledge the object must be present; but in sense-perception there are only images of things perceived, the things themselves being at a distance, in intelligence the primary intelligibles themselves are present, in soul there are only images, it is true, but images so closely linked with the originals that the surfaces could be said to touch.

89. [65b11] The deceit is caused partly by the objects of perception, which contain a strong admixture of unreality, partly by the senses, whose reproductive power does not function faultlessly, partly by the organs of sense, which add passive elements to the activities of the senses.

90. [65c5-9] Thought is free from the body, which is by its very nature ignorant of everything, while sense-perception is mixed up with it; thought achieves knowledge of the cause, sense-perception is naturally incapable of inquiring into causes; thought grasps the essence, sense-perception reports affects; thought belongs to soul in relation to itself only, sense-perception to soul in relation to other things, so that its knowledge is severed from its object by otherness and separateness. For this reason intellection is the truest perception, because it is indivisible from the intelligible.

---

§ 87. Ol. 4 § 14 and note. – On the relation between λογισμός and νοῦς cf. Pr., *Tim.* I 399.8-28 (ref. the λογίζεσθαι of the Demiurge, *Tim.* 30b1).

§ 88. The lemma is the word ἅπτεται, 65b9. Intuitive knowledge can be compared either to sight (the intelligence as the eye of the mind, Pl., *Rep.* VII 533d2) or to touch. On touch: Epicurus, frg. 134 (p. 462) Arrighetti τῆς αὐτῆς ποιότητος ἐπαφὴ καὶ ἀντίληψις. Plot. I 2, 6.13 νοῦς δὲ τῇ ἐπαφῇ, V 3, 10.42 (without succession or variety no intellection), ἀλλὰ θίξις καὶ οἷον ἐπαφὴ μόνον ἄρρητος καὶ ἀνόητος, VI 6, 8.13-14 οὗ τὸ ἐφαψάμενον ἔχει ταῦτα κατὰ λόγον τῆς ἐπαφῆς, VI 7, 36.4 ἡ τοῦ ἀγαθοῦ εἴτε γνῶσις εἴτε ἐπαφή, VI 9, 9.18-19 τῇ πρὸς ἐκεῖνο ἐπαφῇ. Iambl., *comm. math.* 33.19-20 τάς τε γὰρ ἰδέας οἱονεὶ κατ' ἐπαφὴν ἔχει ὁ νοῦς τὰ ὄντως ὄντα οὔσας. Pr., *Tim.* II 300.12-13 (explaining Pl., *Tim.* 37a6 ἐφάπτηται): τῆς ἐπαφῆς τὴν ἐναργῆ καὶ ἄμεσον καὶ κατ' ἐπιβολὴν ὡρισμένην ἑστῶσαν γνῶσιν δηλούσης. Pr., *prov.* 30.14-23 "etenim ille [i.e. qui ut vere intellectus] videns intellectualia, magis autem ens, una, inquit, epibole (id est iniectione vel intuitu) et attactu intellectorum se ipsumque intelligentem et illa in se ipso entia conspicit ... hunc igitur imitans ... anima fit et ipsa

πε'. – Ὅτι αἱ μὲν καὶ ἐν οὐρανῷ εἰσιν, αἱ δὲ κατιούσῃ προσγίνονται. **86**

πς'. – [65c2-9] Ὅτι ὁ λογισμὸς νοῦς ἐστι διεξοδικός, ταύτῃ μὲν τοῦ νοῦ **87** ἀπολειπόμενος, ᾗ δὲ νοῦς τῆς αἰσθήσεώς τε καὶ φαντασίας ὑπερέχων· καὶ ἔστι ψυχῆς ἐνέργεια λογικῆς. διὸ πρὸς μὲν τὸν νοῦν ἀνατεινόμενος ἐπιλαμπρύνεται τῷ φωτὶ τῆς νοερᾶς ἀληθείας, εἰς δὲ τὴν ἄλογον γνῶσιν κατατεινόμενος ἐπιθολοῦται τῷ σκότῳ τοῦ συμφύτου ταῖς αἰσθήσεσι ψεύδους. 5

πζ'. – [65b9] Ὅτι τὴν νόησιν ὡς μὲν ἐνέργειαν ἀπαθῆ καλοῦσιν ὄψιν, ὡς **88** δὲ τοῖς νοητοῖς ἡνωμένην καλοῦσιν ἁφήν, οἷον αὐτὰ σχεδὸν οὖσαν τὰ νοητά. δεῖ μὲν γὰρ ἐν τῇ γνώσει τὸ γνωστὸν ἐγγίγνεσθαι· ἀλλ' ἐν μὲν τῇ αἰσθήσει μιμήματα τῶν αἰσθητῶν πόρρω κειμένων, ἐν δὲ τῷ νῷ αὐτὰ τὰ πρῶτα γνωστά, ἐν δὲ τῇ ψυχῇ μιμήματα μέν, ἀλλὰ συμπαγῆ τοῖς ἀρχετύποις, ὡς οἷον ἅμα τὰ 5 ἐπίπεδα ἔχειν.

πη'. – [65b11] Ὅτι γίνεται ἡ ἀπάτη καὶ παρὰ τὰ αἰσθητὰ πολλῷ τῷ μὴ **89** ὄντι συγκεκραμένα καὶ παρὰ τὰς αἰσθήσεις οὐκ ἀκριβούσας τὴν εἰδοποιὸν δύναμιν καὶ παρὰ τὰ αἰσθητήρια πάθη συνεισφέροντα ταῖς ἐνεργείαις.

πθ'. – [65c5-9] Ὅτι ὁ μὲν λογισμὸς καθαρός ἐστι τοῦ φύσει πάντα ἀγνοοῦντος **90** σώματος, ἡ δὲ αἴσθησις τούτῳ συμμιγής· καὶ ὁ μὲν αἰτίας ἐπήβολος, ἡ δὲ οὐ πέφυκεν τὴν αἰτίαν ἐπιζητεῖν· καὶ ὁ μὲν οὐσίας ἐστὶ συναιρέτης, ἡ δὲ παθῶν ἄγγελος· καὶ | ὁ μὲν αὐτῆς πρὸς ἑαυτὴν τῆς ψυχῆς, ἡ δὲ αὐτῆς πρὸς ἄλλα, (103) διόπερ ἡ γνῶσις τῇ ἑτερότητι καὶ τῷ διασπασμῷ διακόπτεται. ὅθεν ἡ τοῦ νοῦ 5 νόησις ἀληθεστάτη, διότι ἀμέριστος πρὸς τὰ νοητά.

---

§ 87. 4–5 ἐπιθολοῦται τῶι σκότωι M^c : τῶι σκότωι ἐπιθολοῦται M¹

---

intellectus ... et oculum erigens ad entia, contingentia [i.e. θίξει] quidem et ipsa intelligens sicut et intellectus, contingens autem alias alia, que omnia ille simul." Pr., *Eucl.* 4.2; 179.18.

§ 89. 1–2. Cf. Dam., *Phil.* § 166.7 πολλῷ δὲ τῷ μὴ ὄντι κεκραμένον, and note.

§ 90. 3. συναιρέτης in this sense is an *addendum lexicis* (*LSJ* f.l. in a different sense; two more meanings in *PGL*); possibly coined for the purpose of the present passage. Cf. συναιρεῖν 'compress, comprise' I § 41.6; § 130.4; § 176.12; *princ.* 274.8; 275.5; 8; συναίρεσις I § 167.8; *princ.* 144.3; συναιρετικός *princ.* 276.8; *Parm.* 11.14–15. 3–4. ἡ δὲ παθῶν ἄγγελος : cf. Plot. V 3, 3.44–45 αἴσθησις δὲ ἡμῖν ἄγγελος, βασιλεὺς δὲ πρὸς ἡμᾶς ἐκεῖνος, cited by Pr., *Tim.* I 251.18–19; *prov.* 59.10–11; Ol. 4 § 8.6. 5. τῷ διασπασμῷ : *infra* I § 344.4; *princ.* 164.25. Obviously derived from the myth of Dionysus, cf. Pr., *Tim.* I 173.2 μετὰ τὸν τοῦ Διονύσου διασπασμόν and Pr., *Parm.* 875.27–28 τὸν Τιτανικὸν ὑπομένειν διασπασμόν. Examples of the verb in Index; further Pr., *Alc.* 57.3; 13; 105.1; 313.15; *elem.* 98.

91. The beauty of the soul is knowledge because of its 'brilliance' and its 'loveliness' [*Phaedr*. 250d7–e1], the soul that is free from the ugliness of matter and ignorance is even more beautiful, but 'most beautiful of all' is the soul that has blended itself with the light of intelligence. Here, however, he uses the superlative in a comparison with the knowledge that depends on sense-perception.

92. [65c7–9] Though the soul has a separate existence, it is said to reside in the head; this is borne out by the fact that diseases of the brain cause insanity. How, then, can it still be separate? — Because the head has a certain affinity with the soul, in so far as it is primarily fit to receive the light of knowledge that the soul eradiates, just as the heart receives its life-giving power; in a similar way one might say that God is in heaven, though he is everywhere or nowhere.

§§ 93–99. The third point: forms can be apprehended only by pure thought. 65d4–66a10

93. Just as the soul while tied to the senses seems to be material and inseparable from the body, so, when in contact with intelligible and immaterial realities, it can be thought of in no other way than as separable.

94. If there is knowledge more exact than sense-perception, there ought to be also objects of knowledge more real than the objects of sense-perception; and if realities must exist prior to their images, the immaterial must exist prior to the material; and if the perfect comes before the imperfect, the intelligible world is necessarily prior to the sensible world. For material forms are broken up by matter and are mixed with their own privation.

95. [65d4–5] The word 'itself' added to the names of kinds denotes the authentic as against the imitation, the unmixed as against that which is mixed with matter, the universal and unique as against the qualified and the particular, and the primary as against the relative.

96. [65d4–8] Justice is the cause of order in forms, to beauty they owe

---

§ 92. 1–3. Pl., *Tim*. 44d3–6; 69d6–e3; cf. 86e5–87a7.

5. Porph., *sent*. § 31 (16.13) ὁ θεὸς πανταχοῦ ὅτι οὐδαμοῦ. Pr., *elem*. 98 (Dodds pp. 251–252); Simpl., *phys*. 1355.2–3. Cf. Pr. *Parm*.1135.17-21, *Theol*. V, 40, p. 335.35-36.

§§ 93–94. Introduction to the third point: the soul's contact with the transcendent world proves its transcendent character (§ 93); three concise proofs of the reality of transcendent forms (§ 94).

§ 94. 2–3. Cf. Ol. 12 § 1.8–9.

3–4. Cf. Ol. 5 § 5; 12 § 1.9–12.

5. συγχεῖται πρὸς τὰς οἰκείας στερήσεις: cf. I § 153.2; 246.3–4; 301.5–6; *Phil*. § 166.6–8; § 221.2–3; Ol. 13 § 2.46.

§ 95. A survey of the usages of αὐτός, (1) and (2) taken from current Greek

ρ'. — Ὅτι κάλλος ἐστὶ τῆς ψυχῆς ἡ γνῶσις διὰ τὸ 'ἐκφανὲς καὶ ἐράσμιον' **91**
[Phaedr. 250d7–e1], ἡ δὲ καθαρὰ τοῦ αἴσχους τῆς ὕλης καὶ τῆς ἀγνοίας ἔτι
μειζόνως καλή, 'καλλίστη' δὲ ἡ τῷ νοερῷ φωτὶ συγκεκραμένη. τοῦτο δὲ νῦν
ἔφη ὡς πρὸς τὴν μετ' αἰσθήσεως γνῶσιν.

ρα'. — [65c7–9] Ὅτι χωριστὴ οὖσα ἡ ψυχὴ ὅμως ἐν τῇ κεφαλῇ ἱδρῦσθαι **92**
λέγεται· καὶ μαρτυροῦσιν αἱ νόσοι τοῦ ἐγκεφάλου παράφρονας τοὺς ἀνθρώπους
ἀποτελοῦσαι. πῶς οὖν χωριστή; — Ἡ τοσοῦτόν γε προσῳκείωται ἡ κεφαλὴ τῇ
ψυχῇ ὅσον πρώτη δέχεσθαι αὐτῆς τὴν γνωστικὴν ἔλλαμψιν, ὡς ἡ καρδία τὴν
ζωοποιόν· οἷον εἴ τις λέγοι ἐν οὐρανῷ τὸν θεόν, καίτοι πανταχοῦ ἢ οὐδαμοῦ. 5

§§ 93–99. The third point: forms can be apprehended only by pure thought. 65d4–66a10

ρβ'. — Ὅτι ὥσπερ ἡ ψυχὴ ταῖς αἰσθήσεσι συμπαγὴς οὖσα σωματοειδὴς εἶναι **93**
δοκεῖ καὶ ἀχώριστος, οὕτω τοῖς νοητοῖς ὁμιλοῦσα καὶ ἀύλοις οὐκ ἂν ὑπονοοῖτο
ἄλλως ἔχειν ἢ χωριστῶς.

ργ'. — Ὅτι εἰ ἔστι γνῶσις ἀκριβεστέρα τῆς αἰσθήσεως, εἴη ἂν καὶ γνωστὰ **94**
ἀληθέστερα τῶν αἰσθητῶν· καὶ εἰ δεῖ τὰ ἀληθῆ πρὸ τῶν εἰδώλων εἶναι, δεῖ πρὸ
τῶν ἐνύλων εἶναι τὰ ἄυλα· καὶ εἰ τὰ τέλεια πρὸ τῶν ἀτελῶν ὑφίσταται, πῶς
οὐκ ἂν εἴη τὰ νοητὰ πρὸ τῶν αἰσθητῶν; τὰ γὰρ ἐν ὕλῃ παραθραύεται ὑπὸ τῆς
ὕλης καὶ συγχεῖται πρὸς τὰς οἰκείας στερήσεις. 5

ρδ'. — [65d4–5] Ὅτι τὸ 'αὐτὸ' τοῖς εἴδεσιν ἐπικείμενον δηλοῖ τό τε κύριον **95**
ὡς πρὸς μίμημα καὶ τὸ ἀμιγὲς πρὸς τὸ ὕλῃ μεμιγμένον | καὶ τὸ καθόλου καὶ (104)
μονοειδὲς πρὸς τὸ πῇ καὶ τὶ καὶ τὸ πρωτουργὸν ⟨πρὸς τὸ⟩ κατὰ ⟦τὴν⟧ ἀναφοράν.

ρε'. — [65d4–8] Ὅτι κατὰ μὲν τὸ δίκαιον τέτακται τὰ εἴδη, κατὰ δὲ τὸ **96**

---

§ 92. 3 ἀποτελοῦσαι Wk: ἀπαγγέλλουσαι M
§ 95. 3 πρὸς τὸ κατὰ schol.: κατὰ τὴν M

---

idiom, (3) and (4) technical. Some examples from Pl.: (1) οὐκοῦν καὶ Σιμμίαν ἰδόντα γεγραμμένον αὐτοῦ Σιμμίου ἀναμνησθῆναι; (Ph. 73e9–10). (2) ὅστις ... αὐτῇ τῇ διανοίᾳ ἴοι ἐφ' ἕκαστον μήτε τιν' ὄψιν παρατιθέμενος ... μήτε ἄλλην αἴσθησιν (Ph. 65e6–66a1); αὐτῇ τῇ ψυχῇ θεατέον (Ph. 66e1–2). (3) αὐτὸ τὸ ἴσον, αὐτὸ τὸ καλόν, αὐτὸ ἕκαστον δ ἔστιν, τὸ ὄν, μή ποτε μεταβολὴν καὶ ἡντινοῦν ἐνδέχεται; ἢ ἀεὶ αὐτῶν ἕκαστον δ ἔστι, μονοειδὲς ὂν αὐτὸ καθ' αὑτό, ὡσαύτως κατὰ ταὐτὰ ἔχει ...; (Ph. 78d3–6). (4) εἴ τί ἐστιν ἄλλο καλὸν πλὴν αὐτὸ τὸ καλόν, οὐδὲ δι' ἓν ἄλλο καλὸν εἶναι ἢ διότι μετέχει ἐκείνου τοῦ καλοῦ (Ph. 100c4–6).

§§ 96–97. Ol. 5 § 2. Dam. returns to the natural classification of the examples as three relating to the mind, three to the body, which is cited as the opinion of 'some' and rejected as erroneous by Ol. (i.e. Pr.), who says that all six 'pervade all being'.

the desire to mingle with each other, and goodness causes them to preserve and perfect each other. This triad belongs to soul in the first place.

97. [65d12-13] The second triad is more closely connected with the body: magnitude, health, strength. We have an *a fortiori* argumentation here: if even corporeal forms are grasped by thought, how much more certainly is this true of incorporeal forms.

98. [65d12] Two corollaries: first, magnitude is meant in the absolute sense here, not as the opposite of smallness; secondly, matter must be incorporeal, if absolute magnitude is a form.

99. [65e3-66a2] Opinion is directed on the sensible, intelligence on the intelligible, discursive reason taken by itself is directed on itself, whereas in cooperation with opinion it creates political theory, and with intelligence dialectical theory; consequently when directed on itself, it creates the theory of purification, and this is the reason why Socrates mentions it so often.

§§ 100-118. The reflections of the true philosophers. 66b1-67a6

100. Who are the interlocutors in this passage? If they are the 'true philosophers', how can they be subject to the emotions of the crowd? If, on the other hand, they are learners only, how can they be called 'true philosophers'? — The latter view is taken by Onetor and Atticus [frg. 44], the former by Paterius and Plutarch. According to Proclus himself the speakers are the true philosophers, but the words refer to men in general who are liable to emotions of this kind.

But is there a difference at all? Every word that is said is true of those who are still being purified: they still experience these emotions, since their purification is not yet completed. This way of life, as has been said before, should be regarded as a preparation.

101. [66b4] What is the 'trail'? — It is the corollary, so to speak, which emerges from the preceding argument: if the philosopher detaches himself from the body and thus enters into contact with truth, he can enjoy this truth completely only by complete detachment. This is the gift bestowed

---

§ 97. 2. ἐκ περιουσίας: a phrase of rhetorical origin, often used by Dam., cf. index *Phil.*

§ 98. 1-2. Ar. (*cat.* 6, 5b11-6a11) recognizes great and small as correlatives only; Plotinus VI 3, 11 holds that magnitude is not relative; Iambl. ap. Simpl., *cat.* 144.7-146.21 distinguishes between relative and absolute magnitude, the latter pertaining to immaterial form.

2-3. The second corollary does not serve to refute any Platonist view, since there was complete agreement on the point. It may be directed against Aristotle's identification of the χώρα of *Tim.* 52a8 with space (*phys.* IV 2, 209b11-13; 209b33-210a2); Simpl., *phys.* 539.6-542.14, tries to explain that Ar. is dealing with a mis-

καλὸν ἐρᾷ τῆς πρὸς ἄλληλα συγκράσεως, κατὰ δὲ τὸ ἀγαθὸν σῴζει ἄλληλα καὶ τελειοῖ. περὶ ψυχὴν δὲ μᾶλλον αὕτη ἡ τριάς.

ρς'. — [65d12–13] Ὅτι ἡ δευτέρα τριὰς περὶ σῶμα μᾶλλον, μέγεθος, ὑγίεια, 97 ἰσχύς. καὶ ἔστιν ἐκ περιουσίας ὁ λόγος· εἰ γὰρ καὶ τὰ σωματικὰ εἴδη λογισμῷ αἱροῦμεν, πῶς οὐχὶ μᾶλλον τὰ ἀσώματα;

ρζ'. — [65d12] Ὅτι ποριστέον, ἓν μὲν ὡς νῦν μὲν μέγεθος λέγει τὸ ἁπλῶς, 98 ἀλλ' οὐχ ὅπερ ἀντίκειται τῷ μικρῷ· ἕτερον δὲ ὅτι ἀσώματος ἡ ὕλη, εἴπερ τὸ ἁπλῶς μέγεθος εἶδος.

ρη'. — [65e3–66a2] Ὅτι ἡ μὲν δόξα πρὸς τὸ αἰσθητὸν ἀποτείνεται, ὁ δὲ 99 νοῦς πρὸς τὸ νοητόν, ἡ δὲ διάνοια καθ' ἑαυτὴν μὲν πρὸς ἑαυτήν, μετὰ δὲ δόξης ποιεῖ τὴν πολιτικήν, μετὰ δὲ νοῦ τὴν διαλεκτικὴν θεωρίαν· ὥστε τὴν καθαρτικὴν πρὸς ἑαυτήν, διὸ πολλάκις αὐτὴν ὀνομάζει.

§§ 100–118. The reflections of the true philosophers. 66b1–67a6

ρθ'. — Τίνες οἱ νῦν διαλεγόμενοι πρὸς ἀλλήλους; εἰ μὲν γὰρ οἱ 'γνήσιοι 100 φιλόσοφοι', πῶς ὑπομένουσι τὰ τῶν πολλῶν πάθη; εἰ δὲ οἱ προκόπτοντες, πῶς 'γνήσιοι' καλοῦνται; — Τοῦτο μὲν οὖν φασιν Ὀνήτωρ καὶ Ἀττικός [frg. 44], ἐκεῖνο δὲ Πατέριος καὶ Πλούταρχος. αὐτὸς δὲ ὁ Πρόκλος τῶν μὲν γνησίων εἶναι τὸν λόγον, περὶ ἀνθρώπων δὲ κοινῶς λέγεσθαι τοιαῦτα πασχόντων. 5

Μήποτε δὲ οὐδὲ διαφέρονται· οἱ γὰρ καθαιρόμενοι ἔτι ἄξιοι τῶν λεγομένων (105) ἁπάντων, ἔτι γὰρ πειρῶνται τῶν τοιούτων παθῶν ἅτε οὔπω κεκαθαρμένοι. εἴρηται γὰρ οὗτος ὁ βίος ἐν παρασκευῇ θεωρεῖσθαι.

ρ'. — [66b4] Τίς ἡ 'ἀτραπός'; — Ἢ τὸ ἀναφαινόμενον ἐκ τῶν εἰρημένων 101 οἷον πόρισμα, ὡς, εἰ χωρίζει ὁ φιλόσοφος καὶ ταύτῃ ἅπτεται τοῦ ἀληθοῦς, οὐκ ἂν ἀπολαύσειεν αὐτοῦ τελέως, εἰ μὴ τελέως χωρισθείη· τοῦτο δὲ ἡμῖν ὁ

---

§ 97. 2 ἐκ] in ras. M^c — 3 αἱροῦμεν] αἱ- in ras. M^c
§ 100. 3 ὀνήτωρ M — 7 κεκαρθαμένοι M

interpretation of Pl.
§ 99. Ol. 5 § 8; cf. 7 § 9.1–2.
§ 100. Ol. 5 § 13.3; § 15. — The term προκόπτοντες, which though occasionally used by the Neoplatonists does not fit in the Plotinian scheme of virtues, must come directly from Atticus, who is known to have undergone Stoic influence (CAG XX 248.24–26, cited by Ueberweg-Praechter 549–550). On Onetor see Introduction to Ol., pp. 11–12. Atticus' interpretation is rejected, and consequently presupposed, by Paterius and Plutarch, apparently the Athenian.
7–8. εἴρηται: possibly above, I § 51. Infra § 121.4.

on us by perfect death, and in view of this it is obvious that such a death will be welcome when it comes. The reasoning is called a 'trail', because the philosopher, following the Pythagorean maxim, does not 'tread the highways'.

102. [66b6] How can the body be an evil, when it is an integrating part of the world and a work of God and has been given to souls as a help towards recollection? — It is an evil relatively, for souls on the way to purification.

103. [66b2] What is the nature of the 'belief' of the philosophers mentioned here? — It does not originate from sense-perception; this, says the commentator, is obvious from the whole context; nor does it relate to things sensible, but on the contrary to life without the body. It is therefore rather like a *doctrine* arrived at by discursive thought and rational knowledge.

104. 'Genuine' is any form when it is unmixed with its own privation, and it is also 'true' because unmixed with falsehood. That is how we should practice philosophy, not diluting it with any element of the unphilosophical way of life, at least not voluntarily, but avoiding it as far as possible.

105. [66b5] What is the 'contamination' with the body? — A partnership that brings about an abnormal condition both for the body and for the soul, whereas in the case of perfect souls the partnership preserves each of the two in its natural state.

106. [66b2-3] 'To each other' in a context dealing with purification should be understood as 'soul to soul'.

107. [66b7] In what way is truth the goal? — In so far as it brings the philosopher home to his final destination, as beauty does the lover and proportion the musician.

108. [66b7-d3] First Socrates enumerates the obstacles to philosophy that are indispensable to natural life [b7-c1]; secondly those that are adventitious and against nature [c1-2]; thirdly the affects of appetitive life [c2-3]; fourthly the phantoms and triflings of sensory and imaginative life

---

§ 101. 5–6. Ol. 5 § 4. 5–11. – Aelian., *var. hist.* 4,17; Diog. Laert. 8,17; Porph., *vit. Pyth.* 42; Iambl., *vit. Pyth.* 18,83; *protr.* 21, p. 111.17–28; Eustath., *Il.* 23.585.

§ 102. Ol. 5 § 16.

§ 103. Ol. 5 § 13.

§ 105. 1. φύρσις, a correction for the φύσις of the MS., provides the link with the text of Pl. (66b5–6 ἕως ... συμπεφυρμένη ᾖ ἡμῶν ἡ ψυχὴ μετὰ τοιούτου κακοῦ). Pr., *Parm.* 770.30–31, uses the word σύμφυρσις. Vitelli once proposed the same correction at Iambl., *protr.* 15.17–18 ἀπήλλακται τοῦ σώματος καὶ τῶν τῷ σώματι συνηρτημένων φύσεων, and 16.2–3 μεταλλάττειν καὶ τὴν ἀνθρωπίνην φύσιν εἰς τὴν τῶν θεῶν καθαρότητα, but thought better of it later (Pistelli's preface, p. IX). In the

παντελὴς παρέχεται θάνατος, ᾧ καὶ γίγνεται δῆλον ὡς ἀσπάσιος παραγίνεται. 'ἀτραπὸς' δὲ ὁ λόγος, ἐπειδὴ οὐ βαδίζει τὰς λεωφόρους ὁ φιλόσοφος κατὰ τὸ Πυθαγόρειον.

ρα'. — [66b6] Πῶς 'κακὸν' τὸ σῶμα, ὅ γε συμπληροῖ τὸν κόσμον καὶ θεοῦ 102 ποίημά ἐστιν καὶ δέδοται πρὸς ἀνάμνησιν ταῖς ψυχαῖς; — *Η πρός τι κακόν, ταῖς γὰρ καθαιρομέναις.

ρβ'. — [66b2] Τίς ἡ νῦν 'δόξα' τῶν φιλοσόφων; — Ὅτι οὐκ ἀπὸ αἰσθήσεως· 103 ἐκ πάντων γάρ, φησί, τοῦτο δῆλον τῶν εἰρημένων. οὐδὲ περὶ τῶν αἰσθητῶν, τοὐναντίον δὲ περὶ τῆς χωριστῆς ζωῆς. ἔστιν οὖν οἷον δόγμα τῆς διανοίας καὶ τῆς ἐπιστήμης.

ργ'. — Ὅτι 'γνήσιόν' ἐστιν εἶδος τὸ ἀμιγὲς πρὸς τὴν οἰκείαν στέρησιν, 104 τοῦτο δὲ καὶ ἀληθὲς ὡς ἀμιγὲς πρὸς τὸ ψεῦδος. οὕτω δὲ χρὴ φιλοσοφίαν μεταχειρίζεσθαι, μὴ παραμιγνύντας τι τῆς ἀφιλοσόφου ζωῆς ἐκ προαιρέσεώς γε, καθόσον δὲ οἷόν τε φεύγειν τὸ τοιοῦτον.

ρδ'. — [66b5] Τίς ἡ ἐν τῷ σώματι 'φύσις'; — *Η κοινωνία παρὰ φύσιν 105 ἑκάτερον ποιοῦσα, τό τε σῶμα καὶ τὴν ψυχήν, ὡς ἥ γε τῶν τελείων ψυχῶν ἑκάτερον διασῴζει κατὰ φύσιν ἔχον.

ρε'. — [66b2–3] Ὅτι τὸ 'πρὸς ἀλλήλους' καθαρτικῶς ἀκουστέον, 'ψυχαὶ 106 πρὸς ψυχάς'.

ρς'. — [66b7] Πῶς τέλος ἡ ἀλήθεια; — *Η ὡς ὁρμίζουσα τὸν φιλόσοφον 107 ἐν τῷ τέλει, καθὰ τὸν ἐρωτικὸν ἡ καλλονὴ καὶ τὸν μουσικὸν ἡ συμμετρία.

ρζ'. — [66b7–d3] Ὅτι πρῶτα διαριθμεῖται τῶν ἐμποδίων ὅσα τῇ φυσικῇ 108(106) ζωῇ ἀναγκαῖα [b7–c1]· δεύτερα ὅσα ἐπισυμβαίνει παρὰ φύσιν [c1–2]· τρίτα ὅσα πάθη τῆς ὀρεκτικῆς ζωῆς [c2–3]· τέταρτα ὅσα τῆς αἰσθητικῆς καὶ

---

§ 101. 4 παραγίνεται Fh: περιγίνεται M
§ 105. 1 φύρσις Wk: φύσις M

---

present passage, however, ἡ ἐν τῷ σώματι φύσις, defined as a partnership παρὰ φύσιν between body and soul, is hardly possible, and besides there is no lemma in Pl. to which it can be referred; 67a5 μηδὲ ἀναπιμπλώμεθα τῆς τούτου φύσεως is too far away and does not explain the preposition ἐν.

§ 107. 'Truth' is viewed as an element of the triad of *Phil.* 64a7–65a6, truth-beauty-proportion, which is then paralleled with the triad philosopher-lover-musician (*Phaedr.* 248d2–4 in the form made canonical by Plot. I 3, 1–3; a different view in Hermias 166.18–24, where the parallel triad is the beautiful-wise-good of *Phaedr.* 246e1).

§ 108. 1–4. Ol. 6 § 1 and note.

[c3–5]; fifthly all external things that distract the mind, e.g. war and commerce [c5–d2]. For in each case the garment the soul has put on first must be cast off last.

109. [66c1–2] Does it now follow that health is an integrating part of happiness, if sickness is an obstacle to it? — The wise man will use both in a way conducive to happiness.

It is better to say that health, though not an essential part of our happiness, at least does not stand in its way, and in so far it is preferable.

110. [66c7–8] How can he maintain that all wars are for the sake of wealth? Many have evidently had other causes. — We can answer with Harpocration [frg. 3], either that it holds good as a general rule, or that the hope of loot stimulates war; or, with Longinus, that Plato calls all external things wealth; or, with the Attic commentators, that all belligerents use money as an instrument.

It is preferable to understand by war necessary war (hence Socrates continues 'we are compelled' [66d1]), such as that first war which he postulates in the *Republic* [II 373d7–e8]: according as the city increases it will need more land to feed its inhabitants, so that they have to wage war against their neighbors. This means that all wars that are necessary and, in a way, just, have wealth as their cause.

111. [66d3–7] The 'last' garment and the most difficult to cast off is, on the appetitive level, ambition, and, on the cognitive level, imagination. Hence even the majority of philosophers are hampered by these, and especially by imagination. Therefore Plato here bids the philosopher to strip himself even of this last garment; the first he took away from him when he took away 'loves and desires' [b2], using the commonest appetites as examples.

112. The existence of non-imaginative knowledge is proved by knowledge of indivisible things, such as the unit, the point, the now, as well as by the knowledge of universals (any definite shape is already individual and already 'this'); it is proved also by those realities which we cannot visualize, e.g. justice and temperance; it appears also from the fact that transcendent forms can be shown to be indivisible and incorporeal and from the proofs of the existence of incorporeal things generally. This is the way to handle this passage, not to reduce it to sense-perception and imagination

---

5–6. Ol. 6 § 2.2; cf. *infra* § 111.

§ 109. 1. συμπληρώσει: a technical term of the Stoics: *SVF* III frg. 106 (p. 25.27–29) αἱ δ᾽ ἀρεταὶ πᾶσαι καὶ ποιητικά εἰσιν ἀγαθὰ καὶ τελικά, καὶ γὰρ ἀπογεννῶσι τὴν εὐδαιμονίαν καὶ συμπληροῦσι, μέρη αὐτῆς γινόμεναι. So is χρῆσις εὐδαιμονική (III frg. 205).

§ 110. 1–5. Ol. 6 § 8. Ol. begins by rejecting the solution of the 'Attic commentators' as not agreeing with the text, then decides for the solution of Longinus, and finally mentions Harpocratio's second answer, which he says does

φανταστικῆς γνώσεως εἴδωλα καὶ φλυαρήματα [c3–5]· πέμπτα ὅσα ἐκτὸς ὄντα περισπᾷ τὴν ψυχήν, οἷον πόλεμοι καὶ χρηματισμοί [c5–d2]. ἃ γὰρ ἀεὶ πρότερα 5
ἐνεδύσατο, ταῦτα ὕστερα ἀποδυτέον.

ρη′. – [66c1–2] Πῶς οὐ συμπληρώσει ἡ ὑγίεια τὴν εὐδαιμονίαν, εἴπερ 109
ἐμποδίζει ἡ νόσος; — Ἡ ἑκατέρα χρήσεται ὁ σπουδαῖος εὐδαιμονικῶς.
Κάλλιον δὲ λέγειν ὡς οὐ συμπληροῖ μέν, οὐ μὴν ἐμποδίζει, καὶ ταύτῃ αἱρετωτέρα.

ρθ′. – [66c7–8] Πῶς 'διὰ τὰ χρήματα πάντες οἱ πόλεμοι γίνονται'; πολλοὶ 110
γὰρ καὶ δι᾽ ἄλλας αἰτίας ἐγένοντο. — Ῥητέον οὖν, ὡς μὲν Ἁρποκρατίων [frg. 3],
ἢ ὅτι ἐπὶ τὸ πλεῖστον, ἢ ὅτι καὶ ἡ τῶν λαφύρων ἐλπὶς ἐπιτείνει τὸν πόλεμον·
ὡς δὲ Λογγῖνος, τὰ ἐκτὸς πάντα χρήματα καλεῖ· οἱ δὲ Ἀττικοὶ ἐξηγηταί,
ἐπειδὴ ὀργάνοις χρῶνται τοῖς χρήμασι πάντες οἱ πολεμοῦντες. 5
Κάλλιον δὲ πόλεμον ἀκούειν τὸν ἀναγκαῖον (διὸ τὸ 'ἀναγκαζόμεθα' προσέθηκεν
[66d1]), οἷον καὶ τὸν ἐν Πολιτείᾳ πρῶτον [II 373d7–e8] ὑποτίθεται· τῆς γὰρ
πόλεως αὐξομένης δεήσει πλείονος τῆς τρεφούσης χώρας, ὥστε πολεμητέον τοῖς
ὁμόροις. πάντες οὖν οἱ ἀναγκαῖοι πόλεμοι καὶ τρόπον τινὰ δίκαιοι διὰ τὰ χρήματα.

ρι′. – [66d3–7] Ὅτι 'ἔσχατος' χιτὼν καὶ μάλιστα δυσαφαίρετος κατὰ μὲν 111
ὄρεξιν ἡ φιλοτιμία, κατὰ δὲ γνῶσιν ἡ φαντασία. διὸ καὶ οἱ πολλοὶ τῶν
φιλοσοφούντων ἐνέχονται τούτοις, καὶ μάλιστα τῇ φαντασίᾳ. διὸ νῦν καὶ τοῦτον
ἀποδύσασθαι ἀξιοῖ τὸν φιλόσοφον· τὸν δὲ πρῶτον ἀπέδυσε διὰ τῶν ἐρώτων καὶ
τῶν ἐπιθυμιῶν [b2], τὰς γὰρ κοινὰς ὀρέξεις παρέλαβεν. 5

ρια′. – Ὅτι ἔστιν ἀμόρφωτος γνῶσις, δηλοῖ μὲν ἡ τῶν ἀμερῶν, οἷον μονάδος, 112
σημείου, τοῦ νῦν· δηλοῖ δὲ καὶ ἡ τῶν | καθόλου (πᾶς γὰρ τύπος ἤδη ἄτομος (107)
καὶ ἤδη οὗτος)· δηλοῖ δὲ καὶ ὧν μορφὰς οὐκ ἔχομεν, οἷον δικαιοσύνη καὶ
σωφροσύνη· δηλοῖ δὲ καὶ τὰ χωριστὰ εἴδη ἀμέριστα καὶ ἀσώματα ἐπιδεικνύμενα
καὶ ὅλως αἱ τῶν ἀσωμάτων ἀποδείξεις. οὕτως ἔδει μεταχειρίσασθαι τὸν λόγον, 5

---

§ 111. 3 ἐνέχονται] ἐ- in ras. M^x — 4 ἀπέδυσε] -δ- in ras., λ sscr., M^c (i.e. ἀπέλυσε M¹)

---

not fit the facts. He may report Pr.
§ 111. Ol. 6 § 2 and note.
 1–2. An allusion to a dictum of Pl., cited by Dioscurides (Athen. XI 507D).
§§ 112–113. Ol. 6 § 2.15–17. Ol. has only a brief note on intellection being free from imagination when it has universals for its objects (cf. Dam. § 112.2–3). The criticism at § 112.5–7 must be aimed at Proclus, though the nature of the objection is not clear. It is conceivable that Pr., following one of his favorite procedures, had dealt with ἀμερὴς ἀντίληψις at every level of knowledge, including that of sense-perception and imagination.

on the ground that these can operate by indivisible apprehension; for these are precisely the kinds of knowledge it would have us avoid.

113. How is it that we cannot think without imagination? — Because imagination accompanies thought, not as a constituent, but rather as a disturbing element, as a gale during a voyage. For there are three kinds of necessary accompaniments: (1) those that cause harm, as for instance imagination; (2) those that contribute something, such as matter; (3) those that neither harm nor contribute, e.g. a shadow.

114. [66e1] So long as the soul is in sympathy with the body, it belongs to another; when it exercises the civic virtues, to itself *and* another (however, it is better to speak of belonging to another in this case, as has been shown in the *Republic*); when following the purifying virtues, it belongs to itself; and in the contemplative life it *is* itself.

115. [66e2–67a2] The question is raised whether a life of detachment or contemplation in the world of genesis is possible, if this is true. — The commentator says that in its perfect form it cannot be attained here, but only beyond genesis.

It is better to recognize the existence of all the three modes of life both here and in the hereafter, though in the hereafter they have an excellence far higher than here.

116. How can truth belong to the invisible world only? In that case everything here below is false. — Things of this world are also true, but yonder truth is pure; here, as Plato says [a3] we can only come 'as near as possible'.

117. If the soul is separable, how do we explain that it is not active in sleep and insanity? And how can 'the orbit of the identical be impeded' [*Tim.* 43d2]? How can 'diseases handicap' the soul [66c1]?

To all questions of this kind a better answer is in any case that we have not actualized the separate life.

118. [66e4–6] The proof must proceed by division: either it is impossible to know the truth, a supposition proved false by our natural

---

§ 113. 2–3. τῶν ... οὐκ ἄνευ : the term is from Ar., *phys.* II 9, 200a5–6 ἀλλ' ὅμως οὐκ ἄνευ μὲν τούτων γέγονεν, οὐ μέντοι διὰ ταῦτα πλὴν ὡς δι' ὕλην, ἀλλ' ἕνεκα τοῦ κρύπτειν ἄττα καὶ σῴζειν. ὁμοίως δὲ καὶ ἐν τοῖς ἄλλοις πᾶσιν, ἐν ὅσοις τὸ ἕνεκά του ἔστιν, οὐκ ἄνευ μὲν τῶν ἀναγκαίαν ἐχόντων τὴν φύσιν, οὐ μέντοι γε διὰ ταῦτα ἀλλ' ἢ ὡς ὕλην, ἀλλ' ἕνεκά του (cf. Simpl., *phys.* 388.9). Hence τὸν ὧν οὐκ ἄνευ λόγον ἔχειν Alex., *an. mant.* 160.12; 161.31; Hermias 106.22–23; Pr., *Alc.* 8.14; 169.6; Ol., *Alc.* 54.5–7; 57.22; 60.12.

§ 114. 2–3. ὡς ἐν Πολιτείᾳ δέδεικται : Norvin's reference, *Rep.* VI 497b1–7, deals with the philosopher's position in an uncongenial society, which is not the point here. VII 520b5–6 (ὑμᾶς δ' ἡμεῖς ὑμῖν τε αὐτοῖς τῇ τε ἄλλῃ πόλει ὥσπερ ἐν σμήνεσιν ἡγεμόνας τε καὶ βασιλέας ἐγεννήσαμεν) comes closer to meeting the requirements, but it supports Pr.'s ἑαυτοῦ καὶ ἄλλου rather than Dam.'s ἄλλου. In explaining the passage, however, Dam. may have argued that ὑμῖν αὐτοῖς relates to the contemplative life, τῇ ἄλλῃ πόλει to life in society. The words ὡς ἐν Π. δέδεικται

ἀλλὰ μὴ εἰς αἴσθησιν καὶ φαντασίαν αὐτὸν περιαγαγεῖν κατὰ τὴν ἀμερῆ ἀντίληψιν· ἀπὸ γὰρ τούτων ἔφευγεν.

ριβ΄. - Πῶς οὐκ ἄνευ φαντασίας νοοῦμεν; — Ἢ ὅτι παρέπεται καὶ φαντασία, 113 οὐ συμπληροῦσα τὴν νόησιν, ἀλλὰ καὶ ἐπιθολοῦσα, ὡς πλέοντα χειμών. τῶν γὰρ οὐκ ἄνευ τριττὸν τὸ γένος· ἢ γὰρ ὡς βλάπτον, ὡς ἡ φαντασία, ἢ ὥς τι συνεισφέρον, ὡς ἡ ὕλη, ἢ ὡς οὐδέτερον, οὔτε βλάπτον οὔτε συνεισφέρον, οἷον ἡ σκιά. 5

ριγ΄. - [66e1] Ὅτι ἡ ψυχὴ συμπάσχουσα μὲν τῷ σώματι ἄλλου γίγνεται, 114 πολιτικῶς δὲ ἐνεργοῦσα ἑαυτῆς καὶ ἄλλου (κάλλιον δὲ ἄλλου τοῦτο φάναι, ὡς ἐν Πολιτείᾳ δέδεικται), καθαρτικῶς δὲ ἑαυτῆς, θεωρητικῶς δὲ αὐτή.

ριδ΄. - [66e2-67a2] Ὅτι ζητοῦσιν εἰ ἔστιν ἐν τῇ γενέσει βίος κεκαθαρμένος 115 ἢ θεωρητικός, εἴπερ ταῦτα οὕτως ἔχει. — Καὶ φησὶν ὅτι τελέως οὐκ ἔστιν, ἐκτὸς δὲ γενέσεως.

Ἄμεινον δὲ καὶ ἐνταῦθα τοὺς τρεῖς ποιεῖν καὶ ἐκεῖ, διαφέρειν δὲ πολλῷ τοὺς ἐκεῖ τῶν τῇδε. 5

ριε΄. - Πῶς ἐκεῖ τὸ ἀληθές; οὕτω γὰρ τὰ τῇδε πάντα ψευδῆ. — Ἢ ἀληθῆ 116(108) μὲν καὶ ταῦτα, ἐκεῖ δὲ ἀποκεκαθαρμένη γίνεται ἡ ἀλήθεια· ἐνταῦθα δέ, φησίν, 'ἐγγυτάτω' [a3].

ριϛ΄. - Εἰ χωριστὴ ἡ ψυχή, πῶς ἐν τοῖς ὕπνοις οὐκ ἐνεργεῖ οὐδὲ ἐν ταῖς 117 παραφοραῖς; πῶς δὲ 'πεδᾶται ὁ ταὐτοῦ κύκλος' [Tim. 43d2]; πῶς δὲ 'νόσοι ἐμποδίζουσιν' [66c1];

Πρὸς πάντα δ' οὖν τὰ τοιαῦτα κάλλιον εἰπεῖν, ὅτι οὐ προκεχείρισται ἡμῖν ἡ χωριστὴ ζωή. 5

ριζ΄. - Ὅτι ἐκ διαιρέσεως συλλογιστέον· ἢ γὰρ ἀδύνατον γνῶναι τὸ ἀληθές, 118 ὅπερ ἡ κατὰ φύσιν ὄρεξις ἀπελέγχει, ἢ δυνατὸν ἐνθάδε, ὅπερ οὐ δυνατὸν δέδεικται,

---

§ 113. 4 οὔτε¹ ins. M^c: om. M¹ | οὔτε² M^c: οὐ M¹

---

sound less like a reference to Pl. than to a commentary or a course; cf. Introduction p. 11.

§ 115. Ol. 6 § 3 and note.

§ 116. 2–3. Cf. Ol. 6 § 11.

§ 117. The questions contain reminiscences of *Tim.* 71e4–5 ἀλλ' ἢ καθ' ὕπνον τὴν τῆς φρονήσεως πεδηθεὶς δύναμιν ἢ διὰ νόσον, of *Tim.* 43d2 and of the present *Ph.* passage. The 'orbit of the identical' (*Tim.* 43d2) is explained as διάνοια (Hermias 89.25–28; Pr., *Tim.* III 333.2–9; Dam., *Parm.* 254.12–18). The questions raised must be those of Pr., at least in substance, but probably also in the wording; the discussion is cut short impatiently by Dam., who in this case does not even trouble to report the answers of Pr.

§ 118. Ol. 6 § 10. See note on Ol., where it is shown that the argument as presented here is Pr.'s, corresponding to his position in § 115.1–3. The way in which

desire for it, or it is possible here below, which has been shown not to be the case, or, thirdly, it can be known only in the hereafter, so that this argument is at the same time a proof of immortality.

§§ 119-124. Purification the way to God. 67a6-b2

119. The final goal for the philosopher committed to social life is contact with the God who extends his providence to all things, for the one on the way to purification contact with the God who transcends all things and is with himself alone, for the contemplative philosopher contact with the God who is united with the principles superior to himself and wishes to be theirs rather than his own; therefore Plato says: 'to touch the Pure without being pure [b2].

120. One who is purifying himself and endeavoring to assimilate himself to the Pure must in the first place discard pleasure and pain as far as possible; secondly, the food of which he partakes should be simple, avoiding all luxury, and it should also be in accordance with the laws of justice and temperance (that is to say, free from the taint of bloodshed) and with divine command and ancestral custom (for a diet that, in defiance of religious law, offends against animal life and coarsens the vital spirit, will make the body unruly towards the soul and unfit to enter into contact with God): thirdly, he must suppress the aimless motion of irrational appetite (what indeed could arouse desire or anger in one who has disengaged himself from all external things?), but if anything of the kind should ever stir in waking or sleeping, it must be quelled speedily by reason; fourthly, he must detach himself from sense-perception and imagination, except in so far as it is necessary to make use of them; in the fifth place, the man who wants to be set free from the plurality of genesis must dissociate himself from the multifarious variety of opinion; the sixth and last precept is to

---

Dam. qualified this view at § 115.4–5 does not make it strictly necessary for him to drop the present section, or to change its purport, as Ol. did.

§ 119. Cf. Ol. 1 § 5.1–7, where the same correlation is found: civic virtue belongs to the domain of Zeus the King, the Demiurge of the *Timaeus*, purificatory virtue to that of Kronos (=κορόνους or καθαρὸς νοῦς) and contemplative virtue to that of Uranus (παρὰ τὸ τὰ ἄνω ὁρᾶν, Uranus representing the intelligible-intellective order, which is oriented toward the purely intelligible, Pr., *theol.* IV 5; 8). The καθαρόν (or καθαρός) of Ph. 67b2 is identified as Kronos, Pure Intelligence.

§§ 120–123. Several elements in this disquisition on ritual and moral purity seem to point to Porphyry: the protreptic tirade in the manner of Plotinus, § 120 (cf. Porph., *abst.* 1,30–33 and the extract from Amelius in Dam., *Phil.* § 152), the argument for vegetarianism, coinciding in many respects with Porphyry's (however, Pr. was also a vegetarian, cf. Marin., *vit. Pr.* 12), the role of evil demons in § 123, and some verbal correspondences indicated below.

ἢ τὸ τρίτον ἐξ ἀνάγκης ἐκεῖ, ὥστε καὶ τῷ λόγῳ τούτῳ συναποδείκνυσθαι τὴν ἀθανασίαν.

§§ 119-124. Purification the way to God. 67a6-b2

δ ριη'. – Ὅτι τέλος τῷ μὲν πολιτικῷ συναφθῆναι τῷ πάντων προνοοῦντι θεῷ, 119
καθαρτικῷ δὲ τῷ πάντων ἐξῃρημένῳ καὶ ἑαυτῷ συνόντι, τῷ θεωρητικῷ δὲ ⟨τῷ⟩
ἡνωμένῳ τοῖς πρὸ ἑαυτοῦ καὶ ἐκείνων εἶναι μᾶλλον ἢ ἑαυτοῦ βουλομένῳ· διόπερ
φησὶ 'μὴ καθαρῷ καθαροῦ ἐφάπτεσθαι' [b2].

ριθ'. – Ὅτι χρὴ τὸν καθαιρόμενον καὶ τῷ καθαρῷ σπουδάζοντα ὁμοιοῦσθαι 120
α'β' πρῶτον μὲν ἡδονὰς καὶ λύπας ἀποσκευάζεσθαι κατὰ δύναμιν· δεύτερον δὲ τροφὴν
ἀπέριττον τρέφεσθαι τρυφῆς ἔξω οὖσαν, ἔτι δὲ καὶ ὅση δικαία καὶ σώφρων
(αὕτη δέ ἐστιν ἡ ἀναίμακτος καὶ ἀκηλίδωτος) ὅση τε ὁσία καὶ πατριάζουσα
(ἡ γὰρ ἀσεβὴς καὶ ἀδικοῦσα τὰ ζῷα καὶ παχύνουσα τὸ πνεῦμα δύσχρηστον 5
γ' τῇ ψυχῇ τὸ σῶμα παρέχεται καὶ ἀνεπιτήδειον πρὸς θεοῦ συναφήν)· τρίτον τὴν
πλημμελῆ κίνησιν ἀποκόπτειν τῆς ὀρεκτικῆς ἀλογίας (τίνος γὰρ ἂν ἐπιθυμήσειεν
ἢ ἐπὶ τίνι ἂν ὀργισθείη ὁ τῶν ἔξω πάντων ἀφιστάμενος;), εἰ δέ ποτε κινηθείη
τι τοιοῦτον ὕπαρ ἢ ὄναρ, ταχίστην αὐτοῦ γίγνεσθαι τὴν καταστολὴν ἀπὸ τοῦ
δ' λόγου· τέταρτον ἀφίστα|σθαι τῶν αἰσθήσεων καὶ τῶν φαντασιῶν, ὅσον μὴ 10(109)
ε' ἀναγκαῖον χρῆσθαι αὐταῖς· πέμπτον χωρίζεσθαι τῶν παντοδαπῶν δοξῶν τὸν
ς' ἀπαλλαγῆναι βουλόμενον τοῦ πλήθους τῆς γενέσεως· ἕκτον ἐπὶ πᾶσι παράγγελμα,

---

§ 118. 3 ἀνάγκης] -κ- ins. M^c
§ 119. 2 τῷ³ Nv: om. M — 3 βουλομένῳ Fh: -οις M
§ 120. 1 καθαιρόμενον] -ό- in ras. M^c — 8 ἐπὶ τίνι μ : ἐπί τινι M

---

§ 120. 4. ἀκηλίδωτος : used by Porph., abst. 2,46.
ibid. πατριάζουσα : in this meaning ('following ancestral usage') addendum lexicis; LSJ and PGL have only 'resemble one's father'. Cf., however, Porph., abst. 2,20, where the noun πάτρια is used in arguing the same thesis, that the ancestral cult practices were vegetarian: διὰ πολλῶν δὲ ὁ Θεόφραστος ⟨ἐκ⟩ τῶν παρ' ἑκάστοις πατρίων ἐπιδείξας ὅτι τὸ παλαιὸν τῶν θυσιῶν διὰ τῶν καρπῶν ἦν, and 2,59 ἐπεὶ καὶ 'Απόλλων παραινῶν θύειν κατὰ τὰ πάτρια..., ἐπανάγειν ἔοικεν εἰς τὸ παλαιὸν ἔθος· τὸ δὲ παλαιὸν διὰ ποπάνων καὶ καρπῶν ἦν.
5. ἀσεβής : abst. 3,26 δικαίως ἄν τις ἀσεβὴς κρίνοιτο τῶν οἰκείων ... μὴ ἀπεχόμενος.
ibid. ἀδικοῦσα τὰ ζῷα : abst. book 3, esp. 18–19.
ibid. παχύνουσα τὸ πνεῦμα : Porph., de antro 11 καὶ τάς γε φιλοσωμάτους ὑγρὸν τὸ πνεῦμα ἐφελκομένας παχύνειν τοῦτο ὡς νέφος.
6–10. Cf. Plot. I 2, 5.21-31; Porph., sent. 32 (p. 34.11–19).
10–11. Cf. Porph., abst. 4,20 μιαίνεται τοίνυν ἡ διάνοια, μᾶλλον δὲ ὁ διανοούμενος, ὅταν ἢ φανταστικῇ ἢ δοξαστικῇ ἀναμίγνυται.

escape from the complexity of discursive reason and seek the simpler forms of demonstration and division as a preparation for the undivided activity of the intellect.

121. The same relation that exists between education and life in society (the function of education being to quiet down the wild turmoil of birth and to make the soul fit to attain complete harmony), exists also between the life of purification and the life of contemplation: purification checks the downward trend to prepare us for the effort of ascension, and this is also the aim of the purifying ceremonies that precede sacred rites. If one is to be united with the higher powers, it is necessary to detach oneself from lower influences first.

122. Any disposition on our part inevitably assimilates us to one particular category of beings in the universe. If we are pure, we join the pure, if impure, the impure, i.e. matter-bound demons in the latter case, the Gods in the former, or, if our condition is intermediate, the intermediate kinds. In each case similarity is the binding force that unites things of one kind to form a continuous whole, as water does with water and air with air. Therefore, when approaching God, we should strengthen our likeness to him, as far as it lies in our power, through purity; for, as Plato says, 'it is unlawful to touch the Pure without being pure'. It is called 'unlawful', because God must not be soiled by an impure contact; at the same time it is impossible, since darkness can never approach light.

123. Purity is threefold: of the soul, of the body, of external things. We must strive for all of these, so that everything, not only ourselves, but our tools also, may be flooded by divine illumination, that no demoniac darkness may settle on our soiled tools, turning away our sight from the Gods, and that our soul may travel lighter on her way to the divine and, so far from being burdened by those tools, may derive strength from them for the upward journey, since she is still tied to them as far as natural life is concerned. If, on the other hand, we come to God with an impure mind, though pure externally, we lose our pains; for then the soul by her way of life remains chained to the evil genii she resembles.

---

14. πρὸς συνεθισμὸν τῆς ἀμερίστου νοήσεως : from Plot. I 3, 3.5–7 τὰ μὲν δὴ μαθήματα δοτέον πρὸς συνεθισμὸν κατανοήσεως καὶ πίστεως ἀσωμάτου. The later standard form of the quotation, apparently deriving from Proclus, is πρὸς συνεθισμὸν τῆς ἀσωμάτου φύσεως (Pr., *Eucl.* 21.20–22; Amm., *isag.* 12.26–27; Philop., *isag.* 6.15–16; *an.* 3.12–13; etc., see Henry-Schwyzer, *ed. maior*; Ps.-El. 18,29).

§ 121. 1–2. Pl., *Tim.* 42c5–d1 συνεπισπώμενος τὸν πολὺν ὄχλον καὶ ὕστερον προσφύντα ἐκ πυρὸς καὶ ὕδατος καὶ ἀέρος καὶ γῆς, θορυβώδη καὶ ἄλογον ὄντα.

§§ 122–123. An attempt to translate moral, ritual and physical purity into terms of metaphysics: purity=transcendence. Some related passages: Porph., *abst.* 4,20; Iambl., *myst.* 241.1–242.17; Hierocl., *carm. aur.* 478–482; Pr., *Alc.* 301.7–15.

τὴν ποικιλίαν τῆς διανοίας ἐκφεύγειν καὶ τὰς ἁπλουστέρας μεταδιώκειν ἀποδείξεις καὶ διαιρέσεις πρὸς συνεθισμὸν τῆς ἀμερίστου νοήσεως.

ϱκ΄. – Ὅτι ὃν ἔχει λόγον ἡ παιδεία πρὸς τὴν πολιτικὴν ζωήν, τὸν πολὺν θόρυβον συστέλλουσα τῆς γενέσεως καὶ ἐπιτήδειον ποιοῦσα τὴν ψυχὴν εἰς τὴν τελείαν κατακόσμησιν, τοῦτον ἔχει τὸν λόγον ἡ καθαρτικὴ πρὸς τὴν θεωρητικήν, λύουσα τὴν κάτω νεῦσιν εἰς παρασκευὴν τῆς πρὸς τὸ ἄνω ἀνατάσεως· ὃ βούλονται καὶ οἱ καθαρμοὶ ποιεῖν πρὸ τῶν ἱερῶν. ἀνάγκη γὰρ τὸν μέλλοντα συναφθῆναι τοῖς κρείττοσι πρότερον χωρισθῆναι τῶν χειρόνων.

ϱκα΄. – Ὅτι πᾶσα ἡμῶν διάθεσις ἐξομοιοῖ πάντως ἡμᾶς πρός τι τῶν κοσμικῶν γενῶν. ἐὰν μὲν οὖν καθαροὶ ὦμεν, τοῖς καθαροῖς συναπτόμεθα, ἐὰν δὲ ἀκάθαρτοι, τοῖς ἀκαθάρτοις· οὕτω μὲν δαίμοσιν ἐνύλοις, ἐκείνως δὲ τοῖς θεοῖς· εἰ δὲ μέσως ἔχομεν, τοῖς μέσοις. ἀεὶ γὰρ ἡ ὁμοιότης συνάπτει καὶ εἰς μίαν συνέχειαν ἄγει τὰ ὁμοειδῆ, καθάπερ ὕδωρ ὕδατι καὶ ἀὴρ ἀέρι. διὸ προσιόντα θεῷ τὴν πρὸς αὐτὸν ὁμοιότητα εἰς δύναμιν αὐξητέον διὰ τῆς καθαρότητος. 'οὐ γὰρ θεμιτόν', φησί, 'τὸ μὴ καθαρὸν ἅπτεσθαι τοῦ καθαροῦ'. τὸ μὲν οὖν ἀθέμιτον, ὅτι οὐ θέμις μολύνεσθαι τὸν θεόν· τὸ δὲ αὐτὸ καὶ ἀδύνατον, οὐ γὰρ ἂν πελάσειεν τῷ φωτὶ τὸ σκότος.

ϱκβ΄. – Ὅτι τριπλῆ ἡ καθαρότης, ἡ μὲν ψυχῆς, ἡ δὲ σώματος, ἡ δὲ τῶν ἐκτός. ἀντιποιητέον οὖν ἁπάσης, ἵνα καὶ πάντα, ἡμεῖς τε καὶ τὰ ἡμέτερα ὄργανα, θείας ἐλλάμψεως πληρωθῇ, καὶ ἵνα μὴ τοῖς ῥυπαροῖς ἡμῶν ὀργάνοις ἐνιζάνῃ δαι|μόνιόν τι σκότος, ἀποστρέφον ἡμῶν τὴν ὄψιν ἀπὸ τῶν θεῶν, καὶ ἵνα κουφότερον ἡ ψυχὴ πρὸς τὸ θεῖον ἀνατείνηται μὴ βαρυνομένη ὑπὸ τῶν ὀργάνων, τοὐναντίον δὲ καὶ συνεπιρρωννύηται ὑπ' αὐτῶν εἰς ἀναγωγήν, ἅτε συνδεδεμένη ἔτι αὐτοῖς τὸν φυσικὸν τρόπον. εἰ δὲ ψυχῇ μὲν ἀκαθάρτῳ, τοῖς δὲ ἔξω καθαροῖς προσίωμεν, μάταιος ὁ πόνος· ἡ γὰρ ψυχὴ κατὰ τὴν ζωὴν συγκεκόλληται δαίμοσι πονηροῖς κατὰ τὴν ὁμοιότητα.

---

§ 121. 1 τὸν] in ras. 2 litt. M^c
§ 122. 4 ἔχομεν μ: -ω- M
§ 123. 6 συνεπιρωννύηται M — 8 πόνος] πόν- in ras. M¹ | γὰρ in ras. M^x

---

§ 122. 4–5. Cf. Pr., elem. 32 πᾶσα δὲ κοινωνία καὶ συναφὴ πᾶσα δι' ὁμοιότητος (with Dodds' note, p. 219).
7–8. Porph., abst. 4,20 καὶ γάρ πως καὶ ὁ μολυσμὸς καὶ ἡ μίανσις δηλοῖ τὴν μῖξιν τὴν ἑτέρου γένους πρὸς ἕτερον. Iambl., myst. 242.8–10 διότι τῷ ζῶντι τὸ μὴ ζῶν, ὥσπερ τῷ καθαρῷ τὸ ῥυπαρὸν καὶ τῷ ἐν ἕξει τὸ ἐν στερήσει, μολυσμόν τινα ἐντίθησιν. Simpl., Epict. 115.6 μολυσμὸς γάρ ἐστι τῷ καθαρῷ ἡ τοῦ ἀκαθάρτου μῖξις.
8–9. Iambl., myst. 204.7–13 ἃ δ' οὔτε ὅλως ἔχει φύσιν διαιρετὴν οὔτε δύναμιν κέκτηται τοῦ εἰσδέχεσθαι εἰς ἑαυτὰ τὰ ἀπὸ τῆς ὕλης πάθη, τί ἂν ἀπὸ τῶν ἐνύλων μιανθείη; πῶς δ' ἔνεστιν ἀπὸ τῶν ἐμῶν παθημάτων ἢ ἄλλου του τῶν ἀνθρώπων ἐπιβολοῦσθαι τὸ θεῖον, ὃ μηδὲν ἔχει κοινὸν πρὸς ἡμᾶς τῆς ἀνθρωπίνης ἀσθενείας κρεῖττον προϋπάρχον;
§ 123. 8–9. δαίμοσι πονηροῖς : cf. infra, note on § 486.

124. [67b1] Are pure and true identical, as Plato says? — 'Pure' means that a thing is separate from everything else, and 'true' that it is exactly what it is, and this is apparently the reason why it is necessary to become pure first, before we can attain truth. Therefore, since we are not yet pure, because we have not yet died, it is said that 'we shall know the truth when he have arrived yonder' [69d5–6].

§ 125. On hope. 67b8

125. Corresponding to the two kinds of opinion, which may come from below or from above, the one certain, the other uncertain, there is hope resulting from knowledge (the kind referred to here) as well as one derived from sense-perception and surmise.

§§ 126–137. On separation, purification, death: Socrates' conclusion. 67c5–68c4

126. [67c5–d2] Separation is not the same thing as purification; the body, indeed, is not purified when separated from the soul, but rather it becomes unclean and therefore causes uncleanness.

The statement made above [§124.1–2] also needs correction: in current usage a thing does not become cleaner when it is separated from the superior. The fact is expressed clearly in the *Sophist* [227d6–7]: 'Purification is, of course, keeping the rest, while discarding anything that might be inferior'. The Curetes, too, surround the creative Gods, because they stoop to a lower level of being.

127. [67d4–5] Death is not identical with purification, only the death that detaches from the inferior is. For death is a process of separation, as

---

§ 124. The point is that the pure and the true are really identical, not that they are different successive stages, as the wording might seem to imply.

§ 125. Ol. 7 § 1.9–13, cf. § 6.1–10, and notes.

1–2. See Ol. 5 § 13, and above § 103.

§§ 126–127. Ol. 7 § 2.12–15. On the relation between purification, separation, and death: (§ 126) not all separation is purification, despite *Ph.* 67c5–d2; (§ 127) not all death is purification, despite *Ph.* 67d4–5.

§ 126.1–2. Iambl., *myst.* 241.12–17 ἔτι τοίνυν τῶν μὲν ἀνθρωπείων σωμάτων, ἐπειδὰν ἀπολίπῃ αὐτὰ ἡ ψυχή, οὐκ ἔξεστι θιγγάνειν· τῆς γὰρ θείας ζωῆς ἴχνος τι ἢ εἴδωλον ἢ ἔμφασις ἐναποσβέννυται ἐν τῷ σώματι κατὰ τὸν θάνατον· τῶν δὲ ἄλλων ζῴων οὐκέτι ἀνόσιον ἅπτεσθαι τεθνηκότων, ἐπειδὴ οὐδὲ κεκοινωνήκασι τῆς θειοτέρας ζωῆς. This is an attempt to explain *why* the dead body becomes ritually unclean.

3–6. The use of ἀλλά, in spite of the fact that lines 3–6 simply confirm lines 1–2, indicates that this is an observation by Dam., who thinks that in view of lines 1–2 the preceding statement in § 124.1–2 should be revised also.

6–7. The Curetes found their way into Neoplatonic metaphysics via the *Orphica* (frgs. 150–151, 185–186). They are interpreted by Pr., *theol.* V 3, 253.36–51, and esp. V 35, 322.22–324.46, as the second triad of the intellective (or demiurgic)

ρκγ'. – [67b1] *Ἆρα ταὐτὸν καθαρόν τε καὶ ἀληθές, ὥς φησιν; — *Ἢ τὸ μὲν 124
καθαρὸν ὡς τῶν ἄλλων κεχωρισμένον σημαίνει, τὸ δὲ ἀληθὲς αὐτὸ ὅπερ ἐστίν,
καὶ μήποτε διὰ τοῦτο δεῖ καθαρθῆναι πρότερον καὶ οὕτως ἐντυχεῖν τῷ ἀληθεῖ.
ἐπειδὴ οὖν οὔπω κεκαθάρμεθα, οὔπω γὰρ τεθνήκαμεν, διὰ τοῦτο ʽἐκεῖσε ἐλθόντες
τὸ ἀληθὲς εἰσόμεθα' [69d5–6]. 5

§ 125. On hope. 67b8

ρκδ'. – "Ὅτι ὥσπερ ἡ δόξα διττή, ἡ μὲν κάτωθεν, ἡ δὲ ἄνωθεν, αὕτη μὲν 125
βέβαιος, ἐκείνη δὲ ἀβέβαιος, οὕτω καὶ ἐλπὶς ἡ μὲν τῆς ἐπιστήμης ἔκγονος,
ὡς ἡ νῦν λεγομένη, ἡ δὲ αἰσθήσεώς τε καὶ τοῦ εἰκότος.

§§ 126–137. On separation, purification, death:
Socrates' conclusion. 67c5–68c4

ρκε'. – [67c5–d2] "Ὅτι οὐ ταὐτὸν χωρισμὸς καὶ κάθαρσις· οὐ γὰρ δὴ 126
καθαίρεται τὸ σῶμα χωρισθὲν τῆς ψυχῆς, ἀλλὰ καὶ μολύνεται, διὸ καὶ μολύνει.
Ἀλλὰ καὶ τὸ προειρημένον [§ 124.1–2] διορθωτέον· οὐ γὰρ καθαρώτερον τὸ
καὶ τοῦ κρείττονος κεχωρισμένον, ὅσον ἐπὶ τῷ συνήθει δηλώματι. σαφῶς γὰρ
ἐν Σοφιστῇ φησιν [227d6–7]· ʽκαθαρμὸς δὲ ἦν τὸ καταλείπειν θάτερον, ἐκβαλεῖν 5
δὲ ὅσον ἂν ᾖ πού τι χεῖρον'. καὶ οἱ Κουρῆτες περὶ τοὺς δημιουργικοὺς θεούς,
ὅτι νενεύκασι πρὸς τὸ χεῖρον.

ρκϛ'. – [67d4–5] "Ὅτι οὐ ταὐτὸν θάνατος καὶ κάθαρσις, ἀλλὰ ὁ ἀπὸ τοῦ 127
χείρονος θάνατος. χωριστικὸς γὰρ ὁ θάνατος, ὡς ἐδήλου ὁ προρρηθεὶς ὁρισμός

---

order, the first being formed by Kronos (Pure Intelligence), Rhea (Intellective Life) and Zeus (Creative Form). The real purpose in introducing them was no doubt to expand the original intellective triad into a heptad with material taken from the same myth (the Seventh God is the τομή of Kronos), thus establishing the numerical pattern 1, 3, 7, 12, 10, corresponding to the intelligible, intelligible-intellective, intellective, supra-mundane and mundane orders respectively. Since in the myth the Curetes play the part of bodyguards, Pr. derives their name from the supposed adjective κορός=καθαρός and assigns to them the function of protecting the transcendent world from contamination by genesis. They are identified with the ἀμείλικτος τάξις of the Chaldean Oracles, another Neoplatonic flight of fancy (see Kroll p. 21). The text speaks of creative Gods generally (line 6), because in the *Orphica* the Curetes are also the bodyguard of Dionysus (frg. 34) and of Kore (frg. 151).

§ 127. The rather condensed argument can be summarized as follows: (1–3) death is purification only as far as the higher component is concerned; (3–5) separation and death differ in so far as death presupposes a prior union; (5–7) in the case of permanent separation, the 'death of everlasting beings' discussed in § 62, death does still not coincide with otherness, because death presupposes the existence of the other, which otherness brings about (otherness being a productive principle that constitutes things rather than supposes them already there: Dam., *Parm.*

it was said in the definition given above [64c7–8]; this is why we speak of death from above and death from below. Is being separate identical, then, with being dead? No, for the latter follows a period of union, which union is dissolved by death. But if there is permanent separation, there is permanent dissolution and permanent death; then what difference is there between death and otherness? Death severs mutual relations, and so those other things must exist already. And what has death still to do with life? That both inclination towards a thing and withdrawal from it are vital processes; now it is relations of this kind that are severed by death.

128. [67c5–d2] First, the soul must constitute an image of herself in the body (that is what animating the body means); secondly, she must be in sympathy with her phantom because of the likeness, since every form is drawn towards its replica as a result of its innate concentration upon itself; thirdly, having entered into the divided body, she must be torn asunder with it and end in utter disintegration; until through a life of purification she gathers herself from her dispersed state, unties the bond of sympathy, and actualizes the primal life within her that exists by itself without the phantom.

129. The myth [*Orph.* frg. 209] describes the same events as taking place in the prototype of the soul. When Dionysus had projected his reflection into the mirror, he followed it and was thus scattered over the universe. Apollo gathers him and brings him back to heaven, for he is the purifying God and truly the savior of Dionysus, and therefore he is celebrated as the 'Dionysus-Giver'.

130. Like Kore, the soul descends into genesis, like Dionysus she is scattered by generation, like Prometheus and the Titans she is chained to

---

103.7–8 ἔστι γὰρ γόνιμος πρόοδος καὶ προόδου πάσης αἰτία); (7–8) death thus understood remains nevertheless related to life, since the processes of integration and differentiation are precisely those characterizing transcendent life.

3. ὁ ἄνωθεν ... θάνατος καὶ ὁ κάτωθεν : the idea is discussed *supra* § 62, the phrase does not occur elsewhere, as far as I know, so that it is not even clear whether 'death from above' means separation *from* the superior or *brought about by* the superior (the soul). In view of § 125.1, the latter is more likely.

6. ἄλληλα : though, logically, one expects ἄλλα (referred back to in the next line), ἄλληλα is at least understandable.

§ 128. Ol. 7 § 10.1–5. The three phases of the downfall of the soul: descent, imprisonment, disruption; corresponding to these, in reverse order, the three phases of redemption: redintegration (συναγείρεσθαί τε καὶ ἀθροίζεσθαι, c8), deliverance (ἐκλυομένην ὥσπερ ἐκ δεσμῶν, d1), return to itself (οἰκεῖν ... καθ' ἑαυτήν, c8–9).

§§ 129–130. Ol. 7 § 10.5–10.

§ 129.1. ἐν τῷ παραδείγματι : Dionysus, usually the cosmic intelligence, is sometimes the prototype of the human soul: Dam., *Phil.* § 228.7–8.

2. Dionysus and the mirror: texts from Plotinus (IV 3, 12.1–2) and Proclus collected by Kern, *Orphica* frg. 209. Cf. Pépin 202, n. 1.

4. Διονυσοδότης : Pausanias I 31,4 mentions an altar Ἀπόλλωνος Διονυσοδότου

[64c7–8]· διὸ καὶ ὁ ἄνωθεν λέγεται θάνατος καὶ ὁ κάτωθεν. ἆρα οὖν ταὐτὸν χωρὶς εἶναι καὶ τεθνάναι; ἀλλὰ τοῦτο μετὰ τὴν σύζευξιν, διάλυσις γὰρ τῆς συζεύξεως. καὶ εἰ ἀεὶ χωρίς, ἀεὶ διαλέλυται καὶ ἀεὶ τέθνηκεν· τί οὖν ἑτερότητος διαφέρει; ἢ ὅτι τῶν πρὸς ἄλληλα σχέσεών ἐστι δια|κοπτικός, δεῖ οὖν πρότερον εἶναι τὰ ἄλλα. καὶ πῶς περὶ ζωὴν ὁ θάνατος; ἢ ὅτι καὶ αἱ προσνεύσεις καὶ αἱ ἀπονεύσεις ζωτικαί εἰσι· τῶν γὰρ τοιούτων διάλυσις ὁ θάνατος.

ρκζ'. – [67c5–d2] Ὅτι δεῖ πρῶτον ὑποστῆσαι εἰκόνα τὴν ψυχὴν ἑαυτῆς ἐν τῷ σώματι (τοῦτο γάρ ἐστι ψυχῶσαι τὸ σῶμα), δεύτερον δὲ συμπαθεῖν τῷ εἰδώλῳ κατὰ τὴν ὁμοείδειαν (πᾶν γὰρ εἶδος ἐπείγεται εἰς τὴν πρὸς ἑαυτὸ ταὐτότητα διὰ τὴν πρὸς ἑαυτὸ σύννευσιν ἔμφυτον), τρίτον ἐν τῷ μεριστῷ γενομένην συνδιασπασθῆναι αὐτῷ καὶ εἰς τὸν ἔσχατον ἐκπεσεῖν μερισμόν, ἕως ἂν διὰ τῆς καθαρτικῆς ζωῆς συναγείρῃ μὲν ἑαυτὴν ἀπὸ τοῦ σκορπισμοῦ, λύσῃ δὲ τὸν δεσμὸν τῆς συμπαθείας, προβάληται δὲ τὴν ἄνευ τοῦ εἰδώλου καθ' ἑαυτὴν ἑστῶσαν πρωτουργὸν ζωήν.

ρκη'. – Ὅτι τὰ ὅμοια μυθεύεται [Orph. frg. 209] καὶ ἐν τῷ παραδείγματι. ὁ γὰρ Διόνυσος, ὅτε τὸ εἴδωλον ἐνέθηκε τῷ ἐσόπτρῳ, τούτῳ ἐφέσπετο καὶ οὕτως εἰς τὸ πᾶν ἐμερίσθη. ὁ δὲ Ἀπόλλων συναγείρει τε αὐτὸν καὶ ἀνάγει καθαρτικὸς ὢν θεὸς καὶ τοῦ Διονύσου σωτὴρ ὡς ἀληθῶς, καὶ διὰ τοῦτο Διονυσοδότης ἀνυμνεῖται.

ρκθ'. – Ὅτι Κορικῶς μὲν εἰς γένεσιν κάτεισιν ἡ ψυχή, Διονυσιακῶς δὲ μερίζεται ὑπὸ τῆς γενέσεως, Προμηθείως δὲ καὶ Τιτανικῶς ἐγκαταδεῖται τῷ

---

§ 129. 4 post Διονυσοδότης] ÷ ÷ ÷ ÷ in ras. M^x | ἀνυμνεῖται M^c: εὐφημεῖται M¹

---

in the Attic deme Phlya, which is generally taken to be the genitive from Διονυσόδοτος, 'gift of Dionysus' (Jessen, *RE*, art. *Dionysodotos*, vol. 5, 1007. 5–21; Nilsson I 669). Proclus, to whom the present note is probably due, may have known the genitive only, in which case we may assume that he deliberately (and perhaps rightly) preferred the nominative in -της because of a supposed connection with the Orphic myth.

ibid. ἀνυμνεῖται: this is the reading of M¹, erased but preserved *supra lineam* by M^c. The word can be used of any divine attribute and does not necessarily point to Orphic poetry.

§ 130. The three phases of § 128 expressed in mythical symbols: descent and return (Kore/Demeter), imprisonment and deliverance (Prometheus/Hercules), disruption and redintegration (Dionysus/Apollo and Athena). There is no express evidence that the chained Prometheus figured in the *Orphica*; he may have been introduced here because no other instance of a delivered Titan was available, and mentioned again at § 132 because the word προμηθοῦνται (*Ph.* 67d7) suggested his name. However, the Orphic epic did refer to the theft of the fire (frg. 143); Servius, *Aen.* VI 392, cites Orpheus for an account of Hercules' descent to Hades and Charon's punishment for admitting him (frg. 296, from the Κατάβασις εἰς Ἅιδου according to Kern). – Prometheus as Providence unbound by its own power: Plotinus IV 3, 14.12–16; Pépin 200–201.

the body. She frees herself by acquiring the strength of Hercules, gathers herself together through the help of Apollo and of Athena the Savior, i.e. by truly purifying philosophy, and she elevates herself to the causes of her being with Demeter.

131. [67c5–d11] The syllogism can be constructed as follows:
The philos- purifies frees himself separates prepares
opher   himself from the body himself for death.

132. [67d7–8] 'Only to those who practice philosophy in the right way', that is to say, steadfastly and in a spirit of purification, 'their own deliverance is a matter of intense and incessant care', the 'care' [*prométheia*] coming to them from Prometheus, the constancy and intensity from Hercules; for it is to unceasing endeavor that the effort of liberation owes its strength.

133. [67d12–68a3] We grieve both when we lose the good and when we encounter evil; consequently we rejoice both when we are delivered from evil and when we find the good; on both scores we should rejoice at death, because it sets us free from the detested body as well as because it enables us to enjoy the truth for which we longed.

134. Fire can be made to sink down by a certain compulsion and artificially, but of its own nature it tends upward, because its totality is also there; this is what happens to the soul, too, in its descent into the body and its return to reality, because in this case, too, the transcendent totality is yonder.

135. [68a3–b6] The second argument is an *a fortiori* reasoning and is meant to convince outsiders that it would be ridiculous for philosophers to be annoyed at the prospect of death.

However, it seems likely that this argument too is intended for philosophers who live in accordance with reason, proving to them that even the irrational soul detaches itself from the body, when it hopes to find the object of its love in the hereafter; so it would be absurd to think that this faculty, while existing in irrational soul, which is incapable of reverting upon itself, is absent from rational soul, though it can revert both upon itself and upon reality.

136. [68b8–c1] If a man is a philosopher, he is fearless in the face of death, if he is not fearless, he is not a philosopher; the inference is valid

---

4. τῆς Σωτείρας 'Αθηνᾶς : cf. the Orphic line in Pr., *Alc.* 44.3 ἐξ οὗπερ Σώτειρ' ἐπεκλήθη Παλλὰς 'Αθήνη (not recognized as a hexameter by Kern, frg. 210, p. 229).
§ 132. Ol. 7 § 11.
2–4. On Prometheus and Hercules above § 130. On Prometheus and πρόνοια Plotinus cited *ibid.*
§ 134. Ol. 7 § 12.
2. ἡ ὁλότης : the element in its totality (cf. e.g. Pr., *Tim* I. 138.30–139.4), but

σώματι. λύει μὲν οὖν ἑαυτὴν Ἡρακλείως ἰσχύσασα, συναιρεῖ δὲ διὰ Ἀπόλλωνος καὶ τῆς Σωτείρας Ἀθηνᾶς καθαρτικῶς τῷ ὄντι φιλοσοφοῦσα, ἀνάγει δὲ εἰς τὰ οἰκεῖα αἴτια ἑαυτὴν μετὰ τῆς Δήμητρος.

—. - [67c5–d11] Ὁ συλλογισμὸς τοιοῦτος ἂν συλλεγείη· **131**
ὁ φιλό- καθαίρει λύει ἀπὸ τοῦ χωρί- θάνατον
σοφος ἑαυτόν σώματος ζει μελετᾷ.

ρλ΄. - [67d7–8] Ὅτι 'μόνοι οἱ φιλοσοφοῦντες ὀρθῶς', ὅ ἐστιν ἀκλινῶς τε **132**
καὶ καθαρτικῶς, οὗτοι 'μάλιστα καὶ ἀεὶ λύειν προμηθοῦν|ται', τὸ μὲν **(112)**
'προμηθεύεσθαι' παρὰ τοῦ Προμηθέως ἔχοντες, τὸ δὲ 'ἀεὶ' καὶ 'μάλιστα' παρὰ τοῦ Ἡρακλέους· τὸ γὰρ ἀδιάλειπτον καὶ σύντονον ἰσχυροποιεῖ τὴν λύσιν.

ρλα΄. - [67d12–68a3] Ὅτι καὶ τοῦ ἀγαθοῦ στερόμενοι λυπούμεθα καὶ τῷ **133**
κακῷ περιπίπτοντες· ἡδόμεθα ἄρα τοῦ τε κακοῦ ἀπαλλαττόμενοι καὶ τῷ ἀγαθῷ ἐντυγχάνοντες. ὥστε καθ᾽ ἑκάτερον ἐπὶ τῷ θανάτῳ εὐφραίνεσθαι δεῖ, καὶ ὡς ἀπολύοντι τοῦ μισουμένου σώματος καὶ ὡς ἀπόλαυσιν παρεχομένῳ τοῦ ποθουμένου ἀληθοῦς.

ρλβ΄. - Ὅτι ὡς τὸ πῦρ εἰς μὲν τὸ κάτω βρίθει βιαιότερον καὶ διά τινος **134**
μηχανῆς, αὐτοφυῶς δὲ εἰς τὸ ἄνω χωρεῖ, ὅτι ἄνω αὐτῷ καὶ ἡ ὁλότης, οὕτω καὶ ἡ ψυχὴ πάσχει πρός τε τὴν εἰς τὸ σῶμα κάθοδον καὶ τὴν εἰς τὸ ὂν ἐπάνοδον, ἐπειδὴ καὶ αὐτῆς ἡ χωριστὴ ὁλότης ἐκεῖ.

ρλγ΄. - [68a3–b6] Ὅτι ἡ δευτέρα ἐπιχείρησις ἀπὸ τοῦ μᾶλλον καὶ ἧττον **135**
εἰλημμένη καὶ τοὺς πολλοὺς βούλεται πεῖσαι ὅτι γελοῖον τοὺς φιλοσόφους ἐπὶ τῷ θανάτῳ δυσχεραίνειν.

Μήποτε δὲ καὶ αὕτη γίνεται πρὸς τοὺς φιλοσόφους κατὰ λόγον ζῶντας, ἐνδεικνυμένη ὅτι καὶ ἡ ἄλογος ψυχὴ χωρίζει ἑαυτήν, ὅταν ἐκεῖ τῷ ἐραστῷ ἐντυχεῖν ἐλπίσῃ· γελοῖον οὖν τὴν μὲν ἄλογον καὶ οὐδέποτε πρὸς ἑαυτὴν ἐπιστρεφομένην οὕτως ἔχειν, τὴν δὲ λογικὴν ἐναντίως, καὶ ταῦτα εἰς ἑαυτὴν καὶ εἰς τὸ ὂν ἐπιστρέφεσθαι δυναμένην.

ρλδ΄. - [68b8–c1] Ὅτι εἰ φιλόσοφος, ἀδεὴς πρὸς τὸν θάνατον, εἰ δὲ μὴ ἀδεής, **136**
οὐ φιλόσοφος· σὺν ἀντιθέσει γὰρ ἀντιστρέφει. οὐ μέντοι, εἰ ἀδεής, πάντως

---

§ 135. 4 αὕτη Nv: αὐτὴ M

---

also its main agglomeration: the sky for fire, the Earth for earth.
4. The ὁλότης of souls is their monad, cf. Pr., elem. 21 καὶ τῇ τάξει τῶν ψυχῶν πάρεστιν ἐκ μιᾶς τε ἄρχεσθαι ψυχῆς τῆς πρώτης καὶ εἰς πλῆθος ψυχῶν ὑποβαίνειν καὶ τὸ πλῆθος εἰς τὴν μίαν ἀνάγειν.
§ 135. Irrational soul, though not immortal, is considered separable by Pr. (II § 29, note).
§ 136. Ol. 7 § 4.13–17.
2. σὺν ἀντιθέσει γὰρ ἀντιστρέφει: on the theory of this see Ol. 2 § 4.3–4 and note.

because made by negation and conversion. On the other hand, if a man is fearless, he is not necessarily a philosopher; for the negation of the consequent makes the conversion valid because of the resulting negation of the antecedent, but its affirmation does not imply affirmation of the antecedent. This is probably all that the syllogism is meant to convey.

137. [68c1–3] Why does Plato fail to mention pleasure-seeking, when a lover of the body would obviously be a pleasure-seeker too? — An answer is that he *is* the 'lover of the body', and the others are mentioned separately; or that he has been dealt with above [64d2–e3], and the present passage mentions only those omitted then. This is Harpocratio's interpretation [frg. 4]; Paterius escapes the difficulty by saying that a man who *pretends* to be a philosopher does so for the sake either of honor or of gain, none however for the sake of pleasure, because of the severe attitude philosophy imposes; in that case 'this man' is to be understood to apply, not to the lover of the body, but to the sham philosopher.

By this interpretation we avoid another problem too: how can the man who seeks honor be a lover of the body, since he is willing to sacrifice it for the sake of honor? The commentator's solution of this is rather weak, and it seems as if he had forgotten the explanation of Paterius, which was the second; the first, against which the objections were raised, was Harpocratio's.

§§ 138–151. On virtues: general survey. 68c5–69c3

138. First among virtues are the natural virtues, which we have in common with the animals and which are inextricably linked with the bodily temperament and frequently clash with each other; either they belong mainly to the animate body, or they are reflexes of reason when not impeded by temperamental disorder, or they may be due to routine acquired in a previous life. Plato discusses them in the *Statesman* [306a5–308b9] and in the *Laws* [XII 963c3–e9].

139. Above them are the ethical virtues, which we acquire by habituation and by a sort of true opinion; they are the virtues of well-bred

---

§ 137. Ol. 7 § 5. See note on Ol., esp. Beutler's discussion in *RE* cited there. To sum up: (1–2) the problem; (2–4) two solutions, apparently *both* put forward by Harpocratio, since at line 11 they are together called the 'first' solution; the second, according to Ol., was adopted by Pr.; (4–8) solution of Paterius, adopted by Ammonius (Ol.) and Dam. (line 9); (9–11) Paterius' solution also takes care of the problem how the lover of honor can be a lover of the body, a point insufficiently explained by Pr.

7. τὸν πλαστὸν φιλόσοφον : cf. Pl., *Soph.* 216c5–6 οἱ μὴ πλαστῶς ἀλλ' ὄντως φιλόσοφοι.

11–12. πρὸς ἣν αἱ ἀπορίαι : the objections raised, apparently by Paterius, against Harpocratio's interpretation, one of which is cited at lines 9–10.

§§ 138–144. Ol. 8 §§ 2–3; cf. also 1 § 5.1–9. The scale of virtues, though actually the result of a long development, is supposed to be Platonic in most of its essentials, and accordingly an attempt is made to identify its several degrees in the dialogues.

φιλόσοφος· ἡ γὰρ τοῦ ἑπομένου ἀναίρεσις ποιεῖ τὴν ἀντιστροφὴν συναναιροῦσα τὸ ἡγούμενον, ἀλλ' οὐχὶ ἡ θέσις τιθεῖσα. καὶ μήποτε τὸ ὅλον βούλημα τοῦ συλλογισμοῦ τοῦτό ἐστιν.

ρλε'. - [68c1–3] Διὰ τί παρέλιπεν τὸ φιλήδονον; ὁ γὰρ φιλοσώματος εἴη ἂν 137(113) καὶ φιλήδονος. — Ἢ ὅτι ὁ φιλοσώματος οὗτός ἐστιν, προστίθενται δὲ καὶ οἱ ἄλλοι· ἢ ἐν τοῖς πρόσθεν [64d2–e3] τοῦτον ἀπεσκευάσατο, νῦν δὲ παρατίθεται τοὺς τότε παραλειφθέντας. οὕτως μὲν Ἁρποκρατίων ἐξηγεῖται [frg. 4]· ὁ δὲ Πατέριος ἐκφεύγει τὴν ἀπορίαν λέγων τὸν φιλοσοφεῖν προσποιούμενον ἢ διὰ τιμὴν ἢ διὰ κέρδος προσποιεῖσθαι, οὐδεὶς δὲ δι' ἡδονήν, διὰ τὸ σεμνὸν τῆς φιλοσοφίας· τὸ οὖν 'οὗτος' οὐ τὸν φιλοσώματον, ἀλλὰ τὸν πλαστὸν φιλόσοφον νοητέον.

Διαφεύγει δὲ αὕτη ἡ ἐξήγησις καὶ ἄλλην ἀπορίαν· πῶς γὰρ φιλοσώματος ὁ φιλότιμος; προῖεται γὰρ τὸ σῶμα διὰ τιμήν. ἣν ἐπιλύεται μαλακώτερον, ὡς ἐπιλαθόμενος τῆς Πατερίου ἐξηγήσεως, ἢ ἦν δευτέρα· ἡ γὰρ πρώτη, πρὸς ἣν αἱ ἀπορίαι, Ἁρποκρατίωνος.

§§ 138–151. On virtues: general survey. 68c5–69c3

ρλς'. — Ὅτι πρῶται τῶν ἀρετῶν αἱ φυσικαί, κοιναὶ πρὸς τὰ θηρία, 138 συμπεφυρμέναι ταῖς κράσεσιν, ἐναντίαι ἀλλήλαις ὡς τὰ πολλά· ἢ μᾶλλον οὖσαι τοῦ ζῴου, ἢ καὶ ἀπὸ τοῦ λόγου μὴ ἐμποδιζομένου ὑπό τινος δυσκρασίας ἐκλάμπουσαι, ἢ καὶ ἀπὸ προβιοτῆς γεγυμνασμέναι. περὶ δὲ τούτων ἔν τε Πολιτικῷ φησιν [306a5–308b9] καὶ ἐν Νόμοις [XII 963c3–e9].

ρλζ'. — Ὅτι αἱ ἠθικαὶ ὑπὲρ ταύτας, ἐθισμῷ καὶ ὀρθοδοξίᾳ τινὶ ἐγγιγνόμεναι, 139 παίδων οὖσαι ἀρεταὶ ἀγομένων εὖ καὶ τῶν θηρίων ἐνίοις ὑπάρχουσαι, τῶν κράσεων

---

§ 136. 3 συναναιροῦσα M
§ 137. 1 παρέλιπε μ: παρέλειπεν M

The natural virtues (§ 138) are said to be discussed in the *Statesman* and the *Laws*. In the *Statesman*, 306a5–308b9, Pl. contrasts swift and violent action of body and mind (ἀνδρεία) with slow and weak action (σωφροσύνη) and concludes that the statesman should make the corresponding characters the warp and the woof of the texture of society. They answer the description given here of natural virtues in so far as they are qualities of the body also; their value is not absolute, but depends on the circumstances and the congeniality of the critic; they will frequently conflict with each other. The use of φύσις at 306e11 and 307c3 seems to support this interpretation. Yet Pl. says that these qualities are also passed on to the next generation by the example of the parents (307e8–9); he is speaking in a general way of character material to be shaped by the lawgiver. In *Laws* XII 963c3–e9 the context is a similar one: intelligence is the standard for all virtue; in the commonwealth it is represented by the leaders, who should therefore understand

children and are also found in certain animals; being beyond the influence of temperament they do not clash with each other. Plato deals with them in the *Laws* [II 653a5–c4]. They belong to reason and to the irrational faculties simultaneously.

140. Third beyond these are the civic virtues, which belong to reason only, since they are based on knowledge; but of reason in so far as it regulates irrational being and uses it as its own instrument: by prudence it governs the cognitive faculty, by fortitude the spirit, by temperance desire, and all together by justice. These are treated more fully in the *Republic* [IV 434d2–445b4]. They actually imply each other.

141. Above them are the purifying virtues, which belong only to reason, but to reason in so far as it withdraws from everything external into itself, discards the instruments as useless and restrains the activities that depend on them; they deliver the soul from the bonds of genesis. The main passage dealing with them is the present one.

142. Before these are the contemplative virtues, when the soul has finally abandoned even itself, or rather has joined the superior, not in the way of knowledge only, as the word might seem to suggest, but in the way of appetition as well: it is as if the soul aspires to become intelligence instead of soul, and intelligence is both cognition and appetition. They are the counterpart of the civic virtues; the action of the latter is directed on the inferior and proceeds by reason, while the contemplative virtues are directed on the superior and proceed by intellection. Plato treats of them in the *Theaetetus* [173c6–177c2].

143. Archetypal virtues are those of the soul when it no longer contemplates the intelligence (contemplation involving separateness), but has already reached the stage of being by participation the intelligence that is the archetype of all things; therefore these virtues too are called 'archetypal', inasmuch as virtues belong primarily to intelligence itself. This category is added by Iamblichus in his treatise *On Virtues*.

144. Lastly, there are the hieratic virtues, which belong to the Godlike part of the soul; they correspond to all the categories mentioned above, with

---

the relationship that makes qualities as different as courage (found also in animals and in very young children) and prudence (found only in rational beings) nevertheless one thing, virtue. The words ἄνευ γὰρ λόγου καὶ φύσει γίγνεται ἀνδρεία ψυχή (e5–6; cf. *Rep.* VII 518d9–519a1) justified regarding this as a passage on natural virtue. The moral virtues (§ 139) in the *Laws* probably include the whole educational program of books I–II and VII 788a1–VIII 842a3, where ὀρθῶς ἐθίζειν is declared to be the only course applicable to an age not mature enough for rational behavior. The civic virtues (§ 140) are of course those of *Rep.* IV, the purifying virtues (§ 141) those of the *Phaedo*, the contemplative virtues (§ 142) those of *Theaet.* 173c6–177c2; here we are on the familiar ground covered by Plotinus (I 2) and Porphyry (*sent.* 32). It is slightly surprising that no Platonic authority should be claimed for the archetypal virtues (§ 143); for the hieratic virtues there was always the excuse that they are beyond the range of philosophy. The archetypal virtues had already

ὑπερανέχουσαι καὶ διὰ τοῦτο οὐκ ἐναντιούμεναι ἀλλήλαις· ἃς παραδίδωσιν ἐν Νόμοις [II 653a5–c4]. εἰσὶ δὲ ὁμοῦ λόγου τε καὶ ἀλογίας.

ρλη'. – Ὅτι τρίται ὑπὲρ ταύτας αἱ πολιτικαί, μόνου οὖσαι τοῦ λόγου (ἐπιστημονικαὶ γάρ), ἀλλὰ λόγου κοσμοῦντος τὴν ἀλογίαν ὡς ὄργανον ἑαυτοῦ· διὰ μὲν φρονήσεως τὸ γνωστικόν, διὰ δὲ ἀνδρείας τὸ θυμοειδές, τὸ δὲ ἐπιθυμητικὸν σω|φροσύνῃ, πάντα δὲ δικαιοσύνῃ· περὶ ὧν πλείω λέγει ἐν Πολιτείᾳ [IV 434d2–445b4]. αὗται δὲ καὶ ἀντακολουθοῦσιν ἀλλήλαις. 140 (114) 5

ρλθ'. – Ὅτι ὑπὲρ ταύτας αἱ καθαρτικαί, τοῦ λόγου μόνου οὖσαι καὶ ἀπὸ τῶν ἄλλων ἀναχωροῦντος εἰς ἑαυτὸν καὶ τὰ ὄργανα ῥιπτοῦντος ὡς μάταια καὶ τὰς δι' ὀργάνων ἐνεργείας ἀναστέλλοντος, ἀναλύουσαι τὴν ψυχὴν ἀπὸ τῶν δεσμῶν τῆς γενέσεως· ἃς διαφερόντως ἐνταῦθα παραδίδωσιν. 141

ρμ'. – Ὅτι πρὸ τούτων αἱ θεωρητικαί, τῆς ψυχῆς ἤδη καὶ ἑαυτὴν ἀφιείσης, μᾶλλον δὲ τοῖς πρὸ αὐτῆς ἑαυτὴν προσαγούσης, οὐ γνωστικῶς, ὡς ἂν οἰηθείη τις μόνον τὸ ὄνομα δηλοῦν, ἀλλὰ καὶ ὀρεκτικῶς· οἷον γὰρ νοῦς ἀντὶ ψυχῆς ἐπείγεται γενέσθαι, ὁ δὲ νοῦς ἅμα τὸ συναμφότερον. ἀντίστροφοι αὗται ταῖς πολιτικαῖς, ὡς ἐκεῖναι περὶ τὰ χείρω κατὰ λόγον ἐνεργοῦσαι, αὗται περὶ τὰ κρείττω κατὰ νοῦν· ἃς παραδίδωσιν ἐν Θεαιτήτῳ [173c6–177c2]. 142 5

ρμα'. – Ὅτι παραδειγματικαὶ ἀρεταὶ αἱ μηκέτι θεωρούσης τὸν νοῦν τῆς ψυχῆς (τὸ γὰρ θεωρεῖν σὺν ἀποστάσει γίνεται), ἀλλ' ἤδη στάσης ἐν τῷ νοῦν εἶναι κατὰ μέθεξιν ὅς ἐστι παράδειγμα πάντων· διὸ καὶ αὗται παραδειγματικαί, ὅτι προηγουμένως αὐτοῦ εἰσιν τοῦ νοῦ αἱ ἀρεταί. ταύτας δὲ προστίθησιν ὁ Ἰάμβλιχος ἐν τοῖς Περὶ ἀρετῶν. 143 5

ρμβ'. – Ὅτι εἰσὶ καὶ αἱ ἱερατικαὶ ἀρεταί, κατὰ τὸ θεοειδὲς ὑφιστάμεναι τῆς ψυχῆς, ἀντιπαρήκουσαι πάσαις ταῖς εἰρημέναις οὐσιώδεσιν οὔσαις ἑνιαῖαί γε 144

---

§ 139. 3 ἃς Mˣ: ἃ M¹
§ 140. 1 τρίται Mˣ: τριτταὶ M¹
§ 141. 1 μόνου] -υ in ras. Mᶜ (μόνον ut vid. M¹)
§ 144. 1 αἱ] del. Fh — 2 οὖσαις] accent. acut. add., 1 litt. post σ eras. Mˣ (οὐσίαις M¹)

---

been added by Porphyry as the fourth degree (virtues of intelligence: pp. 28.6–29.7) and somehow been linked with theurgy (ὁ δὲ κατὰ τὰς παραδειγματικὰς [ἐνεργῶν] θεῶν πατήρ, p. 31.8; cf. Lewy 465); Iamblichus' innovation may have consisted in making them qualities of the human intelligence by participation, and thus distinguishing them from the ἱερατικαί (or θεουργικαί or μανικαί) ἀρεταί, which completed the scale as the virtues proper to the 'divine' or 'one-like' element in the soul (§ 144.1). §§ 145–146, finally, supply some footnotes on the 'slavish' virtues of Ph. 69b7.

§ 140. What Pl. calls πολιτικαὶ ἀρεταί at Ph. 82a11–b3 are really the moral virtues of § 139: ... οἱ τὴν δημοτικὴν καὶ πολιτικὴν ἀρετὴν ἐπιτετηδευκότες, ἣν δὴ καλοῦσι σωφροσύνην τε καὶ δικαιοσύνην, ἐξ ἔθους τε καὶ μελέτης γεγονυῖαν ἄνευ φιλοσοφίας τε καὶ νοῦ. Cf. also Apol. 20b4–5.

5. ἀντακολουθοῦσιν: see note on Ol. 1 § 5.9.

this difference that while the others are existential, these are unitary. This kind, too, has been outlined by Iamblichus, and discussed more explicitly by the school of Proclus.

145. These are virtues not attended by vices, but there are also certain so-called virtues that are mixed with the contrasting vices; these Plato calls 'servile' [69b7], because they are of no value whatever and can be found even in slaves. For this reason we do not include them in the series of virtues.

146. [68d2–69b8] Some people become courageous and temperant for the sake of honor, or under the pressure of a law that punishes those who behave otherwise, or through ignorance of the evil that awaits them, or through experience of the dangers, or through brutish recklessness and unreasoned instinct, or by changing one affect for another.

147. [68c5–69c3] Plato's object is to isolate the purifying virtues and literally 'purify' them from all the lower virtues, not only from pretended virtues, as Harpocratio [frg. 5] thinks, but also from the 'illusory' ones, i.e. natural and ethical virtues, and not from these only, but also from the perfect civic virtues. After first eliminating vices his obvious next step is now to discard the lower virtues also.

148. The object is partly to prove purifying virtue superior to what is commonly so called, but at the same time it is to make it clear that purifying virtue cannot be insight alone, as the Peripatetics think, but that it includes the other three.

---

§§ 144. 3. οἱ ... περὶ Πρόκλον : Syrianus and Proclus, probably.

§§ 145–148. Ol. 8 § 4.5–§ 6.17 and note. In contrast with the view adopted by Ol. and his successors, Pr. and Dam. deny the identity of 'slavish' virtues (which are spurious ones) with natural virtues (which are after all genuine virtues).

§ 146. This is Ar.'s enumeration of the five inferior kinds of courage, *eth. Nic.* III 11: δοκοῦσι γὰρ ὑπομένειν τοὺς κινδύνους οἱ πολῖται διὰ τὰ ἐκ τῶν νόμων ἐπιτίμια καὶ τὰ ὀνείδη καὶ διὰ τὰς τιμάς (1116a18–19)· δοκεῖ δὲ καὶ ἡ ἐμπειρία ἡ περὶ ἕκαστα ἀνδρεία τις εἶναι (b3–4)· ἀνδρεῖοι εἶναι δοκοῦσι καὶ οἱ διὰ θυμὸν ὥσπερ τὰ θηρία ἐπὶ τοὺς τρώσαντας φερόμενα (b24–25)· ἀνδρεῖοι δὲ φαίνονται καὶ οἱ ἀγνοοῦντες (1117a22–23). The ἀλλαγή of *Ph.* 69a6–8 is added to these as a sixth possibility.

§ 147. The purport of the passage 68d2–69d2 according to Pr. (see analysis in note on Ol.).

3. On Harpocratio's interpretation of Pl.'s ethics see following note.

§§ 148–149. jointly with § 164, provide some (additional) information on the doctrine of the degrees of virtue in the Middle Platonic period. The opinions reviewed are those of the Peripatos, of Harpocratio (end of 2nd cent. A.D.) and of the "Attic commentators" (§ 164), who, being anterior to Pr., must be the official representatives of Athenian Platonism either in Harpocratio's or in Porphyry's days. In the discussion, Porphyry's distinction between purificatory and contemplative virtues (based on Plotinus) does not yet exist; the virtues of the *Ph.* are understood as virtues of the soul by itself. According to the ethics of the Peripatos (*eth. Nic.* X 8),

ὑπάρχουσαι. καὶ ταύτας δὲ ὁ Ἰάμβλιχος ἐνδείκνυται, οἱ δὲ περὶ Πρόκλον καὶ σαφέστερον.

ρμγ'. – "Ότι αὗται μέν εἰσιν ἀρεταὶ κακίας ἐκτός, εἰσὶ δέ τινες καλούμεναι 145 ἀρεταὶ συμμιγεῖς ταῖς ἀντικειμέναις κακίαις· διὸ καλεῖ αὐτὰς 'ἀνδραποδώδεις' [69b7] ὡς οὐδενὸς λόγου ἀξίας, δυ|ναμένας δὲ καὶ ἀνδραπόδοις ὑπάρχειν. (115) διὸ ταύτας οὐ καταλέγομεν ἐν τῷ χορῷ τῶν ἀρετῶν.

ρμε'. – [68d2–69b8] "Ότι γίνονται ἄνθρωποι ἀνδρεῖοι καὶ σώφρονες ἢ διὰ 146 τιμὴν ἢ διὰ νόμον κολάζοντα τοὺς μὴ τοιούτους ἢ διὰ ἄγνοιαν τῶν ἐσομένων κακῶν ἢ διὰ ἐμπειρίαν τῶν κινδύνων ἢ διὰ ἀπόνοιαν θηριώδη καὶ ἄλογον ὁρμὴν ἢ ἀλλαττόμενοι ἄλλα ἀντὶ ἄλλων.

ρμϛ'. – [68c5–69c3] "Ότι σκοπὸς αὐτῷ ἀποδιακρῖναι καὶ ὡς ἀληθῶς καθᾶραι 147 τὰς καθαρτικὰς ἀρετὰς τῶν καταδεεστέρων πασῶν ἀρετῶν, οὐ μόνον τῶν ψευδωνύμων, ὡς Ἁρποκρατίων [frg. 5], ἀλλὰ καὶ τῶν 'ἐσκιαγραφημένων', οἷον τῶν φυσικῶν τε καὶ ἠθικῶν, οὐδὲ τούτων μόνον, ἀλλὰ καὶ τῶν τελείων πολιτικῶν. ἀποκρίνας γὰρ τὰς κακίας εἰκότως νῦν καὶ τὰς χείρους ἀρετὰς ἀποκαθαίρει. 5

ρμζ'. – "Ότι πρόκειται μὲν καὶ τῶν ἐν συνηθείᾳ λεγομένων ἀρετῶν ὑπερέχουσαν 148 ἀποφῆναι τὴν καθαρτικήν, ἤδη δὲ καὶ ἐκεῖνο παραστῆσαι, ὡς οὐ μόνη φρόνησις αὕτη ἂν εἴη κατὰ τοὺς ἀπὸ τοῦ Περιπάτου, ἀλλὰ καὶ αἱ ἄλλαι τρεῖς ἀρεταί.

---

§ 148. 1 post πρόκειται] ~ M˟

---

these can be only the dianoetic virtues; all others necessarily relate to man's social behavior and should be classified as ἠθικαὶ ἀρεταί. Harpocratio, yielding to this argument, held that the virtues described in the Ph. do not go beyond those of the Rep. (correct behavior based on insight); the expression used, τὰς ἐν Πολιτείᾳ, very probably represents Harpocratio's actual words. By implication, the possibility of a higher plane of virtues is admitted, which *may* mean that Harpocratio knew and rejected the view attributed to the 'Attic commentators', according to which these virtues as well as the corresponding affects exist also in a form transcending physical and social relationships (§ 164), a view which thus leads up to the classification of Plotinus and Porphyry. The opinion labeled 'ours' at § 149.7–12 actually does not go beyond the teaching of Porphyry, *sent*. § 32.3, and may come from Porphyry's commentary together with the doxographical information. – Further Middle Platonic material is found in Plutarch, *de virtute morali* (the Aristotelian classification) and Alcinous, *did*. 28–30 (man becomes like God not only through the 'justice and piety together with wisdom' of *Theaet*. 176b2–3 and the 'justice' of *Rep*. X 613a7–b1, but also through the 'popular social virtues' of *Ph*. 82a10–b3, 'which people will call temperance and justice, and which are the result of training and habituation without philosophical insight,' in other words, the 'ethical virtues' of the Neoplatonic scale; virtue as 'a perfect disposition' of the soul is described in the terms of the four cardinal virtues of the *Rep*.; natural disposition and moral progress, the virtues of the προκόπτων, may lead up to them).

§ 148. 2. φρόνησις: not in the limited Aristotelian sense, but in the wider Platonic acceptation of reason in its perfect state.

149. The Peripatetics ask what purpose the other three virtues can serve for a man who is going to devote himself to contemplation, when in that field there are neither unruly emotions nor irrational emotions of any kind whatever, nor activities of reason that descend to this level and therefore need the armor of virtues in the war of genesis; for the same reason they deny these virtues to the Gods, because they do not need them.

Harpocratio [frg. 5] yields to these arguments and says that the virtues discussed here are the same as those in the *Republic* [IV434d2–445b4]. We, however, should rather say that they all reveal their constant universal character in a way peculiar to each level: thus the character of courage is unwavering firmness towards the inferior, of temperance the turning away from the inferior, of justice an activity which is proper to the subject and truly 'belonging' to it, and of prudence the ability to choose the good and reject the bad. Hence the qualifying word 'especially' [68c6].

150. All the virtues are found also in the Gods: (1) many Gods are honored by the names of virtues; (2) all goodness originates with the Gods; (3) prior to those who participate in virtues *sometimes*, there must be those who participate in them *always*, and prior to the participating there must be the participated; therefore, since the 'companions of the Gods' belong to those who participate, the things participated, i.e. the virtues themselves, must be Gods.

151. In what divine order do the virtues first manifest themselves? — Evidently in the same order as soul, since virtue is perfection of the soul, as choice and decision are its activities and actualization; therefore the Chaldean Oracles [frg. 52] line primal virtue with primal soul. Also, one

---

§ 149. 1–2. τῷ στελλομένῳ πρὸς θεωρίαν : an allusion to the line of Pindar quoted below at § 151.7 (on the basis of the reading ἔστειλαν). Cf. Pr., *Rep.* I 59.14–15 εἰς τὴν θέαν τῶν νοητῶν ... στελλόμενον.

5. Cf. Ar., *eth. Nic.* X 8, 1178b7–22: perfect happiness must be contemplative in character; the other virtues, justice, courage, generosity, temperance, are beneath the dignity of the Gods.

7–12. Cf. *infra* § 152.4–6.

§§ 150–151. A digression on the much-discussed topic of the virtues of the Gods, occasioned by § 149.5. Pl. (*Laws* X 900d2–3) pronounced ὡς ἀγαθοί γε ὄντες πᾶσαν ἀρετὴν τὴν τῶν πάντων ἐπιμέλειαν οἰκειοτάτην αὐτῶν οὖσαν κέκτηνται, and went on to specify that this includes σωφρονεῖν and ἀνδρεία (d5–e9). Ar. (cited above; cf. also VII 1, 1145a25–27) holds the opposite view. The Stoics since Cleanthes (*SVF* I frgs. 529 and 564; cf. Chrysippus III frgs. 149 and 245–252) believe that the virtue of the Gods is not essentially different from man's. This is one of the contexts in which the point is raised later: Plut., *de comm. not.* 33, 1076A, and Alexander, *de fato* 37, p. 211.13–17, argue indignantly that the virtue of the Gods is as far superior to ours as their being is; so also Pr., *Tim.* I 351.11–14; *Alc.* 3.12–4.2. A second context is that of becoming like God through virtue, originating in Pl., *Theaet.* 176b2–3 ὁμοίωσις δὲ δίκαιον καὶ ὅσιον μετὰ φρονήσεως γενέσθαι. Alcinous, *did.* 28 explains this: ἀκόλουθον οὖν τῇ ἀρχῇ τὸ τέλος εἴη ἂν τὸ ἐξομοιωθῆναι θεῷ, θεῷ δηλονότι

ρμη'. – Ὅτι ἀποροῦσιν οἱ Περιπατητικοί, πῶς ἂν τῷ στελλομένῳ πρὸς 149
θεωρίαν ἁρμόζοιεν αἱ ἄλλαι τρεῖς, οὔτε ἀταξίας τῶν παθῶν ἐκεῖ ὑποκειμένης
οὔτε ὅλως ἀλογίας παθῶν, ἀλλ' οὐδὲ ἐνεργειῶν τοῦ λόγου τῶν πρὸς ταῦτα
κατιουσῶν καὶ δεομένων διὰ τοῦτο καθάπερ ὅπλων τῶν ἀρετῶν εἰς τὸν τῆς
γενέσεως πόλεμον· διὸ μηδὲ τοῖς θεοῖς αὐτὰς ἐνεῖναι ἅτε | μηδὲν αὐτῶν δεομένοις. 5(116)
Ὁ μὲν οὖν Ἁρποκρατίων [frg. 5] εἴξας καὶ ἐνταῦθα τὰς ἐν Πολιτείᾳ
[IV 434d2–445b4] φησὶ παραδίδοσθαι. ἡμῖν δὲ ῥητέον ὅτι πᾶσαι τοὺς οἰκείους
χαρακτῆρας ἐπιδείκνυνται πανταχοῦ κοινοὺς ὄντας ἰδίως ἐν ἑκάστοις· ἔστι γὰρ
τῆς μὲν ἀνδρείας τὸ ἀρρεπὲς πρὸς τὰ χείρω, τῆς δὲ σωφροσύνης τὸ ἀποστρέφειν
ἀπὸ τοῦ χείρονος, τῆς δὲ δικαιοσύνης ἡ ἴδιος ἐνέργεια καὶ τῷ ὄντι προσήκουσα, 10
τῆς δὲ φρονήσεως τὸ ἐκλεκτικόν τε καὶ ἀπεκλεκτικὸν ἀγαθῶν τε καὶ κακῶν.
διὸ τὸ ʽμάλισταʼ πρόσκειται [68c6].

ρμθ'. – Ὅτι καὶ ἐν θεοῖς εἰσιν αἱ ἀρεταὶ πᾶσαι. καὶ γὰρ πολλοὶ θεοὶ ταῖς 150
αὐτῶν κοσμοῦνται ἐπωνυμίαις· καὶ ἀπὸ θεῶν πᾶσα ἀγαθότης ἄρχεται· καὶ πρὸ
μὲν τῶν ποτὲ μετεχόντων ἀναγκαῖον εἶναι τὰ ἀεὶ μετέχοντα τῶν ἀρετῶν, πρὸ
δὲ τῶν μετεχόντων τὰ μετεχόμενα, τῶν δὲ μετεχόντων οἱ ὀπαδοί, θεοὶ ἄρα τὰ
μετεχόμενα, αὐταὶ δήπου αἱ ἀρεταί. 5

ρν'. – Ἐν ποίᾳ τάξει αἱ ἀρεταὶ ἀναφαίνονται; — Ἢ ὅπου αἱ ψυχαί. τελειότης 151
γάρ ἐστι τῆς ψυχῆς ἡ ἀρετή, καὶ γὰρ ἡ αἵρεσις καὶ ἡ προαίρεσις ψυχῆς ἐνέργειαί
τε καὶ προβολαί· διὸ καὶ τὰ λόγια [frg. 52] τῇ πηγαίᾳ ψυχῇ τὴν πηγαίαν

---

§ 149. 3 οὐδὲ] -έ in ras. Mᶜ
§ 150. 4 ὀπαδοί (ut semper) M

τῷ ἐπουρανίῳ, μὴ τῷ μὰ Δία ὑπερουρανίῳ, ὃς οὐκ ἀρετὴν ἔχει, ἀμείνων δ' ἐστὶ ταύτης. Plot. I 2, 1–3, commenting on the same passage, says that the World Soul is the first divinity to be considered, then questions this on the grounds adduced by Ar. and concludes that we can become like God through virtue without God's possessing virtue, which is found in Soul only, not in Intelligence nor in the One. Proclus, interpreting a text of the Chaldean Oracles (frgs. 51–52), locates both the 'source of souls' and the 'source of virtues' in Rhea-Hecate, i.e. intellective Life (theol. V 32, 316.31–35; cf. Tim. I 208.20–21; Crat. 105.18–106.24), so that soul itself and virtue itself appear at the level immediately below this. This is the opinion expressed in § 151.

§ 150. 1–2. Divinities with the names of virtues: Δικαιοσύνη, Ὑγεία (Orph.), Ἀρετά, Αἰδώς, Νέμεσις, Ἐλευθερία, Ἀλήθεια (taking as the criterion the existence of a cult, or at least of a hymn; cf. Dam., Phil. § 19.4–5).

4. Pl., Phil. 63e5–7 καὶ δὴ καὶ συμπάσης ἀρετῆς ὁπόσαι [scil. ἡδοναί] καθάπερ θεοῦ ὀπαδοὶ γιγνόμεναι αὐτῇ συνακολουθοῦσι πάντη, ταύτας μείγνυ. On ὀπαδοί see note on § 477, esp. the passage from Pr., elem. 185, which shows that it is practically interchangeable with μετέχων, a usage mainly based on Phaedr. 252c3.

§ 151. 1–2. Virtue as τελειότης : see note on Dam., Phil. § 81.
3. On the meaning of πηγαῖος see the index of Dam., Phil. s.v. Here, as usually, it denotes the demiurgic or intellective order.

might observe that the natural function of virtues is to impose order on the chaotic, and that for this reason they first appear in the creative order. But how to reconcile this with their purifying function? The answer is that the Creator himself in the act of creation 'stayed in his own natural abode' [*Tim.* 42e5-6] and even 'takes the road to the Castle of Kronos' [Pind. *Ol.* 2.126-127]; indeed, he himself constituted the soul from three elements, one part that inclines toward the lower world, one that naturally reverts upon itself, and one that can lift itself up towards its cause. Then why is it said in the *Phaedrus* [247d5-e2] that certain virtues exist already in the supra-celestial region? In that passage the virtues serve to describe by analogy the intelligible entities of that level, in the same way as 'meadow' [248c1], 'plain' [b6], 'pasture' [b7], etc., do.

§§ 152-164. On virtues: discussion of the text. 68c5-69c3

152. [68c5-6] Why does he mention courage first? — Because it is the characteristic feature of the purificatory life, just as temperance determines the life of ethical virtue, justice social life, insight contemplative life.

Rather we should go by the natural order of the essential features of each: first, one has to stand firm against the inferior powers, then revert upon oneself, then develop one's own natural activity, finally, by means of this very activity, distinguish between good and evil.

153. [68d2-3] Why is this kind of courage and temperance 'preposterous'? — Because it is mixed with its own privation and is not what it purports to be and puts on the appearance of what it is not.

154. [68c8; d2; 5] Why are those without a philosophical education called 'the others' and the 'many'? — The 'many' as farthest apart from

---

4. βούλονται : on this usage cf. index Dam., *Phil.*; *infra* § 253.3; § 256.3; § 382.9; § 412.4.

6-8. The three phases of remaining, procession and reversion (Pr., *elem.* 35) are found also in the Demiurge. The last, reversion, is expressed in a line from Pindar (*Ol.* 2.124-127) ὅσοι δ' ἐτόλμασαν ἐς τρὶς ἑκατέρωθι μείναντες ἀπὸ πάμπαν ἀδίκων ἔχειν ψυχάν, ἔτειλαν (v.l. ἔστειλαν) Διὸς ὁδὸν παρὰ Κρόνου τύρσιν. According to Turyn, ἔτειλαν is a Byzantine conjecture (Moschopulus and Triclinius), ἔστειλαν being the traditional text (older MSS., scholia, Hermias 168.28, Dam., *Parm.* 152.19 and h.l.; see also *supra*, § 149.1-2 note). The scholiast (92.23-24 Drachmann) explains: ἐστάλησαν ἣν ὁδὸν ἔταξεν ὁ Ζεύς, ἣν μακάρων νῆσον ὀνομάζουσιν· ἣν δὴ Κρόνου τύρσιν προσηγόρευσεν. On Διὸς ὁδόν ibid. 93.16-20: the road ordained or shown by Zeus. Dam., however, obviously understands it as the road taken by Zeus, symbolizing the return of the Creative Intelligence to its origin, the Pure Intelligence; cf. Dam.,

παραζεύγνυσιν ἀρετήν. καὶ μήποτε τακτικαὶ βούλονται εἶναι φύσει τῆς ἀταξίας αἱ ἀρεταί· διόπερ ἀπὸ τῆς δημιουργικῆς ἄρχονται τάξεως. πῶς οὖν καθαρτικαί; 5
ἢ ὅτι καὶ ὁ δημιουργὸς κατὰ τὴν ἑαυτοῦ δημιουργίαν ʽἔμενεν ἐν τῷ ἑαυτοῦ κατὰ τρόπον ἤθει' [Tim. 42e5-6] καὶ ἔτι μέντοι ʽστέλλεται παρὰ Κρόνου τύρσιν' [Pind. Ol. 2.126-127]· καὶ γὰρ τὴν ψυχὴν | τρισὶ πληρώμασι συνεπλήρωσεν αὐτός, (117) τῷ τε πρὸς τὰ μεθ' ἑαυτὴν ῥέποντι καὶ ⟨τῷ⟩ πρὸς ἑαυτὴν ἐπιστρέφεσθαι πεφυκότι καὶ τῷ πρὸς τὰ αἴτια ἀνατείνεσθαι δυναμένῳ. πῶς οὖν ἐν Φαίδρῳ [247d5-e2] 10
λέγονταί τινες ἀρεταὶ ἐν τῷ ὑπερουρανίῳ τόπῳ; ἢ κατὰ ἀναλογίαν ἐνδείκνυται διὰ τῶν ἀρετῶν τὰ ἐκεῖ νοητά, ὡς διὰ ʽλειμῶνος' [248c1] καὶ ʽπεδίον' [b6] καὶ ʽνομῆς' [b7] καὶ τοιούτων τινῶν.

§§ 152-164. On virtues: discussion of the text. 68c5-69c3

ρνα'. - [68c5-6] Διὰ τί περὶ ἀνδρείας πρῶτόν φησιν; — Ἢ ὅτι αὕτη τὴν 152
καθαρτικὴν εἰδοποιεῖ ζωήν, ὡς τὴν ἠθικὴν ἡ σωφροσύνη, τὴν δὲ πολιτικὴν ἡ δικαιοσύνη, τὴν δὲ θεωρητικὴν ἡ φρόνησις.
Κάλλιον δὲ τῇ τάξει τῶν χαρακτήρων ἀκολουθῆσαι· πρῶτον γὰρ δεῖ μὴ ἡττᾶσθαι ὑπὸ τοῦ χείρονος, εἶτα πρὸς ἑαυτὸν ἐπιστρέφειν, εἶτα προβάλλεσθαι 5
τὴν οἰκείαν ἐνέργειαν, εἶτα κρίνειν τὰ ἀγαθὰ δι' αὐτῆς ἐκείνης καὶ τὰ κακά.
ρνβ'. - [68d2-3] Διὰ τί ʽἄτοπος' ἡ ἀνδρεία καὶ ἡ σωφροσύνη; — Ἢ ὅτι 153
συμμιγὴς τῇ οἰκείᾳ στερήσει, καὶ οὐκ ἔστιν ὃ βούλεται εἶναι, καὶ φαντάζεται εἶναι ὃ μή ἐστιν.
ρνγ'. - [68c8; d2; 5] Διὰ τί ʽἄλλοι' καὶ ʽπολλοὶ' οἱ ἀπαίδευτοι; — Ἢ ʽπολλοὶ' 154
μὲν ὡς πορρωτάτω τοῦ ἑνός, ʽἄλλοι' δὲ ὡς πορρωτάτω τοῦ οἰκείου παραδείγματος.

---

§ 151. 9 τῷ² Wk: om. M | ἐπιστρέφεσθαι] -σθαι in ras. M^x — 13 τοιούτων] -ι- in ras. M^c

---

Parm. 152.16-24.
10-11. On the 'virtues' in the ὑπερουράνιος τόπος of the Phaedrus, which in the interpretation of Pr. and Dam. represents the highest level of the intelligible-and-intellective order, cf. Hermias 153.29-154.14; Pr., theol. IV 14.
12-13. On the 'meadow', the 'plain' and the 'pasture': Hermias 160.21-161.9; Pr., theol. IV 15.
§ 152. 1-3. Ol. 8 § 3.8-10, cf. § 1.7-9. Both Dam. h.l. and Ol. report Proclus, see Rep. I 12.25-13.5 καὶ γὰρ αὖ καὶ ὡς ἐν ἄλλοις διείλομεν, ἡ μὲν σωφροσύνη μάλιστα χαρακτηρίζει τὴν ἠθικὴν ἀρετήν..., ἡ δὲ δικαιοσύνη τὴν πολιτικήν..., ἡ δὲ ἀνδρεία τὴν καθαρτικήν..., ἡ ⟨δὲ⟩ φρόνησις τὴν θεωρητικήν. The reference ἐν ἄλλοις is without any doubt to Pr.'s commentary on the Phaedo.
4-6. Dam. returns to the characteristic of the virtues given in § 149.7-12.
§ 153. 2. συμμιγὴς τῇ οἰκείᾳ στερήσει: cf. note on § 94.5.

94   DAMASCIUS I §§ 154-158

the One, the 'others' as farthest apart from their own archetype. In this sense Plato calls the objects of sense-perception 'the other things' in the *Parmenides* [157b7–c4], intelligible reality being 'things themselves.'

155. [68d5–13] The whole doctrine is deduced as follows:
The non-philosopher considers death an evil of a greater evil faces it for fear faces it out of cowardice.

156. Ordinary people regard death as a terrible thing, as terrible as non-existence, and even if they are naturally brave they look upon it as the destruction of their own selves. Those whose standard is conventional morals, even though they may believe in the immortality of the soul, still think the living body necessary to attain perfection in their own kind of virtue, and therefore they have misgivings about death. Those whose standard is life in the community admit that they cannot do without the body as an instrument, so that they, too, consider death a kind of evil. It follows that only the man whose aim is purification can believe that death is good, since it helps him to achieve his end. In this way the first proposition is proved true; the second is evident: when we have to choose between evils we prefer the lesser evil to the greater. The third is that the same man will be a coward and a hero; for he *is* afraid; consequently the only brave man is the man on the way to purification, who considers death a boon.

157. How can the word 'brave' apply to such a man? If he faces death as a terrifying fate, he can no longer be said to have freed himself from the body; if he regards it as beneficent, he may be free from the body, but he is no longer brave, courage being confidence in the midst of dangers. — It can be replied that this is the notion of courage as a social virtue, while on the level of purification it is total separation from the inferior and rather impassibility than emotional balance in dangers.

A more correct explanation is that purifying virtue in general is contempt of all that is painful or pleasant, not to oneself (for in this stage nothing is), but to all other men.

158. The average man chooses death in preference to a greater evil, the

---

§ 154. 3. The ἄλλα of the *Parm.* are the 'other things' of the fourth hypothesis (157b6–159b1), which according to the unanimous opinion of the exegetes since Plutarch of Athens is to be regarded as dealing with materialized form (Pr., *theol.* I, Introd. pp. LXXXV–LXXXVII S.-W.). Dam., *Parm.* 274.9–12, comments: πρὸς δὲ τούτοις πᾶν τὸ ἐν ὕλῃ ὂν καὶ αὐτὴν τὴν ὕλην 'ἄλλα' καλεῖ ὁ ἐν Φαίδωνι Σωκράτης, καὶ πρὸ αὐτοῦ οἱ Πυθαγόρειοι, πρὸς ἀντιδιαίρεσιν τῶν αὐτῶν (read ἀΰλων) εἰδῶν λεγομένων (perh. λεγόμενα). The *Ph.* citation does not refer to the present passage, but to 83b2–3, as is shown by the fuller discussion *ibid.* 172.16–22, where Dam. differs from Pr. in the interpretation of *Parm.* 146d4–5: βέλτιον ἄρα τῷ διορισμῷ αὐτοῦ ἐμμένειν κατὰ τὴν Πυθαγορικὴν συνήθειαν καὶ τὴν αὐτοῦ τοῦ Πλάτωνος, 'ἄλλα' νοοῦντας τὰ ἔνυλα πράγματα καὶ αὐτὴν τὴν ὕλην. ἔν τε γὰρ τῷ Φαίδωνι οὕτως ὀνομάζει τὰ 'ἄλλα' τὰ εἴδη τὰ αἰσθητά, λέγων 'ἄλλα καὶ ἐν ἄλλοις'. Ἀριστοτέλης δὲ ἐν τοῖς Ἀρχυτείοις ἱστορεῖ καὶ Πυθαγόραν 'ἄλλο' τὴν ὕλην καλεῖν ὡς ῥευστὴν καὶ ἀεὶ ἄλλο καὶ ἄλλο γιγνόμενον.

οὕτω γὰρ 'ἄλλα' καλεῖ τὰ αἰσθητὰ ἐν Παρμενίδῃ [157b7–c4], ἐπειδὴ καὶ τὰ νοητὰ 'αὐτὰ' καλεῖ.

—. – [68d5–13] Ὅτι ὁ συλλογισμὸς τοῦ ὅλου δόγματος τοιοῦτος· **155**
ὁ μὴ φιλό- κακὸν ἡγεῖται φόβῳ μείζονος δέει ὑπο-
σοφος τὸν θάνατον κακοῦ ὑπομένει μένει.

ρνδ'. – Ὅτι καὶ οἱ πολλοὶ ἄνθρωποι δεινὸν ἡγοῦνται τὸν θάνατον ἴσα γε τῷ **156**(118)
μὴ ὄντι, κἂν φύσει ὦσιν ἀνδρεῖοι, φθορὰν ἑαυτῶν ἡγοῦνται αὐτόν. οἱ δὲ ἠθικοί,
κἂν δοξάζωσιν ἀθάνατον τὴν ψυχήν, ἀλλὰ δεῖσθαι νομίζουσι τοῦ ζῴου πρὸς
τελέωσιν τῆς οἰκείας ἀρετῆς, ὥστε κακὸν ὑποπτεύουσι τὸν θάνατον. οἱ δὲ
πολιτικοὶ δεῖσθαι τοῦ ὀργάνου ὁμολογοῦσιν, ὥστε καὶ αὐτοὶ κακόν τι ἥγηνται 5
αὐτόν. μόνοι ἄρα οἱ καθαρτικοὶ ἀγαθὸν οἴονται τὸν θάνατον ἅτε συλλήπτορα
τοῦ οἰκείου τέλους. οὕτω μὲν ἡ πρώτη πρότασις ἀληθής· ἡ δὲ δευτέρα σαφής,
ἐν γὰρ αἱρέσει κακῶν τὸ ἔλαττον αἱρούμεθα ἀντὶ τοῦ μείζονος. ἡ δὲ τρίτη ὅτι
δειλὸς ὁ αὐτὸς καὶ ἀνδρεῖος· δέδιεν γάρ· μόνος ἄρα ἀνδρεῖος ὁ καθαρτικὸς ὁ
καὶ ἀγαθὸν αὐτὸν τιθέμενος. 10

ρνε'. – Πῶς ἀνδρεῖος ὁ καθαρτικός; εἰ μὲν γὰρ ὑπομένει ὡς δεινὸν τὸν **157**
θάνατον, οὐκέτι καθαρτικός· εἰ δὲ ὡς ἀγαθόν, καθαρτικὸς μέν, οὐ μὴν ἀνδρεῖος,
ἐν γὰρ τοῖς δεινοῖς ἡ ἀνδρεία θαρραλεότης. — Ἤ ῥητέον ὡς αὕτη μὲν πολιτικῆς
ἀνδρείας ἔννοια, ἡ δὲ καθαρτικὴ τελέα τῶν χειρόνων ἀπόστασις καὶ ἀπάθεια
μᾶλλον ἢ μετριοπάθεια ἐν δεινοῖς. 5
Κάλλιον δὲ τὴν καθαρτικὴν ὅλως ἀρετὴν ὑπεροψίαν εἶναι λυπηρῶν καὶ ἡδέων,
οὐ τῶν ἑαυτῷ (οὐδὲν γὰρ αὐτῷ τοιοῦτον), ἀλλὰ τῶν τοῖς ἄλλοις ἀνθρώποις ἅπασιν.

ρνϛ'. – Ὅτι ὁ μὲν πολὺς ἀντὶ μείζονος κακοῦ αἱρεῖται τὸν θάνατον, ὁ δὲ **158**

---

§ 154. 3 παρμενείδηι M
§ 157. 2 καθαρτικός¹] κα- ins. M^c — 4 post ἀπόστασις ∸ 26ies in ras. M^x

---

ὥστε δῆλός ἐστι καὶ ὁ Πλάτων ταύτῃ τὰ ἄλλα ἀφοριζόμενος. Cf. also Pr., *Parm.* 1059.5–11, discussing Plutarch's view of the hypotheses: τὴν δὲ τετάρτην περὶ τοῦ ἐνύλου εἴδους, τὴν δὲ πέμπτην περὶ τῆς ὕλης, ἐν αἷς τὰ ἄλλα ὑπόκειται τοῦ ἑνός· ἔθος γὰρ ἦν, ὡς εἴπομεν (1048.6–8), καὶ τοῖς Πυθαγορείοις 'ἓν' μὲν προσαγορεύειν πᾶσαν τὴν ἀσώματον καὶ χωριστὴν οὐσίαν, 'ἄλλα' δὲ τὴν σωματικὴν καὶ ἐν σώμασιν ὑφεστηκυῖαν.

3–4. τὰ νοητὰ 'αὐτὰ' καλεῖ : not in the *Parm.* passage, where τὰ ἄλλα is contrasted with τὸ ἕν (see the last quotation from Pr.), but in such well-known texts as *Ph.* 65d5, *Phaedr.* 247d6.

§ 156. 7–9. The three propositions are those shown in the diagram of § 155.

§ 157. Ol. 8 § 10. Ol. offers the "better" solution of lines 6–7; since he occasionally follows Dam. (see *infra* § 163), the κάλλιον may still, as usual, introduce Dam.'s answer.

philosopher-citizen, too, chooses it as a lesser evil in exchange for a greater good, the philosopher in search of purification chooses it as preferable without reserve and for its own sake. This gives us three kinds of courage.

159. [68d2–69a5] On the face of it, courage conquers pain and temperance pleasure, but in reality both conquer both. What is the difference, then? — That courage does so by undaunted resistance to both pleasure and pain, temperance by turning away from them; justice, too, in fact, shuns them as alien activities or affects, and prudence because it recognizes both as harmful.

160. A man whose courage is such that he becomes a hero out of a sort of fear, is a hero in action only: he does not choose courage because he considers it a good, but because it is necessary. The same holds good of a man who is temperant in a comparable way.

161. [68e2–69a5] The ordinary man chooses greater pleasures in preference to lesser ones, and smaller discomforts in preference to greater ones; a man who is still imperfect in virtue prefers the more honorable pleasures to those that are less decorous; the philosopher-statesman accepts pleasure that is necessary for the attainment of a good. The man whose aim is purification, however, is in no way accessible to pleasure, and he is aware of it in the same way as Socrates felt the pain localized in his leg [60b1–c7]; therefore only his temperance is true temperance.

162. [69a6–c3] Formulating a general rule to distinguish between imperfect and perfect virtues, Socrates postulates that virtue is not exchange, but total extirpation of affects. If it is to be an exchange, it should not consist in choosing one affect instead of another, greater for smaller, more respectable for less honorable, nor, in Epicurean terminology, 'stationary' pleasures for erratic ones, nor, in accordance with Stoic doctrine, natural pleasures for those against nature, but insight in exchange for all affects, so that instead of the emotions we acquire insight, which can judge the emotions themselves, because it belongs to reason only and is naturally willing and able to dominate.

163. [68d2–69a5] Why does Plato omit justice from the list of spurious and imperfect virtues? — Because there are no bodily affects in which it can manifest itself.

(Or rather because, as we know, it is a quality of all the three parts of the soul.)

---

§ 162. 4–5. Epicurus: Diog. Laert. 10,136 (=frg. 2 Usener=frg. [7] Arrighetti).

5–6. In Stoic doctrine, pleasure is an affect, and as such by definition παρὰ φύσιν (e.g. *SVF* III frg. 391 ἡδονὴ ἄλογος ἔπαρσις); its counterpart, joy (χαρά) is defined as εὔλογος ἔπαρσις (III frg. 431). These are presumably meant by pleasure παρὰ φύσιν and κατὰ φύσιν.

§ 163. Ol. 8 § 9; § 1.4–5. Ol. refers twice to the point raised here: in his θεωρία at 8 § 1 he says that prudence as a purificatory virtue has already been dealt with before (65a9), that courage and temperance are now added to it, and that justice is not mentioned because it superimposes itself necessarily on the other three

πολιτικὸς ἀντὶ μείζονος ἀγαθοῦ ὡς κακὸν ἔλαττον καὶ αὐτός, ὁ δὲ καθαρτικὸς ὡς αὐτόθεν αἱρετὸν καὶ δι' ἑαυτόν. ὥστε τριττὴ κατὰ γένος ἡ ἀνδρεία.

ρνζ'. – [68d2–69a5] Ὅτι δοκεῖ ἡ μὲν ἀνδρεία τῶν λυπῶν κρατεῖν, ἡ δὲ **159** σωφροσύνη τῶν ἡδονῶν, κατὰ δὲ τὸ ἀληθὲς ἑκατέρα ἑκατέρων. τίς οὖν ἡ διαφορά; — Ἢ ὅτι ἡ μὲν ὡς ἀήττητος ὑφ' ἑκατέρων, | ἡ δὲ ὡς ἐπιστρέφουσα ἀφ' ἑκατέρων· **(119)** ἐπεὶ καὶ ἡ δικαιοσύνη φεύγει αὐτὰς ὡς ἀλλότρια ἐνεργήματα ἢ παθήματα καὶ ἡ φρόνησις ὡς κακὰ ἑκάτερα. 5

ρνη'. – Ὅτι ὁ οὕτως ἀνδρεῖος ὡς δέει τινὶ ἀνδρεΐζεσθαι ἐν ταῖς ἐνεργείαις **160** ἀνδρεΐζεται· οὐ γὰρ ὡς ἀγαθὸν αἱρεῖται τὴν ἀνδρείαν, ἀλλ' ὡς ἀναγκαῖον. οὕτω δὲ καὶ ὁ τούτῳ σώφρων ἀναλογῶν.

ρνθ'. – [68e2–69a5] Ὅτι ὁ μὲν πολὺς τὰς μείζους ἡδονὰς αἱρεῖται ἀντὶ τῶν **161** ἐλαττόνων, ὡς τὰς ἐλάττους λύπας ἀντὶ τῶν μειζόνων· ὁ δὲ ἀτελὴς τὴν ἀρετὴν τὰς καλλίους ἀντὶ τῶν ἀσχημονεστέρων· ὁ δὲ πολιτικὸς ἡδονὴν ἀναγκαίαν ὑπὲρ ἀγαθοῦ. ὁ δὲ καθαρτικὸς οὐδένα τρόπον προσίεται τὴν ἡδονήν, οὕτω δὲ αὐτῆς ἐπαισθάνεται ὡς καὶ ἐν τῷ σκέλει ἦν τὸ ἀλγεῖν [60b1–c7]· ἀληθὴς ἄρα σωφροσύνη 5 ἡ τοῦ καθαρτικοῦ.

ρξ'. – [69a6–c3] Ὅτι κοινὸν ἐκφέρων κανόνα τῶν τε ἀτελῶν ἀρετῶν καὶ **162** τῶν τελείων οὐκ ἀλλαγὴν παθῶν ἀξιοῖ τὴν ἀρετὴν εἶναι, ἀλλὰ ὅλως παθῶν ἐξαίρεσιν. εἰ δὲ ἀλλαγήν, οὐ παθῶν ἄλλων ἀντὶ ἄλλων, οὔτε μειζόνων ἀντὶ ἐλαττόνων, οὔτε καλλιόνων ἀντὶ αἰσχροτέρων, ἀλλ' οὐδὲ κατὰ Ἐπικουρείους καταστηματικῶν ἀντὶ πλημμελῶν ἡδονῶν, οὔτε κατὰ τοὺς Στωικοὺς τῶν κατὰ 5 φύσιν ἀντὶ τῶν παρὰ φύσιν, ἀλλὰ φρονήσεως ἀντὶ πάντων παθῶν, ἵνα ἀντ' ἐκείνων κτησώμεθα φρόνησιν, ἢ καὶ ἐκείνων ἔσται κριτική, ἴδιος οὖσα τοῦ λόγου καὶ φύσει ἄρχειν βουλομένη καὶ δυναμένη.

ρξα'. – [68d2–69a5] Διὰ τί τὴν δικαιοσύνην παρέλιπεν ἐν ταῖς ψευδωνύμοις **163** καὶ ἀτελέσιν; — Ἢ ὅτι οὐκ ἔχει πάθη σωματικὰ οἷς ἐμφαντάζεται.
(*Ἢ ὅτι μᾶλλον τῶν τριῶν ἦν μορίων.*)

---

§ 158. 2 ἀγαθοῦ] ἀγαθ- in ras. M^x — 3 τριττὴ M^x: τρίτη M¹
§ 159. 2 ἑκατέρα μ: ἑκάτερα M
§ 162. 4 ἐπικουρίους M
§ 163. 1 παρέλιπεν Wk: παρέλειπεν M

---

virtues. In the λέξις (8 § 9) he says that Pr. accounted for the omission of justice by pointing out that it does not correspond to any particular temperament, as the others do, then expresses his own preference for the solution of § 1 (justice accompanies the other three), adding that it is Dam.'s. In the very much condensed note which we have here, Dam.'s amendment is inserted at line 3 in a not very clear form; lines 4–5 make sense only if taken as continuing lines 1–2 (prudence too is left out because it has no association with any physical temperament). Another example of such a correction *in parenthesi* is found in § 114.

For the same reason he leaves out insight also, because it is a quality of reason; among the perfect virtues, however, these are included too [69b8-c3].

164. [69a6-c3] The Attic commentators make all the perfect virtues mentioned here purifying virtues and understand by the affects [b4-5] those that can attend a life of purification, e.g. by pleasure the joy of being free from the body, by fear complete avoidance of all that is extraneous; Harpocratio [frg. 5], on the contrary, takes all the virtues as social virtues, and therefore he understands the affects as those of life in society.

In our opinion, the passage should be read as consisting of two parts, the first of which [a9-b5] deals with the social virtues, in which prudence takes the place of the affects, the second [b8-c3] with the purificatory virtues. Socrates indeed is apparently still referring to the same affects; then he continues 'but really and truly virtue is a purification from those,' i.e. evidently from the irrational affects, from which purificatory virtue is said to cleanse us completely. Therefore he adds the article to the several virtues [c1-2] and says that 'really and truly virtue is a purification from affects.'

§§ 165-172. Philosophy is initiation. 69c3-d2

165. Dialectical thought should either start from the divine riddles, developing the mysterious truth in them, or come to rest in them and derive its final confirmation from their symbolical indications, or it should combine the two, as Socrates does here. The whole discussion consisting of two problems, the ban on suicide, and, in spite of this, the necessity of detaching oneself from the body, he makes the divine mysteries the starting-point for the first [62b2-6] and the final point of the second.

166. In this, he imitates the mystic and cosmic cycle of souls. Having fled the undivided Dionysian life and fixed their actual existence on the level of the Titanic and confined way of life, they are in shackles and in 'custody' [62b4]; but when they submit to their punishment and take care of themselves, then, cleansed from the taints of Titanic existence and gathered together, they become Bacchus, that is to say, they become whole again, as the Dionysus who remains above is whole.

---

§ 164. 1-5. On the probable issue of the debate between the Attic commentators and Harpocratio see above, note on §§ 148-149.

6-12. Ol. 8 § 4.5-§ 6.17 and note: Dam. follows Pr., who read into the passage 68d2-69d2 the whole scale of virtues, from natural to contemplative.

8. ὡς γὰρ περὶ τῶν αὐτῶν παθῶν διαλέγεται ὁ Σωκράτης : i.e. the pleasures and fears of b4-5 are still the same as the affects of a7-8.

10-11. μετὰ τῶν ἄρθρων : the absence of the article at b2-3 (ἀνδρεία καὶ σωφροσύνη καὶ δικαιοσύνη . . . μετὰ φρονήσεως) supposedly serves to distinguish the civic virtues from the purifying virtues at c1-2, which are preceded by the article (καὶ ἡ σωφροσύνη

Διὸ καὶ τὴν φρόνησιν ἀφίησιν ὡς τοῦ λόγου οὖσαν· ἐν δὲ ταῖς τελείαις καὶ ταῦτα συναριθμεῖται [69b8-c3].

ρξβ'. - [69a6-c3] Ὅτι οἱ μὲν Ἀττικοὶ ἐξηγηταὶ πάσας τὰς ἐνταῦθα τελείας καθαρτικὰς ποιοῦσιν, καὶ τὰ πάθη [b4-5] νοοῦσιν ὅσα συνεῖναι δύναται τῇ καθαρτικῇ ζωῇ, οἷον ἡδονὴν μὲν τὴν ἐπὶ τῷ χωρισμῷ εὐφροσύνην, φόβον δὲ τὴν τελέαν φυγὴν τῶν ἐκτός· ὁ δὲ Ἁρποκρατίων [frg. 5] πάσας πολιτικάς, διὸ τὰ πάθη ἀκούει πολιτικῶς.

Ἡμῖν δὲ μεριστέον τὸν λόγον εἰς δύο, καὶ τὸν μὲν πρῶτον [a9-b5] παριστάνειν τὰς πολιτικάς, ἅτε φρονήσεως ἀντικαταλλαττομένων τῶν παθῶν, τὸν δὲ δεύτερον [b8-c3] τὰς καθαρτικάς. ὡς γὰρ περὶ τῶν αὐτῶν παθῶν διαλέγεται ὁ Σωκράτης· εἶτα καὶ ἐπάγει 'τὸ δὲ ἀληθὲς τῷ ὄντι ᾖ κάθαρσις ἐκείνων', καὶ δῆλον ὅτι τῶν ἀλόγων παθῶν, ὧν τελεία κάθαρσις εἴρηται ἡ καθαρτικὴ ἀρετή. διὸ καὶ μετὰ τῶν ἄρθρων ὀνομάζει τὰς ἀρετάς [c1-2], καὶ 'τῷ ὄντι' φησὶν 'ἀληθὲς ᾖ κάθαρσιν εἶναι παθῶν'.

§§ 165-172. Philosophy is initiation. 69c3-d2

ρξγ'. - Ὅτι χρὴ τὰς διαλεκτικὰς νοήσεις ἢ ἀπὸ τῶν θείων ἄρχεσθαι αἰνιγμάτων, τὸ ἐν αὐτοῖς ἀπόρρητον τῆς ἀληθείας ἀναπτυσσούσας, ἢ εἰς αὐτὰ ὁρμίζεσθαι καὶ ἐπαναπαύεσθαι ταῖς ἐκείνων ἐνδείξεσιν, ἢ τὸ συναμφότερον, ὃ καὶ νῦν ὁ Σωκράτης ἐποίησεν. τοῦ γὰρ παντὸς λόγου δύο προβλήμασι συμπεπλεγμένου, ὅτι τε μὴ δεῖ ἐξάγειν καὶ ὅτι οὐδὲν ἧττον προσήκει χωρίζειν, τοῦ μὲν πρώτου ἐκ τῶν ἀπορρήτων ἤρξατο [62b2-6], τὸν δὲ δεύτερον εἰς τὰ ἀπόρρητα ἐπανήγαγεν.

ρξδ'. - Ὅτι τὸν μυστικόν τε καὶ κοσμικὸν τῶν ψυχῶν ἐμιμήσατο κύκλον. φυγοῦσαι μὲν γὰρ ἀπὸ τῆς ἀμερίστου ζωῆς καὶ τῆς Διονυσιακῆς προβαλόμεναί τε τὴν Τιτανικήν τε καὶ ἀπεστενωμένην ἐν τῇ φρουρᾷ [62b4] κατεδέθησαν· ἐμμείνασαι δὲ τῇ ποινῇ καὶ σφῶν αὐτῶν ἐπιμεληθεῖσαι, καθαρθεῖσαι τῶν Τιτανικῶν μολυσμῶν καὶ συναγερθεῖσαι γίνονται Βάκχοι, ὅ ἐστιν ὁλόκληροι κατὰ τὸν ἄνω μένοντα Διόνυσον.

καὶ ἡ δικαιοσύνη καὶ ἡ [TWY, Iambl., protr. p. 67.7: om. B, Stob.] ἀνδρεία, καὶ αὐτὴ ἡ φρόνησις).

§§ 165-166. Ol. 8 § 7. Socrates' speech, by beginning and ending with the mysteries of Dionysus, has described a perfect circle, analogous to the cycle of the soul. On Dionysus see note on §§ 1-13.

§ 166. 1. *μυστικόν*: symbolized in the mysteries.
ibid. *ἐμιμήσατο κύκλον*: see note on Ol. 8 § 7.9-12.
5. *Βάκχοι*: not 'Bacchants', but the God himself, cf. *supra* § 9.7 *Διόνυσοι γινόμεθα*, infra § 171, *Vit. Isid.* frg. 172, Ol. 8 § 7.6-9.
6. *τὸν ἄνω μένοντα Διόνυσον*: cf. *infra* § 168.3-4.

167. In the mysteries the first stage used to be general purifying ceremonies, followed by more secret ones, after which conjunction took place, then initiation, and finally vision. Analogous to these stages are the several degrees of virtues, the ethical and social virtues corresponding to the public purifying rites, the purificatory virtues, in which all the extraneous is discarded, to the more secret purifications, speculative activity on the reflective level to conjunction, integration of its results to form an indivisible whole to initiation, simple intuition of simple forms to vision.

168. The object of the initiatory rites is to take souls back to a final destination, which was also the starting-point from which they first set out on their downward journey, and where Dionysus gave them being, seated on his father's throne, that is to say, firmly established in the integral Zeusian life. It follows necessarily that the initiate will 'live with the Gods,' in accordance with the design of the initiating Gods. Initiatory rites are twofold: those here below, which are a kind of preparation, and those in the hereafter, of which there are, in my opinion, again two kinds, those that purify the pneumatic body (as rites here below do the 'shell-like' body) and those that purify the astral body. In other words, the way upward through initiation has three degrees, as also has the way through philosophy: the philosophers' way to perfection takes three thousand years, as it is said in the *Phaedrus* [249a3–5], the number thousand representing a full life and a complete period. Therefore the 'uninitiated,' because farthest remote from his destination, 'lies in slime,' both here and even more hereafter, where his place is in the 'dregs of creation,' Tartarus itself. Of course the text mentions only the extremes, but there is also a wide range of intermediate states. The ways by which philosophy leads us upwards can be

---

§ 167. Norvin cites another passage paralleling philosophy and initiation from Theo Smyrn. (14.18–16.2). Theo's stages are: 1 purification (mathematics); 2 instruction (logic, politics, physics); 3 ἐποπτεία (dialectic); 4 coronation (teaching ability); 5 happiness by living with the Gods (assimilation to God). Hermias 178.14–20 compares the terms τελετή, μύησις and ἐποπτεία as applied to the philosophical life. Correspondences between the three texts are not particularly striking, they must have taken their cues independently from Pl. (*Phaedr.* 249b6–d3; 250b5–c6; *Symp.* 209e5–210a2; *Epin.* 986c5–d4). Cf. Pr., *theol.* IV 26, 77.9–19.

2. συστάσεις : see *LSJ* s.v. I 2 and esp. Lewy 228–238, who gives the following description: "The term derives from the current vocabulary of the magical science and applies to the 'conjunction' of a magician with a god or with one of his ministering spirits ..., who aids the theurgist by granting him the superhuman powers required for the accomplishment of the magical act. Thus the 'conjunction' precedes the main magical operation." Examples from magical papyri in *LSJ*; principal occurrences in Neoplatonic texts: Porphyry, ap. Iambl., *myst.* 132.6; Iambl., *ibid.* 133.15–134.2; Pr., *Tim.* III 89.16–20; Marin., *vit. Pr.* 28.

§ 168. 1–2. Cf. the similar etymology of τελετή in Hermias 178.9–10 τελετὴ ἐκλήθη ... παρὰ τὸ τελέαν τὴν ψυχὴν ἀποτελεῖν.

3. ἱδρυμένος ἐν τῷ θρόνῳ τοῦ οἰκείου πατρός : cf. *Orphica*, frg. 208 (Pr., *Crat.* 55.5–11).

6–7. τὸν πνευματικὸν χιτῶνα, ... τὸν ὀστρέϊνον, ... τὸν αὐγοειδῆ : on the three

ρξε'. – Ὅτι ἐν τοῖς ἱεροῖς ἡγοῦντο μὲν αἱ πάνδημοι καθάρ|σεις, εἶτα 167(121)
ἐπὶ ταύταις ἀπορρητότεραι, μετὰ δὲ ταύτας συστάσεις παρελαμβάνοντο καὶ ἐπὶ
ταύταις μυήσεις, ἐν τέλει δὲ ἐποπτεῖαι. ἀναλογοῦσι τοίνυν αἱ μὲν ἠθικαί τε καὶ
πολιτικαὶ ἀρεταὶ τοῖς ἐμφανέσι καθαρμοῖς, αἱ δὲ καθαρτικαί, ὅσαι ἀποσκευάζονται
πάντα τὰ ἐκτός, τοῖς ἀπορρητοτέροις, αἱ δὲ περὶ τὰ διανοητὰ θεωρητικαὶ ἐνέργειαι 5
ταῖς συστάσεσιν, αἱ δὲ τούτων συναιρέσεις εἰς τὸ ἀμέριστον ταῖς μυήσεσιν,
αἱ δὲ ἁπλαῖ τῶν ἁπλῶν εἰδῶν αὐτοψίαι ταῖς ἐποπτείαις.

ρξϛ'. – Ὅτι σκοπὸς τῶν τελετῶν ἐστιν εἰς τέλος ἀναγαγεῖν τὰς ψυχὰς ἐκεῖνο 168
ἀφ' οὗ τὴν πρώτην ἐποιήσαντο κάθοδον ὡς ἀπ' ἀρχῆς, ἐν ᾗ καὶ ὁ Διόνυσος
αὐτὰς ὑπέστησεν ἱδρυμένος ἐν τῷ θρόνῳ τοῦ οἰκείου πατρός, ὅ ἐστιν ἐν τῇ ὅλῃ
ζωῇ τῇ Διΐῳ. ἀναγκαίως ἄρα ὁ τετελεσμένος ʻοἰκεῖ μετὰ θεῶνʼ, κατὰ τὸν σκοπὸν
τῶν τελούντων θεῶν. διτταὶ δὲ αἱ τελεταί, αἱ μὲν ἐνθάδε, προπαρασκευαί τινες οὖσαι, 5
αἱ δὲ ἐκεῖ· διτταὶ δὲ οἶμαι καὶ αὗται, αἱ μὲν περὶ τὸν πνευματικὸν χιτῶνα, ὡς αἱ
ἐνθάδε περὶ τὸν ὀστρέινον, αἱ δὲ περὶ τὸν αὐγοειδῆ. τρεῖς γὰρ οἱ βαθμοὶ τῆς
ἀνόδου τῆς τελεστικῆς, ὡς καὶ τῆς φιλοσόφου· τρισχιλιοστῷ γὰρ ἔτει οἱ φιλόσοφοι
ἀνάγονται, ὡς ἐν Φαίδρῳ εἴρηται [249a3–5], βίος γὰρ τέλειος καὶ περιοδικὸς
ἡ χιλιάς. ὁ ἄρα ʻἀτέλεστοςʼ ἅτε πορρωτάτω μένων τοῦ οἰκείου τέλους ʻἐν βορβόρῳ 10
κεῖταιʼ καὶ ἐνταῦθα καὶ πλέον ἐκεῖ, ἐν γὰρ τῇ τρυγὶ τῆς γενέσεως, αὐτῷ τῷ
Ταρτάρῳ. καὶ δῆλον ὅτι τὰ ἄκρα ὁ λόγος παρείληφεν, πολὺ δὲ καὶ τὸ ἐν μέσῳ
πλάτος. ἀνάλογον | δέ μοι σκόπει καὶ τὰς διὰ φιλοσοφίας ἀνόδους, εἰ καὶ μὴ (122)

§ 167. 4 ὅσαι] fort. ὅσῳ
§ 168. 3 ἱδρυμένος Wk: -ας M

kinds of living body see Dodds, elem. pp. 306–309, 319–321, 347–348, with the
main references. For occurrences in the present texts cf. the indices s.v. αὐγοειδής,
ὀστρέινος, ὄστρεον, πνεῦμα, πνευματικός. The fleshly body (called ὄστρεον because of
Pl., Phaedr. 250c6) lives once only, the pneumatic body an indefinite but limited
number of times, the luminous body is immortal.
9–10. Cf. Hermias 168.13–14 καὶ ἔφατο τὴν ὑπὸ γῆς πορείαν τῇ ψυχῇ, τουτέστι
τὴν ἀπὸ γενέσεως εἰς γένεσιν, χιλιετῆ εἶναι. 169.22–25 καὶ ὁ χίλια δὲ μέτρον τι δηλοῖ
τελειότητος τῆς ὑπὸ γῆν καθαιρομένης ψυχῆς, ὃ ἔχουσα ἔρχεται πάλιν εἰς γένεσιν, καὶ
πάλιν ἐνταῦθα ἢ εὖ ἢ κακῶς διαζήσασα τυγχάνει ὑπὸ γῆν τῆς ὀφειλομένης τελειότητος.
Pr., Rep. II 161.11–14 ὥστε ἡ χιλιέτης πορεία κοινὴ πάσαις ἐστὶν ταύταις, καὶ ἔοικεν
ἡ χιλιὰς χρόνος εἶναί τις περιοδικὸς ἀπὸ γενέσεως ἐπὶ γένεσιν ἄγων τὰς ψυχάς, οὐχ ἁπλῶς,
ἀλλὰ πρὸ τῆς τελέας ἀποκαταστάσεως.
11. τῇ τρυγὶ τῆς γενέσεως: see Theiler p. 285. The word τρύξ can be applied
to the earth, to its lower strata, or to matter: Metrodorus, Vors. 70 A20=Doxogr. 376
(Plut., Plac. III 9,5) γῆν ὑπόστασιν εἶναι καὶ τρύγα τοῦ ὕδατος, τὸν δὲ ἥλιον τοῦ ἀέρος.
Julian, Or. 5, 170D τὸ δοκοῦν ἄζωον καὶ ἄγονον καὶ σκύβαλον καὶ τῶν ὄντων οἷον ἂν
εἴποι τις ἀποκάθαρμα καὶ τρύγα καὶ ὑποστάθμην. Macrob., somn. Scip. I 14,15 "a summo
deo usque ad ultimam rerum faecem." Dam., Parm. II 282.5 καὶ γὰρ ὡς ὕλην καὶ
τρύγα καὶ ὑποστάθμην αὐτὴν ὀνομάζομεν. Infra § 522.27–28 καὶ αὕτη πρὸς ἐκείνην
οἷον τρὺξ καὶ βόρβορος. Ol., Gorg. 244.3–4 ἡμεῖς γὰρ τρύξ ἐσμεν τοῦ παντός. Ibid. 255.27

thought of in analogous terms, though the communion achieved through them is not perfect nor equal to the mystic union. If it is true that a man who pursues philosophy without eagerness will not have the benefit of its results, it is no less true that neither will a man who follows the way of initiation without total commitment reap its fruits.

169. [69c6] The word 'to lie' describes the helplessness that makes the soul dependent on external impulses, because it has become like a body, while 'living with the Gods' means belonging to their community and sharing in their government. But if so, what is the sense of the Oracle [frg. 130.2]

'They rest in God, breathing the midday rays'?

Here the condition is a higher one, surpassing all power of self-movement, as it were a supernatural form of being moved from without.

170. [69c8–d1] The fennel-stalk symbolizes matter-bound and divided creation, because it is a spurious form, being 'a tree, yet not a tree.'

A better reason is its utterly broken continuity, which has made the plant an attribute of the Titans: they offer it to Dionysus instead of his paternal sceptre, and thus they entice him into divided existence; further, the Titans are represented as bearing the fennel-stalk and Prometheus steals the fire in one, which means either that he forces down the celestial light into the world of process, or that he leads forth the soul to incarnation, or that he calls forth into the generated world the whole of divine illumination, which is itself ungenerated. This is, in fact, why Socrates too calls the

---

ἐχρῆν οὖν καὶ τρύγα καὶ ἔσχατον ἔχειν τὸν κόσμον. Kroll (*Orac*. p. 62) thinks that the Neoplatonists derived the expression from the Chaldean Oracles, but Lewy (385, n. 275) is more probably right in considering it as a substitute for the ὑποστάθμη of *Ph*. 109c2. The two words appear jointly in Julian and Dam. *loc. cit.* (also in the general meaning of sediment in Plut., *aet. phys.* 10, 914E); ὑποστάθμη alone in direct allusions to the *Ph*. in Plut., *de facie* 25, 940E τὴν γῆν οἷον ὑποστάθμην καὶ ἰλὺν τοῦ παντός, Ol., *Gorg*. 42.11–12 τελευταία δὲ [scil. ἡ γῆ] ὡς ὑποστάθμη τοῦ παντός (but also as a report of Stoic doctrine, Diog. Laert. 7,137). Of matter: Plot. II 3, 17.24; Pr., *Alc*. 181.16–17. The application to Tartarus is not found elsewhere.

§ 169. 4. The text continues ἐκ πατρόθεν κατιόντας, ἀφ' ὧν ψυχὴ κατιόντων ἐμπυρίων δρέπεται καρπῶν ψυχοτρόφον ἄνθος, so that πυρσοὺς ... ἀκμαίους is most naturally understood of sunbeams at high noon, the general idea being that of feeding on sunlight (cf. I § 530 and II § 138); ἕλκειν in that case is either 'breathe' or 'drink'. Festugière (*Tim*. V 141) translates "tirant à elles les feux impétueux...", Des Places "tirant à elles des torches florissantes".

5. Cf. Ol. 2 § 9 and note.

§ 170. 1–2. The well-known riddle, Diehl, *Anthol. lyr.*, fasc. 3, p. 76 (=schol. Pl., *Rep*. 479c): αἶνός τίς ἐστιν ὡς ἀνήρ τε κοὐκ ἀνὴρ ὄρνιθα κοὐκ ὄρνιθ' ἰδών τε κοὐκ ἰδὼν ἐπὶ ξύλου τε κοὐ ξύλου καθημένην λίθῳ τε κοὐ λίθῳ βάλοι τε κοὐ βάλοι (answer: εὐνοῦχος νυκτερίδα ἐπὶ νάρθηκος κισήρει). Dav. 42.11; Ps.-El. 16,6–10. – The narthex as a symbol of the visible world: Pr., *Hes*. 33.20–22.

1. σύμβολος: Finckh, following Cousin, wrote σύμβολον, and it is true that the

ἀκριβῆ μηδὲ κατὰ τὴν ἀπόρρητον ἕνωσιν ποιοῦνται τὴν συναφήν. εἰ δὲ μετιών
τις φιλοσοφίαν μαλακώτερον οὐ καρποῦται τὸ τέλος αὐτῆς, δῆλον ὡς καὶ 15
τελεστικῇ ἐνδιατρίβων ἰδιωτικῶς οὐκ ἀμήσει τὸν καρπὸν αὐτῆς οὐδὲ οὗτος.

ρξζ'. – [69c6] "Ὅτι τὸ μὲν 'κεῖσθαι' τὴν εἰς ἑτεροκίνητον πάρεσιν δηλοῖ τῆς 169
ψυχῆς οἷον σῶμα γενομένης, τὸ δὲ 'μετὰ θεῶν οἰκεῖν' συμπολιτεύεσθαί φησι
τοῖς θεοῖς καὶ συνοικονομεῖν. τί οὖν τὸ λόγιον βούλεται [frg. 130.2]
'ἐν δὲ θεῷ κεῖνται πυρσοὺς ἕλκοντες ἀκμαίους';
ἢ τοῦτο μεῖζον καὶ παντὸς αὐτοκινήτου τελεώτερον, οἷον ὑπερφυὲς ἑτεροκίνητον. 5

ρξη'. – [69c8–d1] "Ὅτι ὁ νάρθηξ σύμβολός ἐστι τῆς ἐνύλου δημιουργίας καὶ 170
μεριστῆς ὡς ψευδώνυμον εἶδος· 'ξύλον' γὰρ 'καὶ οὐ ξύλον'.

Κάλλιον δὲ διὰ τὴν ὅτι μάλιστα διεσπασμένην συνέχειαν, ὅθεν καὶ Τιτανικὸν
τὸ φυτόν· καὶ γὰρ τῷ Διονύσῳ προτείνουσιν αὐτὸν ἀντὶ τοῦ πατρικοῦ σκήπτρου,
καὶ ταύτῃ προκαλοῦνται αὐτὸν εἰς τὸν μερισμόν. καὶ μέντοι καὶ ναρθηκοφοροῦσιν 5
οἱ Τιτᾶνες· καὶ ὁ Προμηθεὺς ἐν νάρθηκι κλέπτει τὸ πῦρ, εἴτε τὸ οὐράνιον φῶς
εἰς τὴν γένεσιν κατασπῶν, εἴτε τὴν ψυχὴν εἰς τὸ σῶμα προάγων, εἴτε τὴν θείαν
ἔλλαμψιν ὅλην ἀγένητον οὖσαν εἰς τὴν γένεσιν προκαλούμενος. διὰ δὴ τοῦτο καὶ

---

§ 169. 2 συμπολιτεύεσθαι M^c: πολιτεύεσθαι M¹
§ 170. 8 προκαλούμενος] post -ο-¹ ∼ in ras. M^x (προσκαλούμενος M¹)

---

masculine is cited only in the sense of 'omen, presage' (LSJ; Marin., Vit. Pr. 10);
however, since so common a word as σύμβολον is not very liable to being corrupted,
it seems safer to allow for the possibility that the masculine was used here on purpose.

3–6. Cf. Orphica, frg. 235. The present passage adds to the story of the murder
of Dionysus two elements not found in Kern: first, the handing of the narthex
to Dionysus instead of the sceptre of Zeus, apparently to take away his royal power
(cf. Pr., Hes. 33.23 καὶ προσάγεται ὑπὸ τῶν Τιτάνων τῷ Διονύσῳ); secondly, the fact
that the Titans themselves carry the narthex, which combined with the quotation
from Nonnus at the end of frg. 209 (where they are said to have painted their
faces white) raises the question whether this masquerade can have provided the
original, sinister context for the line "Many carry the thyrsus, few are Bacchants."
See also Dam., Parm. 316.21–317.1, where the Titans are said to present themselves
as Dionysus (i.e. as Bakchoi). The sense suggested by Pl. (and confirmed by
Hermias 172.7–10) is of course the proverbial one, "Many are called but few
are chosen."

6–9. (1) Τὸ οὐράνιον φῶς must be natural light, since the three possibilities are
arranged in an ascending scale. (2) Soul: Pr., Rep. II 53.8–11 καὶ Ὀρφεὺς καὶ
Ἡσίοδος διὰ τῆς κλοπῆς τοῦ πυρὸς καὶ τῆς εἰς ἀνθρώπους δόσεως ἐνδείκνυνται τὴν ψυχὴν
ἀπὸ τοῦ νοητοῦ κατάγειν εἰς τὴν γένεσιν. (3) Divine illumination of the world: Dam.,
Phil. § 57.1–2 ὁ μὲν Προμηθεὺς τὰς εἰς τὴν φύσιν τῶν θεῶν ἐκφαίνει προόδους.

6. ἐν νάρθηκι: Hes., Op. 50–52 κρύψε δὲ πῦρ· τὸ μὲν αὖθις ἐὺς πάϊς Ἰαπετοῖο ἔκλεψ'
ἀνθρώποισι Διὸς πάρα μητιόεντος ἐν κοίλῳ νάρθηκι λαθὼν Δία τερπικέραυνον.

masses 'bearers of the fennel-stalk' with the Orphic term, because they lead the Titanic life.

171. The first Bacchus is Dionysus, whose ecstasy manifests itself in dancing [*basis*] and shouting [*iachê*], that is, in every form of movement, of which he is the cause according to the *Laws* [II 672a5–d4]; but one who has dedicated himself to Dionysus, having become his image, shares his name also. And when a man leads a Dionysian life, his troubles are already ended and he is free from his bonds and released from custody, or rather from the confined form of life; such a man is the philosopher in the stage of purification.

172. To some philosophy is primary, as to Porphyry and Plotinus and a great many other philosophers; to others hieratic practice, as to Iamblichus, Syrianus, Proclus, and the hieratic school generally. Plato, however, recognizing that strong arguments can be advanced from both sides, has united the two into one single truth by calling the philosopher a 'Bacchus'; for by using the notion of a man who has detached himself from genesis as an intermediate term, we can identify the one with the other. Still, it remains evident that he intends to honor the philosopher by the title of Bacchus, as we honor the Intelligence by calling it God, or profane light by giving it the same name as to mystic light.

§§ 173–175. The summing-up. 69d2–e5

173. [69d5–6] As the soul has a double origin, for it is constituted both by itself and by God, so it owes its perfection to two causes. Accordingly Socrates indicates both in the words 'We shall know when we have arrived there, God willing': he makes transition characteristic of the soul, and the power of directing all things solely by his will, of God.

174. [69d7–e5] There are two Defenses of Socrates, one addressed to the Athenian judges, the other to his most faithful friends; in the one he fights to save the living organism, in the other for the life free from the body

---

§ 171. On man becoming Dionysus cf. *supra* § 166 note. There are several echoes of §§ 8, 11 and 12 (Dionysus Lyaeus).

§ 172. Cf. I § 496; II § 109. Iamblichus, *myst.* 96.7–10, already points out the contrast between the two currents in Neoplatonism, represented by Porphyry and himself: διότι φιλοσόφως μᾶλλον καὶ λογικῶς, ἀλλ' οὐχὶ κατὰ τὴν ἐνεργὸν τῶν ἱερέων τέχνην τὸν ἀπολογισμὸν ποιεῖται, διὰ τοῦτο οἶμαι δεῖν θεουργικώτερον εἰπεῖν τι περὶ αὐτῶν. Dam., in spite of his attempt at impartiality, evidently prefers the 'hieratic school' (lines 6–7; cf. *supra* § 168.13–14). The group designed as ἱερατικοί are precisely those whom he mentions as Isidorus's favorites (*vit. Isid.* frg. 77): προσεῖχε δὲ τὸν νοῦν ἐς τὰ μάλιστα μετὰ Πλάτωνα τῷ Ἰαμβλίχῳ καὶ τοῖς Ἰαμβλίχου φίλοις δὴ καὶ ὀπαδοῖς. ὧν ἄριστον εἶναι διισχυρίζετο τὸν ἑαυτοῦ πολίτην Συριανόν, τὸν Πρόκλου διδάσκαλον.

7. The ἀπόρρητον φῶς must be the light of *Rep.* VI 509a1; cf. Pr., *Rep.* I 294.8–10

ὁ Σωκράτης τοὺς πολλοὺς καλεῖ 'ναρθηκοφόρους' Ὀρφικῶς, ὡς ζῶντας Τιτανικῶς.

ρξθ'. - Ὅτι ὁ μὲν πρῶτος Βάκχος ὁ Διόνυσός ἐστιν, ἐνθουσιῶν βάσει τε 171
καὶ ἰαχῇ, ὅ ἐστι πάσῃ κινήσει, ἧς δὴ καὶ αἴτιος, ὡς ἐν Νόμοις [II 672a5–d4]·
ὁ δὲ τῷ Διονύσῳ καθιερωθεὶς ἅτε ὁμοιωθεὶς αὐτῷ μετέχει καὶ τοῦ ὀνόματος.
ὁ δὲ ζῶν Διονυσιακῶς ἤδη πέπαυται πόνων καὶ λέλυται τῶν δεσμῶν, ἀφεθεὶς|
τῆς φρουρᾶς, μᾶλλον δὲ τῆς ἀπεστενωμένης ζωῆς· ὁ δὲ τοιοῦτος ὁ καθαρ- 5(123)
τικός ἐστι φιλόσοφος.

ρο'. - Ὅτι οἱ μὲν τὴν φιλοσοφίαν προτιμῶσιν, ὡς Πορφύριος καὶ Πλωτῖνος 172
καὶ ἄλλοι πολλοὶ φιλόσοφοι· οἱ δὲ τὴν ἱερατικήν, ὡς Ἰάμβλιχος καὶ Συριανὸς καὶ
Πρόκλος καὶ οἱ ἱερατικοὶ πάντες. ὁ δὲ Πλάτων τὰς ἑκατέρωθεν συνηγορίας
ἐννοήσας πολλὰς οὔσας εἰς μίαν αὐτὰς συνήγαγεν ἀλήθειαν, τὸν φιλόσοφον 'Βάκχον'
ὀνομάζων· καὶ γὰρ ὁ χωρίσας ἑαυτὸν τῆς γενέσεως εἰ τεθείη μέσος εἰς ταὐτὸν 5
ἄξει τῷ ἑτέρῳ τὸν ἕτερον. πλὴν δῆλός ἐστιν ὅμως τῷ Βάκχῳ σεμνύνων τὸν
φιλόσοφον, ὡς θεῷ τὸν νοῦν ἢ τῷ ἀπορρήτῳ φωτὶ τὸ ῥητόν.

§§ 173–175. The summing-up. 69d2–e5

ροα'. - [69d5–6] Ὅτι διχόθεν ὑποστᾶσα ἡ ψυχή, καὶ ὑφ' ἑαυτῆς καὶ ὑπὸ 173
θεοῦ, διχόθεν καὶ τελειοῦται. διόπερ ἑκάτερον ἐνδεικνύμενος 'ἐκεῖσέ' φησιν
'ἐλθόντες εἰσόμεθα, ἐὰν θεὸς ἐθέλῃ'· καὶ τὸ μὲν μεταβατικὸν τῇ ψυχῇ ἀποδέδωκεν,
τὸ δὲ θελήσει μόνῃ πάντα κατευθῦνον τῷ θεῷ.

ροβ'. - [69d7–e5] Ὅτι διττὴ ἡ ἀπολογία, ἀλλ' ἡ μὲν πρὸς τοὺς Ἀθηναίων 174
δικαστάς, ἡ δὲ πρὸς τῶν ἑταίρων τοὺς γνησιωτάτους· καὶ ἡ μὲν ὑπὲρ τῆς τοῦ ζῴου
σωτηρίας ἀγωνιζομένη, ἡ δὲ ὑπὲρ αὐτῆς τῆς χωριστῆς οἰκείας ζωῆς· καὶ ἡ μὲν

ὡς γὰρ ταῦτα ἡλιοειδῆ διὰ τὸ ἀφ' ἡλίου φῶς, οὕτως ἐκεῖνα θεῖα πάντα διὰ τὸ ἐκ τἀγαθοῦ φῶς.
§ 173. 2–3. Cf. Ol. 7 § 6.10–16 and note.
4. θελήσει μόνῃ : Pl., *Tim.* 41b4, uses βούλησις for the Divine Will; cf. Pr., *Tim.* III 219.20, who alludes to the use of the corresponding verb at *Tim.* 29e3, 30a2, d3. In Stoic terminology θέλησις is distinct from βούλησις (*SVF* III frg. 173). Plotinus uses θέλησις, VI 8, 13.27; 30; 38; 45; 16.23; so does Iambl., *myst.* 97.16. Θέλημα, frequent in LXX and N.T., appears in the title of Plot. VI 8 (also in Porphyry's second list, *vit. Plot.* 26.24, but omitted 5.45). Proclus uses it *Tim.* I 318.3 (τὸν δὲ πρῶτον θελήματι μόνῳ τὰ πάντα κατασκευάσαντα), a passage depending on the *Hyphegetica* of Julian the Theurgist, and in a Platonic, yet related context, ibid. III 209.15–16 ταῦτα οὖν πάντα ἄλυτά ἐστι διὰ τὸ θέλημα τοῦ πατρός. In the fragments of the Chaldean Oracles themselves θέλημα does not occur, but instead we find twice the substitute τὸ θέλειν (22.3 and 109.1).
§ 174. Ol. 8 § 18.

that is really his own; in the one belief and opinion have their share, the other is based on intellection and knowledge; the starting-point is in the one case life in the community, in the other the life of detachment; in the one apparent death is stated to be a good thing, in the other real death.

175. [69e2] If he is to encounter divine 'masters' and human 'friends,' he is evidently to be a man among men under the guidance of the Gods in the hereafter. It is therefore an un-Platonic notion to make souls pass into genii or angels or Gods.

PART TWO: ON IMMORTALITY

I. THE ARGUMENT FROM OPPOSITES

§§ 176-182. Cebes' question. 69e6-70c5

176. Socrates comprised in one conception the detached life and immortal life; rightly, for the two are convertible, as even Aristotle [*an.* III 5, 430a22-23] admits. Generally speaking, anything that attains higher perfection in being separated cannot be inseparable as regards its essence, because in that case it would deteriorate in the process of separation. Further, if the soul can perfect itself as regards its activity, it is *a fortiori* evident that it strengthens itself as regards its essence and reverts upon itself constituting its own being; therefore, as master of its own being it cannot be destroyed by anything but itself nor degenerate unless through its own fault; no form can destroy itself, it can only assimilate itself to the inferior and thus deteriorate as far as its outward manifestations are concerned. Thus Socrates had comprised the one and identical truth; Cebes however, breaking it up, demands that immortality should be proved separately as if it were a hypothesis on which the demonstration of the detached life was based.

177. Some philosophers extend immortality from rational soul to the animate condition of the body, e.g. Numenius [frg. 46a]; others as far as nature, e.g. Plotinus in certain passages [IV 7, 14]; others, again, as far as

---

5-6. τὸν φαινόμενον θάνατον ἀγαθὸν ἀποφαινομένη : *Apol.* 40b6-41c7.

§ 175. 2-3. The belief that man can become a demon is as old as Hesiod, *Op.* 121-126. It was revived in Middle Platonism: Plut., *de facie* 29, 944C; *def. orac.* 10, 415B-C; Max. Tyr. IX 6 (=XV 6 D.); Stob., *ecl.* I 1064. Iambl., *myst.* 69.7-14, says that the soul can rise to the *rank* of an angel. Proclus rejects the doctrine, *Alc.* 73.9-10; cf. also Psellus, *omnif. doctr.* 48 (probably from Pr.).

§ 176. 2-3. Ar., *an.* III 5, 430a22-23 χωρισθεὶς δ' ἐστὶ μόνον τοῦθ' ὅπερ ἐστί, καὶ τοῦτο μόνον ἀθάνατον καὶ ἀΐδιον.

§ 177. See H. Dörrie, *Kontroversen um die Seelenwanderung im kaiserzeitlichen Platonismus*, Hermes 85, 1957, 414-435 (420-421). The passage is not displaced, as Dörrie thinks; with § 176, it serves as a general introduction to the whole of Part II. Dörrie adds some more material from parallel texts with the same origin: Nemesius ch. 2, Hermias 102.10-15 (on *Phaedr.* 245c5), Pr., *Tim.* III 234.6-238.23.

πίστει καὶ δόξῃ συμμιγής, ἡ δὲ νῷ τε καὶ ἐπιστήμῃ· καὶ ἡ μὲν ἀπὸ ζωῆς πολιτικῆς
προϊοῦσα, ἡ δὲ ἀπὸ καθαρτικῆς· καὶ ἡ μὲν τὸν φαινόμενον θάνατον ἀγαθὸν 5
ἀποφαινομένη, ἡ δὲ τὸν ἀληθινόν.

ρογ΄. - [69e2] "Ὅτι εἰ παρὰ θεοὺς 'δεσπότας' ἀφίξεται καὶ 'ἑταίρους', καὶ 175
ἐκεῖ ἂν ἄνθρωπος εἴη καὶ συνὼν ἀνθρώποις ὑπὸ θεοῖς. οὐκ ἄρα Πλατωνικῶς
δοξάζουσιν οἱ εἰς δαίμονα ἢ ἄγγελον ἢ θεὸν ἀναχέοντες τὰς ψυχάς.

PART TWO: ON IMMORTALITY

I. THE ARGUMENT FROM OPPOSITES

§§ 176–182. Cebes' question. 69e6–70c5

ροδ΄. - "Ὅτι ὁ μὲν Σωκράτης ἐν μιᾷ νοήσει συνεῖχεν τήν τε καθαρτικὴν 176
ζωὴν καὶ τὴν ἀθάνατον· ἀντιστρέφει γάρ, ὡς καὶ Ἀριστοτέλης [an. III 5,
430a22-23] ὁμολογεῖ. καὶ ὅλως τὸ ἐν τῷ χωρισμῷ τελειούμε|νον οὐκ ἂν (124)
ἔχοι τὴν οὐσίαν ἀχώριστον, ἐγίγνετο γὰρ ἂν ἀτελέστερον χωριζόμενον. καὶ ἔτι
πρὸς τούτοις, εἰ τελειοῖ ἑαυτὴν κατὰ ἐνέργειαν, πολλῷ πρότερον κατὰ οὐσίαν 5
ἑαυτὴν βεβαιοῖ καὶ ἐπιστρέφει πρὸς ἑαυτὴν οὐσιοῦσα ἑαυτήν, ὥστε κυρία τοῦ
εἶναι ἑαυτῆς οὖσα ὑπ' οὐδενὸς ἂν φθείροιτο ἀλλ' ἢ ὑφ' ἑαυτῆς, ὥσπερ οὐδὲ
κακύνεται ἀλλ' ἢ ὑφ' ἑαυτῆς· οὐδὲν δὲ ἑαυτὸ πέφυκε φθείρειν τῶν εἰδῶν,
ὁμοιοῦσθαι δὲ μόνον πρὸς τὸ χεῖρον καὶ ταύτῃ κακύνεσθαι κατὰ τὴν ἔξω
προβολήν. οὕτω μὲν οὖν ὁ Σωκράτης συνῃρήκει τὴν μίαν ἀλήθειαν, ὁ δὲ Κέβης 10
διαιρῶν ἀπαιτεῖ προσαποδειχθῆναι τὴν ἀθανασίαν ὡς ἂν ὑπόθεσιν τῆς καθαρτικῆς
ζωῆς γενομένην πρὸς τὴν ἀπόδειξιν.

ροε΄. - "Ὅτι οἱ μὲν ἀπὸ τῆς λογικῆς ψυχῆς ἄχρι τῆς ἐμψύχου ἕξεως 177
ἀπαθανατίζουσιν, ὡς Νουμήνιος [frg. 46a]· οἱ δὲ μέχρι τῆς φύσεως, ὡς
Πλωτῖνος ἔνι ὅπου [IV 7, 14]· οἱ δὲ μέχρι τῆς ἀλογίας, ὡς τῶν μὲν παλαιῶν

---

§ 174. 4 πίστει Wk: αἰσθήσει Bühler, ἐπιστήμῃ M.
§ 176. 3 τελειούμενον Fh: τεχνούμενον M — 10 μίαν] -ίαν in ras. Mˣ
§ 177. 1 ἐμψύχου] ἀψύχου Bernays

Cf. further Pr., elem. 207–209 (with Dodds' notes and Appendix II); Iambl., de anima in Stob. I 49.43.

1. τῆς ἐμψύχου ἕξεως : identical with the ἐμψυχία of Pr., Tim. III 285.3; 287.10; 324.29; Rep. II 90.11; Ol. 10 § 9.7; 13 § 8.6. It is the life of the body and a phantom (εἴδωλον) of the soul.

2. μέχρι τῆς φύσεως : including vegetative life (Plot. IV 7,14) and probably also that of the lower animals, cf. Hermias 102.13–14 (on Phaedr. 245c5 "all soul is immortal") οἱ δὲ περὶ πάσης ψυχῆς ἁπλῶς, καὶ τῆς τοῦ μύρμηκος καὶ μυίας, ὧν ἐστιν Ἁρποκρατίων.

3. μέχρι τῆς ἀλογίας : more particularly the irrational soul in man; thus Iambl. according to Pr., Tim. III 234.32–235.9; on animals see note on § 199.2–3. Plutarch's position is dealt with by R. Beutler, RE, art. Plutarchos von Athen, vol. 21, 969.60–970.17. Paterius instead of Plutarch in the margin of the MS. (infra p. 376) does not

irrational life, e.g. of the ancients Xenocrates [frg. 75] and Speusippus [frg. 55] and, of more recent authorities, Iamblichus and Plutarch; others confine it to rational soul, such as Proclus and Porphyry; others limit it further to intelligence alone, making the opinative function perishable, as many Peripatetics do; others to the universal soul, by which they think individual souls are absorbed.

178. The soul is either (1) inseparable from the body, as Simmias will suppose presently [85e3–86d4], or (2) separable, in which case either (a) it will dissolve at the moment of separation, as Cebes suggests here [69e6–70a6], or (b) continue to exist for some time, a theory which he is going to advance later on [86e6–88b8] or (c) it is completely everlasting, as Socrates will prove ultimately [102a10–107a1]. The reason to take the first view was the affinity with the body; the second was prompted by the fact that the soul pervades the whole (divisible) body and that, further, composite bodies are surpassed in excellence by the simple body, and simple bodies by spirit, which has a strong resemblance to soul in many ways; the ground for the third was the greater strength of soul as compared to body, while Socrates

---

look like a copyist's error, since the name resembles Plutarch's neither in sound nor in lettering and is too unfamiliar to substitute itself for it. Probably, therefore, the scholion is a survey drawn up either by the lecturer or by the *reportator*, so that both Plutarch and Paterius may be correct; see Beutler, *RE*, art. Paterios, vol. 18, 2563.31–36.

5. Proclus' opinion is presented in the same simple form e.g. *Rep.* I 215.5–6 ἄμφω [i.e. θυμός and ἐπιθυμία] θνητὰ καὶ μετ' ἀλλήλων ὄντα ἢ μὴ ὄντα, λόγος δὲ ἀθάνατον. He qualifies it *Tim.* III 236.31–237.1, where he approves of Syrianus' view that the ἀκρότητες of irrational life, and with them the (first) vehicle of the soul, are created by the supreme Demiurge and therefore everlasting. In the same section (on *Tim.* 41d1–2) he cites Porphyry as holding that, though only the rational soul is immortal, the lower elements (the vehicle and the irrational functions) do not perish, but are restored to the spheres from where they came, an elaboration of *Tim.* 42e7–43a1. Proclus attributes this view in its strict form (only rational soul survives) to some older Platonists, τοὺς 'Αττικοὺς λέγω καὶ 'Αλβίνους (*Tim.* III 234.17–18 = Atticus frg. 15). Unfortunately he has confused the issue by introducing, on the one hand, the pneumatic vehicle as the carrier of irrational soul and, on the other hand, νοῦς as the equivalent of rational soul. On the former point see Dodds (*elem.*, p. 306, n. 3); on the latter, Dörrie p. 422, n. 1, who states a contradiction with a *verbatim* quotation from Atticus in Euseb., *praep. evang.* XV 9 [=frg. 7], where Aristotle's doctrine of the separability and immortality of intelligence (νοῦς) is angrily rejected. For this reason Dörrie interprets τοὺς 'Αττικούς as the 'Attic commentators' (see above §§ 148–149), which seems hardly possible without actually changing the text to τοὺς 'Αττικοὺς ⟨ἐξηγητὰς⟩ λέγω καὶ 'Αλβῖνον. However, Atticus' attack is directed against the assumption (un-Platonic to him) of intelligence as a separate entity rather than as a function of the soul, but it does not follow that he cannot have regarded only rational soul as immortal. On the contrary, the fragment in Eusebius may point in this direction, when at § 8, paraphrasing Pl., *Laws* X 897a1–3, on the primary motions of soul, Atticus includes τὸ βουλεύσασθαι, τὸ διανοηθῆναι, τὸ προσδοκῆσαι, τὸ μνημονεῦσαι, τὸ λογίσασθαι, while omitting from

Ξενοκράτης [frg. 75] καὶ Σπεύσιππος [frg. 55], τῶν δὲ νεωτέρων Ἰάμβλιχος καὶ Πλούταρχος· οἱ δὲ μέχρι μόνης τῆς λογικῆς, ὡς Πρόκλος καὶ Πορφύριος· 5
οἱ δὲ μέχρι μόνου τοῦ νοῦ, φθείρουσι γὰρ τὴν δόξαν, ὡς πολλοὶ τῶν Περιπατητικῶν·
οἱ δὲ μέχρι τῆς ὅλης ψυχῆς, φθείρουσι γὰρ τὰς μερικὰς εἰς τὴν ὅλην.

ροςʹ. — Ὅτι ἢ ἀχώριστος ἡ ψυχὴ τοῦ σώματος, ὡς ὑποθήσεται ὁ Σιμμίας 178(125)
[85e3–86d4], ἢ χωριστή· καὶ εἰ τοῦτο, ἢ χωριζομένη διασκεδάννυται, ὡς νῦν
ὑποτίθεται ὁ Κέβης [69e6–70a6], ἢ ἐπιδιαμένει πλείω χρόνον, ὡς αὖθις
ὑποθήσεται [86e6–88b8], ἢ τελέως ἐστὶν ἀίδιος, ὡς ἀποδείξει Σωκράτης τὸ
ἔσχατον [102a10–107a1]. ἔπεισε δὲ τοὺς μὲν πρώτους ἡ πρὸς τὸ σῶμα 5
συμπάθεια· τοὺς δὲ δευτέρους ἡ διὰ παντὸς τοῦ σώματος δίηξις μεριστοῦ ὄντος
(προκέκριται δὲ τῶν μὲν συνθέτων σωμάτων τὸ ἁπλοῦν, τῶν δὲ ἁπλῶν τὸ
πνεῦμα ὡς ὁμοιότατον τῇ ψυχῇ πολλαχῶς)· τοὺς δὲ τρίτους τὸ ἰσχυρότερον εἶναι

Plato's list joy and grief, courage and fear, hatred and love. His view is therefore not an Aristotelizing one, but, as Pr. explains (III 234.15–16), the result of close adherence to the text of Pl., *Tim.* 41d1–2. As regards Albinus, cf. Alcin., *did.* 25: the survival of irrational soul is controversial, but in view of its entirely different character there is a good case for considering it as mortal.

6. Ar., *an.* III 5, 430a17–18 καὶ οὗτος ὁ νοῦς χωριστὸς καὶ ἀπαθὴς καὶ ἀμιγής, τῇ οὐσίᾳ ὢν ἐνεργείᾳ. Pr., *Tim.* III 234.9–15 equates this doctrine with the preceding one: καὶ οἱ μὲν τὴν λογικὴν ψυχὴν μόνην ἀθάνατον ἀπολείποντες φθείρουσι τήν τε ἄλογον ζωὴν σύμπασαν καὶ τὸ πνευματικὸν ὄχημα τῆς ψυχῆς, κατὰ τὴν εἰς γένεσιν ῥοπὴν τῆς ψυχῆς τὴν ὑπόστασιν διδόντες αὐτοῖς μόνον τε τὸν νοῦν ἀθάνατον διατηροῦντες ὡς μόνον καὶ μένοντα καὶ ὁμοιούμενον τοῖς θεοῖς καὶ μὴ φθειρόμενον (e.g. Atticus and Albinus).

8. φθείρουσι γὰρ τὰς μερικὰς εἰς τὴν ὅλην: according to Hermias 102.10–13 Posidonius explained the πᾶσα ψυχή of *Phaedr.* 245c5 as the world soul. Arius Didymus (*SVF* II frg. 821), after stating the Stoic view that the souls of the dead are ἐν τῷ περιέχοντι, adds that some believe they are absorbed by the world soul: ἔνιοι δὲ τὴν μὲν τοῦ ὅλου ἀίδιον, τὰς δὲ λοιπὰς συμμίγνυσθαι ἐπὶ τελευτῇ εἰς ἐκείνην.

§ 178. Ol. 10 § 2. Cf. *infra* § 183.6–8; § 222.1–4. A diaeresis comprising all the doctrines on the soul that will eventually come up for discussion in the *Ph.*: (1) the theory of soul as a harmony, propounded by Simmias 85e3–86d4, based on the observation that the soul's condition corresponds to that of the body; (2) the theory that soul is *pneuma*, 69e6–70a6, resting on the observation that the soul is present throughout the body and on the consideration that if soul is a body it should be a non-composite body, *pneuma* or air being chosen on account of its resemblance to soul (Xenophanes A 8); (3) the belief that soul is of superior and therefore stronger material, so that it outlasts the body, 86e6–88b8 (held by the Stoics, *SVF* II frgs. 809–822); (4) the Platonic doctrine of transcendent soul, cause of life.

6. δίηξις: on the form see Pr., *theol.* I 15, 76.19 note (p. 149).
7–8. τὸ πνεῦμα: cf. *infra* § 222.1–4.

is going to found his proof, eventually [105d3-4], on the argument that soul is the source of life.

179. It is not true that Socrates' argument on purification is hypothetical, as Cebes believes [70a6-8], rather it rests on the essence of soul itself. If, indeed, the soul strives to detach itself and actually does so, its purpose is of necessity to *be* separate, and this explains the desire; otherwise the desire would be aimless, but nothing is aimless. Besides, since desire has as its object something desirable, i.e. something good, if we suppose this good unattainable, and if the unattainable is useless, the good will be useless, and thus not good. Finally, as it has been shown in the *Gorgias* [469c8-470a12], power belongs to the good, as impotence does to evil; therefore whatever is good has by its own nature the power to be; therefore all desire is directed toward the possible, since it is directed toward the good. Now if even an apparent good can be realized, can we doubt that the true good has a still higher degree of reality?

180. [70b1-4] The three questions raised by Cebes, whether the soul exists in Hades, whether it has a certain power, and whether it has understanding, derive from the all-pervading triad of subsistence, potency and intelligence.

Or better, his starting-point is that in the hereafter the soul must be complete as regards essence, potency and activity. It is only by means of these three that the life of purification can be preserved in Hades, since purification implies activity.

181. [70b5-c5] Socrates gives a clear definition of the first problem, that it is not concerned with everlasting existence absolutely, but only with the proof that our souls continue to exist in Hades, which will enable him also to show that their life yonder is a life of purification. For the present he prefers to split the problem in this way, making his hearers familiar with the notion of separate existence.

182. [70b7] Why 'likely'? — As compared to the certainty of transcendental truth. Or because the proof rests on inference, as Harpocratio says [frg. 6]. Or, as the commentator said already [§ 181?], because

---

§ 179. Cf. Ol. 6 § 10. The point made at § 176.10-12 is taken up again.
4. Ar., *cael.* I 4, 271a33.
6-10. The equivocation between δυνατός 'possible' and 'powerful' is obvious.
§ 180. Plato has ἔστι τε ἡ ψυχὴ ... καί τινα δύναμιν ἔχει καὶ φρόνησιν. Pr. (lines 1-3) has not much difficulty in translating this into the 'Chaldean triad' of ὕπαρξις (=πατήρ)-δύναμις-νοῦς (*infra* II § 142.2; cf. Beutler, art. Pr. 214.63-215.68). Because the emphasis is on the condition of the soul, Dam. (lines 4-6) prefers the triad οὐσία-δύναμις-ἐνέργεια, which, however, if applied to a thinking subject, is identical with the first.
§ 181. 1-3. This point, here derived directly from the text, is developed at § 183 as an introduction to the argument from opposites.
3-4. The separation of the issues of detachability and immortality is a concession to Cebes: cf. § 176.10-12.

σώματος ψυχήν· τὸν δὲ Σωκράτην τὸ πηγὴν εἶναι ζωῆς τὴν ψυχήν, ὡς ἐρεῖ [105d3-4].

ροζ'. – Ὅτι οὐκ ἐξ ὑποθέσεως ἀπέδειξε τὴν κάθαρσιν ὁ Σωκράτης, ὡς ὑπονοεῖ ὁ Κέβης [70a6-8], ἀλλ' ἐξ αὐτῆς τῆς ψυχικῆς οὐσίας. εἰ γὰρ ἐφίεται χωρίζειν καὶ χωρίζει τῷ ὄντι, πάντως εἶναι χωρὶς ἐπείγεται, διὸ καὶ ἐφίεται· εἰ δὲ μή, μάτην ἔσται ἡ ἔφεσις, οὐδὲν δὲ μάτην γίγνεται. ἐπεὶ καί, εἰ ἡ ἔφεσις ἐφετοῦ, ὅ ἐστιν ἀγαθοῦ, τοῦτο δὲ ἀδύνατον εἴη, τὸ δὲ ἀδύνατον ἀνωφελές, τὸ ἀγαθὸν ἄρα ἀνωφελές, ὅ ἐστιν οὐκ ἀγαθόν. ἔτι δέ, ὡς ἐν Γοργίᾳ [469c8-470a12] δέδεικται, τοῦ ἀγαθοῦ ἡ δύναμις, ἐπειδὴ καὶ τοῦ κακοῦ ἡ ἀδυναμία· πᾶν ἄρα ἀγαθὸν δυνατὸν τῇ ἑαυτοῦ φύσει· πᾶσα ἄρα ἔφεσις τοῦ δυνατοῦ, εἴπερ τοῦ ἀγαθοῦ. εἰ δὲ καὶ τὸ φαινόμενον ἀγαθὸν δυνατόν, τί δεῖ ἡγεῖσθαι περὶ τοῦ ἀληθοῦς; οὐχ ὅτι ἀληθέστερον ἀγαθόν;

ροη'. – [70b1-4] Ὅτι τρία ζητεῖ ὁ Κέβης, εἰ ἔστιν ἐν Ἅιδου καὶ εἰ δύναμιν ἔχει τινὰ καὶ εἰ φρόνησιν, ἀπὸ τῆς διὰ πάντων χωρούσης τριάδος ὁρμώμενος, ὑπάρξεως δυνάμεως νοῦ.

Κάλλιον δὲ ἀπὸ τοῦ τελείαν εἶναι δεῖν ἐκεῖ τὴν ψυχὴν οὐσίᾳ καὶ δυνάμει καὶ ἐνεργείᾳ. τρισὶ γὰρ τούτοις ἡ καθαρτικὴ ζωὴ ἐν Ἅιδου σωθήσεται· καὶ γὰρ μετὰ τῆς ἐνεργείας ἡ κάθαρσις.

ροθ'. – [70b5-c5] Ὅτι σαφῶς ὁ Σωκράτης ἀφορίζεται τὸ πρῶτον πρόβλημα, ὡς οὐκ ἔστι περὶ τῆς ὅλης ἀιδιότητος, ἀλλ' ὅτι εἰσὶν ἐν Ἅιδου ἡμῶν αἱ ψυχαί, ἵνα δείξῃ καὶ ὅτι ζῶσιν ἐκεῖ καθαρτικῶς. τέως γὰρ δοκεῖ οὕτως μερίσαι τὸ πρόβλημα καὶ προσυνεθίσαι τοὺς ἀκροατὰς πρὸς τὴν χωριστὴν ὑπόστασιν.

ρπ'. – [70b7] Διὰ τί 'εἰκὸς' ἔφη; — Ἤ ὡς πρὸς τὴν ἐκεῖ ἀλήθειαν. ἢ ὅτι ἀπὸ τεκμηρίου, ὡς Ἁρποκρατίων [frg. 6]. ἤ, ὡς ἔφη [§ 181?], ὅτι ἐνδέχεται

---

§ 178. 9 τὸ ins. M^c: om. M^1

---

§ 182. The first explanation of the word 'probably' is a commonplace; cf. Ol. 2 § 6.7-11 with note, and esp. the long essay on οἴμαι (Pl., Alc. I 103a1) in Pr., Alc. 21.8-24.9. The other three are all key issues in the subsequent discussion by the commentators: (2) the proof is ἀπὸ τεκμηρίου (explained § 216.3-4, § 229.21 and Phil. § 68.2; see also Ol. 9 § 8); (3) it is ἐνδεχόμενον : only the possibility of survival is proved; (4) only limited survival is proved. The reference ὡς ἔφη is not clear; it cannot be to Plato, who has made no statement of the kind so far, but neither is there any trace in the preceding sections of such an opinion expressed by either Pr. or Syrianus (cf. I § 207.12). It may have disappeared from § 181 in the process of abridging. The position that the first argument does not go beyond possible survival and limited survival is shared by Syrianus-Pr. (§ 207.12 and § 216) and Dam.; Dam.'s contribution at lines 4-5 consists only in giving the εἰκός a different application.

existence in Hades is proved possible only, not necessary: if we suppose an infinite number of souls, the created world may continue to exist.

It is better to attribute the uncertainty to the fact that survival is not forever; even if there is a chance of survival for some time, it does not follow that it is for good.

§§ 183-192. The argument from opposites reviewed by Syrianus: analysis and preliminaries. 70c5-72e2

183. The purport of the first argument is not to prove that the soul is immortal; this appears from the form in which Cebes propounds his question [69e6-70b4] and the way in which Socrates defines the problem [70c4-5], as well as from his conclusion [72d6-e2] and from the promise of the proof of immortality at the end of the fourth problem [95b8-e3]. For the moment, however, his only point is if the soul survives in Hades; whether for a short or a long time or for good, does not yet become apparent. The same can be inferred from the division of the problems, which could be arranged more clearly as follows: either the soul is inseparable as a harmony, or it is separable as air in a bag, or it survives for a considerable time, or it is immortal altogether.

184. The reasoning is as follows: 'If the living and the dead proceed from each other, our souls exist in Hades; the antecedent is true; therefore so is the consequent.' The minor is proved in the form of a categorical syllogism:

The living and the dead ⎯⎯opposites⎯⎯ proceed from each other, if at all.

185. There is agreement as to the minor premise, because it is granted and implicit in the definition of death. For if the soul can be separated from the body, as air can be let out of a bag, this is a process of disjunction,

---

§§ 183-206 are a summary of Syrianus' monograph on the argument from opposites, cited by Ol. 9 § 2.8-10, criticized and rectified by Dam. I §§ 207-252. The limits of the monograph are indicated by Dam. § 207.12-13: ἐνδεχόμενον εἶναι τὸν λόγον προειπών (§ 183 ?) ἐτελεύτησεν αὐτοῦ εἰς τὴν ἀνάγκην, ἴσην γε ἀνάγκην τῇ τοῦ κόσμου συστάσει (§§ 205-206); further there are references to § 185 at § 209.1 and to § 205 at § 216.1. The word προειπών is puzzling, since neither the term contingency (ἐνδεχόμενον) nor the notion is found in §§ 183-207; unless it was lost in our version of the report, the explanation may be that Dam. had § 182 in mind (προειπών might even mean 'before the beginning of the monograph'). However this may be, it is not advisable to add §§ 176-182 to Syrianus' monograph, for they have clearly the character of a running commentary, and § 183 is a formal new start. – The contents of Syrianus' treatise are: (§ 183) introduction to the σκοπός of the argument; (§§ 184-186) analysis of the argument; (§§ 187-192) definitions of the terms used: 'living,' 'dead,' 'opposites,' 'from each other'; (§§ 193-200) questions and answers, a selection including only Nos. iii-x of Syrianus, i.e. precisely those which Dam. discusses in §§ 243-251; (§§ 201-206) some further observations. No better evaluation of the treatise could be given than that by Dam. in § 207: Syrianus wisely limits the claims made for the scope of the argument,

εἶναι ἐν Ἅιδου· οὐ γὰρ πάντως· εἰ γὰρ ἄπειροι αἱ ψυχαί, μένει ἡ γένεσις. Βέλτιον δὲ τὸ μὴ ἀεὶ τοῦ εἰκότος αἰτιᾶσθαι· οὐ γάρ, εἰ ποτὲ διαμένειν ἐνδέχεται, ἤδη καὶ ἀεὶ διαμένει.

§§ 183–192. The argument from opposites reviewed by Syrianus: analysis and preliminaries. 70c5–72e2

ϱπη′. – Ὅτι ὁ σκοπὸς τοῦ πρώτου λόγου οὐ δεῖξαι ἀθάνατον τὴν ψυχήν, 183(128) ὡς δηλοῖ ὁ Κέβης προτείνων [69e6–70b4] καὶ ὁ Σωκράτης διοριζόμενος τὸ πρόβλημα [70c4–5] καὶ ἔτι συμπεραινόμενος [72d6–e2] καὶ ἐπὶ τέλει τοῦ τετάρτου προβλήματος τὴν ἀθανασίαν ἐπαγγελλόμενος [95b8–e3]· ἀλλὰ μόνον ἐν τούτοις ζητεῖ εἰ ἐν Ἅιδου ἡ ψυχὴ ἐπιδιαμένει, εἴτε δὲ ὀλίγον χρόνον εἴτε 5 τινὰ καὶ πολὺν εἴτε ἄπειρον, οὔπω δείκνυται. δηλοῖ δὲ καὶ ἡ τῶν ζητημάτων διαίρεσις οὕτως ἂν ταχθεῖσα σαφέστερον· ἢ ἀχώριστος ἡ ψυχή, ὡς ἁρμονία, ἢ χωριστή, ὡς πνεῦμα ἀπὸ ἀσκοῦ, ἢ ἐπιδιαμένει πολὺν χρόνον, ἢ πάντῃ ἀθάνατος.

ϱπθ′. – Ὅτι τοιάδε ἡ λογικὴ ἀγωγή· ʽεἰ τὸ ζῶν καὶ τὸ τεθνηκὸς ἐξ ἀλλήλων, 184 εἰσὶν ἡμῶν αἱ ψυχαὶ ἐν Ἅιδου· ἀλλὰ μὴν τὸ πρῶτον· τὸ ἄρα δεύτερονʼ. ὁ δὲ τῆς προσλήψεως συλλογισμός ἐστι κατηγορικός·

τὸ ζῶν καὶ τὸ τεθνη-ⵧἐναντίαⵧἐξ ἀλλήλων γίνε-
κὸς ⎯⎯⎯⎯⎯⎯⎯⎯⎯⎯⎯⎯ται, εἰ γίνεται. 5

ϱϙ′. – Ὅτι ἡ μὲν ἐλάττων πρότασις ὁμολογεῖται διά τε τοῦ δεδομένου καὶ 185 τοῦ ὁρισμοῦ τοῦ θανάτου. εἰ γὰρ χωρίζεται ἡ ψυχὴ τοῦ σώματος ὡς πνεῦμα ἀσκοῦ, διακρίνεται ἄρα, ἐκ συγκεκριμένου ἄρα· καὶ ἔστι συγκεκρίσθαι μὲν τὸ

---

§§ 183–190. post § 197 habet M
§ 183. 6 δείκνυται Nv: δεικνύναι M
§ 184. 4–5 in spat. vac. M^c

---

his definitions and assumptions are helpful, but he complicates the argument by introducing extraneous matter and ends nevertheless by greatly overestimating its demonstrative force. – The interchange of two lectures, §§ 183–190 (ϱπη′–ϱϙε′) and §§ 191–197 (ϱϙα′–ϱπζ′), as directed in the margin of the MS. at § 183.1 and § 191.1 (below p. 377), restores the correct order; Syrianus' ἀπορίαι in §§ 193–201 now run exactly parallel with Dam. §§ 243–251.

§ 183. 1–6. Dam. II § 1. Ol. 10 § 1.11–20. Simpl., phys. 440.35–441.2 ἐκεῖνο δὲ ἐπισημαίνομαι διὰ τοὺς ἀληθείας ἐρῶντας, ὅτι ὁ ἀπὸ τῶν ἐναντίων ἐν Φαίδωνι λόγος οὐ τὴν ἀθανασίαν αὐτόθεν ἐπαγγέλλεται καταδεῖξαι τῆς ψυχῆς, ἀλλὰ τὸ προϋπάρχειν μόνον τοῦ τῇδε βίου ψυχὴν καὶ τὸ ἐπιδιαμένειν.

6–8. Ol. 10 § 2. The same diaeresis as at § 178.1–5; here it serves to show that there is no room for a complete proof of immortality, since the plan of the whole requires only a refutation of possibility two, that the soul is dissolved at the moment of separation.

§ 184. Ol. 10 § 3.6–8 and note; 9 § 1.8–10.
1–2. εἰ – Ἅιδου: Pr.'s formula has been passed on without a change to Dam. on the one hand, to Ol. (10 § 3.6–7) and Philoponus (anal. pr. 358.14–15) on the other.
§ 185. Ol. 10 § 3.19–22; 9 § 2.9–11; § 3.4–10.

which must have been preceded by a state of being joined; being joined is life in the body, disjunction is death; these two are opposites, therefore life and death are opposites too.

186. Socrates establishes the major by three methods: (1) by induction (the characteristic of which is clearness) [70d7–71a11]; (2) by the argument from processes of becoming (processes of becoming, when mutually opposed, proceed from each other, consequently the same is true of the extremes to which these processes lead [71a12–72a10]; (3) by the argument that the world of becoming owes its everlasting existence to a cycle of opposites: if genesis is to continue, opposites must have equal power, for if either of a pair should fail, the whole will perish; therefore the balance must be restored by a cycle of opposites proceeding from each other [72a11–d5].

187. Of the terms used, 'living' has three meanings: (1) life itself; (2) anything participating in a life that is present in it, yet separable, or (3) inseparable. Of these, the second applies here, for the first has no opposite, while the third has no separate existence.

188. 'Dead' has two meanings: (1) what is separated from separable life; (2) what remains when inseparable life is extinct. The former is referred to here, for Socrates argues on the hypothesis that the soul is separated from the body.

189. 'Opposites' can be taken in two ways: (1) what participates; (2) the participated. The latter is meant here, as Socrates himself points out later on [103a11–c2].

190. 'From each other' has a double sense; it may be used (1) loosely of the things participated, which are strictly speaking *after* each other, or (2) of the participants, of which something remains, and which therefore proceed *from* each other in the strict sense of the word. Here, again, there are three possibilities: (1) there may be one substrate (e.g. the same body may become hot and cold), or (2) there may be two, namely when things join and part, in which case we see that either (a) both survive, or (b) at least the stronger of the two, as in the example of a bag of air, of which the bag remains to be filled again with different air, whereas the air is dispersed. The third meaning applies here, since soul is stronger than body and is the force that holds together its dissolving substance.

191. The question rises to what kind of opposites he is referring, opposites in the proper sense or contraries generally. In the latter case it is

---

§ 186. Ol. 10 § 4.1–11.

2. ἧς ἴδιον τὸ σαφές : Ar., *anal. pr.* II 23, 68b36–37; *anal. post.* I 3, 72b29–30; *top.* I 12, 105a16–18; *infra* § 226.8–9.

7. τῷ : this slight correction for τὸ gives an intelligible construction and makes it possible to understand ἀποδίδοσθαι in the sense which it has also in Plato.

§ 188. 1. χωριστῆς : the MS. has χωρισθείσης, the scholion ἀχωρίστου. Since the two possible acceptations for 'the dead' should correspond to the second and third

ζῆν μετὰ τοῦ σώματος, διακεκρίσθαι δὲ τὸ τεθνάναι· ταῦτα δὲ ἐναντία ἐστίν·
ἐναντία ἄρα καὶ τὸ ζῆν καὶ τεθνάναι.

ρρα'. – Ὅτι τὴν μείζω πρότασιν κατασκευάζει τριχῶς· ἔκ τε τῆς ἐπαγωγῆς 186
(ἧς ἴδιον τὸ σαφές) [70d7–71a11], καὶ ἐκ τῶν γενέσεων (αἱ γὰρ ἐναντίαι
γενέσεις ἀλλήλας διαδεχόμεναι ἐξ ἀλλήλων γίνονται, | ὥστε καὶ τὰ ἄκρα ἐξ (129)
ἀλλήλων, εἰς ταῦτα γὰρ ἄγουσιν αἱ γενέσεις) [71a12–72a10]· καὶ τρίτον ἐκ
τῆς κατὰ κύκλον ἀεὶ συνεστώσης γενέσεως ἀπὸ τῶν ἐναντίων. εἰ γὰρ δεῖ μένειν
τὴν γένεσιν, ἰσοκρατῆ δεῖ εἶναι τὰ ἐναντία· εἰ γὰρ ἀπολείψει θάτερον, ἀπολεῖται
τὸ πᾶν· δεῖ ἄρα ἀνταποδίδοσθαι τῷ τὰ ἐναντία ἐξ ἀλλήλων γίνεσθαι κύκλῳ
[72a11–d5].

ρρβ'. – Ὅτι τῶν εἰλημμένων ὅρων τὸ ζῶν τριχῶς· ἢ ὅπερ ἐστὶ ζωή, ἢ ὃ 187
μετέχει ζωῆς παρούσης μὲν χωριστῆς δέ, ἢ ἀχωρίστου. τούτων δὲ εἴληπται
τὸ μέσον· οὔτε γὰρ τῷ πρώτῳ ἐστί τι ἐναντίον οὔτε τὸ τρίτον ἐστὶ χωριστόν.

ρργ'. – Ὅτι τὸ τεθνηκὸς διχῶς· ἢ γὰρ τὸ χωρισθὲν ἀπὸ τῆς χωριστῆς ζωῆς, 188
ἢ τῆς ἀχωρίστου σβεσθείσης. ὧν τὸ πρῶτον εἴληπται· ὑπόκειται γὰρ ἡ ψυχὴ
χωριζομένη.

ρρδ'. – Ὅτι τὰ ἐναντία διχῶς· ἢ τὰ μετεχόμενα, ἢ τὰ μετέχοντα. ἃ νῦν 189
εἴληπται, ὡς αὐτὸς ὁ Σωκράτης ὕστερον ἡμᾶς ἐπέστησεν [103a11–c2].

ρρε'. – Ὅτι τὸ ἐξ ἀλλήλων διχῶς· ἢ ὡς ἐπὶ τῶν μετεχομένων | ἁπλῶς, 190(130)
ἅπερ ἐστὶ κυρίως μετ' ἄλληλα, ἢ ὡς ἐπὶ τῶν μετεχόντων· τούτων γὰρ μένει τι,
α' διὸ κυρίως ἐξ ἀλλήλων. τριχῶς δὲ ταῦτα· ἢ γὰρ ἑνὸς ὄντος τοῦ ὑποκειμένου,
ὡς θερμὸν καὶ ψυχρὸν τὸ αὐτὸ σῶμα, ἢ ὡς δυεῖν, ὡς ἐπὶ τῶν συνιόντων καὶ
β'γ' διισταμένων, διχῶς δὲ τούτων δρωμένων, ἢ ἑκατέρου σῳζομένου, ἢ τοῦ
ἰσχυροτέρου πάντως, οἷον ἀσκοῦ καὶ πνεύματος· τούτων γὰρ ὁ μὲν ἀσκὸς μένει
πρὸς ὑποδοχὴν ἄλλου πνεύματος, τὸ δὲ πνεῦμα διεσκέδασται. τὸ δὴ τρίτον
εἴληπται, εἴπερ ἰσχυρότερον ψυχὴ σώματος καὶ συνεκτικὸν τοῦ διαρρέοντος.

⟨δ⟩ ρπα'. – Ὅτι ζητητέον τίνα τὰ ἐναντία λαμβάνει, πότερον τὰ κυρίως ἢ τὰ 191(126)
ἁπλῶς ἀντικείμενα. εἰ μὲν γὰρ τοῦτο, πῶς ἐξ ἀλλήλων ἕξις καὶ στέρησις; εἰ

---

§ 186. 6 δεῖ ∼ εἶναι] ∼ εἶναι in ras. M^x — 7 τῷ Wk: τὸ M
§ 187. 1 ζωή M^c: ζῶν M¹
§ 188. 1 χωριστῆς Wk: χωρισθείσης M
§ 190. 1 ἁπλῶς Nv (schol.): ἁπλῶν M — 4 δυεῖν] -εῖ- ex -οῖ- M^x

for 'the living' in § 187, the ending -θείσης must be an error due to the influence of σβεσθείσης.
§ 189. Ol. 9 § 2.1–3.
§ 190. 1–3. Ol. 9 § 2.3–7.
3–8. Ol. 9 § 2.12–15.
7–8. This gratuitous assumption is the weakest point in Syrianus' version of the argument; see Dam. I § 215.
§ 191. Ol. 10 § 8.11–18 and note.

difficult to understand how positives and privatives can proceed from each other; but if the former is correct, why does Plato cite relatives as examples [70e6–71a7]? — The answer: the relatives are included by virtue of the opposition they contain.

192. Another question: what kind of opposites should we take to be meant, those without or those with intermediate terms? If there are intermediates, there are obviously more than the 'two transitions' [71a13]; if not, why does he speak of opposites generally? — As a matter of fact Plato does not even acknowledge the existence of opposites without intermediate terms, as in the *Parmenides*. But even if we admit intermediates there are two transitions, whether we take the opposites absolutely or relatively, for an intermediate term is also in a way an opposite, as Aristotle thinks too [*phys.* V 1, 224b30–35].

§§ 193–200. Questions raised and answered by Syrianus. 70c5–72e2

193. (iii) How can the ungenerated and the generated, the immortal and the mortal proceed from each other? Yet they are certainly opposites. — First and foremost they are not opposites, since the one makes and perfects the other. Secondly, Socrates has specified expressly that only those opposites proceed from each other, which are 'subject to process' at all [70d9].

194. (iv) How can we escape the consequence that the incorporeal and body proceed from each other also? Yet there will be a void, if either of these is to proceed from the other. — We distinguish three meanings of 'incorporeal,' and in none of these is it the opposite of body: (1) the tran-

---

3–4. E.g. in δικαιότερον-ἀδικώτερον (71a7) it is not the comparative that is relevant, but the opposites δίκαιον-ἄδικον.

§ 192. Ol. 10 § 10.4–11 and note. The notion of ἄμεσα ἐναντία in Ar., *cat.* 11b38–12a25. Alcinous, summing up the argument from opposites, *did.* 25, decides for ἄμεσα, without saying why; as the examples given by Pl. do not exclude ἔμμεσα, his reason must have been the point raised here, that Pl. speaks of two 'transitions'. At that stage, the discussion may have gone no farther than this. Plotinus, dealing with the category of quality (VI 3, 20) still acknowledges both kinds. It was apparently Pr. who rejected the notion of ἄμεσα ἐναντία, no doubt on the ground of his theory of μεσότητες (*elem.* 132). Amm., *int.* 92.3–15 says that their existence is controversial; Ol., *Ph.* 10 § 10, *mete.* 242.26–31, El., *cat.* 181.9–32 declare the whole concept for un-Platonic.

4. ὡς ἐν Παρμενίδῃ : as there is nothing in Plato's *Parm.* that can be construed as a statement to this effect, the reference must be either to Pr.'s commentary or to Dam.'s. The extant portions of the two commentaries complement each other almost exactly, Pr. covering 126a1–142a8–9, Dam. ca. 142d–166c5; in this work, too, Dam. follows Pr. closely, so that there are probably few important points made by Pr. which he does not mention. Pr.'s commentary does contain a theory of opposites (739–742), but does not touch upon the question of ἔμμεσα or ἄμεσα. The only remaining possibility is the introduction to the second hypothesis, which is missing from both commentaries. The reference to μεσότητες at the very beginning

δὲ ἐκεῖνο, πῶς τὰ πρός τι παρήγαγεν [70e6–71a7]; — Ἢ καὶ τὰ πρός τι κατὰ τὴν ἐναντίωσιν εἴληπται.

ρπβ΄. - Ὅτι ζητητέον ποῖα ἐναντία ληπτέον, ἄμεσα ἢ ἔμμεσα. εἰ μὲν γὰρ τοῦτο, πῶς ἔτι ʽδύο γενέσεις᾽ αἱ μεταξύ [71a13]; πλείους γάρ. εἰ δὲ ἐκεῖνο, πῶς ἁπλῶς τὰ ἐναντία εἴρηται; — Ἢ οὐδὲ ἔστι κατὰ Πλάτωνα ἄμεσα ἐναντία, ὡς ἐν Παρμενίδῃ. εἰ δὲ καὶ ἔμμεσα, δύο αἱ γενέσεις τῶν ἐναντίων λαμβανομένων ἢ ἁπλῶς ἢ πῇ. καὶ γὰρ τὸ μέσον πῇ ἐναντίον, ὡς καὶ Ἀριστοτέλης [phys. V 1, 224b30–35].

§§ 193–200. Questions raised and answered by Syrianus. 70c5–72e2

ρπγ΄. - (iii) Πῶς τὸ ἀγένητον καὶ γενητὸν καὶ ἀθάνατον καὶ θνητὸν ἐξ ἀλλήλων, ἐναντία γε ὄντα; — Ἢ μάλιστα μὲν οὐκ ἐναντία, εἴ γε τὸ ἕτερον τοῦ ἑτέρου ποιητικόν τε καὶ τελεωτικόν. ἔπειτα διωρίσατο σαφῶς ἐκεῖνα γίνεσθαι ἐξ ἀλλήλων ἐναντία, ʽὅσα γένεσιν ἔχει᾽ [70d9].

ρπδ΄. - (iv) Πῶς οὐχὶ καὶ τὸ ἀσώματον καὶ σῶμα ἐξ ἀλλήλων; ἔσται γὰρ κενόν, εἰ ὁπότερον οὖν γένοιτο ἐκ τοῦ ἑτέρου. — Ἢ τριχῶς τὸ ἀσώματον,
α΄ οὐδὲν δὲ τούτων ἐναντίον τῷ σώματι. οὔτε γὰρ τὸ χωριστόν, ἔξω γὰρ τοῦτο
β΄ γενέσεως· οὔτε τὸ ἐν ὑποκειμένῳ τῷ σώματι, πῶς γὰρ ἂν ἐν τῷ ἐναντίῳ τὸ

§ 192. 4 παρμενείδηι M
§ 193. 2 γε²] γ- in ras. Mˣ
§ 194. 2 οὖν ins. Mᶜ: om. M¹ (cf. § 474.5)

of the extant text in Dam. (5.4) is not relevant to the present issue, since it applies to intermediates linking the higher with the lower. However, elsewhere (Phil. § 66.19–20), Dam. speaks of intermediates ἐν τῷ πλάτει, and these could have been mentioned in the Parm. commentary at that particular point in connection with the fact that Parmenides' argument proceeds by pairs of opposites (one-many, whole-parts, in itself – in another, unmoved-moving, identical-different, similar-dissimilar, etc.), one of each pair belonging to the series of limit, the other to that of infinitude (cf. Pr., Parm. 753.32–757.12; 1118.2–1123.21; 1126.13–22; Dam., Phil. § 66.15–17).

5–6. Ar., phys. V 1, 224b30–32 ἐκ δὲ τοῦ μεταξὺ μεταβάλλει· χρῆται γὰρ αὐτῷ ὡς ἐναντίῳ ὄντι πρὸς ἑκάτερον· ἔστι γάρ πως τὸ μεταξὺ τὰ ἄκρα. Cf. also ibid. V 5, 229b14–22. Ol.'s quotation (10 § 10.9–10) shows that these passages are intended, rather than e.g. eth. Nic. II 8, 1108b13–14, as Plot. VI 3, 20.2–3 might suggest.

§§ 193–200. These questions are reviewed again, from his own point of view, by Dam. I §§ 244–251, where the numbers are given (iii–x). In the introductory section (§ 243) Dam. says that the selection is his own, and consequently this holds also for their first occurrence here.

§ 194. 2–3. Porph., cat. 106.25–33, argues on entirely different grounds that body and the incorporeal are not opposites. Simpl., cat. 77.28–30 ἢ διττὸν τὸ ἀσώματον, τὸ μὲν ὡς φύσις ὡρισμένη καὶ ἀντικειμένη τῇ σωματικῇ, τὸ δὲ ὡς ἀπόφασις αἰτία καὶ τῆς σωματικῆς καὶ τῆς ἀσωμάτου τῆς ἀντικειμένης αὐτῇ.

scendent, which is beyond genesis; (2) that which has a body as its substrate; obviously nothing can have its own opposite as substrate; (3) the constituents of body, i.e. matter and form; the part cannot be opposed to the whole, rather it is its component.

195. (v) How is it that an animal that is born waking has not passed from the sleeping to the waking state? — The being born waking is not essential, but accidental; what comes into being is primarily the animal as such, after which the states of sleeping and waking succeed each other.

196. (vi) Why does the younger not proceed from the older? — In the first place there is no process of becoming younger; if there were, it would certainly have being older as its starting-point. Another solution: the child is born from the parent, i.e. younger from older.

Besides, the commentator observes, it is doubtful if they *are* opposites, since youth is a positive, old age a privative term. Finally, if you consider that anything that is older in relation to the past becomes young in relation to the future, you will find that the rule holds even here.

197. (vii) Why do earth and fire not proceed from each other, although they are opposites and subject to the process of coming-to-be? — Fire does not come into being at all, except in so far as it is sharp and rarefied, for the quality of mobility remains the same in three of the elements, so that fire as a whole does not proceed either from earth or from anything else.

But even granting that something remains, in the opposites under discussion there is no remaining quality. Besides, why should the rarefaction of fire not proceed from the density of earth and its sharpness from the obtuseness of earth? And why should the mobility of any of the three others not proceed from the stability of earth? Then, this argument would eliminate also the possibility of the three other sets of qualities passing into each other, whereas Timaeus [55e1] makes only earth unchangeable.

---

§ 195. Ol. 9 § 4.1–7; § 5.1–7 : πρὸς μὲν οὖν τὸ πρῶτον . . . φησιν ὁ Πρόκλος ἤτοι ὁ Συριανὸς ὅτι τὸ ἐγρηγορὸς οὐ κατὰ πρῶτον λόγον ἐκ τῆς φύσεως γίνεται, ἀλλὰ παρέπεται τοῦτο κτλ.

§ 196. Ol. 9 § 4.8–11; § 5.10–23. At 10 § 5.7–13 Ol., recapitulating from memory his own joint discussion of points v and vi at 9 §§ 4–5, attributes to Syrianus a solution of both, which was meant to apply to point v (= § 195) only: ὅτι οὐ κατὰ προηγούμενον σκοπὸν ταῦτα ὑπὸ τῆς φύσεως γίνεται, ἀλλὰ παρέπεται.

4–6. The subject of φησίν, as usual, is Proclus, who is here adding his own solutions to those of Syrianus. So, too, in the additions to §§ 197–198, which do not take into account the completely different approach of Dam.

5–6. Cf. Pr., *Parm.* 1231.5–14 (quoted at Ol. 9 § 5.10–23).

§ 197. How do we explain that earth and fire according to Pl., *Tim.* 55e1, do not proceed from each other, though they are opposites (*Tim.* 30b8–c1 as explained by Pr., *Tim.* II 17.23–18.3) and though they also satisfy the requirement (*Ph.* 70d9) of being subject to coming-to-be? — Syrianus' answer (lines 2–4) is based on the interpretation of *Tim.* 31c2–32c4 set forth by Pr., *Tim.* II 40.22–41.9, which therefore evidently states Syrianus' view of the passage (the ἡμεῖς ibid. 37.14, though Pr. does not say so expressly, must include Syrianus). This "three-quality

γ' ἐναντίον ὑφίσταιτο; οὔτε τὸ ἐξ οὗ τὸ σῶμα, οἷον ἡ ὕλη ἢ τὸ εἶδος, οὐ γὰρ τὸ μέρος 5
τῷ ὅλῳ ἐναντίον, ὅ γε συμπληροῖ τὸ ὅλον.

ρπε'. - (v) Πῶς τὸ τεχθὲν ζῷον ἐγρηγορὸς ἐκ τοῦ καθεύδοντος οὐ γέγονεν; 195(127)
— Ἤ ὅτι οὐ καθ' αὐτὸ γέγονεν ἐγρηγορός, ἀλλὰ κατὰ συμβεβηκός· ἡ γὰρ
γένεσις ἡ πρώτη τοῦ ζῴου καθ' αὐτό, μετὰ δὲ ταῦτα γίγνεται τὸ καθεῦδον καὶ τὸ
ἐγρηγορὸς ἐξ ἀλλήλων.

ρπς'. - (vi) Πῶς οὐχὶ καὶ τὸ νεώτερον ἐκ τοῦ πρεσβυτέρου; — Ἤ μάλιστα 196
μὲν οὐ γίγνεται· εἰ γὰρ ἐγίγνετο, πάντως ἂν ἐκ τοῦ πρεσβυτέρου ἐγίγνετο.
ἔπειτα ὁ παῖς ἐκ τοῦ πατρὸς ὡς νεώτερος ἐκ πρεσβυτέρου γίγνεται.
Μήποτε δέ, φησίν, οὐδὲ ἐναντία· ἡ μὲν γὰρ νεότης ἕξις, τὸ δὲ γῆρας στέρησις.
εἰ δέ τις ἐννοήσειεν ὅτι τὸ ἀεὶ λαμβανόμενον πρεσβύτερον πρὸς τὸ παρῳχημένον 5
γίγνεται νέον πρὸς τὸ μέλλον, ὄψεται καὶ ἐπὶ τούτων ἀληθῆ τὸν λόγον.

ρπζ'. - (vii) Πῶς οὐ γίγνεται γῆ καὶ πῦρ ἐξ ἀλλήλων καίτοι ἐναντία καὶ 197
γιγνόμενα; — Ἤ οὐδὲ γένεσιν ἔχει τὸ πῦρ, ἀλλὰ καθὸ μόνον ὀξὺ καὶ λεπτόν·
τὸ γὰρ εὐκίνητον μένει ἐν τοῖς τρισίν· οὐκ ἄρα ὅλον γίγνεται τὸ πῦρ οὔτε ἐκ
γῆς οὔτε ἐξ ἄλλου τινός.

Ἀλλ' οὐδέν, εἰ καὶ μένοι τι, καὶ μένει ἐπὶ τῶν ὑποκειμένων ἐναντίων. ἔπειτα 5
τὸ λεπτὸν διὰ τί μὴ ἐκ τοῦ γεώδους παχέος, καὶ ἐκ τοῦ γεώδους ἀμβλέος τὸ
ὀξύ; ἔτι δὲ τὸ εὐκίνητον ὁτουοῦν τῶν τριῶν διὰ τί μὴ ἐκ τοῦ δυσκινήτου τοῦ
γεώδους; ἀναιρήσει δὲ ὁ λόγος καὶ τὴν τῶν τριῶν συστοιχιῶν ἐξ ἀλλήλων
γένεσιν, ἀλλ' ὁ Τίμαιος [55e1] μόνην ποιεῖ τὴν γῆν ἀμετάβλητον. μήποτε οὖν

---

§ 197. 1 οὐ Fh: οὖν M — 5 οὐδέν] fort. οὐδέ | μένει Nv: μένειν M — 8 συστοιχιῶν M^c: -είων M¹

---

theory" (on the origin of which see J. H. Waszink, *Studien zum Timaioskommentar des Calcidius*, Leiden 1964, 74–82, and W. Marg, *Timaeus Locrus* 97–99) replaces the usual system of one or two qualities (Ar., gener. et corr. II 3, 331a1–6: fire *hot* and *dry*, air *liquid* and *hot*, water *cold* and *liquid*, earth *dry* and *cold*) by a three-dimensional system based on the three qualities of *Tim.* 55d8–56b6, arranged on the following pattern, so that each of the intermediate elements has two qualities in common with those next to it:

fire	ὀξύ	λεπτόν	εὐκίνητον
air	ἀμβλύ	λεπτόν	εὐκίνητον
water	ἀμβλύ	παχύ	εὐκίνητον
earth	ἀμβλύ	παχύ	δυσκίνητον

Syrianus' point is that there is no coming-to-be of the elements as such, but only partial change of the qualities. – Pr. (lines 5–12) objects that ultimately the two extremes have nothing in common and are complete opposites; there is no reason why their three qualities, forming three pairs of opposites, should be exceptions to Plato's rule; finally, on this line of argument, there could be no transition between fire, air and water either (against *Tim.* 54c3–5). His solution is that the rule excludes pairs of opposites of which *neither* passes into the other.

The solution may be that if the one proceeds from the other, the other must also proceed from the one, and in the present instance neither happens; at least, Socrates bases his conviction that the living proceed from the dead on the manifest fact that the dead proceed from the living.

198. (viii) Why does not the body also return to existence, if the soul does? — As a matter of fact, body too is indestructible, as it is stated in the *Laws* [X 904a8–9].

But what ought to be restored is the body with these individual peculiarities, since it was with this that the soul was united. It may be answered that in an infinite span of time the elements will combine to form such a body too. This, however, is not true in the first place, and besides there would be no numerical identity, as in the case of the soul. A better answer is therefore that the change takes place only where there is also a constant factor, and this is the stronger of the two, i.e. the soul; consequently it is the soul that remains and keeps the cycle going.

199. (ix) Does not the argument necessarily apply to irrational animals as well? — Indeed, even their souls survive, at least those that can be detached from the body. But if the body is a substrate in which they exist, how can the rule hold good? In that case the body is the stronger and survives as body (for it is as such that it is stronger) to become again organic and animate body. But how if the body too should perish? Then the cyclic motion manifests itself in the species.

200. (x) What if life and death have one and the same substrate? — In these cases there is more than one.

§§ 201–206. Final observations by Syrianus. 70c5–72e2

201. All things move in cycles, but in some cases the two terms remain numerically identical, as in the heavens; in other cases they remain specifically identical, as in the rest of creation; in others again the one

---

§ 198. Syrianus cites *Laws* X 904a8–9: ἀνώλεθρον δὲ ὂν γενόμενον, ἀλλ' οὐκ αἰώνιον, ψυχὴν καὶ σῶμα, referring to body in general (cf. b1–2). Pr. (lines 3–7) says that in the present context only the individual body (τὸ τοιόνδε) is relevant. He rejects the tentative solution that, given infinite time, an identical body will be formed, on two grounds: first, the assumed fact is not true (this point is not argued); secondly, even granting that the materials return to the same position, there would be no numerical identity. His own solution is that the rule holds only when there is a constant factor, which in this case is soul as the stronger. See Dam.'s criticism at § 249.

§ 199. Ol. 10 § 1.19–20; § 5.1–6; 9 § 6.6–13.

2–3. ὅσαι διακρίνεσθαι δύνανται τῶν σωμάτων: Pr. admits, with certain qualifications, incarnation of a human soul in an animal body (*Tim.* III 294.22–295.32; *Rep.* II 309.28–312.5); cf. Beutler, art. Pr. 237.14–29; Dörrie (art. cited at § 177) 432–433. He also believes that the irrational part of the human soul, together with the 'pneumatic vehicle', survives the body (cf. at § 168.6–7 and

DAMASCIUS I 127, 130 N. (Β ρπζ', ρϟ'-ρϟθ') 121

εἰ τὸ ἕτερον ἐκ θατέρου γίγνεται, δεῖ καὶ τὸ ἕτερον ἐκ τοῦ ἑτέρου γίγνεσθαι, 10
ἐπὶ δὲ τούτων οὐδέτερον· ἀναγκάζει γοῦν ἐκ τῶν τεθνεώτων εἶναι τοὺς ζῶντας,
ἐπειδὴ σαφῶς ἐκ τῶν ζώντων οἱ τεθνεῶτες.

d ρϟϛ'. – (viii) Πῶς οὐχὶ καὶ τὸ σῶμα ἐπάνεισιν, εἴπερ ἡ ψυχή; — Ἢ καὶ τὸ 198(130)
σῶμα ἀνώλεθρον, ὡς καὶ ἐν Νόμοις [X 904a8–9].
Ἀλλὰ τὸ τοιόνδε ἐχρῆν· πρὸς τοῦτο γὰρ ἡ σύνοδος. ἢ καὶ τὰ στοιχεῖά ποτε
ἐν τῷ ἀπείρῳ χρόνῳ ποιήσει καὶ τὸ τοιόνδε. ἀλλ᾽ οὔτε ἀληθὲς οὔτε ἀριθμῷ
ταὐτόν, ὡς ἐπὶ ψυχῆς. βέλτιον οὖν τῆς μεταβολῆς οὔσης ἐν τοῖς ἔχουσί τι καὶ 5
ὑπομένον, τοῦτο δὲ εἶναι τὸ ἰσχυρότερον, ἰσχυρότερον δὲ εἶναι τὴν ψυχήν·
ταύτην ἄρα καὶ ὑπομένουσαν ἀποσῴζειν τὸν κύκλον.

ρϟζ'. – (ix) Πῶς οὐχὶ καὶ ἐπὶ τῶν ἀλόγων ζῴων συμβήσεται ὁ λόγος; 199
— Ἢ καὶ αἱ τούτων ψυχαὶ ἐπιδιαμένουσιν, ὅσαι διακρίνεσθαι δύνανται τῶν
σωμάτων. εἰ δὲ ἐν ὑποκειμένῳ εἰσίν, πῶς ἐν τούτοις ὁ λόγος σωθήσεται; ἢ τὸ
σῶμα ἐπὶ τούτων ἰσχυρότερον ὂν ἐπιδιαμένει ἢ σῶμα· ταύτῃ γὰρ ἰσχυρότερον·
καὶ γίγνεται πάλιν τοιόνδε καὶ ἔμψυχον. εἰ δὲ καὶ τοῦτο φθείροιτο, τί ἐροῦμεν; 5
ἢ ὅτι κατ᾽ εἶδος ὁ κύκλος.

ρϟη'. – (x) Τί οὖν, εἴπερ ἓν ὑποκείμενον τῷ θανάτῳ καὶ τῇ ζωῇ; — Ἢ πλείω 200
ἐπὶ τῶν τοιούτων.

§§ 201–206. Final observations by Syrianus. 70c5–72e2

ρϟθ'. – Ὅτι πάντα μὲν κυκλίζεται, ἀλλὰ τὰ μὲν ἐκ μενόντων τῶν δύο ἀριθμῷ 201
τῶν αὐτῶν, ὡς ἐν οὐρανῷ· τὰ δὲ κατ᾽ εἶδος, ὡς ἐν τῇ ἄλλῃ γενέσει· τὰ δὲ τοῦ

---

§ 197. 11 γοῦν Mᶜ : οὖν M¹
§ 201. 1 ἀριθμῶι] -ι in ras. Mᶜ (ἀριθμῶν M¹ ?)

---

§ 177.5). Apart from this, it is difficult to draw a parting line through animal life below which it would be inseparable; theoretically, possession of the higher senses is a conceivable criterion.

5. τοιόνδε : not in the sense of § 198.3, but in that of Aristotle's short phrase for φυσικὸν δυνάμει ζωὴν ἔχον (an. II 1, 412b11; met. Z 10, 1035b16). The idea is probably that of a dead body producing lower forms of life, as at § 234.14–15.

§ 200. The question of life and death as qualities of an organic body, already dealt with in § 199.2–6, is raised here again in its most general form; Syrianus answers that in the cases covered by his definitions (§§ 187–188) there is more than one substance involved.

§ 201. This, the first of Syrianus' supplementary remarks, relates more specifically to the problem discussed in § 200. One could even consider merging the two sections into one (the numbers being late additions; cf. Phil. § 212) by writing ... τῶν τοιούτων, ὅτι..., but I think that the connection is too loose to warrant this.

survives and the other perishes, the latter being permanent specifically, the former individually, as in the present instance.

202. The argument is based on three postulates: (1) that all things move in circles, imitating intelligence; (2) that soul is stronger than body; (3) that all things long for the good and aspire to everlasting existence, either as individuals, or as kinds, or in a mode that participates of both. In other words, it is based on the three primal hypostases, Intelligence, Potency, the Good.

203. [70c5-8] The tradition is 'old,' because it hails back to Orpheus and Pythagoras – the tradition according to which souls return to the body and are again lifted up above the body, and this cycle repeats itself many times.

204. [70c5-72e2] From the argument it follows that (1) every soul everlastingly is sometimes above, sometimes below, and has its descents and its ascents; (2) should incorporeality be added to separability, the soul would be proven immortal, because it could perish neither in the way of the corporeal, being incorporeal, nor in the way of the incorporeal, being separable; (3) it is without a beginning in time, for if we think of it as coming into being at a certain moment and then descending into body, it will no longer proceed from the dead, or, if one should call the state of separation death, the dead will not have proceeded from the living.

205. In what respect is the argument not a complete proof of immortmortality? In so far as it is valid only on the assumption that genesis is everlasting, but as soon as we remove genesis, we invalidate the argument also.

206. Even though the argument does not prove the soul immortal, it does prove that it has no beginning in time; for if the living proceeds from the dead, there can be no initial coming-into-being of the soul.

Obviously, however, this also depends on the same hypothesis.

---

§ 202. 1-2. Plot. II 2, 1.1 (of the sky) διὰ τί κύκλῳ κινεῖται; ὅτι νοῦν μιμεῖται (*Tim.* 34a1-4).

2. From Ol. 10 § 9 it appears that Syrianus and Pr. tried to find authority for this assumption in Plato's example καὶ μὴν ἐξ ἰσχυροτέρου γε τὸ ἀσθενέστερον (71a3).

3-4. The three forms of permanency correspond to those of § 201. On the desire for existence as desire for the Good see *Phil.* § 258.3; also Ar., *an.* II 4, 415a26-b8.

3. Ar., *eth. Nic.* I 1, 1094a2-3 διὸ καλῶς ἀπεφήναντο τἀγαθόν, οὗ πάντα ἐφίεται.

4-5. νοῦ, δυνάμεως, ἀγαθοῦ: identified with the 'Chaldean triad' νοῦς-δύναμις-πατήρ, cf. note on § 180. The expression τρεῖς ἀρχικαὶ ὑποστάσεις first occurs in

μὲν μένοντος, τοῦ δὲ φθει|ρομένου, καὶ τούτου μὲν κατ' εἶδος, ἐκείνου δὲ κατὰ (131) ἀριθμόν, ὡς ἐπὶ τοῦ προκειμένου.

σ'. - Ὅτι ὥρμηται ὁ λόγος ἀπὸ τριῶν ἀξιωμάτων· πρῶτον μὲν τοῦ πάντα 202 κυκλίζεσθαι μιμούμενα τὸν νοῦν, δεύτερον δὲ τοῦ ἰσχυροτέραν εἶναι τὴν ψυχήν, τρίτον δὲ τοῦ πάντα ἐφίεσθαι τοῦ ἀγαθοῦ καὶ βούλεσθαι ἀεὶ διαμένειν ἢ κατὰ ἀριθμὸν ἢ κατὰ εἶδος ἤ τινα μικτὸν τρόπον· ὥστε καὶ ἀπὸ τῶν τριῶν ἀρχικῶν ὑποστάσεων, νοῦ δυνάμεως ἀγαθοῦ. 5

σα'. - [70c5-8] Ὅτι 'παλαιὸς' ὁ λόγος, Ὀρφικός τε γὰρ καὶ Πυθαγόρειος, 203 ὁ πάλιν ἄγων τὰς ψυχὰς εἰς τὸ σῶμα καὶ πάλιν ἀπὸ τοῦ σώματος ἀνάγων, καὶ τοῦτο κύκλῳ πολλάκις.

σβ'. - [70c5-72e2] Ὅτι ἕπεται τῷ λόγῳ, ἓν μὲν τὸ πᾶσαν ἀεὶ ψυχὴν ποτὲ 204 μὲν ἄνω μένειν, ποτὲ δὲ κάτω, καὶ καθόδους ἀποδιδόναι καὶ ἀνόδους· ἕτερον δέ, εἰ προστεθείη τὸ ἀσώματον εἶναι πρὸς τῷ χωριστῷ, τὴν ψυχὴν ἀθάνατον εἶναι ἄν (οὔτε γὰρ ὡς σωματικὴ φθαρείη ἄν, εἴπερ ἀσώματος, οὔτε ὡς ἀσώματος, εἴπερ χωριστή)· τρίτον τὸ ἀγένητον αὐτὴν εἶναι, εἰ γάρ ποτε γενομένη κατέλθοι 5 εἰς σῶμα, οὐκ ἔσται οὕτως ἐκ τοῦ τεθνηκότος. εἰ δὲ καὶ τὸ χωρὶς εἶναι φαίη τις τεθνάναι, ἀλλ' οὐκέτι τὸ τεθνηκὸς ἀπὸ ζῶντος ἔσται.

σγ'. - Πῶς οὐ πάντῃ δείκνυσιν αὐτὴν ἀθάνατον ὁ λόγος; — Ἢ ὅτι οὔσης 205 ἀεὶ τῆς γενέσεως ἰσχύει, ἀνελὼν δέ τις τὴν γένεσιν ἀναιρεῖ καὶ τὸν λόγον.

σδ'. - Ὅτι εἰ μὴ καὶ ἀθάνατον δείκνυσιν ὁ λόγος, ἀλλὰ ἀγένητον ἀποδείκνυσιν. 206 εἰ γὰρ τὸ ζῶν ἐκ τοῦ τεθνηκότος, οὐκ ἔσται αὐτῆς πρώτη γένεσις. Ἀλλὰ δῆλον ὅτι καὶ τοῦτο τῆς ὑποθέσεως ἤρτηται.

---

§ 203. 1 πυθαγόριος (et sim. hinc semper) M
§ 204. 5 γεγομένη M — 7 ante ἀλλ'] ∻ ∻ in ras. Mᶜ
§ 205. 1 ante πῶς] ∻ Mˣ

Plot. V 1 title (not in the text), referring to the One, Intelligence and Soul; in the same way Pr., *Tim.* III 165.12-13 (ταῖς τρισὶν ἀρχικαῖς αἰτίαις) and Dam., *Phil.* § 244.9-10.
§ 203. Ol. 10 § 6.
§ 204. 1-2. Ol. 10 § 14. On the rejection of eternal salvation and eternal damnation see *infra* on §§ 547-548, and Ol. *loc. cit.*
2-5. This is the argument attributed to Plotinus by Ol. 13 § 4, Dam. I § 311 and II § 29; it occurs in this precise form in Pr., *elem.* 187. On a restriction made by Pr. himself see note on II § 29.
§ 206. 3. Comment by Pr. or by Dam.?

§§ 207-252. **A monograph on the argument from opposites by Damascius. 69e6-72e2**

The argument from opposites: an account by our professor, preserving both the contingent character and the validity of the argument

207. Dealing with Plato's argument from opposites in the *Phaedo*, the older commentators have not even been able to defend its validity nor to parry the attacks launched against it from the side of the other schools. The great Iamblichus, however, in a way characteristic of 'that spirit of his,' overshoots the mark by attempting to lend it such completeness as to constitute absolute proof of the immortality of the soul, which is more than Socrates himself dared to presume it could do. Then Syrianus, with that balance and proportion which he shows in all things, avoiding on the one hand the amateurish perplexity of earlier generations and moderating the boldness of Iamblichus on the other, tried to keep within the limits of Socrates' professed intention while at the same time refuting those who ridicule the argumentation and proving them guilty of chicanery. On the whole, he has defined the problems and stated the assumptions in a way satisfactory to me and in accordance with his usual high standard, 'yet has he not reached the final end of words.' For he needs many extraneous elements not expressed in the text, and after saying first that the argument proves a possibility, he ends by lending it compulsive force, a force as strong as the necessity that holds the world together; and besides, he does not show this force at work in all cases, which was Socrates' claim [70d7-e6], but in the generation of human beings only, and even there not without restriction, but only as far as the soul is concerned. Therefore I wish to add a few remarks and to define more precisely what the cycle is and what things are subject to it, and to show that the argument is true in the sense that it proves a possibility.

208. For the sake both of shortness and clearness I shall state in summary form (I) the objections against the argument that remain after the intelligent interpretation of Syrianus; (II) the preliminary assumptions

---

§§ 207-252. On Dam.'s monograph see Introd. p. 16. His analysis reduces the argument to the one point that a substance is normally more durable than its (alternating) accidents, and therefore soul as a substance may be expected to survive the accidents of union with and separation from the body.

§ 207. 1-6. Ol. 10 § 1.11-16 (Iambl., *Ph.* frg. 1); cf. 11 § 2.1-5; 13 § 4.6-18.
4. Hom., *Il.* 15.94; 18.262; *Od.* 15.212.
ibid. *CPG* I 168 (Zenob. 6,23); I 375 (Georg. Cypr. 3,89); II 224 (Macar. 8,67); II 702 (Apostol. 17.62). In Pl., *Crat.* 413a8-b1, the expression is ὑπὲρ τὰ ἐσκαμμένα ἄλλεσθαι.
6. Cf. Pl., *Rep.* VI 498e3 ἄνδρα δὲ ἀρετῇ παρισωμένον καὶ ὡμοιωμένον. Pl. alludes

§§ 207-252. A monograph on the argument from opposites by Damascius. 69e6-72e2

Περὶ τοῦ ἀπὸ τῶν ἐναντίων λόγου διάταξις τοῦ ἡμετέρου (132)
καθηγεμόνος, τό τε ἐνδεχόμενον τό τε ἀληθὲς τοῦ λόγου διασῴζουσα

α'. – Τὸν ἀπὸ τῶν ἐναντίων τοῦ Πλάτωνος ἐν Φαίδωνι λόγον οἱ μὲν παλαιότεροι 207
τῶν ἐξηγητῶν οὐδὲ ὡς ἐρρωμένον ὄντα διασῴζειν ἠδυνήθησαν οὐδὲ ἀμύνεσθαι
τὰς κατ' αὐτοῦ φερομένας τῶν ἑτεροφύλων αἱρέσεων βολάς. ὁ δὲ μέγας Ἰάμβλιχος,
'οἷος ἐκείνου θυμός', ὑπὲρ τὰ ἐσκαμμένα πηδήσας ἐσπούδασεν αὐτὸν τελεώσασθαι
εἰς τοσοῦτον, εἰς ὅσον ἀποδεῖξαι παντελῆ τὴν ψυχῆς ἀθανασίαν, οὐδὲ Σωκράτους 5
αὐτοῦ τηλικοῦτον ἐπ' αὐτῷ φρονήσαντος. ὁ δὲ ἐν πᾶσι συμμετρίᾳ παρισωμένος
Συριανὸς τῶν τε προτέρων τὸ ἰδιωτικόν τε καὶ ἄπορον φυλαξάμενος καὶ τοῦ
Ἰαμβλίχου τὸ μέγα χαλάσας ἐπειράθη καὶ ταῖς Σωκράτους ἐπαγγελίαις ἐμμένειν
καὶ τοὺς διακωμῳδοῦντας τὴν ἐπιχείρησιν ἐξελέγχειν ὡς συκοφαντοῦντας. τὰ
μὲν οὖν ἄλλα διωρίσατο καὶ προωμολογήσατο κατὰ νοῦν τε ἐμοὶ καὶ ἑαυτῷ 10
εἰωθότως, 'ἀτὰρ οὐ τέλος ἵκετο μύθων'. πολλῶν τε γὰρ ἐπεισοδίων ἐδεήθη μὴ
κειμένων ἐν τῷ λόγῳ, καὶ ἐνδεχόμενον εἶναι τὸν λόγον προειπὼν ἐτελεύτησεν
αὐτοῦ προϊὼν εἰς τὴν ἀνάγκην, ἴσην γε ἀνάγκην τῇ τοῦ κόσμου συστάσει· καὶ οὐδὲ
ταύτην κοινὴν ἐπὶ πάντων ἀπέφηνεν, | ὥσπερ ὁ Σωκράτης ἠξίωσεν [70d7–e6], (133)
ἀλλ' ἐπὶ μόνων τῶν ἀνθρωπίνων γενέσεων, οὐδὲ τούτων ὅλων, ἀλλὰ μόνον τῶν 15
περὶ ψυχήν. διὸ καὶ ἐγὼ μικρὰ ἄττα προσθεῖναι βούλομαι, καὶ προσδιορίσασθαι
ὅστις ὁ κύκλος καὶ τίνων, ὡς ἀληθής τέ ἐστι καὶ ἐνδεχομένως ἀληθής.

β'. – Συντομίας δὲ εἵνεκεν ἅμα καὶ εὐκρινείας ἐπὶ κεφαλαίων ἐκθήσομαι τάς 208
τε ἀπορίας ὅσας ἄν τις ἀπορήσειε πρὸς τὸν λόγον καὶ τῆς Συριανοῦ τυχόντα
νουνεχοῦς ἐξηγήσεως, καὶ τὰς προομολογήσεις δι' ὧν ἀπαντησόμεθα πρὸς τοὺς

---

§ 207. 1 ἐν φαίδωνι λόγον Mᶜ: λόγον ἐν φαίδωνι M¹ — 2 ἐξηγητῶν μ: ἐξητῶν M

---

to the πάρισα of the rhetoricians.
10–11. καὶ ἑαυτῷ εἰωθότως=Pl., *Symp.* 218b6–7, the reading of Y (Vindob. phil. gr. 21); the other MSS. have ἑαυτοῦ τε καὶ for ἑαυτῷ.
11. Hom., *Il.* 9.56.
11–13. See note on §§ 183–206.
13. ἴσην γε ἀνάγκην τῇ τοῦ κόσμου συστάσει: if the eternity of the world is assumed, the argument, according to Syrianus (§§ 205–206), will be full proof of immortality.
§ 208. 1. ἐπὶ κεφαλαίων ἐκθήσομαι: cf. Pr., *Rep.* II 1.5–8 τὴν ... κεφαλαιώδη ... ἔκθεσιν (in short extract-like sections, many of them with introductory ὅτι).

which will enable us to answer the objections and to present our proofs of the correctness of the argument as a contingent one; (III) the answers themselves to the objections and the interpretation on a basis of probability, in accordance with Socrates' own announcement: 'What shall we do? Shall we talk it over together, whether it is likely or not?' [70b5–7]. I shall take it that the reader has first studied the divine thoughts of my great predecessor, since I see no sense in repeating what has once been well said.

(I) Objections

209. (1) Even if, as the philosopher requires us to do [§ 185], we define life and death as consisting in the union and separation of two entities, soul and body, it does not follow necessarily that what has been separated is joined together again nor that what has been joined together is separated. For instance, after meeting a person for the first time I do not see him again, or, in the terms of Cebes' example [70a5] (an objection which remains unanswered), air caught in a bag and then let out cannot be caught in it again, and smoke, which owes its origin to decomposition, is never recomposed to make wood.

210. (The criticism that in the case of smoke there is separation, but no recomposition, is not valid; for here we do not have to do with separation at all, but with generation, since only that which is already present can be separated, whereas the smoke was neither potentially nor actually present in the wood, being the product of the dissolution of the wood.)

211. (2) Even in one and the same substratum the cycle of opposites is not maintained: the newly born who sleeps for the first time will not necessarily be awake again, though the fact that the waking state is not preceded by sleep may be accounted for on the lines indicated by the commentator [§ 195]; for the child may die in its first sleep, or it may not live long enough to sleep at all. An even more frequent contingency is for a man who was born with a light complexion to remain so for a long time; although he *can* become dark, this may well never happen until his death.

212. (3) The argument requires that, just as the soul that returns to be united with the body is the identical one, so it should be also the identical body that is united with the soul, but we do not see this happen (living bodies do not proceed from dead ones); therefore neither will souls after

---

8. τὸν ἐντευξόμενον : proves that this is a written treatise for separate circulation, which did not include the preceding survey by Syrianus.

§§ 209–220. Eleven points for which Syrianus' solution fails to account, and which are settled by Dam. in §§ 231–242.

§ 209. 3. πρῶτος : Norvin proposes πρώτως here and § 211.1; cf. § 242.1, 3 and 17, where πρώτως is the MS. reading. The change would be a very slight one in these two cases, since most uncorrected copies of the transliteration period are

ἀποροῦντας καὶ τὰς ἀποδείξεις ποιησόμεθα τῆς ἐνδεχομένης ἀληθείας, ἔτι δὲ ἐκ τρίτων τὰς ἐπιλύσεις αὐτὰς τῶν ἀποριῶν καὶ τὰς μετὰ τοῦ εἰκότος ἐξηγήσεις, ὡς αὐτὸς ὑπέσχετο ὁ Σωκράτης· 'ἀλλὰ τί δὴ ποιῶμεν; ἢ περὶ αὐτῶν τούτων βούλει διαμυθολογῶμεν, εἴτε εἰκὸς οὕτως ἔχειν εἴτε μή;' [70b5-7]. ἀξιῶ δὲ ἐγὼ τὸν ἐντευξόμενον γεγυμνάσθαι πρότερον ἐν τοῖς ἐκείνου τοῦ ἀνδρὸς ἱεροῖς σκέμμασι· τὰ γὰρ καλῶς εἰρημένα μεταγράφειν οὐκ εὔλογον εἶναί μοι δοκεῖ.

(I) Ἀπορίαι

α΄   γ΄. – Ὅτι κἂν ὁρισώμεθα, ὡς ὁ φιλόσοφος ἀξιοῖ [§ 185], συγκρίσει καὶ 209 διακρίσει τὸ ζῆν καὶ τεθνάναι δυεῖν οὐσιῶν, ψυχῆς καὶ σώματος, οὐδὲ ὡς ἀνάγκη τὸ διακριθὲν συγκρίνεσθαι πάλιν οὐδέ γε διακρίνεσθαι τὸ συγκριθέν. πρῶτος γὰρ φέρε τινὶ ἐντυχὼν οὐκέτι αὖθις ἐνέτυχον, καὶ ὅ φησι Κέβης [70a5] (ἔτι γὰρ ἐν τῷ αὐτῷ στρεφόμεθα τῆς ἀπορίας), τὸ πνεῦμα κατακλεισθὲν ἐν ἀσκῷ, 5 ἔπειτα διαπνευσθέν, οὐκέτι κατακλείεται πάλιν, ὁ δὲ καπνὸς ἐν διακρίσει τὴν πρώτην λαβὼν ὑπόστασιν οὐκέτι οὐδὲ ἅπαξ εἰς τὸ ξύλον συγκρίνεται.

δ΄. – Ὅτι μὴ καλῶς ἐλέγχει ἀπὸ τοῦ τὸν καπνὸν διακρίνεσθαι μέν, μὴ 210 συγκρίνεσθαι δέ. οὐδὲ γὰρ ὅλως διάκρισίς ἐστιν ἡ τοῦ καπνοῦ, ἀλλὰ γένεσις· διακρίνεται γὰρ δὴ τὸ ἐνυπάρχον, οὐκ ἐνυπῆρχε δὲ τῷ ξύλῳ ὁ καπνὸς οὔτε δυνάμει οὔτε ἐνεργείᾳ, ἀπὸ γὰρ τῆς τοῦ ξύλου διαλύσεως γεννᾶται.

β΄   ε΄. – Ὅτι οὐδὲ περὶ ἓν ὑποκείμενον τὰ ἐναντία κυκλίζεται. οὐδὲ γὰρ ὁ πρῶτος 211 καθευδήσας ὁ νεογενὴς ἔσται πάλιν ἐγρη|γορώς, εἰ καὶ μὴ ἀπὸ καθεύδοντος, (134) ὥς φησι [§ 195], γίγνοιτο· τάχα γὰρ ἂν ἐναποθάνοι τῷ πρώτῳ ὕπνῳ ὁ γεννηθείς, ἢ οὐδ᾽ ἂν εἰς ὕπνον αὐτὸν διαρκέσειεν. ἔτι δὲ συχνότερον τὸν γεννηθέντα λευκὸν ἐπὶ χρόνον ἐνδέχεται διαμεῖναι, μελαίνεσθαι μὲν δυνάμενον, οὐ μελαινόμενον δὲ 5 οὐδὲ ἅπαξ πρὸ τελευτῆς.

γ΄   ς΄. – Ὅτι ἀπαιτεῖ ὁ λόγος, ὡς τὴν ψυχὴν ἐπανιέναι πρὸς τὸ σῶμα 212 συγκρινομένην ἀριθμῷ τὴν αὐτήν, οὕτω καὶ τὸ σῶμα πρὸς τὴν ψυχὴν τὸ αὐτὸ κατ᾽ ἀριθμόν, ὅπερ οὐχ ὁρῶμεν γιγνόμενον (οὐ γὰρ ἐκ τῶν τεθνεώτων σωμάτων

---

§ 212.   3 οὐ γὰρ Wk: οὐκ ἄρα M

---

negligent in the use of o or ω. Yet the adjective is well protected by § 242.15 τοῦ πρώτου ζῶντος, § 246.2 τῶν πρώτων ὑφισταμένων, 5 τὸ πρῶτον μέλαν, 6 τὸ πρῶτον ἐγρηγορός, 7 τὸ πρῶτον ζῶν, § 252.2 τὸν πρῶτον ἄνθρωπον, II § 12.1 ἃ πρῶτα δοκοῦμεν μανθάνειν, Phil. § 163.1 ὁ πρῶτος ἐπιθυμήσας.

§ 210. This section is *extra ordinem*, as already observed by the scholiast (who also skipped it in numbering the objections, as does Dam. § 233.1); it is a criticism of § 209, possibly by the redactor. Dam. makes this point himself at § 232.10-12.

death receive a new life, unless as a species, individuals succeeding each other.

213. (4) It is apparent that Socrates does not limit himself to the case of things being joined together, for he distinctly states that his principle of cyclical movement is true of all opposites: 'Well then, Socrates said, do not consider this point in relation to man only, if you want to have a clearer view, but to all animals and plants, and in short, to everything that comes into being; let us see with regard to all these things, if it is true that each can come to be only by proceeding from its own opposite, in so far as they have such a thing as an opposite' [70d7–e2]; and the examples speak for themselves. We should therefore find confirmation for the cycle of genesis in general, not only for that of composition and decomposition, even further limited to the case where two or more substances are involved.

214. (5) Socrates does not illustrate his rule by means of two or more substances joining and separating in cyclic motion or showing an alternation of other pairs of opposites; rather, he refers to one substance that receives the opposites by turns. Not only do the other examples deal with cases of one substratum, but even that of composition and decomposition, as Plato shows by mentioning cooling and heating next: 'Between larger and smaller are increase and decrease, and we say that one thing increases, the other decreases? — Yes. — Does this not apply also to composition and decomposition, to cooling and heating . . .?' [71b2–7]. Obviously when the same body is heated and cooled it is also this same body which is subjected to decomposition (expansion) and composition (contraction).

215. (6) Nor does Socrates adduce the greater strength of the soul in support of his argument. It is true, to be sure, but nevertheless he does not need it for his proof; for even if the soul were weaker than the body, it still would necessarily be stronger than the opposites that pertain to it and therefore able to sustain the cyclical course of these opposites. However, the point has not yet been proved nor even assumed; on the contrary, it is probably assumed that the soul is weaker, in the same way as the air is more easily dispersed than the bag [70a4–5]. It will be proved stronger afterwards, in the argument from similarity [80b8–e1], and it is with reference to this that Cebes will say then that he does not go back on his admission that the soul is stronger than the body [87a5–7].

216. (7) If we follow the philosopher's interpretation, we cannot escape the claim of presenting complete proof of its immortality; for even though the soul lasts no longer than creation, it is still everlasting, as the universe is.

---

§ 213. 7–9. ἀλλ' οὐ μόνον - πλειόνων : as Syrianus does in § 190. – Σύγκρισις and διάκρισις can take place in the same body in the form of contraction and expansion. See the next section.

§ 214. Dam. may be right in believing that Pl. is thinking throughout of one

τὰ ζῶντα)· οὐδὲ ἄρα αἱ ψυχαὶ μετὰ θάνατον διαδέξονται τὴν ζωήν, εἰ μὴ ἄρα κατ' εἶδος ἄλλαι καὶ ἄλλαι γινόμεναι.

δ' ζ'. — Ὅτι οὐ μόνῃ τῇ συγκρίσει φαίνεται χρώμενος ὁ Σωκράτης· διωρίσατο 213 γὰρ σαφῶς ὡς κοινὸν ποιεῖται τὸν λόγον τῆς ἐπανακυκλήσεως ἐπὶ πάντων ἐναντίων· 'μὴ τοίνυν κατὰ ἄνθρωπον, ἦ δ' ὅς, σκόπει μόνον τοῦτο, εἰ βούλει ῥᾷον μαθεῖν, ἀλλὰ καὶ κατὰ ζώων πάντων καὶ φυτῶν, καὶ ξυλλήβδην ὅσαπερ ἔχει γένεσιν, περὶ πάντων ἴδωμεν, οὑτωσὶ ἄρα γίγνεται πάντα, οὐκ ἄλλοθεν ἢ ἐκ τῶν ἐναντίων τὰ ἐναντία, ὅσοις τυγχάνει ὂν τοιοῦτόν τι' [70d7–e2]· καὶ δῆλα τὰ παραδείγματα. τὸν οὖν κοινὸν ἔδει κρατῦναι τῆς γενέσεως κύκλον, ἀλλ' οὐ μόνον τὸν συγκρινόμενον καὶ διακρινόμενον, καὶ τοῦτον μέντοι τὸν ἐπὶ δυεῖν οὐσιῶν ἢ πλειόνων.

3' η'. — Ὅτι ὁ Σωκράτης οὐκ ἐπὶ δυεῖν οὐσιῶν οὐδὲ πλειόνων συγκρινομένων 214 καὶ διακρινομένων ἐν κύκλῳ γυμνάζει τὸν λόγον οὐδὲ ἄλλοις ἐναντίοις κυκλιζομένων, ἀλλ' ἐπὶ μιᾶς τὰ ἐναντία παρὰ μέρος δεχομένης. τά τε γὰρ ἄλλα παραδείγματα ἐφ' ἑνὸς παράκειται ὑποκειμένου καὶ αὐτὸ τὸ συγκρίνεσθαι καὶ διακρίνεσθαι· δηλοῖ γοῦν τούτοις ἐπισυνάψας τὸ ψύχεσθαι καὶ θερμαίνεσθαι· 'μείζονος μὲν γὰρ καὶ ἐλάττονος μεταξὺ αὔξη καὶ φθίσις, καὶ καλοῦμεν οὕτω τὸ μὲν αὐξάνεσθαι, τὸ | δὲ φθίνειν; ναί, ἔφη. οὐκοῦν καὶ τὸ διακρίνεσθαι καὶ (135) τὸ συγκρίνεσθαι καὶ τὸ ψύχεσθαι καὶ θερμαίνεσθαι' [71b2–7]. δῆλον γὰρ ὅτι τὸ αὐτὸ σῶμα θερμαινόμενον καὶ ψυχόμενον τὸ αὐτὸ διακρίνεται καὶ συγκρίνεται.

ς' θ'. — Ὅτι οὐδὲ τὸ ἰσχυροτέραν σώματος εἶναι ψυχὴν προστίθησιν ὁ Σωκράτης 215 εἰς βοήθειαν τῷ λόγῳ. καίτοι ἀληθές ἐστιν, ἀλλ' ὅμως οὐδὲν αὐτοῦ προσεδεήθη εἰς τὴν ἀπόδειξιν· καὶ γὰρ εἰ ἀσθενεστέρα τοῦ γε σώματος ἔτυχεν οὖσα, τῶν γε περὶ ἑαυτὴν ἐναντίων οὖσαν ἰσχυροτέραν ἔδει πάντως ὑπομένειν τὴν τῶν ἐναντίων ἐπανακύκλησιν. οὐ μὴν οὐδὲ ἀποδέδεικταί πω οὐδὲ ὑπόκειται, τοὐναντίον δὲ ἴσως ἀσθενεστέρα, καθάπερ τοῦ ἀσκοῦ τὸ πνεῦμά ἐστιν εὐθρυπτότερον [70a4–5]. ἀποδειχθήσεται δὲ εἰσαῦθις ἐν τῷ ἀπὸ τῆς ὁμοιότητος λόγῳ [80b8–e1], πρὸς ὃν καὶ τότε ὁ Κέβης ἐρεῖ ὡς οὐκ ἀνατίθεται τὸ μὴ ἰσχυρότερον εἶναι ψυχὴν σώματος [87a5–7].

ζ' ι'. — Ὅτι οὕτως ἐξηγούμενοι ὡς ὁ φιλόσοφος οὐκ ἐκφευξούμεθα τὸ μὴ οὐκ 216 ἀθάνατον αὐτὴν ἀποδεικνύναι τὸ πάμπαν· εἰ γὰρ καὶ ἐφ' ὅσον ἡ γένεσις, ἀλλὰ καὶ οὕτως ἀίδιος, ἴσα γε τῷ παντὶ καὶ ὅλῳ. εἰ δὲ διὰ τοῦτο ἐνδεχομένη ἡ ἀπόδειξις,

---

§ 213. 3 ἀνθρώπων Pl. — 5 οὑτωσὶ ἄρα M¹: ἄρα οὑτωσὶ Mᶜ (Pl.) — 7 ante ἔδει] ∴ ∴ ∴ ∴ in ras. Mᶜ | ἔδει] ἔ- ins. Mᶜ

---

and the same subject going through these various processes. He evidently forces the text, however, when he tries to make 'cooling and heating' equivalent to 'composition and decomposition' (and to this end in line 9 changes the order in which Pl. names them).

§ 216. 1. ὡς ὁ φιλόσοφος : cf. § 205.

If, on the other hand, the proof is to be considered contingent in character because it rests on inference, yet even the fact on which this inference rests is not merely 'probable,' but something indestructible and necessary.

217. (8) As far as this argument goes, the irrational soul jointly with its pneumatic body will also have complete immortality. Here, too, there will be the cycle of life and death revolving endlessly (or perhaps as long as creation holds together – but then it holds together always, since God continues always to shape matter); for this organism, too, is alive when united with the 'oysterlike' body and dies when separated from it by a process of decomposition.

218. (9) Where the body as instrument is concerned we say that there is regeneration of the species only, and this is true of all beings that come to be and pass away, e.g. humans and horses: now supposing that similarly each individual man has a soul of his own, which dies immediately after the organism in any way one chooses to think it happens, how can we still save the compelling force of the argument, when the soul would last long enough just for one union and one separation? This is more or less what Cebes' objection about the air in the bag [70a4–5] suggested, except that in the present objection we view the body as the instrument of the soul.

219. (10) Nor is it true that everything will eventually be asleep, or dead, so long as living individuals continue to be born, and so long as there is an ever fresh supply of waking people, as in the instance of beings that come to be and pass away [§ 218]. Only then would there be a problem, if, with the living already fixed at a given number, and birth excluded, the transition from the living to the dead took place, so that all the material from which individual living beings are shaped would be spent.

220. (11) Finally one could wonder why the argument is said to prove only a continued existence of the soul in Hades, as Socrates states here in his conclusion [72d8–e2], and as he specifies afterwards [77c6–d4] in his answer to Simmias' question, the one with which he is going to deal in the argument from similarity; surely the pre-existence of the soul is proved at the same time, if it is true that the living always proceed from the dead?

(II) Points granted and assumptions made

221. The soul is supposed to be a substance, if it is to be 'dispersed like air or smoke' [70a4–5]; later on, in fact, it will be supposed to be present in a substrate and no longer a substrate itself, viz. when it is thought of as harmony [85e3–86d4].

---

4. ὅτι τεκμηριώδης : this was Harpocratio's explanation of the εἰκός at *Ph.* 70b7 (*supra* § 182).

§ 217. 1. τὸ πνευματικὸν ἄλογον ζῷον : cf. *supra* § 168.6–7, note, and *infra* II § 29.

§ 218. 3. ἀνθρώπων : the mortal individual, not, in accordance with the current Platonic definition, the soul (e.g. Pr., *Alc.* 18.4–5).

ὅτι τεκμηριώδης, ἀλλ' οὐκ 'εἰκὸς' οὐδὲ τὸ τεκμήριον, ἄλυτον δέ τι καὶ ἀναγκαῖον.

η'   ια'. — Ὅτι καὶ τὸ πνευματικὸν ἄλογον ζῷον ἀθάνατον ἔσται τελέως ἔκ γε   217
τοῦ λόγου. καὶ περὶ αὐτὸ γὰρ ὁ κύκλος τοῦ ζῆν καὶ τεθνάναι ἀνελιχθήσεται
ἐπ' ἄπειρον (ἴσως δὲ μέχρι οὗ συνέστηκεν ἡ γένεσις — ἀεὶ δὲ συνέστηκεν, ἀεὶ
τοῦ θεοῦ δημιουργοῦντος), εἴ γε καὶ αὐτὸ ζῇ μὲν συγκεκριμένον τῷ ὀστρέῳ,
θνῄσκει δὲ χωριζόμενον ἀπ' αὐτοῦ κατὰ διάκρισιν.   5

θ'   ιβ'. — Ὅτι ὡς ἐπὶ τοῦ ὀργάνου φαμὲν τὴν κατ' εἶδος μόνην σῴζεσθαι   218
παλιγγενεσίαν, καὶ ὅλως ἐπὶ τῶν γιγνομένων καὶ φθειρομένων οὐσιῶν οἷον
ἀνθρώπων καὶ ἵππων, εἰ οὕτω καθ' ἕκαστον ἄνθρωπον γίγνοιτο ψυχὴ ἄλλη
καὶ ἄλλη, φθειρομένη καὶ αὐτὴ ἐπὶ τῷ ζῴῳ τρόπον ὃν ἄν τις ὑποθοῖτο, | πῶς (136)
ἂν ἡμῖν περιγένοιτο καὶ ὡς ἡ τοῦ λόγου ἀνάγκη πρὸς μίαν μόνην σύζευξιν καὶ   5
μίαν διάζευξιν τῆς ψυχῆς ἀρκούσης; οἷόν τι καὶ ἡ Κέβητος ἀπορία κατὰ τὸ
πνεῦμα τοῦ ἀσκοῦ [70a4–5] ἐνεδείκνυτο, πλὴν ὅτι νῦν ἀπὸ τοῦ σώματος
ἠπορήκαμεν ὡς ὀργάνου.

ι'   ιγ'. — Ὅτι οὐδὲ πάντα καθεύδοντα γενήσεται οὐδὲ πάντα τεθνεῶτα τῶν τε   219
ζώντων ἀεὶ γιγνομένων καὶ τῶν ἐγρηγορότων ἄλλων καὶ ἄλλων ἐπαγομένων,
ὡς ἐπὶ τῶν γενητῶν καὶ φθαρτῶν οὐσιῶν [§ 218]. τότε δὲ ἂν συνέβαινεν ἄτοπον,
εἰ ἑστώτων ἤδη καὶ οὐ γινομένων τῶν ζώντων, οἷον τοσῶνδε ὄντων, ἡ μεταχώρησις
εἰς τοὺς τεθνεῶτας αὐτῶν ἐγίγνετο, καὶ ἀνάλωτο ἂν ἡ οὐσία πᾶσα ἀφ' ἧς τὰ   5
ζῶντα κατὰ μέρος ἐπλάττετο.

ια'   ιδ'. — Ὅτι ἀπορήσειεν ἄν τις καὶ διὰ τί μόνον ἀποδεικνύναι λέγεται ὁ λόγος   220
τὸ μετὰ θάνατον ἐν Ἅιδου τὴν ψυχὴν ἐπιδιαμένειν, ὡς νῦν τε συμπεραίνεται
ὁ Σωκράτης [72d8–e1] καὶ ἐς ὕστερον [77c6–d4] διορίζεται πρὸς ἀποροῦντα
Σιμμίαν, πρὸς ὃν τὸν ἀπὸ τῆς ὁμοιότητος κινήσει λόγον· καίτοι καὶ τὸ πρὸ
τοῦ σώματος εἶναι αὐτὴν συναποδείκνυται, εἴπερ ἐκ τῶν τεθνεώτων οἱ ζῶντες ἀεί.   5

(II) Ὁμολογήματα καὶ ὑποθέσεις

ιε'. — Ὅτι οὐσία ὑπόκειται ἡ ψυχή, εἴπερ 'ὡς πνεῦμα ἢ καπνὸς διαπταμένη   221
οἰχήσεται' [70a4–5]· ἐπεὶ καὶ αὖθις ὡς ἐν ὑποκειμένῳ ὑποτεθήσεται, ἀλλ' οὐκέτι
ὑποκείμενον, ἁρμονία γε ὑποτιθεμένη [85e3–86d4].

---

§ 217. 1 γε Fh: τε (an γε?) M
§ 218. 7 ὅτι Wk: ἔτι M
§ 219. 1 τε revera M — 4 εἰ Fh: ἦ M — 5 ἀνάλωτο Fh: ἀνάλογον M

---

§ 220. Syrianus (§ 204.5–6) actually concludes that the argument proves preexistence as well.
§§ 221–230. What starts as a list of assumptions gradually expands into a full discussion of Dam.'s interpretation; in §§ 231–251 it is shown that this interpretation solves all the problems; § 252 is not the conclusion, but a recapitulation.
§ 221. Dam. II § 2.1–2.

222. So far as the examples cited in his question go, Cebes supposes the soul to be corporeal, air, as the commentator also says, or breath; he argues that it cannot be thought to be any other element, fire being excluded because of its destructiveness, water because of its liquidity, earth because of its inertia. I believe, however, that it can also be incorporeal, though subject in a different way to the same process as air; he does not call it air, but says that it perishes 'like air.' I would go even farther and say that it should definitely be supposed to be incorporeal 'like a shadow or a dream,' as Homer describes it [*Od.* 11. 207]; in this way there is a contrast between body in general and soul, not between different kinds of bodies. Also, that which animates the body cannot be a body itself, for if inanimate, how can it bestow life? And then, if Cebes regarded the soul as corporeal, why does not Socrates refute this anywhere? It must have been obvious that Cebes was convinced by the speeches on purification that the soul is incorporeal, and also that it is a kind of substance, since nothing that is present in a substratum can exist by itself or be separated from its substratum.

223. It is assumed that the soul is separable, as air is from the bag and smoke from the log. Accordingly, when answering Simmias' question if soul might not be harmony, Socrates builds his refutation of this theory on the grounds that the soul can be separated [92a6–b2] and that it can resist the body [94b4–c7]; and again, in dealing with Cebes' objection, the one based on the comparison with the weaver, he specifies the same point [95c4–9].

224. Socrates calls substances opposites in virtue of alternate participation in opposites, i.e. in opposites present in a substratum; this appears from the examples as well as from the way in which Socrates later [103a11–c2] corrects the opinion of the unnamed questioner, saying that the subject of the present passage is not participated, but participating opposites, in other words the substrata, which participate in the qualities present in them.

---

§ 222. 1–4. A fuller report of Pr.'s view already stated in § 178, cf. Ol. 10 § 2.4–11. The καί at line 2 is somewhat vague: the ἐξηγητής may be either Pr. conforming to the opinion of Syrianus, or Syrianus himself (as at §§ 235.2, 236.1, 237.1, 243.2) following certain unnamed predecessors. He probably already quoted the lines of Homer included in Ol. *loc. cit.*, esp. *Il.* 23.100–101 ᾤχετο τετριγυῖα κατὰ χθονὸς ἠΰτε καπνός, to illustrate this primitive belief. In reply, Dam. cites another line of Homer, in which the soul is compared to a shadow and a dream, apparently to show that the description 'like smoke', too, is intended to convey the notion of insubstantiality, i.e. incorporeality.

6–9. The text in the original used by M was blurred; the scribe (M¹) left some gaps, which were later filled in by Mᶜ with the help of the original (as is proved by the meaningless ἂν καὶ αἱρεῖσθαι at line 7, which cannot be a conjecture, but must represent a half-legible ἀντιδιαιρεῖσθαι). In lines 6–7 the scribe read ὡς σκιὰ ἢ

ις΄. – Ὅτι ὅσον μὲν ἐπὶ τοῖς παραδείγμασιν τῆς ἀπορίας σῶμα τὴν ψυχὴν 222
ὑποτίθεται, ἀέρα, φησὶν καὶ ὁ ἐξηγητής, ἢ πνεῦμα· τῶν γὰρ ἄλλων στοιχείων μηδὲν
δύνασθαι ὑποτεθῆναι, πῦρ μὲν διὰ τὸ φθαρτικόν, ὕδωρ δὲ διὰ τὸ ῥευστόν, γῆν | δὲ (137)
διὰ τὸ δυσκίνητον. οἴομαι δὲ καὶ ἀσώματον εἶναι δύνασθαι, πάσχουσαν μέντοι ἄλλον
τρόπον τὸ τοῦ πνεύματος πάθος· οὐ γὰρ ἔφη πνεῦμα, ἀλλ᾽ ʽὥσπερ πνεῦμα᾽ ποιεῖσθαι 5
τὴν φθοράν. μᾶλλον δὲ αὐτόθεν καὶ ἀσώματον ὑποθετέον αὐτὴν ὡς σκιὰν ⟨ἢ καὶ
ὄνειρον⟩, ὡς καὶ Ὅμηρος ἀπήγγειλεν [λ 207]· οὕτω γὰρ ἀντιδιαιρεῖσθαι πρὸς
σῶμα ἁπλῶς ψυχήν, ἀλλ᾽ οὐ τοιόνδε σῶμα πρὸς τοιόνδε. καὶ τὸ ψυχοῦν οὐχ
οἷόν τε εἶναι σῶμα· ἄψυχον γὰρ ὂν πῶς τι ψυχώσειεν; τὸ δὲ εἰ σῶμα τὴν ψυχὴν
ὁ Κέβης ὑπέλαβεν, πῶς οὐδαμοῦ τοῦτο διήλεγξεν ὁ Σωκράτης; ἀλλὰ δῆλος ἦν 10
ὁ Κέβης ἐκ τῶν καθαρτικῶν λόγων πεπεισμένος ὅτι ἀσώματός ἐστι, καθάπερ
καὶ οὐσία τις· οὐδὲν γὰρ τῶν ἐν ὑποκειμένῳ χωρὶς εἶναι δύναται ἢ χωρίζεσθαι
τοῦ ⟦εἶναι⟧ ἐν ᾧ ἐστιν.

ιζ΄. – Ὅτι χωριστὴ ὑπόκειται, ὡς τοῦ ἀσκοῦ πνεῦμα καὶ τοῦ ξύλου καπνός. 223
ἀμέλει ἐν τῇ Σιμμίου ἀπορίᾳ τῇ ἀπὸ τῆς ἁρμονίας ἀπὸ τοῦ χωρίζεσθαι ἐπιχειρεῖ
ὁ Σωκράτης ἐλέγχειν τὴν ἁρμονίαν [92a6–b2] καὶ ἀπὸ τοῦ ἐναντιοῦσθαι τῷ
σώματι [94b4–e7]· καὶ αὖθις ἐν τῇ Κέβητος τὸ αὐτὸ διορίζεται [95c4–9] τῇ
ἀπὸ τοῦ ὑφάντου εἰσηγμένῃ. 5

ιη΄. – Ὅτι ἐναντίας καλεῖ τὰς οὐσίας κατὰ τὴν παρὰ μέρος τῶν ἐναντίων 224
μέθεξιν, τῶν ἐν ὑποκειμένῳ φημὶ ἐναντίων, ὡς τά τε παραδείγματα δηλοῖ καὶ ὁ
Σωκράτης ἐπανορθοῦται τὴν τοῦ ἀνωνύμου ἀποροῦντος εἰς ὕστερον [103a11–c2]
ὑπόληψιν, ὅτι οὐκ ἄρα περὶ τῶν μετεχομένων ὁ προκείμενος γίνεται λόγος ἐναντίων,
ἀλλὰ περὶ τῶν μετεχόντων· μετέχει δὲ τῶν ἐν ὑποκειμένῳ τὰ ὑποκείμενα. 5

§ 222. 5 ποιεῖσθαι (seq. ~) Mᶜ: spat. vac. M¹ — 6 καὶ ἀσώματον] καὶ ἀσώ- Mᶜ: spat. vac. M¹ — 6–7 σκιὰν ⟨ἢ καὶ ὄνειρον⟩, ὡς καὶ Ὅμηρος Wk: σκιαν· ὡς καὶ ὅμηρος, -αν ὡς ex corr., ʺ ex ʺ, -μη- in ras., sscr. νει Mᶜ (ergo σκιὰ ἢ καὶ ὄνειρον M¹, σκιὰν ὡς καὶ ὅμηρος Mᶜ) — 7 ἀπήγγειλεν Wk: ἐπήγγειλεν M | γὰρ ἀντιδιαιρεῖσθαι Wk: γὰρ ἂν καὶ αἱρεῖσθαι Mᶜ: spat. vac. et αἱρεῖσθαι M¹ — 8 ψυχῇ μ: ψυχή, ~ Mᶜ: spat. vac. M¹ | τοιόνδε καὶ] -ιόνδε καὶ Mᶜ: spat. vac. M¹ — 9 σῶμα¹] σῶμα· ~ Mᶜ: spat. vac. M¹ | ὄν, πῶς τι M¹: ὄν πως, τί Mᶜ — 13 εἶναι M: del. Wk (cf. § 226.3)
§ 223. 1 ξύλου Mᶜ: spat. vac. M¹ — 5 ὑφαντοῦ M

καὶ ὄνειρος ἐπήγγειλεν, which the corrector changed into ὡς σκιὰν ὡς καὶ Ὅμηρος ἐπήγγειλεν. I have combined the two readings, because both are necessary, the ἢ καὶ ὄνειρος to complete the reference to Hom., Od. 11.207 (σκιῇ εἴκελον ἢ καὶ ὀνείρῳ), the ὡς καὶ Ὅμηρος to make sense of the whole sentence. Perhaps the original had ἢ καὶ ὄνειρον inserted above ὡς καὶ Ὅμηρος, making it look like a lectio duplex.
7. ἐπήγγειλεν gives no satisfactory sense, while ἀπήγγειλεν can be understood of a report on things seen in Hades, the line being from the Nekyia (cf. Pl., Rep. X 619e2 ἐκ τῶν ἐκεῖθεν ἀπαγγελλομένων).
8–9. The issue being what Cebes thought, not what the real state of things is, these remarks can be relevant only if meant to imply that no reasonable person (such as Cebes was) could fail to see this point.
§ 223. Cf. Dam. II § 2.2–3. Ol. 9 § 3.4–10.
§ 224. 4–5. Cf. supra § 189 (Syrianus' definition of the opposites intended here).

225. Any substance is stronger and more permanent than its accidents, those, that is to say, that come and go; for as all such accidents have their being in the substance, they are necessarily weaker by nature. Therefore the substance remains while the accidents change.

226. Any substance, while remaining numerically the same, is capable of receiving a succession of numerically different opposites, which come and go; for they can have no existence apart from their substratum, but each time their coming and going, or rather, their being there and not being there, is a new one. Thus the soul, too, is receptive of vice and virtue (in its imperfect form, that is), without losing its identity: it can change both ways again and again, sometimes in the course of one day. This is also a necessary consequence of the assumption that the substance is more permanent than its accidents [§ 225], but the inductive proof is more manifest than any argument *a priori*: normally it outlasts its accidents, unless some kind of unusual violence should interfere.

227. What exists in a substratum is and is-not only once, even if we consider it with reference to everlasting substances: in the case of the heavenly bodies, for instance, we find that their recurring movements are identical in kind only; the substrata, however, i.e. the substances, remain numerically the same, the everlasting ones forever, the more durable ones a maximum number of times, but even those substances that are weaker outlast at least two or three recurrences of specifically identical accidents such as they are apt to receive, since they must be stronger than that which depends on them for its existence. For neither the appearance nor the disappearance of the accidents is a change or a being ousted of the substances themselves, so that, as far as their own power is concerned, they can endure the cyclic change of the accidents.

228. Recurrence of the same forms may occur in many ways. The identity may be either specific or numerical; in the latter case, the repetition may go on infinitely, or it may take place a number of times, as we established just now [§ 227]; in the former case, the cycle may be one of substances or of accidents. The present argument is concerned only with recurrence of the numerically identical, achieved a limited number of times through the alternation of accidents that are each other's opposites specifically. This is made abundantly clear by the examples of Socrates, which refer to accidents replacing each other more than once in one and the same substratum [70e4–71a11].

---

§ 225. 2. τῶν γινομένων φημὶ καὶ ἀπογιγνομένων : Porphyry, *isag.* 12.24–25, defines accident in general as ὃ γίνεται καὶ ἀπογίνεται χωρὶς τῆς τοῦ ὑποκειμένου φθορᾶς, but his commentators (Amm. 111.7–18, El. 91.27–92.6) limit this to χωριστὰ συμβεβηκότα.

§ 226. Cf. Dam. II § 2.5–10.

1–2. Ar., *cat.* 5, 4a10–12 μάλιστα δὲ ἴδιον τῆς οὐσίας δοκεῖ εἶναι τὸ ταὐτὸν καὶ

ιθ'. – Ὅτι πᾶσα οὐσία τῶν ἐν αὐτῇ συμβεβηκότων ἐστὶ μονιμωτέρα καὶ 225
ἰσχυροτέρα, τῶν γινομένων φημὶ καὶ ἀπογιγνομένων· ἐν γὰρ αὐτῇ τὰ τοιαῦτα τὸ
εἶναι ἔχοντα πάντως ὅτι ἀσθενέστερα αὐτῆς ἐστι φύσει. διὸ μένει αὕτη
μεταβαλλομένων ἐκείνων.

κ'. – Ὅτι πᾶσα οὐσία δεκτικὴ τῶν ἐναντίων ἐστὶν παρὰ μέρος ἡ αὐτὴ κατὰ 226
ἀριθμὸν μένουσα τῶν μὴ ἐν ὄντων ἀριθμῷ | προσγινομένων καὶ ἀπογιγνομένων· (138)
οὐ γὰρ οἷόν τε ταῦτα χωρὶς εἶναι τοῦ ἐν ᾧ ἐστιν, ἀλλ' ἄλλην ἑκάστοτε ποιεῖται
τὴν πρόσοδόν τε καὶ ἄφοδον, μᾶλλον δὲ τὸ εἶναι καὶ τὸ μὴ εἶναι. οὕτως οὖν καὶ
ἡ ψυχὴ δέχεται κακίαν καὶ ἀρετήν, ἀτελῆ φάναι, μένουσα ἡ αὐτή, πολλάκις 5
ἐφ' ἑκάτερα μεταβάλλουσα καὶ μιᾶς ἡμέρας ἐνίοτε. ἀπαιτεῖται μὲν οὖν τοῦτο
καὶ ὁ λόγος ὁ τὴν οὐσίαν μονιμωτέραν τῶν συμβεβηκότων ὁμολογῶν [§ 225],
ἡ δὲ ἐπαγωγὴ παντὸς λόγου ἐναργεστέρα· φύσει γὰρ ἐπιμένει, πλὴν εἰ μή τι
βιαιότερον ἀπαντήσειεν.

κα'. – Ὅτι τὰ μὲν ἐν ὑποκειμένῳ μόνον εἰσάπαξ ἔστι τε καὶ οὐκ ἔστιν, 227
κἂν ἐπὶ τῶν ἀιδίων οὐσιῶν θεωρῇ τις αὐτά, καθάπερ ἐπὶ τῶν οὐρανίων σωμάτων
τὰς κινήσεις εὑρίσκομεν εἴδει μόνῳ τὰς αὐτὰς ἀνακαμπτούσας· τὰ δὲ ὑποκείμενα
καὶ αἱ οὐσίαι μένουσι κατὰ ἀριθμόν, ἀεὶ μὲν αἱ ἀΐδιοι, πλειστάκις δὲ αἱ πολυχρονιώτεραι, τὸ δὲ ἐλάχιστον, ὅσαι καὶ ἀσθενέστεραι τῶν οὐσιῶν εἰσιν, δὶς 5
ἢ τρὶς ὑπομένουσι τὰ κατ' εἶδος ἀνακυκλούμενα τῶν περὶ αὐτὰς ὑφίστασθαι
πεφυκότων συμβεβηκότων, εἴπερ ἰσχυρότεραί εἰσι τῶν ἐν αὐταῖς τὸ εἶναι
ἐχόντων. οὔτε γὰρ ἡ γένεσις αὐτῶν οὔτε ἡ φθορὰ αὐτῶν τίς ἐστι τῶν οὐσιῶν
μεταβολή τε καὶ ἔκστασις· ὥστε ὅσον ἐπὶ τῇ οἰκείᾳ δυνάμει περιμένοιεν ἂν τὴν
τῶν συμβεβηκότων ἐπανακύκλησιν. 10

κβ'. – Ὅτι πολλαχῶς ἡ τῶν αὐτῶν εἰδῶν ἐπανακύκλησις, ἡ μὲν κατὰ εἶδος, 228
ἡ δὲ κατὰ ἀριθμόν. τούτων μὲν τοίνυν ἡ μὲν ἀπειράκις, ἡ δὲ πλεονάκις, ὡς δὴ
νῦν πεπαύμεθα διοριζόμενοι [§ 227]· ἐκείνων δὲ ἡ μὲν οὐσιῶν, ἡ δὲ συμβεβηκότων.
χρῆται οὖν ὁ λόγος μόνῃ τῇ πλεονάκις κατὰ ἀριθμὸν ἀποτελουμένῃ κατὰ τὴν
τῶν ἐναντίων εἴδει περὶ αὐτὴν ἀνταπόδοσιν. δηλοῖ δὴ σαφῶς τὰ τοῦ Σωκράτους 5
παραδείγματα περὶ ἓν ὑποκείμενον πολλάκις ἀνακυκλούμενα τὰ ἐν ὑποκειμένῳ
παράγοντα [70e4–71a11].

---

§ 225. 1 αὐτῇ] -ῇι~ in ras. M^c | μονιμωτέρα Fh (M¹ ut vid.): γονιμωτέρα, γ-
in ras. M^c — 3 αὕτη] ″ ex ', post -η ras. 1 litt. M^x
§ 226. 3 ἀλλ' ἄλλην Wk: ἀλλαμην M — 7 μονιμωτέραν Fh: γονιμωτέραν M
§ 227. 8 αὐτῶν² ins. M^c: om. M¹ | οὐσιῶν Fh: οὐ M
§ 228. 2-3 δὴ νῦν M¹: νῦν δὴ M^c — 3 πεπαύμεθα Fh: πεπαυμένα M — 5 δηλοῖ δὴ
Wk: δηλαδὴ M

ἐν ἀριθμῷ ὂν τῶν ἐναντίων εἶναι δεκτικόν.
5. ἀτελῆ φάναι : because perfect virtue cannot be lost.
8. ἡ δὲ ἐπαγωγή : Socrates' induction at 70d7–71a11; cf. supra § 186.1–2.
§ 228. Dam. II § 2.11–13. – Instances of numerical identity: (infinite recurrence)
the rising and setting *sun*; (limited recurrence) the sleeping and waking *Socrates*.
Of specific identity: (of substances) *horses* are born and die; (of accidents) the sun
rises and sets, Socrates *sleeps and wakes*.

229. The eternity of creation as a whole is due, strictly speaking, to the immutability of its causes; a more immediate ground is the circular motion of the heavenly bodies; in the third place come the principles that act as contributory causes, matter, which has an everlasting aptitude to receive forms, however fleeting, and form, whose very essence is bound up with the cyclic course of creation. For immaterial form is a self-generated whole, but materialized form, having its origin in division, is split into the generating and the generated in individuals: man begets man, and similarly all animals, and plants also, produce their own likes. Even inanimate forms, each in the measure of its possibilities, strive to multiply themselves and by their own power to change others into themselves; their instrument is nature, which always moves and is moved. Whatever the mode, all things endeavor to complete the cycle as far as possible; but in the case of sempiternal beings this is a cycle of motions, for the others the substances are also involved: so long as the substances themselves remain numerically the same, there is a cyclic succession of actions and other accidents; the actions, however, and anything that cannot survive individually in the cyclic process, is or is-not for once only. Any attempt, therefore, to eliminate cyclic succession from genesis is an attempt to upset the principle of everlasting generation and to prove the immutable causes idle; on the other hand, any one who admits the universal cycle, will admit also that those substances which last for a limited time imitate, as long as they exist, the everlasting ones by the alternation of the accidents appearing in them. Consequently he who denies this last cycle, which is the lowest in the scale of being, has eliminated the first also; for if the first exists, the lowest will exist too, because the latter proceeds from the former. It is true *a priori* that, given the highest, the lowest will exist also, derived from it through the intermediate stages; *a posteriori*, given the lowest levels of being, the highest can be inferred through the intermediate terms. This, then, is the reason why Socrates assumes as a recognized fact that if the living does not in like manner arise from the dead by a cyclic process, everything will eventually be dead [72c5–d3].

230. If we suppose that the number of the living is limited and that they continuously pass on to join the number of the dead, the absurdity will come to pass that creation must spend itself because no new living beings are born, since the cycle has been eliminated. The answer can be that the cycle of specifically identical substances replacing each other has not been eliminated: let us assume that the living proceed from what is not alive and even non-existent, but not from the dead; e.g. a man's previous state is not a dead man, but non-existence, yet it remains true

---

§ 230. 3. φαίης ἄν : this is not a possible objection to disprove Socrates' *reductio ad absurdum* on the ground that the species survives in any case, but the beginning of Dam.'s explanation of Socrates' real point: individuals of one kind continue

κγ'. – Ὅτι ἀίδιος μὲν ἡ ὅλη γένεσις κυρίως διὰ τὰς ἀκινήτους αἰτίας· 229(139)
προσεχέστερον δὲ διὰ τὰς κινουμένας κατὰ κύκλον οὐρανίας περιφοράς· ἐν τρίτῃ
δὲ τάξει καὶ διὰ τὰς συναιτίους ἀρχάς, τήν τε ὕλην ἀεὶ πεφυκυῖαν δέχεσθαι
τὰ εἴδη, κἂν ἀπορρέῃ, καὶ τὸ εἶδος αὐτῷ τῷ κύκλῳ συνουσιωμένον τῆς γενέσεως.
τὸ μὲν γὰρ ἄυλον εἶδος αὐτόγονον πᾶν, τὸ δὲ ἔνυλον ἐν μερισμῷ γενόμενον 5
εἰς γεννῶν καὶ γεννώμενον διῄρηται ⟨ἐπὶ⟩ τῶν ἀτόμων· ἄνθρωπος γὰρ ἄνθρωπον
γεννᾷ καὶ ζῷον ἅπαν καὶ φυτὸν ὁμοίως τὸ ὅμοιον. ἀλλὰ καὶ τῶν ἀψύχων εἰδῶν
ἕκαστον ὡς δύναται πολλαπλασιάζειν ἑαυτὸ βούλεται καὶ ἑαυτῷ τὰ ἄλλα πρὸς
ἑαυτὸ μεταβάλλειν· ὄργανον δὲ ἡ φύσις ἀεὶ κινοῦσα καὶ κινουμένη. ὁ δ' οὖν
κύκλος ἐσπούδασται πᾶσιν εἰς δύναμιν, ἀλλὰ τοῖς μὲν ἀιδίοις ὁ τῶν κινήσεων, 10
τοῖς δὲ μὴ καὶ ὁ τῶν οὐσιῶν· ἔστ' ἂν δὲ μένωσιν αἱ οὐσίαι αὐταὶ κατὰ ἀριθμόν,
καὶ αὗται κυκλίζονται ταῖς ἐνεργείαις καὶ τοῖς ἄλλοις συμβεβηκόσιν· αἱ δὲ
ἐνέργειαι καὶ τὰ μένειν κατὰ ἀριθμὸν ἐν τῷ κύκλῳ μὴ δυνάμενα, ταῦτα εἰσάπαξ
ἔστιν ἢ οὐκ ἔστιν. ὁ τοίνυν τὸν κύκλον ἀναιρεῖν ἐπιχειρῶν ἀπὸ τῆς γενέσεως
αὐτὴν ἀνατρέπειν ἐπιχειρεῖ τὴν ὅλην ἀειγενεσίαν καὶ ματαίους ἀποφαίνειν τὰς 15
ἀκινήτους αἰτίας· συγχωρῶν δὲ τὸν καθόλου κύκλον συγχωρήσει καὶ τὰς μέχρι
τινὸς ὑπομενούσας οὐσίας μιμεῖσθαι τὰς ἀιδίους, ἐφ' ὅσον εἰσί, τῇ ἀνακυκλήσει
τῶν περὶ αὐτὰς μεταβαλλομένων. ὥστε ὁ τοῦτον ἀνελὼν τὸν κύκλον ἔσχατον
ὄντα ἀνῄρηκε καὶ τὸν πρῶτον· ὄντος γὰρ τοῦ πρώτου καὶ ὁ ἔσχατος ἔσται διὰ
τὴν ἀπ' ἐκείνου εἰς τοῦτον πρόοδον. ἀπ' αἰτίας μὲν γὰρ ἀληθές, εἰ ἔστι τὰ πρῶτα, 20
εἶναι καὶ τὰ ἔσχατα διὰ τῶν μέσων· ἀπὸ δὲ τεκμηρίου, εἰ τὰ ἔσχατα, | καὶ (140)
τὰ πρῶτα διὰ τῶν μέσων. διὰ ταῦτα τοίνυν ὡς ὁμολογούμενον ἠξίωσεν ὁ
Σωκράτης, εἰ μὴ καὶ ἀπὸ τῶν τεθνεώτων τὰ ζῶντα γίγνοιτο κατὰ κύκλον,
ὅτι πάντα τεθνεῶτα γενήσεται [72c5–d3].

κδ'. – Ὅτι πεπερασμένων τῶν ζώντων ὑποκειμένων, ἀεὶ δὲ εἰς τὰ τεθνεῶτα 230
προχωρούντων, συμβήσεται τὸ ἄτοπον ἀναλωθῆναι τὴν γένεσιν ἄλλων ζώντων
μὴ γιγνομένων, ἅτε ἀνῃρημένου τοῦ κύκλου. ἀλλ' οὐκ ἀνῄρηται, φαίης ἄν, ὁ
τῶν κατ' εἶδος ἀεὶ κυκλιζομένων οὐσιῶν· γιγνέσθω γοῦν τὰ ζῶντα ἀπὸ τῶν μὴ
ζώντων μηδέ γε ὄντων, οὐ μὴν ἀπὸ τῶν τεθνεώτων· οὐδὲ γὰρ ἄνθρωπος ἐκ 5
τοῦ τεθνεῶτος ἀνθρώπου, ἀλλ' ἐκ τοῦ μὴ ὄντος, ἀεὶ δὲ ὅμως ἄνθρωπος ἐκ μὴ

---

§ 229. 5 μερι~σμῶι, -ι~ M^c — 6 ἐπὶ Wk (ὑπὸ Nv): om. M — 9 ἑαυτὸ~μεταβάλλειν] ~μετα- in ras. M^x — 17 εἰσί] in ras. M^x

---

to replace each other, therefore presumably the replacement of accidents in relation to the same individual will also continue, and such accidents are life (being joined to a body) and death (being separated from it).

that man proceeds from not-man. Now if the cycle is maintained, the cycle of replacement in relation to the substratum, this is probably also true of the cycle of the numerically identical, in which the same substances survive, not only the everlasting ones, but also those which undergo the alternation of accidents only for a certain time. We actually observe that these show the cycle of alternating accidents: a man, while remaining his own self, becomes hot and cold a great number of times; consequently, the living and the dead also are substances of this nature, subject to a great number of changes from one opposite to the other, e.g. being joined together and being separated. If, however, after the first separation they are not united again, they have ceased to be what they are, so that neither do subsequent living substances possess this quality of being subject to a cycle of alternating accidents. Therefore the existence of such substances will come to an end as soon as the remaining individuals of this kind are spent.

(III) Brief answers to the preceding objections

231. Now that we have thus clearly defined these points, it will be easy to answer the objections in a few words.

232. (1) To counter the first objection [§ 209] we will say that a substance can outlast the cyclic alternation of accidents that come and go, such as composition and decomposition, or joining the body and leaving the body, and it is possible for substances to pass through this a great number of times, precisely because they are substances and can endure the frequent repetition of external processes. It is possible, I repeat, as far as the substances are concerned, though there are other causes of a more violent kind by which they are destroyed or recurrence of the same accidents is prevented; even the dissipated air, considered by itself, could have been enclosed in the bag again, if it were possible at all to catch it: in fact, we sometimes breathe the same air in and out, caught under a blanket. Smoke is not a case in point, but falls under generation and destruction of substances, whereas we are now concerned with the alternation of accidents in one and the same substratum. It follows that the substance of the soul, considered by itself, when it has been separated from the body and has survived this as a substance, *can* undergo the opposite process also, i.e. being united with the body. This is, in my opinion, the conclusion to which this argument leads, a possibility and even a probability, since in the majority of cases substances are naturally capable of outlasting a succession of accidents.

233. (2) Against the second objection [§ 211] the same answer will serve: the substance of animals is naturally capable of being awake and

---

§§ 231–242. Discussion of the "remaining difficulties" of §§ 209–220.
§ 232. 1–3. Cf. Dam., *princ.* 28.11–13 τῶν γὰρ συμβεβηκότων ἐπιγιγνομένων ἕκαστα

ἀνθρώπου. οὐκοῦν εἰ σῴζοιτο ὁ κύκλος οὗτος, φημὶ δὲ ὁ τῶν μεταβαλλομένων περὶ τὸ ὑποκείμενον, σῴζοιτο ἂν καὶ ὁ κατὰ ἀριθμόν, τῶν αὐτῶν οὐσιῶν μενουσῶν, οὐ μόνον τῶν ἀιδίων, ἀλλὰ καὶ τῶν ἄχρι τινὸς τὰ μεταβάλλοντα κύκλῳ δεχομένων. αὗται γὰρ νῦν οὕτω κυκλίζονται ταῖς μεταβολαῖς, ἄνθρωπος γὰρ ὁ αὐτὸς ὑπομένων θερμαίνεταί τε καὶ ψύχεται πολλάκις· ὥστε καὶ τὰ ζῶντα καὶ τὰ τεθνεῶτα τοιαῦται οὐσίαι οἷαι δεκτικαὶ τῶν ἐναντίων εἶναι πολλάκις μεταβολῶν, οἷον συζεύξεών τε καὶ διαζεύξεων. εἰ δὲ ἅπαξ διαζυγεῖσαι μηκέτι συζεύγνυνται, ἀπώλεσαν τὸ εἶναι ὅ εἰσιν, ὥστε καὶ αἱ ἐπιγιγνόμεναι τῶν ζώντων οὐκέτι τοιαῦται οἷαι κυκλίζεσθαι ταῖς τῶν συμβεβηκότων μεταβολαῖς. ἀπολεῖται οὖν ἡ τῶν τοιούτων οὐσιῶν ὑπόστασις, ἀναλωμένων τῶν γε ὑπολελειμμένων τοιούτων.

(III) Ἐπιλύσεις τῶν προηπορημένων σύντομοι

—. - Τούτων ἡμῖν οὕτως διωρισμένων σαφῶς οὐ πολὺ ἔργον ἔτι τὰς ἀπορίας ταῖς λύσεσιν ἐπιδραμεῖν.

α' κε'. - Ὅτι πρὸς τὴν πρώτην [§ 209] ἀπαντῶντες λέγωμεν ὡς δύναται μὲν ὑπομένειν ἡ οὐσία τὴν κύκλῳ μεταβολὴν τῶν περὶ αὐτὴν γιγνομένων καὶ ἀπογιγνομένων συμβεβηκότων, οἷον | τοῦ συγκρίνεσθαι καὶ διακρίνεσθαι ἢ τῷ σώματι προσιέναι καὶ ἀπιέναι ἀπὸ τοῦ σώματος, καὶ ἐνδέχεται τοῦτο πάσχειν πολλάκις οὐσίας γε οὔσας καὶ ὑπομενούσας τὴν τῶν παθῶν πολλάκις ἐπανακύκλησιν. ἐνδέχεται μὲν οὖν, ὅπερ ἔφην, ὅσον ἐπὶ ταῖς οὐσίαις, δι' ἄλλας δὲ αἰτίας ἢ φθείρονται βιαιότερον ἢ ἐμποδίζονται πρὸς τὴν τῶν αὐτῶν ἐπάνοδον· ἐπεὶ καὶ ὁ διαπνευσθεὶς ἀήρ, ὅσον ἐφ' ἑαυτῷ, πάλιν ἂν ἐν τῷ ἀσκῷ κατεκλείσθη, εἴπερ οὖν ἦν πιεστός· ἀμέλει ποτὲ τὸν αὐτὸν ἱματίῳ συμπιέζοντες εἰσπνέομέν τε καὶ ἐκπνέομεν. ὁ δὲ καπνὸς οὐκ ἔστι τῆς ὑποθέσεως, ἀλλὰ γενέσεώς τε καὶ φθορᾶς τῶν οὐσιῶν, ὑπόκειται δὲ ὁ περὶ ἓν ὑποκείμενον τῶν ἐν ὑποκειμένῳ κυκλισμός. ὥστε καὶ ἡ ψυχῆς οὐσία, τὸ ὅσον ἐφ' ἑαυτῇ, διαζευχθεῖσα τοῦ σώματος, εἶτα ὑπομείνασα ὡς οὐσία, δύναται καὶ τὸ ἐναντίον πάθος παθεῖν, συζυγῆναι τῷ σώματι. καὶ τοῦτο εἶναί φημι τὸ δεικνύμενον ἐν τῷ λόγῳ συμπέρασμα, ἐνδεχόμενον καὶ ‛εἰκός'· ὡς γὰρ ἐπὶ τὸ πλεῖστον ὑπομένουσιν αἱ οὐσίαι κατὰ φύσιν τὴν ἑαυτῶν τὴν πολλάκις ἐπανακύκλησιν τῶν παθῶν.

β' κς'. - Ὅτι καὶ πρὸς τὴν δευτέραν [§ 211] ἀπορίαν τὰ αὐτὰ φήσομεν. καὶ γὰρ πέφυκεν ἡ οὐσία τῶν ζώων ἐγρηγορέναι καὶ καθεύδειν πλεονάκις, βεβαιοτέρα

---

§ 232. 4 προσιέναι M^c: προϊέναι M¹ — 9 εἴπερ οὖν ἦν πιεστός] εἴπερ οὖν ἦν-̇ -̇πι- M^c: spat. vac. M¹

μένει τὰ εἴδη..., περὶ ἃ μένοντα ἡ μεταβολὴ θεωρεῖται τῶν συμβεβηκότων.
15. εἰκός : 70b7 (supra § 182).

asleep a number of times, because it is more stable and more enduring than one single change of one opposite into the other, and this is obviously true in the majority of cases, while the exceptions are abnormal events.

234. (3) Against the third objection [§ 212] we will say that the soul is supposed to be an incorporeal substance with the power of animating bodies and giving them life, as long as it exists, just as fire has the power of heating; therefore, as long as it remains what it is, fire, it cannot lose its intrinsic heat. Neither can the soul be bereft of its life-giving activity, as long as it remains what it is, soul; the body, on the contrary, at some time loses its life, since it is adventitious. Now after undergoing privation nothing returns to possession, blindness does not return to sight nor bodily death to bodily life; the cycle here assumed is not a cycle of these pairs, but of opposites, e.g. sight and ophthalmia and the rest of the so-called privative and possessive forms. Hence the body can return to the soul from the last stage of the death struggle and people have even been known to return to life after burial, because necrosis was not complete; soul, however, never dies, no more than fire becomes cold, but both either are such or do not exist at all. Therefore, as long as each of the two remains what it is, it can in its turn heat, or animate, other substances. Still, if there is a kind of life to which the body is not dead, it can be joined to that form of life again in the production of other living beings, e.g. maggots and that sort of animals.

235. (4) As regards the fourth objection [§ 213] we must observe that it is directed against the commentator, not against Plato's argument. Accordingly our own claim is that the law of repeated recurrence should be found to apply to all accidents, whether more than one substance is involved or one only, just as Plato's argument deals with the repeated union with and separation from the body of a soul that remains numerically the same.

236. (5) The fifth objection [§ 214] also concerns the commentator; our point of view as well as Plato's is that there is only one substance, the soul, to which we should make the cycle of opposite processes incident.

237. (6) The sixth [§ 215], also regarding the commentator alone, can be disposed of on similar grounds, if accepted for the moment as relevant: we are not comparing the soul with the body, neither as stronger nor as weaker, but examining it by itself as a substance and as such more enduring than all its accidents, in the sense that it outlasts not only each of any pair of opposites by itself, but also a single change from each into the other, since a substance realizes all such changes normally, that is to say, unless an external factor prevents this.

---

§ 234. 8–9. τῶν ... εἰδῶν τῶν στερητικῶν οὕτω λεγομένων καὶ τῶν ἑκτικῶν : I have found no example of the adjectives applied to form (εἶδος). Both are used by Simpl., cat. 394.23 and 32, in the context of cat. 10.

9–15. Dam. II § 2.17–19.

10–11. καὶ ταφέντες ἤδη τινὲς ἀνεβίωσαν : a list of such cases Pr., Rep. II 113.6–

γε οὖσα καὶ πολυχρονιωτέρα τῆς ἅπαξ τῶν ἐναντίων εἰς ἄλληλα μεταβολῆς·
καὶ ἡ ἐνάργεια τῶν πραγμάτων οὕτως ἔχει ὡς ἐπὶ τὸ πλεῖστον, τὸ δὲ ὡς
ἐπ' ἔλαττον παρὰ φύσιν.

γ' κζ'. - Ὅτι πρὸς τὴν τρίτην [§ 212] ἐροῦμεν ὅτι ἡ μὲν ψυχὴ ἀσώματος οὐσία 234
ὑπόκειται ψυχωτικὴ τῶν σωμάτων καὶ ζωοποιός, ἕως ἂν ᾖ, καθάπερ τὸ πῦρ
θερμαντικόν· οὐ τοίνυν μένον ὅ ἐστι, πῦρ, στερίσκεται τῆς οἰκείας θερμότητος.
οὐδὲ ἄρα ἡ ψυχὴ τῆς ζωτικῆς ἐνεργείας ἐν στερήσει γίγνεται, μένουσα ὅ ἐστι,
ψυχή· τὸ δὲ σῶμα στερεῖταί ποτε τῆς ζωῆς, ἅτε ἐπεισάκτου οὔσης. παθὸν δὲ
οὐδὲν τὴν στέρησιν ἀνακάμπτει πρὸς | τὴν ἕξιν, οὔτε γὰρ τυφλότης εἰς ὄψιν (142)
οὔτε νέκρωσις σώματος εἰς τὴν ζώωσιν· ὑπόκειται γὰρ οὐ τούτων ὁ κύκλος,
ἀλλὰ τῶν ἐναντίων, οἷον ὄψεως καὶ ὀφθαλμίας καὶ τῶν ἄλλων εἰδῶν τῶν
στερητικῶν οὕτω λεγομένων καὶ τῶν ἑκτικῶν. τοιγαροῦν ἀπὸ τῆς ἐσχάτης
ψυχορραγίας ἀνακάμψειεν ἂν πρὸς τὴν ψυχὴν τὸ σῶμα, καὶ ταφέντες ἤδη τινὲς 10
ἀνεβίωσαν διὰ τὸ μὴ τελέαν ἀποβῆναι τὴν νέκρωσιν· ἡ μέντοι ψυχὴ οὐ νεκροῦταί
ποτε, ὥσπερ οὐδὲ τὸ πῦρ ψύχεται, ἀλλ' ἑκάτερον ἢ ἔστι τοιοῦτον ἢ οὐκ ἔστι.
μένον ἄρα ὅ ἐστιν, ἐφ' ὅσον μένει, δύναται πάλιν ἕτερα τὸ μὲν θερμαίνειν, ἡ δὲ
ψυχοῦν. πρὸς ὃ δὲ οὐ νενέκρωται τὸ σῶμα ζωῆς εἶδος, πρὸς τοῦτο συνάπτεται
πάλιν ἐν ἄλλων ζῴων γενέσεσιν, οἷον εὐλῶν καὶ τῶν τοιούτων θηρίων. 15

δ' κη'. - Ὅτι πρὸς τὴν τετάρτην [§ 213] ῥητέον ὡς ἔστι πρὸς τὸν ἐξηγητήν, 235
ἀλλ' οὐ πρὸς τὸν Πλάτωνος λόγον. τοιγαροῦν ἡμεῖς ἐπὶ τῶν ἐν ὑποκειμένῳ
πάντων ἀξιοῦμεν σῴζεσθαι τὴν πολλάκις ἐπανακύκλησιν, εἴτε περὶ πλείους οὐσίας
εἴτε περὶ μίαν, ὡς λαμβάνει ὁ λόγος τὴν περὶ ψυχὴν μένουσαν κατὰ ἀριθμὸν
τὴν αὐτὴν ἀπόζευξίν τε καὶ σύζευξιν πρὸς σῶμα γιγνομένην πολλάκις. 5

κθ'. - Ὅτι καὶ ἡ πέμπτη [§ 214] πρὸς τὸν ἐξηγητήν· ἡμῖν δὲ καὶ Πλάτωνι 236
ὁ λόγος ἐστὶν περὶ μίαν οὐσίαν τὴν ψυχὴν ἀποδοῦναι τὸν κύκλον τῶν ἐν αὐτῇ
συμβαινόντων παθῶν ἐναντίων.

λ'. - Ὅτι ἡ ἕκτη [§ 215] καὶ αὐτὴ οὖσα πρὸς τὸν ἐξηγησάμενον τῶν ὁμοίων 237
τεύξεται ἀπολογισμῶν κατὰ συνδρομήν. οὐ γὰρ πρὸς τὸ σῶμα τὴν ψυχὴν
παραβάλλομεν, οὔτε ὡς ἰσχυροτέραν οὔτε ὡς ἀσθενεστέραν αὐτοῦ, ἀλλὰ καθ'
ἑαυτὴν ὡς οὐσίαν καὶ ταύτῃ μονιμωτέραν τῶν οἰκείων παθῶν ἁπάντων, οὐ μόνον
ἑκατέρου καθ' ἑαυτό, ἀλλὰ καὶ τῆς εἰσάπαξ ἀμφοῖν μεταβολῆς, ὡς προχειριζομένην 5
δηλονότι ἑκάστην ὡς ἐπὶ τὸ πλεῖστον, εἰ μηδὲν γὰρ ἔξωθεν ἐμποδίσειεν.

---

§ 234. 2 τῶν] ex corr. Mᶜ — 5 ἄτε ἐπεισάκτου] ἄτε ἐ- in ras. Mᶜ | δὲ²] in ras. Mᶜ —
15 εὐλῶν Fh: ἐνύλων M
§ 235. 3 πλείους] post -ί- ras. M (πλείστους ut vid. M¹)
§ 237. 1 αὐτὴ M¹: αὕτη Mᶜ | ἐξηγησάμενον] -σά- in ras. Mᶜ — 5 ἑαυτὸ] ἑαυ- in
ras. 2 litt. Mᶜ | προχειριζομένην Wk: -ῃι M

116.18; cf. 122.17–123.16; Phlegon, mirab. 1-2 (pp. 117–125 Westermann); Philostr.,
vit. Ap. 4, 45.
14–15. Cf. infra § 249.5–6. Lucret. III 717–729 (vermes, vermiculi).
§ 237. 2. κατὰ συνδρομήν: in the rhetorical sense (LSJ s.v. 3), from συντρέχειν
'concur'.

238. (7) The seventh [§ 216] is in accordance with our own interpretation, which concludes nothing else from the argument but that it is possible for a numerically identical substance to be disjoined and to be joined, and, as regards the soul, for the same soul to be alive and to be dead, more often than once.

239. (8) The eighth [§ 217] will show the same accordance with our view. We do admit that the animated pneumatic body repeatedly enters and leaves this 'oyster-like' body. The philosophers themselves hold that the pneumatic body accompanies the rational soul until its complete deliverance from genesis. What is more, Socrates is going to say a little later [81c9–e2] that what he describes as 'the shadowy phantom' remains joined to the soul after death, 'until the soul, yielding to the compulsion of the corporeal, is imprisoned again in the earthly body.' Its cycle continues until the time when this vehicle, too, suffers privation of life. Nor will it ever be restored to possession of life, just as we asserted above [§ 234] with regard to this earthly body, once it has died; for complete immortality is not proved for the pneumatic body, any more than for the soul, but only continuance longer than a repeated or at least than a single recurrence of its accidents.

240. (9) To the ninth objection [§ 218] we may answer that substances after continuing to exist for a long time and then suffering privation, are destroyed and come into being again only by mere identity in kind, but it remains nevertheless true that in each, as long as it continues to exist, the cycle of opposites is consummated. Consequently we shall admit the same with regard to the substance of soul: different substances belonging to one species may come to be at different times, but each substance, being of longer duration than its opposite accidents, can undergo their alternation a greater number of times.

241. (10) The tenth objection [§ 219] can be met as follows: if the relation between substances and accidents is what it is, i.e. if substances are naturally more constant and enduring than accidents, then the argument from the opposites is true contingently. For there is no question of their being more stable than some, less so than others; they must be more lasting than all their opposite accidents without exception, since accidents come and go, and so this is also true of separation from and conjunction with the body, these too being accidents with the soul as a substratum. If, as I said, substances have this property, the argument is saved; if, however, in the future substances should be produced without this property, which they

---

§ 239. 3–5. On Pr.'s belief in the survival (not: immortality) of the pneumatic body cf. note on II § 29.

7–8. The MSS. of Pl. have ἕως ἂν τῇ τοῦ ξυνεπακολουθοῦντος, τοῦ σωματοειδοῦς, ἐπιθυμίᾳ πάλιν ἐνδεθῶσιν εἰς σῶμα. Euseb., *praep. evang.* XIII 16,4 reads ἕως ἂν τῇ τοῦ σωματοειδοῦς τοῦ ξυνεπακολουθοῦντος ἐπιθυμίᾳ etc. Dam. seems to have read, or remembered, the text as ἕως ἂν τῇ τοῦ σωματοειδοῦς ξυνεπακολουθοῦσαι ἐπιθυμίᾳ ...

ζ´ λα´. – Ὅτι ἡ ἑβδόμη [§ 216] συνομολογεῖ ταῖς ἡμετέραις ἐξηγήσεσιν οὐδὲν 238(143) ἄλλο συναγούσαις ἐκ τοῦ λόγου ἢ τὸ πλεονάκις ἢ ἅπαξ ἐνδέχεσθαι διακρίνεσθαί τε καὶ συγκρίνεσθαι τὴν αὐτὴν κατὰ ἀριθμὸν οὐσίαν, ζῆν τε καὶ τεθνάναι τὴν αὐτήν, αὐτήν γε ψυχήν.

η´ λβ´. – Ὅτι καὶ ἡ ὀγδόη [§ 217] τὴν αὐτὴν ἡμῖν ὁμολογίαν παρέξεται. καὶ 239 γὰρ τὸ πνευματικὸν ζῷον ὁμολογοῦμεν πολλάκις ἐγγίγνεσθαι τῷδε τῷ ὀστρέῳ καὶ πολλάκις αὐτοῦ ἀπογίγνεσθαι. φασὶ γοῦν καὶ αὐτοὶ οἱ φιλόσοφοι τὸν πνευματικὸν χιτῶνα τοῦτον τῇ λογικῇ ψυχῇ συνεῖναι μέχρι τελείας ἀποκαταστάσεως ἀπὸ τοῦ γενητοῦ. μᾶλλον δὲ καὶ αὐτὸς ὁ Σωκράτης ἐρεῖ μικρὸν ὕστερον 5 [81c9–e2] ὡς τὸ σκιοειδὲς τοῦτο δὴ φάντασμα τῇ ψυχῇ συνέζευκται μετὰ θάνατον, ἕως ἂν τῇ τοῦ σωματοειδοῦς ἀνάγκῃ συνεπομένη πάλιν ἐνδεθῇ τῷ ὀστρεώδει σώματι'. καὶ μένει τούτου ὁ κύκλος, ἕως ὅτε καὶ τοῦτο τὸ ὄχημα πάθῃ τὴν στέρησιν. τοῦτο δὲ οὐκέτι πρὸς τὴν ἕξιν ἐπαναχθήσεται, καθάπερ ἐπὶ τῷδε τῷ σώματι νεκρουμένῳ πρότερον [§ 234] ἠξιοῦμεν· οὐ γὰρ οὐδὲ ἐπὶ τούτου τὸ 10 πάμπαν ἀθάνατον ἀποδείκνυται, ἀλλ᾿ ὡς ἐπὶ τῆς ψυχῆς τὸ πολυχρονιώτερον τῆς τῶν ἐν αὐτῷ συμβεβηκότων ἐπανακυκλήσεως πλεονάκις ἢ ἅπαξ τοὐλάχιστον γιγνομένης.

θ´ λγ´. – Ὅτι πρὸς τὴν ἐνάτην [§ 218] ῥητέον ἐκεῖνο, ὡς αἱ μὲν οὐσίαι πολὺν 240 ἐπιμένουσαι χρόνον, ἔπειτα παθοῦσαι στέρησιν ἀπόλλυνται καὶ γίγνονται πάλιν αἱ αὐταὶ κατ᾿ εἶδος, οὐδὲν μέντοι ἧττον περὶ ἑκάστην, ἕως ὅτε μένει, τῶν ἐναντίων ὁ κύκλος ἐπιτελεῖται. τὸ αὐτὸ τοίνυν ὁμολογήσομεν καὶ τὴν ψυχῆς οὐσίαν γίγνεσθαι μὲν κατ᾿ εἶδος ἀεὶ ἄλλην καὶ ἄλλην, μένουσαν δὲ ἐπὶ πλείω 5 χρόνον ἢ τὰ περὶ αὐτὴν ἐναντία δέχεσθαι τὴν τούτων ἐν κύκλῳ μεταβολὴν πλεονάκις.

ι´ λδ´. – Ὅτι πρὸς τὴν δεκάτην [§ 219] ἀπαντησόμεθα λέγοντες· εἰ μὲν τοιαῦταί 241(144) εἰσιν αἱ οὐσίαι πρὸς τὰ συμβεβηκότα οἷαι καὶ εἰσί, μονιμώτεραι καὶ πολυχρονιώτεραι κατὰ φύσιν ἐκείνων, ἔστιν ὁ λόγος ἀληθὴς ἐνδεχομένως ὁ ἀπὸ τῶν ἐναντίων. οὐ γὰρ τῶν μέν, τῶν δὲ οὐ βεβαιότεραι, ἀλλὰ πάντων ἁπλῶς τῶν περὶ αὐτὰς ἐναντίων ἅτε γιγνομένων καὶ ἀπογιγνομένων, ὥστε καὶ τοῦ διαζεύγνυσθαι καὶ συζεύγνυσθαι 5 πρὸς τὸ σῶμα· συμβέβηκε γὰρ καὶ ταῦτα ταῖς ψυχαῖς οὐσίαις οὔσαις. εἰ μὲν οὖν, ὅπερ ἔφην, αἱ οὐσίαι τοιαῦται, σῴζεται ὁ λόγος· εἰ δὲ τὸ λοιπὸν γένοιτο μὴ τοιαῦται, ὡς μέχρι γε τήμερόν εἰσιν, ἀναλωθήσονται αἱ νῦν οὖσαι τοιαῦται

---

§ 238. 2 ἐνδέχεσθαι Mᶜ: -εται ut vid. M¹ — 4 αὐτήν, αὐτήν] -τὴν αὐ- ins. Mᶜ
§ 239. 13 γιγνομένης] -ς in ras. Mᶜ
§ 240. 5 πλείω Fh: πλεῖον M

---

§ 240. 5. γίγνεσθαι μὲν κατ᾿ εἶδος ἄλλην καὶ ἄλλην: a confused way of saying that only identity *in kind* is preserved (cf. § 218.1 κατ᾿ εἶδος), the *individuals* being different each time (cf. § 218.3–4 ἄλλη καὶ ἄλλη).

§ 241. 7–8. εἰ δὲ τὸ λοιπὸν γένοιτο μὴ τοιαῦται: comparison of this restatement of the argument with its counterpart in the *Ph.* (72a11–d3: if opposites did not alternate, one of each pair would disappear) shows the gap between Pl. and Dam.

have had to this day, those that are such now will eventually be spent and eventually substances will not be more lasting than their accidents. For if this happens in relation to one kind of accident, viz. separation and conjunction, the same follows logically for all, so that, once any change of accident takes place, the substratum itself will be destroyed. Now accidents change several times every hour, so that before long everything will perish, not to be revived even as regards kind. For generation could not keep pace with destruction, if substances disappear at the same rate as their contrasting accidents; the individual substance will perish even before it has been able to reproduce itself, since it will be destroyed at the moment of the first change of any accident whatsoever into its opposite. For instance, if on the very first day, or even in the first hour after its birth a being passes from hot to cold, it is gone, and if it passes from moist to dry, it is gone, and if it passes from waking to sleep, it is gone, and whatever else the change may be, it dies at once while still in its infancy. In this way how can there be a new generation to preserve the race? The result will be that ultimately everything will pass away. In order to make this clear Socrates uses examples that leave no room for doubt: if sleepers did not wake up, when would waking individuals be born fast enough to equal the number of those who are asleep, every night and every day? How could the everflowing stream of birth run swiftly enough to prevent a state of affairs in which beings that become (let us say) hot and then cold again many times within a single hour, would all have acquired either heat or cold, either walking or sitting, or any other of a pair of opposites, as permanent characteristics? If this is improbable and even downright impossible, it is obviously also impossible for all things to be eventually dead and nothing else or, similarly, living and nothing else. For those, too, are accidents, and not unchangeable ones; and further, we are still relying on the reasonable assumption made above [§ 229], that if cyclic recurrence is not possible in the case of this particular substance, neither will it be possible in the case of another, by the rule that substrata outlast the alternation of this kind of opposites. But if there is no cyclic motion in the case of short-lived substances, as long as they exist, no more will it be possible for the lasting, long-lived ones nor for those who have a life-span of many generations, and consequently not even for everlasting beings, Neither, therefore, will substances manifest a frequent recurrence of identical pairs of opposite actions. The result will be that everything will 'collapse and come to a standstill,' and it will not be raised again, because otherwise we should surreptitiously reintroduce the cycle of opposite accidents in a constant substance.

τῷ χρόνῳ καὶ ἔσονται τῷ χρόνῳ τῶν συμβεβηκότων οὐκέτι πολυχρονιώτεραι. εἰ γὰρ ἑνὸς εἴδους, οἷον τοῦ διαζεύγνυσθαι καὶ συζεύγνυσθαι, τῷ αὐτῷ λόγῳ καὶ πάντων· ὥστε ἐὰν ἅπαξ μόνον ὁτιοῦν τῶν ἐν ὑποκειμένῳ μεταβληθῇ, καὶ αὐτὴ φθαρήσεται ἡ ὑποκειμένη οὐσία. πολλάκις δὲ ὥρας ἑκάστης ταῦτα μεταβάλλεται· οὐκ ἂν οὖν φθάνοι πάντα φθειρόμενα καὶ οὐκέτι ἀναβιωσκόμενα οὐδὲ κατὰ εἶδος. οὐ γὰρ ἂν καταλαμβάνοι τὴν φθορὰν ἡ γένεσις, τοσαύτης οὔσης τῶν οὐσιῶν ὑπορροῆς ὅση ἐστὶ τῶν περὶ αὐτὰς ἐναντίων· πρὸ γὰρ τοῦ καὶ γεννῆσαι τὸ ὅμοιον ἑκάστη οὐσία φθαρήσεται· εὐθὺς γὰρ ἀπολεῖται ἐπὶ τῇ πρώτῃ μεταβολῇ παντὸς ὁτουοῦν ἐναντίου εἰς τὸ ἐναντίον. οἷον εἰ κατὰ τὴν πρώτην ἡμέραν, μᾶλλον δὲ ὥραν, ἐν ᾗ ἐγεννήθη, ψυχθῇ ἀπὸ τοῦ θερμοῦ, ἀπώλετο, καὶ εἰ ξηρανθῇ ἀπὸ τοῦ ὑγροῦ, ἀπώλετο, καὶ εἰ καθευδήσειεν ἀπὸ ἐγρηγορότος, ἀπώλετο, κἂν ὁτιοῦν κατὰ ἄλλο, παραχρῆμα οἴχεται ἔτι βρέφος. τίς οὖν ἔτι ὁ τεξόμενος καὶ τὴν εἰς ἀεὶ διαδοχὴν τοῦ γένους διατηρήσων; πάντα ἄρα τελευτῶντα φθαρήσεται. καὶ ταῦτα ἐνδείξασθαι βουλόμενος ἐχρήσατο παραδείγμασιν ἐναργεστάτοις· εἰ γὰρ τὰ καθεύδοντα οὐκ ἠγείρετο, πότε ἂν ἔφθη τῶν ἐγρηγορότων ἡ γένεσις ἀντανισῶσαι τὸν ἀριθμὸν τῶν καθευδόντων ἐπὶ νυκτός τε καὶ ἡμέρας ἑκάστης; ἢ πῶς ἂν ἐξῄ|κεσεν ὁ τῆς γενέσεως ἀέναος ποταμὸς τοὺς πολλάκις ἐν ὥρᾳ μιᾷ τυχὸν θερμαινομένους καὶ αὖθις ψυχομένους μὴ πάντας ἐᾶσαι γενέσθαι θερμοὺς ἢ ψυχροὺς ἢ βαδίζοντας ἢ καθημένους ἢ καθ᾽ ὁτιοῦν τῶν ἐναντίων χαρακτηριζομένους; εἰ δὴ ταῦτα ἄτοπα καὶ ἀδύνατα διαρρήδην, πῶς οὐχὶ καὶ τεθνεῶτα πάντα γενέσθαι μόνον, ὁμοίως δὲ καὶ ζῶντα μόνον; καὶ ταῦτα γὰρ τῶν ἐν ὑποκειμένῳ ἐστὶ καὶ οὐκ ἀμεταβλήτων· ἐπεὶ καὶ τὰ πρότερον [§ 229] ὑποτεθέντα μετρίως ὑπόκειται, ὅτι, εἰ μὴ ἐπὶ ταύτης ὁ κυκλισμός ἐστι δυνατός, οὐδὲ ἐπὶ ἄλλης ἐνδεχόμενος ἔσται, ὑπομενουσῶν τῶν ὑποκειμένων οὐσιῶν τὸν ἐν τοῖς τοιούτοις ἐναντίοις κύκλον. εἰ δὲ ἐπὶ τῶν ὀλιγοχρονίων οὐσιῶν οὐδεὶς ἔσται κύκλος, ἐφ᾽ ὅσον χρόνον εἰσίν, οὐδὲ ἐπὶ τῶν πολυχρονίων ἔσται καὶ μακροβίων οὐδὲ μακραιώνων, ὥστε οὐδὲ ἐπὶ τῶν ἀϊδίων οὐσιῶν. οὐδὲ ἄρα τὰς ἐναντίας ἐνεργείας αἱ οὐσίαι προβαλοῦνται τὰς αὐτὰς πολλάκις κυκλιζομένας. πάντα ἄρα ʿσυμπεσόντα στήσεταιʾ καὶ οὐκέτι ἀνεγερθήσεται, ἵνα μὴ λάθωμεν τὰ ἐναντία περὶ τὴν μένουσαν οὐσίαν κυκλίζοντες.

---

§ 241. 13 φθάνοι] -ι in ras. M^c | ἀναβιοσκόμενα M — 19 καθευδήσειεν] -εν in ras. M^c — 33 οὐδεὶς ἔσται M^c: οὐδείς ἐστι M¹

36–37. Cf. Pl., Phaedr. 245d8–e1 πάντα τε οὐρανὸν πᾶσάν τε γῆν εἰς ἓν συμπεσοῦσαν στῆναι

242. (11) Our answer to the eleventh point [§ 220] is this: the case as stated deals with men who live for the first time and who were born, not from the dead, but from what is neither alive nor existent, just as, according to Syrianus' shrewd observation [§ 195], those who are awake for the first time do not come into being from the sleeping; in fact, as he says, they do not come into being at all as waking individuals, but as humans, and the waking state is only an accident. In our opinion, though, even that is a case of coming into being as such, but from a state of being neither awake nor existent, because the first genesis of anything is not from the opposite form, but from what is not-such; and this is certainly true as regards generation of the living from the not-living. Now when in the living being the soul has been united with a body, to be separated from it afterwards in death, from that time onward the cycle of alternating opposites continues, or rather, it *may* continue, with one identical soul as its constant center, as long as this soul exists; but it does not exist infinitely, sometimes not even for a long time, though necessarily longer than a single recurrence of its contrasting accidents. Consequently it is not shown that the soul is immortal, but only that is survives sometimes; it had also a beginning in time, viz. the moment when the living individual came into being. This explains why it did not exist prior to the original living being, and yet survives the dissolution of the living being into its two elements. The argument from recollection, on the contrary, will show also that the soul must exist before the original living being; only thus can it be reminded of pure reality through the senses and with the help of things sensible.

(IV) Solutions, on the basis of our own assumptions, of the more pertinent questions raised by the philosopher

243. These, then, will be the answers to the questions from which we started ourselves. Since, however, the commentator too begins by raising some relevant objections and then arrives at solutions satisfactory to himself, some of which are adequate, while others might be improved with the help of our own assumptions stated above, we will now take these one by one and answer them briefly on the principles just set forth. Only the more pertinent questions raised in his work call for an answer.

244. (iii) To the third of his questions [§ 193] our reply must be that the generated and the ungenerated, the mortal and immortal are not accidents that alternate with each other in one substance, nor indeed accidents at all, but constituents of the substance itself, wherever these phenomena occur. Socrates derives his argument not from these, but from real accidents, as we have shown [§ 224].

ια' λε'. – Ὅτι πρὸς τὴν ἑνδεκάτην [§ 220] λέγομεν ὡς τοὺς ζῶντας πρώτως 242
ἀνθρώπους τὸ πρόβλημα ἔλαβεν οὐκ ἐκ τεθνεώτων γενομένους, ἀλλ' ἐκ μὴ
ζώντων μηδὲ ὄντων, ὡς τοὺς πρώτως ἐγρηγορότας αὐτὸς ἐπέστησεν ἐντρεχῶς
ὁ Συριανὸς [§ 195] μὴ ἐκ καθευδόντων γιγνομένους· ἀλλὰ μηδὲ γιγνομένους,
φησίν, ᾗ ἐγρηγορότας, ἀλλ' ᾗ ἀνθρώπους· ᾗ δὲ ἐγρηγορότας, κατὰ συμβεβηκός. 5
ἡμεῖς δὲ ἐροῦμεν καθ' αὐτὸ μὲν καὶ τούτους, ἀλλ' ἐκ μὴ ἐγρηγορότων μηδὲ
ὄντων· παντὸς γὰρ ἡ πρώτη γένεσις οὐκ ἐκ τοῦ ἐναντίου εἴδους, ἀλλ' ἐκ τοῦ
μὴ τοιούτου· οὕτω δ' οὖν καὶ τοῦ ζῶντος ἐκ τοῦ μὴ ζῶντος. ἐπειδὴ δὲ ἐν τῷ
ζῶντι συνέζευκται σώματι ἡ ψυχή, εἶτα διαζεύγνυται ἐν τῷ θανάτῳ, τότε
κυκλίζεται τῶν ἐναντίων ἡ μεταβολή, μᾶλλον δὲ ἐνδέχεται αὐτὴν κυκλίζεσθαι, 10
περὶ μίαν κατὰ ἀριθμὸν ὑπομένουσαν τὴν ψυχήν, ἐφ' ὅσον ἔστι χρόνον· ἔστι δὲ
οὐκ ἐπ' ἄπειρον οὐδὲ ἐπὶ πολὺν ἐνίοτε, ἐπὶ πλείω δὲ τῆς εἰσάπαξ | μόνον τῶν (146)
ἐναντίων περὶ αὐτὴν συνισταμένης ἐν κύκλῳ μεταβολῆς. οὐκ ἄρα δείκνυται
ἀθάνατος, ἀλλὰ ποτέ· καὶ γὰρ ἀπὸ χρόνου ἤρξατο, ἐν ᾧ καὶ τὸ ζῶν ὑπέστη.
διόπερ οὐ προϋπῆρχε τοῦ πρώτου ζῶντος, ἐπιδιαμένει δὲ ὅμως μετὰ τὴν τοῦ 15
ζῶντος εἰς δύο διάλυσιν. ὁ μέντοι ἀπὸ τῶν ἀναμνήσεων λόγος ἀποδείξει καὶ ὅτι
προϋπάρχειν ἀναγκαῖον αὐτὴν καὶ τοῦ πρώτως ζῶντος· [καὶ] τότε γὰρ ἂν τῶν
ὄντως ὄντων ἀναμνησθείη διὰ τῶν αἰσθήσεων καὶ ἀπὸ τῶν αἰσθητῶν.

*(IV) Ἐπιλύσεις τῶν τοῦ φιλοσόφου ἀποριῶν κατὰ τὰς
ἡμετέρας ὑποθέσεις τῶν γενναιοτέρων*

λϛ'. – Τὰ μὲν οὖν ἡμῖν προηπορημένα καὶ δὴ λελύσθω τοῦτον τὸν τρόπον. 243
ἐπειδὴ δὲ καὶ ὁ ἐξηγητὴς προαπορήσας καλῶς ἐπελύσατο κατὰ τὸν ἑαυτοῦ νοῦν τὰς
ἀπορίας, ἐνίας μὲν ἱκανῶς, ἐνίας δὲ καλλιόνως ἂν λυθείσας κατὰ τὰς ἐκκειμένας
ἡμῖν ὑποθέσεις, φέρε ταύτας γε μόνας ἀπολαβόντες ἐπιδράμωμεν λύοντες ὃν
ἄρτι διεξῄειμεν τρόπον. εἰσὶ δὲ αἱ γενναιότεραι τῶν παρ' αὐτῷ γεγραμμένων 5
ἃς ἐπιλυτέον.

λζ'. – (iii) Ὅτι πρὸς τὴν τρίτην [§ 193] αὐτοῦ τῶν ἀποριῶν λεκτέον ὡς τὸ 244
γενητὸν καὶ ἀγένητον καὶ θνητὸν καὶ ἀθάνατον οὐκ ἔστι τῶν περὶ μίαν οὐσίαν
κυκλιζομένων συμβεβηκότων, οὐδὲ ὅλως συμβεβηκότων ἀλλὰ τὴν οὐσίαν αὐτὴν
συμπληρούντων, ἐν οἷς καὶ εἰσὶν αἱ τοιαῦται φύσεις. οὐκ ἀπὸ τούτων δέ, ἀλλὰ
ἀπ' ἐκείνων ποιεῖται τὴν ἐπιχείρησιν ὁ Σωκράτης, ὡς δέδεικται [§ 224]. 5

---

§ 242. 6 ἀλλ' ἐκ μὴ ἐγρηγορότων] ἐκ in ras. 1 litt., ἐ- in ras. 2 litt., M^c (i.e. ἀλλὰ
μὴ ἐκ γρηγορότων M^1) — 12 μόνον Fh: -ων M — 14 γὰρ] s.l. M^1 — 17 καὶ M: del. Wk
§ 243. 3 ἐκκειμένας] ἐκ- in ras. M^c — 4 ἀπολαβόντες Fh: ἐπιλαβόντες M —
5 διεξῄειμεν μ: διεξείημεν M
§ 244. 2 οὐκ] -κ in ras. 2 litt. M^c — 4 οἷς Nv: αἷς M

---

§§ 243-251. Syrianus' ἀπορίαι (§§ 193-200) reviewed and answered by Dam.
On the numbering see note at §§ 193-200.

245. (iv) The same answer applies to the fourth [§ 194]: the body and the incorporeal, too, are substances; anything incorporeal that is not a substance but an accident, is not opposed to body. Consequently, not being opposites, they do not proceed from each other either.

246. (v) Against the fifth [§ 195] we just before [§ 242] adduced this argument, which holds good of all things that come into being for the first time, whether substances or accidents, that they do not proceed from opposite forms, but from their own privation; from a privation not posterior to form, but anterior to it, as it were their own non-existence. The originally black has not proceeded from white, but from not-black; similarly what begins by being awake has proceeded from the not-awake, not from the sleeping; and in the same way the assumption is now that what is alive first, has not proceeded from something dead, but from the not-alive. Thus as far as we are concerned there will be no need for the concession that its coming-to-be is a mere accident.

247. (vi) Against the sixth objection [§ 196] we will say that time, if taken as an accident, will present the kind of cyclic recurrence meant in the proof. 'In this way, too, faster comes from slower,' as Socrates will say presently [71a3–4], and so, of course, will slower from faster; consequently the same action, for example, and the same motion, could take place in a longer or a shorter time; and therefore this can be said also of the thing in motion: being a substance it will, while remaining the same, be measured by a longer and a shorter time according as it moves slower or faster. Age, on the contrary, is an essential attribute inherent in generated substances, and thus, with the substance itself, it proceeds in forward direction only, for age is a kind of progression and retrogression of *substances*. In the same way, then, as the time of coming-to-be and passing away should be left out of account, because they are not included in the argument, so we should leave out increase and decrease of the substance as such. Plato says, it is true, that smaller and larger make a pair of opposites [71b2–4], but this applies to cases where large and small are accidents. All qualities, as Plotinus says [II 6, 1.18–20], are in some cases constitutive of substances, in others incidental to them; even white and black, as essential characteristics, do not proceed from each other.

248. (vii) The answer to the seventh problem [§ 197] is the same: we do not admit as evidence the passing of the elements into each other, because the elements are substances and their specific differences are essential differences. Why should we then complicate things by dragging in, quite needlessly, the question whether fire or earth pass, or do not pass, into each other? That Socrates is referring to the cyclic alternation of

---

§ 246. Cf. Ol. 9 § 4.1–7.
8. ἡμεῖς γε : in contradistinction from Syrianus (§ 195.2).

λη'. – (iv) "Ότι καὶ πρὸς τὴν τετάρτην [§ 194] τὰ αὐτὰ λέγομεν· οὐσία γὰρ καὶ τὸ σῶμα καὶ τὸ ἀσώματον. εἰ δέ τι ἀσώματον οὐκ οὐσία ἀλλὰ συμβεβηκός, οὐκ ἔστι τοῦτό γε ἐναντίον τῷ σώματι. οὐκοῦν οὐδὲ γίγνεται ἐξ ἀλλήλων τά γε μὴ ἐναντία.

λθ'. – (v) "Ότι πρὸς τὴν πέμπτην [§ 195] καὶ ὀλίγῳ πρότερον [§ 242] εἴρηται κοινὸς οὗτος λόγος περὶ πάντων τῶν πρώτων ὑφισταμένων εἴτε οὐσιῶν εἴτε συμβεβηκότων, ὅτι οὐκ ἐκ τῶν ἐναντίων εἰ|δῶν γίγνεται, ἀλλ' ἐκ τῶν οἰκείων στερήσεων, οὐ τῶν μετὰ τὸ εἶδος, ἀλλὰ τῶν πρὸ εἴδους λεγομένων, οἷον ἐκ τῶν οἰκείων μὴ ὄντων. οὐδὲ γὰρ τὸ πρῶτον μέλαν ἐκ λευκοῦ γέγονεν, ἀλλ' ἐκ μὴ μέλανος· οὕτως οὖν καὶ τὸ πρῶτον ἐγρηγορὸς ἐκ τοῦ μὴ ἐγρηγορότος, ἀλλ' οὐκ ἐκ τοῦ καθεύδοντος· οὕτω δὲ καὶ τὸ πρῶτον ζῶν οὐκ ἐκ τεθνεῶτος ὑπόκειται, ἀλλ' ἐκ μὴ ζῶντος. οὕτω δὲ οὐδὲ κατὰ συμβεβηκὸς ἡμεῖς γε ὁμολογήσομεν γίγνεσθαι.

μ'. – (vi) "Ότι πρὸς τὴν ἕκτην [§ 196] ἐροῦμεν ὡς ὁ χρόνος, εἰ μὲν ἐπισυμβαίνων ληφθείη, ποιήσει τὸν κύκλον τῆς ἀποδείξεως. 'καὶ μὴν ἐκ βραδυτέρου τὸ θᾶττον', φήσει [71a3–4]· καὶ δῆλον ὅτι καὶ ἐκ θάττονος τὸ βραδύτερον· ὥστε καὶ ἡ πρᾶξις φέρε καὶ διὰ πλείονος καὶ δι' ἐλάττονος χρόνου γένοιτο ἂν ἡ αὐτὴ καὶ ἡ κίνησις· ὥστε καὶ τὸ κινούμενον, οὐσία γε ὄν, βράδιον καὶ θᾶττον κινούμενον τὸ αὐτὸ μετρηθήσεται χρόνῳ πλείονι καὶ ἐλάττονι. ὁ μέντοι τῶν ἡλικιῶν χρόνος οὐσιώδης ἐστὶ καὶ ταῖς γενηταῖς οὐσίαις συμπεφυκώς, ᾗ καὶ σὺν τῇ οὐσίᾳ μονοειδῶς εἰς τὸ πρόσω χωρεῖ, τῶν γὰρ οὐσιῶν αἱ ἡλικίαι προποδισμοί τινές εἰσι καὶ ἀναποδισμοί. ὥσπερ οὖν οὐ παραληπτέον χρόνον τὸν τῆς γενέσεως καὶ φθορᾶς, ὅτι μηδὲ ταύτας ἡ ἀπόδειξις περιείληφεν, οὕτως οὐδὲ τὸν τῆς οὐσιώδους αὐξήσεως ἢ μειώσεως. εἰ δὲ ἐξ ἐλάττονος καὶ μείζονος γίγνεσθαι λέγει τὸ ἐναντίον [71b2–4], ἀλλ' ὧν τὸ μέγα καὶ μικρὸν συμβεβηκότα. πάντα γάρ, ὥς φησι Πλωτῖνος [II 6, 1.18–20], τοῖς μὲν συμπληροῖ τὰς οὐσίας, τοῖς δὲ ἐπισυμβαίνει περὶ τὰς οὐσίας· οὐδὲ γὰρ τὸ λευκὸν καὶ μέλαν ἐξ ἀλλήλων τὰ οὐσιώδη.

μα'. – (vii) "Ότι πρὸς τὴν ἑβδόμην [§ 197] [ὅτι] ὁ αὐτὸς ἀπαντήσεται λόγος μὴ συγχωρῶν ἐν τῷ λόγῳ παραλαμβάνεσθαι τὸν τῶν στοιχείων εἰς ἄλληλα κυκλισμόν· οὐσίαι γὰρ τὰ στοιχεῖα, καὶ αἱ εἰδοποιοὶ αὐτῶν διαφοραὶ οὐσιώδεις εἰσί. τί οὖν πράγματα ἔχομεν τὴν πυρὸς ἢ γῆς εἰς ἄλληλα μεταβολὴν ἢ οὐ μεταβολὴν παρεισκυκλοῦντες οὐδεμιᾷ σὺν ἀνάγκῃ; δῆλος γάρ ἐστιν ὁ Σωκράτης καὶ διὰ τῶν παραδειγμάτων ἁπάντων τὴν περὶ τὰς οὐσίας τῶν συμβεβηκότων

---

§ 246. 2 πρώτων Mᶜ: -ως M¹ — 5 ἐκ λευκοῦ] -κ λευκ- in ras., accent. add., Mᶜ
§ 247. 5 ἄν] -ν in ras. Mᶜ — 14 ἀλλήλων μ: ἄλλων M
§ 248. 1 ὅτι² M: del. Wk — 3 εἰδοποιοί Wk: -αὶ M

§ 247. Cf. Ol. 9 § 4.8–11.
15. τὰ οὐσιώδη : the standard classroom examples are the crow and the Ethiopian (Porph., isag. 13.1–2).

accidents in the same substance is evident, first, from all the examples, and secondly from the form of the objection now under discussion [69e6–70a6], viz. whether the soul after being separated from the body is again united with it.

249. (viii) Against the eighth objection [§ 198] we have already pointed out [§§ 215, 225, 237] that it is not necessary for the soul to be stronger than the body, so that thanks to the soul the cycle of opposites can be preserved; the nature of substance in general requires it, even though the soul should be weaker than the body. The body, too, would be joined to another soul, if it had not suffered the loss of its own essence; in fact, it can be animated anew by the kind of soul for which it has not lost its aptitude, since all sorts of animals grow in it. If, however, its elements could be freed from this negative condition, they might receive also another human soul, unless they have already decayed; even body devoid of quality, if it should continue to exist, either as indestructible or as resisting decay for a long stretch of time, can receive a soul again, just as it can receive qualities.

250. (ix) With regard to the ninth [§ 199] we have already said [§ 239] that irrational soul survives and is reincarnated in an earthly body, as long as it can continue to exist, whether always or for a very long time.

251. (x) If we must say something as to the tenth point also [§ 200], we may observe that both Cebes in his objection and Socrates in his reply to it deal with the alternation of opposite accidents in one substance; the substance in this case is the soul and the question is whether it returns to the body after being severed from it, in other words, whether the soul itself is capable of being absent from the body and present in the body by turns.

(V) Summary of the argument

252. The purport of the argument is to show that the soul, once it has been brought forth with its 'instrument' and has for the first time formed a man, from not-man, not from a dead man, will then constitute him again

---

§ 249. 8. τὸ ἄποιον σῶμα: the term comes from the Stoics, who identify it with matter, or substance, as the bearer of qualities (*SVF* III frgs. 320 and 326). The identification is rejected by Plot. II 4, 1.6–14 and by Simpl., *phys.* 227.23–230.33, who cites Proclus' friend Pericles as an isolated champion of this doctrine. In the later Neoplatonists it appears as the intermediate stage between primary matter and fully qualified body. It is the common substratum of the elements (Syr., *met.* 49. 13–15; Pr. *Parm.* 735.34; Ascl.,*met.* 99.11–14; El., *cat.* 199.28–31; Philop., *aet.* 346.7–11; 408.25-409.25), which is devoid of quality, but already three-dimensional (Simpl., *cat.* 120.33; Philop., *aet.* 409.22–23; 426. 21–24); like matter, it is indestructible (cf. Syr. *loc. cit.*; Philop., *aet.* 434.2–4; Dav. 205.34–35; 206.13). It is also called δεύτερον ὑποκείμενον (by Alexander ? see Simpl., *cael.* 599.4–5, with *var. lect.*; further Dam., *princ.* 27.12–28.13; Philop., *aet.* 409.23–24; 426.22–23; also Pr., *Tim.* I 387.12–14,

ἐπανακύκλησιν εἰσηγούμενος | καὶ διὰ τῆς τοῦ ζητουμένου ἐνστάσεως [69e6– (148)
70a6], εἰ διαζευγνυμένη ἡ ψυχὴ πάλιν συζεύγνυται τῷ σώματι.

μβ'. - (viii) Ὅτι πρὸς τὴν ὀγδόην [§ 198] εἴρηται πρότερον [§§ 215, 225, 237] 249
ὡς οὐ χρεία τοῦ εἶναι τὴν ψυχὴν τοῦ σώματος ἰσχυροτέραν πρὸς τὸ δι' αὐτῆς
ἀποσῴζεσθαι τὸν κυκλισμὸν τῶν ἐναντίων, ἀλλ' ἡ κοινὴ τῆς οὐσίας φύσις τοῦτον
ἀπαιτεῖ, καὶ εἰ τοῦ σώματος εἴη ἀσθενεστέρα ἡ ψυχή. καὶ γὰρ τὸ σῶμα συνεζύγη
ἂν ἄλλῃ ψυχῇ, εἰ μὴ ἐπεπόνθει τὴν στέρησιν· πρὸς ἣν γοῦν οὐ πέπονθεν, ψυχοῦται 5
ταύτῃ, φύεται γὰρ ἐν αὐτῷ πολλὰ θηρία. εἰ δὲ τὰ στοιχεῖα καθαρθείη τῆς
στερήσεως, ψυχωθείη ἂν ἄλλῃ ψυχῇ καὶ ἀνθρωπίνῃ, πλὴν εἰ μὴ φθαίη διαφθαρέντα·
ἐπεὶ καὶ τὸ ἄποιον σῶμα, εἰ διαμένοι εἴτε ὡς ἄφθαρτον εἴτε ὡς πολυχρόνιον,
ψυχωθῆναι πάλιν ἐνδέχεται, ὥσπερ καὶ ποιωθῆναι.

μγ'. - (ix) Ὅτι πρὸς τὴν ἐνάτην [§ 199] ἤδη λέλεκται [§ 239] ὡς ἐπιδιαμένει 250
ἡ ἄλογος καὶ πάλιν εἰσκρίνεται εἰς τὸ ὄστρεον, ἕως ἂν δύνηται διαμένειν, εἴτε
ἀεὶ εἴτε ὡς χρόνον ἐπὶ πλεῖστον.

μδ'. - (x) Ὅτι πρὸς τὴν δεκάτην [§ 200], εἴ τι δεῖ καὶ πρὸς ταύτην εἰπεῖν, 251
ἐκεῖνο ῥητέον, ὡς καὶ ἡ ἀπορία τοῦ Κέβητος καὶ ὁ λόγος τοῦ Σωκράτους πρὸς
τὴν ἀπορίαν τὴν περὶ μίαν οὐσίαν τῶν ἐναντίων συμβεβηκότων παρατίθεται
συμβαίνουσαν ἐπανακύκλησιν, οἷον περὶ ψυχήν, εἰ χωρισθεῖσα τοῦ σώματος πάλιν
αὐτῷ πρόσεισιν, ὅ ἐστιν, εἰ αὐτὴ δεκτικὴ παρὰ μέρος ἀπουσίας καὶ παρουσίας 5
τῆς πρὸς τὸ σῶμα.

(V) Συναγωγὴ τοῦ λόγου διὰ βραχέων

με'. - Σκοπὸς μέν ἐστι τῷ λόγῳ τὴν ψυχὴν σὺν τῷ ὀργάνῳ γεννηθεῖσαν καὶ 252
τὸν πρῶτον ἄνθρωπον ἐκ μὴ ἀνθρώπου συστησαμένην, ἀλλ' οὐκ ἐκ τεθνεῶτος,
ἐπιδεῖξαι πάλιν αὐτὸν | ὑποστήσουσαν ἐκ τεθνεῶτος, ἵνα δειχθῇ ἐπιδιαμένουσα (149)

---

§ 248. 8 εἰ Fh: ἢ M
§ 251. 2 ὡς Mᶜ: ὧι M¹

---

where Festugière mistakenly explains it as "la matière entièrement qualifiée"). It is not clear, who revived the term, or why; Proclus, on two separate occasions (*Tim.* I 387.12–14; *mal. subs.* 34.14–24) argues that the κινούμενον πλημμελῶς καὶ ἀτάκτως of *Tim.* 30a4–5 cannot be identified with the ἄποιον σῶμα or δεύτερον ὑποκείμενον, and though in his lengthy account of the *Tim.* passage he does not cite anyone in particular as holding that view, this may well have been the starting-point. To Porphyry (Pr., *Parm.* 1054.5) the subject of the 5th hypothesis is ἀκόσμητον σῶμα (opposed to the σῶμα κεκοσμημένον of the fourth, and followed by ὕλη κεκοσμημένη and ὕλη ἀκόσμητος for the 6th and the 7th); its relation to the κινούμενον πλημμελῶς καὶ ἀτάκτως on the one hand, and to ὕλη κεκοσμημένη on the other, remains unexplained. See Baltes I pp. 151-157.
§ 250. Ol. 10 § 1.19–20; § 5; 9 § 6.6–13.
§ 252. 1–6. Dam. II § 1. Ol. 11 § 1. Cf. *supra* I § 183.

from a dead man, the object being to prove that the soul survives after death; similarly, the purport of the argument from recollection is to show that the soul is prior to the living man and has primary reality, even if it should not survive after death. Against the opinion of the others that the soul is born and dies with the body, Socrates proves by the first argument that it does not die with the body, by the second that it is not born with the body, and the conclusive force of each of the two arguments goes no further than this. As for the first, then, it runs as follows: since soul is an incorporeal substance productive of life in bodies and therefore not subject to loss of life; since, furthermore, in each substance there is the cyclic alternation of contrasting accidents, the accidents themselves remaining the same in kind, the substance remaining numerically the same — if forever, the cycle is infinite and everlasting; if for a maximum period, it completes a maximum number of cyclic changes; if for a short period, a small number; but in any case there will be more than one recurrence, both because this is what manifestly happens and because any substance must be more durable than its own accidents, unless destroyed before its time by unusual violence; — since this is true, as has been shown before, it must necessarily be true of soul also: if the soul is immortal, it will leave the body and return to it sooner or later an infinite number of times, and if it has a life that lasts many ages or at least a long time, or else a short time only, it will continue its cycle of descent and ascent as long as it survives, but at least it will undergo the alternation of opposite accidents several times, as far as this depends on its own staying power. Which was the thing to proved.

II. THE ARGUMENT FROM RECOLLECTION

§§ 253–261. On recollection in general. 72e3–78b3

253. Recollection is an activity, not of an appetitive, but of a cognitive faculty; further, it is not a first, but a second taking in of the object; nor does it occur when memory has remained unbroken, but only after forgetting (for *anamnêsis* really means a renewal of memory, so that it must follow a state of obsolescence, i.e. of forgetting, which is the old age of knowledge); and finally, it cannot take place without recognition, for unless it recalls its object and 'recognizes' it, as we say, there is a first act of cognition, but no recollection.

254. To sum up: recollection is a second cognitive activity of the soul, which, after oblivion, takes up its object again and recognizes it as its own.

9–10. The same assumption above § 234.1–2.

§§ 253–265. In the MS., §§ 262–265 (α'–γ') precede §§ 253–261 (δ'–ιγ'), but this is set right in marginal notes at § 253.1 and § 262.1 (*infra* p. 378). The corrected text runs parallel with Dam. II §§ 4–14.

§ 253. Cf. Dam. II § 4. Ol. 11 § 5.

1. οὐκ ... ὀρεκτικῆς: it does not seem likely that anyone actually expressed

μετὰ θάνατον· ὥσπερ τῷ ἀπὸ τῆς ἀναμνήσεως λόγῳ τὸ δεῖξαι πρὸ τοῦ ἀνθρώπου τοῦ ζῶντος καὶ πρώτως οὖσαν τὴν ψυχήν, καὶ εἰ μὴ ἐπιδιαμένειν μέλλοι μετὰ θάνατον. καὶ γὰρ τῶν ἄλλων οἰομένων καὶ συγγεννᾶσθαι τῷ σώματι τὴν ψυχὴν καὶ συμφθείρεσθαι, ὁ Σωκράτης δείκνυσιν διὰ μὲν τοῦ πρώτου ὅτι οὐ συμφθείρεται, διὰ δὲ τοῦ δευτέρου ὅτι οὐ συγγεννᾶται, καὶ τοσοῦτόν γε ἰσχύει τῶν λόγων ἑκάτερος. ὁ δ' οὖν πρῶτός φησιν· εἰ ἡ ψυχὴ οὐσία ἐστὶν ἀσώματος ζωοποιὸς τῶν σωμάτων καὶ διὰ τοῦτο μὴ πάσχουσα στέρησιν ζωῆς, περὶ δὲ ἑκάστην οὐσίαν ἐπιτελεῖται τῶν ἐναντίων συμβεβηκότων ὁ κυκλισμός, αὐτῶν μὲν κατ' εἶδος, τῆς δὲ οὐσίας κατὰ ἀριθμὸν ὑπομενούσης, εἰ μὲν ἀεί, τὸν ἄπειρον καὶ ἐπ' ἄπειρον χρόνον, εἰ δὲ ἐπὶ χρόνον ὡς πλεῖστον, τὸν πλειστάκις περὶ αὐτὴν κυκλιζόμενον, εἰ δὲ ὀλίγον, τὸν ὀλιγάκις, πάντως δὲ πλεονάκις ἢ ἅπαξ, καὶ διὰ τὸ ἐναργὲς οὕτως ἔχον καὶ διὰ τὸ μονιμωτέραν ἑκάστην οὐσίαν εἶναι τῶν οἰκείων συμβεβηκότων, εἰ μὴ βιαιότερον φθαίη διαφθαρεῖσα· — εἰ δὴ ταῦτα οὕτως ἔχει, ὡς δέδεικται πρότερον, ἀναγκαῖον οὕτως ἔχειν καὶ τὰ περὶ ψυχήν· εἰ μὲν ἀθάνατός ἐστιν, ἀπειράκις ἀπιέναι τε ἀπὸ τοῦ σώματος καὶ ἰέναι πάλιν πρὸς αὐτὸ εἴτε θᾶττον εἴτε βράδιον ἀνακάμπτουσαν, εἰ δὲ μακραίων τις ἢ ἄλλως πολυχρόνιος ἢ καὶ ὀλιγοχρόνιος, ἐφ' ὅσον ἀρκεῖ χρόνον, ἐπὶ τοσοῦτον τῇ καθόδῳ καὶ ἀνόδῳ κυκλιζομένην, πάντως δὲ ὑπομένουσαν τὴν εἰς ἄλληλα τῶν ἐναντίων μεταβολὴν πλεονάκις, ὅσον ἐπὶ τῇ δυνάμει τῆς οἰκείας φύσεως. ὅπερ ἔδει δεῖξαι.

II. THE ARGUMENT FROM RECOLLECTION

§§ 253-261. On recollection in general. 72e3-78b3

δ δ'. — Ὅτι ἡ ἀνάμνησις οὐκ ἔστιν ὀρεκτικῆς, ἀλλὰ γνωστικῆς δυνάμεως 253(151) ἐνέργεια· οὐ μὴν οὐδὲ πρώτη, ἀλλὰ δευτέρα τοῦ γνωστοῦ ἀνάληψις· οὐδὲ σωζομένης ἀδιακόπου τῆς μνήμης, ἀλλὰ μετὰ λήθην (βούλεται γὰρ ἀνανέωσις εἶναι τῆς μνήμης, ὥστε μετὰ παλαίωσιν, ὅ ἐστι λήθη· ἔστι γὰρ ἡ λήθη γνώσεως γῆρας)· ἀλλὰ μὴν οὐδὲ χωρὶς γνωρισμοῦ, εἰ γὰρ μὴ ἀναπολήσειεν τὸ γνωστὸν καὶ ὁ λέγεται γνωρίσειεν, πρώτη γίνεται γνῶσις, ἀλλ' οὐχὶ ἀνάμνησις.

ε'. — Ὅτι συνάγεται ἀνάμνησιν εἶναι ψυχῆς ἐνέργειαν γνωστικὴν δευτέραν 254(152) μετὰ λήθην ἀναλαμβάνουσαν τὸ γνωστὸν καὶ ὡς οἰκεῖον γνωρίζουσαν.

---

§ 252. 5 μέλλοι] -ο- in ras. M¹ — 6 συγγενᾶσθαι M — 14 διὰ Mᶜ: δὶς ut vid. M¹ — 18 τε] -ε in ras. Mᶜ
§§ 253-261. post § 265 habet M
§ 253. 1 ὀρεκτικῆς ... γνωστικῆς Mᶜ: -κὴ ... -κὴ M¹ — 6 γίνεται] γίν- in ras. Mᶜ

---

this opinion; Dam. is leading up to the point of appetitive renewal, discussed in § 255. This means that, though the definition of recollection in § 254 is presented as summing up the results attained in § 253, this section is in reality a comment on the definition.

3. βούλεται : see note on § 151.4.
4-5. Cf. Pl., Phaedr. 276d3-4 εἰς τὸ λήθης γῆρας ἐὰν ἵκηται.

255. In the appetitive faculty, too, there is something analogous to recollection in the cognitive faculty, though there is no word for it: there exists a renewal of virtue after it has been lost.

256. What imperishability is to being and immortality to life, memory is to knowledge. Therefore memory, as the other attributes, exists primarily in intelligence, not, however, in so far as it thinks itself (since the thing remembered is by its very nature an object present in a different subject), but by virtue of the activity by which it preserves forever unchanged the participation in the intelligible reality that is prior to it.

257. Here we must question if the counterpart of being and life is really knowledge, rather than the entire nature of the living being; secondly, if the analogue of the two other attributes mentioned is really memory, rather than the negation of ignorance (for which we have no word), as the others are the negations of death and destruction. Furthermore, even granting that each is a kind of permanence, surely continuance of knowledge, which consists in knowing always the same thing, is different from memory: intelligence constantly knows itself, and yet, as the commentator says [§ 256], it does not remember itself. Besides, memory is characterized by a certain distance from the object, being apprehension and preservation of a kind of imprint of it, as Plato himself says [*Theaet.* 191c8–e1], whereas intelligence is also united forever with the intelligible reality beyond it, even more so than with itself, and instead of an imprint of that reality possesses that reality itself. Therefore there is no memory in intelligence; there is only intellection, not memory of it, except in the measure in which intelligence is separated and exists apart from its prior. Even the commentator himself realizes that memory in the proper sense belongs primarily to souls, because in them having thought is separated from thinking. The first souls, which know no oblivion, evidently have everlasting memory of all things, though their momentary activities extend to different objects at different times.

---

§ 255. To recovery of knowledge corresponds recovery of the right disposition of the appetitive faculty. It does not appear whether its loss is here supposed to result from the downfall of the soul, or to occur in the course of life on earth.

§§ 256–257. On memory cf. Dam., *Phil.* §§ 71 and 158–159, where it is said to exist on all planes, from the divine down to sense-perception; Pr., *Tim.* I 27.2–5. In his commentary on the *Ph.*, Pr. limited memory in the strict sense to soul (§ 257.11–13), and this point is stressed by Dam.

§ 256. Dam. II § 8.3–5. Ol. 11 § 3.6–9. The whole section, including lines 2–4, reports the view of Pr., which is qualified by Dam. in § 257. Cf. Simpl., *cael.* 369.3–5 λέγεται δὲ ἡ μὲν ἀθανασία κατὰ τὸ ἀνέκλειπτον τῆς ζωῆς, ἡ δὲ ἀϊδιότης κατὰ τὸ ἀνέκλειπτον τῆς οὐσίας, ὡς καὶ ἐν τῷ τοῦ Πλάτωνος Φαίδωνι μεμαθήκαμεν. Simpl. omits memory as not relevant to his purpose. The reference is either to Dam.'s commentary or to one by Simpl. himself.

ς'. – Ὅτι ἔστι τι καὶ περὶ τὴν ὀρεκτικὴν δύναμιν τοιοῦτον οἷον ἡ ἀνάμνησις 255 ἦν περὶ τὴν γνωστικήν, εἰ καὶ ἀνώνυμόν ἐστιν· ἔσται γὰρ καὶ ἀρετῆς ἀνανέωσις μετὰ ἀποβολὴν αὐτῆς.

ζ'. – Ὅτι ὅ ἐστι περὶ οὐσίαν ἡ ἀφθαρσία καὶ περὶ ζωὴν ἡ ἀθανασία, τοῦτο 256 περὶ γνῶσιν ἡ μνήμη. διὸ καὶ αὕτη πρώτως ἐν νῷ, καθάπερ αἱ ἄλλαι, οὐ μὴν ὡς ἑαυτὸν νοοῦντι (βούλεται γὰρ τὸ μνημονευτὸν ἄλλο ἐν ἄλλῳ εἶναι), ἀλλ' ὡς ἀεὶ σῴζοντι ἐν ταὐτῷ τὴν μέθεξιν τοῦ πρὸ αὐτοῦ νοητοῦ.

η'. – Ὅτι ἐπιστῆσαι χρὴ εἰ τῇ οὐσίᾳ καὶ τῇ ζωῇ τὴν γνῶσιν ἀντιδιαιρετέον, 257 ἀλλ' οὐχ ὅλην ὁμοῦ τὴν τοῦ ζῴου φύσιν· καὶ δεύτερον εἰ μνήμη ταῖς ἄλλαις ἀναλογεῖ, ἀλλὰ μὴ ἀγνοίας ἀπόφασις, εἰ καὶ ἀνώνυμος, ὡς ἐκεῖ θανάτου καὶ φθορᾶς ἀπόφασις. ἔτι δέ, εἰ καὶ μονιμότης ἑκάστη, ἄλλο ἂν εἴη μονὴ γνώσεως, ἐν τῷ γιγνώσκειν ἀεὶ τὸ αὐτὸ θεωρουμένη, ἄλλο ἡ μνήμη, ἐπεὶ καὶ νοῶν ἑαυτὸν 5 ὁ νοῦς μένει, ἀλλ' ὅμως, ὥς φησιν, οὐ μέμνηται [§ 256]. πρὸς δὲ τούτοις ἐν ἀποστάσει τοῦ γνωστοῦ ἡ μνήμη, τύπου τινὸς αὐτοῦ ἀντίληψις οὖσα καὶ συνοχή, ὡς καὶ αὐτὸς λέγει [Theaet. 191c8–e1]· ὁ δὲ νοῦς καὶ τῷ πρὸ αὐτοῦ νοητῷ ἀεὶ συνήνωται καὶ μᾶλλον ἢ ἑαυτῷ, καὶ οὐκ ἐκείνου τύπον ἔχει, ἀλλ' αὐτὸ ἐκεῖνο. οὐκ ἄρα μνήμη ἐν νῷ· μόνη γὰρ νόησις, ἀλλ' οὐ μνήμη νοήσεως, εἰ μὴ ἄρα κατὰ 10 ἀναλογίαν τῆς ἀπὸ τοῦ πρὸ αὐτοῦ διαστάσεως καὶ ἀποστάσεως. καὶ αὐτὸς δὲ συννοεῖ κυρίως ἐν ψυχαῖς πρώταις εἶναι τὴν μνήμην διὰ τὸ διεζεῦχθαι τοῦ νοεῖν τὸ νενοηκέναι. αἱ δὲ πρῶται ψυχαὶ λήθην οὐκ ἴσχουσαι δῆλον ὡς ἀεὶ μέμνηνται πάντων, εἰ καὶ ἄλλοτε περὶ ἄλλα κατὰ τὸ παρὸν ἐνεργοῦσιν.

§ 255. 2 ἀνώνυμόν Fh: -ός (-ς puncto notatum) M | ἔσται] ἔστι Fh
§ 256. 3 ἐν ἄλλῳ Wk: ὃν ἄλλως M
§ 257. 10 μνήμη ἐν νῷ μ: μνήμηενῶι M^c: μνημησνῶι (?) M¹ | μόνη M¹, accent. eras. M^x (μονὴ Fh) | μνήμη² Fh: μὴν μὴ M

3. βούλεται: see note on § 151.4.
§ 257. Cf. Dam. II § 6. – The intention can hardly be to substitute a series οὐσία-ζωή-ζῷον for the familiar one οὐσία-ζωή-νοῦς. Rather, we have to do with careless wording, the meaning being ἀλλ' οὐχ ὅλην ὁμοῦ τὴν τοῦ ζῴου φύσιν (=ζωή and γνῶσις) τῇ οὐσίᾳ, cf. note on § 31.4–7.
4. ἑκάστη: i.e. imperishability, immortality, memory.
6. ὁ νοῦς μένει: allusion to the etymology μνήμη=μονὴ τοῦ νοῦ (Ol. 11 § 3.4 and note).
8. It is unlikely that Proclus, who is criticized for identifying the constant possession of intelligence with memory, should have made this sharp distinction; therefore Norvin must be right in taking the reference to be to Pl., Theaet. 191c8–e1 θὲς ... ἐν ταῖς ψυχαῖς ἡμῶν ἐνὸν κήρινον ἐκμαγεῖον ... καὶ εἰς τοῦτο ὅτι ἂν βουληθῶμεν μνημονεῦσαι ... ἀποτυποῦσθαι. The next καὶ αὐτός (line 11) of course designates Pr.
10–14. Dam. II § 6.1–5. Ol. 11 § 4.9–13.

258. Where oblivion first occurs, is the beginning of recollection also, since renewal of memory is possible only after loss of it.

259. Knowledge proceeds by degrees: from single intellection, in which all its objects are forever present, to double intellection of things partly present, partly absent; from double to triple intellection, of things present, absent, or lost. Accordingly, knowledge is primary, secondary, or tertiary.

260. Its efficient cause is the God who is the source of all renascence and, in a more divided way, the genius subordinate of him (or, better, a particular God); its exemplary cause is the prototype existing in an intelligence of this kind; its final cause, a renewed endeavor to assimilate oneself to intelligence and, through this, to unite oneself with the Good.

261. The instrumental cause should also have been mentioned: this would be the whole of philosophy.

§§ 262–265. Analysis of the argument. 72e3–77a5

Main points of the argument from recollection

262. Socrates makes five assumptions preliminary to the whole argument: (1) Anyone who recollects anything necessarily has previous knowledge of the thing he recollects [73c1–2]. This point will serve him to prove the major of the hypothetical syllogism; through it the soul will be shown to be pre-existent. — (2) If anyone derives knowledge of one thing from another, this is recollecting the thing of which he gains actual knowledge [73c4–d11]. — (3) Recollection occurs after a state of forgetting brought about either by time or by lack of attention [73e1–3]. — (4) The starting-point of recollection is either a similar object, or one which, though dissimilar, has some relationship with the thing remembered [73e5–74a4]. — (5) When recollection starts from similar objects, it is possible to correct a detail of the copy with the help of the prototype of which it reminded [74a5–8]. These last four points he uses to prove the minor.

---

§ 258. Dam. II § 6.5–6. Ol. 11 § 4.15–16.
1. ὅπου λήθη πρώτως : i.e., of course, in the human soul. On the etymology (Pr.'s ?) cf. Ol. 11 § 3.3.
§ 259. Ol. 11 § 4.9–13.
§§ 260–261. Dam. II §§ 7–11. On the standard list of three causes (final, exemplary, efficient) and three concomitant causes (formal, material, instrumental) see the passages cited at Ol., *Gorg.* 3.24–4.1. In the present instance, Pr. had apparently listed the three main causes only; Dam. adds the instrumental cause in § 261 (II § 11), the material cause in II § 10.
§ 260. 2. κάλλιον δέ τινα θεόν : the ultimate efficient cause is at each level a Demiurge, in this case Dionysus, the guardian of palingenesis (on whose identity see II § 8.1–2). Pr.'s addition καὶ μερικώτερον ὁ ὑπὸ τοῦτον δαίμων relates to the genius in charge of the individual as the immediate cause of his return to transcendent reality, i.e. the εἰληχὼς δαίμων of 107d6–7 or e3–4, who is responsible for the

θ'. - Ὅτι ὅπου λήθη πρώτως, ἐκεῖ καὶ ἀνάμνησις, εἴπερ μετὰ μνήμης 258
ἀποβολὴν ἡ ταύτης ἀνανέωσις.
ι'. - Ὅτι ὁδῷ πρόεισιν ἡ γνῶσις· ἀπὸ τῆς ἀεὶ πάντων παρόντων μιᾶς νοήσεως 259
ἡ διπλῆ, τῶν μὲν παρόντων τῶν δὲ | ἀπόντων· καὶ ἀπὸ τῆς διπλῆς ἡ τριπλῆ, (153)
παρόντων ἀπόντων ἀποβληθέντων. διὸ ἡ μὲν γνῶσις πρώτη, ἡ δὲ δευτέρα,
ἡ δὲ τρίτη.
ια'. - Ὅτι ποιητικὸν μὲν ὁ καὶ τῆς παλιγγενεσίας ὅλης αἴτιος καὶ μερικώτερον 260
ὁ ὑπὸ τοῦτον δαίμων (κάλλιον δέ τινα θεόν)· παραδειγματικὸν δὲ τὸ ἐν νῷ
τῷ τοιούτῳ τούτου παράδειγμα· τελικὸν δὲ ἡ ἀνάληψις τῆς πρὸς νοῦν ὁμοιώσεως,
δι' ἧς καὶ ἡ πρὸς τὸ ἀγαθὸν ἕνωσις.
ιβ'. - Ὅτι ἔδει καὶ τὸ ὄργανον εἰπεῖν· εἴη δὲ ἂν ἡ ὅλη φιλοσοφία. 261

§§ 262-265. Analysis of the argument. 72e3-77a5

Κεφάλαια τοῦ ἐκ τῶν ἀναμνήσεων λόγου (149)
⟨δ⟩ α'. - Ὅτι πέντε ὑποθέσεις προλαμβάνει τοῦ παντὸς λόγου· | α'. τὸν 262(150)
ἀναμιμνησκόμενον προεγνωκέναι τοῦτο πάντως δεῖν οὗ ἀναμιμνήσκεται [73c1-2].
συντελεῖ δὲ αὐτῷ πρὸς τὸ συνημμένον· διὰ τούτου γὰρ ἡ ψυχὴ προϋπάρχουσα
δειχθήσεται. — β'. τὸν ἀπὸ ἄλλου ἄλλου γνῶσιν λαμβάνοντα ἀναμιμνήσκεσθαι
τούτου οὗ τὴν γνῶσιν προὐβάλετο [73c4–d11]. — γ'. τὴν ἀνάμνησιν γίγνεσθαι 5
μετὰ λήθην ἢ τὴν ὑπὸ χρόνου ἢ τὴν ὑπὸ ἀνεπισκεψίας γενομένην [73e1-3].
— δ'. τὴν ἀνάμνησιν γίγνεσθαι ἢ ἀπὸ ὁμοίων ἢ ἀπὸ ἀνομοίων, ἐχόντων δέ τι
πρὸς τὸ ἀναμνηστὸν οἰκεῖον [73e5-74a4]. — ε'. τὸν ἀπὸ ὁμοίων ἀναμιμνησκόμενον
ἔχειν τι διορθοῦσθαι τὴν εἰκόνα ἀπὸ τοῦ πρωτοτύπου οὗ ἡ ἀνάμνησις [74a5-8].
τοῖς δὲ δ' χρῆται πρὸς ἀπόδειξιν τῆς προσλήψεως. 10

---

§ 259. 2 ἀπόντων μ: ἀπὸ τῶν M
§ 260. 2 τὸ Fh: τὸν M
§ 262. 5 τούτου Nv: τοῦτον M — 10 τοῖς in spat. vac. Mᶜ | δ M¹, σι sscr. Mᶜ

---

well-being of the soul in every respect (Pr., Alc. 78.1-6). Dam., however, seems to take the word μερικώτερον to mean, not 'in the case of the individual person,' but 'in relation to the specific issue of revival of memory,' cf. II § 8.3 εἴη δὲ ἂν τι καὶ ἴδιον τῆς γνωστικῆς παλιγγενεσίας. This would necessarily be a universal, and therefore a divine cause.

2-3. ἐν νῷ τῷ τοιούτῳ : i.e. in (an) intramundane intelligence; Dam. II § 7 does not specify (ἐν τῷ νῷ).

3-4. A condensed statement combining the views of Pr. and Dam., cf. II § 9.
§ 261. More fully developed in II § 11.
§ 262. Dam. II § 13. Ol. 11 § 5.
9. ἔχειν τι διορθοῦσθαι : τι, if it is to stand, must be an accus. of respect (cf. Pl. 74a5-6 εἴτε τι ἐλλείπει τοῦτο); otherwise we should have to read τὸν ἀναμιμνησκόμενόν τι ἔχειν διορθοῦσθαι ("when recollection of something starts ..., it is possible to correct the copy ...").

263. What is the gist of the argument? That the soul is stimulated by the sensa to actualize its universal notions, which are there, though undeveloped. For everyone will say that a thing is just or not just, equal or not equal, etc.; now it is impossible, if we did not have certain notions prior to sense-perceptions, to know anything besides the sensa, or to correct them as not true, since we would have no notion of the truth.

264. The syllogisms in logical order

(i) Every human as soon as born — uses sense-perception — acquires notions of the non-sensible from the sensible — either possesses developed knowledge of each thing or possessed it once.

(ii) Every human — either possesses developed knowledge of each thing, or possessed it once and has undeveloped knowledge now — but he does not possess it now, therefore he possessed it once.

(iii) Every human — possessed developed knowledge, but does not possess it now — when receiving knowledge now, recollects.

(iv) Every human — when receiving knowledge, recollects — forgot what he knew — must have known either before birth or during it or after it.

(v) Every human — acquired his knowledge either before birth or during it or after it — neither the second nor the third is true; therefore the first is.

(vi) Every soul before birth — had knowledge of what it learns now — existed before the body.

265. Of these six syllogisms, the first three establish the minor, showing that learning is recollection; the second three the major, by proving that if things learned are things recollected, our souls existed before birth.

§§ 266–273. Various questions concerning the argument. 72e3–77a5

266. Can it not be with souls as it is with individual natures, that they receive their formative principles in the process of coming-to-be? — No; for if souls have these principles as part of their essence, how can they lose them? and if they acquire them by learning, how can they do so during

---

§ 264. Dam. II § 14 (where a' corresponds to $a' + \beta'$ here, and $\beta' + \gamma'$ to γ').
§ 266. Dam. II § 16.

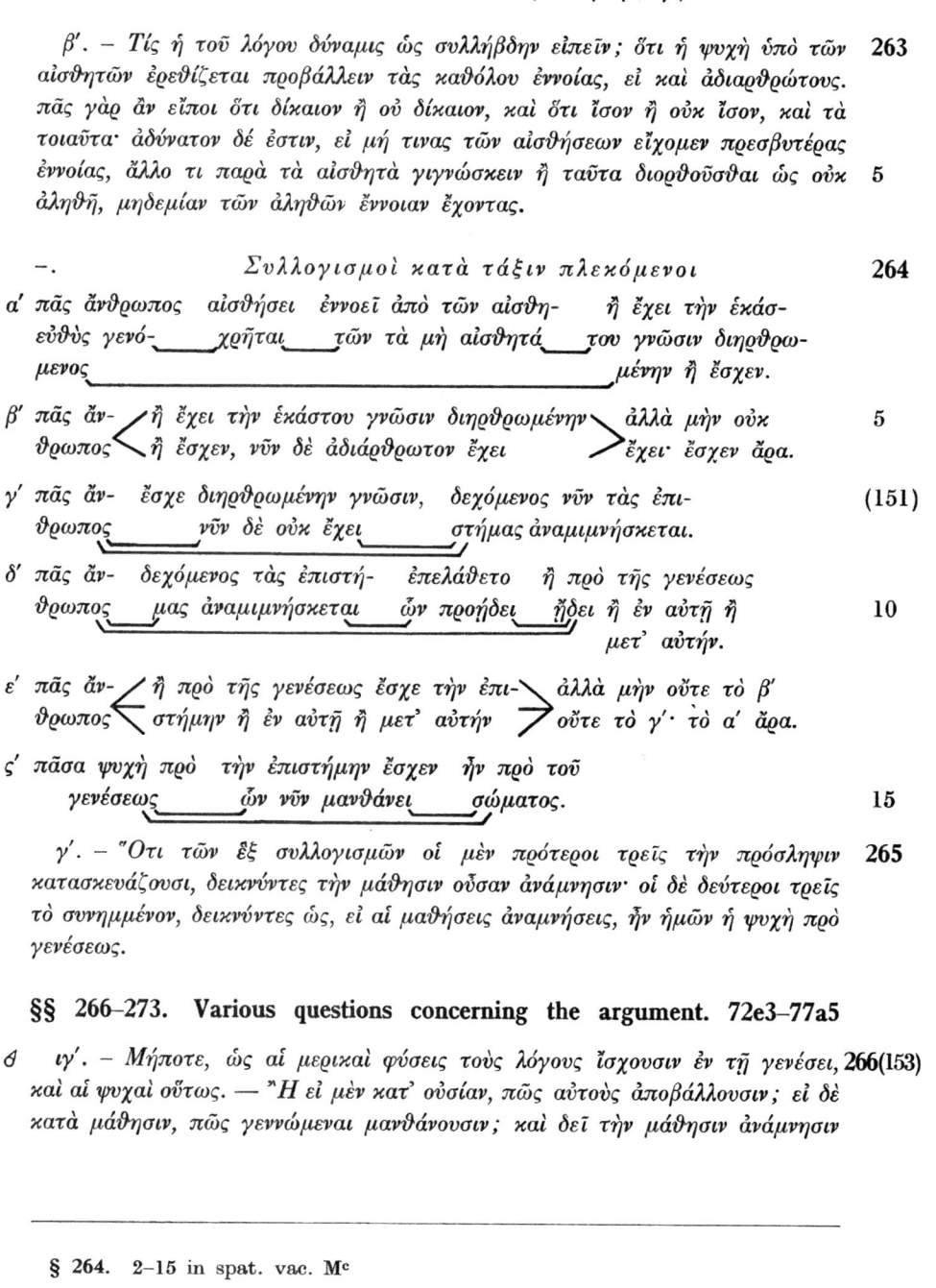

β'. — Τίς ή τοῦ λόγου δύναμις ὡς συλλήβδην εἰπεῖν; ὅτι ή ψυχή ὑπό τῶν 263
αἰσθητῶν ἐρεθίζεται προβάλλειν τὰς καθόλου ἐννοίας, εἰ καὶ ἀδιαρθρώτους.
πᾶς γὰρ ἂν εἴποι ὅτι δίκαιον ἢ οὐ δίκαιον, καὶ ὅτι ἴσον ἢ οὐκ ἴσον, καὶ τὰ
τοιαῦτα· ἀδύνατον δέ ἐστιν, εἰ μή τινας τῶν αἰσθήσεων εἴχομεν πρεσβυτέρας
ἐννοίας, ἄλλο τι παρὰ τὰ αἰσθητὰ γιγνώσκειν ἢ ταῦτα διορθοῦσθαι ὡς οὐκ 5
ἀληθῆ, μηδεμίαν τῶν ἀληθῶν ἔννοιαν ἔχοντας.

—. Συλλογισμοὶ κατὰ τάξιν πλεκόμενοι 264

α' πᾶς ἄνθρωπος αἰσθήσει ἐννοεῖ ἀπὸ τῶν αἰσθη- ἢ ἔχει τὴν ἑκάσ-
εὐθὺς γενό- χρῆται τῶν τὰ μὴ αἰσθητά του γνῶσιν διηρθρω-
μενος μένην ἢ ἔσχεν.

β' πᾶς ἄν- ⟨ ἢ ἔχει τὴν ἑκάστου γνῶσιν διηρθρωμένην ⟩ ἀλλὰ μὴν οὐκ 5
θρωπος ⟨ ἢ ἔσχεν, νῦν δὲ ἀδιάρθρωτον ἔχει ⟩ ἔχει· ἔσχεν ἄρα.

γ' πᾶς ἄν- ἔσχε διηρθρωμένην γνῶσιν, δεχόμενος νῦν τὰς ἐπι- (151)
θρωπος νῦν δὲ οὐκ ἔχει στήμας ἀναμιμνῄσκεται.

δ' πᾶς ἄν- δεχόμενος τὰς ἐπιστή- ἐπελάθετο ἢ πρὸ τῆς γενέσεως
θρωπος μας ἀναμιμνῄσκεται ὧν προῄδει ᾔδει ἢ ἐν αὐτῇ ἢ 10
μετ' αὐτήν.

ε' πᾶς ἄν- ⟨ ἢ πρὸ τῆς γενέσεως ἔσχε τὴν ἐπι- ⟩ ἀλλὰ μὴν οὔτε τὸ β'
θρωπος ⟨ στήμην ἢ ἐν αὐτῇ ἢ μετ' αὐτήν ⟩ οὔτε τὸ γ'· τὸ α' ἄρα.

ς' πᾶσα ψυχὴ πρὸ τὴν ἐπιστήμην ἔσχεν ἣν πρὸ τοῦ
γενέσεως ὧν νῦν μανθάνει σώματος. 15

γ'. — Ὅτι τῶν ἓξ συλλογισμῶν οἱ μὲν πρότεροι τρεῖς τὴν πρόσληψιν 265
κατασκευάζουσι, δεικνύντες τὴν μάθησιν οὖσαν ἀνάμνησιν· οἱ δὲ δεύτεροι τρεῖς
τὸ συνημμένον, δεικνύντες ὡς, εἰ αἱ μαθήσεις ἀναμνήσεις, ἦν ἡμῶν ἡ ψυχὴ πρὸ
γενέσεως.

§§ 266–273. Various questions concerning the argument. 72e3–77a5

δ ιγ'. — Μήποτε, ὡς αἱ μερικαὶ φύσεις τοὺς λόγους ἴσχουσιν ἐν τῇ γενέσει, 266(153)
καὶ αἱ ψυχαὶ οὕτως. — Ἤ εἰ μὲν κατ' οὐσίαν, πῶς αὐτοὺς ἀποβάλλουσιν; εἰ δὲ
κατὰ μάθησιν, πῶς γεννώμεναι μανθάνουσιν; καὶ δεῖ τὴν μάθησιν ἀνάμνησιν

---

§ 264. 2–15 in spat. vac. M^c

---

1. A μερικὴ φύσις is the total of immanent λόγοι in any corporeal unit, organic or anorganic, their monad is universal Nature. Pr., elem. 21 (Dodds pp. 208–209); Tim. III 193.20–22.

birth? Besides, learning must be recollection, and recollection must follow forgetting. Also, what sense is there in their acquiring this knowledge during birth, if they are to lose it after birth? For this much is evident, that children are ignorant from the moment of their birth until well on in age.

267. Perhaps we are born with the common notions implanted in us by nature, as irrational animals have their instincts. — But in that case everybody would have them, whereas in fact many people lose even these, at least a great part of them, through gross ignorance. And how, in that case, can man correct his natural irrational instincts? For the judging faculty, supposing it judges on the basis of reason, must have knowledge of these notions; if it can do so without reason, it must have possessed them and lost them, as critics who judge a literary work, but without remembering the standards by which they judge.

268. Why do we not remember the time together with the facts? — The same often happens in this life: no wonder, then, if after so radical a change the interior forces, i.e. universal notions, should still continue to act upon us, when the external and ever-changing influences have ceased to do so.

269. Why do we not realize, when recollecting, that it *is* recollection? In the present life this awareness comes with recollection itself. — In the first place, even this is not always true (often remembrance presents itself to us as newly acquired knowledge, since remembrance comes about more easily than awareness of it; for self-consciousness is apt to be diverted owing to its constantly varying direction, also because such awareness is attended with reversion upon oneself, while all other knowledge seems to go straight to its object); and there is all the more reason why it should be different after that deep fall the soul has made. Thus sick people, too, sometimes forget what happened to them while in good health, but those in good health are certain to remember what happened during their illness.

270. Why are conscious memories from former lives so rare? — Because conscious perceptions of particular things are external as regards their objects and their origins, while those of universals arise from within and

---

§ 267. Dam. II § 18. On *notiones communes* see the note in Pr., *theol.* vol. I, pp. 159–161 S.-W. In Neoplatonic literature they are spoken of as propositions, not as terms; here, Dam. seems to make no distinction between *notiones communes* and innate forms. When there is question of their being lost, this means becoming inactive or latent; complete loss is impossible, for it would destroy the substance of the soul (Pr., *Rep.* I 23.10–25).

§ 268. Dam. II § 17 and notes.

§ 269. Dam. II § 19. Ol. 12 § 2.15–18.

εἶναι καὶ τὴν ἀνάμνησιν μετὰ λήθην. ἔτι δὲ διὰ τί ἴσχουσιν ἐν τῇ γενέσει τὴν γνῶσιν, μέλλουσαί γε αὐτὴν ἀποβάλλειν μετὰ τὴν γένεσιν; φαίνονται γοῦν ἀμαθεῖς εὐθὺς γεννηθεῖσαι ἕως πόρρω τῆς ἡλικίας.

ιδ'. - Μήποτε φύσει γεννώμεθα τὰς κοινὰς ἐννοίας ἔχοντες, ὡς τὰ ἄλογα 267 τὰς ὁρμάς. — Ἢ ἔδει πάντας ἔχειν αὐτάς· πολλοὶ δὲ καὶ ταύτας ἀποβάλλουσι διὰ πολλὴν ἀμαθίαν ἢ πλείστας αὐτῶν. πῶς δὲ ἄνθρωπος διορθοῦται τὰς φυσικὰς καὶ ἀλόγους ὁρμάς; ὁ γὰρ κριτής, εἰ μὲν μετὰ λόγου κρίνοι, ἔχει τὴν ἐπιστήμην· εἰ δὲ ἄνευ λόγου, ἔχων ἀπέβαλεν, ὡς οἱ κρίνοντες λόγον ῥητορικόν, οὐκέτι δὲ μεμνημένοι τῶν καθ' οὓς κρίνουσι κανόνων.

ιε'. - Διὰ τί μὴ συναναφέρομεν τὸν χρόνον; — Ἢ καὶ ἐν τῷδε τῷ βίῳ 268 πολλάκις τοῦτο πάσχομεν· τί οὖν θαυμαστόν, εἰ καὶ τοσαύτης μεταβολῆς γινομένης ἔτι τὰ ἔνδον ὄντα δρᾷ εἰς ἡμᾶς, οἷα τὰ καθόλου, τὰ δὲ ἐκτὸς οὐκέτι καὶ ὄντα ἄλλοτε ἄλλα;

ις'. - Διὰ τί ἀναμιμνησκόμενοι οὐκ ἐφιστάνομεν ὅτι ἀναμιμνησκόμεθα; καὶ 269 γὰρ ἐν τῷδε τῷ βίῳ πρόσεστι τοῦτο τῇ ἀνα|μνήσει. — Ἢ μάλιστα μὲν οὐδὲ (154) τοῦτο ἀεί (πολλάκις γὰρ ἀναμνησθέντες ὅμως οἰόμεθα πρώτην ποιεῖσθαι τὴν γνῶσιν, ῥᾷον γάρ τινος ἀνάμνησις γίνεται ἢ ἐπίστασις τῆς ἀναμνήσεως· ἐκκρούεται γὰρ τὸ προσεκτικὸν ὡς ἄλλοτε πρὸς ἄλλοις ἀεὶ γιγνόμενον, διότι καὶ μετὰ ἐπιστροφῆς ἡ ἐπίστασις, ἡ δὲ ἄλλη γνῶσις οἷον κατὰ εὐθυωρίαν)· ἄλλως τε καὶ τῆς ψυχῆς πτῶμα τηλικοῦτον πιπτούσης. καὶ γὰρ οἱ μὲν νοσοῦντες ἐπιλανθάνονται ἐνίοτε τῶν ἐν τῇ ὑγείᾳ, οἱ δὲ ὑγιαζόμενοι τῶν ἐν τῇ νόσῳ μέμνηνται πάντως.

ιζ'. - Διὰ τί σπάνιοι αἱ τῆς προβιοτῆς ἐπιστάσεις; — Ἢ ὅτι ἀλλοτρίων εἰσὶ 270 καὶ ἀπὸ ἀλλοτρίων αἱ τῶν μερικῶν ἐπιστάσεις, αἱ δὲ τῶν καθόλου ἔνδοθεν

---

§ 268. 3 ἔνδον] mg. ins. M¹
§ 269. 8 τῶν¹ μ: τῶι M
§ 270. 1 σπάνιοι] accent. add., -νι- in ras., Mᶜ

---

1. ἐφιστάνειν, with the cognate nouns ἐπίστασις and ἐπιστασία, is mostly used of awareness of external facts or objects (Pr., Rep. II 353.28–29; Tim. I 348.6; III 9.2–3; 58.24; 85.24; dec. dub. 55.24); application to self-consciousness in the present text and its parallels (see indices) is exceptional and incidental. For ἐπιστασία (§ 270.3) cf. dec. dub. 9.2; elsewhere in Pr. it is always 'control, supervision' (so, too, Plot. IV 9, 4.4); Pr., Parm. 74.20–26k.
5. τὸ προσεκτικόν: see note on § 271.
6–9. Dam. II § 17.2–6. Cf. Ol. 12 § 2.8–18.
§ 270. Dam. II § 20. Also Pr., Rep. II 350.15–22.

are our own and at the same time present themselves to our consciousness with a less strong impact because they are familiar and not strange. Besides, those of universals are more numerous.

271. What is that which remembers that it remembers? — It is a faculty by itself beside all the others, which always acts as a kind of witness to some one of the others, as conscience to the appetitive faculties, as self-consciousness to the cognitive ones. Therefore it is not surprising that we should remember without being aware of it, just as we sometimes read without realizing the fact.

3. ἀπληκτότεραι πρὸς ἐπιστασίαν: cf. Pr., dec. dub. 46.12–13 πληττούσας αὐτῶν τὴν ἐπίστασιν and Crat. 37.2–3 πληρούντων δ' ἀπλήκτως καὶ ἀναφῶς τὴν ἀκοὴν τῆς οἰκείας γνώσεως.
4. πλείους αἱ τῶν καθόλου: see note on II § 5.
§ 271. Dam. II § 21. Προσοχή, apart from its current meaning of 'attention' generally, appears in Stoic terminology in the moral sense of 'supervision of one's own thoughts and actions': SVF III frg. 111; Epict., man. 33,6 and esp. diss. IV 12 (Περὶ προσοχῆς); also in Plut., prof. in virt. 12, 83B; de garr. 23, 514E. Προσεκτικόν in the corresponding sense Epict., frg. 27. Instances of προσοχή meaning 'awareness, observation' of any object: Atticus cited by Pr., Tim. II 306.1 [=frg. 36]; Iambl., myst. 133.3. Only in late Neoplatonism (from Pr. onward?) are the words used in the context of a theory of self-consciousness. It is stated most explicitly by Steph., an. 462–467 (cf. also 555.11–17). The terminological distinction made here by Dam. is formulated at 465.11–16: τοῦτο γὰρ τὸ προσεκτικὸν διὰ πάντων φοιτᾷ τῶν δυνάμεων, καὶ τῶν γνωστικῶν καὶ τῶν ζωτικῶν. ἀλλ' εἰ μὲν διὰ τῶν γνωστικῶν φοιτᾷ, λέγεται προσεκτικόν, ὅθεν ὅτε κατὰ τὰς γνωστικὰς ἐνεργείας ῥεμβομένῳ τινὶ θέλομεν ἐπιπλῆξαι, φαμὲν αὐτῷ 'πρόσεχε σαυτῷ'· εἰ δὲ διὰ τῶν ζωτικῶν χωρεῖ, λέγεται συνειδός, ὅθεν ἡ τραγῳδία φησὶν 'ἡ σύνεσις, ὅτι σύνοιδα ἐμαυτῷ δεινὰ εἰργασμένῳ' (Eurip., Or. 396). Ol., Alc. 23.16–17 should be corrected accordingly: ἰστέον δὲ ὅτι τοῦ συνειδότος τὸ μὲν ἐπὶ ταῖς γνωστικαῖς ἡμῶν δυνάμεσι λέγεται ⟨προσεκτικόν, τὸ δὲ ἐπὶ ταῖς ὀρεκτικαῖς δυνάμεσι λέγεται⟩ συνειδὸς ὁμωνύμως τῷ γένει (the quotation from Euripides occurs just before at lines 10–13; that συνειδός has become the comprehensive term may be a mistake of Ol., who in this passage is dealing with conscience). – Stephanus is explaining Ar., an. III 2, 425b16 ff., which tries to determine the subject that is aware of any act of sense-perception as such. According to Plutarch of Athens, this is opinion (δόξα), the "newer commentators", however, argue that the ego should be the same for any act of the mind, otherwise the unity of the person would be lost; now since opinion can never perform an act proper to intelligence, the faculty of self-observation, while active at all levels, must belong to the highest (rational) level of the soul. – In Pr., the subject is rarely touched upon; his fullest discussion of it occurs, in a lengthy parenthesis, Parm. 957.28–958.11: καὶ γὰρ ἄλλως τῆς ἀκοῆς τὰ ἀκουστά, καὶ τῆς κοινῆς αἰσθήσεως ἄλλως πρὸ τούτων τὰ αἰσθητὰ πάντα· πρὸ ταύτης πάλιν ἄλλως ὁ λόγος καὶ ταῦτα καὶ τὰ ἄλλα γιγνώσκει ὅσα μὴ αἴσθησις. καὶ αὖ πάλιν τῆς ἐπιθυμίας ἄλλων ὀρεγομένης, τοῦ θυμοῦ δὲ ἄλλων ἐφιεμένου καὶ τῆς προαιρέσεως εἰς ἄλληλα (read ἄλλα) κινούσης, ἔστι τις μία ζωὴ πρὸς πάντα ταῦτα κινοῦσα τὴν ψυχήν, δι' ἣν φαμεν 'ἐγὼ ἐπιθυμῶ' καὶ 'ἐγὼ θυμοῦμαι' καὶ 'ἐγὼ προαιροῦμαι'·

ἐγείρονται καὶ εἰσὶν ἡμέτεραι καὶ ἅμα ἀπληκτότεραι πρὸς ἐπιστασίαν διὰ τὸ οἰκεῖαι εἶναι καὶ μὴ ξενίζειν. ἄλλως δὲ πλείους αἱ τῶν καθόλου.

ιη'. - Τί τὸ ἀναμιμνησκόμενον ὅτι ἀναμιμνήσκεται; — Ἡ ἄλλη δύναμις παρὰ 271 τὰς ἄλλας ἁπάσας, ἀεί γέ τινι τῶν ἄλλων οἷον ἐπιμαρτυροῦσα, ὡς μὲν συνειδὸς ταῖς ὀρεκτικαῖς, ὡς δὲ προσεκτικὸν ταῖς γνωστικαῖς. διόπερ οὐ θαυμαστὸν εἰ καὶ ἀναμιμνησκόμενοι οὐκ ἐφιστάνομεν, ὥσπερ οὐδὲ ἀναγιγνώσκοντες ἐνίοτε.

§ 271. 1 ἢ Mᶜ: ἡ M¹

συνεπινεύει γὰρ ἐκείνη πάσαις καὶ συζῇ μετὰ πασῶν, οὖσα δύναμις ὁρμητικὴ πρὸς πᾶν ὀρεκτόν. καὶ δὴ καὶ πρὸ τούτων ἀμφοτέρων ἔστι τῆς ψυχῆς ἕν, ὃ δὴ λέγει πολλάκις 'ἐγὼ αἰσθάνομαι' καὶ 'ἐγὼ λογίζομαι' καὶ 'ἐγὼ ἐπιθυμῶ' καὶ 'ἐγὼ βούλομαι', καὶ παρακολουθοῦν πάσαις ταύταις ταῖς ἐνεργείαις καὶ συνεργοῦν αὐταῖς· ἢ οὐκ ἂν ἐγιγνώσκομεν πάσας οὐδ' ἂν εἴποιμεν ὅτῳ διαφέρουσι μὴ ἑνός τινος τοῦ γιγνώσκοντος πάσας ἀμεροῦς ὄντος ἐν ἡμῖν, ὃ δὴ καὶ ἐπὶ τῆς κοινῆς αἰσθήσεως καὶ πρὸ δόξης καὶ πρὸ ἐπιθυμίας καὶ πρὸ βουλήσεως ὂν καὶ τὰς ἐκείνων οἶδε γνώσεις καὶ τὰς ὀρέξεις αὐτῶν ἀμερῶς συνήρηκεν, ἐφ' ἑκάστῳ λέγον τὸ 'ἐγὼ' καὶ τὸ 'ἐνεργῶ'. In this passage, the question of self-consciousness is subordinate to that of the identity of the subject, the main point being that all our appetitive functions have one common subject, and so have all our functions, cognitive or appetitive, taken together; self-consciousness appears only as the evidence of this identity. The ego is indivisible and comprises without partition all our knowledge and impulses. - In the extant work of Pr., there is no theory of self-consciousness as a separate faculty, nor are the terms προσοχή or προσεκτικόν found in this sense; but προσοχή does appear in four closely related extracts from Pr., all in some way connected with Psellus, viz.: (1) Extracts from the commentary on the Chaldean Oracles, p. 211.1-4 Des Places οὐ γάρ ἐσμεν νοῦς μόνον, ἀλλὰ καὶ διάνοια καὶ δόξα καὶ προσοχὴ καὶ προαίρεσις, καὶ πρὸ τῶν δυνάμεων τούτων οὐσία μία τε καὶ πολλὴ καὶ μεριστή τε καὶ ἀμερής. (2) Extracts from the commentary on Plotinus, Byz. Zeitschr. 52, 1959, 7, § 16 περὶ δὲ τοῦ ζητοῦντος ἀκριβούμενος, τὸ μὲν δὴ ζητοῦν, φησίν, ἐν ἡμῖν ἡ διάνοια, τὸ δὲ παρακολουθοῦν ὅτι ζητεῖ τὸ προσεκτικὸν μέρος τῆς ψυχῆς ἄνω καὶ κάτω φερόμενον, ⟨ὃ⟩ καὶ πάσαις συντάττεται ταῖς ἐν ἡμῖν ζωαῖς. (3) Psellus, omnif. doctr. 63-62: (63.2) μέσαι δυνάμεις εἰσὶ τῆς ψυχῆς προσοχὴ καὶ προαίρεσις... (6–10) προσοχὴ δέ ἐστι καθ' ἣν προσέχομεν τοῖς ἔργοις οἷς πράττομεν καὶ τοῖς λόγοις οἷς λέγομεν· αὕτη γαρ ποτὲ μὲν τὰ τῆς ψυχῆς ἤθη ἀνασκοπεῖται τίνα τέ ἐστι καὶ πῶς ἔχει πρὸς ἄλληλα, ποτὲ δὲ αὖ τὸ ζῷον θεωρεῖ τί πράττει καὶ πῇ παραβαίνει καὶ τί ἐλλείπει. (4) Psellus, cod. Sinait. 1864, f. 166ᵛ: οὕτω μὲν οὖν τριμερὴς καὶ οὕτω τριδύναμος παρὰ τοῖς φιλοσόφοις ὠνόμασται· εἰ δὲ μὴ κατὰ τὸ μέτρον ὧν ἔχει μερῶν ἢ δυνάμεων κἀκεῖνοι ταύτην διηριθμήσαντο, ἀλλὰ τὸ φανταστικὸν ἀφέντες, τὸ διανοητικόν, τὸ φυσικόν, τὴν προσοχήν, τὴν συνείδησιν, τἆλλα, τῷ λογιστικῷ ταύτην καὶ θυμικῷ καὶ ἐπιθυμητικῷ διῃρήκασι, θαυμάζειν οὐ χρή. - The "newer commentators" of Stephanus cannot be identified: though traces of the doctrine are found in Pr., Dam. and Ol., for none of them is a commentary on the De anima attested. Note that Ol. seems to have taken his information directly from Pr. or Dam., for Ammonius' classification of faculties (Philop., an. 1.5-9.2) does not include the προσεκτικόν.

4. Cf. Plotinus' famous example, I 4, 10.24-26.

272. Do irrational animals also have recollection? — If they forget a thing after having had a memory of it and then get knowledge of it again, there is a renewal of memory, but no awareness of it; for this is reserved for a soul that can revert upon itself.

273. There are as many kinds of recollection as of knowledge: intellective, as in the *Phaedrus* [249b6–c6]; discursive, as in the *Meno* [81c5–d5]; and on the level of opinion, as in the case of those who recollect former lives.

§ 274. The forms referred to at 74a9–77a5

274. We do not judge particulars by themselves; for such as we apprehend them, they are faulty, and we are aware of their faultiness. Nor do we measure them by the standard of what is common in them; for the common elements in faulty particulars are themselves faulty, since their being rests precisely on the faulty particulars. Neither can concepts deduced from these common elements by abstraction serve, since abstraction starting from faulty data will lead to faulty notions. Necessarily, therefore, the standards must be prior to the things judged. A first possibility is that they exist in nature; nature, however, is itself matter-bound, and it does not produce forms with a clearly defined essence, being divided and corporeal. Prior to nature we must assume soul as a self-moved cause, whereas nature is moved from outside: accordingly, forms in the soul are prior to those in nature; and then, beyond self-moved forms we have immovable forms. But those that are proper to us and closest to us are easiest to set in motion, and from the objects of sense-perception the transition to these is a more gradual one; indeed, it is only through these that with patience and toil we pass on to intelligible forms. For this reason Socrates here shows us the way up from things sensible to forms in soul through recollection. That this is what he intends to do appears from the fact that he calls the 'substance' of these forms 'our own' [76e1].

---

§ 272. Dam. II § 22. Ol. 11 § 4.16–18. Further, the direct quotation from Pr. on the *Ph.* in Elias, *isag.* 2.10–25, printed in the note on Ol.

2. ἀνανεοῦται τὴν μνήμην: i.e. ἀναμιμνήσκεται, according to the definition of § 253.3–4.

§ 273. Dam. II § 23. Cf. the division of memory Dam., *Phil.* §§ 71 and 159: ἄλογος (φανταστική, αἰσθητική), λογική (διανοητική, δοξαστική), νοερά (οὐσιώδης, θεία).

§ 274. Dam. II § 15. Cf. Ol. 12 § 1.2–3. The same question "What forms are meant?" is asked again in connection with the argument from similarity (78d1–7) at I § 330 (II § 35; Ol. 13 § 5).

1–6. Cf. Hermias 171.8–13 δεῖ γὰρ τὸν ἄνθρωπον δύνασθαι ... ἀπὸ τῶν ἐν τοῖς

ιθ'. — *Ἆρα καὶ τὰ ἄλογα ἀναμιμνήσκεται; — Ἤ εἰ ἐπιλήθεται μετὰ μνήμην, 272
εἶτα πάλιν γιγνώσκει, ἀνανεοῦται τὴν μνήμην, οὐ μὴν καὶ ἐφιστάνει· τοῦτο γὰρ
ἤδη ψυχῆς ἐπιστρεφούσης εἰς ἑαυτήν.

κ'. — Ὅτι τοσαῦται αἱ ἀναμνήσεις κατὰ εἶδος, ὅσαι αἱ γνώσεις· νοερά, ὡς 273
ἐν Φαίδρῳ [249b6–c6]· διανοητική, ὡς ἐν Μένωνι [81c5–d5]· δοξαστική, ὡς
ἐπὶ τῶν ἀναμιμνησκομένων τῆς προβιοτῆς.

§ 274. The forms referred to at 74a9–77a5

δ κα'. — Ὅτι οὐ τὰ καθ' ἕκαστα δι' ἑαυτῶν αὐτὰ κρίνομεν· ἐσφαλμένα γὰρ 274
ταῦτα καταλαμβάνομεν, καὶ ὅτι ἔσφαλται ταῦτα καταλαμβάνομεν. ἀλλ' οὐδὲ
πρὸς τὰ ἐν τούτοις κοινὰ ἀναφέρομεν· τὰ γὰρ τῶν ἐσφαλμένων κοινὰ καὶ αὐτὰ
ἐσφαλμένα, | ἐν αὑτοῖς ἔχοντα τὸ εἶναι τοῖς ἐσφαλμένοις. οὐ τοίνυν οὐδὲ τὰ (155)
ὑστερογενῆ· τῶν γὰρ ἐσφαλμένων ἡ ἀφαίρεσις ἐσφαλμένα παρέχεται. ἀνάγκη 5
ἄρα τοὺς κανόνας εἶναι πρὸ τῶν κρινομένων. ἤτοι οὖν ἐν τῇ φύσει· ἔνυλος δὲ
καὶ ἡ φύσις, καὶ οὐκ ἀκριβοῖ τὴν τῶν εἰδῶν οὐσίαν ἅτε μεριστὴ καὶ σωματοειδής.
ὥσπερ δὲ πρὸ τῆς φύσεως ἀνάγκη τὴν ψυχὴν ὑποτίθεσθαι ὡς αὐτοκίνητον
ἑτεροκινήτου, οὕτω καὶ τὰ τῆς ψυχῆς εἴδη τῶν φυσικῶν προγενέστερα· καὶ δὴ
καὶ πρὸ τῶν αὐτοκινήτων τὰ ἀκίνητα. κινεῖται δὲ πρῶτα ἐν ἡμῖν τὰ οἰκεῖα 10
καὶ προσεχῆ καὶ ἡ ἀπὸ τῶν αἰσθητῶν μετάβασις εἰς ταῦτα συμμετροτέρα·
καὶ γὰρ διὰ τούτων εἰς τὰ νοητὰ μεταβαίνομεν ὀψέ ποτε καὶ μόλις. ὅθεν δὴ
καὶ ὁ Σωκράτης εἰς τὰ ψυχικὰ ἡμᾶς ἀνάγει ἐν τούτοις ἀπὸ τῶν αἰσθητῶν
δι' ἀναμνήσεως. καὶ δῆλός ἐστι τοῦτο ποιῶν· 'ἡμετέραν' γὰρ εἶναί φησι τὴν
τῶν εἰδῶν τούτων οὐσίαν [76e1]. 15

---

§ 273. 1 νοερά Fh: -αί M
§ 274. 2 ὅτι] in ras. M^c — 5 ὑστερογενῆ] ὑστε- in ras. M^c — 11 συμμετρωτέρα M

καθέκαστα κατατεταγμένων κοινοτήτων συναθροίζειν τῇ διανοίᾳ ἀπὸ τοῦ ἐν τῷ Σωκράτει
καὶ Πλάτωνι καὶ τῶν ὁμοίων κοινοῦ τὸ καθόλου τὸ ὑστερογενές, καὶ ἀπὸ τούτων προβαλεῖν
τὰ κατ' οὐσίαν ἐνυπάρχοντα τῇ ψυχῇ καθόλου, δι' ὧν ὡς εἰκόνων ἀναμνησθήσεται τῶν
ἐν τῷ νοητῷ εἰδῶν. The process is, accordingly: (1) observation of common elements
in individuals; (2) formation of a universal concept from these; (3) confrontation
of the concept *a posteriori* with the form that exists in the soul *a priori*; (4) reduction
of the form in the soul to transcendent form.
5. ὑστερογενές : the word in the general meaning of 'posterior in the order of
being' is as old as Ar., *met.* N 4, 1091a33; cf. e.g. Porphyry, *isag.* 21.14; Iambl.,
comm. math. 42.16. Of general concepts, as opposed to individuals on the one hand,
to pre-existent forms on the other: Syr., *met.* 7.22; 29.23; 35.32; 53.9; etc.; Hermias
171.11; 15; 20; Pr., *Eucl.* 14.21; 15.1; 18; *Tim.* II 151.20; *Rep.* I 260.21; 28.

§§ 275-292. Extracts from Plutarch on recollection. 72e3-77a5

From Plutarch of Chaeronea

275. The object of knowledge is not its cause, as Arcesilaus said, for in this way ignorance itself will become the cause of knowledge.

276. It is not the soul that turns itself towards the apprehension of reality and towards error, as the Stoics hold [*SVF* II 846]; for how can the soul become the cause of knowledge and ignorance to itself even before it possesses them?

277. To Plato alone the explanation presents no problem at all, since he reduces knowledge and ignorance to oblivion and recollection.

278. Knowledge of things is present within us, but it is hidden by other extraneous elements, as the writing on the tablet of Demaratus.

279. Both our seeking and our finding prove the fact of recollection: no one can search for a thing he has never thought of, nor find such a thing, at least by seeking; of course the word finding is also used for a chance discovery.

280. To answer the problem raised in the *Meno* [80d5–e5], whether it is possible to seek and to find (we cannot seek for what we know already, because this is pointless, nor for what we do not know, because even if we chance upon it, we fail to distinguish it from any other object), the Peripatetics have invented the 'potential intellect' — however, we set the

---

§§ 275-292. Dam. II § 28. Dübner (*Plutarchi Opera*, ed. Didot., vol. V pp. 11-15) and Bernardakis (*Plutarchi Moralia* VII pp. 28-36) print §§ 275-310 (plus II § 28) as fragments of Plutarch Περὶ ψυχῆς. However, §§ 298-310, which make sense only in a running commentary, are obviously out of the question. Finckh and Norvin regard only I §§ 275-292 (and II § 28) as extracts from Plutarch; Sandbach (*Plutarchus, Moralia* VII pp. 133-138=frgs. 215-217) adds §§ 293 and 294 marked with an asterisk. So much is certain, that §§ 293-297 no longer fall under the heading Παρὰ τοῦ αὐτοῦ συστάσεις ἕτεραι, since in Dam. II the corresponding sections occur in the reverse order: first §§ 24-27 (I §§ 293-297), then § 28 (I §§ 275-292); in other words, the group of sections headed in the present edition "A few questions and observations" precedes the extracts from Plut. in Dam. II. Yet in §§ 293-297 there is so much that reminds of Plutarch (see notes below; in particular, the point of § 294 is listed as Plutarch's in II § 28.9) that pure coincidence is hardly possible. It was therefore already Pr. or Dam. (or an even earlier commentator) who, after using some material from Plutarch, then appended a survey of his arguments. The lecture mark at § 288 shows that the extracts are not a later addition to Dam., but part of his commentary; in the controversial sections (I § 297, II §§ 25 and 27) there are also references to Proclus. The insertion might even go back as far as Plutarch of Athens, or Porphyry. However, even if it is no earlier than Dam., the double condensation process, first by Dam., then by the *reportator*, makes it pointless to look for stylistic criteria and such details as the avoidance of hiatus, as Ziegler does (*RE*, art. *Plutarch*, vol. 21, 752-753); his conclusion that the fragments might be notes jotted down by Plutarch for future use cannot be right, since the

§§ 275-292. Extracts from Plutarch on recollection. 72e3-77a5

'Εκ τῶν τοῦ Χαιρωνέως

κβ'. - Ὅτι οὐ τὸ ἐπιστητὸν αἴτιον τῆς ἐπιστήμης, ὡς Ἀρκεσίλαος· οὕτω 275
γὰρ καὶ ἡ ἀνεπιστημοσύνη τῆς ἐπιστήμης αἰτία φανεῖται.

κγ'. - Ὅτι οὐχ ἡ ψυχὴ τρέπει ἑαυτὴν εἰς τὴν τῶν πραγμάτων κατάληψιν καὶ 276
ἀπάτην κατὰ τοὺς ἀπὸ τῆς Στοᾶς [SVF II 846]· πῶς γὰρ αἰτία ἑαυτῇ γνώσεως
ἡ ψυχὴ καὶ ἀγνοίας, μήπω αὐτὰς ἔχουσα ἀρχήν;

κδ'. - Ὅτι μόνῳ τῷ Πλάτωνι ῥᾷστον ἀποδοῦναι τὸν λόγον, εἰς λήθην καὶ 277
ἀνάμνησιν ἀναφέροντι τὴν γνῶσιν καὶ τὴν ἄγνοιαν.

κε'. - Ὅτι ἔνεισιν μὲν αἱ ἐπιστῆμαι, κρύπτονται δὲ ὑπὸ τῶν ἄλλων ἐπεισοδίων 278
ὁμοίως τῇ ὑπὸ Δημαράτου πεμφθείσῃ δέλτῳ.

κς'. - Ὅτι καὶ τὸ ζητεῖν καὶ τὸ εὑρίσκειν δηλοῖ τὴν ἀνάμνησιν· οὔτε γὰρ 279
ζητήσειεν ἄν τις οὗ ἐστιν ἀνεννόητος οὔτε ἀνεύροι, διά γε ζητήσεως· λέγεται
γὰρ εὑρίσκειν καὶ ὁ κατὰ περίπτωσιν.

κζ'. - Ὅτι ἀπόρου ὄντος εἰ οἷόν τε ζητεῖν καὶ εὑρίσκειν, ὡς ἐν Μένωνι 280 (156)
[80d5-e5] προβέβληται (οὔτε γὰρ ἃ ἴσμεν, μάταιον γάρ, οὔτε ἃ μὴ ἴσμεν,
κἂν γὰρ περιπέσωμεν αὐτοῖς, ἀγνοοῦμεν ὡς τοῖς τυχοῦσιν), οἱ μὲν [γὰρ]
Περιπατητικοὶ τὸν δυνάμει νοῦν ἐπενόησαν· — ἡμεῖς δὲ ἠπορίοῦμεν ἀπὸ τοῦ

---

§ 279. 2 fort. ἂν εὕροι
§ 280. 3 γὰρ² M: del. Wk

Neoplatonists would hardly have had that kind of material at their disposal. – The work from which they were taken must have been a dialogue, certainly not a running commentary. Everything points to this: the wealth of examples, stories and anecdotes; the type of argument (etymology, §§ 281 and 283, also in the Stobaeus frgs. 177-178; incidental observations, §§ 291-292); the lively presentation, § 290. All this fits very well with the Περὶ ψυχῆς (frgs. 173-178), which according to Origen was full of miraculous stories. Some kind of discussion of the reasons for believing in immortality would be almost inevitable in it, though a different, otherwise unknown dialogue remains possible. – The new heading at § 288 does not necessarily indicate a new series of extracts, it may simply be due to the fact that a new lecture begins here. The order of the items differs from II § 28, and is therefore arbitrary in at least one of the two versions, possibly in both.

§ 275. τοῦ Χαιρωνέως: cf. Introd. Ol. p. 10, n. 9.
1. Arcesilaus may have adopted this view in opposing the Stoic doctrine of συγκατάθεσις, cf. Sext. Emp., adv. dogm. 7,153-157.
§ 276. The passage figures in SVF II as frg. 846. There is, however, nothing else closely resembling the present statement, which may well be Plutarch's own inference from the doctrine of κατάληψις, in which Sextus (adv. dogm. 8,397 = SVF II frg. 91) distinguishes a passive element (the φαντασία presented to us) and an active one (our assent). The latter being decisive, Plutarch concludes that 'the soul turns itself towards the apprehension of reality and towards error.'
§ 278. Herod. 7,239,4.
§ 280. 1-3. Dam. II § 28 η' (14-15).
3-4. Ar., an. III 4, 429a15-18.

problem in terms of actual knowledge and actual ignorance; even granting that potential intellect exists, the question remains the same: how does it apprehend? Surely the object can be only a known or an unknown one. The Stoics, on the other hand, use natural notions as an explanation — but if these are to be thought of as potential, the same answer will apply; if as actual, why do we seek for what we know already? Or, if we start from them to find other unknowns, how can we identify what we do not already know? The Epicureans, finally, appeal to 'preconceptions' — if, by this, they mean fully developed notions, seeking is superfluous; if undeveloped ones, what motive do we have to search for something else in addition to those preconceptions, something of which we do not have a preconception at all?

281. The very word *alêtheia* ('truth') expresses that knowledge is a getting rid of oblivion (*lêthê*), in other words, that it is recollection.

282. This is also indicated by those who called Mnemosyne the mother of the Muses: seeking is a gift of the Muses, finding of Mnemosyne.

283. Common usage confirms this, when it describes ignorance in terms of forgetting: we say that a thing 'escapes' us, if we do not know it, and we speak of things 'escaping notice' (*lathraios*), if they remain unknown.

284. Also, there are cases of recollection of a former life on record, as for instance that of Myro.

285. Other examples are those who are afraid of weasels, lizards or turtles, some of whom Plutarch says he knew himself. The nephew of Tiberius, who hunted bears and lions, yet could not stand the sight of a rooster. Plutarch tells he knew a druggist who was immune from vipers and snakes, but frightened of gadflies to the point of shouting and losing all self-control. The physician Themison could handle all other diseases, but

---

6–9. *SVF* II frg. 104.
7. τὰς φυσικὰς ἐννοίας : defined *SVF* II frg. 83.
9. Epicurus, frg. [1] 33 Arrighetti (=Diog. Laert. 10,33); cf. frg. 255 Usener (=Clem. Alex., *strom.* 2,4).
§ 281. **Dam. II § 28 θ' (16–17).** This section and the following offer some arguments based on etymology, with which compare Plutarch frg. 177 Sandbach (p. 106.25–28). The underlying ground for this type of argument is that the etymology is supposed to represent *communis opinio*; cf. οἱ πολλοί, *infra* § 283.1, and Ar., *eth. Nic.* VII 12, 1152b6–8 οἱ πλεῖστοι in a similar context. The one proposed here is different from Pl.'s, *Crat.* 421b1–3.
§ 282. **Dam. II § 28 ι' (18–19).** The Muses stand for ζήτησις Pl., *Crat.* 406a3–5: τὰς δὲ Μούσας καὶ ὅλως τὴν μουσικὴν ἀπὸ τοῦ μῶσθαι, ὡς ἔοικεν, καὶ τῆς ζητήσεώς τε καὶ φιλοσοφίας τὸ ὄνομα τοῦτο ἐπωνόμασαν. Mnemosyne as Platonic anamnesis Plut., *lib. educ.* 13, 9E; Max. Tyr. X 9 (=XVI 9 D.).
§ 284. Aeneas Gaz., *Theophr.* p. 18.14–19 Ἱεροκλῆς δέ, οὐχ ὁ διδάσκαλος ἀλλ' ὁ προβαλλόμενος τὰ θαυμάσια, ἄπιστον καὶ τοῦτο προσέθηκεν ὅτι νέος ἡταιρηκὼς (Κερκυραῖος δὲ ὁ νέος) μετὰ ἐραστοῦ Μύρωνος ἔπλει. καθορμισθείσης δὲ τῆς νεὼς εἰς

ἐνεργεία εἰδέναι καὶ μὴ εἰδέναι, ἔστω γὰρ εἶναι τὸν δυνάμει νοῦν, ἀλλ' ἔτι 5
ἀπορία ἡ αὐτή· πῶς γὰρ οὗτος νοεῖ; ἢ γὰρ ἃ οἶδεν ἢ ἃ οὐκ οἶδεν. οἱ δὲ ἀπὸ
τῆς Στοᾶς τὰς φυσικὰς ἐννοίας αἰτιῶνται· — εἰ μὲν δὴ δυνάμει, τὸ αὐτὸ ἐροῦμεν·
εἰ δὲ ἐνεργεία, διὰ τί ζητοῦμεν ἃ ἴσμεν; εἰ δὲ ἀπὸ τούτων ἄλλα ἀγνοούμενα,
πῶς ἅπερ οὐκ ἴσμεν; οἱ δὲ Ἐπικούρειοι τὰς προλήψεις· — ἃς εἰ μὲν διηρθρωμένας
φασί, περιττὴ ἡ ζήτησις· εἰ δὲ ἀδιαρθρώτους, πῶς ἄλλο τι παρὰ τὰς προλήψεις 10
ἐπιζητοῦμεν, ὅ γε οὐδὲ προειλήφαμεν;

κη'. - Ὅτι καὶ ἡ ἀλήθεια τὸ ὄνομα δηλοῖ λήθης ἐκβολὴν εἶναι τὴν ἐπιστήμην, 281
ὅ ἐστιν ἀνάμνησις.

κθ'. - Ὅτι καὶ οἱ μητέρα τῶν Μουσῶν τὴν Μνημοσύνην εἰπόντες αὐτὸ 282
τοῦτο ἐνδείκνυνται· αἱ μὲν γὰρ Μοῦσαι τὸ ζητεῖν παρέχονται, ἡ δὲ Μνημοσύνη
τὸ εὑρίσκειν.

λ'. - Ὅτι καὶ οἱ πολλοὶ τὸ ἀγνοεῖν ἐπιλελῆσθαι λέγοντες τῷ αὐτῷ μαρτυροῦσιν· 283
'λανθάνειν' γὰρ ἡμᾶς φαμεν ἅπερ ἀγνοοῦμεν καὶ 'λαθραῖα' πράγματα καλοῦμεν
τὰ ἀγνοούμενα.

λα'. - Ὅτι καὶ προβιοτῆς ἀναμνήσεις ἱστοροῦνται, οἷα καὶ ἡ τοῦ Μύρωνος. 284

λβ'. - Ὅτι καὶ ὅσοι γαλῆν φοβοῦνται ἢ σαυρὸν ἢ χελώνην, οὓς εἰδέναι 285
αὐτός. καὶ ὁ Τιβερίου ἀδελφιδοῦς ἄρκτους θηρῶν καὶ λέοντας ὅμως ἀλεκτρυόνα
οὐδὲ ἰδεῖν ἠδύνατο. φαρμακο|πώλην δέ τινα εἰδέναι ὑπὸ μὲν ἀσπίδων καὶ (157)
δρακόντων μηδὲν πάσχειν, μύωπα δὲ φεύγειν μέχρι βοῆς καὶ ἐκστάσεως.
Θεμίσων δὲ ὁ ἰατρὸς τὰ μὲν ἄλλα πάθη πάντα μετεχειρίζετο, τὸν δὲ ὑδροφόβαν 5

---

§ 280. 9 οὐκ ἴσμεν] -κ ἴ- in ras. Mˣ
§ 281. 1 δηλοῖ ins. Mᶜ: om. M¹ | ἐκβολὴν Mᶜ: εἰσβολὴν ut vid. M¹ | post ἐπιστήμην] ⸱⸱ ⸱⸱ in ras. Mᶜ
§ 283. 2 post πράγματα] ⸱⸱ ⸱⸱ ⸱⸱ in ras. Mᶜ
§ 284. 1 post καὶ¹] ⸱⸱ in ras. Mᶜ
§ 285. 2 ἀλεκτρυῶνα M

τινα χῶρον ἔρημον ἀποχωρήσας ὀλοφύρεται, ἀναμνησθεὶς ὅτιπερ ἐκεῖ τῶν ἐραστῶν τις ἐν τῷ πρὸ τοῦ βίῳ τῆς ὥρας τοῦ νέου διαμαρτὼν ἀπεπνίγη καὶ δακρύει ὅτι μὴ αὐτῷ πρότερον ἐχαρίσατο. It is not quite certain that this is the same story, since in Aeneas it is not Myro, but the young man from Corcyra who has this recollection of a former life; this would have to be accounted for as the result of careless quoting on Plutarch's part, or of careless abridging later. On Hierocles the paradoxographer see *RE*, art. *Hierokles* 16 (F. Jacoby). Datings vary from the 1st cent. A.D. (Praechter) to the 5th (Jacoby); of course, Hierocles may have depended on Plutarch, or conversely, or both on a common source.

§ 285. Dam. II § 28 ζ' (12–13).
1. Cf. Ar., *eth. Nic.* VII 6, 1149a8–9 ὁ δὲ τὴν γαλῆν ἐδεδίει διὰ νόσον.
1–3. Plut., *inv. et od.* 3, 537B δεύτερον δὲ τὸ μισεῖν γίγνεται καὶ πρὸς ἄλογα ζῷα· καὶ γὰρ γαλᾶς καὶ κανθαρίδας ἔνιοι μισοῦσι καὶ φρύνους καὶ ὄφεις· Γερμανικὸς δ' ἀλεκτρυόνος οὔτε φωνὴν οὔτ' ὄψιν ὑπέμενεν.
5–7. Themison: probably the founder of the 'methodical' school (*RE*, art. Themison 7), who belongs to the reign of Augustus. Plutarch cannot have known him personally.

if one only mentioned hydrophobia, he would become agitated and show what looked like symptoms of the disease. The cause of this, Plutarch believes, is recollection of a previous experience.

286. When previous experiences are particularly strong, they impress themselves on the memory for two lives, as for example in the case of Polemarchus, of the people of Corinth in the great earthquake, and the event described in the epitaph of Demetrius in Amorgos.

287. Something similar happens to persons who are more scared of rivers than of the sea, and in cases of acrophobia.

Further proofs from the same source

288. Newly born children are unsmiling and angry-looking until the age of about three weeks, during which period they sleep most of the time; yet sometimes, in their sleep, they will laugh again and again and look happy. How else can this be explained than by assuming that the soul then recovers from the turmoil of life in the body and feels the emotions connected with its previous experiences?

289. Natural aptitude for this or that has the same origin.

290. To say that there is a natural predisposition is a simplistic and unphilosophical answer, which will fit any question; we still have to ask ourselves what the character of such a natural predisposition is, for it differs from case to case; thus rational soul is naturally predisposed to identify things now present by means of things known before.

291. That we bring forth from within ourselves the knowledge that solves our problems is proved by the fact that, in the effort of finding them, we look inward.

292. Further, our joy at our discoveries indicates recognition of a truth which is very much our own, but had been lost as it were in the intervening time.

§§ 293–297. A few questions and observations. 72e3–77a5

293. Bion asked the question whether falsehood too is a result of recollection, as its opposite is, or not, pointing out the absurdity of this. — The solution is that falsehood, too, owes its origin to a semblance of truth and that this semblance is something one would not take for the truth, if one did not know the truth somehow.

---

§ 286. No particulars are known about the persons and events mentioned in this section. Polemarchus without any further qualification is probably the brother of Lysias (Plut., *de esu carn.* II 4, 998B, refers to him as Πολέμαρχον τὸν φιλόσοφον); his tragic death may have given rise to a story of this kind. The "great earthquake" can be either that of 420 B.C. (Thuc. 5,50,5) or that of 77 A.D. (Malalas p. 261 ed. Bonn); see *RE*, art. *Erdbebenforschung*, Suppl. 4, 350. The second is only barely possible because of the supposed interval of two generations, or more. The inscription

εἴ τις καὶ ὠνόμασε μόνον, ἐταράττετο καὶ ὅμοια ἔπασχε τοῖς ὑπ' αὐτοῦ κατεχομένοις. ὧν αἰτίαν εἶναι τὴν ἀνάμνησιν τῆς προπαθείας.

λγ'. – Ὅτι αἱ τῶν προπαθειῶν σφοδρότεραι τυποῦσι τὰς μνήμας εἰς δύο 286 γενέσεις· οἷον τὸ Πολεμάρχου καὶ τῶν ἐν Κορίνθῳ ὑπὸ τῷ μεγάλῳ σεισμῷ καὶ τὸ ἐν Ἀμόργῳ τοῦ Δημητρίου ἐγγεγραμμένον τῷ τάφῳ.

λδ'. – Ὅτι ὅμοια πάσχουσι καὶ οἱ ποταμοὺς μᾶλλον ἢ θάλατταν δεδοικότες 287 καὶ οἱ πρὸς τὰ ὕψη ταραττόμενοι.

Παρὰ τοῦ αὐτοῦ συστάσεις ἕτεραι

λε'. – Ὅτι τὰ νεογενῆ παιδία ἀμειδῆ ἐστι καὶ ἄγριον βλέπει μέχρι τριῶν 288 σχεδὸν ἑβδομάδων ὑπνώττοντα τὸν πλείω χρόνον· ἀλλ' ὅμως ποτὲ καθ' ὕπνους καὶ πολλάκις γελᾷ καὶ διαχεῖται. τίνα οὖν τρόπον ἄλλον τοῦτο συμβαίνει ἢ τῆς ψυχῆς τότε ἀπὸ τῆς δίνης τοῦ ζῴου ἀναφερούσης καὶ κατὰ τὰς ἑαυτῆς προπαθείας κινουμένης; 5

λς'. – Ὅτι καὶ αἱ πρὸς τάδε ἢ τάδε εὐφυΐαι τοῦτον ἀποβαίνουσι τὸν τρόπον. 289

λζ'. – Ὅτι τὸ μὲν λέγειν οὕτω πεφυκέναι παχύ τε καὶ ἰδιωτικὸν καὶ ἀρκοῦν 290 πρὸς πᾶσαν ἀπόκρισιν· ἀλλὰ οἷον τὸ πεφυκέναι ζητητέον ὅμως· ἄλλο γὰρ ἄλλον, ὡς τῆς λογικῆς ψυχῆς τὸ ἀπὸ τῶν προεγνωσμένων τὰ παρόντα ἀναγνωρίζειν.

λη'. – Ὅτι ἔσωθεν ἐκφέρομεν τὰς τῶν ζητημάτων ἐπιστήμας, δηλοῖ τὸ πρὸς 291 τὴν εὕρεσιν συντεινομένους εἴσω βλέπειν.

λθ'. – Ὅτι καὶ ἡ εὐφροσύνη ἐπὶ τοῖς εὑρήμασι δηλοῖ τὸν ἀναγνωρισμὸν τῆς 292 ὅτι μάλιστα οἰκείας ἡμῖν ἀληθείας ἐν τῷ μέσῳ χρόνῳ οἷον ἀπολομένης.

§§ 293–297. A few questions and observations. 72e3–77a5

μ'. – Ὅτι Βίων ἠπόρει περὶ τοῦ ψεύδους, εἰ καὶ αὐτὸ κατὰ ἀνάμνησιν, ὡς 293(158) τὸ ἐναντίον γε, ἢ οὔ· καὶ τίς ἡ ἀλογία; — Ἡ ῥητέον ὡς καὶ τοῦτο γίνεται κατὰ τὸ εἴδωλον τοῦ ἀληθοῦς· τὸ δὲ εἴδωλον εἶναι τοῦτο ὅπερ ἀληθὲς οὐκ ἄν τις νομίσειεν, εἰ μή πῃ εἰδείη τὸ ἀληθές.

---

§ 288. tit. συστάσεις Μ

---

on Demetrius' grave in Amorgos is otherwise unknown.
§ 288. Dam. II § 28 ς' (10–11).
4. ἀπὸ τῆς δίνης τοῦ ζῴου : as described Pl., Tim. 43a6–44c4 (the word ζῷον 43b1).
§ 289. Dam. II § 28 δ' (8).
§ 292. On the joy of discovery cf. Ascl., Nicom. I κθ'; Philop., Nicom. I κθ'.
§ 293. Dam. II § 24. Much of what we know about Bio comes from Plutarch: see O. Hense's Index Bioneus in: Teletis reliquiae, ²Tübingen 1909 (repr. Hildesheim 1969) 100–102.

294. Strato [frg. 126] wondered why, if the theory of recollection holds, we do not acquire knowledge without proof, and how it is that nobody has ever learnt to play the flute or the cither without practice. — In the first place, there have been self-taught men, such as Heraclitus, the Egyptian farmer, Phemius in Homer [*Od*. 22.347], the painter Agatharchus. In the second place, souls overcome by the torpor of genesis cannot be roused to recollection without a great effort; and therefore they need the support of sensible things.

295. Just as the imagination, starting from one name, can call up the story of a whole life, e.g. of Alcibiades, so rational memory, starting from any given point, can expand its knowledge.

296. The union with the body is like an epileptic fit; there, too, the mind needs a long time to regain consciousness of its normal situation.

297. If learning is always by reference to previous knowledge through recollection, the existence of souls reaches back into the past to infinity; the other direction still remains to be considered, and therefore immortality is not yet proved. If, on the other hand, the soul has its origin in time and is born with knowledge as part of her being, how can she lose it at the same moment? This is a better solution than the commentator's, who loses himself in a great number of various possibilities.

§§ 298–310. Notes on the text. 72e3–77e9

298. [72e3–73a3] It is evident that Cebes is not adding another argument that leads to the same conclusion, but he is thinking of the counterpart of the first and reminds Socrates that the soul can be shown to exist before the body. So he says that the soul is 'something immortal' also in this sense that it has a separate prior existence.

299. While the others thought that the soul is born with the body and perishes with it, the first argument refutes the latter view, the second argument the former.

300. [73a7–b2] The 'obstetrical' method of questioning, which elicits

---

§ 294. Dam. II § 25. Strato, too, is quoted a number of times by Plutarch, who himself at II § 28 ε´ uses the argument that some people are self-taught.
  3. Heraclitus, frg. A 1 (5), cf. B 101.
  4. ὁ Αἰγύπτιος γεωργός : collectively, it seems, since the Egyptians were supposed to be the inventors of agriculture, Dion. Perieg. 232–235.
  ibid. Hom., *Od*. 22.347–348 αὐτοδίδακτος δ᾽ εἰμί, θεὸς δέ μοι ἐν φρεσὶν οἴμας παντοίας ἐνέφυσεν.
  ibid. Agatharchus: mentioned twice by Plut. (*Alcib*. 16, *Pericl*. 13), though in a different context.
  6. διὸ καὶ τῶν αἰσθητῶν χρῄζουσιν : cf. II § 26.
§ 297. Dam. II § 27. The argument proves either eternal pre-existence only

μα'. - Ὅτι Στράτων [frg. 126] ἠπόρει, εἰ ἔστιν ἀνάμνησις, πῶς ἄνευ ἀποδείξεων οὐ γιγνόμεθα ἐπιστήμονες, πῶς δὲ οὐδεὶς αὐλητὴς ἢ κιθαριστὴς γέγονεν ἄνευ μελέτης. — Ἡ μάλιστα μὲν γεγόνασί τινες καὶ αὐτοδίδακτοι, Ἡράκλειτος, ὁ Αἰγύπτιος γεωργός, Φήμιος ὁ Ὁμήρου [X 347], Ἀγάθαρχος ὁ γραφεύς. εἶτα καὶ αἱ ψυχαὶ πολλῷ τῷ κάρῳ κατεχόμεναι τῆς γενέσεως πολλῆς πρὸς ἀνάμνησιν δέονται τῆς μοχλείας· διὸ καὶ τῶν αἰσθητῶν χρῄζουσιν.

μβ'. - Ὅτι ὡς ἡ φαντασία ἀφ' ἑνός τινος ὀνόματος ὅλου ἀναμιμνήσκεται βίου, οἷον τοῦ Ἀλκιβιάδου, οὕτω καὶ ἡ λογικὴ μνήμη ἀπὸ τῆς τυχούσης ἀφορμῆς προσεξευρίσκει πλείονα.

μγ'. - Ὅτι ἔοικεν ἡ πρὸς τὸ σῶμα σύνδεσις ἐπιληψίᾳ· καὶ γὰρ ἐν ἐκείνῃ ὀψέ ποτε ἀναφέρουσιν αἱ ψυχαὶ τὰ καθεστῶτα.

μδ'. - Ὅτι εἰ μὲν ἀεὶ πρὸς τὰ πρόσθεν διὰ ἀναμνήσεων αἱ μαθήσεις, ἐπ' ἄπειρόν εἰσιν αἱ ψυχαὶ ἐπὶ τὰ πρόσω· λείπει δὲ καὶ τὸ ἐπὶ θάτερον μέρος, διόπερ οὔπω ἀθάνατοι. εἰ δὲ ἀπὸ χρόνου γενομένῃ μετὰ τῆς ἐπιστήμης γέγονεν ⟨κατὰ οὐσίαν⟩, πῶς ἀποβάλλει αὐτὴν εὐθέως [κατὰ οὐσίαν]; οὕτω γὰρ κάλλιον ἐπιλύσασθαι ἤπερ ὡς ὁ ἐξηγητής· εἰς γὰρ ποικιλίαν ἐξηνέχθη πολλήν.

§§ 298-310. Notes on the text. 72e3-77e9

με'. - [72e3-73a3] Ὅτι σαφῶς ὁ Κέβης οὐ τοῦ αὐτοῦ συμπεράσματος ἐπάγει ἄλλην ἐπιχείρησιν, ἀλλὰ τὸ ἀντίστροφον ἐννοεῖ τε καὶ τὸν Σωκράτη ὑπομιμνήσκει δειχθῆναι δυνάμενον τὸ πρὸ τοῦ σώματος εἶναι τὴν ψυχήν. καὶ ταύτῃ οὖν λέγει τὴν ψυχὴν ἀθάνατόν τι εἶναι, ᾖ προϋπάρχει χωριστή.

μϛ'. - Ὅτι τῶν ἄλλων οἰομένων τὴν ψυχὴν καὶ συγγίνεσθαι τῷ σώματι καὶ συμφθείρεσθαι, τοῦτο μὲν ἀνασκευάζει ὁ πρῶτος λόγος, ἐκεῖνο δὲ ὁ δεύτερος.

μζ'. - [73a7-b2] Ὅτι ἡ μαιευτικὴ ἐρώτησις πρόκλησις οὖσα τῆς κυουμένης

---

§ 297. 4 κατὰ οὐσίαν transp. Wk | post πῶς] ÷ in ras. M^c

(and this is as it should be: none of the arguments preceding the final and decisive one must contain complete proof of immortality: cf. § 298) or even a limited pre-existence, which latter alternative now has to be eliminated. The way in which Pr. does this (II § 27.4-6) is rejected by Dam. as too complicated and irrelevant. He prefers the argument used above (I § 266, II § 16), that the soul cannot have acquired the reason-principles at birth.

4. I have transposed the words κατὰ οὐσίαν because ἀποβάλλειν κατὰ οὐσίαν is meaningless. Cf. I § 266.2 ἢ εἰ μὲν κατ' οὐσίαν, πῶς αὐτοὺς ἀποβάλλουσιν; II § 16.5-6 ἔτι δέ, εἰ μὲν κατ' οὐσίαν λαμβάνει τὰς ἐπιστήμας, πῶς ἀποβάλλει ὅτε δήποτε;

§§ 298-310. No parallel text in Dam. II, from which this entire lecture is missing (after § 28).

§ 300. Ol. 11 § 9.3-7.

latent knowledge, is unanswerable proof of the soul's pre-existence, as Socrates demonstrates by a practical test in the *Meno* [82a7–86a11].

301. [74a9–c6] Socrates proves the existence of forms more or less incidentally, assuming it but adding a demonstration at the same time: if there are many equal things, this manifold must derive its common character from one equal, which must obviously be real and obviously cannot exist in any of the individual things in which the many equals are found; it is therefore prior to them, since they are derived from it, and this is expressed by saying that they are 'different' from it [b7]. Then he outlines a second proof [b7–c6] observing that equals existing in matter are contaminated with their own privation, but those existing by themselves are pure; and the perfect is necessarily prior to the imperfect.

302. He speaks now of 'the equal' [74a10–12; c4–5], then of 'the equals themselves' [74c1], either because he is thinking of the plurality of intelligences, each of which possesses equality itself; — or else the one should be related to intelligence, the plural to soul, in which even the one is many, because there it adapts itself to the level of soul.

303. [74d9–75a4] The image that expresses a thing's essence is in sympathy with its original and 'tends' toward it as its cause; indeed, even artificial images by the mere fact of their likeness receive the illumination of the Gods.

304. [75a5–8] What does it mean that intelligible reality 'cannot be apprehended' unless through things sensible? — For the majority of souls this is the case.

305. [75a1–3] By 'tending towards them' things prove their descent from forms, by 'falling short' their separateness.

306. [75b1–2] The formula 'that which is' denotes, first, its real-existence, secondly, its being free from the accretions of genesis.

307. [75b4–d6] If objects of knowledge are prior to objects of sense-perception, knowledge is necessarily prior to sense-perception, and therefore so are subjects of knowledge to subjects of sense-perception, and therefore so is each of us as a knowing subject prior to himself as a perceiving subject; sense-perception begins immediately after birth; it follows that we possessed knowledge before birth. This is why Socrates says that this reasoning is a hypothetical one [76d7–e7].

308. [75e2–3] At the moment when we first enter into life, the most radical change takes place, which disturbs the memory and by confusing it causes oblivion. Therefore we cannot have received knowledge then; so it must have been before we entered the body: either immediately

---

§ 301. Ol. 12 § 1.7–13.

§ 303. 2–3. The theory of cult statues was worked out in Iamblichus' Περὶ ἀγαλμάτων, which, however, is known only from a report by Photius (*Bibl.* 215) on Philoponus' criticism of it. Some fragmentary information in Pr., *Rep.* II 241.4–5

ἐπιστήμης ἀναγκαίως δείκνυσιν αὐτὴν προϋπάρχουσαν, ὡς ἔργῳ δείκνυσιν καὶ ὁ Σωκράτης ἐν τῷ Μένωνι [82a7–86a11].

μη'. – [74a9–c6] Ὅτι ἔστιν τὰ εἴδη παρενδείκνυταί πως, ὑποτιθέμενος αὐτὰ 301 σὺν ἀποδείξει· εἰ γὰρ πολλὰ τὰ ἴσα, ἀφ' ἑνὸς ἂν εἴη τοῖς πολλοῖς τὸ αὐτό, καὶ δῆλον ὅτι ὄντος, καὶ δῆλον ὅτι ἐν οὐδενὶ τῶν καθ' ἕκαστα ἐν οἷς τὰ πολλὰ ἴσα· πρὸ αὐτῶν ἄρα, εἴπερ ταῦτα ἀπ' αὐτοῦ, διὸ καὶ ‛ἕτερα᾽ αὐτοῦ εἴρηται [b7]. εἶτα δευτέραν ἐνδείκνυται ἀπόδειξιν [b7–c6] τὰ ἐν ὕλῃ ἴσα παραχραινόμενα 5 λέγων τῇ οἰκείᾳ στερήσει, τὰ δὲ αὐτὰ καθ' ἑαυτὰ ἀκραιφνῆ· πάντως δὲ ὅτι τὰ τέλεια τῶν μὴ τελείων πρεσβύτερα.

μθ'. – Ὅτι ποτὲ μὲν ‛ἴσον᾽ [74a10–12; c4–5], ποτὲ δὲ ‛αὐτὰ ⟨τὰ⟩ ἴσα᾽ [74c1] 302 λέγει, ἢ εἰς τοὺς πολλοὺς ἀποβλέπων νόας, ὧν ἐν ἑκάστῳ τὸ αὐτοῖσον· ἢ τὸ μὲν ἓν τῷ νῷ ἀποδοτέον, τὸ δὲ πεπληθυσμένον τῇ ψυχῇ, ἐν ταύτῃ γὰρ καὶ τὸ ἓν πολλὰ διὰ τὴν ἐν αὐτῇ πρὸς αὐτὴν ὑπόβασιν.

ν'. – [74d9–75a4] Ὅτι κατ' οὐσίαν ἡ εἰκὼν οὖσα συμπάσχει τῷ οἰκείῳ 303 παραδείγματι καὶ ‛ὀρέγεται᾽ αὐτοῦ ὡς αἰτίου, ὅπου γε καὶ αἱ τεχνηταὶ εἰκόνες κατὰ ψιλὴν ἀφομοίωσιν ὅμως ἐλλάμπονται ὑπὸ θεῶν.

να'. – [75a5–8] Πῶς ‛οὐ δυνατὸν ἐννοῆσαι᾽ μὴ διὰ τῶν αἰσθητῶν τὰ νοητά; 304 – Ἤ τάς γε πλείστας τῶν ψυχῶν.

νβ'. – [75a1–3] Ὅτι ᾗ μὲν ‛ὀρέγεται᾽, ἀπ' αὐτῶν, ᾗ δὲ ‛ἐνδεῖ᾽, ἐκτὸς αὐτῶν. 305

νγ'. – [75b1–2] Ὅτι τὸ ‛ὅ ἐστι᾽ δηλοῖ μὲν καὶ τὸ ὄντως ὄν, δηλοῖ δὲ καὶ 306 τὸ ἀπηλλαγμένον τῶν ἐν τῇ γενέσει περιφυομένων.

νδ'. – [75b4–d6] Εἰ τὰ ἐπιστητὰ πρὸ τῶν αἰσθητῶν, ἀνάγκη καὶ τὰς 307 ἐπιστήμας εἶναι πρὸ τῶν αἰσθήσεων, ὥστε καὶ τοὺς ἐπισταμένους πρὸ τῶν αἰσθανομένων, ὥστε καὶ ἕκαστος ἐπιστάμενος πρὸ αἰσθανομένου αὐτὸς ἑαυτοῦ· εὐθὺς δὲ γεννηθέντες αἰσθανόμεθα· πρὸ τοῦ γεννηθῆναι ἄρα ἠπιστάμεθα. διό φησιν ἐξ ὑποθέσεως εἶναι ταῦτα [76d7–e7]. 5

νε'. – [75e2–3] Ὅτι ἐν τῇ πρώτῃ γενέσει ἡ σφοδροτάτη μεταβολή ἐστιν· 308 αὕτη δὲ ἐκπλήσσει τὴν μνήμην καὶ ταράττουσα λήθην ἐμποιεῖ. τότε ἄρα οὐκ ἂν ἐλάβομεν ἐπιστήμην· πρότερον ἄρα τοῦ σώ|ματος· ἤτοι δὲ προσεχῶς, (160)

---

§ 301. 4 εἴπερ Fh: ἤπερ M
§ 302. 1 τὰ Wk (Pl.): om. M — 3 ἓν¹ μ: ἐν M — 4 αὐτὴν Wk: ἑαυτὴν M
§ 304. 1 ⟨εἰ⟩ μὴ Nv
§ 305. 1 ᾗ (bis) Wk: ἡ M
§ 306. 1 δηλοῖ Mᶜ: δῆλον M¹
§ 308. 2 αὕτη Mᶜ: αὐτὴ M¹

(οὐδὲ γὰρ οἱ τὰ τῇδε ἀγάλματα ἐλλάμποντες ἄνευ ζωῆς ἐλλάμπουσιν); *Tim.* I 51.25–27; 330.31–331.3; III 4.32–5.2; 6.24–7.26; 155.18–22; *Crat.* 19.12–15; 108.9–12.

§ 304. 1. Norvin's insertion of ⟨εἰ⟩ before μή is not strictly necessary; the meaning remains the same; cf. *theol.* II 3, 30.10 S.-W.

before, as in the case of the 'newly initiated' [*Phaedr.* 250e1] or of those who have a philosophical life behind them [*ib.* 248d2–3], or else from earlier lives.

309. [77a8–b9] Thinking of the second argument Simmias says that it does not prove our continued existence in Hades; nor indeed did the first prove our pre-existence. Therefore Socrates combines the two arguments to make one complete proof.

310. [77e5] For the 'child' in reason ignorance is abnormal, in the irrational faculties it is normal, in the body it is a matter of age.

III. THE ARGUMENT FROM SIMILARITY TO THINGS INTELLIGIBLE

§ 311. Plotinus' proof of immortality and the argument from similarity. 78b4–85b9

311. The great Plotinus [IV 7?] shows the immortality of the soul by demonstrating its incorporeality and separability; but he took his inspiration from the present passage, the notion of uncompoundedness [78c1–9] suggesting that of incorporeality, and mastery over the body [79e8–80a5] that of separability.

It is preferable, however, not to identify the arguments; Plato does not start from the two modes of death or destruction as Plotinus does, nor does he set out to prove the same thing, but only that the substance of soul is more enduring than that of body because it shows a stronger resemblance to things immortal. On the other hand, even if the argument were identical, this is no reason to reject it as a complete proof of immortality (since it is shown on the same ground that soul is separable from *all* body); a valid reason is that there remains a possibility of its becoming exhausted at last, even while existing by itself, as appears from the conclusion of the argument [80d5–e1] and from the position of Cebes later on [86e6–88b8].

---

§ 308. 4. The 'newly initiated' of *Phaedr.* 250e1 are those who have recently seen transcendent reality (250b5–c6); Pr., *Tim.* III 295.15.

§ 311. Dam. II § 29. Ol. 13 § 4. See note on Ol., where it has been shown that (1) the argument in this form is not found in Plot. IV 7; (2) Pr. accepts it as a correct report of the argument of Plot. and (3) as equivalent to the argument of Pl.; but (4) does not consider it complete proof of immortality because it is conceivable that the soul, though separable from this earthly body, may be inseparable from the pneumatic body and perish with it; (5) Dam. denies the identity of the two arguments and (6) limits the range of the argument in order to keep closer to

ὡς ἐπὶ τῶν 'νεοτελῶν' [*Phaedr*. 250e1] ἢ τῶν ἐκ φιλοσοφίας [ib. 248d2–3], ἢ καὶ ἐκ προγενεστέρων ἔτι βίων.

νς'. – [77a8–b9] *Ὅτι ὡς πρὸς τὸν δεύτερον λόγον ἀπιδὼν ὁ Σιμμίας οὐκ ἀποδεικνύναι φησὶν αὐτὸν τὸ καὶ ἐπιδιαμένειν ἐν Ἅιδου· οὐδὲ γὰρ ἐκεῖνος τὸ πρὸ τῆς γενέσεως. διόπερ ὁ Σωκράτης ἐκ τῶν δύο λόγων συνάγει τὴν μίαν ὅλην ἀπόδειξιν.* **309**

νζ'. – [77e5] *Ὅτι ὁ παῖς ἐν μὲν τῷ λόγῳ παρὰ φύσιν ἀπαίδευτος, ἐν δὲ τῷ ἀλόγῳ κατὰ φύσιν τὴν ἑαυτοῦ, ἐν δὲ τῷ σώματι καθ' ἡλικίαν.* **310**

III. THE ARGUMENT FROM SIMILARITY TO THINGS INTELLIGIBLE

§ 311. **Plotinus' proof of immortality and the argument from similarity. 78b4–85b9**

νη'. – *Ὅτι Πλωτῖνος ὁ μέγας* [IV 7?] *ἀθάνατον ἀποφαίνει τὴν ψυχὴν ἀσώματόν τε ἀποδείξας καὶ χωριστήν· τὰς δὲ τοῦ λόγου ἀφορμὰς οὗτος ὁ λόγος αὐτῷ παρέδωκεν, τὸ μὲν ἀσύνθετον* [78c1–9], *ὅτι ἀσώματος, τὸ δὲ δεσποτικόν* [79e8–80a5], *ὅτι χωριστή.* **311**

Κάλλιον δέ, μήτε τὸν αὐτὸν λόγον ποιεῖν· οὐ γὰρ τοῖς δύο τοῦ θανάτου τρόποις ἢ τῆς φθορᾶς ὁ Πλάτων κέχρηται οἷς ὁ Πλωτῖνος, οὐδὲ τὸν αὐτὸν ποιεῖται σκοπὸν τῆς ἀποδείξεως, ἀλλ' ὅτι πολυχρονιωτέρα τοῦ σώματος ἡ ψυχῆς οὐσία ἅτε ὁμοιοτέρα τοῖς ἀθανάτοις· καὶ εἰ ἦν δὲ ὁ αὐτὸς λόγος, οὐ διὰ τοῦτο ἀτιμαστέος πρὸς τὴν τελέαν ἀθανασίαν (παντὸς γὰρ σώματος ἀποδείκνυται χωριστὴ τῷ αὐτῷ λόγῳ), ἀλλ' ὅτι ἴσως ὑπολείπεται καὶ καθ' ἑαυτὴν οὖσαν ὅμως ἐν χρόνῳ πολλῷ ἀπαγορεύειν, ὡς δηλοῖ καὶ τὸ συμπέρασμα τοῦ λόγου [80d5–e1] *καὶ ὁ Κέβης ὕστερον ὑποτιθέμενος* [86e6–88b8].

---

§ 308. 4 ἢ M: del. Wyttenbach
§ 309. 2 ἀποδεικνύ~ναι] accent. in -εί- eras., ∸ in ras. 2 litt. Mˣ

---

the text of the *Ph*.
5. μήτε: Norvin's μηδὲ is wrong, since the μήτε refers forward to the καί in line 8 (cf. II § 29.12 μήτε and 16 ἔπειτα δέ).
8. οὐ διὰ τοῦτο: i.e. if Plato's argument were really the one ascribed here to Plot., we could not call it incomplete proof (with Pr.) on the ground that the premise of the separability of the soul is valid only as far as the 'earthly' body is concerned and does not necessarily hold for the pneumatic body. Dam. thinks that the argument on which this premise rests holds true for any kind of body, and the only possible remaining flaw in the proof is that the soul, while separate, might nevertheless wear out.

§§ 312–324. A survey of, and comment upon, 80b1–5

312. What does the argument presuppose? First, that there are two kinds of forms, real-existents and things in process; secondly that the number and nature of what might be called the elements of each are the following:

Real-existents:	Things in process:
divine	corporeal
immortal	not immortal
intelligential	non-intelligential
having a single form	multifarious
indissoluble	dissoluble
of the same condition and nature	ever changing

313. Things that have true being are 'divine' because dependent on Gods before them.

314. They are 'immortal' because their nature is eternal; for since they do not lack anything, neither can they ever lack life.

315. They are 'intelligential' in the sense that they are capable of thought; this is proved by the contrasting attribute of things in process, 'non-intelligential' (*anoêton*). In the *Timaeus* the word is used in the same meaning.

316. They 'have a single form' because they are form only and are simple forms, indivisible because of their unity.

317. They are 'indissoluble' as a consequence of being indivisible, without parts and absolutely non-dimensional; for anything that is dissolved, is dissolved into its components.

318. Existents as such are 'always of the same condition and quality';

---

§§ 312–318. Dam. II § 30. The six attributes of real-existence are discussed also by Pr., *theol*. I 26–27, but as attributes of the divine, which causes a certain amount of distortion.

§ 312. Ol. 13 § 1.

4–5. In the second column the explanatory synonyms σωματικόν and οὐκ ἀθάνατον have taken the place of ἀνθρώπινον and θνητόν, cf. *infra* §§ 319–320 (II § 30.4–5).

§§ 313–324. Ol. 13 § 2.

§ 313. Cf. Pr., *theol*. I 26, 114.16–18 S.-W. νῦν δὲ ὅτι τὸ θεῖον τοιοῦτόν ἐστι διορισώμεθα, τὸ ὂν τὸ τοῦ ἑνὸς μετέχον ἢ τὸ ἓν συνῃρημένως μετὰ τοῦ ὄντος.

§ 315. Pr. lists the different applications of νοητός *theol*. I 26, 117.18–118.9 S.-W.: (1) soul, (2) intelligence, (3) real-existence, i.e. the prototype of *Tim.* 27d5–31b3, (4) the divine. Similarly, *Tim.* I 230.22–28 καὶ γὰρ τὸ νοητὸν ποτὲ μὲν κατὰ πάσης φέρουσι τῆς ἀειδοῦς καὶ ἀοράτου φύσεως, ὥσπερ ὅταν καὶ τὴν ψυχὴν νοητὴν λέγωσιν, ὡς ὁ ἐν Φαίδωνι Σωκράτης (=1+2+3), ποτὲ δὲ κατὰ τῶν κρειττόνων ἁπάντων τῆς ψυχικῆς οὐσίας, ὡς ἡ ἐν Πολιτείᾳ δηλοῖ διαίρεσις (=2+3), ποτέ γε μὴν κατὰ τῶν πρωτίστων τοῦ ὄντος τριάδων, ὡς μικρὸν ὕστερον [28a1–2] ὁ Τίμαιος ἀποκαλέσει (=3). In other words, he acknowledges Pl.'s use of νοητόν as the object of thought generally (opp. the visible), whereas in Procline terminology it is set apart for the reality beyond intelligence. The obvious inference from the correspondence between νοητός

§§ 312-324. A survey of, and comment upon, 80b1-5

νθ'. - Τίνες αἱ τοῦ λόγου ὑποθέσεις; μία μέν, διττὰ εἶναι τὰ εἴδη, τὰ μὲν 312
ὄντα τὰ δὲ γιγνόμενα· ἑτέρα δέ, τοσάδε εἶναι καὶ τοιάδε τὰ ἑκατέρων οἶον στοιχεῖα·

ὄντων	γιγνομένων
θεῖον	σωματικόν
ἀθάνατον	οὐκ ἀθάνατον 5
νοητόν	ἀνόητον
μονοειδές	πολυειδές
ἀδιάλυτον	διαλυτόν
κατὰ τὰ αὐτὰ καὶ ὡσαύτως ἔχον	ἄλλοτε ἄλλως ἔχον

ξ'. - Ὅτι 'θεῖα' τὰ ὄντα ὡς θεῶν ἐξημμένα προϋπαρχόντων. 313(161)
ξα'. - Ὅτι 'ἀθάνατα' ὡς κατὰ φύσιν αἰώνια· ὧν γὰρ οὐδὲν ἄπεστιν, οὐδὲ 314
ζωή ποτε ἂν ἀπείη.
ξβ'. - Ὅτι 'νοητά' ἐστιν ὡς νοητικά· δηλοῖ δὲ τὸ ἀντικείμενον τοῖς 315
γιγνομένοις ὑπάρχον, τὸ ἀνόητον. εἴρηται δὲ καὶ ἐν Τιμαίῳ ἡ λέξις ἐπὶ τῆσδε
τῆς σημασίας.
ξγ'. - Ὅτι 'μονοειδῆ' ὡς μόνον εἴδη καὶ ἁπλᾶ εἴδη καὶ ἀμέριστα ὡς ἓν μόνον. 316
ξδ'. - Ὅτι τὸ 'ἀδιάλυτον' ὡς ἑπόμενον τῷ ἀμερίστῳ καὶ ἀμερεῖ καὶ πάμπαν 317
ἀδιαστάτῳ· τὸ γὰρ διαλυόμενον εἰς τὰ ἐξ ὧν ἐστι διαλύεται.
ξε'. - Ὅτι τὰ ὄντα [νοητὰ] ᾗ ὄντα 'ἀεὶ κατὰ τὰ αὐτὰ καὶ ὡσαύτως ἔχει'· 318

---

§ 312. 1-2 μὲν ὄντα Mᶜ: μένοντα M¹
§ 316. 1 ἓν μόνον Mᶜ: ἓν M¹
§ 317. 1 ἀμερεῖ] -εῖ in ras. Mᶜ
§ 318. 1 νοητὰ M: del. Wk (v.l. ad ᾗ ὄντα)

---

and ἀνόητος would be that the latter is also passive (as in Plot. V 3, 10.42). The active sense and the synonym νοητικός seem to have been chosen (here and II § 30.9) to make the resemblance between soul and real-existence more manifest. Cf. Pr., Tim. I 452.8-9; III 226.15-16; elem. 20, p. 22.23.

2. ἐν Τιμαίῳ : the reference is problematic. Practically all the instances of the word in the Tim. are connected with the αὐτοζῷον, which, for Pr. and Dam., represents the νοητόν in the strict sense, the intelligible world (30c7, 31a5, 39e1, 48e6, 92c7). The two remaining cases can be taken into consideration: 37a1, of which Pr., Tim. II 293.3-295.25, offers three different interpretations, relating the word (1) to soul, (2) to the Demiurge, (3) to the intelligible world; and 51b1, of the ideal forms, which in Pr.'s system are manifested completely only in the intelligence, cf. Pr., Tim. I 245.31, where the passage is linked with the νοήσει μετὰ λόγου of 28a1.

§ 316. The explanation of μονοειδῆ as μόνον εἴδη is against Greek derivation, ἁπλᾶ εἴδη on the contrary expresses the obvious meaning of 'having one form only' (cf. the opposite πολυειδῆ). It is connected with ἀμέριστος by Pl., Theaet. 205d1-2.

§ 318. 1. νοητά (ΝΟΗΤΑ) is probably a conjecture made in an uncial copy for ΗΟΝΤΑ (=ᾗ ὄντα). Cf. below § 338.2, where M¹ had νοῦ δὲ (=ΝΟΥΔΕ) for ᾗ οὐδὲ (ΗΟΥΔΕ).

for in that which is real in the proper and primary sense there neither was nor will be anything that is not; therefore they are entirely invariable.

319. Things in process are described by the narrower term 'human things'; elsewhere [*Laws* I 631b6–d1] Plato contradistinguishes the human as corporeal from the divine, inasmuch as the divine participates in the Gods, whereas human nature on its lower level is participated by the body.

Rather we should contrast the divine as the most completely united with the human as the most radically disintegrated.

320. They are all without exception 'not immortal' according to the *Timaeus* [41b2]; here, however, in combination with 'human' things, he applies the term 'mortal.'

321. Corporeal things have no 'thought'; nor even perception, taken by themselves.

322. It is 'multifarious' inasmuch as each part of it is an aggregate of many things and inasmuch as it is divided and material.

323. It is 'dissoluble' because it is composed of many parts; the way in which it is dissolved is the same in which it was composed, either as regards its essence only, or also in time.

324. It is 'never of the same condition and nature,' because it is forever changing either in activity or in substance as well.

§§ 325–329. Analysis of the argument. 78b4–80c1

325. Socrates adduces three points to prove that the bodily part of our being is more like sensible reality, the psychic part more like intelligible reality: visibility and invisibility [79b1–c1], thought and perception [79c2–e7], sovereignty and subjection [79e8–80a9]. The last point concerns practical power and activity, the second cognitive power and activity, the first being, sensible and intelligible.

326. [79b1–c1] If the body is visible and the soul invisible, i.e. apprehensible only by thought, the soul is obviously more like the intelligible world, the body more like the sensible world.

---

§ 319. 1–2. Strictly, man, i.e. the human soul (*Ph*. 115c4–e4) belongs to the intelligible world; more loosely, humanity is a part of the visible world. At *Laws* I 631b6–d1, the human goods are material advantages, the divine goods are the virtues. Accordingly, the ἐπεί here must mean, not '⟨this is a sense peculiar to this passage,⟩ for elsewhere . . .,' but '⟨this must be the sense,⟩ since elsewhere ⟨too⟩ . . .' Cf. § 312.4, where σωματικόν appears as the equivalent of ἀνθρώπινον.

3. μετεχόμενα κάτωθεν ὑπὸ σωμάτων : not applicable to the 'human goods' of the *Laws*, but to the human situation in general.

4. Dam. reduces the double contrast 'participat*ing in* the *divine*' – 'participat*ed by* the *corporeal*' to one pair of opposites 'completely united' – 'radically dissipated'. On disintegration (the 'Titanic life') as the characteristic of human existence see § 8; cf. II § 30.4–5, where τῷ ἀνθρωπίνῳ is paraphrased ὡς ἂν εἰ λέγοι τῷ ἐσχάτῳ εἴδει.

ἐν γὰρ τῷ κυρίως ὄντι καὶ πρώτως οὐδὲν μὴ ὂν οὔτε ἦν οὔτε ἔσται· πάντῃ οὖν ἀπαράλλακτα.

ξϛ'. - Ὅτι τὰ γιγνόμενα μερικώτερον εἴρηται 'ἀνθρώπινα', ἐπεὶ ἐν ἄλλοις 319 [Laws I 631b6–d1] ὡς σωματικὰ ἀντιδιαιρεῖ τοῖς θείοις ὡς μετέχουσι θεῶν μετεχόμενα 〚δὲ〛 κάτωθεν ὑπὸ σωμάτων.
Κάλλιον δέ, ὡς μάλιστα ἡνωμένοις μάλιστα διεσκεδασμένα.
ξζ'. - Ὅτι ἁπλῶς μὲν πάντα 'οὐκ ἀθάνατα' κατὰ τὸν Τίμαιον [41b2], νῦν 320 δὲ τοῖς 'ἀνθρωπίνοις' τὸ 'θνητὸν' συνέζευξεν.
ξη'. - Ὅτι οὐκ ἔχει 'νοῦν' τὰ σωματικά· οὐδὲ γὰρ αἴσθησιν, ὅσον ἐφ' ἑαυτοῖς. 321
ξθ'. - Ὅτι 'πολυειδὲς' ὡς ἐκ πολλῶν συμπεφορημένον ἕκαστον καὶ ὡς μεριστὸν 322 καὶ ὡς ἔνυλον.
ο'. - Ὅτι 'διαλυτὸν' ὡς σύνθετον ἐκ πολλῶν· διαλύεται δὲ ᾗ συνετέθη, ἢ λόγῳ 323 μόνον ἢ χρόνῳ.
οα'. - Ὅτι 'οὐδέποτε κατὰ τὰ αὐτὰ καὶ ὡσαύτως'· μεταβάλλεται γὰρ ἢ 324 ταῖς ἐνεργείαις ἢ καὶ ταῖς οὐσίαις.

§§ 325–329. Analysis of the argument. 78b4–80c1

δ οβ'. - Ὅτι διὰ τριῶν ἀφορμῶν δείκνυσι τὸ μὲν σωματικὸν ἡμῶν τῷ αἰσθητῷ 325 ὁμοιότερον, τὸ δὲ ψυχικὸν τῷ νοητῷ· ἀπὸ τοῦ ὁρατοῦ καὶ ἀοράτου [79b1–c1], ἀπὸ τῆς νοήσεως καὶ αἰσθήσεως [79c2–e7], ἀπὸ τοῦ ἄρχειν καὶ ἄρχεσθαι [79e8–80a9]· ἔστι δὲ τοῦτο μὲν τῆς πρακτικῆς | δυνάμεως καὶ ἐνεργείας, τὸ (162) δὲ δεύτερον ἀπὸ τῆς γνωστικῆς, τὸ δὲ πρῶτον ἀπὸ τῆς οὐσίας, αἰσθητῆς τε 5 καὶ νοητῆς.

ογ'. - [79b1–c1] Εἰ τὸ μὲν σῶμα ὁρατόν, ἡ δὲ ψυχὴ ἀόρατον, ὅ ἐστι λογισμῷ 326 ληπτὴ μόνῳ, δῆλον ὡς ἡ μὲν τοῖς νοητοῖς ὁμοιοτέρα, τὸ δὲ τοῖς αἰσθητοῖς.

---

§ 318. 2 ἔσται] -αι in ras. M^c
§ 319. 3 δὲ M: del. Wk
§ 325. 5 πρῶτον ins. M^c: om. M¹

---

§ 320. Pr., Tim. III 215.25–216.20 gives a narrower sense to the 'not immortal' of Tim. 41b2: 'immortal' is what owes unending life to itself, 'not immortal' what derives immortal life from another, 'mortal' is what does not possess unending life. Here (as well as II § 30.5 and 31.2) 'not immortal' is used as the more comprehensive term including the lifeless.
§ 323. The point is developed more fully in § 331.
§ 324. According to II § 30.11–12, the attribute κατὰ τὰ αὐτὰ καὶ ὡσαύτως ἔχον more especially concerns activities, whereas the preceding one (ἀδιάλυτον) concerns substance, a distinction made neither supra § 318 nor by Ol. 13 § 2.
§§ 325–328. Dam. II §§ 32–33. Ol. 13 § 3.1–10.
§ 325. One of Pr.'s favorite triads (cf. § 256); see Dam.'s criticism in II § 33.5–7. The three approaches are worked out in the next three sections.

327. [79c2-e7] If intellection lifts the soul up to the level of intelligence and brings it to its natural condition, while sense-perception brings it down to the level of the body and to an abnormal state, there can be no doubt as to the conclusion.

328. [79e8-80a9] If the soul rules, as intelligence does, and the body is ruled, as the world of process is, the inference is once more obvious.

329. The more like the   more like   more immortal, lasting
      soul intelligible   the immortal longer than the body

§§ 330–339. Some difficulties in 78c1-80e1

330. [78d1-7] One may ask to what kind of forms Socrates is referring here as indissoluble. If to those in ourselves, which are component parts of the soul, why is the soul said to be more like them instead of actually the same? And what right has Socrates to suppose them immortal, in order to prove that the soul lasts longer than the body? If, on the other hand, he means the intelligible forms, how can he say that they are discussed in questions and answers? For of intelligible things there is neither knowledge, according to the *Letters* [VII 342a7–343d2], nor definition nor name. — The answer is that the discussion does deal with intelligible forms, though its direct concern is with their derivatives; for somehow it establishes contact with the forms themselves too, if it achieves its object.

331. [78c1-4] Does it not follow that the world can also be dissolved, being composite? — It can be dissolved by the one who bound it, if he is so inclined, which he is not. For the world was well joined together, and therefore, since he is good, he will not dissolve it, nor did he make it dissoluble.

⟨It is more correct to say that he did make it dissoluble:⟩ he made it an everlasting composite whole, and consequently an everlasting dissoluble whole, because what is composite is necessarily dissoluble; in fact, it is always in process of being dissolved, since it is also always in process of being joined together. In the same way as the universe is simultaneously coming-to-be and passing away, so it is also being joined together and being dissolved, integration and decomposition exist side by side in it:

'How I shall make all things one and each by itself' [*Orph.* frg. 165.1].

332. [79a1-4] Why does he make it a specific property of things intelligible that we do not use sense-perception to apprehend them, when the same holds good of the objects of discursive reason? — In apprehending

---

§ 329. Dam. II § 34. Ol. 13 § 3.16–20. Dam. II and Ol. prove that the step from 'more indissoluble' to 'lasting longer' forms a separate syllogism. The diagram here should be corrected accordingly.

§ 330. Dam. II § 35. Ol. 13 § 5. See note on Ol., and *supra* § 274.

§ 331. Dam. II § 36. Ol. 13 § 2.32–40; § 9. See note on Ol.

οδ'. - [79c2-e7] Εἰ ἡ μὲν νόησις εἰς νοῦν αὐτὴν ἀνάγει καὶ διατίθησι κατὰ 327 φύσιν, ἡ δὲ αἴσθησις εἰς σῶμα καὶ παρὰ φύσιν, δῆλον τὸ συμπέρασμα.

οε'. - [79e8-80a9] Εἰ αὐτὴ μὲν ἄρχει, ὥσπερ ὁ νοῦς, τὸ δὲ σῶμα ἄρχεται, 328 ὡς ἡ γένεσις, καὶ τοῦτο δῆλον.

—. - ἡ ψυ- ὁμοιοτέρα ὁμοιοτέρα μᾶλλον ἀθάνατον, πολυ- 329
χὴ τῷ νοητῷ τῷ ἀθανάτῳ χρονιώτερον τοῦ σώματος.

§§ 330–339. Some difficulties in 78c1–80e1

ος'. - [78d1-7] Ὅτι ζητήσειεν ἄν τις, περὶ ποίων λέγει εἰδῶν ὡς ἀδιαλύτων. 330 εἰ μὲν γὰρ περὶ τῶν ἐν ἡμῖν καὶ τὴν ψυχὴν συμπληρούντων, πῶς τούτοις ὁμοιοτέρα ἡ ψυχή, ἀλλ᾽ οὐκ ἄντικρυς ἡ αὐτή; πῶς δὲ ὑποτίθεται ἀθάνατα, ἵνα δειχθῇ ἡ ψυχὴ πολυχρονιωτέρα; εἰ δὲ τὰ νοητά, πῶς περὶ τούτων αἱ ἐρωτήσεις καὶ ἀποκρίσεις γίγνονται; οὐδεμία γὰρ τῶν νοητῶν ἐπιστήμη, ὡς ἐν Ἐπιστολαῖς 5 [VII 342a7-343d2] εἴρηται, οὐδὲ λόγος, οὐδὲ ὄνομα. — Ἢ ῥητέον ὅτι περὶ αὐτῶν, εἰ καὶ περὶ τῶν ἀπ᾽ αὐτῶν· ἐφαπτόμενος γάρ πως καὶ ἐκείνων, εἴπερ κατορθοῖ.

οζ'. - [78c1-4] Πῶς οὐχὶ καὶ ὁ κόσμος ἔσται λυτός, εἴπερ σύνθετος; 331
— Ἢ τῷ δήσαντι λυτός, εἴπερ ἐκεῖνος λυτικός, ὅπερ οὐκ ἔστι. συνετέθη γὰρ καλῶς, ὥστε ἀγαθὸς ὢν οὐ λύσει, οὐδὲ λυτὸν ἐποίησε.
⟨Κάλλιον δὲ λέγειν ὅτι καὶ λυτὸν ἐποίησε·⟩ σύνθετον γὰρ ἀΐδιον ἐποίησεν, ὥστε καὶ λυτὸν ἀΐδιον, εἴπερ λυτὸν πάντως τὸ σύνθετον· καὶ λυόμενόν γε ἀεί, 5 καὶ γὰρ ἀεὶ συντιθέμενον. ὡς γὰρ ὁμοῦ τὸ πᾶν γινόμενον καὶ ἀπολλύμενον, οὕτω συντιθέμενον καὶ λυόμενον· ἅμα γὰρ τῇ συγκρίσει καὶ ἡ διάκρισις ἐν αὐτῷ. ʽπῶς δέ μοι ἕν τε τὰ πάντα ἔσται καὶ χωρὶς ἕκαστα᾽ [Orph. frg. 165.1].

οη'. - [79a1-4] Πῶς ὡς ἐξαίρετόν φησι τῶν νοητῶν τὸ μὴ χρῆσθαι αἰσθήσει; 332(163) οὐδὲ γὰρ πρὸς τὰ διανοητά. — Ἢ πρὸς μὲν ταῦτα κατὰ γοῦν ἀνάμνησιν ἡ χρῆσις

---

§ 329. in spat. vac. Mᶜ
§ 331. 4 Κάλλιον - ἐποίησε Wk: om. M

1-3. Pl., Tim. 41a7-b2.
4. The supplement is justified by II § 36.9-14.
8. The line is spoken by Zeus, who consults the oracle of Night on the creation of the world; cf. Kern pp. 198-199.
§ 332. Dam. II § 37. Ol. 13 §§ 12-13.

these, however, sensible things can at least serve to stir the memory, a function which, where intelligible reality is concerned, is taken over by the objects of discursive thought, the result being 'ap-prehension' [a further grasp, a3], not prehension simply.

333. [79b7–8] In what sense is the soul invisible 'to men'? Even if it were visible to other, higher beings, it would have to be corporeal. — The answer: anything that is visible is at some time visible also to men, in one out of four ways: (1) by ordinary perception; (2) by a special natural disposition; (3) by a disposition brought about artificially through natural means; (4) by second sight.

334. [79d6] How can insight be called an 'affect,' when it unites us with the intelligible world? — Because it is not only an activity of the soul, but is also subject to the assimilating influence of intelligence.

335. [79c2–9] How can the senses be causes of error, the senses 'through which we have received the gift of philosophy' [*Tim.* 47a7–b1]? — The latter is true of those who, having achieved recollection, then abandon the senses, the former of those who abide by them and rely on them.

336. [80a10–c1] Why should anything that resembles an indissoluble substance be indissoluble itself? Surely resemblance excludes identity? — Yes, but the conclusion goes no farther than that soul is less dissoluble than body.

337. If that which is more like intelligible reality is more permanent, how is it that matter is more permanent than forms? — The commentator's explanation is that they do not dominate.

Nevertheless, matter *is* less like the intelligible than form is, since, after all, it is not characterized by intelligence. It is therefore better to say that form separated from matter has a more real existence than matter not mastered by form.

338. How do we explain that the life which has the body as its substratum is not more permanent, though it is certainly more like the intelligible than the body is? — The commentator's solution is again that it does not dominate, nor does it have knowledge.

3–4. Based on the division of the line in *Rep.* VI 510b2–511e5, where the objects of διάνοια are the copy through which the νοητόν is known. This meaning is here lent to the words οὐκ ἔστιν ὅτῳ ποτ' ἂν ἄλλῳ ἐπιλάβοιο ἢ τῷ τῆς διανοίας λογισμῷ, *Ph.* 79a2–3.

§ 333. Dam. II § 38. Ol. 13 § 15. (With notes).

§ 334. Dam. II § 39. Ol. 13 § 19. See note on Ol.

§§ 335–337. On the (remote) possibility that these objections might derive from Strato, see Introduction to Ol., pp. 7–8.

§ 335. Dam. II § 40. Same question and same answer Ol. 4 § 7.1–4; § 8.

§ 336. Dam. II § 41. Ol. 13 § 6.1–6.

§ 337. Dam. II § 42. Ol. 13 § 6.7–12.

2. οὐ δεσπόζει : Ol. and Dam. II have ἐν ὑποκειμένῳ (ἐστί), which can be reduced

ἂν παραληφθείη τῶν αἰσθητῶν, πρὸς δὲ ἐκεῖνα ἀπὸ τῶν διανοητῶν ἡ ἀνάμνησις καὶ ἀπὸ τούτων 'ἐπίληψις' [a3], ἀλλ' οὐ λῆψις ἁπλῶς.

οθ'. - [79b7–8] *Πῶς ἀόρατον ἡ ψυχὴ 'ὑπὸ ἀνθρώπων'; εἰ γὰρ καὶ ὑπὸ ἄλλων κρειττόνων, σωματικὴ ἂν εἴη.* — Ἢ πᾶν ὁρατὸν καὶ ὑπὸ ἀνθρώπων ποτὲ ὁρατόν, τετραχῶς· ἢ κατὰ τὴν κοινὴν αἴσθησιν, ἢ κατὰ φυσικὴν τοιάνδε κατασκευήν, ἢ διὰ τῶν φυσικῶν δυνάμεων τετεχνασμένην, ἢ ἐνθουσιῶσαν. 333

π'. - [79d6] *Πῶς 'πάθος' ἡ φρόνησις, καίτοι συνάπτουσα πρὸς τὰ νοητά;* — Ἢ ὅτι οὐ μόνον ἐνέργεια τῆς ψυχῆς, ἀλλὰ καὶ πεπονθυῖα τὸν νοῦν κατὰ ἀφομοίωσιν. 334

πα'. - [79c2–9] *Πῶς αἰτίαι πλάνης αἱ αἰσθήσεις, 'δι' ὧν τὸ φιλοσοφίας ἐπορισάμεθα γένος' [Tim. 47a7–b1];* — Ἢ τοῖς μὲν ἀναμιμνησκομένοις εἶτα ἀφισταμένοις τοῦτο ἀληθές, τοῖς δὲ ἐγκαταμένουσι καὶ πιστεύουσιν ἐκεῖνο. 335

πβ'. - [80a10–c1] *Πῶς τὸ ὅμοιον τῷ ἀδιαλύτῳ ἀδιάλυτον; οὐδὲν γὰρ ὅμοιον ταὐτὸν ᾧ ἐστιν ὅμοιον.* — Ἢ μᾶλλόν γε τοῦ σώματος ἀδιάλυτον συμπεραίνεται. 336

πγ'. - *Εἰ τὸ ὁμοιότερον πρὸς τὸ νοητὸν μονιμώτερον, πῶς ἡ ὕλη μονιμωτέρα τῶν εἰδῶν;* — Ἢ ὅτι, φησίν, οὐ δεσπόζει. 337

'Αλλ' ὅμως ἧττον ὁμοία τοῦ εἴδους, ἐπεὶ οὐδὲ νοερά. κάλλιον οὖν εἰπεῖν ὅτι μᾶλλον τὸ εἶδος ἔστι χωριζόμενον ὕλης ἢ ἡ ὕλη μὴ διακρατουμένη ὑπὸ τοῦ εἴδους.

πδ'. - *Πῶς ἡ ἐν ὑποκειμένῳ ζωὴ οὐ μονιμωτέρα, καίτοι οὖσα ὁμοιοτέρα τῷ νοητῷ τοῦ γε σώματος;* — Ἢ οὐδὲ αὕτη δεσπόζει, φησίν, οὐδὲ γιγνώσκει. 338

---

§ 335. 2 ἐπορισάμεθα M^c (Pl.): ἐποιησάμεθα M¹
§ 338. 2 ἢ οὐδὲ M^c: νοῦ δὲ M¹

---

to the same terms, cf. § 311.3–4. The subject must be immanent form (the argument being that it lacks the third characteristic of § 325), whereas that of ἧττον ὁμοία τοῦ εἴδους (line 3) is matter.

3. *ἐπεὶ οὐδὲ νοερά*: as it is rather superfluous to state that matter is not characterized by intelligence, these words should perhaps be transferred after line 2 *οὐ δεσπόζει*, where they would have τὰ (ἔνυλα) εἴδη, immanent forms, as their subject, and would provide an exact parallel with the οὐδὲ γιγνώσκει at § 338.2.

§ 338. Dam. II § 43. Ol. 13 § 6.12–15. Instead of ἡ ἐν ὑποκειμένῳ ζωή, Dam. II has ἡ μερικὴ ζωή, which amounts to the same thing, Ol. ἡ φύσις, which is different, but is discussed here in passing (line 4). Pr.'s answer to the objection is that immanent life lacks the third and second characteristics of § 325; Dam. observes that it does at least have the first. His solution is that in assigning to intermediate entities

Yet the fact remains that it is invisible, so that the first reason [§ 325] should apply. A better way out is therefore that all things of this kind (life in a substratum, nature, form) belong to the world of process, to which intermediate entities may show similarity, as some others do to the intelligible world. If anyone should want to divide these still further and look for resemblances, let him realize that his comparison is not applicable throughout, but to life on the one hand, to body on the other. Now if life holds together the body in spite of its state of flux, that which holds together must be more permanent than that which is so held.

339. [79e8–80a9] How can it be shown that the soul rules the body? — On the basis of the seven qualifications of the ruler as given in the *Laws* [III 690a1–c9]; soul is: (1) a contributory cause; (2) nobler than the body, because descended from an immutable cause; (3) older, because preexistent; (4) dominant, because it imparts motion; (5) stronger, since it holds the body together; (6) wiser, inasmuch as it looks ahead; (7) more fortunate, because it has received an allotment, rather than being given out as an allotment itself.

§§ 340–348. Observations on 78c1–80e1

340. [78c1–5] Non-composite is not necessarily the non-pluralized, but that in which the one prevails over plurality, so that the manifold belongs to the one; composite is that in which the one is dominated by the many, so that the one is a kind of bond of the manifold, whereas in the other case the manifold is a kind of procession of the one. In this sense intelligence is non-composite, and in the sense that it answers the other description all materialized form is composite. Soul holds an intermediate position between compositeness and non-compositeness, but still it is prevailingly non-composite; for though it lives on two planes, it attains its highest excellence when taking refuge in the non-composite, and the form of each thing is determined by its superior part.

341. [78c6–9] The one presents no change whatever, for change can exist only in a manifold, since it means that one thing follows another. Therefore Socrates uses 'being always of the same condition and nature' as

---

a place between the two poles of the intelligible and the generated, we should remember that the instances now under discussion (immanent life, nature, immanent form) are already classified as γενητά to begin with. Anyone who wants to distinguish two different constituents in them should make it clear to himself, to which of the two he is referring. The final point of the argument (lines 7–8) is explained more fully at II § 43.3–7.

§ 339. Dam. II § 44. The qualifications in the *Laws*, loc. cit., are: (1) τό τε πατρὸς καὶ μητρός, (2) γενναίους ἀγεννῶν ἄρχειν, (3) πρεσβυτέρους μὲν ἄρχειν ..., νεωτέρους δὲ ἄρχεσθαι, (4) δούλους μὲν ἄρχεσθαι, δεσπότας δὲ ἄρχειν, (5) τὸ κρείττονα μὲν ἄρχειν, τὸν ἥττω δὲ ἄρχεσθαι, (6) ἕπεσθαι μὲν τὸν ἀνεπιστήμονα ..., τὸν δὲ φρονοῦντα ἡγεῖσθαί

'Αλλ' ὅμως ἀόρατον· ἔδει οὖν τὸν α' λόγον [§ 325] κρατεῖν. κάλλιον οὖν λέγειν ὅτι τὰ τοιαῦτα πάντα, οἷον ἡ ζωὴ ἡ ἐν ὑποκειμένῳ, ἡ φύσις, τὸ εἶδος, τῶν γενητῶν | ἐστιν, πρὸς ἃ ἡ τῶν μέσων ἀφομοίωσις, ὡς ἐνίων πρὸς τὰ νοητά. 5(164) εἰ δὲ καὶ ταῦτα διαιρῶν τις ἐπιζητοῖ τὰ ὅμοια, μαθέτω μὴ πάντῃ ποιούμενος τὴν ὁμοίωσιν, ἀλλὰ πῇ μὲν τῆς ζωῆς, πῇ δὲ τοῦ σώματος. εἰ δὲ καὶ ἐν ῥοῇ ὂν τὸ σῶμα συνέχει, μονιμωτέρα ἡ συνέχουσα τοῦ συνεχομένου.

πε'. – [79e8–80a9] *Πῶς δείκνυται ἡ ψυχὴ τοῦ σώματος ἄρχουσα;* — Ἢ κατὰ 339 τὰ ἑπτὰ ἀρχικὰ ἀξιώματα τὰ ἐν Νόμοις [III 690a1–c9]· καὶ γὰρ συναιτία, καὶ εὐγενεστέρα ὡς ἀπὸ αἰτίας ἀκινήτου, καὶ πρεσβυτέρα ὡς προϋπάρχουσα, καὶ δεσποτικωτέρα ὡς κινοῦσα, καὶ ἰσχυροτέρα ὡς συνέχουσα, καὶ φρονιμωτέρα ὡς προβουλευομένη, καὶ εὐτυχεστέρα ὡς λαχοῦσα οὐ ληχθεῖσα. 5

§§ 340-348. Observations on 78c1-80e1

πς'. – [78c1–5] *Ὅτι ἀσύνθετόν ἐστιν οὐ τὸ ἀπλήθυντον πάντως, ἀλλ' ἐν ᾧ* 340 *τὸ ἓν ἐπικρατεῖ τῶν πολλῶν, ὥστε τοῦ ἑνὸς εἶναι τὸ πλῆθος·* σύνθετον δέ, ἐν ᾧ κρατεῖται τὸ ἓν ὑπὸ τῶν πολλῶν, ὥστε τῶν πολλῶν εἶναι τὸ ἓν οἷον συνοχήν, ἐκεῖ δὲ τὰ πολλὰ τοῦ ἑνὸς οἷον πρόοδος. οὕτω μὲν οὖν ὁ νοῦς ἀσύνθετος, ἐκείνως δὲ τὸ ἔνυλον εἶδος σύνθετον ἅπαν. ἡ δὲ ψυχὴ μέσως μὲν ἔχει συνθέσεως καὶ 5 ἀσυνθεσίας, ὅμως δὲ μᾶλλον ἀσύνθετος· εἰ γὰρ καὶ ἀμφίβιος, ἀλλὰ κρείττων αὐτή γε ἑαυτῆς εἰς τὸ ἀσύνθετον ἀναφεύγουσα, κατὰ δὲ τὸ κρεῖττον ἕκαστον εἰδοποιεῖται.

πζ'. – [78c6–9] *Ὅτι οὐδεμίαν μεταβολὴν τὸ ἓν παρέχεται·* ἐν πλήθει γὰρ 341 ἡ μεταβολή, ἄλλο γὰρ μετ' ἄλλο. διὸ τὸ 'κατὰ τὰ αὐτὰ καὶ ὡσαύτως ἔχειν'

---

§ 338. 3 α' λόγον Wk: ἄλογον M
§ 340. 3 συνοχήν Mᶜ: -ή M¹

τε καὶ ἄρχειν, (7) λαχόντα μὲν ἄρχειν, δυσκληροῦντα δὲ ἀπιόντα ἄρχεσθαι.

2. *συναιτία*: soul is emphatically αἰτία, not συναιτία (I § 409, II § 66); yet the text is probably correct, soul being called a contributory cause in relation to intelligence as the cause proper (cf. the next lines). We know nothing about the usual interpretation of the passage in the *Laws*, but it seems that for the present purpose Intelligence is assigned the role of Father, Soul that of Mother. – For the feminine form συναιτία cf. § 407.5 (Pl. has the fem. adj. συναιτίας *Polit.* 281c4, otherwise -ους : 281e4; 9; 287c8; d2).

§§ 340–360. These two lectures are missing from Dam. II.

§ 340. 5–6. Cf. Pr., *Tim.* II 117.16–20: the intelligible is non-composite, the generated is composite, soul is intermediate.

evidence that the one prevails, that is to say, a non-composite one, and 'continual change' as proof that not the one dominates, but plurality.

342. The pluralization that causes change affects the substances of things united in substance, and the activities of things united in activity. Those substances that have reached the lowest margin of the realm of the one betray this coming down to the lowest point in their activities by drawing away somewhat from their own being towards the external and at the same time towards change.

343. [78d1–9] Any form that 'is only what it is, existing in a single form by itself,' by reason of its being by itself and only what it is, is self-sufficient and rests in itself and is saturated with itself, and by reason of its existing in a single form, is indivisible and therefore proof against change.

344. [78d10–e5] Any individual reproduced form is manifold, for, being divisible, it will in the normal course of things be divided and thereby change. It is not manifold because present in many; even in one thing it is manifold, because it is divided and as it were crippled. This is why it never remains in the same condition: it has become distant with respect to itself, and the result is otherness, or rather disintegration.

345. [78e2] Copies are 'homonymous' with their prototypes, as if the identity is preserved by the name only, the reality having passed from original to image.

346. How can we say that words belong primarily to the prototypes, which cannot be expressed in words? — Words apply properly to intermediate forms, the objects of discursive reason; but as they somehow point to intelligible forms as well, they seem, however inadequately, to express something of those at the same time.

347. [80c2–e1] If the soul holds the body together and thus gives it being, it has a higher degree of reality and is stronger than the body, since for its own part it does not need the body. So if the body continues to exist for a considerable time after death, how much more will this be true of the soul?

348. [80d7] Pluto is praised as 'good and wise' because he gives back to souls the ethical perfection and the knowledge which they lost in genesis. Hence his name Pluto ['the Rich One'], because he heals them from the bereavement of matter; and the other name, Hades ['the Invisible One'],

---

§ 342. The 'realm of the one' is the intelligible (cf. § 340); the 'marginal substances' are souls, whose activities detach them from their essence (Pr., *elem.* 191).

§ 345. According to Ar.'s definition, *cat.* 1, 1a1–2 ὁμώνυμα λέγεται ὧν ὄνομα μόνον κοινόν, ὁ δὲ κατὰ τοὔνομα λόγος τῆς οὐσίας ἕτερος.

τεκμήριον ποιεῖται τοῦ ἐπικρατεῖν τὸ ἕν, ὅ ἐστιν ἀσύνθετον ἕν, καὶ τὸ 'ἄλλοτε ἄλλως' τοῦ μὴ ἐπικρατεῖν τὸ ἕν, ἀλλὰ τὸ πλῆθος.

πη'. – "Ότι ὁ μεταβολῆς αἴτιος πληθυσμὸς τῶν μὲν ἐν ταῖς οὐσίαις ἡνωμένων 342 μεταβάλλει τὰς οὐσίας, τῶν δὲ ἐν ταῖς ἐνεργείαις τὰς ἐνεργείας. αἱ γὰρ ἐπὶ τὸ ἔσχατον ἐλθοῦσαι τῆς τοῦ ἑνὸς ἐπικρατείας οὐσίαι ἐν ταῖς ἐνεργείαις ἐλέγχουσιν τοῦτο τὸ ἔσχατον μικρὸν ἀπὸ τῶν οὐσιῶν ἀποστᾶσαι εἰς τὸ ἐκτὸς ἅμα καὶ εἰς μεταβολήν. 5

πθ'. – [78d1–9] "Ότι πᾶν εἶδος 'αὐτὸ ὂν ὅ ἐστι μονοειδὲς καθ' αὑτό', διότι 343(165) μὲν καθ' αὑτὸ καὶ αὐτὸ ὅ ἐστιν, αὔταρκές ἐστι καὶ ἐν ἑαυτῷ καὶ ἑαυτοῦ διακορές, διότι δὲ μονοειδές, ἀδιαίρετον εἰς μεταβολήν.

ρ'. – [78d10–e5] "Ότι πᾶν εἶδος εἰκονικὸν πολλὰ ἕκαστον· μεριστὸν γὰρ 344 πεφυκὸς ἄρα μερίζεσθαι εἰς μεταβολήν. οὐ γὰρ πολλὰ τῷ ἐν πολλοῖς, ἀλλὰ καὶ τὸ ἐν ἑνὶ πολλὰ ὡς μεμερισμένον καὶ οἷον παραλελυμένον. διόπερ οὐδέποτε κατὰ τὰ αὐτὰ ἔχει· διέστηκε γὰρ αὐτὸ πρὸς ἑαυτὸ εἰς ἑτερότητα, μᾶλλον δὲ διασπασμόν.

ρα'. – [78e2] "Ότι 'ὁμώνυμοί' τοῖς παραδείγμασιν αἱ εἰκόνες, ὡς μόνου τοῦ 345 ὀνόματος τὴν ταὐτότητα σῴζοντος, τοῦ δὲ πράγματος ἐκστάντος ἀπὸ τοῦ παραδείγματος εἰς εἰκόνα.

ρβ'. – Πῶς ἐκείνων τὰ ὀνόματα πρώτων, εἴπερ οὐκ ἔστιν αὐτῶν ὀνόματα; 346 – Ἢ ἔστι μὲν τὰ ὀνόματα κυρίως τῶν διανοητῶν καὶ μέσων εἰδῶν· ἐπειδὴ δὲ ἐνδείκνυταί πως καὶ ἐκεῖνα, ὁπωσοῦν δοκεῖ τι καὶ ἐκείνων παρασημαίνειν.

ργ'. – [80c2–e1] "Ότι εἰ ἡ ψυχὴ συνέχει τὸ σῶμα πρὸς τὸ εἶναι, οὐσιωδεστέρα 347 ἐστὶν αὐτοῦ καὶ ἰσχυροτέρα, ἅτε μηδὲ δεομένη τι αὐτοῦ. εἰ τοίνυν τοῦτο ἐπιμένει πλείω χρόνον μετὰ θάνατον, πόσῳ γε μᾶλλον ἐκείνη;

ρδ'. – [80d7] "Ότι ὁ Πλούτων 'ἀγαθὸς καὶ φρόνιμος' ἀνυμνεῖται ὡς ἀποδιδοὺς 348 ταῖς ψυχαῖς τὴν ἀρετὴν καὶ ἐπιστήμην, ἣν κατὰ τὴν γένεσιν ἀπώλεσαν. διὸ καὶ Πλούτων, ὅτι ἐξιᾶται αὐτῶν τὴν ὑλικὴν χρησμοσύνην· καὶ ἔτι Ἅιδης, ὅτι

---

§ 341. 3 τὸ² Mˣ: τῶι M¹ — 4 τοῦ Fh: τῶι M
§ 342. 4 ἀποστᾶσαι] -ι in ras. Mˣ (ἀποστᾶσαν M¹?)

---

§ 346. 1. εἴπερ αὐτῶν οὐκ ἔστιν ὀνόματα: according to the well-known passage in Ep. VII, 342a7–343d2, cited above § 330.
§ 348. 2–4. Pluto 'the Rich One', Hades 'the Invisible': Pl., Crat. 403a3–8; Pr., Crat. 87.5–18.

because he takes away all the marks of visibility with which they have been branded (this is the meaning of the story of the helmet of Hades) and purifies them from the evil consequences of living in sympathy with the visible world.

§§ 349-360. The fate of the soul. Observations on 81a4-85b9

349. [81a4-5] What does it mean that the soul 'departs for what resembles it'? In what sense, indeed, does the intelligible resemble the content of discursive reason? We do not say, either, that Socrates looks like his own portrait. — Perhaps, however, the original does resemble its copy in so far as it assimilates the copy to itself. Just as a blow is twofold, in the striking force and in the object struck, so it is with resemblance too.

350. [81a5-6] That 'blessed' [*eudaimôn*] is used here in the sense of 'receiving the good [*eu*] from the Godhead [*daimôn*],' appears from Plato's phrase 'When she has arrived there, happiness is her lot.'

351. [81a8-9] Those who 'have their abode with the Gods' are the 'truly initiated,' that is, men who have taken refuge in their own oneness and the oneness of the Gods; uninitiated are those in the contrary state, who share in the multiplicity of the body and are mesmerized by it, so that they may be expected to go to that which they resemble.

352. [81c4-d4] The 'body-like' is different from the body: it is an affect of the soul, brought about in it by the body. Body-like is also the 'phantom' formed by such a kind of life-force and a more rarefied bodily substance, of which Plato says that it is 'weighed down' and that it is 'seen in the neighborhood of graves'; hence it is said to 'accompany' the soul [e1]. It is 'produced by those souls' that are still tied to the visible; this is why they can be seen, through participation in the visible or through affinity with it.

353. [81d7-9] They are not only willing, but are also 'compelled' to haunt the graves, to 'do penance' for their affinity with the body.

354. [81d9-e2] This phantom, which has a natural craving for the earthly body, eventually drags the soul towards it, justice permitting, and in some cases becomes instrumental in its improvement.

355. [81e2-82c1] Reincarnation in another species is explained (1) by the older Platonists in the sense that the soul becomes an integrating part

---

4. ἡ Ἄϊδος κυνῇ : both here and Ol., *Gorg.* 225.14, the reading of the first hand in M seems to have been κυανῇ, the 'dark cloud of Hades'. This is also the explanation given for κυνέη in schol. Pl., *Rep.* 612b νέφος τὴν Ἄϊδος κυνέην φασὶν ἀθάνατον καὶ ἀφανές, ἤτοι ἀορασίαν ... Eustath., *Il.* 5.845 ἔστι δὲ κατὰ τοὺς παλαιοὺς νέφος τι πυκνότατον ἡ τοῦ Ἄϊδου κυνέη (cf. *Il.* 16.66 κυάνεον Τρώων νέφος, 20.417-418 νεφέλη δέ μιν ἀμφεκάλυψε κυανέη, in death). The question arises whether Dam. and Ol. may actually have used the quasi-etymological form κυανῇ, and whether it may have been corrected away in other cases as well.

ἀποτρίβεται αὐτῶν ὅσον ἐγκέκαυται ὁρατόν, ὡς δηλοῖ ἡ ῎Αϊδος κυνῆ λεγομένη, ἀποκαθαίρει δὲ ἀπὸ τῶν ἑπομένων κακῶν τῇ πρὸς τὸ ὁρατὸν συμπαθείᾳ.

§§ 349-360. The fate of the soul. Observations on 81a4-85b9

δ ρε′. – [81a4-5] *Πῶς λέγεται 'εἰς τὸ ὅμοιον ἀπιέναι'; πῶς γὰρ τὸ νοητὸν* 349 *τῷ διανοητῷ ὅμοιον; οὐδὲ γὰρ ὁ Σωκράτης ἐοικέναι λέγεται τῇ ἑαυτοῦ εἰκόνι.* — ῍Η τάχα καὶ τὸ παράδειγμα τῇ εἰκόνι ὅμοιον ὡς ἐξομοιοῦν ἑαυτῷ τὴν εἰκόνα. ὡς γὰρ ἡ πληγὴ διτ|τή, ἡ μὲν τοῦ πλήττοντος, ἡ δὲ τοῦ πληττομένου, οὕτω (166) καὶ ἡ ὁμοίωσις.

ρϛ′. – [81a5-6] *῞Οτι τὸ εὔδαιμον κατὰ τὴν τοῦ εὖ μέθεξιν ἀπὸ τοῦ κρείττονος* 350 *εἴληπται, δηλοῖ εἰπὼν 'οἷ ἀφικομένῃ ὑπάρχει εὐδαίμονι εἶναι'.*

ρζ′. – [81a8-9] *῞Οτι 'μετὰ θεῶν διάγουσιν' οἱ 'ὡς ἀληθῶς μεμυημένοι',* 351 *τουτέστιν εἰς τὸ ἓν τό τε ἑαυτῶν καὶ τὸ ἐκείνων ἀναφυγόντες. ἀμύητοι δέ εἰσιν οἱ ἀντιστρόφως διακείμενοι, οἱ τῷ σώματι συμπεπληθυσμένοι καὶ πρὸς τοῦτο διαχαίνοντες· ὅθεν οὗτοι κἂν χωροῖεν πρὸς τὸ ὅμοιον.*

ρη′. – [81c4-d4] *῞Οτι ἄλλο παρὰ τὸ σῶμα τὸ 'σωματοειδές'· τοῦτο γὰρ τῆς* 352 *ψυχῆς ἐστι πάθος ἀπὸ τοῦ σώματος ἐγγενόμενον. ἔστι δὲ καὶ τὸ 'εἴδωλον' σωματοειδές, ἐκ τῆς τοιαύτης ζωῆς καί τινος λεπτοτέρου σώματος, ὃ καὶ 'βαρύνεσθαι' καὶ 'ὁρᾶσθαι' λέγει 'περὶ τοὺς τάφους'· διὸ 'συνακολουθεῖν' αὐτῇ λέγεται* [e1]. *ὃ 'παρέχονται αἱ ψυχαί' ὅσαι ἔτι ἐνδέδενται τῷ ὁρατῷ· διὸ καὶ ὁρῶνται κατὰ μέθεξιν τοῦ ὁρατοῦ ἢ συμπάθειαν τὴν πρὸς αὐτό.*

ρθ′. – [81d7-9] *῞Οτι οὐ μόνον βούλονται, ἀλλὰ καὶ 'διαναγκάζονται' πλανᾶσθαι* 353 *περὶ τὰ μνήματα, 'δίκην τίνουσαι' τῆς περὶ τὸ σῶμα συμπαθείας.*

ρ′. – [81d9-e2] *῞Οτι τὸ εἴδωλον τοῦτο σύμφυτον ἔχον ἐπιθυμίαν πρὸς τὸ* 354 *ὄστρεον ἕλκει ποτὲ πρὸς αὑτὸ τὴν ψυχὴν συγχωρούσης τῆς δίκης, καὶ ἐνίοτε συναίτιον γίγνεται πρὸς τὸ ἄμεινον.*

α′ ρα′. – [81e2-82c1] *῞Οτι τὴν εἰς τὰ ἄλλα εἴδη μετεμψύχωσιν οἱ μὲν παλαιότεροι* 355 *Πλατωνικοὶ κατὰ συμπλήρωσιν ἐξηγοῦνται. οἷς πολλὰ μὲν οἱ ἀκριβέστεροι*

---

§ 348. 4 ῎Αϊδος] άϊδ ≡ ος, accent. in a- add., in -ϊ- eras., M^c (ἀίδιος ut vid. M¹) | κυνῆ] -υ- in ras. 2 litt., ¯ ex ', M^c (κυανή fort. M¹)
§ 350. 2 εὐδαίμονι Fh (Pl.): εὔδαιμον M
§ 352. 4 αὐτῇ] -ῆι in ras. M^x
§ 353. 1 scr. ἀναγκάζονται? (Pl.; infra § 355.13)

---

§ 352. Cf. Porphyry's comment on the *Ph.* passage, *sent.* § 29, and the parallels collected by Lamberz *ad loc.*
§ 353. 1. διαναγκάζονται: the meaningless δι- may be either a dittography of the preceding (κ)αί or anticipation of the following δί(κην).
§ 355. On metempsychosis see Dörrie's paper cited at § 177 and Beutler, art. Pr. 273.14–31. The doxography given here by Dam. can be completed from a passage in Aeneas of Gaza, *Theophrastus* p. 12.1-25, which may derive either from Pr.'s commentary on the *Ph.*, or from that on the *Phaedrus*, in which he says he

of the being in question. The more discerning critics have many arguments to oppose this view, their strongest point being that it will not fit in with Plato's statement that some 'join the Gods': no more than they become parts of Gods do the others become parts of animals. (2) Others say that human beings are metaphorically assigned the form corresponding to their characters, donkeys standing for the donkeyish, Gods for the God-like and so forth. This is disproved by the fact that Plato makes reincarnation in other kinds dependent on habit and training in a particular way of life in the human shape, so that for example those who are like donkeys become donkeys by reincarnation, and the God-like Gods, which is the reverse of what these people make him say. (3) A third group hold that reincarnation consists in an outward association with irrational animals. Their view is supported by Plato's remark that the similar will seek the company of its similar [82a7–8] and by the consideration that the words 'joining the Gods' and 'having their abode with the Gods,' as it was expressed before [69c7], clearly bear this meaning. Besides, if justice 'compels them to haunt graves' [81d7–8], why should it not also compel them to join brute animals, which, though alien to man, are at least less repulsive than corpses?

356. [82a10–b8] Why do those who 'practice the popular virtues' enter into irrational animals? — Because they have immersed themselves deeply in worthless occupations.

357. [83c5–8] From activities we know substances; therefore the substances whose activities we observe most keenly and most often, are the ones of which we are aware most keenly and most often.

---

discussed the whole problem and his own view of it at length (*Tim.* III 295.3–14; cf. also *Rep.* II 329.26–341.4). As representatives of opinion (1) Aeneas lists Plotinus (III 4,2; IV 3,12; VI 7, 6.33–36), Harpocratio (cf. Hermias 102.13–15), Amelius, Boethus (a Peripatetic, who at best could have *cited* the doctrine in this form) and Numenius (frg. 37); for opinion (2), Porphyry (*de regressu*, frg. 11,1 = Aug., *civ.* 10,30) and Iamblichus; opinion (3) is that of Syrianus (Hermias 170.16–19), Proclus (*Tim.* III 294.22–295.14) and Dam.

10. κατὰ ἐπακολούθησιν : Hermias' term (170.17) is συνεπιπλέκεται.

11. *Ph.* 82a8 (κατὰ τὰς αὑτῶν ὁμοιότητας τῆς μελέτης); cf. *Gorg.* 510b2–4; *Lys.* 214b3–4; *Symp.* 195b5; *Rep.* IV 425c2.

§ 356. 2. βαθύνοντες ἐπὶ πολὺ τῆς βαναύσου ζωῆς : intransitive use of the verb Pr., *Alc.* 130.14 ἵνα καὶ προνοῇ τῶν ἀτελεστέρων καὶ μὴ βαθύνῃ περὶ αὐτά, and Dam., *princ.* 206.23–25 ὅσῳ δὲ ἐπικατιέναι συμβαίνει τὴν πρόοδον, βαθύνουσάν τε καὶ ἐποικοδομουμένην ταῖς περιγραφαῖς καὶ τοῖς μερισμοῖς. Otherwise usually in the phrase βαθύνειν τὸ ἐπίπεδον, the origin of which, according to Kroll (Pr., *Rep.* II 51.26), is Pl., *Laws* X 904c9–d1: (animate beings) σμικρότερα μὲν τῶν ἠθῶν μεταβάλλοντα ἐλάττω κατὰ τὸ τῆς χώρας ἐπίπεδον μεταπορεύεται, πλείω δὲ καὶ ἀδικώτερα μεταπεσόντα, εἰς βάθος τά τε κάτω λεγόμενα τῶν τόπων. In the mathematical sense of 'adding a third dimension' Pr., *Tim.* I 146.14–15; transferred to the soul Pr., *Rep.* II 52.4–5 (the soul while directed towards intelligence is one-dimensional, a line; when entering into itself it becomes two-dimensional, a surface) εἰς δὲ τὰ μετ' αὐτὴν

ἀντιλέγουσιν, ἐκεῖνο δὲ μέγιστον τεκμήριον ὅτι μὴ οὕτως εἴρηται τὸ 'εἰς θεῶν γένος ἀφικνεῖσθαι' τινας· ὡς οὖν οὗτοι οὐ συμπληροῦσι θεούς, οὐδὲ ἐκεῖνοι τὰ
β' ἄλλα ζῷα. οἱ δὲ τοῖς ἤθεσι κατὰ μεταφορὰν εἰδοποιεῖσθαι τοὺς ἀνθρώπους,   5
ὄνους μὲν λεγομένους τοὺς ὀνώδεις, θεοὺς | δὲ τοὺς θείους, καὶ τὰ ἄλλα γένη (167)
ὡσαύτως. οὓς διελέγχει εἰπὼν κατὰ συνήθειαν καὶ μελέτην τῆς ἐν ἀνθρωπείῳ
βίῳ ζωῆς μετεμψυχοῦσθαι εἰς τὰ ἄλλα γένη, τοὺς μὲν ὀνώδεις φέρε εἰς τοὺς
γ' ὄνους, τοὺς δὲ θείους εἰς θεούς, ἀνάπαλιν ἢ ὡς οὗτοι λέγουσιν. τρίτοι δὲ οἱ
κατὰ ἐπακολούθησιν τὴν σὺν τοῖς ἀλόγοις ζῴοις ἔξωθεν γιγνομένην. ὧν τὴν 10
δόξαν βεβαιοῖ τό τε ὅμοιον τῷ ὁμοίῳ συνεῖναι βουλόμενον [82a7–8] καὶ τὸ οὕτω
σαφῶς 'εἰς θεοὺς ἀπιέναι' καὶ 'συνδιατρίβειν θεοῖς' οὕτως εἰρημένον πρότερον
[69c7]. καὶ εἰ 'περὶ τὰ μνήματα ἀναγκάζονται πλανᾶσθαι' ὑπὸ τῆς δίκης
[81d7–8], διὰ τί οὐχὶ καὶ περὶ τὰ ἄλογα ζῷα, εἰ καὶ ἀλλότρια ὄντα, ὅμως
καλλίω τῶν νεκρῶν σωμάτων;   15

ρβ'. – [82a10–b8] Πῶς οἱ 'τὴν δημοτικὴν ἀρετὴν ἐπιτηδεύοντες' εἰς ἄλογα 356
φέρονται; – Ἢ ὡς βαθύνοντες ἐπὶ πολὺ τῆς βαναύσου ζωῆς.

ργ'. – [83c5–8] Ὅτι ἐκ τῶν ἐνεργειῶν γιγνώσκομεν τὰς οὐσίας· ὧν τοίνυν 357
μάλιστα ἐνεργειῶν ἀντιλαμβανόμεθα καὶ ὧν πλειστάκις, ταύτας μάλιστα καὶ
πλειστάκις γνωρίζομεν.

§ 355.   9 ἦ] in ras. M^c — 10 post ἔξωθεν] ∼ in ras. M^c

ῥέπουσα βαθύνει τὰ ἐπίπεδα. Hermias 130.25–29 (discussing the 'solid body' of Phaedr. 246c3) στερεὸν δὲ εἰπὼν τὸ ἔνυλον δῆλός ἐστι μὴ ἀξιῶν τὸ ἀίδιον ὄχημα τῆς ψυχῆς στερεὸν καλεῖν, ὃ οὐκ ἔστι τριχῇ διαστατὸν ἀλλὰ ἐπίπεδον ὡς λεπτὸν καὶ ἄυλον· διὸ καὶ παρακελεύεται μὴ βαθύνειν τὸ ἐπίπεδον καὶ ποιεῖν αὐτὸ γεῶδες καὶ ἔνικμον διὰ τῆς ῥυπαρᾶς ζωῆς. The subject of παρακελεύεται can be hardly anyone else than Plato, either in the Laws, loc. cit., or in Ph. 81c8–d4 (where the word βαρύνεται occurs) or both. Hermias' interpretation (the 'surface' is the astral body) is shared by Psellus, de orac. Chald., PG 122, 1137C8–D4 (p. 176 Des Places), who quotes the phrase as part of a Chaldean Oracle: μὴ πνεῦμα μολύνῃς μηδὲ βαθύνῃς τὸ ἐπίπεδον, to which Kroll (followed by Lewy and Des Places, frg. 105) gave the look of hexameter verse by writing τοὐπίπεδον. The first words μὴ πνεῦμα μολύνῃς are well attested as belonging to the Chaldean Oracles, but the rest is open to doubt: (1) the sentence as transmitted is not verse, and it does not become so by the spelling τοὐπίπεδον, (2) neither Pr. nor Hermias indicates that it is from the Oracles, (3) frgs. 105 and 104 (in this, the correct order) are paraphrased by Pr. (Des Places p. 208.19–25) "Cast out envy and jealousy and do not quench them in your heart, lest you soil the spirit," without any reference to a sequel. Rather, the μολύνῃς seems to have ended the line (e.g. ζῆλόν τε φθόνον τε | ἔκβαλε μηδὲ φρενὶ σβέσσαι, μὴ πνεῦμα μολύνῃς). Evidently Psellus was following Pr., but in doing so he may unwittingly have added some extraneous material to the Oracles, as he did in other cases.

358. [84a3–6] In what sense does she 'handle the web in a way opposite to Penelope's'? — In the sense that philosophy invisibly weaves the soul together and unifies it, while ignorance undoes it and tears it apart openly, i.e. in this world of process.

Rather, philosophy undoes the web, and the ignorant life entangles the soul with the body. But then why 'in a way opposite to Penelope's'? The answer is that this applies to Penelope too, because she also handled her web in opposite ways as compared to herself.

359. [84e3–4] Prophecy is divine or demonic or human ('for believe me, my friend, the soul, too, is something prophetic' [*Phaedr.* 242c6–7]), and then there is another, natural kind, which is found in irrational animals also and consists in an inner perception of the future.

360. [85b4–5] Being an Apollonian man by virtue of his purificatory way of life, Socrates justly calls himself 'a fellow servant of the swans'; also, however, as a 'musical man' and as a healer of souls.

IV. THE ARGUMENT ON HARMONY

§§ 361–370. Analysis of the argument. 85b10–95a6

The argument on harmony

361. [91e2–92e3] The first argument to refute the position that soul is harmony is derived from what has already been proved, viz. that the soul

---

§ 358. Modern opinion is still divided between these two choices: ἐναντίως either means 'in a way opposite to Penelope's' (Pr., lines 1–3) or 'in opposite ways, as Penelope first wove, then undid her web' (Dam., lines 4–6). The inaccurate quotation ἐναντίως τῇ Πηνελόπῃ (lines 1 and 5) fits the first solution, but not the second; logically, the question at line 5 should be πῶς οὖν 'ἐναντίως'; cf. Pr., *Tim.* III 332.26–28 τῆς θρεπτικῆς δυνάμεως ... ὃ ἀνέλυσε συντιθείσης πάλιν κατὰ τὸν τῆς Πηνελόπης ἱστόν.

§ 359. Iambl., *myst.* 287.16–290.4, distinguishes (1) natural premonition in animals, (2) human knowledge of the future, either τεχνική or φυσική, (3) divine prophecy. Hermias 70.13–18 opposes divine prophecy to demonic and human. Cf. also *ibid.* 71.2–8 on 242c6–7, the sentence quoted here by Dam.

3. κατὰ προσυναίσθησιν : συναίσθησις as a function of plants Pr., *theol.* III 6, 128.54–129.2; Dam., *Phil.* § 163.4–5.

§ 360. Of the four motifs connected here with the Apollonian status of Socrates, three are also used to prove Plato's Apollonian origin, *Proleg.* 1.21–22; 1.38–39; 6.14–16. Socrates' patron deity, besides Apollo, is also Eros (*Phaedr.* 265c2; Pr., *Alc.* 33.3–5; 234.4–5), Zeus (*Phaedr.* 250b7; cf. Ol., *Alc.* 87.13 and 151.10–12) or Artemis (*Proleg.* 1.44–45).

1. κατὰ τὴν καθαρτικὴν ζωήν : *Proleg.* 1.38–39 οὐ μόνον δὲ τὰ ὀνείρατα ταῦτα δηλοῦσιν αὐτὸν (=Plato) Ἀπολλωνιακὸν ὄντα, ἀλλὰ καὶ τὸ εἶδος τῆς ζωῆς αὐτοῦ, καθαρτικὸν ὄν. Cf. Pr., *Alc.* 5.10 (Apollo as ἡγεμὼν τῆς καθαρτικῆς ζωῆς).

2. ὡς μουσικός : *Ph.* 61a1–4; *Phaedr.* 248d2–4.

2–3. ὡς ἰατρὸς τῶν ψυχῶν : *Proleg.* 6.14–16 (on the epigram cited Ol., *Alc.* 2.166–167=Diog. Laert. 3,45). Philosophy as ἰατρικὴ ψυχῶν El., *isag.* 9.9; 27.14; 31.10.

ρδ'. – [84a3–6] *Πῶς 'ἐναντίως τῇ Πηνελόπῃ ἱστὸν μεταχειρίζεται';* — Ἢ ὅτι 358
ἡ μὲν φιλοσοφία ἐν τῷ ἀφανεῖ συνυφαίνει αὐτὴν καὶ συναθροίζει, ἡ δὲ ἀμαθία
καταλύει καὶ διασπᾷ ἐν τῷ ἐμφανεῖ, τουτέστιν ἐν τῇ γενέσει.

Ἢ κάλλιον, λύειν μὲν τὴν φιλοσοφίαν, συνυφαίνειν δὲ τὴν ἀμαθῆ ζωὴν τῷ
σώματι. πῶς οὖν 'ἐναντίως τῇ Πηνελόπῃ'; ἢ τοῦτο καὶ τῇ Πηνελόπῃ ἁρμόζει· 5
καὶ γὰρ ἐκείνη πρὸς ἑαυτὴν ἐναντίως.

ρε'. – [84e3–4] *Ὅτι ἡ μαντικὴ ἢ θεία ἢ δαιμονία ἢ ἀνθρωπίνη ('ὡς δή τοι,* 359
ὦ ἑταῖρε, μαντικόν γέ τι καὶ ἡ ψυχή' [Phaedr. 242c6–7]*), ἡ δὲ φυσική τις,
οἷα καὶ τοῖς ἀλόγοις ζῴοις ἐγγίγνεται κατὰ προσυναίσθησιν.*

ρϛ'. – [85b4–5] *Ὅτι Ἀπολλωνιακὸς ὢν κατὰ τὴν καθαρτικὴν ζωὴν εἰκότως* 360
*'ὁμόδουλος' εἶναι λέγει 'τοῖς κύκνοις'· ἤδη δὲ καὶ ὡς μουσικὸς καὶ ὡς ἰατρὸς
τῶν ψυχῶν.*

IV. THE ARGUMENT ON HARMONY

§§ 361–370. Analysis of the argument. 85b10–95a6

Ὁ περὶ ἁρμονίας λόγος (168)

δ ρζ'. – [91e2–92e3] *Ὅτι ὁ πρῶτος ἀνασκευάζων λόγος μὴ εἶναι τὴν ψυχὴν* 361
ἁρμονίαν ἀπὸ τῶν προδεδειγμένων συνάγεται, λέγω δὲ τοῦ προϋπάρχειν αὐτὴν

---

§ 358. 2 ἐν ins. M^c: om. M¹
§ 359. 2 τι μ (Pl.): τοι M — 3 οἷα M | προσυναίσθησιν μ: προσσυναίσθησιν M

---

§§ 361–370. Dam. II §§ 45–53. The analysis of the argument on harmony current before Pr. has been preserved by Philop., *an.* 142.4–143.1 and Nemes., *nat. hom.* 83.5–86.11. Philop. distinguishes five isolated 'points': (1) soul exists prior to its recipient, harmony does not (*Ph.* 91e2–92e3); (2) soul can oppose the movements of the body, harmony cannot (94b4–95a3); (3) soul does not admit of gradation, harmony does (93b4–7); (4) soul admits of harmony and disharmony (i.e. virtue and vice), harmony does not (93b8–c10); (5) if soul does not admit of disharmony, all souls are equally perfect (94a8–b3). Nemesius omits point 5, adding instead an argument not derived from the *Ph.*: soul is substance, harmony is quality; the fifth point being really a subdivision of the fourth, its absence is not an important difference. For the rest, the agreement of the two *against* the *Ph.* is too striking to be accidental, even if we take into account that the peculiar position of point (2) is explained by the fact that its major premise (no harmony can oppose its elements) is found at *Ph.* 93a4–10, i.e. between (1) and (3). There must be a common source, which is almost certainly Porphyry (Krause p. 21). See also below § 405.1–2, where Dam. states that until the time of Pr., the proposition 93b4–7 was treated as a separate argument (number 3 in Nemes. and Philop.; cf. also note at § 388, on Strato). The method used is still that of Middle Platonism: the passage is cut up into five supposedly self-contained units, apparently for mnemonic or doxographical purposes. Compared to it, the analyses in the present commentary (I §§ 361–370, §§ 405–406, II §§ 45–53) are considerably more sophisticated. There are now only three separate arguments: (1) soul exists prior to its recipient (*Ph.* 91e2–92e3); (2) soul admits of harmony and disharmony (93b8–94b3); (3) soul can oppose the movements of the body (94b4–95a3). The

exists prior to the body, and the result is a syllogism in the second figure:

existence prior to recipient

den. / \ aff.
harmony / den. \ soul

362. [92e4–93b7] On behalf of his second [93b8–94b3] and his third argument [94b4–95a3] Socrates makes certain previous assumptions on the strength of which he denies that virtue is harmony; they relate partly to the predicate, harmony, partly to the subject, soul.

363. [92e4–93a3] The first assumption is that no harmony, nor indeed anything that is composite, can be conditioned differently from the elements of which it is a harmony or compound: what it is, each is in reference to them, and neither of the two in reference to itself.

364. [93a4–5] A second assumption follows from the preceding (whereas the first concerned the substance, this one regards its active or passive states), viz. that a harmony or a compound can neither exert nor undergo any influence by itself apart from its substratum; or else its substance will also be detachable.

365. [93a6–7] A third assumption, or rather an auxiliary proposition deduced from the preceding ones, is that a harmony cannot be prior to its recipient nor a compound to its constituents, because in that case it will have an activity independent from them, namely the very action of preceding them, once it is granted that, instead of preceding, they come after it.

366. [93a8–10] Socrates deduces a fourth auxiliary proposition from these, that a compound or a harmony cannot oppose its components or its recipient: if it cannot precede them, it is even less capable of opposing them. Preceding can at least be a part of the same action, e.g. if on the same journey the one leads and the other follows, but opposition means complete dissociation from the recipient.

---

intermediate portion of the *Ph.* text consists of assumptions to arguments (2) and (3), in inverse order, those for the third argument (92e4–93a10) preceding those for the second. Hence in Dam. II §§ 50–51 the third and the second argument are counted as the second and the third resp. There is still another way of counting, in § 376.4–5, where the two last arguments are considered together and (2) is counted as the first, (3) as the second. The first argument is dealt with in § 361, the assumptions for the other two jointly in § 362; the assumptions for the third in §§ 363–366, followed by the diagram of the argument in § 367; those for the second in §§ 368–369, with the argument itself in § 370.

σώματος, καὶ γίνεται συλλογισμὸς ἐν β' σχήματι·
προϋπάρχειν τοῦ ἐν ᾧ ἐστιν

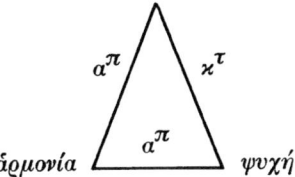

ἁρμονία $a^π$ $κ^τ$ $a^π$ ψυχή

ρη'. - [92e4–93b7] Ὅτι πρὸς τὸν δεύτερον [93b8–94b3] καὶ τρίτον λόγον 362 [94b4–95a3] ὑποθέσεις προλαμβάνει ἐξ ὧν ἀποφάσκει τῆς ψυχῆς τὴν ἁρμονίαν, τὰς μὲν ἀπὸ τοῦ κατηγορουμένου, ὅ ἐστι τῆς ἁρμονίας, τὰς δὲ ἀπὸ τοῦ ὑποκειμένου, ὅ ἐστι τῆς ψυχῆς.

ρθ'. - [92e4–93a3] Ὅτι πρώτη ὑπόθεσις, μηδεμίαν ἁρμονίαν μηδὲ σύνθεσιν 363 ἄλλως ἔχειν ἢ ὡς ἔχει τὰ ὧν ἐστιν ἁρμονία ἢ σύνθεσις· ἐκείνων γάρ ἐστιν ὃ ἔστιν, ἀλλ' οὐχ ἑαυτῆς οὐδετέρα.

ρι'. - [93a4–5] Ὅτι δευτέρα ὑπόθεσις ἑπομένη τῇ πρὸ αὐτῆς (ἐκείνης γὰρ 364 περὶ τὴν ὑπόστασιν οὔσης αὕτη περὶ τὴν ἐνέργειαν ἐξετάζεται ἢ πάθησιν), μηδὲν ποιεῖν μηδὲ πάσχειν τὴν ἁρμονίαν ἢ τὴν σύνθεσιν καθ' ἑαυτὴν χωρὶς τῶν ὑποκειμένων· εἰ δὲ μή, χωριστὴν ἕξει καὶ τὴν οὐσίαν.

ρια'. - [93a6–7] Ὅτι τρίτη ὑπόθεσις, μᾶλλον δὲ λημμάτιον ἐκ τούτων 365 ἀποδεικνύμενον, ὡς οὐκ ἂν ἡγοῖτο τῶν ἐν οἷς ἐστι καὶ ἐξ ὧν· ἐνεργήσει γάρ τι χωρὶς ἐκείνων, αὐτὸ τὸ ἡγεῖσθαι, ἐκείνων μὴ ἡγουμένων γε ἀλλ' ἐπομένων αὐτῇ.

ριβ'. - [93a8–10] Ὅτι δ' λημμάτιον ἀπὸ τῶνδε συνάγει, ὡς οὐκ ἂν τούτοις 366 ἐναντιοῖτο ἐξ ὧν ἐστι καὶ ἐν οἷς· εἰ γὰρ μὴ ἡγοῖτο, πολλῷ μᾶλλον οὐκ ἐναντιώσεται. τὸ μὲν γὰρ ἡγεῖσθαι γένοιτο ἂν κατὰ τὴν αὐτὴν ἐνέργειαν, οἷον κατὰ μίαν ὁδὸν τοῦ | μὲν ἡγουμένου τοῦ δὲ ἑπομένου, τὸ δὲ ἐναντιοῦσθαι καὶ (169) παντάπασίν ἐστιν ἀφίστασθαι τοῦ ἐν ᾧ ἐστιν.

---

§ 361. 3 σχήματι μ: σχήμασι M — 6 $a^π$ M^c: om. M¹
§ 364. 2 αὕτη Fh: αὐτὴ M
§ 365. 3 ἐκείνων¹ - ἡγεῖσθαι mg. M^c: om. M¹
§ 366. 1 δ'] τέταρτον Fh: πρῶτον M

---

§ 361. Dam. II § 45.
§ 362. Only the last assumption for the second argument relates to the subject of the proposition, soul (§ 369; another, 'soul is receptive of virtue and vice,' is added at § 405.4–5); the rest relate to the predicate, harmony.
§§ 363–365. Dam. II §§ 46–48.
§ 366. Dam. II § 49.
1. δ' : Finckh rightly corrects τέταρτον for πρῶτον, but the mistake is attributable of course to the use of figures, δ' in some semi-uncial hands being almost indistinguishable from α'.

367. [94b4–95a3] These premises can be combined to form a syllogism in the second figure, as follows:

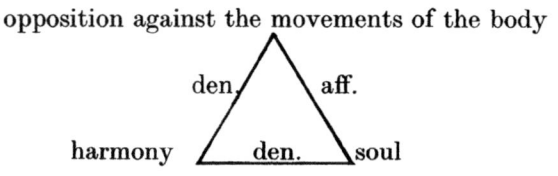

opposition against the movements of the body

```
           den /\ aff.
              /  \
     harmony /den.\ soul
```

368. [93a11–b3] On behalf of his second argument Socrates introduces the assumption that no harmony can be more or less harmony than another, either in quantity or in degree. The former refers to the number of intervals and combinations of intervals (e.g. the fourth cannot extend over more or fewer tones), the latter to less or more tension (as far as the form itself goes no harmony shows differences of intensity). Socrates says that harmonies do admit of differences in degree, then goes on to point out that this does not seem possible in respect of the musical ratios themselves, which are definite, but only in respect of our perception, according to the view of the Aristoxenians, shared in some instances by the Pythagoreans, who call the

---

§ 367. Dam. II § 50.
§§ 368–370. Dam. II §§ 51–54. With I §§ 405–406, this makes three different analyses of the tangled argument 93a11–94b3, which in the *Ph.* proceeds in the following steps. All harmony exists in the way in which it is attuned (93a11–13), in other words, supposing there can be degrees in attunement, there are corresponding degrees in harmony (93a14–b3); one soul cannot be more or less soul than another (93b4–7); soul admits of virtue and vice (93b8–c2), which, to those who hold that soul is harmony, can only mean that another harmony, resp. disharmony, would superimpose itself on the initial harmony (93c3–10); but it was agreed that one soul cannot be more or less soul than another, which would mean that one harmony cannot be more or less harmony than another (93d1–5), i.e. cannot be more or less attuned (93d6–11), consequently no soul could be more or less attuned than another, i.e. possess virtue or vice in a different degree (93d12–e9); or rather, being harmony soul could not share in disharmony, so that all souls of all living beings would be equally good, which is absurd (94a1–b3). – The analysis of §§ 368–370 seems to be substantially that of Pr. (in spite of § 369.1 ὑπόθεσις, against the λημμάτιον at § 405.2); it runs as follows. First assumption: harmony as such does not admit of differences either in quantity or degree (=93a11–b3); second assumption: soul does not admit of differences in degree (=93b4–7). Syllogisms: (1) soul is receptive of virtue and vice, what is receptive of virtue and vice is receptive of harmony and disharmony, therefore soul is receptive of harmony and disharmony (=93b8–c2); (2) no harmony is receptive of harmony and disharmony, all soul is, therefore soul is not harmony (=93c3–e9). The passage 93a11–b7, which was formerly considered a separate argument, has now been recognized as only preparatory to the syllogisms:

ριγ'. — [94b4–95a3] "Ότι ἐκ τούτων γίγνεται συλλογισμὸς ἐν δευτέρῳ 367
σχήματι τοιόσδε·
τὸ ἐναντιοῦσθαι ταῖς τοῦ σώματος κινήσεσιν

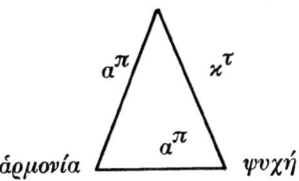

$a^π$ /\ $κ^τ$

ἁρμονία /___$a^π$___\ ψυχή   5

ριδ'. — [93a11–b3] "Ότι πρὸς τὸν β' λόγον ὑποτίθεται μὴ εἶναι ἁρμονίαν 368
ἁρμονίας πλείω μηδὲ ἐλάττω, ἀλλὰ μηδὲ μᾶλλον μηδὲ ἧττον. ἔστι δὲ τὸ μὲν
πρῶτον περὶ τὴν ποσότητα τῶν διαστημάτων καὶ τῶν συστημάτων (ἢ γὰρ διὰ
τεσσάρων οὐκ ἂν γένοιτο οὔτε ἐν πλείοσιν οὔτε ἐν ἐλάττοσιν)· τὸ δὲ δεύτερον
περὶ τὴν ἄνεσιν καὶ τὴν ἐπίτασιν (κατ' αὐτὸ γὰρ τὸ εἶδος οὐδεμία ἁρμονία   5
οὔτε ἀνίεται οὔτε ἐπιτείνεται). λέγει μὲν οὖν ὁ Σωκράτης τὰς ἁρμονίας δέχεσθαι
τὸ μᾶλλον καὶ ἧττον, ἐφίστησι δὲ μὴ οὐ δυνατὸν ᾖ τοῦτο κατ' αὐτούς γε τοὺς
ἁρμονικοὺς λόγους ὡρισμένους ὄντας, εἰ μὴ ἄρα κατὰ τὴν αἴσθησιν, ὡς οἱ
Ἀριστοξένειοι, ἐνίοτε δὲ καὶ ὡς οἱ Πυθαγόρειοι, εἴπερ συλλαβὴν μὲν καλοῦσιν

§ 367. 1–3 in spat. vac. M^c — 2 τοιόσδε Wk: τοῖσδε M^c — 5 $a^π$ M^c: om. M^1 | ψυχή
M^1: -ῃι M^c
§ 368. 1 β'] τρίτον Fh

the first assumption (93a11–b3) will serve as the minor of syllogism (2), while the second (93b4–7) apparently reappears in 93d1–5 to support the proposition that no harmony is receptive of harmony and disharmony. On the whole the analysis follows the *Ph.* text rather closely, which makes it less easy to discern the connection between the assumptions and the syllogisms. Dam. II §§ 51–54 is almost identical (adding 94a1–10 as an additional argument in § 54), except for the puzzling fact that the first assumption there appears in the affirmative form "harmony does admit of differences both in quantity and degree," on which discrepancy see note at § 368. Finally, in I §§ 405–406 there is an entirely new attempt, which must be Damascius' own.

§ 368. Dam. II § 51. The section is clearly divided between Pr. and Dam., who each in his way try to deal with two separate problems: (1) What do the opposites 'greater-smaller' and 'more-less' mean if applied to harmony? (2) Do Socrates' words εἴπερ ἐνδέχεται τοῦτο γίγνεσθαι imply that we should, or that we should *not* assume such a difference in degree? This last question seems to be answered in the affirmative at II § 54, and the formula in which the other possibility is referred to (at lines 6–7 and 16–17) points the same way; but since in the last syllogism (§ 370.3–5) the proposition appears in the negative form, this should be decisive.

1. β' : second or third; see note on §§ 361–370.
3. συστημάτων : a definition of the term Ptol., *harm.* II 4, 50.12–23.
7. ἐφίστησι δέ : the subject is still Socrates, cf. II § 51.9.
8–9. Aristoxenus is supposed to represent empirical music as contrasted with the purely mathematical musical theory of the Pythagoreans: Dam., *Phil.* § 225.13–14.

fourth '*syllaba*' because it is least of all a harmony, and the octave the 'fullest' because it is so most of all.

However, this is not a case of a difference in degree within the same form, since the fourth and the octave are different ratios. It seems better to me, therefore, to take the same interval each time, in lower and higher pitches and different modes; in this way the form will show no difference in degree, but the matter will, for the same ratio (2:1) will sound now low, now high. If nevertheless Socrates expresses a doubt, he does so because harmony does not admit of a more and less absolutely, but only in a particular way.

369. [93b4–7] From the subject the assumption is taken that one soul is not more or less soul than another. For soul is a substance, because (1) it is receptive of opposite accidents; and because (2) it is a part of an animal, and an animal is a substance; and because (3) it preserves the body and is therefore *a fortiori* a substance.

370. [93b8–e10] The second argument proceeds through the following syllogisms:

the soul ⏜ receptive of virtue and vice ⏜ receptive of harmony and disharmony.

anything receptive of harmony and disharmony

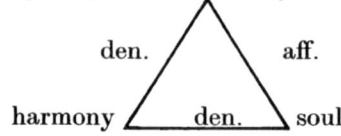

```
           /\
      den./  \aff.
         /    \
  harmony/_den._\soul
```

§§ 371–378. Comment on 93b8–95a6

371. [93c3–10] In what way is virtue a harmony? Let us grant that temperance could be the octave, in so far as it links desire to reason with spirit as the middle term. But how about courage? – Its one aspect, gentleness, could be the fifth, being a relation between reason and spirit;

9–10. On συλλαβή and ἁρμονία : Porph., *Ptol.* III 5, 96.21–23; 96.29–97.2. Cf. Nicom., *harm.* 9, p. 252.5–7 Jan.

10–11. Perhaps we should read or understand ἁρμονίαν δὲ τὴν διὰ πασῶν ὡς κατακορεστάτην.

§ 369. Dam. II § 52.

1–2. Ar., *cat.* 5, 3b33–34 δοκεῖ δὲ ἡ οὐσία οὐκ ἐπιδέχεσθαι τὸ μᾶλλον καὶ τὸ ἧττον.

2. Cf. *ibid.* 4a10–11 μάλιστα δὲ ἴδιον τῆς οὐσίας δοκεῖ εἶναι τὸ ταὐτὸν καὶ ἓν ἀριθμῷ ὂν τῶν ἐναντίων εἶναι δεκτικόν.

§ 370. Dam. II § 53.

§§ 371–372. Dam. II § 55. An attempt is made here, first by Pr., then by Dam., to reduce the Platonic 'parts' of the soul to (musical) harmony, and more specifically to ἁρμονία in the sense of the octave. Cf. Philolaus frg. B 6, where the octave, composed of the fourth (ὑπάτη-μέση) and the fifth (μέση-νήτη), is made the principle that rules the cosmos; so, too, Pr., *Rep.* II 4.15–20, who identifies intelligence with ὑπάτη (the lowest tone!), soul with μέση, and body with νήτη. Applying this to the human soul, Pl. in *Rep.* IV describes justice as the harmony that unites the

τὴν διὰ δ' ἁρμονίαν ὡς ἥκιστα ἁρμονίαν, κατακορεστάτην δὲ τὴν διὰ πασῶν 10
ὡς μάλιστα.
Οὐ μὴν κατὰ ἐπίτασιν καὶ ἄνεσιν γίνεται τοῦτο τοῦ αὐτοῦ εἴδους· ἄλλη γὰρ
ἡ διὰ τεσσάρων πρὸς τὴν διὰ πασῶν. κάλλιον οὖν οἶμαι τὴν αὐτὴν ποιεῖν ἑκάστην
ἐν βαρυτέροις καὶ ὀξυτέροις τόποις τε καὶ τρόποις· οὕτω γὰρ κατὰ μὲν τὸ εἶδος
οὐχ ἕξει τὸ μᾶλλον καὶ ἧττον, κατὰ δὲ τὸ ὑποκείμενον· ὁ γὰρ αὐτὸς λόγος ὁ 15
διπλάσιος νῦν μὲν βαρύς, νῦν δὲ ὀξύς. ἐπέστησε δὲ ὅμως ὁ Σωκράτης διὰ τὸ
μὴ ἁπλῶς ἐπιδέχεσθαι τὸ μᾶλλον καὶ ἧττον, ἀλλά τινα τρόπον.

ριε'. – [93b4–7] *Ὅτι ἀπὸ τοῦ ὑποκειμένου λαμβάνεται ὑπόθεσις, μὴ εἶναι* **369**(170)
ψυχὴν ψυχῆς μᾶλλον καὶ ἧττον. οὐσία γάρ, εἴπερ δεκτικὴ τῶν ἐναντίων· καὶ
ζῴου μέρος, οὐσία δὲ τὸ ζῷον· καὶ συνεκτικὴ τοῦ σώματος, πολλῷ ἄρα
μᾶλλον οὐσία.

ρις'. – [93b8–e10] *Ὅτι ὁ δεύτερος λόγος διὰ τοιούτων πρόεισι συλλογισμῶν·* **370**
ἡ ψυχὴ δεκτικὴ ἀρετῆς καὶ κακίας, δεκτικὸν ἁρμονίας καὶ ἀναρμοστίας.

τὸ ἁρμονίας καὶ ἀναρμοστίας δεκτικόν

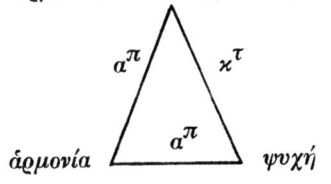

$a^π$ $κ^τ$

ἁρμονία $a^π$ ψυχή 5

§§ 371–378. Comment on 93b8–95a6

ριζ'. – [93c3–10] *Πῶς ἁρμονία ἡ ἀρετή;* ἡ μὲν γὰρ σωφροσύνη ἔστω διὰ **371**
πασῶν ὡς τὴν ἐπιθυμίαν τῷ λόγῳ συνάπτουσα διὰ μέσου τοῦ θυμοῦ. πῶς δὲ
ἡ ἀνδρεία; — *Ἢ ὡς μὲν πραότης διὰ πέντε, λόγου γὰρ καὶ θυμοῦ· ὡς δὲ*

§ 368. 10 ἁρμονίαν¹ Mᶜ: ἁρμ et spat. vac. M¹ | ἁρμονίαν² Mᶜ: ἁρμ̊ M¹
§ 370. 1 δεύτερος] τρίτος Fh — 2–5 in spat. vac. Mᶜ — 5 ψυχή μ: -ῆι Mᶜ
§ 371. 3 ἀνδρία (et sim. hinc semper) M¹

parts of the soul in man, (443d4–e2) ἄρξαντα αὐτὸν αὑτοῦ καὶ κοσμήσαντα καὶ φίλον
γενόμενον ἑαυτῷ καὶ συναρμόσαντα τρία ὄντα, ὥσπερ ὅρους τρεῖς ἁρμονίας ἀτεχνῶς,
νεάτης τε καὶ ὑπάτης καὶ μέσης, καὶ εἰ ἄλλα μεταξὺ τυγχάνει ὄντα, πάντα ταῦτα
συνδήσαντα καὶ παντάπασιν ἕνα γενόμενον ἐκ πολλῶν, σώφρονα καὶ ἡρμοσμένον. Cf.
Ptol., *harm.* III 5, 96.27–32, who makes reason the octave, spirit the fifth, and
desire the fourth.

§ 371. This section is from Pr. (cf. II § 55.7–8). The cardinal virtues being
coextensive, he tries to show that each of them is the octave, with reason as the
νήτη (the highest tone! cf. *Rep.* II 4.15–20 cited above), spirit as the μέση, desire
as the ὑπάτη. Temperance links reason with desire through spirit; courage is composed
of gentleness (i.e. reason dominating spirit – the fifth) and daring (spirit dominating
the desire to live – the fourth); justice unites the parts of the soul as explained
by Pl. Since insight is proper to reason exclusively, the three 'term' method no
longer applies here, it becomes simply concord between the knower and the known
(i.e. again the octave, but this time determined by its two extremes).

3. πραότης: cf. *infra* § 555.2.

the other, daring, the fourth, since it belongs to spirit and desire. — What to say, however, of justice, which is rather a discriminating force? — We can view it as communion without confusion. — And what to do with insight, which is a quality of reason alone? — It is harmony in so far as it is knowledge, and knowledge is concord between the cognitive faculty and its object.

372. Some corrections: (1) insight, too, should be viewed as a moral virtue, the one by which we elect what is good and shun what is evil; (2) insight and courage can also be identified with the octave, since each of the virtues extends through the whole of tripartite soul, bestowing its own specific quality on the entire soul; (3) though it is true that insight is more especially the formative principle of reason and courage of spirit, it should be noted that temperance is similarly peculiar to desire, imposing a certain restraint on its shamelessness and looseness; (4) each virtue is not only common to the whole, spanning the entire soul, but in each part by itself there is also a harmony and a musical proportion, which coordinates the manifold contrary appetites of each several part.

373. [94a2–4] That harmony is not accessible to disharmony is obvious, but neither is it accessible to a different harmony; for thus the same substratum, in the same respect, will be determined by two different harmonies.

374. [93d1–e10] Virtue and vice admit of gradation, and therefore so do harmony and disharmony, the assumption being that such is their character. On the other hand, the harmony that is supposed to be soul does not admit of gradation, because the assumption is that it is a substance; while the harmony that is virtue cannot be soul, since soul admits of harmony and disharmony.

375. [94b4–e7] What if each part by itself is a harmony, and one harmony fights another, instead of the soul fighting the body? — We will still want to know the one harmony that is prior to the many, and what its relationship with the many is. If it fights them, it will be separable from the many and prior to the parts of the soul; if it does not fight them, the only possible reason is that it has permanent control of the parts, which do

---

§ 372. Criticism by Dam. He makes four points: (1) We should stress the moral and practical character of insight, which affects not only reason but the lower functions as well. (2) Not only temperance and justice, but insight and courage too should be identified with the octave, each extending through the entire soul. (3) In defense of the position taken in point two, Dam. observes that after all temperance, too, is primarily the virtue of one function. (4) Each virtue attunes both the entire soul and the particular part to which it belongs. – Only the first point returns in Dam. II § 55.9–11, the other three are rightly omitted, since they are the result of a misunderstanding: Pr. certainly did intend to equate courage and insight, too, with the octave.

§ 375. Dam. II § 56. In the *Rep.*, instead of the soul fighting the body, we have the 'parts' of the soul fighting each other; in view of this, is there any objection

θαρραλεότης διὰ τεσσάρων, θυμοῦ γὰρ καὶ ἐπιθυμίας. — Ἡ δὲ δικαιοσύνη πῶς, διακριτικὴ οὖσα; — Ἡ κοινωνία ἐστὶν ἀσύγχυτος. — Πῶς δὲ ἡ φρόνησις, λόγου μόνου οὖσα; — Ἡ ὡς γνῶσις, συμφωνία γὰρ τοῦ γνωστικοῦ πρὸς τὸ γνωστὸν ἡ γνῶσις.

ριη'. – Ὅτι ἄμεινον, πρῶτον μὲν καὶ τὴν φρόνησιν ὡς ἀρετὴν ἐκλαβεῖν, 372 καθ᾿ ἣν αἱρούμεθα μὲν τὰ ἀγαθά, φεύγομεν δὲ τὰ κακά· δεύτερον δὲ καὶ ταύτην καὶ τὴν ἀνδρείαν διὰ πασῶν ποιεῖν, ἑκάστη γὰρ διὰ πάσης τέταται τῆς τριμερείας τὸ οἰκεῖον τῇ ὅλῃ ψυχῇ παρεχομένη· τρίτον δέ, εἰ καὶ μᾶλλον εἰδοποιεῖ τὸν μὲν λόγον ἡ φρόνησις, τὸν δὲ θυμὸν ἡ ἀνδρεία, ἐπίστησον ὅτι καὶ σωφροσύνη ἴδιός ἐστι τῆς ἐπιθυμίας, τὸ ἀναιδὲς αὐτῆς καὶ διαρρέον εὐσχημοσύνης πληροῦσά τινος· τέταρτον δὲ ὡς ἑκάστη οὐ μόνον κοινή, διατείνουσα διὰ | πάσης, ἀλλὰ καὶ ἐν (171) μέρει ἑκάστῳ ἁρμονία ἐστὶ καὶ λόγος ἁρμονικός, τῶν ὑπὸ ἕκαστον μέρος πολλῶν ὀρέξεων καὶ ἐναντίων ἀλλήλαις ἁρμοστικός.

ριθ'. – [94a2–4] Ὅτι μὲν ἀναρμοστίας ἄδεκτος ἡ ἁρμονία, δῆλον, οὐ μὴν 373 οὐδὲ ἁρμονίας ἄλλης δεκτική· ἔσται γὰρ τὸ αὐτὸ ὑποκείμενον κατὰ τὸ αὐτὸ ἡρμοσμένον β' ἁρμονίαις διαφόροις.

ρκ'. – [93d1–e10] Ὅτι ἡ ἀρετὴ καὶ ἡ κακία ἐπιδέχεται τὸ μᾶλλον καὶ ἧττον, 374 ὥστε καὶ ἁρμονία καὶ ἀναρμοστία· τοιαῦται γὰρ ὑπόκεινται. ἀλλ᾿ ἡ ὡς ψυχὴ ἁρμονία οὐ δέχεται, ὑπόκειται γὰρ οὐσία· ἡ δὲ ὡς ἀρετὴ ἁρμονία οὐκ ἂν εἴη ψυχή, δέχεται γὰρ αὕτη ἁρμονίαν καὶ ἀναρμοστίαν.

ρκα'. – [94b4–e7] Τί δέ, εἰ καθ᾿ ἕκαστον μόριον ἁρμονία, ἄλλη δὲ πρὸς 375 ἄλλην μάχεται, ἀλλ᾿ οὐχ ἡ ψυχὴ τῷ σώματι; — Ἡ ζητήσομεν καὶ τὴν μίαν πρὸ τῶν πολλῶν ἁρμονιῶν, πῶς ἔχει πρὸς τὰς πολλάς. εἰ μὲν γὰρ μάχεται, χωριστὴ ἂν εἴη τῶν πολλῶν καὶ πρὸ ⟨τῶν⟩ μερῶν γε ἔσται· εἰ δὲ μὴ μάχεται,

§ 372. 7 πάσης Mᶜ: πασῶν ut vid. M¹
§ 374. 3 ἡ Fh: εἰ M | ἀρετὴ μ: -ῆι M — 4 αὕτη Fh: αὐτὴ M
§ 375. 2 ψυχὴ ins. Mᶜ: om. M¹ — 4 τῶν² Wk: om. M

against the assumption of one 'harmony' fighting another? The parallel text in II specifies Pr.'s twofold answer to this suggestion: (1) the substratum being different, these harmonies would have no awareness of each other; (2) if each of the 'harmonies' has a substratum of its own, where and in what substratum can we find a joint harmony to unite them? Dam. (ibid.) condemns the first answer as superficial, the second as not solving the problem; the common substratum, for that matter, could be the body as a whole. He then gives, in different terms, the solution propounded here: reason opposes and dominates the whole physical organism, which is therefore not its substratum. It is apparently the second solution of Pr. which Dam. here (line 6) describes as a 'circular argument' because it begs the question by assuming that there can be no common harmony which is soul.
4–5. On ὁλότης πρὸ τῶν μερῶν, ἐκ τῶν μερῶν, ἐν τῷ μέρει see Pr., elem. 67–69.

not even have the natural power to resist. This is a better solution than the circular argument propounded by the commentator.

376. [94a8–11] Why are irrational animals also included in the argument, so as to show that the soul of no being is harmony? On this showing the soul of every animal will be separable. — The answer is that without being harmony the soul can be inseparable in a different way, inseparability being the more comprehensive term. Hence Socrates mentions irrational animals only in the demonstration that soul is not harmony, i.e. in the first of the two arguments [93b8–94b3], but no longer in the second [94b4–95a3], in which the soul is further shown to be separable on the ground of its resistance to the body.

377. [95a4–5] Socrates mentions Harmonia of Thebes, the Goddess, to convey that it is also possible to conceive of a transcendent harmony, represented by the daughter of Ares and Aphrodite; in this sense the soul too could be called a harmony, as set forth by Timaeus [34b10–36d7]. When he says that he has 'propitiated' the Goddess, he means that he has detached the phantom from the true harmony of the soul; otherwise, as far as current opinion goes, even the Goddess herself could be thought of as an inseparable harmony.

378. [95a5–6] 'And what about Cadmus, how shall we propitiate him?' Cadmus is the sublunary world as belonging to the domain of Dionysus; therefore he is wedded to the Goddess Harmonia and father of the four Bacchae. This is made clear also by Pisander [frg. 21], who deals with the theology of Cadmus in the myth where he represents Cadmus as advising

---

§ 376. Dam. II § 62.
4–5. On the numbering of the arguments see note on §§ 361–370.

§ 377. Dam. II § 57. Three levels of harmony are considered: (1) the divine henad heading the σειρά, symbolized in mythology by Harmonia daughter of Cadmus; (2) the transcendent harmonious proportion in soul, as in the *Timaeus*; (3) proportion in the body, a 'reflection' of the true harmony in soul.

1–3. Hes., *theog.* 933–937 αὐτὰρ ῎Αρηι ῥινοτόρῳ Κυθέρεια Φόβον καὶ Δεῖμον ἔτικτε ... ‛Αρμονίην θ᾽, ἣν Κάδμος ὑπέρθυμος θέτ᾽ ἄκοιτιν.

4–5. A Platonic God is propitiated by true insight in his being; cf. *Phaedr.* 257a6–8.

5–6. ἣ – ἁρμονία : the argument really concerns only harmonies (2) and (3); but then confusion between these might also preclude a true understanding of Harmony (1).

6. ἀχώριστος : M has χωριστός, which, in spite of a similar case in Ol., *Gorg.* 7.17, seems grammatically unacceptable; the choice being between ἀχώριστος and χωριστή, the context clearly favors the former.

§ 378. Cadmus is identified with the sublunary world simply on the strength of his association with Dionysus; the grandfather-grandson relation as such is not taken into account. On Cadmus' share in the defeat of Typhon see K. Latte, *RE* art. *Kadmos*, vol. 10, 1469–70. The story is here explained as symbolizing how the universal Demiurge (Zeus) makes use of the intramundane Intelligence (Dionysus-Cadmus) to dominate the lowest and most refractory elements in creation (I § 539;

πῶς οὐκ ἀεὶ τάττει τὰ μέρη, ἅ γε μηδὲ ἐναντιοῦσθαι πέφυκεν; κάλλιον γὰρ οὕτως ἐπιλύσασθαι ἢ ὡς αὐτὸς κύκλῳ περιών.

ρκβ'. — [94a8–11] Πῶς καὶ ἐπὶ τῶν ἀλόγων ὁ λόγος κινεῖται, τὸ μηδενὸς ἁρμονίαν εἶναι τὴν ψυχήν; οὕτω γὰρ ἔσται ἑκάστου ἡ ψυχὴ χωριστή. — Ἡ δύναται καὶ μὴ οὖσα ἁρμονία ἄλλως ἀχώριστος εἶναι, ἐπὶ πλέον γὰρ τὸ ἀχώριστον. διὸ τῶν ἀλόγων μέμνηται ἐν ἐκείνῳ μόνῳ ἐν ᾧ δείκνυται ὅτι οὐχ ἁρμονία, ἐν τῷ πρώτῳ τοῖν δυοῖν [93b8–94b3], ἐν δὲ τῷ δευτέρῳ [94b4–95a3] οὐκέτι, ἐν ᾧ δείκνυται καὶ χωριστὴ ἡ ψυχὴ κατὰ τὸ ἐναντιοῦσθαι.

ρκγ'. — [95a4–5] Ὅτι μέμνηται τῆς Θηβαϊκῆς Ἁρμονίας τῆς θεοῦ, ἐνδεικνύμενος ὅτι ἐστὶ νοεῖν καὶ χωριστὴν ἁρμονίαν, ὡς τὴν Ἄρεως παῖδα καὶ Ἀφροδίτης· οὕτω γάρ πως καὶ ἡ ψυχὴ λέγοιτο ἂν ἁρμονία κατὰ τὸν Τίμαιον [34b10–36d7]. 'ἱλάσασθαι' δέ φησι τὴν θεόν, τὸ εἴδωλον χωρίσας ἀπὸ τῆς ἀληθοῦς ψυχικῆς ἁρμονίας· ἢ ὅσον γε ἐπὶ ταῖς δόξαις τῶν πολλῶν καὶ ἡ θεὸς ἀχώριστος εἶναι δόξειεν ἁρμονία.

ρκδ'. — [95a5–6] 'Τί δὲ δὴ τὰ Κάδμου, πῶς ἱλασόμεθα;' ἢ Κάδμος μὲν ὁ ὑποσέληνος κόσμος ὡς Διονυσιακός· διὸ καὶ Ἁρμονίᾳ σύνεστι τῇ θεῷ καὶ τῶν τεττάρων Βακχῶν πατήρ. δηλοῖ δὲ καὶ ὁ Πείσανδρος [frg. 21] θεολογῶν τὰ κατὰ Κάδμον ἐν τῷ μύθῳ ἐν ᾧ φησιν τὸν Κάδμον ὑποτίθεσθαι τῷ Διί, πῶς

---

§ 377. 3 οὕτω∼ M^x — 6 ἀχώριστος Wk: χωριστὸς M
§ 378. 3 πατήρ] πα- s.l. ins. M^c

II § 142).
1. ἤ: since the preceding question is Plato's, not the commentator's, the particle is meaningless; I have not deleted it, because the mistake may be the redactor's.
2–7. Hes., theog. 975–978 Κάδμῳ δ' Ἁρμονίη, θυγάτηρ χρυσέης Ἀφροδίτης, Ἰνὼ καὶ Σεμέλην καὶ Ἀγαυὴν καλλιπάρηον Αὐτονόην θ', ἣν γῆμεν Ἀρισταῖος βαθυχαίτης, γείνατο. I know no other instance of the sisters being called 'the four Bacchae'; Semele, of course, having died before the God's birth, can qualify neither as a devotee of the cult nor as a character in Euripides' play (the other three are mentioned together 229–230 and 681–682). The phrase may have been coined for the purpose of the present argument: the interpretation of the four sisters as the elements under the sway of cosmic Intelligence.
3–5. There were two epic poets Pisander, an older one of Rhodes (6th cent. B.C.), who wrote a Heraclea in two books, and a quite late one of Laranda in Lycaonia (3rd cent. A.D.), who wrote Ἡρωϊκαὶ θεογαμίαι in sixty books (see Keydell, RE art. Peisandros 11–12, vol. 19, 144–147); edition of the fragments in Asii, Pisandri, ... fragmenta (appendix to Dübner's Hesiod, Paris 1840) pp. 5–12. Another reference to a Pisander by Proclus is found Ol., Alc. 156.15–157.4. The present one, because of its content, must be assigned to the younger of the two, and the obvious probability is that the fragment in Ol., in spite of the fact that it refers to Hercules, has the same origin. It is surprising to find a poet of so late an age added to the distinguished company of the θεολόγοι, the carriers of the Greek religious tradition (Orpheus, Homer, Hesiod), and one is apt to wonder if Pr.,

Zeus how to defeat Typhon. The four Bacchae subject the four elements to the power of Dionysus: Semele fire, Agaue earth (because she lacerates her own children), Ino, as a Sea-goddess, water, and the remaining one, Autonoe, air. Socrates 'propitiates' Cadmus by proving that the soul is completely immortal, so that this universe is an abode, not of mortal nor even of longeval beings only, but also of the altogether immortal.

§§ 379–382. Objections against the argument on harmony. 92e4–95a6

379. [93a11–94b3] Using the argument from gradation one can prove that the swan is not white. — Our reply is that it does yield the legitimate conclusion that whiteness itself is not a swan:

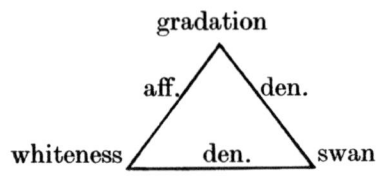

```
                    gradation
                       /\
                  aff./  \den.
                     /    \
          whiteness /_den._\ swan
```

380. [93b8–94b3] What is there against the supposition that soul is a harmony of the body on the one hand, while having, on the other hand, virtue as a harmony of its own activities and vice as a disharmony? — The commentator argues that in that case there will be a harmony of one ratio, rather than of a number of elements that are opposed to each other and by themselves irrational; for the soul that is supposed to be a harmony is the one ratio of the many elements of the body.

This, however, is beside the point, the assumption being that virtue is a harmony of *activities*. The right answer is that the soul, while being the harmony of the four elements, is at the same time the perfection of their activities, so that it will not need another perfection ruling its own activities; otherwise we shall go on *ad infinitum* assuming perfection of perfection as we proceed to consider one activity after another.

381. What does he mean by saying that the harmony 'is attuned' [93a12]? What is really attuned is the substratum. — It 'is attuned' in so far as it is a harmony that has its cause elsewhere.

---

though in his time some precise information was available (Hesychius=*Suda* II 1465 and 1466) can have confused him with his namesake; Macrobius, *Sat.* V 2,5, considers him older than Virgil. Otherwise he must have been accepted as an authority in religious tradition on the same footing as prose writers on cult practices, such as Proclus of Laodicea.

§ 379. Dam. II § 58. The argument is ascribed to Epicurus and analyzed at

ἂν καταγωνίσαιτο τὸν Τυφῶνα. αἱ δὲ τὰ τέσσαρα στοιχεῖα Διονυσιακὰ ποιοῦσιν, Σεμέλη μὲν τὸ πῦρ, Ἀγαύη δὲ τὴν γῆν διασπῶσα τὰ οἰκεῖα γεννήματα, Ἰνὼ δὲ τὸ ὕδωρ ἐνάλιος οὖσα, καὶ Αὐτονόη δὲ τὸν ἀέρα ἡ λοιπή. ἱλάσκεται᾽ δὲ τὸν Κάδμον ἀποδεικνὺς τὴν ψυχὴν πάμπαν ἀθάνατον καὶ τόδε τὸ πᾶν οὐ θνητῶν μόνων οὐσιῶν οὐδὲ μακραιώνων δεκτικόν, ἀλλὰ καὶ παντάπασιν ἀθανάτων.

§§ 379–382. Objections against the argument on harmony. 92e4–95a6

ρκε΄. – [93a11–94b3] Ὅτι τῷ ἀπὸ τοῦ μᾶλλον καὶ ἧττον λόγῳ χρώμενός 379 τις δείξει μὴ ὄντα τὸν κύκνον λευκόν. — Ἦ καὶ συμπεραίνεται ἀληθῶς μὴ εἶναι κύκνον τὸ λευκὸν αὐτό·

τὸ μᾶλλον καὶ ἧττον
⟨κ^τ⟩ ⟨α^π⟩
λευκοῦ ⟨α^π⟩ κύκνου

ρκϛ΄. – [93b8–94b3] Τί κωλύει ἁρμονίαν μὲν εἶναι τὴν ψυχὴν τοῦ σώματος, 380 ἔχειν δὲ ἁρμονίαν τῶν οἰκείων ἐνεργειῶν τὴν ἀρετὴν καὶ ἀναρμοστίαν τὴν κακίαν; — Ἤ, φησίν, ἔσται τις ἁρμονία λόγου ἑνός, ἀλλ᾽ οὐχὶ τῶν ἐναντίων καὶ ἀλόγων καθ᾽ ἑαυτούς· ἡ γὰρ ὑποτιθεμένη ψυχὴ ἁρμονία λόγος εἷς ἐστι τῶν πολλῶν στοιχείων τοῦ σώματος.
Ἀλλὰ παρὰ θύρας· ἐνεργειῶν γὰρ ἡ ἀρετὴ ὑπόκειται ἁρμονία. ἀλλὰ ῥητέον ὡς ἡ ψυχὴ τῶν δ᾽ | στοιχείων οὖσα ἁρμονία καὶ τῶν ἐνεργειῶν αὐτῶν ἐστι (173) τελειότης· οὔκουν δεήσεται ἄλλης τελειότητος ἐπὶ ταῖς οἰκείαις ἐνεργείαις· εἰ γὰρ μή, ἐπ᾽ ἄπειρον ἥξομεν ἀεὶ τελειότητα τελειότητος ὑποτιθέμενοι κατὰ τὰς ἐνεργείας τὰς ἀεὶ λαμβανομένας.
ρκζ΄. – Πῶς ἡρμόσθαι᾽ [93a12] λέγει τὴν ἁρμονίαν; τὸ γὰρ ὑποκείμενον 381 ἁρμόζεται. — Ἤ οὕτως ἡρμόσθαι λέγεται ὡς ὑφισταμένη ἑτέρωθεν ἁρμονία.

---

§ 378. 6 ἀγαύη] ita M — 7 Αὐτονόη] post -ό- ras. 1 litt., accent. add., -η ex corr. M^c
§ 379. 2 ἦ Wk: ἢ M (εἰ Fh) — 5–6 suppl. Wk
§ 380. 6 παρὰ] ex corr. M^c — 8 οὔκουν Fh: οὐκ οὖν M

---

length by Philop., an. 143.1–144.19, with "sweet" and "honey" instead of "white" and "swan". At the end, 144.10–12, the same solution that is proposed here.
§ 380. 1–5. Dam. II § 60. Dam.'s correction (lines 6–10) is omitted in Dam. II.
6. παρὰ θύρας ἀπαντᾶν : 'come to the wrong door,' i.e. answer the wrong question; or, more vaguely, probably owing to a confusion with ἀπαντᾶν 'answer': 'give the wrong answer,' a number of times in Ol., Gorg. (see index).
§ 381. Cf. Dam. II § 61, with a small correction by Dam.

382. In what sense is the soul called a harmony in the *Timaeus* [35b1–36b5] and by Timaeus himself [95e1–96c3]? — The soul is not only one, but also manifold; now any manifold, unless ruled by harmony, is chaotic and contrary to nature.

It is better to think of the intermediate position of soul; after all, intelligence is also manifold and so is body, but while body is a plurality of parts divided from one another, intelligence is everything indivisibly, and while intelligence is superior to the blending that is harmony, body is inferior to it and too much broken up; the soul, however, is neither so completely unified nor dispersed to such a degree, but in virtue of its essential intermediacy it is rightly described as harmony. This is characteristic of audible harmony also, that it is neither one nor many, but a kind of fusion between the two.

§§ 383–387. Aristotle's arguments in support of Plato. 92e4–95a6

383. Aristotle in the *Eudemus* [frg. 45 R.[3]] reasons as follows: the opposite of harmony is disharmony, soul, being a substance, has no opposite, and the conclusion is obvious. Secondly, since disharmony between the elements of an animal is sickness, harmony between them would be health, not soul.

384. In the *De Anima* [I 4] he uses these arguments: (1) each animal has only one soul, but many harmonies, one for each part, consequently etc. [407b32–34].

385. (2) Soul moves body; harmony, on the contrary, *is* moved, though accidentally; therefore harmony is not soul [407b34–408a1].

386. (3) As the second argument of the *Eudemus* [408a1–3].

387. (4) If sense-perception, spirit, desire, imagination, opinion, discursive reason or intelligence are none of them harmony, because each,

---

§ 382. **Dam. II § 59.** See the note on Dam. II, where the same material appears distributed in a different way. The answer that seems to be marked as Dam.'s here (lines 4–10), is there attributed to Porphyry, while the answer described as "closer to the truth" at II § 59.5–8 is a slightly expanded version of the one rejected here as less satisfactory (lines 1–4). There may be an error in either one of the reports, but on the other hand there is no reason to think that Dam. was always consistent in his preferences.

1–2. The word ἁρμονία occurs neither in *Tim.* nor in Ps.-Tim., but cf. Pr., *Tim.* II 29.14–15 (διὸ καὶ ὁ Τίμαιος ἁρμονίαν ἐκάλεσε τὴν τοιαύτην σύνδεσιν) and *infra* II 57.4–5.

9. βούλεται: see note on § 151.4.

§§ 383–406. No corresponding text in Dam. II.

§§ 383–387. The material comes from the commentaries on Ar., *an.* I 4, where Ar. himself refers to the *Eudemus* (407b28–29). See Themistius, Simplicius, Philoponus.

§ 383=Philop., *an.* 144.22–145.9.

§ 384. Ar., *an.* I 4, 407b32–34 says καίτοι γε ἡ μὲν ἁρμονία λόγος τίς ἐστι τῶν

ρκη'. – Πῶς ἁρμονία λέγεται ἐν Τιμαίῳ τε [35b1–36b5] καὶ παρὰ Τιμαίῳ 382
[95e1–96c3]; – ῎Η ὅτι οὐχ ἓν ἡ ψυχὴ ἀλλὰ καὶ πολλά· πᾶν δὲ πλῆθος, εἰ μὴ
εἴη ἡρμοσμένον, ἄτακτον ἔσται καὶ παρὰ φύσιν.

Κάλλιον δὲ τὴν μεσότητα τῆς ψυχῆς ἐννοεῖν· ἐπεὶ καὶ ὁ νοῦς πολλὰ καὶ τὸ
σῶμα πολλά, ἀλλὰ τοῦτο μὲν μεμερισμένα ἀπ' ἀλλήλων, ἐκεῖνος δὲ ἐν ἀμερεῖ 5
πάντα, καὶ ὁ μὲν νοῦς κρείττων ἢ κατὰ τὴν ἁρμονικὴν σύγκρασιν, τὸ δὲ σῶμα
χεῖρον καὶ ἐπὶ μᾶλλον διεσπασμένον· ἡ μέντοι ψυχὴ οὔτε ἡνωμένη οὕτως οὔτε
διεσπασμένη εἰς τοσοῦτον, ἀλλ' ἔχουσα μέσως κατ' οὐσίαν, εἰκότως ἁρμονία
ἐστίν. βούλεται γοῦν καὶ ἡ φαινομένη ἁρμονία οὔτε ἓν εἶναι οὔτε πολλά, ἀλλ'
οἷόν τι σύγκραμα μέσον. 10

§§ 383–387. Aristotle's arguments in support of Plato. 92e4–95a6

ρκθ'. – ῞Οτι ὁ Ἀριστοτέλης ἐν τῷ Εὐδήμῳ [frg. 45 R.³] οὕτως ἐπιχειρεῖ· 383
τῇ ἁρμονίᾳ ἐναντίον ἐστὶν ἡ ἀναρμοστία, τῇ δὲ ψυχῇ οὐδὲν ἐναντίον (οὐσία γάρ),
καὶ τὸ συμπέρασμα δῆλον. ἔτι, εἰ ἀναρμοστία τῶν στοιχείων τοῦ ζῴου νόσος,
ἡ ἁρμονία εἴη ἂν ὑγίεια, ἀλλ' οὐχὶ ψυχή.

ρλ'. – ῞Οτι ἐν τοῖς περὶ ψυχῆς [I 4] οὕτως· ἡ ψυχὴ τοῦ ζῴου μία ἑκάστου, 384
αἱ δὲ ἁρμονίαι πολλαί (καθ' ἕκαστον γὰρ μέρος), καὶ τὸ συμπέρασμα [407b32–34].

ρλα'. – Ἡ ψυχὴ κινεῖ τὸ σῶμα· ἡ δὲ ἁρμονία κινεῖται, καὶ εἰ κατὰ συμβεβηκός· 385
οὐκ ἄρα ψυχή [407b34–408a1].

ρλβ'. – Τὸ τρίτον ταὐτὸν τῷ ἐν Εὐδήμῳ δευτέρῳ [408a1–3]. 386

ρλγ'. – Τέταρτον δέ, εἰ μὴ ἁρμονία αἴσθησις ἢ θυμὸς ἢ ἐπιθυμία ἢ φαντασία 387
ἢ δόξα ἢ διάνοια ἢ νοῦς (ἁπλοῦν γάρ τι | ἑκάστη, ἑκάστη ⟨γὰρ⟩ ἐνέργεια· καὶ (174)

---

§ 382. 7 διεσπασμένον] post -ι- ∸ in ras. Mᶜ
§ 386. 1 δευτέρωι Mᶜ: δεύτερον ut vid. M¹
§ 387. 2 τι ins. Mᶜ: om. M¹ | ἑκάστη²] in fine lin. suppl. M¹ | γὰρ Wk: om. M

μιχθέντων ἢ σύνθεσις, τὴν δὲ ψυχὴν οὐδέτερον οἷόν τ' εἶναι τούτων. Since the arguments purport to be given in the original order, this should be the corresponding passage in Ar.; if so, it has been distorted so as to become scarcely recognizable.
§ 385. Ar. 407b34–408a1 ἔτι δὲ τὸ κινεῖν οὐκ ἔστιν ἁρμονίας, ψυχῇ δὲ πάντες ἀπονέμουσι τοῦτο μάλισθ' ὡς εἰπεῖν.
§ 386. Ar. 408a1–3 ἁρμόζει δὲ μᾶλλον καθ' ὑγιείας λέγειν ἁρμονίαν, καὶ ὅλως τῶν σωματικῶν ἀρετῶν, ἢ κατὰ ψυχῆς. Eudemus: above § 383.3–4; cf. Philop., an. 145.9–10 ... ὧν τὸ τρίτον ἐστὶ τὸ εἰρημένον ἐν τῷ Εὐδήμῳ δεύτερον. 147.8 τοῦτο τρίτον ἐπιχείρημα· ἔστι δὲ τὸ δεύτερον τῶν ἐν Εὐδήμῳ.
§ 387. Ar. 408a3–5 φανερώτερον δ' εἴ τις ἀποδιδόναι πειραθείη τὰ πάθη καὶ τὰ ἔργα τῆς ψυχῆς ἁρμονίᾳ τινί· χαλεπὸν γὰρ ἐφαρμόζειν.
1–2. The same examples in Philop. 147.17–18: ποία οὖν ἁρμονία ὁ θυμὸς ἢ ἡ ἐπιθυμία ἢ ἡ αἴσθησις ἢ τὰ λοιπά;
2. Syntactically, it is hardly possible to save the second ἑκάστη without inserting a γάρ. Since M has added it ex corr., it must have been in its original.
ibid. ἐνέργεια: Simpl., an. 54.3–7, uses the same word to include both πάθη and ἔργα.

being an activity, is a single thing, and also because it would be a problem even to define what kind of harmony each of these would have to be, it follows that the whole soul cannot be harmony either [408a3–5].

§ 388. An objection by Strato. 93a11–b6

388. Just as one harmony is sharper or flatter than another, so one soul, Strato says [frg. 118] is sharper or duller than another. — Let him explain, then, what is the origin of knowledge and appetition, both rational and irrational; it can be neither the body and its temperament, these being inferior to them, nor knowledge and appetition themselves, since they are supposed inseparable from the body, nor chance; it remains that they come from above and therefore must be separable on account of their superiority. Besides, since intelligence knows itself, must it not be separable? And since soul initiates motion as being itself the subject that handles the instrument, must it not be outside the instrument?

§§ 389–402. Notes on the introductory passage 85b10–90d8

389. [85c3–4] Why is it said to be 'either impossible or extremely difficult to acquire any clear knowledge in this life'? — By 'clearness' we must understand that final vision which dialectic descries when rushing toward the end of its long search; hence it is unattainable to the many, and extremely difficult to attain even to the selected few.

390. [85c5–6] What is 'wearing oneself out examining it from every angle'? — It means exploring the whole problem by dialectical methods, and yet wearing oneself out, because no dialectical approach is left to which we can turn, while the sight of the object has not yet flashed upon us.

---

§ 388. Strato's argument refers directly to the passage in the *Ph.* on gradation in soul; it is therefore part of the attack on the *Ph.* (frgs. 122–127 Wehrli). He tries to show that in soul there is a "more and less" corresponding to the difference in pitch in harmony. This *may* indicate, incidentally, that he, too, already read 93b4–7 as a separate argument (cf. above, note on §§ 361–370). – The answer at lines 2–7, instead of refuting the point, adduces three independent arguments to establish the transcendence of the soul: (1) knowledge and appetition remain unexplained by the harmony theory; (2) intelligence knows itself; (3) soul is the cause of motion.

6–7. Two different points, soul as the cause of motion (*Phaedr.* 245c5–246a2) and soul as the user of the instrument (*Alc. I* 129b5–130a4) are merged here. This, as well as the awkward ὡς αὐτὸ χρώμενον, can be explained from the condensed form of the statement; it remains possible, however, that some of the text has been lost, e.g. ὡς αὐτο⟨κίνητος ἡ ψυχή, πῶς οὐ προτέρα τοῦ κινουμένου; καὶ εἰ αὐτὴ τὸ⟩ χρώμενον, ... In any case, the subject of the whole sentence is ἡ ψυχή (not the

τίς ἂν εἴη ἑκάστῃ ἁρμονία, οὐκ ἂν ἔχοι τις ἀφορίσαι ῥᾳδίως), οὐδὲ ἄρα ἡ ὅλη ψυχή [408a3–5].

§ 388. An objection by Strato. 93a11–b6

ρλδ′. – "Ὅτι ὡς ἁρμονία ἁρμονίας ὀξυτέρα καὶ βαρυτέρα, οὕτω καὶ ψυχὴ 388 ψυχῆς, φησὶν ὁ Στράτων [frg. 118], ὀξυτέρα καὶ νωθεστέρα. – Οὐκοῦν εἰπάτω πόθεν γνῶσις καὶ ὄρεξις ἥκει, ἥ τε λογικὴ καὶ ἡ ἄλογος· οὔτε γὰρ ἀπὸ τοῦ σώματος καὶ τῆς κράσεως αὐτοῦ (χείρω γὰρ ταῦτα) οὔτε ἀφ' ἑαυτῶν (ἀχώριστα γάρ) οὔτε ἀπὸ ταὐτομάτου· ἄνωθεν ἄρα· χωριστὰ ἄρα· κρείττω γάρ. ἔπειτα ὁ 5 νοῦς ἑαυτὸν γιγνώσκων πῶς οὐ χωριστός; καὶ εἰ προκατάρχει τῆς κινήσεως ὡς αὐτὸ χρώμενον, πῶς οὐκ ἔξω τοῦ ὀργάνου;

§§ 389–402. Notes on the introductory passage 85b10–90d8

d ρλε′. – [85c3–4] Πῶς ἐν τῷ βίῳ τούτῳ 'σαφές τι εἰδέναι ἢ ἀδύνατον ἢ 389 παγχάλεπον' λέγεται; — Ἢ τὸ σαφὲς ἐκεῖνο λεκτέον, ὃ διοπτεύει θέουσα πρὸς τέλος ἡ διαλεκτικὴ πᾶσα διέξοδος· διόπερ ἀδύνατον μὲν τοῖς πολλοῖς, παγχάλεπον δὲ τοῖς ἐλαχίστοις.

ρλϛ′. – [85c5–6] Τί τὸ 'ἀπειπεῖν πανταχοῦ σκοποῦντα'; — Ἢ διαλεκτικῶς 390 ὅλον τὸ πρᾶγμα περιδραμεῖν, ἀπειπεῖν δὲ ὅμως, ὡς οὐκ οὔσης ἄλλης ἀναστροφῆς διαλεκτικῆς, οὔπω δὲ τῆς διόψεως ἐπιστάσης οἷον ἀστραπῆς. τὸ δὲ οὔπω γνῶναι

---

§ 388. 3 ἥκει Wk: ἡ ἐκεῖ M
§ 389. 2 ἤ] in ras. M^c
§ 390. 3 οὔπω¹ Wk: ὅπου M | διόψεως Wk: δι' ὄψεως M

νοῦς of line 6).

§ 389. 2. Both διοπτεύει here and δίοψις at § 390.3 describe the apprehension of truth in terms of the sighting of a star with the *dioptra* or a similar instrument. The main point of the metaphor is that the observer, however close to the discovery of the object (Plato's πανταχοῦ σκοποῦντα and the commentator's περιδραμεῖν) does not discern it at all until the actual sighting. But cf. *Parm.* 136c5 and Pr. *Parm.* 1015.41-1016.3.

§ 390. 3. οἷον ἀστραπῆς: the sudden flash of illumination, as described by Pl., *Symp.* 210e3–5 πρὸς τέλος ἤδη ἰὼν τῶν ἐρωτικῶν ἐξαίφνης κατόψεταί τι θαυμαστὸν τὴν φύσιν καλόν. *Ep.* VII 341c5–d2 ῥητὸν γὰρ οὐδαμῶς ἐστιν ὡς ἄλλα μαθήματα, ἀλλ' ἐκ πολλῆς συνουσίας γιγνομένης περὶ τὸ πρᾶγμα αὐτὸ καὶ τοῦ συζῆν ἐξαίφνης, οἷον ἀπὸ πυρὸς πηδήσαντος ἐξαφθὲν φῶς, ἐν τῇ ψυχῇ γενόμενον αὐτὸ ἑαυτὸ ἤδη τρέφει. Plot. V 5, 3.12–13 and VI 7, 36.18-19 uses ἐξαίφνης in a similar way. Dam., *princ.* 179.27, 305.7–10 (human knowledge of the intelligible, however faulty and warped, is yet all we have) ἄλλως μὲν γὰρ οὐκ ἔστιν, ὡς νῦν ἔχομεν ἔχοντα, ἐννοεῖν περὶ αὐτῶν, ἀγαπητέον δὲ καὶ πόρρωθεν καὶ μόλις καὶ ἀμυδρότατά πῃ παράπτεσθαι (ita cod.: παραπτέσθαι ed.) ἢ παρυπονοεῖν τι ἴχνος οἷον ἀστράπτον ἐξαίφνης περὶ τοῖς ἡμετέροις ὄμμασιν, κἂν αὐτόθεν ποθὲν ἐγείρηται ἀπὸ τῆς ψυχῆς ἡ ἀστραπή. Porph., ad Gaur. 11,3, p. 49.13, uses the lightning metaphor to illustrate the timeless character of incarnation. cf. Pr.*Rep.* II 353.1–7.

That we do not yet achieve knowledge is because our longing for that vision is still imperfect and because we despair of attaining it by dialectical methods, though it is there at the end of them.

391. [85c7–d5] The noblest part of our being is intelligence with its direct intuition of reality; so long as this has not been stirred to action, the dialectical argument must suffice, which is called the 'most irrefutable', not because it *can* be refuted as false, but because it does not yet have the evidence of that other, divine account. It is 'human' and therefore 'risky' and comparable to a 'raft,' inasmuch as it does not offer the best crossing possible.

392. [85d2–4] What is this 'safer, less risky and more reliable divine account'? — Surely not, as it is maintained, that given out by God, for such knowledge rests on opinion; rather it is the intuitive intelligence of which we spoke [§ 391], which truly remains in the presence of God, as the *Phaedrus* says [250b5–c4].

393. [85e1–2] Why does Socrates say that it is 'perhaps not conclusive'? — In view of a higher kind of truth or of complete immortality; or else he may simply be thinking of the objections of the young men.

394. [85e3–88b8] The soul not only creates the body (the mortal body in particular), but is also the cause of the harmony of its elements; both are proved by the fact that when the soul leaves the body, it falls into disharmony and decay. Simmias in his objection starts from the soul as the cause of harmony, Cebes from the soul as the principle of existence, each using an example of his own.

395. [88c1–7] At first the soul is easily convinced by specious arguments, because she thirsts for truth and is at the same time unwilling to exert herself. When finding that these are proved false, she lapses 'into scepticism,' and this is the second stage, which many people never outgrow. The third stage is that in which a man can answer the objections, becomes aware of the truth, and recognizes the reliability of dialectic; this is the

---

4. ἐνδεεῖ πόθῳ : the most questionable of the emendations in this section, since the theme of ἐνδεὴς πόθος is not exactly frequent; however, on Neoplatonic lines there can be hardly any other way to explain why illumination does not happen, but the imperfect ἐπιτηδειότης of the subject.

§ 391. 1. αὐτοπτῶν (and § 392.3 αὐτοπτικός): the translations given by *LSJ* for these words and their cognates (including αὐτοψία) in Neoplatonic and magical literature all relate to direct manifestations of the divine. To be added is the meaning '(to know by) intuition,' which stems from the legal sense '(to be an) eye-witness,' though it has certainly picked up some of the mystical associations of the other usage. Syr., *met.* 180.7 γυμνάζουσα τὴν ψυχὴν πρὸς αὐτοπτικὴν τοῦ παραδείγματος ἐπιβολήν. Pr., *Tim.* I 302.12–13 κατὰ τὴν ἐπιβολὴν τὴν αὐτοπτικὴν καὶ τὴν ἐπαφὴν τοῦ νοητοῦ. 247.7 τὸν δὲ νοῦν ἁπλουστέραν (scil. ἔχειν ἐνέργειαν), αὐτοπτικῶς τὰ ὄντα θεωμένην. *Rep.* II 122.4–5 αὐτοπτικαὶ τῶν ὄντων . . . καταλήψεις. Dam., *Phil.* § 225.27 τῶν λογικῶς αὐτοπτουσῶν τὰ ὄντα. Ol., *Ph.* 10 § 3.3 μὴ αὐτοπτουσῶν τὰ

ἐνδεεῖ πόθῳ ἐκείνης καὶ ἀπορρήσει τοῦ μὴ θηράσειν αὐτὴν διὰ τῶν διαλεκτικῶν ὁδῶν, ἀλλ' ἐπ' αὐταῖς.

ϱλζ'. – [85c7–d2] Ὅτι κάλλιστον μὲν ἐν ἡμῖν ὁ αὐτοπτῶν τὰ ὄντα νοῦς· 391 εἰ δὲ μὴ οὗτος κεκίνηται, ὁ λόγος ἀρκεῖ ʽδυσελεγκτότατοςʼ ὢν ὁ διαλεκτικός· οὐχ ὅτι ψευδὴς ὢν ἐλέγχεται, ἀλλ' ὅτι οὔπω ὁ σαφὴς ἐκεῖνος ὁ θεῖος. οὗτος γὰρ ʽἀνθρώπινοςʼ καὶ διὰ τοῦτο ʽκινδυνώδηςʼ καὶ ʽσχεδίᾳʼ παρεοικώς, ἅτε οὐ τὸν πρῶτον πλοῦν παρεχόμενος.

ϱλη'. – [85d2–4] Τίς ὁ ʽἀσφαλέστερος καὶ ἀκινδυνότερος καὶ βεβαιότερος 392 καὶ θεῖος λόγοςʼ; — Οὐ δήπου, ὥς φασιν, ὁ θεόθεν ἐκδοθείς, δοξαστικὸς γὰρ ὅ γε τοιοῦτος· ἀλλ' ἔστιν ὁ εἰρημένος αὐτοπτικὸς νοῦς [§ 391] ὁ θεῷ τῷ ὄντι συνών, ὡς ἐν Φαίδρῳ [250b5–c4].

ϱλθ'. – [85e1–2] Πῶς ʽἴσως οὐχ ἱκανῶςʼ φησὶν ὁ Σωκράτης; — Ἢ πρὸς 393 (175) μεῖζόν τι μέγεθος ἀληθείας ἢ πρὸς τὴν ὅλην ἀθανασίαν ἢ καὶ πρὸς αὐτὰς ἀπεῖδεν τὰς τῶν νεανίσκων ἀπορίας.

ϱμ'. – [85e3–88b8] Ὅτι ἡ ψυχὴ καὶ ὑφίστησι τὸ σῶμα ἄλλως τε καὶ τὸ 394 θνητόν, καὶ ἁρμόζει αὐτοῦ τὰ στοιχεῖα· δηλοῖ δὲ ἑκάτερον ἀφεῖσα τὸ σῶμα εἴς τε ἀναρμοστίαν καὶ φθορὰν ὑποφερόμενον. ὡς μὲν οὖν ἀπὸ ἁρμοζούσης ὁ Σιμμίας, ὡς δὲ ὑφιστώσης ὁ Κέβης ἀπορεῖ οἰκείῳ παραδείγματι χρώμενος.

ϱμα'. – [88c1–7] Ὅτι πρῶτον μὲν ἡ ψυχὴ τοῖς πιθανῶς λεγομένοις 395 ἀποπιστεύει ῥᾳδίως, ἅτε διψῶσα ἀληθείας καὶ ἔτι μέντοι ἀταλαίπωρος οὖσα. τούτων δὲ ἐλεγχομένων ἐπαισθανομένη ʽεἰς ἀπιστίανʼ φέρεται, καὶ δεύτερος οὗτος βαθμός, ἐν ᾧ καὶ πολλοὶ κατέμειναν. τρίτος δὲ ὁ τὰς ἐνστάσεις δυνηθεὶς ἐπιλύσασθαι καὶ τοῦ ὄντος αἰσθόμενος καὶ τῆς διαλεκτικῆς τὸ βέβαιον ἐπιγνούς·

---

§ 390. 4 ἐνδεεῖ Wk: ἐνδεῖ (sequente puncto) M
§ 391. 4 παρεοικώς] -εοι- in ras. M^c

πράγματα.
§ 392. 2–3. This would apply to any revealed creed or philosophy, including the Chaldean Oracles; cf. the expression used by Pr., *Tim.* II 50.20–21 ἡ τῶν Ἀσσυρίων θεολογία τὰ αὐτὰ παραδίδωσι θεόθεν ἐκφανθέντα. They are λόγος, because expressed in human language, and δοξαστικός because not demonstrated. This low assessment of sacred texts is noteworthy; of course, it does not affect Dam.'s estimate of the higher knowledge gained in theurgical practice (above § 172).

3–4. There is no *verbatim* correspondence with the *Phaedrus*; besides 250b5–c4, which is the most likely passage because it combines the notion of the divine presence with that of ἐποπτεία, several others dealing with the vision of true being could be considered (esp. 247c6–e4 and 249c1–6); but the reference may also be to Dam.'s own commentary.

§ 393. 2. τὴν ὅλην ἀθανασίαν: the full proof of immortality, reserved for the fifth argument.

man who finds knowledge and possesses it, the goal to which Socrates invites them [90c8–e3].

396. [89a1–7] Why do we quicker and more easily learn what is true than strive to do what is right and have our appetitive faculties disciplined? — Because the cognitive function reacts more readily, the appetitive function less so, with the result that it will shift to the opposite or back again to the same point. What is the cause of this? That knowledge, being a judgment and as it were a standard, falls under the category of limit, whereas appetition is characterized by infinitude and is the thing measured rather than the measure. For this reason Phaedo feels even more admiration for Socrates' moral greatness than for his insight.

397. [89a2–4] Socrates listens to the objections 'with pleasure' because he is a charming man, 'with benevolence' because he is a good man, and 'with admiration' because he is a just man.

Or otherwise: the first relates to both parties in the conversation, by the second he reveals his own friendly intention, by the third the power of his questioners.

398. Phaedo credits Socrates with three qualities the perfect physician should possess: first ready sympathy, secondly ability to diagnose the trouble, thirdly ability to cure.

399. [89d1–3] Why is there no worse disease than 'hatred of reasoning'? — In the first place because it means that one must hate oneself, as a being naturally gifted with reason. A second consequence is hatred of truth, for it is by reasoning that we arrive at truth, the foremost of all blessings. Thirdly, a man who hates reason is inevitably a lover of unreason, which is a kind of being bestialized.

400. Socrates mentions 'misanthropy' in the same breath with 'misology' because both concern the same nature, our own, and are ultimately the same.

401. [90a4–b3] In the ether the superior predominates, in the Tartarus and in the subterranean places of punishment generally, the inferior, in our world, the intermediate; so that we must adapt our attitude to this intermediate level.

402. [90c8–d8] The blame for the untrustworthiness should be laid, either upon the nature of reality, or upon the ineffectiveness of reasoning, or upon our own lack of training; Socrates chooses the last possibility, with a view to possible correction.

---

§ 396. 4. ἡ μὲν γνῶσις περατοειδής : Pl., *Phil.* 28a4–30e3.

ibid. κρίσις γάρ : cf. Dam., *Phil.* § 86.4 (with note) and § 127.7. The notion is Aristotelian.

§ 397. 1–2. The triad ἀγαθόν-καλόν-δίκαιον : Pl., *Alc. I* 115a1–116d4; Pr., *Alc.* 319.12–322.17; Ol., *Alc.* 109.15–110.13. These kind of structures are typical of Pr.; Dam. returns to the obvious meaning of the text.

§ 398. Cf. the three characteristics of the counselor, Pr., *Alc.* 184.9–18:

οὗτος ἤδη ἐπιστήμων γίνεταί τε καὶ ἔστιν, ἐφ' ὃ καὶ ὁ Σωκράτης αὐτοὺς παρακαλεῖ [90c8–e3].

ρμβ'. – [89a1–7] Διὰ τί θᾶττον γιγνώσκομεν καὶ ῥᾷον τὰ ἀληθῆ ἤπερ 396 ὀρεγόμεθα τῶν δεόντων καὶ παιδευόμεθα τὸ ὀρεκτικόν; — Ἢ ὅτι τὸ γνωστικὸν μὲν εὐκινητότερον, τὸ δὲ ὀρεκτικὸν δυσκινητότερον· διὸ καὶ ἐπὶ τἀναντία ἢ καὶ ἐπὶ ταὐτὰ ἀνάπαλιν. τίς οὖν αἰτία; ἢ ὅτι ἡ μὲν γνῶσις περατοειδής (κρίσις γὰρ καὶ οἷον κανών), ἡ δὲ ὄρεξις ἀπειροειδὴς καὶ μετρουμένη μᾶλλον. διὸ πλέον 5 θαυμάζει τὴν Σωκράτους ἀρετὴν τῆς ἐπιστήμης ὁ Φαίδων.

ρμγ'. – [89a2–4] Ὅτι ἀπεδέξατο τὰς ἀπορίας 'ἡδέως' μὲν ὡς καλός, 'εὐμενῶς' 397 δὲ ὡς ἀγαθός, 'ἀγαμένως' δὲ ὡς δίκαιος.

Ἢ τὸ μὲν πρῶτον κοινόν, τὸ δὲ δεύτερον τὴν ἑαυτοῦ προφαίνων βούλησιν, τὸ δὲ τρίτον τὴν ἐκείνων ἀπορητικὴν ἰσχύν.

ρμδ'. – Ὅτι τρία αὐτῷ ἐμαρτύρησεν ἃ δεῖ ἔχειν τὸν ἄριστον ἰατρόν· πρῶτον 398 προθυμίαν εὐνοϊκήν, δεύτερον διάγνωσιν τοῦ πάθους, τρίτον τὴν ἴασιν.

ρμε'. – [89d1–3] Πῶς οὐδὲν μεῖζον πάθος μισολογίας; — Ἢ πρῶτον μὲν 399 ὅτι μισεῖν ἑαυτὸν ἀνάγκη λογικὸν ὄντα κατὰ φύσιν. ἔπειτα μισεῖν τὴν ἀλήθειαν συμβαίνει· διὰ γὰρ τῶν λόγων ἡ ἀλή|θεια εὑρίσκεται, ἢ πάντων ἡγεῖται τῶν (176) ἀγαθῶν. τρίτον ὁ μισόλογος ἀλογίας πάντως ἐραστής, ὥστε θηριοῦται τρόπον τινά.

ρμς'. – Ὅτι μισανθρωπίαν τῇ μισολογίᾳ συνέζευξεν ὡς περὶ τὴν αὐτὴν φύσιν 400 ἑκατέραν οὖσαν, τὴν ἡμῶν αὐτῶν, καὶ εἰς ἓν ἐρχομένην.

ρμζ'. – [90a4–b3] Ὅτι ἐν μὲν τῷ αἰθέρι πλεῖστον τὸ ἄκρον, ἐν δὲ τῷ 401 Ταρτάρῳ καὶ ὅλως τοῖς ὑπὸ γῆν δικαιωτηρίοις τὸ ἔσχατον, ἐν δὲ τῷ καθ' ἡμᾶς τόπῳ τὸ μέσον εἶδος τῆς ζωῆς· ὥστε προσομιλεῖν χρὴ μέσως.

ρμη'. – [90c8–d8] Ὅτι ἀνάγκη τῆς ἀπιστίας αἰτιᾶσθαι ἢ τὴν τῶν πραγμάτων 402 φύσιν ἢ τὴν τῶν λόγων ἀδυναμίαν ἢ τὴν ἡμετέραν ἀναγωγίαν· ὃ μᾶλλον ἀξιοῖ πρὸς ἐπανόρθωσιν.

---

§ 396. 4 ταὐτὰ Nv: ταῦτα M
§ 398. 1 ante αὐτῷ] ἐν eras. M^c
§ 399. 4 μισολόγος M^c
§ 401. 1 αἰθέρι] accent. add., -ι in ras. 2 litt., M^c

---

benevolence, knowledge, and power, corresponding to God, Intelligence, and Soul. The same pattern may be intended here.

§ 401. Plato explains that extremes are rare everywhere; Pr. (more probably than Dam.) changes the meaning considerably by his "level" theory. Cf. Pr., Alc. 258.6–9: in heaven all souls are good, in Tartarus all are wicked, in genesis, which is nearer Tartarus, most are bad.

2. Pl., Phaedr. 249a6–7 τὰ ὑπὸ γῆς δικαιωτήρια.

§§ 403–404. Notes on 92c11–e3 and 95b5–6

403. [92c11–e3] Like draws to like; therefore the common run of people, superficial and attached to the world of appearances, find pleasure in plausible argument and are persuaded by it, while the more profound thinkers, who scorn the world of the senses and its easy beliefs, rise above plausibilities and are content only with arguments that have a certain measure of cogency.

404. [95b5–6] Nemesis is the Goddess who curbs the excesses of the soul, and her wrath more manifestly visits the boastful, because the humble are more clearly aware where they fall short of the standard; in the lowest regions she must obviously have created jealous, malicious demons, who exert a baleful influence even on seekers for truth, so long as they are still trying to find their way to wisdom, as well as on those who follow the hieratic art. As for Socrates, he is wary of this malicious brood at least for the sake of his disciples.

§§ 405–406. A new analysis of the passage 93a11–94b3

405. The words 'Does this apply to soul . . .' [93b4–6] do not form another syllogism, as the commentator's predecessors thought, nor do they serve to establish an auxiliary proposition, as he himself thinks; as a matter of fact no inference is drawn at all, this is simply one of the previous assumptions relating to the logical subject [§ 362]. This one is the first; the second is that the soul is receptive of vice and virtue [93b8–c2]; then a third, that virtue is harmony, vice disharmony [93c3–10]; and immediately prior to all these is the premise that the nature of every harmony is determined by the way it was arranged [93a11–12]. On these data rests the first of the two arguments. They yield the following syllogisms:

[93d1-5] If harmony and soul are identical, and soul can be in no respect more or less soul than another, then neither can a harmony be more or less a harmony than another; the former is true: therefore so is the latter.

---

§ 404. On Nemesis see Pr., *Hes.* 73.23–74.16, where φθόνος is described as an εἴδωλον νεμέσεως, and unworthy of the deity.

§§ 405–406. Cf. I §§ 368–370; II §§ 51–54. The new analysis may have been prompted by a student's question, since it follows the comments on the last words of this section of the *Ph.* text (95b5–6). Its interest lies, first, in the explicit distinction between the views of Pr.'s predecessors, Pr. himself, and Dam. (see note on §§ 361–370), and, secondly, in its scrupulous adherence to the text of the *Ph.* There are now four assumptions: (preliminary) the nature of each harmony depends on the way in which it is attuned (93a11–12); (1) soul does not admit of differences in degree (93b4–6); (2) soul does admit of virtue and vice (93b8–c2); (3) virtue is harmony, vice disharmony (93c3–10). The proof consists of two steps: (1) if harmony

§§ 403–404. Notes on 92c11–e3 and 95b5–6

ϱμθ′. – [92c11–e3] *Ότι τὸ ὅμοιον τῷ ὁμοίῳ χαίρει· διόπερ οἱ μὲν πολλοὶ* **403**
ἐπιπόλαιοι ὄντες καὶ τῷ φαινομένῳ συζῶντες τοῖς εἰκόσι τῶν λόγων χαίρουσι
καὶ τούτοις ἕπονται, οἱ δὲ βαθύτεροι τὴν διάνοιαν καὶ τῶν ὑπὸ τὴν αἴσθησιν
καὶ προχείρων καταφρονοῦντες τῶν μὲν εἰκότων ὑπερανέχουσιν, ἀγαπῶσι δὲ
τοὺς ἀνάγκῃ τινὶ συνδεδεμένους λόγους. 5

ϱν′. – [95b5–6] *Ότι ἡ Νέμεσις, θεὸς οὖσα κολουστικὴ τῆς τῶν ψυχῶν* **404**
ἀμετρίας καὶ διαφανέστερον νεμεσῶσα τοῖς ὑπεραύχοις διὰ τὸ τοὺς ταπεινοὺς
μᾶλλον συναισθάνεσθαι τῆς οἰκείας ἀμετρίας, εἰκότως ἐπ' ἐσχάτοις δαίμονας
συνεστήσατο φθονερούς καὶ βασκάνους, οἳ καὶ ταῖς τῶν φιλοσόφων ἐνεργείαις
βασκαίνουσιν, ὅσοι ἔτι φιλοσοφεῖν πειρῶνται, ὥσπερ καὶ τοῖς ἱερατικῆς ἁπτο- 5
μένοις. ὁ δ' οὖν Σωκράτης εὐλαβεῖται τὸ βάσκανον γένος διὰ τοὺς ἑταίρους.

§§ 405–406. A new analysis of the passage 93a11–94b3

ϱνα′. – *Ότι λέγων 'ἢ οὖν ἔστι τοῦτο περὶ ψυχήν'* [93b4–6] *οὔτε συλλογισμὸν* **405**
ποιεῖ ἄλλον, ὡς οἱ πρὸ αὐτοῦ, οὔτε, ὡς αὐτὸς ὁ ἐξηγητής, λημμάτιον προκατασκευ-
άζει· ὅλως γὰρ οὐδ' ὁτιοῦν | συμπεραίνεται, ἀλλ' ἔστι μία καὶ αὕτη τῶν ὑποθέσεων (177)
ἀπὸ τοῦ ὑποκειμένου [§ 362]. *καὶ αὕτη πρώτη· δευτέρα δὲ ὅτι δέχεται ψυχὴ*
κακίαν καὶ ἀρετήν [93b8–c2]· *ἐφ' αἷς τρίτη τὸ τὴν μὲν ἀρετὴν ἁρμονίαν εἶναι,* 5
τὴν δὲ κακίαν ἀναρμοστίαν [93c3–10]· *ὧν πασῶν προϋπάρχει προσεχῶς ἡ*
λέγουσα οὕτω πεφυκέναι ἑκάστην ἁρμονίαν ὡς ἂν ἁρμοσθῇ [93a11–12]. *ἐκ δὴ*
τούτων συνάγεται τὸ πρῶτον τῶν δυεῖν ἐπιχειρημάτων. ἐξ ὧν γίγνονται
συλλογισμοὶ οὗτοι·
ϱνβ′ [93d1–5] *εἰ ταὐτὸν ἁρμονία καὶ ψυχή, οὐδὲν δὲ μᾶλλον οὐδὲ ἧττον ψυχὴ* 10
ψυχῆς, οὐδὲ ἁρμονία ἁρμονίας· ἀλλὰ μὴν τὸ πρῶτον· τὸ ἄρα δεύτερον.

---

§ 403. 3 τῶν] -ῶ- in ras. Mᶜ
§ 404. 4 ταῖς] -αῖς ex corr. Mᶜ
§ 405. 3 αὕτη Wk: αὐτὴ M — 4 πρώτη· δευτέρα Fh: πρῶτον· δεύτερον M — 5 τρίτη Fh: -ον M

---

and soul are identical, since no soul is more soul than another, no harmony will be more harmonious than another (93d1–11); (2) therefore, if soul and harmony are identical, no soul will be more perfect than another (93d12–94a7).

§ 405. 2–4. The difference between *λημμάτιον* and *ὑπόθεσις* is that the former is derivative, the latter axiomatic. This is the meaning of "no inference is drawn"; of course, the premise is eventually used at lines 10–11.

8. *τὸ πρῶτον τῶν δυεῖν ἐπιχειρημάτων* : if the wording is correct, this must be the rest of the section (lines 10–21), not lines 10–14, as the second and third assumptions are used only in the second half of the argument (lines 15–21); the second *ἐπιχείρημα* is then § 406.

11. *ἀλλὰ μὴν τὸ πρῶτον* : the adversary's thesis is accepted for the purpose of a *reductio ad absurdum*.

[93d6–11]

| har-
mony | shows no differ-
ence in degree | cannot be more
or less attuned | cannot participate in
harmony more or less. |

[93d12–e3] If soul and harmony are identical, and no harmony can be more or less attuned, then neither can soul; the former is true; therefore so is the latter.

[93e4–10]

| soul | cannot be more
or less attuned | cannot participate in
harmony more or less | cannot have a greater or
smaller share of virtue
and vice. |

[94a1–7] soul harmony inaccessible to disharmony inaccessible to vice.

406. [94a8–b3] Socrates adds another syllogism, which is a reduction to absurdity:

| irrational
soul | soul unqualifiedly | cannot have a greater or smaller
share of virtue. |

V. THE ARGUMENT FROM THE ESSENCE OF SOUL

§§ 407–415. Causes and contributory causes: comment on 95e7–100a7

407. [95e9–96a1] Why is it necessary, before coming to immortality, 'to give a complete account of the cause of coming-to-be and passing-away'? — Because the discussion is a search for the principle of these processes, soul, and an attempt is made to approach the problem from this angle. Or because the soul, if it perishes, also has a beginning in time, and therefore we must first define the way these very processes take place and the causes or contributory causes by which they are brought about. The more immediate reason is that soul, being form and causing a certain effect in other things, must be inaccessible to the contrary of that effect. The same is true of all other things, whether simple or composite. Of both categories there are two kinds: of simple things some are separable, others inseparable; composite things, on the other hand, have simple things either as their elements or as consequents and accidents. However this may be, these are the kinds of subjects with which the discussion will deal.

408. [96a8] 'Sublime' in what sense? — Because it is a search for the cause, which transcends sensible phenomena.

13–14. The first two terms in the diagram should probably be joined so as to read ἁρμονία οὐδὲν μᾶλλον οὐδὲ ἧττον, 'that harmony which shows no difference in degree' (as in *Ph.* 93d6).

§ 406. 1. εἰς ἄτοπον ἀπάγων: this is also the case in the first argument.

§ 407. Dam. II § 66. Three answers to the question in what way the disquisition on causes is relevant to the final argument ("soul is life"). Though Dam. II mentions only the first, it looks as if the last, which is qualified as the "more immediate" reason and is presented in greater detail, is the answer preferred by Dam.

[93d6-11]

ἁρμο-νία   οὐδὲν μᾶλλον   οὐδὲν μᾶλλον οὐδὲ   οὐδὲν μᾶλλον οὐδὲ ἧτ-
         οὐδὲ ἧττον   ἧττον ἥρμοσται   τον ἁρμονίας μετέχει.

ρνγ' [93d12-e3] εἰ ταὐτὸν ψυχὴ καὶ ἁρμονία, ἡ δὲ ἁρμονία οὐδὲν μᾶλλον οὐδὲ 15
ἧττον ἥρμοσται, οὐδὲ ἄρα ἡ ψυχή· ἀλλὰ μὴν τὸ πρῶτον· τὸ ἄρα δεύτερον.
[93e4-10]

ψυχὴ   οὐδὲν μᾶλλον οὐδὲ   οὐδὲν μᾶλλον οὐδὲ ἧτ-   οὐδὲν μᾶλλον οὐδὲ
       ἧττον ἥρμοσται   τον ἁρμονίας μετέχει   ἧττον ἀρετῆς καὶ
                                                    κακίας μετέχει. 20

[94a1-7] ψυχὴ   ἁρμονία   ἀναρμοστίας ἄδεκτος   κακίας ἄδεκτος.

ρνδ'. - [94a8-b3] Ὅτι καὶ εἰς ἄτοπον ἀπάγων προστίθησι καὶ ἄλλον 406
συλλογισμόν·

ἡ ἄλογος   αὐτὸ τοῦτο ψυχὴ   οὐδὲν μᾶλλον οὐδὲ ἧττον
ψυχὴ   ἀρετῆς μετέχει.

V. THE ARGUMENT FROM THE ESSENCE OF SOUL

§§ 407-415. Causes and contributory causes: comment on 95e7-100a7

d ρνε'. - [95e9-96a1] Διὰ τί πρὸ τῆς ἀθανασίας ʽδεῖ περὶ γενέσεως καὶ φθορᾶς 407
τὴν αἰτίαν διαπραγματεύσασθαιʼ; — Ἢ ὅτι τὴν τούτων ἀρχὴν ἐπιζητεῖ ὁ λόγος, (178)
τὴν ψυχήν, καὶ ἀπὸ τούτων αὐτὴν ἐπιχειρεῖ θηρεύειν. ἢ ὅτι, εἰ φθείρεται, καὶ
γίνεται, ὥστε αὐτὰ ταῦτα προδιοριστέον τίνα τρόπον ἐπιτελεῖται καὶ κατὰ τίνας
αἰτίας ἢ συναιτίας. ἤ, τὸ προσεχέστερον, ὅτι εἶδος οὖσα ἡ ψυχὴ καί τινος οἰστικὴ 5
τοῖς ἄλλοις, ἄδεκτος ὀφείλει εἶναι τοῦ ἐναντίου τῷ ἐπιφερομένῳ. οὕτως γὰρ
ἔχει καὶ τὰ ἄλλα πάντα, ὅσα τε ἁπλᾶ καὶ ὅσα σύνθετα. διττὰ δὲ ἑκάτερα· τὰ
μὲν γὰρ χωριστὰ τῶν ἁπλῶν, τὰ δὲ ἀχώριστα, καὶ αὖ τῶν συνθέτων τὰ μὲν
ὡς ἐκ στοιχείων τῶν ἁπλῶν συγκείμενα, τὰ δὲ ὡς ἐπιγιγνομένων καὶ
συμβεβηκότων. τὰ δ' οὖν τοιαῦτα περιέξει ὁ λόγος. 10

ρνς'. - [96a8] Πῶς ʽὑπερήφανοςʼ; — Ἢ κατὰ τὴν ζήτησιν τῆς αἰτίας, οὐκέτι 408
γὰρ τῶν φαινομένων.

---

§ 405. 13-14; 18-406.4 in spat. vac. M^c
§ 407. 1 δεῖ] δ- in ras., ˉ ex ʽ, M^c (ἀεὶ M¹?) — 5 καί τινος μ: καὶ τίνος M

5. συναιτίας : on the form see at § 339.2.
6-10. Forms are either simple (and in that case separable or inseparable), or composite (in which case they have simple forms either as their elements or as accidents). The same classification returns at § 428. It is meant to include the whole range of opposites covered by Socrates' induction at 102d5-105b4.
§ 408. ὑπερήφανος is explained as ὑπὲρ τὰ φαινόμενα, just as ὑπερφυής = ὑπὲρ φύσιν, Ol. 5 § 12. The resemblance with *Etym. Magn.* 778.51-52 ὁ ὑπεράνω πάντων φαινόμενος is accidental.

409. [96b2–8] By depreciating the contributory causes Socrates supports his claim that the soul cannot be classed as such. He also points out in passing the absurdity to which this view leads: what, indeed, can be more preposterous than to derive true knowledge, which is universal, causal, transcendent, and in every respect superior, from sense-perception, which deals with the individual, fails to discern causes, cannot be separated from matter, and is in every respect inferior?

410. [96b8–c7] After we have learnt how to account for things in terms of contributory causes, a necessary step for further progress is to inquire into the higher causes, and the result will be that we unlearn and forget about those others, because we no longer acknowledge them. This is the stage of simple ignorance, which is the beginning of knowledge.

411. [96d8–97b7] With regard to the other contributory causes, too, Socrates includes, by implication, the proofs for their rejection. If forms are only what they are, the one itself can never become two, each form being only the one thing it really is, nor can one and one become two by being added to each other, for when a man and another man meet, the result is simply men and not another form, whereas two is a different form. Further, how can this same form be brought about by contrary processes, viz. addition and division? Nothing can, as such, be the efficient cause of opposite effects, nor a product of opposite causes. And even if we consider addition and division as forms, addition will only add, division only divide, but neither will produce a dyad or a monad.

412. [97b8–98c2] Anaxagoras, though he had a glimpse of the efficient cause, did not make use of it: in his account of the facts he puts forth the irrational, indefinite causes, which will take opposite directions by what appears to be a sudden change of mind. Intelligence, however, is essentially a limit and indeed a standard; it sets itself one goal only, the Good, which it defines by means of its faculty of judgment, and which it is stirred to make its own by its faculty of appetition, both faculties speeding it on its way thither, a way which is aspiration towards the Good with cognition and appetition as fellow-travelers.

---

§ 409. 1–2. Cf. **Dam. II § 66**. The term συναίτιον comes from *Tim.* 46c7 and d1; the idea is already there in the *Ph.* On the three causes proper and the three contributory causes see note at §§ 260–261.

§ 411. 1. καὶ ἐπὶ τῶν ἄλλων συναιτίων : the reference of ἄλλων is not completely certain; it probably means the other two (material and instrumental) besides the formal cause, whose insufficiency is pointed out in the present passage. Cf. II § 68, where *Ph.* 100c8–101c9 is taken to deal with immanent form (the formal cause) as opposed to transcendent form (the exemplary cause).

§ 412. 1. In Plato, νοῦς represents the final cause, in Neoplatonism it is the efficient or creative cause, whereas the Good is the final, the νοητόν the exemplary

ρνζ'. - [96b2-8] *Ότι τὰ συναίτια ἀτιμάζων ἀξιοῖ μηδὲ τὴν ψυχὴν ἐν τοῖς συναιτίοις τάττειν. παρενδείκνυται δὲ καὶ τὸ ἄτοπον ἑπόμενον· τί γὰρ ἂν εἴη ἀτοπώτερον τοῦ τὴν ἐπιστήμην γεννᾶν ἀπὸ τῆς αἰσθήσεως, τὴν καθόλου ἀπὸ τῶν ἀτόμων, τὴν ἀποδοτικὴν τῆς αἰτίας ἀπὸ τῶν ἀναιτίων, τὴν χωριστὴν καὶ ὅλως κρείττω ἀπὸ τῆς ἀχωρίστου καὶ ὅλως χείρονος;

ρνη'. - [96b8-c7] *Ότι μαθόντα τὰς τῶν συναιτίων ἀποδόσεις, εἰ μέλλοι τις προκόπτειν, ἐπιζητεῖν δεῖ τὰς καλλίους, ὥστε ταύτας ἀπομαθεῖν τε καὶ ἀποβαλεῖν διὰ κατάγνωσιν. τοῦτο δέ ἐστιν ἡ ἁπλῆ ἄγνοια, ἀρχὴ δὲ αὕτη τῆς ἐπιστήμης.

ρνθ'. - [96d8-97b7] *Ότι παρενδείκνυται καὶ ἐπὶ τῶν ἄλλων συναιτίων τὰς ἐλεγκτικὰς ἀποδείξεις. εἰ γὰρ τὰ εἴδη αὐτὰ ἅ ἐστι μόνον ἐστίν, οὐκ ἂν τὸ ἓν αὐτό ποτε γένοιτο δύο (ἓν γάρ ἐστι μόνον ὅ ἐστιν ἕκαστον), οὐδ' ἂν τὸ ἓν καὶ τὸ ἓν συνιόντα γένοιτο· καὶ γὰρ ἄνθρωπος καὶ ἄνθρωπος συνελθόντες οὐδὲν ἄλλο ἢ ἄνθρωποι καὶ οὐκ ἄλλο τι εἶδος, ἀλλὰ μὴν τὰ δύο ἄλλο εἶδος. πῶς δὲ τοῦτο διὰ τῶν ἐναντίων γίγνεται τὸ αὐτό, οἷον διὰ συνθέσεώς τε καὶ διαιρέσεως; οὐδὲν γὰρ τῶν ἐναντίων ποιητι|κὸν καθ' αὑτὸ οὐδὲ γέννημα τῶν ἐναντίων. εἰ δὲ καὶ εἶδος ἡ σύνθεσις καὶ ἡ διαίρεσις, ἡ μὲν συνθήσει μόνον, ἡ δὲ διαιρήσει, δυάδα δὲ οὐ ποιήσει οὐδὲ μονάδα.

ρξ'. - [97b8-98c2] *Ότι ὁ 'Αναξαγόρας εἶδεν μὲν εἰς τὸ ποιητικὸν αἴτιον, οὐ μὴν ἐχρήσατό γε αὐτῷ· ἐν γὰρ ταῖς ἀποδόσεσι τὰς ἀλογίστους αἰτίας προβάλλεται καὶ ἀορίστους καὶ ἐπὶ τὰ ἐναντία φερομένας ὑπὸ δόξης παλιμβόλου τινός. ὁ μέντοι νοῦς ὅρος εἶναι βούλεται καὶ ἀτεχνῶς κανών· ἀλλὰ καὶ σκοπὸν ἕνα τίθεται, τὸ ἀγαθόν, ὅπερ τῇ μὲν κρίσει ὁρίζει, τῇ δὲ ὀρέξει ἐγείρεται πρὸς οἰκείωσιν αὐτοῦ, ἀμφοτέραις δὲ ὁμοῦ τὴν πρὸς ἐκεῖνο στέλλεται ὁδόν, καὶ ἔστιν ἡ ὁδὸς ὁρμὴ πρὸς τὸ ἀγαθὸν γνώσει τε καὶ ὀρέξει παραπεμπομένη.

---

§ 411. 2 post ἂν] ∻ ∻ ∻ in ras. M^x — 8 συνθήσει ... διαιρήσει Wk: συνθέσει ... διαιρέσει M (-έ- utrumque puncto not. M^c)

---

cause. The fact is noticed and explained below, § 413.4-6.

3-4. ὑπὸ δόξης παλιμβόλου τινός : not to be joined to προβάλλεται (in which case it would describe a change of mind in Anaxagoras), but to τὰς ἀλογίστους αἰτίας ... καὶ ἐπὶ τὰ ἐναντία φερομένας. Cf. infra § 414.2-3 (the lower causes subject to contrary impulses).

4. βούλεται : see note § 151.4.

5-6. On judgment and appetition in intelligence see note on § 31.4-7.

6. τὴν πρὸς ἐκεῖνο στέλλεται ὁδόν : there may be an allusion to Zeus "taking the road to the castle of Kronos" (the creative Intelligence in its conversion to the transcendent Intelligence), supra § 151.6-8.

413. [97c2–d3] Intelligence is the first to revert to the Good, because it is separated from it and yet closest to it of all separate existents and, in the phrase of the *Philebus*, its 'kinsman' [30e1]; because, having been projected as the 'eye of love' of the Good, it is the first of all beings that have detached themselves and therefore need such an eye. It is for a good reason, then, that Socrates links the efficient cause, intelligence, directly with the final cause, and cannot view intelligence apart from finality.

414. [98c2–99b2] Socrates demonstrates clearly by referring to himself and to human intelligence that the contributory causes tend in opposite directions and subserve contrary opinions, like a blind man, and that Intelligence, which has nothing in view but the Good, is superior to these; if this is already true of human intelligence, how much more of divine.

415. [99c6–100a3] He begins by presenting as the true causes of things sensible the efficient and the final cause. However, since the sensible world is indefinite and in it sense-perceptions and opinions take the place of pure reason, he resorts to 'reasons', i.e. universal forms (the fact that he calls them 'reasons' and considers them superior to sensible things proves that he locates them in rational soul), because on this level he expects to find more easily what he is seeking. So the 'alternative course' is after the final cause the exemplary cause, or after the world of intellection that of discursive thought, or else, starting from below, after the search in the sphere of sense-perception the approach in the sphere of discursive thought.

§§ 416–420. The ideas and the problem of participation: comment on 100a7–102a2

416. It is easier and simpler to assume and posit prototypes as the causes of sensible things and with the help of the copies form a notion of their character (they must, while showing the same qualities, be real, single in form and always constant in their state and condition, because they are prior to their images) than it is to understand the final cause. The latter is truly ineffable and is beyond having visible images (no image of it exists); moreover, in the world of process it disappears because of the indefiniteness which is inherent in process and which causes all the evil that pervades it. On the other hand, the exemplary cause is also easier to

---

§ 413. 2. γενούστης: now generally considered a textual error, but the only reading known to the Neoplatonists and the lexicographers; see Dam., *Phil.* § 134.4; § 135.2.

3. ὄμμα ἐρωτικὸν τοῦ ἀγαθοῦ: the notion is Plotinus's (V 1, 7.5–6 πῶς οὖν νοῦν γεννᾷ; ἢ ὅτι τῇ ἐπιστροφῇ πρὸς ἑαυτὸ ἑώρα, ἡ δὲ ὅρασις αὕτη νοῦς), the phrase is Plato's (*Phaedr.* 253e5), but from a totally different context. The structure of the transcendent world implied in the expression, with the Intelligence as the first emanation from the One, is that of Plotinus rather than of Proclus. Cf. also Dam., *princ.* 188.8–10 καὶ ὁδηγὸς καθίσταται τοῖς ἄνω στελλομένοις ἡ γνῶσις. ἔστι γὰρ οἷον

ρξα'. - [97c2-d3] Ὅτι ὁ νοῦς πρῶτος ἐπιστρέφεται πρὸς τὸ ἀγαθόν, καὶ ὡς 413
διακριθεὶς ἀπ' αὐτοῦ, καὶ ὡς τῶν διακριθέντων ἐγγυτάτω καὶ 'γενούστης', ὡς
ἐν Φιλήβῳ εἴρηται [30e1], καὶ ὡς ὄμμα ἐρωτικὸν τοῦ ἀγαθοῦ προβαλλόμενος
πρῶτος τῶν χωρισθέντων καὶ διὰ τοῦτο δεηθέντων ὄμματος τοιούτου. εἰκότως
ἄρα ὁ Σωκράτης τὸ ποιητικὸν αἴτιον, τὸν νοῦν, εὐθὺς τῷ τελικῷ συνάπτει αἰτίῳ 5
καὶ οὐ δύναται νοῦν ὁρᾶν ἄνευ τοῦ τέλους.

ρξβ'. - [98c2-99b2] Ὅτι ἐναργῶς ἀπέδειξε δι' ἑαυτοῦ καὶ τοῦ ἀνθρωπίνου 414
νοῦ ὅτι τὰ μὲν συναίτια ἐπὶ τἀναντία φέρεται καὶ ταῖς ἐναντίαις δόξαις ὑπηρετεῖ
τυφλοῦ δίκην, ὁ δὲ νοῦς πρὸς μόνον ὁρῶν τὸ ἀγαθὸν ὑπερέχει τούτων· εἰ γὰρ
ὁ ἀνθρώπινος, πολλῷ μᾶλλον ὁ θεῖος.

ρξγ'. - [99c6-100a3] Ὅτι πρότερον ἐξηγεῖται τῶν αἰσθητῶν ἀληθεῖς αἰτίας 415(180)
τήν τε ποιητικὴν καὶ τὴν τελικήν. τῶν δὲ αἰσθητῶν ἀορίστων ὄντων καὶ ἀντὶ
καθαροῦ τοῦ νοῦ ταῖς αἰσθήσεσι χρωμένου καὶ ταῖς δόξαις, ἀνέφυγεν ἐπὶ τοὺς
'λόγους' καὶ τὰ καθόλου εἴδη, ἄπερ 'λόγους' ὀνομάζων καὶ κρείττονα τῶν
αἰσθητῶν εἶναι λέγων δῆλός ἐστιν ἐν τῇ λογικῇ ψυχῇ αὐτὰ τιθέμενος, ὡς ἐν 5
τούτῳ ῥᾷον εὑρήσων ὃ βούλεται. 'δεύτερος' οὖν 'πλοῦς' μετὰ τὸ τελικὸν τὸ
παραδειγματικόν, ἢ μετὰ τὰ νοερὰ τὰ διανοητά, ἢ κάτωθεν μετὰ τὴν ἐν τοῖς
αἰσθητοῖς ζήτησιν ἡ ἐν τοῖς διανοητοῖς.

§§ 416-420. The ideas and the problem of participation: comment on 100a7-102a2

δ ρξδ'. - Ὅτι ῥᾷον καὶ ἁπλούστερον ὑποθέσθαι καὶ θέσθαι τὰ παραδείγματα 416
ὡς αἴτια τῶν αἰσθητῶν καὶ τίνα ταῦτα ἐννοῆσαι ἀπὸ τῶν εἰκόνων, ὅτι τοιαῦτα
ἕτερα ἀληθῆ καὶ μονοειδῆ καὶ ἀεὶ κατὰ τὰ αὐτὰ καὶ ὡσαύτως ἔχοντα ἅτε
προϋπάρχοντα τῶν εἰκόνων, ἤπερ τὸ τελικόν. τοῦτο γὰρ καὶ [ὡς] ἄρρητον ὡς
ἀληθῶς καὶ τῶν φαινομένων εἰκόνων ὑπερανέχον (οὐ γάρ ἐστιν αὐτοῦ εἰκών) 5
καὶ ἔτι μέντοι ἐν τῇ γενέσει ἀφανιζόμενον διὰ τὴν αὐτῆς ἀοριστίαν σύμφυτον,
δι' ἣν καὶ τοῦ κακοῦ πολλοῦ ἀναπέπλησται. ἀλλὰ μὴν καὶ ἥπερ τὸ ποιητικόν,

---

§ 413. 2 γενού~στης, ~σ- in ras. Mᶜ
§ 415. 8 ἡ] in ras. Mᶜ (ἦ M¹ ?)
§ 416. 4 ἥπερ Fh: ἢ περὶ M | ὡς M: del. Wk

ὄμμα προπομπεῦον καὶ ἡγεμονοῦν τῆς ὀρέξεως ἐπ' ἐκεῖνο σπευδούσης, φῶς ἀνάπτουσα τὸ οἰκεῖον. Ol. 13 § 2.18 τὸ γὰρ ὄμμα ⟨νοῦ⟩ σύμβολόν ἐστι.
§ 414. 3. τυφλοῦ δίκην : end of a trimeter, probably by chance.
§ 415. 6-8. Evidently the usual acceptation for δεύτερος πλοῦς ("second best") does not fit the third explanation offered.
§ 416. The explanation why the ideas (exemplary causes) are easier to grasp than either the final or the efficient cause is a makeshift one, serving to fit the present Ph. passage. Normally, the efficient cause, being the closest to us, should be the easiest to understand.
5. οὐ γάρ ἐστιν αὐτοῦ εἰκών : a quotation?

approach than the efficient cause, in the first place because of the association of the efficient cause with the final cause, as shown above [§ 413]; secondly because of the far-reaching changes in the images, which belie the existence of intelligence as a changeless efficient cause, for which reason Aristotle attributes all efficient causality to the celestial beings; and thirdly because it is hidden behind the particular sensible causes, which are all but sufficient to account for the created world, since every form seems to be capable of reproducing itself. Prototypes, then, inasmuch as they are forms, are easier to grasp than the final cause, and inasmuch as they exist by themselves and have no contact with the world of process even for the purpose of creation, being beyond the Creator, they are simpler to understand. For the same reason they are also sooner underrated, because they do not create, but only exist, the assumption being that, as far as mere existence is concerned, the sensible world is sufficient.

417. [100b3–7] Once exemplary causes are posited, the efficient cause is somehow comprehended in them (things here below are what they are by participation in the prototypes), and so is the final cause. For there is also a prototype of the good, that is to say, of goodness as a form, and if we find the useful in this world, it will prove to exist by virtue of participation in that form; I believe that this is the reason why Socrates uses the beautiful as his example, because it includes the profitable, as it is laid down in the *Gorgias* [474d3–475a4].

418. [100d3–6] Plato has often raised the question of the participation of forms, but nowhere is the answer indicated more clearly than here. If it is by presence, then how can forms be separable from particulars, and how can they be indivisible? If by communion, other realities will be needed in which both forms and particulars can communicate, and this *ad infinitum*, so that forms are no longer primary. What Plato says, however, is 'or whatever the way': form *is* present, but only by participation, and there *is* communion, but only in the sense that particulars communicate in forms, not both in a third reality, and they communicate in the way of participation.

10–11. Walzer and Ross make this a fragment of Ar.'s Περὶ φιλοσοφίας (frg. 22); it is at least as likely, however, that it is a reference to *met. Λ* 8 or *cael.* II 12, texts with which Pr. and Dam. were more familiar than with the dialogues.

§ 417. Cf. Dam., *Phil.* § 114.1–4, where the three causes are said to meet in the Demiurge.

3–4. Proclus, in his essay Περὶ τοῦ ἐν Πολιτείᾳ λόγου τοῦ δεικνύντος τί ποτέ ἐστιν τἀγαθόν (*Rep.* I 269–287), distinguishes three levels of the Good: (1) immanent good (*Phil.*; *Rep.* VI 509a5 τὴν τοῦ ἀγαθοῦ ἕξιν); (2) the form of the good (*Ph.* 65d7; *Parm.* 130b7–9; *Rep.* VI 505a2–4); and (3) the transcendent Good (*Rep.* VI 509b6–10 ἔτι ἐπέκεινα τῆς οὐσίας).

3–4. τὸ ὠφέλιμον : according to *Rep.* VI 505a2–4 ἡ τοῦ ἀγαθοῦ ἰδέα . . ., ᾗ δὴ καὶ δίκαια καὶ τἆλλα προσχρησάμενα χρήσιμα καὶ ὠφέλιμα γίγνεται.

πρῶτον μὲν διὰ τὴν πρὸς τὸ τελικὸν συμπλοκήν, ὡς δέδεικται [§ 413]· δεύτερον δὲ διὰ τὴν πολλαχοῦ τῶν εἰκόνων μεταβολὴν ἀναινομένην τὸ τοῦ νοῦ ποιητικὸν ἀκίνητον, διὸ καὶ Ἀριστοτέλης τοῖς οὐρανίοις ζῴοις περιτίθεται τὴν ποίησιν 10 ὅλην· τρίτον δὲ αὖ διὰ τὸ προφαίνεσθαι τὰ μερικὰ αἴτια καὶ αἰσθητὰ σχεδὸν ἀρκοῦντα πρὸς τὴν γένεσιν· πᾶν γὰρ εἶδος εἶναι δοκεῖ τοῦ ὁμοίου γεννητικόν. τὰ τοίνυν παραδείγματα ὡς μὲν εἴδη εὐληπτότερα τοῦ τελικοῦ, ὡς δὲ ἐφ' ἑαυτῶν ἑστῶτα οὐδὲ ἁπτόμενα τῆς γενέσεως οὐδὲ ποιητικῶς, ἅτε ὑπὲρ τὸν ποιητὴν ὄντα, ἁπλούστερον λαμβάνεται. διὸ καὶ θᾶττον ἀτιμάζεται, ὡς οὐ ποιοῦντα, 15 μόνον δὲ ὄντα· ἀρκεῖν δὲ ὄντα εἶναι τὰ αἰσθητά.

ρξε'. – [100b3-7] Ὅτι τὰ παραδείγματα τεθέντα καὶ τὸ ποιητικὸν συνείληφεν **417** τρόπον τινά (μετοχῇ γὰρ αὐτῶν τὰ τῇδέ ἐστιν ἅ | ἐστιν), καὶ ἔτι τὸ τελικόν. (181) ἔστι γὰρ καὶ ἀγαθοῦ παράδειγμα, τοῦ εἰδητικοῦ δηλονότι, κἂν εὕρωμεν τὸ ὠφέλιμον ἐνθάδε, τῇ ἐκείνου μετασχέσει φανήσεται ὄν· διό μοι δοκεῖ ὁ Σωκράτης τῷ καλῷ χρήσασθαι παραδείγματι, ἅτε περιέχοντι καὶ τὸ χρήσιμον, ὡς ἐν 5 Γοργίᾳ διώρισται [474d3-475a4].

ρξς'. – [100d3-6] Ὅτι περὶ τῆς τῶν εἰδῶν μεθέξεως πολλαχοῦ ἀπορήσας **418** ἐνταῦθα μάλιστα τὴν λύσιν ἐνδείκνυται. εἰ μὲν γὰρ παρουσίᾳ, πῶς χωριστὰ ἐκεῖνα τούτων, πῶς δὲ ἀμέριστα; εἰ δὲ κοινωνίᾳ, δεήσει καὶ ἄλλων, ὧν κοινωνήσει ταῦτα καὶ ἐκεῖνα, καὶ τοῦτο ἐπ' ἄπειρον, καὶ οὐκ ἄρα πρῶτα. ὁ δέ φησιν ʿεἴτε ὅπῃ καὶ ὅπως᾽· πάρεστι μὲν γάρ, ἀλλὰ τῇ μετοχῇ, κοινωνεῖ δέ, ἀλλὰ ταῦτα 5 ἐκείνων, ἀλλ' οὐχὶ ἑτέρου ἑκάτερα, κοινωνεῖ δὲ κατὰ μετοχήν.

---

§ 416. 10 περιτίθεται] accent. in -ί- add., in -ε-[2] eras., -τ-[2] in ras. scr., ν sscr. et puncto del. M^c (ergo περιτιθέναι M[1])
§ 417. 1 post τὸ] ∼ in ras. M^c (τὸν M[1] ?) — 3 καὶ] in ras. M^c
§ 418. 2 παρουσίᾳ] -ι add. M^c (sed 3 κοινωνίαι M[1])

---

§ 418. Dam. II § 69. The question of participation or communication is raised by Pl., *Parm.* 128e5–135e4; *Soph.* 253d5–e2; 254b7–d2; *Phil.* 15b4–8; and commented upon by Pr., *Parm.* 878.17–883.9 (the *Ph.* passage); Dam., *Phil.* §§ 46–47. The Neoplatonist solution is that there is neither participation nor communication in the current sense, but a relationship that transcends both, because the form itself is transcendent. This third relationship is supposed to be indicated by Socrates' words εἴτε ὅπῃ δὴ καὶ ὅπως, cf. note on Dam., *Phil.* § 12.

2–3. παρουσία ... κοινωνία : there are three more occurrences of these two words, either in the nom. or in the dat.: II § 69.2 and 4; *Phil.* § 46.4–5. M^c has consistently added the iota, where missing (which is manifestly wrong at II § 69.4); I have followed M[1], only adapting the παρουσία at line 2 to the κοινωνίαι at line 3. There is a case, of course, for writing the nom. throughout (with Pl.).

419. [100e8–101b2] Socrates shows that a man cannot be bigger or smaller than another 'by a head': first, how can the same cause have opposite effects? secondly, how can being bigger be brought about by what is small in itself? The following point might be added: how can one form be caused by another, 'bigger' or 'smaller' by 'head'? Further, if a thing is big by bigness and small by smallness rather than by a head, this must apply also where higher degrees of these qualities are concerned; for a 'higher degree' of a quality means more complete participation in the same form.

420. [101d5–e1] What succession of other grounds can there be beyond the exemplary cause? Surely only one remains, the final cause? — We must look deeper: prototypes are on the level of differentiated reality, so that we must assume as a prior ground that which is in process of being differentiated, a description properly applying to the life that is beyond intelligence; beyond this, again, is the undifferentiated, i.e. existence, which is prior even to life in the degree of its unity. Finally there are the two causes beyond these, that of differentiation and that of unification, and prior to these, as we conceive it, the One Principle.

§§ 421–430. Analysis of the argument. 102a10–107a1

Assumptions

421. [103e5–104b4] Not only detachable form is incapable of receiving its opposite while remaining what it is (this is implied in the notion of receiving), but so are immanent form and form that is detachable or not detachable depending on the point-of-view, such as in the instance given of number, even or odd.

422. [104b6–105b4] Not only opposites are incapable of sustaining each other's approach, but so are things that have either term of a pair of opposites as part of their essence; i.e. all things that carry the opposite quality, viz. that particular opposite quality that belongs to their essence, as heat does to fire, which is the reason why fire always brings heat with it.

---

§ 419. Dam. II 68.5–10. The first two arguments are Pl.'s (101a5–b3), the other two are additional. Numbers 1–3 reappear (in the order 1–3–2) in II.

§ 420. According to the simplified scheme of things as presented so far (§§ 413 and 417: final – exemplary – efficient cause=One – Intelligible – Intelligence), there is only one step beyond the exemplary cause. Here, in order to show that there is still a number of possible further ὑποθέσεις, the complete metaphysical structure of Pr. is used: the exemplary cause, i.e. the αὐτοζῷον of the *Tim.*, is only the third intelligible triad (intelligible Intelligence); the second is intelligible Life, the first intelligible Being. Each of the three triads is characterized by its last component, the first two are in each case Limit and Infinitude. The Limit and Infinitude of the first triad are the "causes of differentiation and unification" mentioned here. On all this see Pr., *theol.* III 7. The series διακεκριμένον – διακρινόμενον – ἀδιάκριτον, corresponding to intelligible Intelligence, Life and Being,

ρξζ'. – [100e8–101b2] Ὅτι οὐ τῇ κεφαλῇ μείζων καὶ ἐλάττων, δείκνυσι. 419
πρῶτον μὲν τῷ αὐτῷ πῶς τὰ ἐναντία γίγνεται; δεύτερον δὲ πῶς τῇ σμικρᾷ
τὸ μεῖζον; λέγοιτο δὲ ἄν τι καὶ τοιοῦτον· πῶς ἄλλῳ εἴδει ἄλλο, τῇ κεφαλῇ
μείζων ἢ ἐλάττων; ἔτι δέ, εἰ μέγα τῷ μεγέθει καὶ σμικρὸν τῇ σμικρότητι,
ἀλλ' οὐ τῇ κεφαλῇ, σαφὲς ὅτι οὐδὲ αἱ ἐπιτάσεις τῶν αὐτῶν· ἡ γὰρ ἐπίτασις 5
πλείων ἐστὶ τοῦ αὐτοῦ μετάσχεσις.

ρξη'. – [101d5–e1] Καὶ τίς ἂν εἴη πρὸ τοῦ παραδειγματικοῦ ἄλλη καὶ ἄλλη 420
ὑπόθεσις; μία γὰρ μόνη ἡ τοῦ τελικοῦ. – Ἡ βαθύτερον αὐτὸ νοητέον· ἐν γὰρ τῷ
διακεκριμένῳ τὰ παραδείγματα, ὥστε πρὸ τούτου ὑποθετέον ⟨τὸ διακρινόμενον⟩,
ὃ μάλιστα τὴν πρὸ νοῦ ζωὴν ἐνδείκνυται, ἀλλὰ πρὸ τούτου τὸ ἀδιάκριτον, ὅπερ
ἐστὶ τὸ ὄν, ὃ καὶ τῆς ζωῆς προϋπάρχει κατὰ τὸ ἡνωμένον. ἀλλὰ καὶ τὰ αἴτια 5
τὰ δύο πρὸ τούτων, τό τε τῆς διακρίσεως καὶ τὸ τῆς ἑνώσεως, ὧν προεῖναι
νοεῖται ἡ μία ἀρχή.

§§ 421–430. Analysis of the argument. 102a10–107a1

Ὑποθέσεις

ρξθ'. – [103e5–104b4] Ὅτι οὐ μόνον τὸ χωριστὸν εἶδος οὐ δέχεται τὸ 421
ἐναντίον μένον ὅ ἐστι (τοῦτο γὰρ τὸ δέχεσθαι), ἀλλὰ καὶ τὸ ἀχώ|ριστον καὶ (182)
τὸ πῶς μέν, πῶς δὲ οὔ, οἷον τὸ ἐν τοῖς ἀριθμοῖς παρακείμενον ὑπόδειγμα,
ἄρτιον ἢ περιττόν.

ρο'. – [104b6–105b4] Ὅτι οὐ μόνον τὰ ἐναντία οὐ δέχεται ἄλληλα ἐπιόντα, 422
ἀλλ' οὐδὲ ὅσα συνουσίωται τῶν ἐναντίων τινί· ταῦτα δέ ἐστιν ὅσα σὺν ἑαυτοῖς
ἐπιφέρει τὸ ἐναντίον, λέγω δὲ ἐναντίον ἐκεῖνο ᾧ συνουσίωται, οἷον τὸ πῦρ τῇ
θερμότητι, διὸ καὶ ἀεὶ συνεπιφέρει τοῦτο.

---

§ 420. 3 τὸ διακρινόμενον Wk: ∻ decies in ras. 22 fere litt. M^c
§ 421. 3 μέν] μ- in ras. M^c

---

appears e.g. Pr., theol. I 11, 54.18–22 S.-W.; Dam., princ. 290.10–13; Phil. § 244.
There can be little doubt as to the supplement in line 3, though nothing of the
original text is legible; the best way to account for its being erased is the hypothesis
of an obviously false reading (for instance τὸ διακεκριμένον, by assimilation to
lines 2–3) having supplanted the correct τὸ διακρινόμενον.

§§ 421–430. There are two analyses of the final argument: the first (paralleled
in Dam. II §§ 75–77) does not attempt to be more than a restatement of Pl.'s
reasoning, and is probably the work of Pr., as we can see from Dam.'s intervention
at II § 76.5–10. After a detailed discussion of Strato's objections, in which a number
of fresh points come to light, Dam. returns to the argument to reformulate it
independently, taking into account the newly-gained insights (§§ 449–457).

§§ 421–425. Dam. II § 75. Dam. II lists only three assumptions, the first two
of which correspond to §§ 421 and 422, the third to Ph. 105b5–c7.

423. [104b6–c1] Anything incapable of receiving its opposite must either perish on its approach or withdraw, whether it be simple or have that particular quality as part of its essence.

424. [105c9–d5] Soul is a substance which always brings life to its recipient; a thing is admittedly animate as soon as soul has taken possession of it, and therefore necessarily alive.

425. [105d6–11] The opposite of life is death, and therefore life, so long as it remains what it is, does not admit death, nor does soul, which always brings life with it.

426.   Syllogisms

Soul⏝always carries life⏝inaccessible to death⏝immortal.

Soul⏝immortal⏝eternal⏝imperishable.

427. If soul is immortal and imperishable merely because it participates in life, then what is superior to soul and communicates life to it is even more certainly immortal and imperishable; the antecedent is true; so, therefore, is the consequent.

428. Socrates includes simple opposites as well as opposites participating in these, inseparable as well as separable opposites, because soul, thanks to its intermediate position, is conceived as being both.

429. Among the assumptions we must also reckon that of Cebes, who took for granted that soul is separable and longer-lasting than body [95b8–e6].

430. Further, the argument proceeds on the assumption that soul is a substance, otherwise Socrates could not have inferred that it is imperishable [105e10–107a1]; besides, already in a preceding passage [105b8–c2] he compares the soul to fire, because it has life as part of its essence, just as fire has heat.

---

§ 423. 1–2. ἢ φθείρεται ... ἢ ὑπεξίσταται : Plato's formula. Dam. II §§ 75.4–5 specifies that the two possibilities apply to inseparable and separable form respectively.

§ 426. Dam. II § 77. The first syllogism covers *Ph.* 105d3–e7, the second 106c9–d4, where 'eternal' appears as a middle term between 'immortal' and 'imperishable'.

§ 427. A corollary establishing that Life itself (i.e. intelligible or intellective

ροα'. - [104b6-c1] Ὅτι τὸ μὴ δεχόμενον τὸ ἐναντίον ἢ φθείρεται ἐπιόντος 423
ἢ ὑπεξίσταται, καὶ ὅταν ἁπλοῦν ᾖ καὶ ὅταν τούτῳ συνουσιωμένον.

ροβ'. - [105c9-d5] Ὅτι ἡ ψυχὴ οὐσία ἐστὶν ἀεὶ συνεπιφέρουσα ἑαυτῇ ζωὴν 424
τῷ δεχομένῳ· τοῦτο γὰρ καὶ ἔμψυχον εὐθὺς ὁμολογεῖται ὃ ἂν ψυχὴ κατάσχῃ,
ὃ καὶ ζῇ πάντως.

ρογ'. - [105d6-11] Ὅτι τῇ ζωῇ ἐναντίον θάνατος, καὶ διὰ τοῦτο οὐδέποτε 425
ἡ ζωὴ μένουσα ὅ ἐστι δέχεται θάνατον, οὐδέ γε ψυχὴ ἡ συνεπιφέρουσα ἀεὶ τὴν ζωήν.

—. Συλλογισμοί 426

ψυχὴ ‿ ἀεὶ ζωὴν ἐπιφέρει ‿ ἄδεκτον θανάτου ‿ ἀθάνατον.

ψυχὴ ‿ ἀθάνατον ‿ ἀίδιον ‿ ἀνώλεθρον.

ροδ'. - Εἰ ἡ ψυχὴ ἀθάνατος καὶ ἀνώλεθρος μετέχουσά γε ζωῆς, πολλῷ μᾶλλον 427
τὸ κρεῖττον αὐτῆς καὶ ὃ μεταδίδωσι τῆς ζωῆς ἀθάνατον καὶ ἀνώλεθρον· ἀλλὰ
μὴν τὸ πρῶτον· τὸ ἄρα δεύτερον.

ροε'. - Ὅτι καὶ τὰ ἁπλᾶ ἐναντία καὶ τὰ μετέχοντα τούτων, ἔτι δὲ ἀχώριστα 428
καὶ χωριστὰ παρέλαβεν, ἐπειδὴ ἡ ψυχὴ μέση οὖσα φαντάζεται ἑκάτερα εἶναι.

ροϛ'. - Ὅτι ἐν ταῖς ὑποθέσεσι τακτέον καὶ τὴν Κέβητος· ὑπέθετο γὰρ τὴν 429
ψυχὴν χωριστὴν καὶ πολυχρονιωτέραν τοῦ σώματος [95b8-e6].

ροζ'. - Ὅτι καὶ ὡς οὐσίας τῆς ψυχῆς οὔσης πρόεισιν ὁ λόγος· ἢ πῶς ἐπῆγεν 430
καὶ τὸ ἀνώλεθρον [105e10-107a1]; καὶ πρότερόν γε [105b8-c2] πυρὶ |
παραβάλλει αὐτήν, συνουσιωμένην τὴν ζωὴν ἔχουσαν ὡς τὸ πῦρ τὴν θερμότητα. (183)

---

§ 424. 2 κατασχῇι M
§ 426. in spat. vac. M^c
§ 428. 2 ἑκάτερα M^c: ἑκατέρα M¹

Life) is *a fortiori* indestructible.

§§ 428-430. Some further comment on the assumptions, the first apparently still by Pr. (II § 76.1-4=§ 428). The second and the third (soul is separable and it is a substance) may be additions by Dam. (cf. §§ 449-450).

§ 428. Cf. Dam. II § 76. Socrates, in the choice of his examples, obviously includes inseparable form: why, when inseparable form is destroyed by its opposite ? Pr. answers that at first sight it is not apparent to which category soul belongs.

§§ 431–448. Strato's objections answered

Thirteen objections against the argument by Strato [frg. 123]

431. (i) Is not every living being immortal on this ground, that it is insusceptible of death? A dead living being will be found as impossible as a dead soul.

432. In this way the composite will never be disjoined, being insusceptible of its opposite; it will never be decomposed so long as it remains composite.

433. Since the negation is open to more than one construction, we can admit that soul is deathless, not in the sense that it is, or possesses, inextinguishable life, but in the sense that it is susceptible of only one of the opposites, and exists, or does not exist, with this.

434. (ii) On this line of reasoning, are not the souls of irrational animals also immortal, since they bestow life and are insusceptible of the opposite of what they bestow?

435. The same could be said of the souls of plants, which also give life to their bodies.

436. It would be equally true of any natural principle: as it bestows natural powers, it cannot be susceptible of that which is against nature, and being insusceptible of this, it can never perish.

437. Whatever is in process of becoming would be imperishable, for it would be equally insusceptible of its opposite: nothing that is in process of becoming can have passed out of existence.

438. (iii) Is it not rash to assume that, if soul is insusceptible of death and in that sense immortal, it is also imperishable? In this sense of the word even a stone is immortal, but it does not follow that it is imperishable.

---

§§ 431–443. Cf. Dam. II § 78. Wehrli (Strato, frg. 123, cf. commentary pp. 75–76) rearranges the arguments as follows, to arrive at a more satisfactory structure for the whole: §§ 431, 436, 437, 432, 433, 435, 434, 438–443; he was followed by Hackforth, *Plato's Phaedo*, appendix. Whatever the *prima facie* advantages of such a proceeding, it ignores the positive information on the grouping of Strato's arguments contained in §§ 444–448 and by doing so disrupts, for instance, the real connection between § 431 and §§ 432–433 as revealed by § 444. Though there is no reason for much optimism concerning the condition of a text which has probably passed through four or more phases of rewording (Porph. [?], Pr., Dam., the *reportator*), our only hope of retrieving something of Strato's plan of attack is in strict adherence to the pattern presupposed in Dam.'s refutation: (i) §§ 431–433: on Pl.'s line of reasoning no living being could die, no compound be dissolved; as it is, the negations ('immortal,' 'indissoluble') mean that each can exist only in conjunction with one term of a pair of opposites (life, composition); (ii) §§ 434–437: animal and vegetative soul, even nature, and finally everything in generation would

§§ 431–448. Strato's objections answered

'Απορίαι Στράτωνος ⟨ι⟩γ' πρὸς τὸν λόγον [frg. 123]

ροη'. – (i) Μήποτε καὶ πᾶν ζῷον οὕτω γε ἀθάνατον· θανάτου γὰρ ἄδεκτον· οὐ γὰρ ἔσται ζῷον τεθνηκὸς οὐδὲ ψυχὴ τεθνηκυῖα. 431

ροθ'. – Οὕτως οὐδὲ τὸ σύνθετόν ποτε διαλυθήσεται· ἄδεκτον γάρ ἐστι τοῦ ἐναντίου· οὐ γὰρ ἔσται ποτὲ διαλυθὲν μένον γε σύνθετον. 432

ρπ'. – Εἰ πολλαχῶς ἡ ἀπόφασις, ἀθάνατος ἡ ψυχὴ ἂν εἴη οὐχ ὡς ζωὴ ἄσβεστος ἢ ζωὴν ἄσβεστον ἔχουσα, ἀλλ' ὡς μόνον ἑνὸς δεκτικὴ τῶν ἐναντίων καὶ μετὰ τούτου οὖσα ἢ μὴ οὖσα. 433

ρπα'. – (ii) Μήποτε καὶ αἱ τῶν ἀλόγων ψυχαὶ οὕτως ἀθάνατοι, ὡς ἐπιφέρουσαι ζωὴν καὶ ἄδεκτοι τοῦ ἐναντίου τῷ ἐπιφερομένῳ. 434

ρπβ'. – Μήποτε οὕτω καὶ αἱ τῶν φυτῶν· ζωοποιοὶ γὰρ καὶ αὗται τῶν σωμάτων. 435

ρπγ'. – Μήποτε οὕτω καὶ ἡ φύσις ἑκάστη· τὸ γὰρ κατὰ φύσιν παρέχουσα πῶς ἂν δέξαιτό γε τὸ παρὰ φύσιν; ἄδεκτος δὲ οὖσα τούτου οὐκ ἄν ποτε φθαρείη. 436

ρπδ'. – Μήποτε πᾶσα γένεσις ἄφθαρτος· ἄδεκτος γὰρ καὶ αὐτὴ τοῦ ἐναντίου· οὐ γὰρ ἔσται τι γιγνόμενον ἐφθαρμένον. 437

ρπε'. – (iii) Μήποτε προχείρως εἴληπται ὡς, εἰ ἄδεκτος θανάτου καὶ ταύτῃ ἀθάνατος, ὅτι καὶ ἀνώλεθρος· ἀθάνατος γὰρ καὶ ὁ λίθος οὕτω γε, ἀλλ' οὐκ ἀνώλεθρος. 438

---

§ 431. tit. ιγ' Wk: γ' M | λόγον] λ- in ras., -όγον in spat. vac. Mᶜ

---

be imperishable, since they are associated with life, growth, coming-to-be, to the exclusion of their opposites); (iii) §§ 438–440: 'deathless' as used in the argument is not equivalent to imperishable; the plea that in the case of the soul the two are identical, because soul is the giver, not the recipient of life, is not valid, as it is unproven; (iv) § 441: if we distinguish between life conferred and life-giving life, there is no reason why the soul should not be subject to the death that is contrary to the latter; (v) § 442: as far as the analogy with fire is concerned, soul would give life only as long as it exists.

§ 431. The heading: Norvin wanted to read the γ' of the MS. as τρίται, i.e. third after those on the argument from opposites and that from recollection. This is impossible because of the following πρὸς τὸν λόγον, which can only be the present argument; besides, Dam. I so far has only Strato's refutation of the argument on harmony (§ 388); if the others were to be added from Dam. II (§§ 63–65), there would be a total of four. A more satisfactory solution is to read the figure as a cardinal and to adapt it to the actual number by writing either ε' (see §§ 444–448) or ιγ' (possibly in the older form γι', which would help to explain the error).

439. What reason do we have to believe that soul confers life, to justify the inference that it is insusceptible of the opposite of what it confers? In some cases soul is life that *is* conferred.

440. The possibility remains that soul is a living thing and that its life is adventitious, so that at a certain moment it may be lost.

441. (iv) How if soul, while not susceptible of the death that is contrary to life conferred from without, is nevertheless subject to another death, the opposite of life-giving life?

442. (v) Fire, so long as it exists, is not subject to cooling: in the same way, perhaps, soul is free from death so long as it exists; for it does bestow life only so long as it exists.

443. Even if we succeed in dealing with all the other difficulties, can we ever refute the objection that soul is limited and has limited power? Granting that she bestows life, that she is essentially separable and that she does not admit of the kind of death contrary to the life she gives, yet during this separate existence the moment will come when she is exhausted and must perish by extinction all by herself, without any external impact.

444. In answer to Strato's first group of objections [§§ 431–433] we will say that neither the animal nor the compound really bestows a quality opposed to another, but they merely exist in conjunction with either one of a pair of opposites; hence in their case the only valid statement is negation of the opposite quality, which is equivalent to affirmation of their existence, since they can exist only with the other opposite; the argument, however, related to things that bring about either one of a pair of opposite qualities.

445. Against the second series of objections [§§ 434–437] we observe that all those kinds of life and genesis itself belong to the lowest fringe of reality and *are* conferred, but do not confer anything, as the substances under discussion did. If, however, in any sense of the word these, too, bestow anything at all, they certainly are inaccessible to the opposite of what they bestow and do not perish with their gifts.

446. In reply to the third series [§§ 438–440] we must point out that it is assumed, and generally admitted as evident, that soul is alive and bestows life on bodies, since anything of which soul takes hold becomes animate, i.e. living. Consequently the soul is not insusceptible of death in the way a stone is; nor is the life that she possesses merely conferred upon her, or adven-

---

§ 442. This argument comes close to that of Boethus cited by Simpl., *an.* 247.23–26 καλῶς γὰρ καὶ τὸ ἀίδιον προστέθεικεν, ὡς ὁ Πλάτων τὸ ἀνώλεθρον ἐν τῷ Φαίδωνι, ἵνα μὴ ὡς ὁ Βοηθὸς οἰηθῶμεν τὴν ψυχὴν ὥσπερ τὴν ἐμψυχίαν ἀθάνατον μὲν εἶναι ὡς αὐτὴν μὴ ὑπομένουσαν τὸν θάνατον ἐπιόντα, ἐξισταμένην δὲ ἐπιόντος ἐκείνου τῷ ζῶντι ἀπόλλυσθαι. However, Boethus' argument is already suggested by the *Ph.*, where it occurs almost *verbatim* at 104b10–c1 and 106c9–d4, and there is no further evidence to link Strato with Boethus.

ρπς'. - Πόθεν ὅτι συνεπιφέρει ζωήν, ἵνα καὶ ἄδεκτος ᾖ τοῦ ἐναντίου τῷ 439 ἐπιφερομένῳ; ἐνίοτε γὰρ ἐπιφερομένη ἐστίν.

ρπζ'. - Μήποτε ζῶν ἐστι καὶ ἐπείσακτον ἔχει τὴν ζωήν, ὥστε ποτὲ καὶ 440 ἀποβάλλειν αὐτήν.

ρπη'. - (iv) Μήποτε τὸν μὲν ἐναντίον θάνατον τῇ ἐπιφερομένῃ ζωῇ οὐ 441 δέχεται, ἄλλον δὲ τὸν τῇ ἐπιφερούσῃ.

ρπθ'. - (v) Μήποτε ὡς τὸ πῦρ, ἔστ' ἂν ᾖ, ἄψυκτον, οὕτω καὶ ἡ ψυχή, 442 ἔστ' ἂν ᾖ, ἀθάνατος· καὶ γὰρ ἐπιφέρει ζωὴν ἔστ' ἂν ᾖ.

ρρ'. - Μήποτε, κἂν πάντα τὰ ἄλλα διαφύγωμεν, τὸ πεπερασμένην εἶναι καὶ 443(184) δύναμιν ἔχειν πεπερασμένην οὐκ ἂν ἐλέγξαιμεν. ἔστω γὰρ καὶ ἐπιφέρουσα ζωὴν καὶ χωριστὴ κατ' οὐσίαν καὶ μὴ δεχομένη τὸν ἐναντίον τῇ ἐπιφερομένῃ ζωῇ θάνατον· καθ' ἑαυτὴν δὲ οὖσα καμεῖταί ποτε καὶ φθαρήσεται σβεσθεῖσα ἐφ' ἑαυτῆς, οὐδενὸς ἔξωθεν ἐπιόντος. 5

ρρα'. - Ὅτι πρὸς τὰς Στράτωνος ⟨α'⟩ ἀπορίας [§§ 431–433] ἐροῦμεν ὅτι 444 οὐδὲ ἐπιφέρει τι ἐναντίον οὔτε τὸ ζῷον οὔτε τὸ σύνθετον, ἀλλ' ἔστι μόνον σὺν θατέρῳ τῶν ἐναντίων· διὸ καὶ τούτοις ἁρμόζει ἡ τοῦ ἐναντίου μόνη ἀπόφασις, ἢ εἰς ταὐτὸν ἔρχεται τῇ τοῦ εἶναι καταφάσει, ἐπειδὴ καὶ σὺν τῷ ἑτέρῳ τὸ εἶναι· ὁ δὲ λόγος ἦν περὶ πραγμάτων ἐπιφερόντων θάτερον τῶν ἐναντίων. 5

ρρβ'. - Ὅτι πρὸς τὰς δευτέρας ἀπορίας [§§ 434–437] ἐροῦμεν ὡς πᾶσαι αἱ 445 τοιαῦται ζωαὶ καὶ ἡ γένεσις ἐπ' ἐσχάτοις ἐπιφερόμεναί εἰσιν, ἀλλ' οὐκ ἐπιφέρουσαι, περὶ οἷων ὁ λόγος. εἰ δέ τι καὶ αὗται ἐπιφέρουσι καὶ ὁπωσοῦν, τοῦ γε ἀντικειμένου τῷ ἐπιφερομένῳ ἄδεκτοί εἰσι καὶ οὐ συναποσβέννυνται τοῖς ἐπιφερομένοις. 5

ρργ'. - Πρὸς τὰς γ' [§§ 438–440] ῥητέον ὅτι ὑπόκειται καὶ ἐκ τῆς ἐναργείας 446 ὁμολογεῖται ὡς ἡ ψυχὴ ζῇ καὶ ζωὴν ἐπιφέρει τοῖς σώμασιν, εἴπερ ἃ ἂν κατάσχῃ, ταῦτα γίνεται ἔμψυχα, ὅ ἐστι ζῶντα. οὐκ ἄρα, ὡς ὁ λίθος, ἄδεκτος θανάτου·

---

§ 444. 1 α' Wk: om. M — 4 ᾖ Mᶜ: ἢ M¹
§ 446. 1 ἐναργείας revera M

---

§ 443. This last objection is no longer Strato's, whose fifth argument consists of a single point, § 442, answered in § 448 (τὴν πέμπτην, in the singular). Rather, it is the last obstacle that remains, according to Dam. II § 78.17-21, 28–29 and § 80.1–2, after all Pr.'s answers to Strato's objections have been taken into account. It is the essence of Cebes' objection (86e6–88b8, cf. 91d2–7), which, as the context both here and in Dam. II indicates, must have been raised again by Dam., and not by Strato, as not sufficiently answered. Dam.'s new analysis will dispose of it (esp. §§ 459 and 461).

titious, for soul never appears without life, no more than fire does without heat.

447. Our answer to the fourth point [§ 441] is that the form of life-giving life and of life conferred is one and the same, as heat is in the case of fire. Hence they have only one opposite, the same cold, which is contrary both to the heat *from* the fire and to the heat *in* the fire; accordingly it destroys both. Besides, supposing that this is a different form of death and a different form of life, if the soul bestows this other kind of life too, it will bestow two forms of life, and then what becomes of the difference? And what is the cause by which the first in its turn is given? In that case there must be two kinds of life-giving life, too, which means that the essential character of the two forms is identical. So there is no need to go beyond the first kind, which is both life-bestowing life and the life bestowed.

448. The fifth objection [§ 442] is dealt with adequately by Socrates' specification [105a1–5]. If the soul which confers life is always insusceptible of death, nothing else remains to extinguish the life that bestows life. What death destroys was the life that *is* given; if it were to destroy also the life that gives life, it could do so only in so far as this life *is* conferred by one thing upon another and exists in a substratum, which will be accessible to the opposite quality. In the analogous case of fire: though fire is not accessible to cold, yet it has a body that is, a body which was also the receptacle of the fire's heat; therefore fire is annihilated on the approach of cold. If, on the contrary, this life should be purely life-giving, it cannot have anything that is accessible to the opposite. Now the truth, *and* the assumption in the present debate, is without any doubt that the soul exists separately, for if it were itself in something else, i.e. in a substance, it would not be life-giving life, but the life given.

§§ 449–465. A new analysis of the argument. 102a10–107a1

Assumptions necessary if the argument is to stand

449. Soul is a substance.

450. It can exist separately from any substratum.

451. Every substance is either accessible to both terms of any pair of opposites or naturally united with the one to the exclusion of the other, as fire is with heat; this is the relation of soul with life.

---

§ 448. 2. The MS. has an erasure after τήν, which makes the situation look very much like that at § 420.3: the erased word could be ἐπιφερομένην, in explicit contrast with the ἐπιφέρουσαν at line 3. However, since in this case it is difficult to see a reason for the correction except the obvious one that the word was not in the exemplar, it seems wiser to leave the text alone.

4–5. The restriction serves to deal with the objection indicated in lines 5–7, but also to eliminate irrational soul.

οὐδὲ ἐπιφερομένην μόνον, ἀλλ᾽ οὐδὲ ἐπείσακτον ἔχει τὴν ζωήν, οὐδέποτε γὰρ ἄνευ ζωῆς ἔρχεται, ὡς οὐδὲ τὸ πῦρ ἄνευ θερμότητος. 5

ρρδ'. - Πρὸς τὴν τετάρτην [§ 441], ὡς ἓν τὸ εἶδος τῆς ἐπιφερούσης καὶ 447 τῆς ἐπιφερομένης, οἷον ἐπὶ τοῦ πυρὸς ἡ θερμότης. διὸ καὶ ἓν τὸ ἀντικείμενον, ἡ ψυχρότης ἡ αὐτή, καὶ τῇ ἀπὸ τοῦ πυρὸς καὶ τῇ ἐν τῷ πυρί· ἀμέλει καὶ ἑκατέραν φθείρει. ἐπεὶ καὶ εἰ ἄλλος τῷ εἴδει θάνατος καὶ ἄλλη τῷ εἴδει ζωή, εἰ μὲν ἐπιφέρει καὶ τοιαύτην, δύο ἐποίσει· καὶ τίς ἡ διαφορά; αὐτὴ δὲ ἡ προτέρα πόθεν ἐπιφέρεται; 5 ἢ β' καὶ αἱ ἐπιφέρουσαι, ὥστε καὶ ὁ λόγος ἐφ᾽ ἑκατέρου εἴδους ὁ αὐτός. ἀρκεῖ ἄρα ἡ προτέρα ἐπιφέρουσά τε καὶ ἐπιφερομένη.

ρρε'. - Πρὸς τὴν πέμπτην [§ 442] ἀρκεῖ ὁ Σωκράτους διορισμός [105a1-5]. 448 εἰ γὰρ ἡ ἐπιφέρουσα τὴν ζωὴν ἄδεκτος ἀεὶ θανάτου, οὐδὲν ἔσται | ἄλλο τὸ (185) σβεννύον αὖ τὴν ἐπιφέρουσαν. ὁ γὰρ θάνατος τῆς ἐπιφερομένης ἦν σβεστικός· εἰ δὲ καὶ τῆς ἐπιφερούσης, ἀλλ᾽ ᾗ ἐπιφέρεται ἄλλῳ ἀπ᾽ ἄλλου καὶ ἐν ἄλλῳ, ὃ καὶ τοῦ ἐναντίου δεκτικὸν ἔσται. οὕτω γὰρ καὶ εἰ μὴ τὸ πῦρ δεκτικὸν ψυχρότητος, 5 ἀλλ᾽ ἔχει σῶμα δεκτικόν, ὃ καὶ τῆς πυρὸς ἦν θερμότητος ὑποδοχή· διὸ καὶ φθείρεται τὸ πῦρ ἐπιούσης. εἰ δὲ μόνον ἐπιφέρουσα εἴη, οὐκ ἂν ἔχοι τι δεκτικὸν τοῦ ἐναντίου. πάντως ⟨δὲ⟩ χωριστὴ καὶ ἔστιν καὶ ὑπόκειται· εἰ γὰρ καὶ αὐτὴ ἐν ἄλλῳ, οἷον ἐν οὐσίᾳ, οὐκ ἔσται ἐπιφέρουσα, ἀλλ᾽ ἐπιφερομένη.

§§ 449-465. A new analysis of the argument. 102a10-107a1

Ὑποθέσεις ἀναγκαῖαι πρὸς τὴν τοῦ λόγου ἀλήθειαν

ρρς'. - Ὅτι οὐσία ἡ ψυχή. 449
ρρζ'. - Ὅτι χωριστὴ παντὸς ὑποκειμένου. 450
ρρη'. - Ὅτι πᾶσα οὐσία ἢ ἑκατέρου δεκτικὴ τῶν ἐναντίων ἢ θατέρῳ 451 συμπέφυκεν ἀφωρισμένως, ὡς θερμότητι τὸ πῦρ· οὕτως ἡ ψυχὴ τῇ ζωῇ.

---

§ 446. 4 ἐπιφερομένην Fh: -όμενος M
§ 447. 6 ἢ Wk: ἡ M
§ 448. 2 post τὴν] ~ sexies in ras. 12 litt. M^c — 8 δὲ Wk (γὰρ Nv): om. M

---

8. πάντως - ὑπόκειται: supra § 429, infra § 450.
§§ 449-465. The method used is very similar to that of the monograph on the argument from opposites (§§ 207-252), though it is applied on a much smaller scale, mainly because the last argument was less controversial and, on the assumptions of Neoplatonism, offered no great difficulty. Dam.'s return to the subject has the double purpose of restating the argument objectively and of expanding it so as to cover also Strato's objections and the difficulty raised in § 443.

452. Substances to which this applies are inaccessible to the other extreme.

453. If they are present in a substratum that is accessible to the other extreme, they are destroyed when the other takes possession of the substratum; otherwise they withdraw, because the substratum has become unfit for them by admitting their opposites.

454. The living does not perish so long as it has life; therefore the body decays only when life is gone from it.

455. Anything that always brings along with itself some particular form to something else, is naturally united with the form it confers.

456. It is not accessible to the opposite of what it confers, i.e. of the form with which it is naturally united, whatever it may be.

457. Whatever is accessible to life bestowed from without as something extraneous, is accessible also to death, so far as its own essence is concerned.

Proofs of immortality

458. If soul is a substance in which life is inherent, which is the reason why she always bestows life upon that which is receptive of the life conferred from without, and if she herself can exist separately from this substratum, which is naturally accessible to the opposite of the life thus conferred, she cannot be subject to death, being the giver of life, nor will she perish when death takes possession of the substratum, being capable of separate existence. Consequently she withdraws, while remaining immune from death — immune from death in the sense that she has life as her inalienable property; and if this be true, she must remain imperishable as well; for even a body having inalienable life would be imperishable.

459. If soul is only the giver of life, she has life by her own nature and produces it from within herself. Therefore as long as she exists, she produces and possesses a life that is innate to her; as long as she has this life, she is immortal; as long as she is immortal, she is imperishable; therefore, as long as she has the gift of producing life, she is imperishable. Now she *always* has this gift of producing life; for she is a fountain of life, so that it cannot be taken away from her; and consequently she is forever what she is.

460. If death, being privation, can only be found in a substratum, and if that in which either one of the opposites, privation or possession, is found, is also the substratum of the other, it follows necessarily that the life that is the opposite of death also exists in a substratum; this is true only of the life given from without, while life-giving life exists by itself and not in a substratum; so that no death can approach it, since this life has no substratum and it is in the nature of death to occur in a substratum.

---

§ 457. 2. ὅσον γε ἐφ' ἑαυτῷ : the qualification is necessary to account for immortal bodies, such as those of the stars and of the universe.

ρρθ'. - Ὅτι αἱ οὕτως ἔχουσαι οὐσίαι ἄδεκτοί εἰσι θατέρου τῶν ἐναντίων. 452
σ'. - Ὅτι εἰ μέν εἰσιν ἐν ἄλλῳ δεκτικῷ τοῦ ἑτέρου, ἐπιόντος ἐκείνου τῷ 453
ὑποκειμένῳ φθείρονται· εἰ δὲ μή, ὑπεξίστανται, ἅτε ἀνεπιτηδείου γεγονότος τοῦ
ὑποκειμένου διὰ τὴν τοῦ ἀντικειμένου παραδοχήν.
σα'. - Ὅτι τὸ ζῶν ἔστ' ἂν ἔχῃ τὴν ζωὴν οὐ φθείρεται· διὸ καὶ τὸ σῶμα 454
τότε φθείρεται, ὅταν στερεθῇ τῆς ζωῆς.
σβ'. - Ὅτι τὸ ἀεὶ σὺν ἑαυτῷ τι φέρον ἑτέρῳ συμπεφυκὸς ἔχει τὸ ἐπιφερόμενον 455
εἶδος.
σγ'. - Ὅτι οὐκ ἐπιδέχεται τὴν τοῦ ἐπιφερομένου ἐναντιότητα, τουτέστιν τοῦ 456
συμπεφυκότος αὐτῷ εἴδους ὁτουοῦν.
σδ'. - Ὅτι τὸ δεκτικὸν τῆς ἐπιφερομένης ζωῆς ἐπείσακτον ἔχον αὐτὴν 457
δεκτικὸν ἂν εἴη καὶ θανάτου, ὅσον γε ἐφ' ἑαυτῷ.

Ἀποδείξεις τῆς ἀθανασίας

σε'. - Εἰ ἡ ψυχὴ οὐσία ζωὴν ἔχουσα συμπεφυκυῖαν, διὸ καὶ ἀεὶ ζωὴν ἐπιφέρει 458
τῷ δεκτικῷ τῆς ἐπιφερομένης ζωῆς, αὐτὴ | δὲ χωριστή ἐστιν ἐκείνου πεφυκότος (186)
γε δέχεσθαι τὸ ἐναντίον τῇ ἐπιφερομένῃ ζωῇ, οὔτ' ἂν δέχοιτο θάνατον ὡς
⟨ζωὴν⟩ ἐπιφέρουσα οὔτ' ἂν φθείροιτο τοῦ θανάτου ἐπιόντος τῷ ὑποκειμένῳ ὡς
χωριστή. ἐξίσταται ἄρα μένουσα ἀθάνατος, οὕτω δὲ ἀθάνατος ὡς ζωὴν 5
ἀναφαίρετον ἔχουσα· εἰ δὲ τοῦτο, καὶ ἀνώλεθρος μένουσα· καὶ γὰρ σῶμα εἴ τι
ζωὴν ἔχοι ἀναφαίρετον, καὶ ἀνώλεθρόν ἐστιν.
σς'. - Εἰ ἐπιφέρουσα μόνον ἐστὶ τὴν ζωήν, οἴκοθεν ἔχει ταύτην καὶ ἀφ' 459
ἑαυτῆς προβάλλεται. ἔστ' ἂν οὖν ᾖ, ζωὴν προβέβληται σύμφυτον· ἔστ' ἂν δὲ
ταύτην ἔχῃ, ἀθάνατός ἐστιν· ἔστ' ἂν δὲ ἀθάνατος, καὶ ἀνώλεθρος· ἔστ' ἂν ἄρα
ᾖ ζωῆς προβλητική, ἀνώλεθρός ἐστιν. ἀεὶ δὲ ζωῆς προβλητική· βρύουσα γὰρ
ζωὴν ἀναφαίρετον ἔχει ταύτην· ὥστε καὶ ἀεί ἐστιν ὅ ἐστιν. 5
σζ'. - Εἰ ἐν ὑποκειμένῳ ὁ θάνατος (στέρησις γάρ), ἐν ᾧ δὲ τὸ ἕτερον τῶν 460
ἐναντίων, ἢ στερήσεως ἢ ἕξεως, ἐν τούτῳ καὶ τὸ ἕτερον, ἀνάγκη ἄρα τὴν
ἀντικειμένην τῷ θανάτῳ ζωὴν ἐν ὑποκειμένῳ καὶ αὐτὴν εἶναι· τοιαύτη δὲ μόνη
ἡ ἐπιφερομένη, ἡ δὲ ἐπιφέρουσα καθ' ἑαυτήν ἐστι καὶ οὐκ ἐν ἄλλῳ· ὥστε οὐδεὶς
αὐτῇ θάνατος πελάσει, μὴ ἐχούσῃ τι ὑποκείμενον, πεφυκὼς δὲ ἐν ὑποκειμένῳ 5
ἐγγίγνεσθαι.

---

§ 454. 1 ζῶν] ζ- in ras. 2 litt., accent. ex corr., M^c
§ 455. 1 ~φέρον, ~ in ras., accent. add., M^x
§ 458. tit. ἀποδείξεις] ἀ- in ras. M^c (ὑποδείξεις M¹?) — 2 αὐτὴ Wk (M¹?): αὕτη M^c — 4 ζωὴν Wk: om. M
§ 459. 3 ἔχῃ μ: ἔχοι M
§ 460. 3 μόνη] -η in ras. M^c — 5 πεφυκὼς μ: -ὸς M

---

§ 459. Cf. Dam. II 80.2-4.

461. If life is essential to the form of soul, soul is alive in virtue of its own form. It is only form: it has nothing that is extraneous, nor does it have its existence in anything extraneous; therefore it is only what it is. Nothing is worn out by existing in accordance with its own form, nor can it be toilsome for a thing to be what it is, only not being itself and the presence of adventitious elements can have this effect; it follows that the soul cannot be wearied out so long as it is only what it is. If it suffers in the world of creation, it suffers because it envelops itself in what it is not, but not by being only what it is. What it is, is soul and nothing else; therefore soul does not suffer from being what it is, a substance in which life is inherent.

462. If that which produces one term of a pair of opposites tends to destroy the other term, as for example what causes light will destroy darkness, it is evident that soul, being the giver of life, destroys approaching death even before it can reach her.

463. If it is the cause of life in the lifeless, it is also the cause of not dying; consequently it is itself alive in virtue of its own substantial character and does not die in virtue of the same character; it follows that not dying, in other words immortality, is also inherent in its essence. Since, then, it bestows both being and not-perishing, it necessarily has imperishability as another substantial characteristic.

464. If soul is substantial life and living essence, and nothing else (being free from matter and having a separate existence of its own, it is not in one respect itself, in another not-itself, since it is pure form; neither, therefore, can it be actually this, potentially that, for in that case it would no longer be only what it is, namely form), it follows that it cannot at the same time be mortal or perishable; therefore it will not die or perish.

465. If soul antecedes all change, being the cause of all change, it must be beyond all change, including the passage from possession to privation, and consequently that from life to death. What it is by its essence, then, it is forever without change; for, as we said, by its essence it is the source of all change, as intelligence is of all changelessness.

PART THREE: THE MYTH

§§ 466–471. Preliminaries to the myth. 107c1–114c8

On the myth

466. The third part of the dialogue deals with the destinations of the soul. It is not entirely a myth, but, as expressed in the conclusion, only in

---

§ 465. On intelligence as the cause of stability see Pr.'s commentary on *Laws* X in *theol.* I 14 (esp. 65.14–17 S.-W.).

§ 466. 1. **Dam. II § 81.** On the structure of the dialogue see introduction Ol., pp. 28–29.

ση'. - Εἰ συνουσίωται τῷ τῆς ψυχῆς εἴδει ζωή, κατὰ εἶδος ζῇ τὸ οἰκεῖον. **461**
ἔστι δὲ μόνον εἶδος οὐδὲν ἔχον ἀλλότριον οὐδὲ ἐν ἀλλοτρίῳ τὸ εἶναι ἔχον· ὃ ἄρα
ἐστί, μόνον ἐστίν. οὐδὲν δὲ κάμνει κατὰ εἶδος ὅ ἐστιν ὄν, οὐδέ τινι τὸ εἶναι
ὅ ἐστιν ἐπίπονον, ἀλλὰ τὸ μὴ εἶναι μόνον καὶ τὸ ἐπείσακτον· ὥστε οὐδὲ καμεῖται
ἡ ψυχὴ τοῦτο μόνον οὖσα ὅ ἐστιν. εἰ γοῦν κάμνοι περὶ τὴν γένεσιν, ἐπειδὴ 5
προσπεριβάλλεται καὶ ὃ μή ἐστι, διὰ τοῦτο κάμνει, οὐ μὴν τοῦτο ὃ μόνον ἐστίν.
ἔστι δὲ μόνον ψυχή· οὐκ ἄρα κάμνει ψυχὴ οὖσα ὅ ἐστιν, οὐσία ζωὴν ἔχουσα
σύμφυτον.

σθ'. - Εἰ τὸ τοῦ ἐναντίου γεννητικὸν ἀναιρετικόν ἐστι τοῦ ἐναντίου, ὡς τὸ **462**
φωτὸς αἴτιον τοῦ σκότους, δῆλον ὡς καὶ ἡ ψυχὴ τὸν θάνατον ἐπιόντα προαναιρεῖ,
ζωῆς οὖσα χορηγός.

σι'. - Εἰ τὸ ζῆν ἐμποιεῖ τοῖς μὴ ζῶσιν, ἐμποιεῖ καὶ τὸ μὴ | ἀποθνῄσκειν· **463(187)**
αὐτὴ ἄρα καθ' ὕπαρξιν ζῇ τὴν ἑαυτῆς καὶ οὐκ ἀποθνῄσκει ἄρα καθ' ὕπαρξιν·
συνουσίωται ἄρα καὶ τῷ μὴ ἀποθνῄσκειν, τῷ ἄρα ἀθανάτῳ. εἰ δὲ καὶ τὸ εἶναι
δίδωσι καὶ τὸ μὴ φθείρεσθαι, πάντως ὅτι καὶ ἄφθαρτός ἐστι καθ' ὕπαρξιν.

σια'. - Εἰ καθ' ὕπαρξιν ζωή ἐστιν ἡ ψυχὴ καὶ οὐσία ζῶσα, καὶ ἔστι τοῦτο **464**
μόνον (ἄνευ γὰρ ὕλης καὶ χωριστὴ καθ' ἑαυτὴν οὐ πῇ μέν ἐστιν ὅ ἐστιν, πῇ
δὲ οὔ, μόνον γὰρ εἶδος· οὐδὲ ἄρα τῇ μὲν ἐνεργείᾳ τοῦτο, τῇ δὲ δυνάμει ἕτερον,
οὐ γὰρ ἔτι μόνον ὅ ἐστιν, εἶδος), οὐδὲ ἄρα θνητὴ οὐδὲ φθαρτή· οὐδὲ ἄρα
τεθνήξεται οὐδὲ φθαρήσεται. 5

σιβ'. - Εἰ πάσης μεταβολῆς ἡ ψυχὴ προκατάρχει, τὸ αἴτιον οὖσα πάσης **465**
μεταβολῆς, ἐπέκεινα ἂν εἴη πάσης μεταβολῆς· ὥστε καὶ τῆς περὶ ἕξιν καὶ
στέρησιν· ὥστε καὶ τῆς περὶ ζωὴν καὶ θάνατον. ὃ ἄρα ἐστὶ κατ' οὐσίαν, ἀεί
ἐστιν ἀμετάβλητος· ἡ γὰρ οὐσία αὐτῆς πηγὴ ἦν πάσης μεταβολῆς, ὡς ὁ νοῦς
πάσης ἀμεταβλησίας. 5

PART THREE: THE MYTH

§§ 466-471. Preliminaries to the myth. 107c1-114c8

Εἰς τὸν μῦθον

α'. - Ὅτι τὸ τρίτον μέρος τοῦ διαλόγου ἐστὶ μὲν περὶ τῶν ψυχικῶν λήξεων· **466**
οὐ πᾶν δὲ μῦθός ἐστιν, ἀλλ' ὅσον συμπεραίνεται λέγων ὡς 'ταῦτα ἢ τὰ τοιαῦτα'

---

§ 463. 2 αὐτὴ Fh (M¹?): αὕτη Mᶜ
§ 464. 3 τῇ...τῇ Wk: πῆι... πῆι M

2-3. **Dam. II § 83.** At II § 129 the word 'myth' of *Ph.* 110b1-2 is limited (correctly) to the immediately following description of the "heights of the earth".

so far that we must believe the situation in Hades to be 'this or something like it' [114d2-3]. Such, it should be remembered, is the character of the Platonic myths, which picture reality 'in the right way,' as he puts it in the *Republic* [II 377d9].

467. A 'destination' is the rank in this universe allotted by Justice to each according to his merits.

468. There are four kinds of destinations: divine, demonic, human, animal. Each of these is twofold: it may be an essential character, and then it is immutable, rooted in the order of the universe; or it may be external and subject to change, a change brought about in the case of divine and demonic destinations by mutation in the allotted portions, and in the case of human and animal destinations by the utter changeability of those to whom they were allotted.

469. The discourse on destinations rests on two assumptions: the separate life of souls, which has already been proved, and the belief in the providence of the Gods, which Plato establishes in the *Laws* [X 899d4–905c4].

470. The destinations of souls are threefold: prior to genesis in the realm of Zeus, in genesis in the realm of Poseidon, after genesis in the realm of Pluto, which is the one discussed here; hence we speak of a 'descent into Hades.'

471. Of the three 'descents into Hades' the present one deals mainly with destinations, the one in the *Gorgias* [523a1–527a4] with the judges, the one in the *Republic* [X 614b2–621d3] with those on trial.

---

4. καλῶς : cf. Pl., *Rep.* II 377d9 ἄλλως τε καὶ ἐάν τις μὴ καλῶς ψεύδηται. The interpretation of the καλόν at 110b1 is Pr.'s, cf. II § 129.4–7; also Ol., *Gorg.* 242.24–243.4; *Proleg.* 7.18–33.

§§ 467–468. The word λῆξις has two special senses: (1) the domain of a God, an idea deriving from the old notion that the Gods have divided the world among them, as men parcel out land; the noun λῆξις used in this way is first found in Pl., *Critias* 109b1–2; c8–9; 113b7–c1 (and in the human sphere 114a1; b1; 116c8); *Laws* V 747e3–5; Hermias 29.30; Pr., *Tim.*, *passim* (see Diehl's index); (2) in the later Neoplatonists: a similar province or task assigned to a soul, but also, by association with the "lots" of *Rep.* X 617d1–621a4 (where the noun is κλῆρος, but the verb λαγχάνειν), the rank or condition of souls, esp. after death, though the definition in § 467 is carefully worded so as to include the present life as well. Julian, *or.* 6, 187c (speaking of Hercules) ὑπὲρ τῶν θεῶν καὶ τῶν εἰς θείαν λῆξιν πορευθέντων εὐφημεῖν ἐθέλων. Hermias 86.25–30 εἰ μὲν αἱ λήξεις τῶν ψυχῶν πᾶσαι ὑποσέληνοί εἰσιν, ἀληθὴς αὐτῶν ἔσται ὁ λόγος, εἰ δέ εἰσι λήξεις ψυχῶν καὶ ὑπὲρ σελήνην (ὥσπερ οὖν εἰσιν· αἱ μὲν γὰρ ἡλίου ὀπαδοί εἰσιν, αἱ δὲ σελήνης, αἱ δὲ Κρόνου· ἔσπειρε γὰρ τὰς μὲν εἰς γῆν, τὰς δὲ εἰς ἥλιον, τὰς δὲ ἄλλας ἀλλαχοῦ), δυνατὸν ἔσται τὴν ψυχὴν καὶ ὑπὲρ σελήνην ἐνεργῆσαι. Pr., *Tim.* I 54.1–3 νῦν μὲν γενέσει προσομιλούσας, νῦν δὲ εἰς δαιμονίαν ἢ θείαν λῆξιν μεθισταμένας. Ibid. 58.22 (ἵνα) . . . κατὰ νοῦν διοικῶσι τὰς ἑαυτῶν λήξεις. Ibid. 58.26–27 πρὸ τῶν μεταβαλλομένων λήξεων τὰς ἀμεταβλήτους. Ibid. 77.11–12 μερικαὶ . . . ψυχαὶ δαιμονίας τυχοῦσαι λήξεως. Pr., *Rep.*, *passim*, see index Kroll; Ol., *Ph.* 2 § 7.2; 5; 9 § 1.4; 10 § 15.4; *Gorg.* 266.23 ἵνα ἐκεῖ θείας λήξεως

χρὴ τὰ ἐν Ἅιδου ἡγεῖσθαι [114d2–3]. τοῦτο γὰρ ἦν καὶ τὸ εἶδος τῶν Πλατωνικῶν μύθων ἅτε καλῶς τὴν ἀλήθειαν μιμουμένων, ὡς ἐν Πολιτείᾳ φησίν [II 377d9].

β'. – Ὅτι λῆξίς ἐστι τάξις ἐν τῷδε τῷ παντὶ κατ' ἀξίαν ἑκάστοις ἀποκληρουμένη 467
παρὰ τῆς Δίκης.

γ'. – Ὅτι τετραχῶς ἡ λῆξις, θεία δαιμονία ἀνθρωπίνη θήρειος. διττὴ δὲ 468
ἑκάστη, ἡ μὲν οὐσιώδης· ἀμετάβλητος αὕτη καὶ τῷ παντὶ κόσμῳ συμπεπηγυῖα·
ἡ δὲ ἔξω μεταβαλλομένη, ἡ μὲν θεία καὶ δαιμονία διὰ τὴν μεταβολὴν τῶν
μετεχουσῶν | λήξεων, ἡ δὲ ἀνθρωπίνη καὶ θήρειος διὰ τὴν τῶν λαγχανόντων (188)
παντοίαν ἐξαλλαγήν. 5

δ'. – Ὅτι ἐκ δύο ὑποθέσεων ἤρτηται ὁ περὶ τῶν λήξεων λόγος· τῆς τε 469
χωριστῆς ζωῆς τῶν ψυχῶν, ἥτις δέδεικται, καὶ τῆς πρόνοιαν θεῶν εἰσηγουμένης,
ἣν καταδεῖται ἐν Νόμοις [X 899d4–905c4].

ε'. – Ὅτι τρεῖς αἱ λήξεις τῶν ψυχῶν· ἡ μὲν πρὸ γενέσεως ἐν Διός, ἡ δὲ ἐν 470
τῇ γενέσει ἐν Ποσειδῶνος, ἡ δὲ μετὰ τὴν γένεσιν ἐν Πλούτωνος, περὶ ἧς ὁ
λόγος· διὸ νέκυια.

ς'. – Ὅτι τριῶν οὐσῶν νεκυιῶν ἡ μὲν ἐνταῦθα μάλιστα περὶ τῶν λήξεων 471
ποιεῖται τὸν λόγον, ἡ δὲ ἐν Γοργίᾳ [523a1–527a4] περὶ τῶν δικαστῶν, ἡ δὲ
ἐν Πολιτείᾳ [X 614b2–621d3] περὶ τῶν δικαζομένων.

---

§ 470. 3 νεκυία M (item infra II 81.1; 85.1)

τύχωμεν, Examples of Christian usage dependent on this *PGL* s.v. λῆξις (A) 5.

§ 468. The "essential destinations" (corresponding to the notion of God or demon κατ' οὐσίαν, cf. Pr., *Alc.* 73.18–75.1) represent the natural and unchangeable categories of Gods, demons, men and animals; external destinations vary as described in the text. Note that reincarnation in animals is implied here, which may point to Porphyry; but Macrob., *somn. Scip.* I 1, 5–6, speaks of "loca" (τόποι) only, as also does Dam. II § 85.3.

§ 469. The same observation is made Ol. 2 § 7 and 9 § 1.

§ 470. Pr., *Rep.* II 140.14–21 ὅτι δὲ καὶ αἱ μὲν μακάρων νῆσοι Πλουτώνειοι λήξεις εἰσίν, αἱ δὲ οὐράνιαι τῆς τοῦ πρώτου τῶν τριῶν Διὸς ἀρχῆς κατὰ τὴν εἰς τρία τῶν Κρονιδῶν τομὴν τοῦ κόσμου, πάλιν ἐν τοῖς αὐτοῖς ἀποδεδείχαμεν λόγοις [on the myth of the *Gorgias*]· καὶ ὡς ἡ μὲν εἰς Πλούτωνός ἐστι τρίοδος ἢ εἰς τὰς μακάρων νήσους ἢ εἰς τὸ δεσμωτήριον τῆς τίσεως ἢ εἰς τοὺς καθαρτικοὺς τόπους, ἡ δὲ εἰς Διὸς μοναδικὴ πρὸς οὐρανὸν ἄγουσα, ἡ δὲ εἰς Ποσειδῶνος †σώζει† (εἰς Kroll) τὰ τῶν χθονίων δικαστῶν. Cf. *ibid.* II 156.12–14. On the three sons of Kronos see note on II § 131.

§ 471. Dam. II § 85. On the three νέκυιαι Pr., *Rep.* I 168.11–23: Ph. τοὺς τόπους ... τοὺς ἐκεῖ καὶ τὰ ὅλα δικαιωτήρια τῶν ψυχῶν, Rep. τὰς παντοίας τῶν κρινομένων τίσεις, Gorg. τῶν δικαστῶν ⟨τὰς⟩ τάξεις. *Ibid.* II 128.12–23: Gorg. τοὺς δικαστάς, Rep. τὸν τόπον τῶν δικαστῶν, Ph. τὰς λήξεις τὰς ὑπ' αὐτῶν ἀφοριζομένας. Ol., *Gorg.* 241.11–28: Ph. περὶ αὐτῶν τῶν κολαστικῶν τόπων, Rep. περὶ τῶν κρινομένων, Gorg. περὶ τῶν δικαστῶν. Ol., *mete.* 144.21–35: Gorg. περὶ τοῦ δικάζοντος, Ph. περὶ τῶν δικαστικῶν τόπων, Rep. περὶ τῶν δικαζομένων. El., *isag.* 33.12–18: Gorg. περὶ τῶν δικαστῶν, Ph. περὶ τῶν δικαστικῶν τόπων, Rep. περὶ τῶν δικαζομένων ψυχῶν. The

§§ 472–476.   Death not the end. 107c1–d5

472. [107c1–4] After the conversation on immortality Socrates says 'it is right to bear in mind,' because true righteousness rests on reason; he adds that our 'care' should be all the greater because it concerns a longer and a more real stretch of life, and because it is an image of the self-perfection of intelligence.

473. [107c3–4] What does it mean that this care extends 'over all time'? Surely it is impossible to lead the right life forever. — No, but it is proposed to us as a final goal, to which we should conform to the best of our ability.

Or, better, it is no longer a matter of mortal life, but of the immortal life that has been established as true.

474. [107c2–8] Why does Socrates make two hypothetical statements without adding a minor? And why is the consequent negatived because the antecedent is? Both are against the rules of logic; thus the statement: 'If death is deliverance from everything, the wicked are freed from their wickedness with the body; the former is not true; therefore neither is the latter.' — The solution is that the two, antecedent and consequent, are convertible, and therefore negativing either one means negativing the other.

475. [107c6–8] If not to be is a godsend for the wicked, it follows that being, if it involves evil, is not a good; if with the good it is a good, then being by itself is neither evil nor good; therefore the Good is beyond being.

476. [107d4–5] We 'are told' so by our innate notions and preconceptions, by the theologians, and, in symbols, by the mysteries themselves.

§§ 477–486.   The guardian spirit and judgment. 107d5–e4

477. The class of spirits fills the gap between divine beings, who have

---

ultimate source is Porphyry, cf. Macrob., *somn. Scip.* I 1, 6–7 "sic in *Phaedone* . . . sequitur *distinctio locorum* quae hanc vitam relinquentibus ea lege debentur quam sibi quisque vivendo sanxerunt. sic in *Gorgia* . . . de *habitu post corpus animarum* . . . admonemur. . . . in illis . . . voluminibus quibus statum *reipublicae* formandum recepit . . . per illam demum fabulam . . . *quo anima post corpus evadat* vel unde ad corpus veniat . . . adseruit, ut iustitiae vel cultae praemium vel spretae poenam . . . servari doceret."

§ 472.   Dam. II § 86.

4. τὴν νοῦ περὶ ἑαυτὸν τελεσιουργίαν : Pr., *elem*. 167 πᾶς νοῦς ἑαυτὸν νοεῖ, i.e. it reverts upon itself, which is why its motion is described as circular (Pl., *Laws* X 897d3–898b4; *Tim*. 34a1–5; Pr., *Tim*. II 94.15–24).

§ 473.   Dam. II §§ 87–89. Pr.'s explanation (lines 2–3) seems to represent a condensed form of II § 89. Dam.'s answer is different from the one proposed at II § 88.6–7.

§ 474.   The two συνημμένα are 107c2–3 εἴπερ ἡ ψυχὴ ἀθάνατος, ἐπιμελείας δὴ δεῖται, etc., and c5–8 εἰ μὲν γὰρ ἦν ὁ θάνατος τοῦ παντὸς ἀπαλλαγή, ἕρμαιον ἂν ἦν τοῖς κακοῖς, etc.

§§ 472-476. Death not the end. 107c1-d5

ζ'. - [107c1-4] "Ότι μετὰ τοὺς περὶ ἀθανασίας λόγους 'δίκαιον' μέν φησι 'διανοηθῆναι' ὡς τῆς ἀληθοῦς δικαιοπραγίας ἐν τῇ διανοίᾳ ἱσταμένης· μείζω δὲ τὴν 'ἐπιμέλειαν' ἅτε πολυχρονιωτέρας ζωῆς γιγνομένην καὶ ἀληθεστέρας καὶ τὴν νοῦ περὶ ἑαυτὸν τελεσιουργίαν μιμουμένην. **472**

η'. - [107c3-4] Πῶς 'ὑπὲρ τοῦ παντὸς χρόνου' ἡ ἐπιμέλεια; οὐ γὰρ οἷόν τε τὸν πάντα χρόνον εὖ ζῆν. — Ἢ ὡς τέλους προκειμένου πρὸς μίμησιν τὴν ὅτι μάλιστα δυνατήν. **473**

Ἢ ἄμεινον ὡς οὐκέτι περὶ θνητῆς ζωῆς, ἀλλὰ τῆς κατὰ τὴν ἀθανασίαν ἀποδεδειγμένης. 5

θ'. - [107c2-8] Πῶς ἔλαβεν δύο συνημμένα ἄνευ προσλήψεως; ἢ πῶς τῷ ἡγουμένῳ συναναιρεῖται τὸ ἑπόμενον; ἑκάτερον γὰρ ἀμέθοδον· οἷον ' εἰ ὁ θάνατος τοῦ παντὸς ἀπαλλαγή, ἀπαλλάττονται οἱ πονηροὶ τῆς πονηρίας μετὰ τοῦ σώματος· ἀλλὰ μὴν οὐ τὸ πρῶτον· οὐδὲ ἄρα τὸ δεύτερον'. — Ἢ δύο ἐστίν, ἡγούμενον καὶ ἑπόμενον, ἀντιστρέφοντα, καὶ διὰ τοῦτο ὁπότερον συναναιρεῖ τὸ ἕτερον. **474** 5

ι'. - [107c6-8] "Ότι εἰ τὸ μὴ εἶναι τοῖς κακοῖς ἕρμαιον, οὐκ ἄρα τὸ εἶναι ἀγαθὸν μετὰ τοῦ κακοῦ· εἰ δὲ μετὰ τοῦ ἀγαθοῦ, αὐτὸ | ἄρα τὸ εἶναι οὔτε κακὸν οὔτε ἀγαθόν· τὸ ἀγαθὸν ἄρα τοῦ ὄντος ἐπέκεινα. **475** (189)

ια'. - [107d4-5] "Ότι 'λέγεται' ταῦτα ὑπὸ τῶν κοινῶν ἐννοιῶν τε καὶ προλήψεων, ὑπὸ τῶν θεολόγων, ὑπ' αὐτῶν ἐνδείκνυται τῶν τελετῶν. **476**

§§ 477-486. The guardian spirit and judgment. 107d5-e4

ιβ'. - "Ότι τὸ δαιμόνιον γένος τὴν μεσότητα συμπληροῖ τῶν θείων ἀειζώων **477**

---

§ 473. 1-2 οἷόν τε τὸν Wk (οἷόν τε Fh): οἴοντο M¹: οἷόν το Mᶜ

The first question (why is there no πρόσληψις, or minor ?) is left unanswered; the answer would obviously be that the last forty pages or so had been devoted to proving the propositions "the soul is immortal," resp. "death is not the end." As regards the second question, see note on Ol. 2 § 4: normally the antecedent is negatived if the consequent is, the opposite procedure, however, is valid when the terms are coextensive.

§ 475. Dam. II § 91.
§ 476. Dam. II § 93 (clearer and more complete).
2. ὑπ' αὐτῶν... τῶν τελετῶν: one would expect αὐτῶν τῶν θεῶν (as at II § 93.3-4); there may be some confusion due to drastic abridging.
§§ 477-486. Treatises on Neoplatonic demonology are found in the commentaries on Pl., Alc. I 103a5-6 (Pr. 67.19-83.16; Ol. 15.5-20.14) and on the present text (Plotinus III 4; Dam. here and II §§ 94-101). Pr.'s commentary at this point seems to have contained a digression on (1) demons generally and (2) the guardian spirit (cf. Pr., Alc., where a third section on the daimonion of Socrates is added).
§ 477. Dam. II § 94.

everlasting life, and those who come into being for a certain time; what we become for a time, they are always; and therefore they pre-eminently deserve the name of 'companions of the Gods.'

478. Every intramundane God has depending on him: matter, before it, body, before this, nature, still higher, soul, and even higher than this, intelligence, all this dominated by divinity; so the spirits who proceed from each God become divine, if determined by his divinity, guardians of matter, if by his material part, and intellective, psychical, physical, or corporeal, if by his intermediate functions.

It should be observed that as many classes of Gods can be distinguished by the same characteristics.

479. There is another classification of spirits according to their 'Divine Herdsmen': celestial, ethereal, aerial, aquatic, terrestrial, subterranean.

480. The spirits 'to whom each is allotted' are the guardians of souls that descend into genesis, and they are not necessarily intellective or ethereal, or belonging to any particular class. We must specify only that inasmuch as there are also guardian Gods in control of these descents and ascents, the companions of these Gods are the spirits to whom souls are allotted, and that they differ in degree from each other in proportion to the depth of the descent.

481. [107d7–e2] The 'seat' of the judges is the space between earth and heaven. This seems to be the ether, since the earth reaches up as far as the ether; it is a sphere adapted to all kinds of souls.

---

3. ὀπαδοί ... τῶν θεῶν: though the words θεοῦ ὀπαδοί occur at *Phil.* 63e5–6, the real source is *Phaedr.* 252c3–4, τῶν ... Διὸς ὀπαδῶν (and similarly, but in different terms, c5 and 253b1; 3), referring back to the pageant of Gods, demons and souls at 246e4–247a1 (cf. a6–7 and 248a1–2). A strictly defined meaning is given to the word by Pr., *elem.* 185, where three classes of souls are distinguished: (1) divine souls=Gods; (2) souls participating in intellective Intelligence, "perpetually attendant upon Gods," apparently=demons (cf. Iambl., *myst.* 36.8–10); (3) souls subject to change, "at certain times attendant upon Gods."

§ 478. Dam. II § 95. Six ranks of demons corresponding to six levels of existence: θεότης, νοῦς, ψυχή, φύσις, σῶμα, ὕλη. Cf. Pr., *Alc.* 71.3–72.12, who distinguishes (1) θεῖοι, (2) οἱ τῆς νοερᾶς ἰδιότητος μετέχοντες, (3) οἱ τῶν θείων ψυχῶν τὰς ... ποιήσεις διανέμοντες, (4) οἱ τῶν ὅλων φύσεων τὰς δυνάμεις ... διαπορθμεύοντες, (5) οἱ σωματοειδεῖς, (6) οἱ περὶ τὴν ὕλην στρεφόμενοι. Ol., *Alc.* 17.10–19.10: demons at the levels of (1) θεότης, (2) νοῦς, (3) ψυχὴ λογική, (4) ψυχὴ ἄλογος, (5) εἶδος, (6) ὕλη. – The observation at line 6 (by Dam.?), that the same six ranks are also those of the Gods, does not conform to the usual divisions of the Gods into (1) νοητοί, (2) νοεροί, (3) ὑπερκόσμιοι, (4) ἐγκόσμιοι, or (1) νοητοί, (2) νοητοὶ καὶ νοεροί, (3) νοεροί, (4) ὑπερκόσμιοι, (5) ἀπόλυτοι, (6) ἐγκόσμιοι, the former of which schemes is followed by Pr., *elem.* and elsewhere, the latter by Pr., *theol.* and Dam., *Parm.*

§ 479. Dam. II § 96. A second way of dividing demons into six classes, this time relating them to parts of the universe, or to the corresponding ἀγελάρχαι,

ὄντων καὶ τῶν ποτὲ γιγνομένων· ὃ γὰρ ἡμεῖς ποτὲ γιγνόμεθα, τοῦτο αὐτοὶ ἀεί· διόπερ ἐξαιρέτως αὐτοὶ ὀπαδοὶ λέγονται τῶν θεῶν.

ιγ΄. – Ὅτι θεοῦ ἑκάστου ἐγκοσμίου συνηρτημένην ἔχοντος ὕλην καὶ πρὸ 478 ταύτης σῶμα καὶ πρὸ τούτου φύσιν καὶ ἔτι πρότερον ψυχὴν καὶ πρότερον ἔτι νοῦν καὶ πάντων θεότητα προκαθημένην, οἱ δαίμονες οἱ ἀπὸ τοῦ θεοῦ προϊόντες οἱ μὲν κατὰ τὴν θεότητα θεῖοι γίγνονται, οἱ δὲ κατὰ τὴν ὕλην ὕλης ἔφοροι, καὶ οἱ μέσοι νοεροὶ ψυχικοὶ φυσικοὶ σωματικοί. 5
Ἐπιστῆσαι δὲ χρὴ ὅτι καὶ θεῶν γένη τοσαῦτα διήρηται κατὰ τὰς αὐτὰς ἰδιότητας.

ιδ΄. – Ὅτι καὶ ἄλλον τρόπον συνδιήρηνται τοῖς ἀγελάρχαις θεοῖς οἱ δαίμονες, 479 οὐράνιοι αἰθέριοι ἀέριοι ὑδραῖοι χθόνιοι ὑποχθόνιοι.

ιε΄. – Ὅτι οἱ εἰληχότες ἔφοροί εἰσι ψυχῶν τῶν εἰς γένεσιν κατιουσῶν, οὔτε 480 δὲ νοεροὶ πάντως οὔτε αἰθέριοι οὔτε ἀφωρισμένως κατ᾿ ἄλλην τινὰ μίαν διαφοράν. τοσοῦτον δὲ προσδιοριστέον, ὅτι καὶ θεῶν ὄντων τῶν ἐφορώντων τὴν τοιαύτην διοίκησιν τῶν καθόδων τε καὶ ἀνόδων οἱ τούτων ὀπαδοὶ τῶν θεῶν δαίμονές εἰσιν οἱ εἰληχότες, ὅση τῆς καθόδου ἡ διαφορότης εἰς βάθος, τοσοῦτον 5 ὑποβαίνοντες καὶ αὐτοὶ πρὸς ἀλλήλους.

ις΄. – [107d7–e2] Ὅτι 'τόπος' τῶν δικαστῶν ὁ μεταξὺ γῆς τε καὶ οὐρανοῦ. 481 εἴη δὲ ἂν ὁ αἰθήρ, εἴπερ ἄχρι τοῦ αἰθέρος ἡ γῆ ἀνα|τείνεται· σύμμετρος γὰρ (190) οὗτος ταῖς πάσαις γίγνεται.

---

§ 480. 5 οἱ Mᶜ: ὁ M¹ | καθόδου Mᶜ: καθόλου M¹
§ 481. 2 ∻ ἄχρι, ∻ et -ι in ras. Mᶜ

---

i.e. the intramundane Gods heading each class (see note on Ol. 7 § 4.4). Ol., *Alc.* gives practically the same classification of the ἐγκόσμιοι θεοί : (1) οὐράνιοι, (2) αἰθέριοι or πύριοι, (3) ἀέριοι, (4) ἐνύδριοι, (5) χθόνιοι, (6) ὑποταρτάριοι. Since this second classification is not found in Pr., *Alc.*, it may have been borrowed from the *Ph.* commentary by Ol. (or by his predecessor Ammonius).

§ 480. **Dam. II §§ 97–98.** Pr., having presented the twofold classification of demons (ontological and cosmological), went on to argue that the guardian spirits belonged to the class of νοεροί by the former, and of αἰθέριοι by the latter division. This appears from Dam. II, where his opinion is formally stated and rejected (cf. Pr., *Alc.* 72.20–73.1). It follows that, here, the first statement (lines 1–2) represents Dam.'s view that guardian spirits do not necessarily belong to any particular level or rank; hence the qualification at lines 3–6 must be also his.

3–4. θεῶν ... ἐφορώντων τὴν τοιαύτην διοίκησιν τῶν καθόδων τε καὶ ἀνόδων : as the demons do (τὰς ἀνόδους αὐτῶν καὶ τὰς καθόδους ἐπιτροπεύουσι Pr., *Alc.* 72.21); cf. note on II § 97.8.

§§ 481–483. **Dam. II §§ 99–100.** The equation of the δικαστικὸς τόπος (=the δαιμόνιος τόπος of *Rep.* X 614c1=the meadow of 614e2-3, 616b2 and *Gorg.* 524a2) with ether is argued at length by Pr., *Rep.* II 128.3–134.23; cf. also *infra* I § 497 and § 499; II § 100, 110. It corresponds to the classing of the εἰληχὼς δαίμων as αἰθέριος, and is rejected with it by Dam.

§ 481. 2. Earth reaching as far as ether: see below § 506, § 522.12–13, § 523.3.

Perhaps, however, we should assume a whole series of judgment seats, because souls belonging to different ranks, first, middle and last, will not appear before the same judges; everywhere order prevails and the different degree of procession is decisive. The commentator himself remarks on this below [§ 482].

482. The series of judgment, too, headed by Justice herself, proceeds through all its successive stages down to inanimate things (ordeals by waters and exhalations).

483. Disembodied souls are not necessarily in Hades; only those souls go there which are being purified of the visible and are privileged to join the Unseen ('that which sheds visibility'). Some, indeed, are at once directed upwards to the palace of Zeus by the judges, some are sent down again into genesis, others go to Hades. It is not strange at all that it should still be Pluto who speeds them all on their way by his Zeusian or Poseidonian powers or by those that characterize himself. The seat of the judges, then, is common to the three sons of Kronos and adapted to all three.

484. [107d6–7] We should not assign one spirit to each individual soul: first because the number of those who are nearer unity is of necessity smaller than that of those who are farther removed; secondly because, when the life is over, the spirit appointed to govern the life of that soul would be idle; thirdly because there is a fixed number of types of life, so that, if several souls adopt the same course, they will share the same guardian spirit as they share the same life. There may be a certain diversity among them, but then the one spirit, though his character is one, also possesses a variety of powers.

485. Nor, on the other hand, can there be more than one spirit in charge of one soul. In that case the number of spirits would be greater than that of souls; besides, one identical type of life requires one identical spirit;

4–7. The objection is by Dam., but it anticipates a qualification by Pr. himself (§ 482).

§ 482. An application of the general principle (Pr., elem. 140) πᾶσαι τῶν θεῶν αἱ δυνάμεις ἄνωθεν ἀρχόμεναι καὶ διὰ τῶν οἰκείων προϊοῦσαι μεσοτήτων μέχρι τῶν ἐσχάτων καθήκουσι καὶ τῶν περὶ γῆν τόπων. The formula returns often, varying according to the different σειραί or ἰδιότητες, in Pr. (e.g. Crat. 48.1–4); in Dam., Phil. § 228.2–4. – For the κριτικὴ ἰδιότης cf. Pr., Tim. III 198.25–30, where the orders of intramundane (as well as of supracelestial) Gods are listed as follows: δημιουργικαὶ ζωογονικαὶ συνοχικαὶ τελεσιουργοὶ φρουρητικαὶ κριτικαὶ καθαρτικαί. In demons: Pr., Rep. I 122.5–6 δαιμόνων δὲ τάξεις διαφόρους ἐφεστώσας, τὰς μὲν τιμωρούς, τὰς δὲ κολαστικάς, τὰς δὲ καθαρτικάς, τὰς δὲ κριτικάς.

2. ὑδάτων κριτικῶν καὶ πνευμάτων: Pr., Tim. III 140.24–28 οὕτως οὖν καὶ Διόνυσον χθόνιον ἐροῦμεν καὶ Ἀπόλλωνα χθόνιον, ὃς καὶ ὕδατα μαντικὰ πολλαχοῦ τῆς γῆς ἀναδίδωσι καὶ στόμια προφητεύοντα τὸ μέλλον. ἄλλους δὲ τόπους αὐτῆς καθαρτικοὺς ἢ κριτικοὺς ἢ ἰατικοὺς ἀποτελοῦσιν αἱ εἰς αὐτὴν καθήκουσαι παιώνιοι καὶ κριτικαὶ δυνάμεις. The connection with Justice proves that the meaning of κριτικός is more specific than Festugière in his note on this passage (vol. IV, p. 179, n. 4) thinks. There

Μήποτε δὲ καὶ τῶν δικαστικῶν τόπων ὅλην πρόοδον ποιητέον. οὐ γὰρ παρὰ τοῖς αὐτοῖς αἱ πρῶται καὶ αἱ μέσαι καὶ αἱ ἔσχαται κριθήσονται· πανταχοῦ γὰρ ἡ τάξις κρατεῖ καὶ τὸ κατὰ πρόοδον ἐξηλλαγμένον. τοῦτο δὲ καὶ αὐτὸς προϊὼν συννοεῖ [§ 482].

ιζ'. – Ὅτι καὶ ἡ δικαστικὴ σειρὰ ἀπὸ τῆς Δίκης ἀρξαμένη διὰ πάσης πρόεισι τῆς οἰκείας προόδου μέχρι καὶ τῶν ἀψύχων, οἷον ὑδάτων κριτικῶν καὶ πνευμάτων. 482

ιη'. – Ὅτι αἱ ἔξω σωμάτων ψυχαὶ οὐ πάντως εἰσὶν ἐν Ἅιδου· ἐκεῖναι γὰρ 483 μόναι, ὅσαι τοῦ ὁρατοῦ καθαίρονται καὶ τοῦ ἀειδοῦς τοῦ ἀποτιθεμένου τὸ ὁρατὸν ἀπολαύουσιν. ἔνιαι γοῦν εὐθὺς εἰς Διὸς ἀνατείνονται ὑπὸ τῶν δικαστῶν, ἔνιαι δὲ πάλιν εἰς γένεσιν καταπέμπονται, αἱ δὲ εἰς Ἅιδου ἀπίασιν. οὐδὲν δὲ θαυμαστὸν καὶ τὸν Πλούτωνα πάσαις συμπράττειν κατὰ τὸ ἑαυτοῦ Δίιον ἢ Ποσειδώνιον ἢ τὸ ἑαυτοῦ ἴδιον. ὁ ἄρα τόπος τῶν δικαστῶν κοινός ἐστι τῶν τριῶν Κρονιδῶν καὶ σύμμετρος τοῖς τρισίν.

ιθ'. – [107d6–7] Ὅτι οὐ καθ' ἑκάστην ψυχὴν εἷς δαίμων τακτέος· πρῶτον 484 μὲν ὅτι ὁ τῶν ἐγγυτέρω τοῦ ἑνὸς ἀριθμὸς ἐλάττων ἐξ ἀνάγκης τῶν πορρωτέρω· δεύτερον ὅτι τοῦ βίου λυθέντος ἀργήσει ὁ λαχὼν ἐκείνης διοικεῖν τὸν βίον· τρίτον ὅτι τῶν βίων τόσων ὄντων καὶ τοίων, ἐὰν πλείους τὸν αὐτὸν προβάλωνται, ὁμόβιοι οὖσαι καὶ ὁμοδαίμονες ἔσονται. εἰ δὲ καὶ τούτων ἐστὶ διαφορά τις, ἀλλὰ καὶ τοῦ ἑνὸς δαίμονος εἷς μὲν ὁ χαρακτήρ, διάφοροι δὲ τοῦ ἑνὸς δυνάμεις.

κ'. – Ὅτι οὐδὲ πλείους δαίμονες τῆς μιᾶς ἐπιστατήσουσιν. ἔσται γὰρ ὁ τῶν 485 δαιμόνων ἀριθμὸς πλείων τοῦ τῶν ψυχῶν· καὶ ὁ εἷς χαρακτὴρ τοῦ βίου ἕνα

---

§ 481. 4 ὅλην M^c: ὅλη M¹
§ 483. 4 ἀπιᾶσιν M — 6 κρονίδων M
§ 484. 6 ∻εἷς, ∻ in ras., accent. add., M^c | τοῦ ἑνὸς in fine lin. ins. M¹

---

are examples of ordeal wells in Philostr., *vit. Ap.* 1, 6 (=Ps.-Ar., *mirab. ausc.* 152; near Tyana) and 3,14 (in India). I have found no instances of vapors in a similar function.

§ 483. Plato's own explanation of Hades as the Invisible (*Ph.* 80d5–7; cf. *supra* § 348) is modified so as to make it an intermediate stage between genesis and the supramundane world ("the palace of Zeus"); this is achieved by using the present tense καθαίρονται, 'are in process of being cleansed from the visible'. In § 470, Zeus represents the pre-incarnation state, Pluto life after death. This idea is taken up in lines 4–7, where it is explained that in a sense all the three categories of the dead belong to the domain of Hades.

§ 484. **Dam. II § 101.** As Dam.'s strictures in II show, the three arguments are Pr.'s. Cf. *elem.* 62 πᾶν πλῆθος ἐγγυτέρω τοῦ ἑνὸς ὂν ποσῷ μέν ἐστι τῶν πορρωτέρω ἔλαττον, τῇ δυνάμει δὲ μεῖζον, with the corollary: therefore souls are more numerous than intelligences. See also *ibid.* 203, and Dodds on both; Pr., *Tim.* III 261.4–263.6 on the numerical relation between particular souls and star souls. The view that there is one demon for each soul is expressed by Iambl., *myst.* 283.1–284.10.

§ 485. The belief of more than one demon for each soul is opposed by Iambl., *ibid.* 281.5–282.5.

finally, if there were more than one, either their action is determined by one common character, so that the only guardian is the one who possesses this common character, or their characters differ, and the question arises to which of them the soul will assimilate herself, for he is the only real guardian spirit.

486. Neither can there be one good, one evil spirit, since no evil being is naturally capable of care or fellowhip, nor will such a spirit cling to us for good; for it is always possible to banish an evil genius by philosophy and by sacrificial devices.

§§ 487–494. The guardian spirit and judgment: notes on the text. 107d5–e4

487. [107d7] The words 'makes ready to lead him' express that there is no compulsion, only activation of our free-will: the spirit governs the soul neither as a thing moved from without nor as a completely self-dependent being.

488. [107d6–7] Souls have spirits allotted to them, as it is said in the *Republic* [X 617e1], by their choice of the kind of life that is under the patronage of these spirits; souls are allotted to spirits, as it is put here, in accordance with the several kinds of life of which they have the guardianship.

489. [107d8] The phrase 'are gathered' shows that many share in the judicial decision simultaneously; the words 'to stand their trial' express the clear discrimination of what is due to each.

490. 'Justice' determines what each deserves, 'judgment' makes the sentence discriminate and free from confusion.

491. [107d5–e4] The spirit to whom each has been allotted leads them to the judges, because it is his task to conclude that life and to add this final part to the whole; the one who conducts them from the judges to

---

§ 486. On the concept of a good and an evil demon accompanying every man cf. Nilsson II 201–202, who cites Menander frg. 550 Koch (=714 Koerte) ἅπαντι δαίμων ἀνδρὶ συμπαρίσταται εὐθὺς γενομένῳ μυσταγωγὸς τοῦ βίου, ἀγαθός· κακὸν γὰρ δαίμον' οὐ νομιστέον εἶναι βίον βλάπτοντα χρηστὸν οὐδ' ἔχειν κακίαν· ἅπαντα δ' ἀγαθὸν εἶναι τὸν θεόν. Censorinus, *de die natali* 3,3 "Euclides autem Socraticus duplicem omnibus omnino nobis genium dicit adpositum." P. Boyancé, *Les deux démons personnels dans l'antiquité*, Rev. philol. 61, 1935, 189–202. Apparently this view had been adopted by an earlier Platonist, who must have found the good demon in 107d6–8, the evil one in 107e1–2 and 108b2–3. – Evil demons are very much in evidence in the Chald. Or. (Lewy 259–279), as well as in Origen the Neoplatonist (Pr., *Tim.* I 76.30–77.3) and Porph. (*abst.* 2,37–43; Pr., *Tim.* I 77.18–24). Iamblichus, who assigns to demons a fixed rank between angels and heroes, disagrees with this, *myst.* 67.1–70.9; 173.9–175.14. Pr., *mal. subs.* 16–17, denies that a demon can be essentially evil, though he may cause harm in some respects. This concerns, in the first place, avenging and chastising demons, but also the lower ranks (chthonic

τὸν δαίμονα ἀπαιτεῖ· καὶ εἰ πλείους, ἢ καθ᾽ ἓν εἶδος τὸ κοινόν, ὥστε εἷς ὁ κατὰ κοινὸν | εἰδοποιούμενος, ἢ κατὰ πλείω, καὶ τίνι ἐξομοιωθήσεται ἡ ψυχή; οὗτος (191) γὰρ ἂν εἴη μόνος.

κα'. – Ὅτι οὐδὲ ὁ μὲν ἀγαθός, ὁ δὲ κακός· οὐδεὶς γὰρ κακὸς ἐπιμελεῖσθαι 486 πέφυκεν οὐδὲ συντάττεται κατὰ φύσιν οὐδὲ ἀναπόστατος ἀεί· τὸν γὰρ κακόν ἐστιν ἀποπέμπεσθαι διὰ φιλοσοφίας καὶ τῆς ἱερατικῆς μηχανῆς.

§§ 487–494. The guardian spirit and judgment: notes on the text. 107d5–e4

κβ'. – [107d7] Ὅτι 'ἄγειν ἐπιχειρεῖ', διότι οὐ βιάζεται, ἀλλὰ κινεῖ τὸ 487 αὐθαίρετον· οὔτε γὰρ ὡς ἑτεροκίνητον διοικεῖ τὴν ψυχὴν οὔτε ὡς αὐτάρκη.

κγ'. – [107d6–7] Ὅτι αἱ μὲν ψυχαὶ λαγχάνουσι τοὺς δαίμονας, ὡς ἐν Πολιτείᾳ 488 [X 617e1], κατὰ τὴν αἵρεσιν τῶν προστατουμένων ὑπ᾽ αὐτῶν βίων· οἱ δὲ δαίμονες τὰς ψυχάς, ὡς νῦν φησι, κατὰ τοὺς βίους ὧν ἀεὶ προστατοῦσιν.

κδ'. – [107d8] Ὅτι τὸ μὲν 'συλλέγεσθαι' δηλοῖ τὴν ὁμοῦ πολλῶν μέθεξιν 489 τῆς δικαστικῆς κρίσεως, τὸ δὲ 'διαδικάσασθαι' τὴν ἀσύγχυτον διάκρισιν τῶν ἑκάστοις ὀφειλομένων.

κε'. – Ὅτι ἡ μὲν δίκη τὰ κατ᾽ ἀξίαν ἑκάστοις ὁρίζει, ἡ δὲ κρίσις τὰ 490 ψηφισθέντα διακεκριμένα ποιεῖ καὶ ἀσύγχυτα.

κϛ'. – [107d5–e4] Ὅτι ὁ μὲν εἰληχὼς ἄγει παρὰ τοὺς δικαστὰς ὡς 491 συμπεραίνων τὸν βίον καὶ ὡς μέρος καὶ τοῦτο τοῦ ὅλου βίου ἀποπληρῶν· ὁ δὲ ἀπὸ τῶν δικαστῶν εἰς Ἅιδου κομίζων δικαστικός ἐστι δαίμων καὶ οἷον ὑπουργῶν

---

§ 486. 3 φιλοσοφίας Mᶜ: φίλον M¹
§ 489. 1 ὅτι τὸ] -τι τὸ ex corr. Mᶜ

---

or material demons), who can interfere with man's higher aspirations (Pr., Alc. 45.7–12; above § 123).

§ 487. Dam. II § 102. On the interplay between divine guidance and human free-will see e.g. Pr., Rep. II 127.25–128.2 (with a reference to the commentary on the Ph.: ὡς ἐν Φαίδωνι μεμαθήκαμεν); Alc. 281.16–282.2.

§ 488. Dam. II § 103. Pr., Rep. II 271.6–273.5.

§ 489. Dam. II § 104.

§ 490. δίκη: as contained in διαδικασαμένους. The word κρίσις, to which it is compared, does not occur in the Ph., but Gorg. 523c6 and e6 (and the verb b7 etc.) and Phaedr. 249a6. Δίκη compared to τίσις Pr., Rep. II 140.6–13; 184.14–19; Ol., Gorg. 248.3–7.

§ 491. Dam. II § 105. The second of the three demons is derived from 107e1–2 and 108b2–3 (cf. note on § 486); he is usually taken to be identical with the first. The third is the εἰληχὼς δαίμων for the new life, who is explicitly called "another" by Pl.

Hades is a spirit of judgment and as it were the executor of the sentence, which is the reason why he is not chosen by the souls; a third, described as 'different' from the latter, is the one who takes the soul back to the world of process, so that he is again a spirit in charge of a life.

492. [107e2–4] It is impossible for any soul, either to remain forever in the intelligible world, as Iamblichus thought it could (the fact that it descended once proves that it is disposed by nature to descend sometimes), or forever in Tartarus, as Socrates will say presently [113e6], since it is also disposed by nature to be sometimes above. The latter statement must be explained otherwise, as we shall show below [§ 547]: here, in any case, Socrates anticipates the answer by saying that 'having stayed there the appointed time' the soul is led back to this world by another spirit: 'appointed' means of course that the time is fixed by providence and destiny in accordance with what we have deserved by our own voluntary actions.

493. [107e4] Perpetual changes are cyclic changes; therefore there is also a cycle of ascents and descents; therefore, too, Plato describes souls as spheres [*Tim.* 36e2–5].

494. Different souls have different periods (Plato does not speak of one only); consequently the cycles of one thousand or three thousand or ten thousand years [*Phaedr.* 248e5–249b3] should not be given a numerical value, but related to a particular type of life.

§§ 495–502. Observations on 107e4–108c5

495. [107e4–108a2] Aeschylus was thinking of the common fate by which all souls leave the body, when he said that there is only one road to Hades [frg. 239 N.]. As a matter of fact, even the leaving of the body is not the same for all: there may be a strong emotional tie, or none at all, or a state between two extremes, and in each case there are many differences. The road to Hades, at all events, varies widely; destinations are different and sometimes contrary, the life-patterns of souls are unlike one another, and the guiding spirits are of many kinds, so that each leads them his own way.

496. [108a2–6] Socrates has two proofs: the philosophical argument that the souls have need of guides (if there were only one road they would

---

§ 492. Iambl., *Ph.* frg. 5. On eternal salvation and eternal damnation see I §§ 547–548; Ol. 10 § 14.

§ 493. Dam. II § 106.

1. τὰ ἀεὶ μεταβάλλοντα κύκλῳ μεταβάλλει: the proposition is demonstrated by Ar., *phys.* VIII 8; cf. *gener. et corr.* II 10, 337a1–7; Pl., *Laws* X 898a3–b3; Pr., *elem.* 198 πᾶν τὸ χρόνου μετέχον, ἀεὶ δὲ κινούμενον, περιόδοις μετρεῖται.

2. σφαῖραι αἱ ψυχαὶ παρὰ Πλάτωνι: the *Tim.* passage refers to the world-soul, and does not mean that the soul itself is spherical. Pr., *Tim.* II 284.18–25 warns against taking this sphericity in a spatial sense.

τῇ ψήφῳ, διὸ τοῦτον αἱ ψυχαὶ οὐχ αἱροῦνται· τρίτος δὲ καὶ ⸌ἄλλος⸍ παρὰ τοῦτον εἰρημένος ὁ δεῦρο πάλιν κομίζων εἰς γένεσιν, διὸ καὶ οὗτος εἰληχώς.

κζ'. – [107e2-4] *Ὅτι οὐκ ἔστιν ἀεί τινα μένειν οὔτε ἐν τῷ νοητῷ, ὡς Ἰάμβλιχος· εἴπερ γὰρ κατῆλθεν, πέφυκεν κατιέναι ποτέ· οὔτε ἐν τῷ Ταρτάρῳ, ὡς νῦν ἐρεῖ ὁ Σωκράτης* [113e6]· *πέφυκε γὰρ καὶ ἄνω ποτὲ εἶναι. ἀλλὰ ταῦτα ἑτέρως νοητέον, ὡς ἐροῦμεν* [§ 547]· *ἐπεὶ νῦν γέ φησι προλαβὼν ὅτι ⸌μείνασαν ὃν χρὴ χρόνον⸍ ἐκεῖ | ἄλλος ἄγει δεῦρο· εἰ δὲ ὃν χρή, δῆλον ὡς κατὰ ἀξίαν τοῦ ἐφ' ἡμῖν ὁ χρόνος ὁρίζεται ὑπὸ τῆς προνοίας καὶ τῆς εἱμαρμένης.* 492

κη'. – [107e4] *Ὅτι τὰ ἀεὶ μεταβάλλοντα κύκλῳ μεταβάλλει· διὸ καὶ ἄνοδοι καὶ κάθοδοι κύκλῳ· διὸ καὶ σφαῖραι αἱ ψυχαὶ παρὰ Πλάτωνι* [*Tim.* 36e2-5]. 493

κθ'. – *Ὅτι ἄλλαι ἄλλων περίοδοι, οὐ γὰρ μίαν φησίν· ἡ ἄρα χιλιέτης ἢ τρισχιλιέτης ἢ μυριέτης* [*Phaedr.* 248e5-249b3] *οὐ κατὰ ἀριθμὸν νοητέα, ἀλλὰ κατὰ ζωῆς τι εἶδος.* 494

§§ 495-502. Observations on 107e4-108c5

λ'. – [107e4-108a2] *Ὅτι ὁ μὲν Αἰσχύλος εἰς τὴν κοινὴν ἔξοδον ἀπὸ τοῦ σώματος τῆς ψυχῆς ἀποβλέψας ἁπλῆν ἔφη τὴν εἰς Ἅιδου πορείαν* [frg. 239 N.]. *ἦν δὲ οὐδὲ ἔξοδος μία, εἴπερ ἡ μὲν ἐμπαθής, ἡ δὲ ἀπαθής, ἡ δὲ μέση, καὶ ἑκάστη πολυειδής. ἀλλ' ἥ γε εἰς Ἅιδου πορεία ποικίλη· καὶ γὰρ λήξεις διάφοροι καί τινες καὶ ἐναντίαι, καὶ ζωαὶ τῶν ψυχῶν οὐχ ὁμότροποι, καὶ οἱ ἄγοντες δαίμονες πολυειδεῖς· ἕκαστος οὖν ἄγει τὴν οἰκείαν ὁδόν.* 495

λα'. – [108a2-6] *Ὅτι ὁ Σωκράτης διχῇ δείκνυσιν· φιλοσόφως μὲν ἀπὸ τοῦ δεῖσθαι τὰς ψυχὰς ἡγεμόνων (μιᾶς γὰρ οὔσης ὁδοῦ μὴ ἂν δεηθῆναι τῶν ἀγόντων),* 496

---

§ 492. 4 post ἐροῦμεν] ∻ undecies in ras. M^c — 5 χρή¹] s.l. M¹
§ 496. 2 ἄν] -ν in ras. M^c

---

§ 494. Dam. II § 107. Pl., *Rep.* X 615a2-3 εἶναι δὲ τὴν πορείαν χιλιέτη, cf. 621d2; *Phaedr.* 248e6 οὐκ ἀφικνεῖται ἐτῶν μυρίων, 249a4-5 τρισχιλιοστῷ ἔτει ἀπέρχονται. Thousand as symbolizing a way of life: Hermias 169.10-12 ἢ οὕτως· οὐ τὸ μαθηματικὸν καὶ ἀριθμητικὸν τῶν ἐτῶν πλῆθος βούλεται δηλοῦν ὁ Πλάτων, ἀλλὰ μέτρα τελειοτήτων καὶ βαθμοὺς βούλεται ἡμῖν σημαίνειν πρώτων τε καὶ μέσων καὶ τελευταίων. Pr., *Rep.* II 172.20-21 ὥστε χρὴ τὸν ἀριθμὸν ἔς τι ζωῆς εἶδος ἀναπέμπειν.
§§ 495-496. Dam. II § 108.
§ 496. 1-3. φιλοσόφως ... ἱερατικῶς : same contrast as § 172, the implication being that Pl. combines the science of both.

not need anybody to lead them), and another derived from sacrificial practice, the cult of Hecate at places where three roads meet. There are many more ways to be certain of this.

497. There is one road forking common to all, the meeting point of the three roads leading from ether upwards, downwards, or to middle earth; each of these branches off in three directions, the upward road to the spheres of the planets, of fixed stars, of Olympus, the downward road to the Acheron, to the Cocytus, to the Pyriphlegethon, the middle road to air, to water, to earth. Orpheus, too, proclaims these truths often and at great length [frg. 123].

498. [108a6–b3] Souls with right insight and right inclinations follow their guide willingly and welcome the verdict, but the undisciplined and ignorant ones resist. Then how can it still be said that they are 'led away'? — In these cases the guide deals with them as objects moved from without.

Or should we say that he treats even those as self-moved beings, by awakening their inborn notions somehow or other, though they may sometimes resist?

499. [108b3–4] Why do they have to gather in the ethereal region? The judges can see everything everywhere, and souls can receive their sentence no matter where they are. — In the first place souls become more amenable to treatment when removed from the influence of the lower regions; secondly, some places are more suited than others to a particular person or a particular form of illumination; thirdly, we prefer to appear before the Gods in holy places, even though they are everywhere.

500. [108b3–c5] Socrates contrasts the extreme kinds of behavior, and

---

3. τριόδοις: the MSS. of Pl. and Stob. read περιόδους, the reading τριόδους has been introduced into the text from Pr., *Rep.* I 85.6 and 11, Dam., *Ph. h. l.*, § 497.1 and II § 108.9.

ibid. πολλαχῶς δὲ καὶ ἄλλως: not referring back to φιλοσόφως ... ἱερατικῶς, but rather to ἀπὸ τῶν θυσιῶν (v.l. ὁσίων) τε καὶ νομίμων τῶν ἐνθάδε τεκμαιρόμενος λέγω, for which Dam. II § 108.6–12 offers a choice of possible explanations.

§ 497. This section, which makes ether the starting-point of the journey, must be from Pr. (see §§ 481–483, note); the division into three triads is also characteristic of him, though in this case it was suggested by the τριόδους πολλάς of the text. Cf. Pr., *Rep.* II 132.5–13, where only the basic triad is mentioned (ἄκρα τῆς γῆς, γένεσις, ὑπόγειος τόπος). Similarly *infra* II § 131.

3. πλανώμενον ... ἀπλανές ... Ὀλύμπιον: this triad and the following (air – water – earth) derive from Julian's *Hyphegetica* (on which see Lewy pp. 123–124 and note 231) cited by Pr., *Tim.* I 317.22–28 δοκεῖ μὲν οὖν ὅσα τῷ τρίτῳ τῶν ἀρχικῶν ὁ θεουργὸς ἀνατίθησι, ταῦτα καὶ οὗτος τῷ κόσμῳ διδόναι καὶ δημιουργεῖν μὲν τὸν οὐρανόν, κυρτῷ σχήματι περικλάσας, πηγνύναι δὲ πολὺν ὅμιλον ἀστέρων ἀπλανῶν, ζώνας δὲ πλανωμένων ὑφιστάνειν ἑπτά, καὶ γῆν ἐν μέσῳ τιθέναι καὶ ὕδωρ ἐν τοῖς κόλποις τῆς γῆς καὶ ἀέρα ἄνωθεν τούτων. Lewy, p. 377, compares Alcin., *did.* 15, to show that this system knows only a twofold sky (fixed stars and planets) enclosing the three remaining elements. Out of it, Pr. has constructed a triadic sky by adding a highest, supramundane level, the Ὀλύμπιον, αἰθέριον or ἐμπύριον, on the ground

ἱερατικῶς δὲ ἀπὸ τῶν ἐν τριόδοις τιμῶν τῆς Ἑκάτης. πολλαχῶς δὲ καὶ ἄλλως εἴσεταί τις.

λβ'. - "Ότι μία μὲν κοινὴ τρίοδος ἡ ἀπὸ τοῦ αἰθέρος ἀπάγουσα ἢ ἄνω ἢ κάτω ἢ εἰς τὸ μεταξύ· καὶ ἑκάστη τούτων ἔσχισται τριαδικῶς, ἡ μὲν ἄνω εἰς τὸ πλανώμενον, εἰς τὸ ἀπλανές, εἰς τὸ Ὀλύμπιον, ἡ δὲ κάτω εἰς τὸν Ἀχέροντα, εἰς τὸν Κωκυτόν, εἰς τὸν Πυριφλεγέθοντα, ἡ δὲ μεταξὺ εἰς ἀέρα, εἰς ὕδωρ, εἰς γῆν. πολὺς δὲ καὶ ὁ Ὀρφεὺς τὰ τοιαῦτα κηρύττων [frg. 123].

λγ'. - [108a6-b3] "Ότι αἱ μὲν καὶ γνώσει καὶ ὀρέξει καλῶς διακείμεναι ἑκουσίως ἕπονται τῷ ἡγεμόνι ἀσμενίζουσαι τὴν δίκην, αἱ δὲ ἀκοσμοῦσαι καὶ ἀγνοοῦσαι ἀντιτείνουσι. πῶς οὖν 'ἄγονται'; | — Ἢ ὡς ἑτεροκινήτοις τότε χρῆται ὁ ἄγων.

Μήποτε δὲ καὶ ταύταις ὡς αὐτοκινήτοις, ὁπωσοῦν ἀνακινῶν τὰς κατὰ φύσιν αὐτῶν ἐννοίας, εἰ καὶ ἐνίοτε ἀντιτείνουσιν.

λδ'. - [108b3-4] Διὰ τί εἰς τὸν αἰθέριον συλλέγονται τόπον; οἵ τε γὰρ δικασταὶ πάντα ὁρῶσι πανταχοῦ καὶ αἱ ψυχαὶ πανταχοῦ οὖσαι δύνανται τυγχάνειν τῆς ψήφου. — Ἢ πρῶτον μὲν αἱ ψυχαὶ ἀπαλλαγεῖσαι τῶν χειρόνων τόπων ἐπιτηδειότεραι γίγνονται· δεύτερον ἄλλοι [δι'] ἄλλων τόπων πρὸς τόνδε ἢ τήνδε τὴν ἔλλαμψιν ἐπιτηδειότεροι· τρίτον ὅτι καὶ μᾶλλον ἐν ἱεροῖς τόποις βουλόμεθα προσιέναι τοῖς θεοῖς, καίτοι πανταχοῦ εἰσιν.

λε'. - [108b3-c5] "Ότι διίστησι τὰς ἀντικειμένας ζωάς, ἐξ ὧν καὶ τὰς μέσας

---

§ 499. 3 ἀπαλλαγεῖσαι] ἀπ- in ras. M^c — 4 ἐπιτηδειότεραι M^c: spat. vac. M¹ | ἄλλοι δι'ἄλλων τρόπων M^c (δι' del. Wk, τόπων Fh): spat. vac. et οπων M¹ — 5 καὶ μᾶλλον ἐν M^c: spat. vac. M¹

---

of the principle that the highest unit in each order has the characteristics of the order preceding it (elem. 112). Tim. II 57.9-14 τί οὖν; φαίη τις ἂν τῶν ἐκ τῆς ὑπερορίου θεοσοφίας ὡρμημένων καὶ τὰ πάντα διαιρουμένων εἰς ἐμπύριον αἰθέριον ὑλαῖον, καὶ μόνον τὸ ἐμφανὲς ὑλαῖον καλούντων· τὰ ὑπὲρ τὸν κόσμον στερεώματα τί φήσομεν, εἴτε Ὄλυμπον χρὴ καλεῖν, εἴτε ἐμπύριον, εἴτε αἰθέρας; Cf. ibid. II 144. 29-30 (ὑπερκόσμιος=αἰθέριος= ἐμπύριος). Ibid. III 186.16-17 τὸν ἀκρότατον [scil. Οὐρανὸν] ... τὸν ἐκπεσόντα τοῦ Ὀλύμπου καὶ ἐκεῖ τεταγμένον.

§ 498. Dam. II § 110. Cf. supra § 487.

§ 499. Dam. II § 111. The assumption that the place of judgment is ether, is Pr.'s. Neither here nor in II does Dam. repeat the dissent expressed in § 481.4-7.

4. ἄλλοι ἄλλων τόπων: the reading filled in by M^c, [ἄλλοι δι' ἄλλων τρ]όπων is not relevant to the argument; Finckh's correction ἄλλοι δι' ἄλλων τόπων would fit Dam.'s belief that judgment can take place on many different levels of existence, but not Pr.'s as explained and defended here. With the δι' dropped, the sense becomes that ether is a particularly favorable medium for receiving the illumination of judgment. Ether being the common place of judgment for all, the τόνδε remains puzzling; perhaps, since the original of M was damaged in any case, we should feel free to supply a noun, e.g. τόνδε ⟨τὸν θεόν⟩.

§ 500. Cf. Dam. II § 112.

1-2. Intermediates are implicit when extremes are stated: a commonplace in the commentaries, e.g. Dam., Phil. § 56.4-5; Ol., Gorg. 260.3-4.

through them enables us to image the intermediate forms as well. There is one kind of souls from which the others shrink back as unclean, another which they admire; none will accompany or guide the one, the Gods themselves are the companions of the other (that is, the good are granted guidance by divine apparitions, while the wicked are scarcely deemed worthy of invisible providence); thirdly and finally, the one kind reach their own chosen destinations immediately, the others after heavy toil and a long lapse of time attain the end destined for them by fate. It is obvious from this that the good are governed by providence, the wicked, because irrational, by fate.

501. [108b4–8] The unclean are avoided by souls, lest they should be affected (to which they are liable by nature), and by the guiding spirits, because they can exert no influence upon the unreceptive.

502. [108b8] They are called 'guides and companions' because they are transcendent as well as co-ordinate.

Or the one should be taken to refer to souls, the other to higher beings.

§§ 503–511. What earth is meant? Its divinity. Its height. 108c5–110b1

503. The earth of which Plato speaks here is incorporeal according to some, corporeal according to others; of the latter, Harpocratio [frg. 8] thinks the whole world is meant, Theodorus [test. 42] the sublunary world; of those who think of it as incorporeal, Democritus believes that it is the idea, Plutarch that it is Nature.

504. To all these views there is one common reply, namely that the earth of which Socrates speaks is simply the earth of our geography books.

505. Against those who believe it to be incorporeal, it should be pointed out that Socrates thinks of its inhabitants as having bodies and ⟨possessing

---

4. αὐτοφανοῦς ... προνοίας : the pure soul is aware of the presence of its guide, the guilty soul is not. Normally, αὐτοφανής has a technical (theurgical) meaning, see Lewy 246–247.

6. μόλις καὶ ἐν μακροῖς χρόνοις εἱμαρμένων : cf., besides 108c1–2, also 107e4 ἐν πολλαῖς χρόνου καὶ μακραῖς περιόδοις and 113a3 καί τινας εἱμαρμένους χρόνους μεῖναι. The εἱμαρμένη here, however, is primarily an equivalent for ὑπ' ἀνάγκης.

6–7. This is Pr.'s doctrine of Fate as stated *prov.* 4 and 14.

§ 502. Dam. II § 113. Dam.'s suggestion (line 3) fits b8 well enough, but clashes with c4.

§§ 503–511. The literalistic approach of Pr. and Dam. to Plato's cosmography is shared by Ar., *mete.* II 2, 355b32–356a14, who criticizes it without even considering the possibility of any but a strictly literal intention. The Platonists felt themselves committed to the view that the description was true, either literally or allegorically, according as they stressed the ταῦτα or the τοιαῦτα in 114d2–3 ὅτι μέντοι ἢ ταῦτ' ἐστὶν ἢ τοιαῦτ' ἄττα περὶ τὰς ψυχὰς ἡμῶν καὶ τὰς οἰκήσεις.

§§ 503–504. Dam. II § 114. Harpocratio's opinion is difficult to account for without further information, since Pl. at several points distinguishes between earth

δίδωσιν ἐννοεῖν. καὶ τὰς μὲν ἐκτρέπονται αἱ ἄλλαι ψυχαὶ ὡς μυσαράς, τὰς δὲ ἄγανται· καὶ ταῖς μὲν οὐδεὶς ἐθέλει συνέμπορος οὐδὲ ἡγεμὼν εἶναι, ταῖς δὲ καὶ θεοὶ συνοδοιποροῦσιν (αὗται μὲν γὰρ καὶ τῆς αὐτοφανοῦς ἀξιοῦνται προνοίας, ἐκεῖναι δὲ μόλις τῆς ἀφανοῦς)· ἔτι τὸ τρίτον αἱ μὲν εὐθὺς τυγχάνουσι τῶν 5 οἰκείων λήξεων, αἱ δὲ μόλις καὶ ἐν μακροῖς χρόνοις εἱμαρμένων. ὅθεν δῆλον ὡς αἱ μὲν κατὰ πρόνοιαν διοικοῦνται οἷα λογικαί, αἱ δὲ κατὰ εἱμαρμένην ὡς ἄλογοι.

λϛ'. - [108b4–8] "Ὅτι τὰς μυσαρὰς αἱ μὲν ψυχαὶ ἐκτρέπονται, ἵνα μὴ πάθωσι, 501 πεφυκυῖαί γε, οἱ δὲ ἡγεμόνες, ὅτι μὴ δύνανται δρᾶσαί τι εἰς τὰς ἀνεπιτηδείους.

λζ'. - [108b8] "Ὅτι ‘ἡγεμόνες καὶ συνέμποροι᾽ λέγονται ὡς ἅμα καὶ ἐξῃρημένοι 502 καὶ συντεταγμένοι.

Ἢ τὸ μὲν ἐπὶ τῶν ψυχῶν, τὸ δὲ ἐπὶ τῶν κρειττόνων ἀκουστέον.

§§ 503–511. What earth is meant? Its divinity. Its height. 108c5–110b1

λη'. - "Ὅτι τὴν γῆν οἱ μὲν ἀσώματόν φασι τὴν ἐνταῦθα λεγομένην, οἱ δὲ 503 σωματικήν· καὶ τούτων ὅλον μὲν τὸν κόσμον ʽΑρποκρατίων [frg. 8], τὸν δὲ ὑπὸ σελήνην Θεόδωρος [test. 42]· τῶν δὲ ἀσώματον τὴν μὲν ἰδέαν Δημόκριτος, τὴν δὲ φύσιν Πλούταρχος.

λθ'. - "Ὅτι πρὸς πάντας ἑνὶ λόγῳ ἀντιρρητέον ὡς περὶ τῆς αὐτῆς τοῖς 504 γεωγράφοις διαλέγεται ὁ Σωκράτης.

μ'. - "Ὅτι πρὸς τοὺς ἀσώματον, ὡς σώματα περιβεβλημένους κα[ὶ αἰσθήσει 505(194) χρω]μένους ὑποτίθεται τοὺς ἐν αὐτῇ οἰκοῦντας, ἔτι δὲ πολυχρονιώτερα ζῷα

§ 502. 1 ἅμα] " et -μ- ex corr. Mᶜ
§ 503. 2 τούτων Mᶜ: τοῦτον M¹
§ 504. 1 ὡς ins. Mᶜ: om. M¹ — 1–2 τοῖς γεωγράφοις Mᶜ: spat. vac. et γραφοις M¹
§ 505. 1 τοὺς Mᶜ: τὸν M¹ | ἀσώματον, ὡς σώματα Mᶜ: ἀσώματ et spat. vac. M¹ — 1–2 κα[ὶ αἰσθήσει χρω]μένους Wk: κα ... (spat. 9 litt.) ... μόνους M — 2 ἐν αὐτῆι ∻ Mᶜ: spat. vac. M¹ | πολυχρονιώτερα Mᶜ: πολυ et spat. vac. M¹

and sky; his main purpose may have been to explain the "heights of the earth" as the higher spheres, which would fit the eschatology of Numenius and Cronius (and Porphyry). Theodorus of Asine must have included the whole sublunary world because of 109b7–c1 αὐτὴν δὲ τὴν γῆν καθαρὰν ἐν καθαρῷ κεῖσθαι τῷ οὐρανῷ ἐν ᾧπέρ ἐστι τὰ ἄστρα, ὃν δὴ αἰθέρα ὀνομάζειν τοὺς πολλοὺς τῶν περὶ τὰ τοιαῦτα εἰωθότων λέγειν. This brings him fairly close to Pr., who held that the ether of the *Ph.* reaches as far as the moon sphere (*Rep.* II 133.4–11). Others, despairing of making literal sense of the description, took refuge in the transcendent: Democritus by τὴν ... ἰδέαν probably means 'the ideal form of Earth'; he must have found confirmation for this in 108d9 τὴν μέντοι ἰδέαν τῆς γῆς οἵαν πέπεισμαι εἶναι ... Plutarch (of Athens, probably) may have interpreted the superior beauty, purity and durability of natural things described in 110c1–111c3 as symbolizing the perfection of the pure λόγοι of Nature, not distorted or dulled by matter, which is the cause of ugliness and corruption (see esp. 110e2–6).

§ 505. 1–2. Norvin's proposed supplement κα[ὶ ἀνόσους] μόνους is not relevant to the point that the earth described by Pl. is material; an obvious argument to use is the keenness of the senses of its inhabitants, 111b3–6.

the faculty of sense-perception⟩ and further says that animals there have a longer span of life. As for the two theories in particular: if it is an idea, how can it be 'whiter than chalk,' or have a temperate climate? If it is nature, how can it be an abode of blessed souls and how can it be 'inhabited by Gods'?

506. Against those who maintain that it is the universe or the sublunary world we observe that Socrates describes it as situated under the heavens and surrounded by ether, as ours is by air.

507. That the size of the earth is 'enormous' [109a9] is indicated by Timaeus, who calls it 'the most venerable being within heaven' [40c2–3], apparently because it approaches heaven and has the other elements as integrating parts of itself; it is further indicated by the story of Atlantis, preserved in Egyptian tradition, according to which the isle of Atlantis alone was larger than Africa and Europe together [*Tim.* 24e6–7; *Criti.* 108e6–7].

508. Earth is a Goddess, according to Timaeus [40c2–3], to authorities on ritual, and to the theologians. Besides, if the world is a total made up of totals, it follows that it is a God made up of Gods; that it is a God is true, therefore so are its parts, therefore so is the Earth as one of its parts. Furthermore, if Earth is contradistinguished from Heaven, and Heaven is a God (as it certainly must be, if the Sun and the Moon are), the same holds true of the Earth. Furthermore, if the subterranean Gods are parts of the Earth, Earth itself is *a fortiori* a Deity. Now this Earth of ours is an intramundane being, since it has this lowest kind of body attached to it; but if even we, human beings, have the luminous body prior to the earthly body, this is all the more certainly true of the whole Earth, and consequently there is also a soul beyond it, and an intelligence beyond the soul.

509. The Pythagoreans, too, make the Earth one of the stars on plausible grounds, and Timaeus [42d4–5] says that the Creator determined the essences of souls by scattering some on the Sun, some on the Moon,

---

§ 507. On Pr.'s contention that Pl.'s description is not (necessarily) at variance with scientific geography see the passage cited at § 510. The subject is dealt with in greater detail at § 522 (II §§ 124–125).

5. Εὐρώπης : Pl. in both passages mentions Asia instead; however, cf. note on § 522.4.

§ 508. Dam. II § 115. The subject is treated also by Pr., *Tim.* III 136.4–28.

1–2. Timaeus: both Plato's (40c2–3) and the Ps.-Timaeus (97e1–2). The ἱερατικοί may represent the Chaldean Oracles and the literature around them (though no references to Earth as a Goddess are extant), or, more generally, any writer on cult practice, e.g. Proclus of Laodicea; the "theologians" are in particular Orpheus (e.g. frg. 109), Homer (*Il.* 3.104 only: sacrifice to Earth and Sun) and Hesiod (*theog.* 44–45; 116–117).

2. ὅλος ἐξ ὅλων : the ὁλότητες (of the spheres and the elements) are Gods, because directly depending on a divine henad, as individual things do not. Cf. also Pl.,

εἶναι. ἰδίως δέ, εἰ μὲν ἰδέα, πῶς γύψου λευκοτέρα, πῶς εὖ κεκραμέναις ταῖς ὥραις; ἢ ὅλως ποία ἐκεῖ σωματικὴ διαίρεσις; εἰ δὲ φύσις, πῶς οἴκησις εὐδαιμόνων ψυχῶν, πῶς δὲ ˊθεοὺς οἰκητὰςˋ ἔχουσα; 5

μα΄. – ˊὍτι πρὸς τοὺς λέγοντας τὸ πᾶν ἢ τὸ ὑπὸ σελήνην ῥητέον ὡς ὑπὸ 506 τὸν οὐρανὸν αὐτὴν ὑποτίθεται καὶ τῷ αἰθέρι περιεχομένην, ὡς ἡ παρ᾽ ἡμῖν ἀέρι.

μβ΄. – ˊὍτιˋπάμμεγά τι᾽ [109a9] ἡ γῆ, δηλοῖ μὲν καὶ ὁ Τίμαιος ˊπρεσβυτάτην· 507 εἰπὼν ˊτῶν ἐντὸς οὐρανοῦˋ [40c2–3], ὡς ἂν αὐτῷ πελάζουσαν, τὰ δὲ ἄλλα στοιχεῖα πληρώματα ἑαυτῆς ἔχουσαν· δηλοῖ δὲ καὶ ὁ ᾽Ατλαντικὸς λόγος ἀπὸ Αἰγύπτου διασωθείς, ὃς καὶ τὴν ᾽Ατλαντίδα νῆσον μείζω γενέσθαι φησὶν ὁμοῦ Λιβύης τε καὶ Εὐρώπης [Tim. 24e6–7; Criti. 108e6–7]. 5

μγ΄. – ˊὍτι θεὸς ἡ γῆ, ὡς ὅ τε Τίμαιος [40c2–3] καὶ οἱ ἱερατικοί φασιν 508 καὶ οἱ θεολόγοι. ἔτι δὲ εἰ ὁ κόσμος ὅλος ἐξ ὅλων, καὶ θεὸς ἄρα ἐκ θεῶν· ἀλλὰ μὴν θεός, καὶ ἐκ θεῶν ἄρα, ὥστε καὶ τῆς γῆς. ἔτι δὲ εἰ ἀντιδιῄρηται τῷ οὐρανῷ, θεὸς δὲ ὁ οὐρανός, εἴπερ καὶ ἥλιος καὶ σελήνη, καὶ ἡ γῆ ἄρα. ἔτι δὲ εἰ οἱ χθόνιοι θεοὶ μέρη αὐτῆς, πολλῷ μᾶλλον αὐτὴ θεός. ἀλλὰ δὴ ἐγκόσμιος αὕτη ἡ γῆ, σῶμα 5 γὰρ αὐτῆς ἐξήρτηται τοῦτο τὸ ἔσχατον· εἰ δὲ πρὸ τοῦ ὀστρέου καὶ ἐφ᾽ ἡμῶν τὸ αὐγοειδές, πολλῷ μειζόνως ἐπὶ τῆς ὅλης γῆς, ὥστε καὶ ψυχὴ πρὸ τούτου, καὶ νοῦς γε πρὸ ταύτης.

μδ΄. – ˊὍτι καὶ οἱ Πυθαγόρειοι τὴν γῆν εἰκότως ἕνα τῶν | ἀστέρων ποιοῦσιν, 509(195) καὶ ὁ Τίμαιος [42d4–5] σπείρειν φησὶ κατ᾽ οὐσίαν τὰς ψυχὰς τὰς μὲν εἰς ἥλιον,

---

§ 505. 3 πῶς¹ Nv: ἡ ὡς Mᶜ: spat. vac. M¹ | γύψου (-ν puncto not.) Mᶜ: γύψο et spat. 1 litt. M¹ | εὖ κεκραμέναις Mᶜ (-ϑ in textu, κεκραμέ- in mg.): ε... (spat. 8 litt.)... ναις M¹
§ 507. 2 τῶν] -ῶ- in ras. Mᶜ (fort. τὴν M¹)
§ 508. 3 post καί²] ἐκ θεοῦ add. Nv — 5 αὕτη Mᶜ: αὐτὴ M¹ (?) — 8 νοῦς γε] -οῦς ex -οῦ, γ- in ras., Mᶜ

Tim. 32c5–33a1, with Pr.'s commentary (II 56.17–57.2).
4–8. The argument is explained by II § 115.5–8: since the Earth comprises [the subterranean] Gods, it must be a Deity; this Deity [being intramundane] has not only an intelligence and a soul dependent upon it, but also a luminous and an earthly body. It is also possible, however, to read lines 5–8 as a separate argument: since the Earth is an intramundane being [but of a higher order than we are,] it must have at least all the higher constituents that we have.
§ 509. 1. See Norvin 1915, 196, n. 3. The source of this statement is Ar., cael. II 13, 293a20–23: (while Earth is usually placed in the center) ἐναντίως οἱ περὶ τὴν ᾽Ιταλίαν, καλούμενοι δὲ Πυθαγόρειοι λέγουσιν· ἐπὶ μὲν γὰρ τοῦ μέσου πῦρ εἶναί φασι, τὴν δὲ γῆν, ἓν τῶν ἄστρων οὖσαν, κύκλῳ φερομένην περὶ τὸ μέσον νύκτα τε καὶ ἡμέραν ποιεῖν. In his commentary on the passage (512.14–17), Simplicius tries to normalize the Pythagorean doctrine: ἄστρον δὲ τὴν γῆν ἔλεγον ὡς ὄργανον καὶ αὐτὴν χρόνου· ἡμερῶν γάρ ἐστιν αὕτη καὶ νυκτῶν αἰτία· ἡμέραν μὲν γὰρ ποιεῖ τὸ πρὸς τῷ ἡλίῳ μέρος καταλαμπομένη, νύκτα δὲ κατὰ τὸν κῶνον τῆς γινομένης ἀπ᾽ αὐτῆς σκιᾶς.

others on the Earth, apparently because he regards Earth also as one of the divine sequences. Blessed, then, are all those souls that make their rounds under the guidance of Earth; so it cannot be this Earth which the more fortunate souls escape.

510. The height of the Earth is confirmed by the so-called Moon Mountains, which reach as high as the Moon; by mountain tops above the clouds, exposed neither to wind nor to rain; and by those ranges on which the sunlight falls at all hours except four, such as the Caucasus, which nevertheless belong to our part of the world.

511. What Socrates says about the Earth is partly seen from below, partly from the middle and in conformity with that level, partly from above, and in so far 'a sight for the blessed to behold' [111a3].

§§ 512–522. The four problems concerning the earth. 108e4–110b1

512. There are four problems concerning the Earth: its position, its shape, its stability, its size. Socrates takes the first two for granted, the other two he demonstrates through them.

513. That the Earth is the center of the universe appears from the fact that it is at all points equidistant from the sky. This is proved by astronomical observations.

514. That it is spherical can be deduced from the rule that all totals conform to the universe, as well as from the fact that at all points heavy objects show an equal downward trend.

---

4. ὅσαι τῇ ἡγεμόνι Γῇ συμπεριπολοῦσιν : the "guides" and the "revolutions" are of course those of the *Phaedrus*, 246b6–7, 246e5–247a7, 252c4–5, where Hestia (247a1) is identified as the Earth by "some" (Pr., *Tim.* III 137.20–138.1; Hermias 141.32–142.6).

4–5. *Ph.* 114b6–7 οἳ δὲ δὴ ἂν δόξωσι διαφερόντως πρὸς τὸ ὁσίως βιῶναι, οὗτοί εἰσιν οἱ τῶνδε μὲν τῶν τόπων τῶν ἐν τῇ γῇ ἐλευθερούμενοί τε καὶ ἀπαλλαττόμενοι ὥσπερ δεσμωτηρίων, ἄνω δὲ εἰς τὴν καθαρὰν οἴκησιν ἀφικνούμενοι καὶ ἐπὶ γῆς οἰκιζόμενοι. Cf. *Theaet.* 176a8–b1 διὸ καὶ πειρᾶσθαι χρὴ ἐνθένδε ἐκεῖσε φεύγειν ὅτι τάχιστα.

§ 510. Norvin 1915, 197–204. Pr., *Tim.* I 180.25–181.28 (referring to the present *Ph.* passage). While maintaining that Pl.'s cosmography is correct, Pr. wisely does not even attempt to verify it in terms of mathematics. Simpl., *cael.* 549.32–550.4, discussing the spherical shape of the Earth, says that the highest mountains (10 stadia according to Eratosthenes) are negligible in proportion to its diameter (57,273 stadia according to Ptolemy).

1. Σεληναῖα ὄρη : Pr., *Tim.* I 181.16–17 ἀλλὰ καὶ Πτολεμαῖος τὰ Σεληναῖα ὄρη τὸ ὕψος ἄπλετον ἔχειν φησί. However, though Ptolemy, *geogr.* IV 8, 2, does mention the mountain as the source of the Nile and indicates its position, there is no question

τὰς δὲ εἰς σελήνην, τὰς δὲ εἰς γῆν, ὡς οὖσαν καὶ ταύτην μίαν τῶν θείων σειρῶν. ὥστε εὐδαίμονες αἱ ψυχαὶ ὅσαι τῇ ἡγεμόνι Γῇ συμπεριπολοῦσιν· οὐκ ἄρα αὕτη ἐστὶν ἣν φεύγουσιν αἱ μακαριώτεραι τῶν ψυχῶν.

με΄. – Ὅτι καὶ τῷ ὕψει αὐτῆς ὁμολογεῖ τά τε Σεληναῖα καλούμενα ὄρη 510 ὡς πρὸς αὐτὴν τὴν σελήνην ἀνατεινόμενα, καὶ τὰ ὑπερνεφῆ μήτε ἀνέμοις μήτε ὄμβροις ὑποκείμενα, καὶ τὰ βαλλόμενα τῷ ἡλίῳ πάσας τὰς ὥρας πλὴν δ΄, ὡς ὁ Καύκασος, καὶ ταῦτα τῆς καθ᾽ ἡμᾶς οἰκουμένης ὄντα.

μς΄. – Ὅτι ὁ Σωκράτης τὰ μὲν λέγει περὶ αὐτῆς ἀπὸ τῶν ἐσχάτων ὁρμώμενος, 511 τὰ δὲ ἀπὸ τῶν μέσων καὶ πρέποντα μέσοις, τὰ δὲ ἀπὸ τῶν ἄκρων, ἄξια ταῦτα 'θεατῶν εὐδαιμόνων' [111a3].

§§ 512–522. The four problems concerning the earth. 108e4–110b1

μζ΄. – Ὅτι τέσσαρα τὰ περὶ γῆς προβλήματα· περὶ τῆς θέσεως αὐτῆς, περὶ 512 τοῦ σχήματος, περὶ μονῆς, περὶ μεγέθους. τὰ μὲν οὖν πρῶτα δύο ὡς ὁμολογούμενα ἔλαβεν, τὰ δὲ λοιπὰ διὰ τούτων δείκνυσιν.

μη΄. – Ὅτι ἐν μέσῳ ἡ γῆ, δηλοῖ ἡ πανταχόθεν αὐτῆς ἀπόστασις ἴση πρὸς 513 τὸν οὐρανόν· τὴν δὲ ἴσην οἱ ἀστρονόμοι τετηρήκασιν.

μθ΄. – Ὅτι περιφερής, δηλοῖ τὸ πάντα ὅσα ὅλα πρὸς τὸ πᾶν ἀφομοιοῦσθαι 514 καὶ τὸ πανταχόθεν ἐπ᾽ ἴσης τὰ βαρέα πρὸς τὸ κάτω χωρεῖν.

---

§ 509. 4 αὕτη M^c: αὐτὴ M¹
§ 510. 3 ὑπο~κείμενα, -ο~ in ras. M^c (ὑπερκείμενα ut vid. M¹) | δ΄] -ας compendio sscr. M^c
§ 513. 1 ἦ² μ: ἦ M | ἀπόστασις μ : ἀποστάσεις M

---

of its height. Ol., mete. 129.28–30 (reporting the old "theologies" as opposed to modern astronomy) καὶ γὰρ τοῦτο τὸ μέγα μέρος ὑποτίθενται τὴν γῆν τοῦ παντὸς διὰ τὰ Σεληναῖα ὄρη, ἅτινα σχεδὸν λέγουσι φαίνειν τῆς σεληνιακῆς σφαίρας (a different account of the name ibid. 105.30–32).

2. ὑπερνεφῆ : Philop., mete. 26.32–33 τὰ γὰρ ὑψηλότατα τῶν ὀρῶν ὑπερνεφῆ τ᾽ ἐστὶ καὶ ὑπερήνεμα. Id., an. 333.1.

3–4. Ar., mete. I 13, 350a28–33 ὁ δὲ Καύκασος μέγιστον ὄρος τῶν πρὸς τὴν ἕω τὴν θερινήν ἐστιν καὶ πλήθει καὶ ὕψει. σημεῖα δὲ τοῦ μὲν ὕψους ὅτι ... ἡλιοῦται τῆς νυκτὸς αὐτοῦ τὰ ἄκρα μέχρι τοῦ τρίτου μέρους ἀπό τε τῆς ἕω καὶ πάλιν ἀπὸ τῆς ἑσπέρας.

§§ 512–522. The four "usual questions" (II § 116) are mentioned by Pl. himself in the order (1) position (2) shape (3) stability (4) size; and treated by Ar. (cael. II 13–14) in the order 1, 3, 2, 4.

§ 512. Dam. II § 116.1–4. Pl. formally proves the third point from the first two; as regards the proof for the fourth, see § 522, and note.

§ 513. 2. Ptolemy, synt. I 5. – Perhaps ταύτην δὲ ἴσην or τὴν δὲ ἰσότητα.

§ 514. Dam. II § 118. The first, purely speculative argument is Neoplatonic (cf. Dam. II and Pr., Tim. III 148.19–20). The second is from Ar., cael. II 14, 297b17–20.

515. If placed in the middle, it may be expected to maintain its natural position round the center. Inasmuch as it is conglomerated round the center, it remains in the same place; inasmuch as it conforms to the universe, in its natural position.

516. The spherical shape of the universe can be proved by an argument from finality, viz. that of all shapes the sphere is the most similar to the One, in other words to the Good, and being the most unitary, it is also the most beneficial. For either the One and the Good are identical (since neither of the two can be superior to the other other or simpler than it, nor can they be equal in rank, because this would mean two first principles) or, better, since the concepts differ, both are approximations of the same reality. So much for the argument from the final cause; another argument, derived from the exemplary cause, is that this cause is 'all-complete' [*Tim.* 31b1], and the closest approach to all-completeness is the most perfect of shapes, i.e. the most comprehensive. Finally there is the argument from the efficient cause: what Intelligence creates is permanent, and the most permanent of shapes is the sphere.

517. Because of its perfect unity the universe is spherical all through, not only on the surface, as a wooden ball is, with the grain inside running straight, whereas the universe is entirely concentric. Therefore its spherical structure does not leave room for any vacuum, so that all the constituent parts must conform to the spherical shape of the whole, including the Earth.

518. That the Earth is in the middle and round the center, the commentator proves at greater length in the following way. If the universe is spherical all through and conglomerated round its center, there are two possibilities: since mortal bodies consist of different kinds of particles, either the fine particles must have sunk to the middle and the coarse ones

---

§ 515. Dam. II § 116.4–7.
2. περὶ τὸ κέντρον ἐσφιγμένη (cf. § 518.2 συνέσφιγκται περὶ τὸ κέντρον). This is an old formula paraphrasing *Tim.* 40b8 ἰλλομένην δὲ περὶ τὸν διὰ παντὸς πόλον τεταμένον, with the purpose of discarding Ar.'s explanation of ἰλλομένην as 'rotating' (*cael.* II 13, 293b30–32). Thus already Alcin., *did.* 15 κεῖται δὲ ἡ μὲν γῆ τῶν ὅλων μέση, περὶ τὸν διὰ παντὸς σφιγγομένη πόλον. Pr., *Tim.* III 137.6–13 ἰλλομένην δὲ τὴν σφιγγομένην δηλοῖ καὶ συνεχομένην· οὐ γάρ, ὡς Ἀριστοτέλης οἴεται, τὴν κινουμένην· διαφερόντως γὰρ ὁ Πλάτων ἀκίνητον φυλάττει τὴν γῆν καὶ τὴν αἰτίαν προστιθεὶς ἐν τῷ Φαίδωνι δι' ἣν ἀκίνητος ἵδρυται· λέγει οὖν 'ἰσόρροπον - κλιθῆναι' [109a4–5]. Cf. Simpl., *cael.* 517.13–22 τὸ δὲ ἰλλομένην, εἴτε διὰ τοῦ ἰῶτα γράφοιτο, τὸ δεδεσμημένην δηλοῖ, ... εἴτε διὰ τῆς ει διφθόγγου γράφοιτο, καὶ οὕτως εἰργομένην δηλοῖ ... · καὶ ὅτι τὸ ἰλλομένην οὕτως ὑπὸ τοῦ Πλάτωνος εἴρηται, δηλοῖ τὰ ἐν Φαίδωνι περὶ τῆς γῆς εἰρημένα, ἐν οἷς φησιν 'ἰσόρροπον - κλιθῆναι'.

§ 516. Dam. II § 117. A selection from the comprehensive account given by Pr., *Tim.* II 68.14–76.29 (on Pl., *Tim.* 33b1–7). He lists: three proofs by Pl. (μία μὲν ἀπὸ τοῦ ἑνός, ἑτέρα δὲ ἀπὸ τοῦ νοητοῦ κάλλους, τρίτη δὲ ἀπὸ τῆς νοερᾶς ποιήσεως); eight arguments of Iamblichus; five of Ar.; four astronomical ones and a mathematical one.

ν'. - Ὅτι εἰ ἐν μέσῳ, μένοι ἂν ἐν τῷ οἰκείῳ τόπῳ καὶ περὶ τὸ κέντρον. 515
ᾗ μὲν γὰρ περὶ τὸ κέντρον ἐσφιγμένη, μένει ἐν τῷ αὐτῷ τόπῳ· ᾗ δὲ πρὸς τὸ πᾶν ὡμοίωται, ἐν τῷ οἰκείῳ.

να'. - Ὅτι σφαιροειδὲς τὸ πᾶν, ἀπὸ μὲν τοῦ τελικοῦ δείξεις ὡς ὁμοιότατον 516
τῷ ἑνί — ταὐτὸν δὲ εἰπεῖν τῷ ἀγαθῷ — σχημάτων | ἁπάντων ἡ σφαῖρα καὶ (196)
ἑνοειδέστατον, ὥστε καὶ ἀγαθώτατον. ἢ γὰρ ταὐτὸν ἕν τε καὶ ἀγαθόν — οὐδέτερον
γὰρ τοῦ ἑτέρου δύναται κρεῖττον εἶναι οὔτε ἁπλούστερον, οὔτε ὁμοταγῆ, δύο
γὰρ αἱ ἀρχαὶ ἔσονται οὕτως· — ἢ κάλλιον, ἐπειδὴ χωρὶς αἱ ἔννοιαι, τοῦ αὐτοῦ 5
ἐνδεικτικὸν εἶναι ἑκάτερον. ταῦτα μὲν οὖν ἀπὸ τοῦ τελικοῦ· ἀπὸ δὲ τοῦ
παραδειγματικοῦ, ὅτι 'παντελές' [Tim. 31b1], ὁμοιότατον δὲ τῷ παντελεῖ τὸ
τελειότατον τῶν σχημάτων, πανδεχέστατον γάρ. ἀπὸ δὲ τοῦ ποιητικοῦ, ὅτι
ἀιδίων δημιουργὸς ὁ νοῦς, ἀιδιώτατον δὲ πάντων σχημάτων ἡ σφαῖρα.

νβ'. - Ὅτι ἑνοειδέστατον ὂν τὸ πᾶν ὅλον δι' ὅλου ἐσφαίρωται, οὐ γὰρ κατὰ 517
μόνην τὴν ἐπιφάνειαν ὡς ἡ ξυλίνη σφαῖρα· εὐθεῖαι γὰρ ἔνδον αἱ τοῦ ξύλου ἶνες·
τὸ δὲ πάντα ἔχει συννεύοντα πρὸς τὴν σφαίρωσιν. οὐδὲν ἄρα κενὸν ἐάσει
παρεμπίπτειν ἡ σφαίρωσις· πάντα ἄρα τὰ πληρώματα τῷ παντὶ συσφαιροῦται,
καὶ ἡ γῆ ἄρα. 5

νγ'. - Ὅτι μέση καὶ περὶ τὸ κέντρον, οὕτως ἀποδείκνυσι πλατύτερον. εἰ γὰρ 518
ὅλον δι' ὅλου ἐσφαίρωται καὶ συνέσφιγκται περὶ τὸ κέντρον, ἀνάγκη τῶν θνητῶν
σωμάτων ἀνομοιομερῶν ὄντων ἤτοι τὰ λεπτομερῆ ὑποκεῖσθαι περὶ τὸ μέσον

§ 516. 7 τῷ μ : τὸ Μ

1-3. Pl.'s first argument according to Pr. II 68.27-69.2 αὐτίκα ἀπὸ τοῦ ἑνὸς εἴποις μὲν ἂν ὅτι καὶ ὁ δημιουργὸς εἷς, εἴποις δ' ἂν ὅτι καὶ τὸ παράδειγμα ἕν, εἴποις δ' ἂν ὅτι καὶ τὸ ἀγαθὸν ἕν ἐστιν, καὶ ἀπὸ τούτων ἂν λάβοις ὅτι καὶ ἐν τοῖς σχήμασι τὸ μάλιστα ἓν τοῦ μὴ ἑνὸς θειότερόν ἐστι καὶ τελειότερον.
3-6. Dam., in a disjunctive sentence, first reports Pr.'s view of the identity of the One and the Good, then adds his own comment, that these two different concepts cannot have the same meaning, but at best symbolize the same reality. On this use of ἐνδείκνυσθαι cf. Dam., Phil. § 62 note and index s.v. ἔνδειξις.
6-8. Cf. Pr. II 70.32-71.5 διὰ τί δὲ συγγενὲς καὶ πρέπον τῷ παντὶ τὸ σφαιρικὸν ἐξηγούμενος ὁ Πλάτων ἐπήνεγκεν, ὅτι τὸ πάντων περιεκτικὸν δεῖ τοιοῦτον ἔχειν σχῆμα· τάχα μὲν ὅτι καὶ τῶν ἰσοπεριμέτρων στερεῶν ἡ σφαῖρα πολυχωρητότερον, ὥς φασιν οἱ τὰ μαθηματικὰ δεινοὶ καὶ ἡμεῖς μικρὸν ὕστερον ἀναλεγόμενοι τὰ ἐκείνων ἐροῦμεν [76.7-29].
8-9. Cf. Iamblichus' eighth argument (Pr. II 73.15-16) ἔτι τὸ ἄτρεπτον καὶ ἄθραυστον καὶ ἀίδιον οἰκειότατά ἐστι τῷ σφαιρικῷ σχήματι.
§ 517. Dam. II § 118.
§ 518. Dam. II § 119. A supplement to § 513 by Pr., who must be the subject of ἀποδείκνυσι, since nothing of this is found in Pl.
3. The heavens are ὁμοιομερῆ : Pr., Tim. II 75.15-17 (as proof of the spherical shape of ether); Simpl., cael. 388.31; 420.25.

must have risen to the circumference, or, this being impossible because the thicker particles cannot pass through the denser ones nor rest on them, only the contrary remains. The coarsest element of all is earth, therefore it must be at the bottom of all the rest, i.e. in the middle.

519. What is closest to the circumference, i.e. to the sky, has circular motion, because it adapts itself to the adjoining element. In the same way the Earth is stationary because it adapts itself to the neighboring center; and just as ether is a sky with characteristics of mortality, so Earth is a visible center with the properties of an element.

520. If the Earth were to swerve from its central position, it would do so either because moved in one direction by the sky − but the sky is entirely symmetrical; or because gravitating to one side by its own force − but the Earth is perfectly balanced, since there is equal pressure of all weight towards the center. So neither factor can cause a deviation. That the Earth is in equilibrium, Socrates deduces also from its spherical shape.

521. If fire had been given the place in the middle, it would not have stayed there, as Aristotle objects [*cael.* II 13, 295b16–19]. 'Equilibrium' means an equal pressure downward, while fire has a natural tendency to rise to the surface, or rather to move in circles at the highest level; straight courses, in fact, are the motions of elements in disorder.

522. [109a9–110b1] For his claim that the Earth is 'of enormous size' [109a9] Socrates adduces no evidence whatever, though the other contentions are adequately proved. − As a matter of fact, he proves this point, too, by an argumentation based on proportion, and that is why he refers so often to the subject of proportion. (1) If the whole European quarter of our part of the world is already so large, and yet is merely a cavity in the whole Earth, of a sort of which there are many everywhere (think of the isle of Atlantis, which once lay outside our part of the world, and was larger

---

§ 519. Dam. II § 120. On the revolution of the sky and the different degrees of participation in it cf. Pr., *Tim.* II 97.10–24.

§ 520. Dam. II §§ 121–122. *Ph.* 109a2–6 paraphrased.

4–5. Socrates does not state his ground for assuming that the earth is in perfect equilibrium; here, it is suggested that such proof is implicit in 108e5 περιφερὴς οὖσα. Since no further proof is offered, the καί seems to be redundant.

§ 521. Dam. II § 123. Ar., *cael.* II 13, 295b11–19 εἰσὶ δέ τινες οἳ διὰ τὴν ὁμοιότητά φασιν αὐτὴν μένειν, ὥσπερ τῶν ἀρχαίων 'Αναξίμανδρος· ... τοῦτο δὲ λέγεται κομψῶς μέν, οὐκ ἀληθῶς δέ· κατὰ γὰρ τοῦτον τὸν λόγον ἀναγκαῖον ἅπαν, ὅ τι ἂν τεθῇ ἐπὶ τοῦ μέσου, μένειν, ὥστε καὶ τὸ πῦρ ἠρεμήσει· τὸ γὰρ εἰρημένον οὐκ ἴδιόν ἐστι τῆς γῆς. Pr., *Tim.* II 11.24–12.5 εἰ δὲ τούτων ὑφ' ἡμῶν λεγομένων ὁ 'Αριστοτέλης ἀπορεῖ, πῶς οὖν, εἰ πῦρ ἐστιν ἐν οὐρανῷ, κύκλῳ κινεῖται καὶ οὐκ ἐπ' εὐθείας, λεκτέον τὸν Πλωτίνειον λόγον [II 2, 1] πρὸς αὐτόν, ὅτι πᾶν σῶμα ἁπλοῦν ἐν τῷ οἰκείῳ τόπῳ ὂν ἀκίνητον μένει ἢ κύκλῳ κινεῖται· ... καὶ γὰρ ὅταν ἐπὶ τὸ ἄνω φέρηται τὸ πῦρ, ἐν ἀλλοτρίῳ τόπῳ ὂν ἐπὶ τὸ ἄνω φέρεται, καὶ ἡ βῶλος ἐπὶ τὸ κάτω ὡσαύτως, καὶ ὅλως τῶν στοιχείων αἱ ἐπ' εὐθείας φοραὶ παρὰ φύσιν εἰσὶ διακειμένων. The same notion attributed to Ptolemy and Plotinus, Pr., *Tim.* III 114.30–115.2; to Plato, Simpl., *cael.* 531.34–532.9.

τὰ δὲ παχυμερῆ ἐπικεῖσθαι κατὰ τὸ πέριξ, ἢ εἰ τοῦτο ἀδύνατον (οὐ γὰρ οἷόν τε διὰ τῶν πυκνοτέρων τὰ παχύτερα διιέναι οὐδὲ ἐνιζάνειν ἐν αὐτοῖς) ἀναγκαῖον, 5
ὅπερ λείπεται, τὸ ἀνάπαλιν εἶναι. παχυμερεστάτη δὲ ἡ γῆ πάντων· πᾶσιν ἄρα καὶ ὑπόκειται· περὶ τὸ μέσον ἄρα.

νδ΄. - Ὅτι τὸ πλησίον τοῦ πέριξ, ὅ ἐστι τοῦ οὐρανοῦ, κύκλῳ κινεῖται, πρὸς   519
τὸ σύνορον ἀφομοιούμενον. οὕτως ἄρα καὶ ἡ γῆ μένει πρὸς τὸ γειτονοῦν κέντρον ἀφομοιουμένη· καὶ ὡς ὁ αἰθὴρ οὐρανὸς θνητοειδής, οὕτως ἡ γῆ κέντρον φαινόμενον καὶ στοιχειῶδες.

νε΄. - Ὅτι παρεκινήθη ἂν ἔξω τοῦ μέσου ἡ γῆ ἢ ὑπὸ τοῦ οὐρανοῦ ἐπὶ θάτερα   520
κινηθεῖσα, — ἀλλὰ πανταχοῦ ὅμοιος ἑαυτῷ ὁ οὐρανός· — ἢ αὐτὴ βαρυνομένη ἐπὶ θάτερα, — ἀλλ᾽ ἰσόρροπος πάντῃ ἐστίν, πανταχόθεν γὰρ ἐπ᾽ ἴσης τὰ βάρη πρὸς τὸ μέσον. οὐδετέρως ἄρα κλιθήσεται. ὅτι δὲ ἰσόρροπος, καὶ ἀπὸ τοῦ σφαιροειδοῦς συλλογίζεται. 5

νϛ΄. - Ὅτι εἰ τὸ πῦρ ἐν μέσῳ ἐτέθη, οὐκ ἂν ἔμεινεν, ὡς Ἀριστοτέλης ἀπορεῖ 521(197)
[cael. II 13, 295b16–19]. τὸ γὰρ ἰσόρροπον ὡς κάτω βρῖθον ἐπ᾽ ἴσης εἴρηται, τὸ δὲ πῦρ εἰς τὸ ἄνω πέφυκε χωρεῖν, μᾶλλον δὲ ἄνω κυκλίζεσθαι· αἱ γὰρ εὐθυπορεῖαι νοσούντων εἰσὶ τῶν στοιχείων κινήσεις.

νζ΄. - [109a9–110b1] Ὅτι 'πάμμεγά τι εἶναι' τὴν γῆν ἀξιῶν οὐδεμίαν   522
παρέχεται πίστιν καίτοι τὰ ἄλλα μετρίως ἀποδείξας. — Ἦ καὶ τοῦτο κατασκευάζει διὰ ἀναλογίας· διὸ καὶ πολὺν περὶ ταύτης πεποίηται λόγον.
α΄ πρῶτον μὲν γάρ, εἰ τὸ Εὐρωπαῖον ὅλον τεταρτημόριον τῆς καθ᾽ ἡμᾶς οἰκουμένης τηλικοῦτόν ἐστιν, ἔστι δὲ τῆς ὅλης γῆς οἷον κοιλάς τις, πολλαὶ δὲ τοιαῦται 5
πολλαχοῦ εἰσιν, ὡς δηλοῖ καὶ ἡ Ἀτλαντὶς νῆσος ἔξω τῆς οἰκουμένης οὖσά ποτε

---

§ 518. 4–5 οἶόν τε] acc. corr., -ε in ras. 2 litt. scr. M^c (οἴονται M¹?)

---

§ 522. Dam. II §§ 124–125. Plato's opinion as to the size of the Earth is contrasted with those of the astronomers also by Pr., *Tim.* I 180.25–182.2, with an implied preference for Pl. In the present interpretation of *Ph.* 109a9–110b1, four "proofs" are distinguished, all of them construed as based on proportion: (1) 109a9–c3: our *oikoumenè* is only a fraction of the Earth; (2) 109c3–d5: at our level the globe is considerably smaller than at its highest level; (3) 109d5–110a1: presumably the ratio between the real earth and the apparent earth is the same as between the real and the apparent sky; (4) 110a1–b1: with the decrease in size goes a decrease in quality.

4. τὸ Εὐρωπαῖον τεταρτημόριον τῆς καθ᾽ ἡμᾶς οἰκουμένης: our "world" is the northern half of the eastern hemisphere, as far as supposed habitable; the four quarters must be Europe, Africa (cf. lines 6–7), and Asia north and south of the Mediterranean-Taurus line (Strabo II 1,31=C. 84), though τεταρτημόριον does not seem to be attested in this sense. At II § 139.7–8 there is a division into only two parts, Europe and Asia. See Norvin 1915, 217–218.

6. ἡ Ἀτλαντὶς νῆσος ἔξω τῆς οἰκουμένης οὖσα: Pl., *Tim.* 24e5–6 νῆσον γὰρ πρὸ τοῦ στόματος εἶχεν ὃ καλεῖτε ... ὑμεῖς Ἡρακλέους στήλας. *Critias* 108e2–3. Pr., *Tim.* I 172.6 ἔξωθέν ποθεν τῆς ἡμετέρας οἰκουμένης.

than two quarters of it) and if each cavity is only a fraction of the entire Earth, which as a whole because of its spherical shape must have a predominantly convex surface, in relation to which such regions as ours are cavities, as proved by the stagnant air, then evidently the size of the Earth must appear to us as enormous. (2) If this Earth is inhabited on three levels, one on the bottom of the sea, one, our own, in the middle, and the highest on the crests of the Earth, the lowest surrounded by water, the middle one by air, the highest by ether, and if, furthermore, the ratio between the surrounding elements equals that between the parts of the Earth which they surround, then it follows, since the sphere of ether, being outermost, is larger than that of air, and the sphere of air, being farther outside, is larger than that of water, that the top level of the Earth is larger than the intermediate level, and the intermediate level larger than the lowest. For as the Earth is a sphere, circles described nearer the center are smaller than those farther from it, and it is manifest that the largest circles that can be described in the outermost surface of a sphere first and foremost determine its form, and it is these that mark the outline of the Earth, as the equator and the meridian mark that of the sky. (3) If the sky is not as small as we see it (for neither is the Sun or the Moon or any other star, and what is true of them is true of the sky itself too), then the Earth must be larger in such a way that, as the apparent Earth is to the apparent sky, the real Earth will be to the real sky, otherwise the same proportion could not prevail between the Earth and the sky as we see them. (4) A fourth argument can be derived from quality: if the dwellers on the heights of the Earth are much more beautiful than those in the middle regions, and if the more beautiful live on a more beautiful earth, and a more beautiful Earth is Earth in a purer form, there can be no doubt that the upper earth is the true one, and ours is only dross and mire in comparison. So one should not measure the great circle of this Earth, as the geographers do, but of the other, which deserves the name more fully. The other practice is no better than if beings living on the bottom of the sea were to make the Earth even smaller, measuring it by the great circle of their own surface.

---

7. μείζων τῶν δύο τεταρτημορίων : Pl., *Tim.* 24e6-7 ἡ δὲ νῆσος ἅμα Λιβύης ἦν καὶ 'Ασίας μείζων. *Critias* 108e6-7 ἦν δὴ Λιβύης καὶ 'Ασίας μείζω ... ἔφαμεν. If, however, Africa and Asia are two quarters (and Europe the third), it is difficult to account for a fourth; probably, therefore, the error of § 507.4-5 (Atlantis larger than Europe and Africa) still persists.

17-18. οἱ δι' αὐτῶν μέγιστοι κύκλοι : the text requires no correction, if αὐτῶν is taken as a loose reference to ἄκρα, which in any case is the only possible explanation. The 'great circle' (in the mathematical sense) of the topmost level determines the

μείζων τῶν δύο τεταρτημορίων, ἐλάχιστον δὲ τῆς ὅλης γῆς ἑκάστη κοιλάς (ἡ γὰρ ὅλη σφαιροειδὴς οὖσα τῷ πλείστῳ ἂν εἴη κυρτὴ τὴν ἐπιφάνειαν, πρὸς ἣν αὗται κοιλάδες εἰσίν, ὡς δηλοῖ ὁ λιμνάζων ἀήρ), φανερὸν ὅτι πάμμεγά τι
β' ἔοικεν ἡ γῆ εἶναι. δεύτερον δέ, εἰ τρεῖς αἱ ἐπὶ ταύτης οἰκήσεις, ἡ μὲν ἐν τῷ 10
πυθμένι τοῦ πελάγους, ἡ δὲ ἡμετέρα ἡ μέση, ἡ δὲ ἄκρα ἐπὶ τῶν νώτων αὐτῆς, καὶ περιέχεται ἡ μὲν ἐσχάτη ὑπὸ τοῦ ὕδατος, ἡ δὲ μέση ὑπὸ τοῦ ἀέρος, ἡ δὲ ἄκρα ὑπὸ τοῦ αἰθέρος, ὡς δὲ ἔχει μεγέθους τὸ περιέχον πρὸς τὸ περιέχον, οὕτως ἕξει τὸ περιεχόμενον πρὸς τὸ περιεχόμενον, μείζων δὲ ὁ αἰθὴρ τοῦ ἀέρος (ἐξωτάτω γάρ) καὶ ὁ ἀὴρ τοῦ ὕδατος (ἐξωτέρω γάρ), δῆλον ὡς καὶ τὰ ἄκρα 15
τῶν μέσων καὶ τὰ μέσα τῶν ἐσχάτων. καὶ γὰρ ὡς σφαίρας οἱ τῷ κέντρῳ πλησιαίτερον γραφόμενοι κύκλοι ἐλάττους τῶν πορρώτερον· καὶ δῆλον ὡς οἱ δι' αὐτῶν μέγιστοι κύκλοι μάλιστα καὶ πρῶτοι τὴν σφαῖραν εἰδοποιοῦσι καὶ κατ' ἐκείνους ἡ γῆ μάλιστα ἕστηκεν, ὥσπερ ὁ οὐρανὸς κατὰ τὸν ἰσημερινὸν
γ' καὶ μεσημβρινόν. τρίτον δέ, εἰ μὴ τηλικοῦτος μόνον ὁ οὐρανὸς ἡλίκος | ὁρᾶται 20(198) — οὐδὲ γὰρ ὁ ἥλιος οὐδὲ ἡ σελήνη οὐδὲ ἄλλος ἀστήρ, ἀλλὰ πολλῷ τινι μείζων ἕκαστος καὶ αὐτός γε ὁ οὐρανός, — ἀναγκαῖον οὕτω μείζω τὴν γῆν εἶναι, ἵνα, ὡς ἡ φαινομένη πρὸς τὸν φαινόμενον ἔχει μεγέθους, οὕτως ἔχῃ καὶ ἡ ἀληθὴς
δ' πρὸς τὸν ἀληθῆ· εἰ γὰρ μή, οὐδὲ ἡ φαινομένη πρὸς τὸν φαινόμενον. τέταρτον τοίνυν ἀπὸ τῆς ποιότητος εἴποις ἄν· εἰ γὰρ οἱ τῶν ἄκρων οἰκήτορες τῶν μέσων 25
πολλῷ καλλίους, οἱ δὲ καλλίους ἐπὶ καλλίονος οἰκοῦσι γῆς, ἡ δὲ καλλίων καθαρώτερόν ἐστιν ὅ ἐστιν, σαφὲς ὅτι μάλιστα γῆ ἐκείνη, καὶ αὕτη πρὸς ἐκείνην οἷον τρὺξ καὶ βόρβορος. οὐκ ἄρα τὸν ταύτης ἀναμετρεῖσθαι δεῖ μέγιστον κύκλον, ὃ ποιοῦσιν οἱ γεωγράφοι, ἀλλὰ τὸν ἐκείνης τῆς ἀληθεστέρας. ὅμοιον γὰρ ὡς εἰ καὶ οἱ ἐν τῷ πυθμένι τοῦ πελάγους ἔτι ἐλάττω φαῖεν αὐτὴν κατὰ τὸν μέγιστον 30
κύκλον τῆς αὐτῶν ἐπιφανείας.

§ 522. 17 post πλησιαίτερον] ∻ ∻ in ras. M^c — 23 ἔχει μ : -ηι M | ἔχῃ μ : -ει M — 27 αὕτη M^c: αὐτὴ M¹ (?)

size of the whole.
19–20. Though this is correct as far as it goes (in the sense of the preceding note), the mention of the meridian and the equator invites comparison with the smaller circles in the *same* sphere (arctic, tropic of Cancer, tropic of Capricorn, antarctic; cf. Pr., *Rep.* II 43. 21–24) and thus prepares the way for the confusion of II § 124.3–6.
20–24. What appears to us as the "sky" is merely the "air" (109d7); the numerical ratio between the apparent and the real sky may be assumed to exist also between the apparent and the real earth (109e7–110a1).
28. τρύξ : see note at § 168.11.

§§ 523–526. The four (three) levels. 109a9–110b4

523. There are four abodes for human souls in the world of process, while on Earth: the three discussed above and the one in Tartarus. Each of these is bounded by its specific element, one of the four: the first by ether, the second by air, the third by water, the fourth by earth itself; those in Tartarus dwell in a kind of cave. From a different point of view, again, there are three levels, one on the heights, one under the earth, one in between, which can be distributed among the three sons of Kronos.

524. [109b8–c1] Plato follows Homer in using the word 'heaven' for the ether, in which shooting stars appear; a heaven subject to process has also stars subject to process. It is by this heaven that the Earth is surrounded, not immediately by the ungenerated heaven. Perhaps it is this mortal heaven also that is the counterpart of earth, with its character of mortality, for generated earth can scarcely be on a par with ungenerated heaven; and perhaps, when Earth is called 'the most venerable Deity within heaven' [*Tim.* 40c3], this heaven is meant.

525. [110b1] Why do we enjoy stories? – Because we have innate notions that are pictures of reality. Or else, because our chosen level of life is dominated by generation and imagination, we have a preference for fictions.

You could also say that stories are a kind of casual and playful earnestness; and the reason why we like play is that we want to have pleasure without pains, in other words, illusory pleasure.

526. [110b1–2] Why this mixture of cosmography and mythology? – To point beyond physical science to a more divine reality, which has a more rightful claim to be the home of souls.

---

§ 523. The four levels are reduced to three, because the bottom of the sea (used as an illustrative parallel by Pl.) is nowhere mentioned as an abode of human souls.

6. τοῖς τρισὶ Κρονίδαις : see note on II § 131.

§ 524. 1–3. Homer, *Il.* 15.192; cf. Eustath., *Od.* 1550.5. – Pr., *Tim.* I 272.17–25 καὶ γὰρ δὴ καὶ αὐτὸ τοῦτο ἰστέον, ὅτι τὰ ὀνόματα ταῦτα πολλὴν ἔσχε παρὰ τοῖς παλαιοῖς ἀμφιβολίαν, τῶν μὲν τὸ ὑπὸ σελήνην μόνον κόσμον καλούντων, τὸ δὲ ὑπὲρ αὐτὴν οὐρανόν, τῶν δὲ τὸν οὐρανὸν μέρος τοῦ κόσμου λεγόντων, καὶ τῶν μὲν ἄχρι σελήνης αὐτὸν ὁριζόντων, τῶν δὲ καὶ τὰ ἄκρα τῆς γενέσεως οὐρανὸν προσειπόντων· 'Ζεὺς δ' ἔλαχ' οὐρανὸν εὐρὺν

§§ 523-526. The four (three) levels. 109a9-110b4

νη'. - "Ότι τέσσαρές εἰσιν αἱ οἰκήσεις τῶν ἐν τῇ γενέσει ψυχῶν ἀνθρωπίνων 523
ἐν γῇ οὐσῶν, αἱ προειρημέναι τρεῖς καὶ ἡ ὑπὸ τῷ Ταρτάρῳ. ἑκάστη δὲ περιέχεται
ὑπὸ ἰδίου στοιχείου τινὸς τῶν τεσσάρων, ἡ μὲν πρώτη ὑπὸ τοῦ αἰθέρος, ἡ δὲ
δευτέρα τοῦ ἀέρος, ἡ δὲ τρίτη τοῦ ὕδατος, ἡ δὲ τετάρτη τῆς γῆς αὐτῆς· οἷον
γὰρ ἐν σπηλαίῳ οἱ ἐν τῷ Ταρτάρῳ οἰκοῦσιν. ἄλλως δὲ αὖ πάλιν τρεῖς, ἡ ἐπὶ 5
τῶν ἄκρων καὶ ἡ ὑπὸ γῆν καὶ ἡ μέση, ἃς τοῖς τρισὶ Κρονίδαις συνδιαιρετέον.

νθ'. - [109b8-c1] "Ότι οὐρανὸν λέγει τὸν αἰθέρα Ὁμηρικῶς, ἐν ᾧ τὰ ἄστρα 524
διάττειν πέφυκε· τοῦ γὰρ γενητοῦ οὐρανοῦ καὶ τὰ ἄστρα γενητά. ἐν τούτῳ γὰρ
κεῖται ἡ γῆ, ἀλλ' οὐκ ἐν τῷ ἀγενήτῳ προσεχῶς. καὶ μήποτε τούτῳ συντάττεται
ἡ θνητοειδὴς γῆ ὡς θνητῷ· πῶς γὰρ ἡ γενητὴ τῷ ἀγενήτῳ; καὶ μήποτε
'πρεσβυτάτη καὶ θεῶν' εἴρηται 'τῶν ἐντὸς οὐρανοῦ' τοῦ τοιούτου [Tim. 40c3]. 5

ξ'. - [110b1] Διὰ τί χαίρομεν τοῖς μύθοις; — Ἢ ὅτι λόγους ἔχομεν τῶν 525
ὄντων εἰκόνας. ἢ ὅτι φιλογένεσιν ζωὴν προβαλλόμενοι καὶ φαντασιώδη τοῖς
πλάσμασι χαίρομεν.
Εἴποις δὲ ἂν ὅτι καὶ σπουδῇ ῥαθύμῳ καὶ οἷον παιζούσῃ ἐοίκασι· φιλοπαίγμονες
δέ ἐσμεν ὡς χαίρειν βουλόμενοι ἀπονητί, ὅ ἐστιν ἐπὶ εἰδώλοις. 5

ξα'. - [110b1-2] Διὰ τί τῇ φυσιολογίᾳ συμπλέκει τὸν μῦθον; — Ἢ ἵνα 526(199)
τινὰ καὶ ὑπὲρ αὐτὴν ἀλήθειαν ἐνδείξηται θειοτέραν, ἐν ᾗ καὶ ψυχὰς ἱδρύεσθαι
δικαιότερον.

---

§ 523. 6 Κρονίδαις] -αις in ras. M^c

ἐν αἰθέρι καὶ νεφέλῃσι' [Hom., Il. 15.192].
3. συντάττεται: as in the mythical marriage of Heaven and Earth.
4-5. Pr., Tim. III 141.1-143.33, does not refer to this possibility; the idea, therefore, is probably Dam.'s.
§ 525. Dam. II § 130. Pr.'s view of the function of myths is developed at greater length Rep. I 67.10-69.19 (cf. II 108.7-10); Proleg. 13.14-20; Ol., Gorg. 236.21-237.23 (esp. 237.14-21). - The comments by Dam. (lines 4-5; II § 130.6-7) are different in the two versions.
§ 526. Dam. II § 129.8-9: Pl.'s description is an 'account' in so far as it conforms to physical reality, a 'myth' in so far as it points beyond this.

§§ 527–533. The heights of the earth. 110b5–111d2

527. [110b6–7] In what sense is the Earth like 'a ball made of twelve pieces of leather'? — Because the dodecahedron, which Timaeus [55c4–6] uses 'to adorn the universe' (see the commentary on that passage), reaches down as far as the Earth. Secondly, because it has twelve parts corresponding to the irradiations of the Twelve Leading Gods, a subject to be discussed in the *Phaedrus*; this concerns, in the first place, its luminous body, but then, within the limits of the possible, also its high places, since even on our own level certain traces of such influxes are visible. Thirdly, the Earth is the twelfth sphere, and as it undergoes all the influences of the higher spheres, it is natural that it should appear in twelve aspects.

528. [110c1–111b1] The description of the heights of the earth *can* be understood as cosmographical reality: pure colors, limpid beauty of stones, plants filled with a life more divine and made of an ether-like substance, animals enveloped in beautiful, long-lived pneumatic bodies, everything in keeping with the elements as they exist at that level; but, on account of the myth interwoven with it, we are also entitled to think of patterns of life and incorporeal creative principles, and of the patron deities of all this, who are referred to by these same names.

529. [111b3] One wonders why men in that abode should be long-lived. If thanks to their godly lives they are ready to be lifted up to a higher plane, why are they not very soon given a place in heaven itself? — However, even in that region not all are seekers for wisdom; some are 'carried up by Justice' from our abode to that higher one who have 'led a life of habitual virtue without philosophy,' as he puts it elsewhere [*Phaedr.* 249a8; *Rep.* X 619c7–d1]. An alternative answer is that a society must

---

§ 527. Dam. II § 132. For earlier opinions see Norvin 1915, 224, nn. 1–2 (Ps.-Timaeus 98d; Alcin., *did.* 13; Plut., *quaest. Plat.* 5,1). The present section appears to consist entirely of new suggestions by Dam. (see II); line 3 λέγεται refers to his published commentary on the *Timaeus*, line 4 ῥηθήσεται to a forthcoming lecture on the *Phaedrus* (the eighth dialogue in Iamblichus' program, in which the *Phaedo* is the third). Cf. *princ.* 123.2.

2. Pl., *Tim.* 55c4–6 ἔτι δὲ οὔσης συστάσεως μιᾶς πέμπτης, ἐπὶ τὸ πᾶν ὁ θεὸς αὐτῇ κατεχρήσατο ἐκεῖνο διαζωγραφῶν. Pr., *Tim.* I 6.31–7.2 (Ar. follows Pl.) καθόσον ἀγένητον τίθεται τὸν οὐρανὸν καὶ πέμπτης οὐσίας – τί γὰρ διαφέρει πέμπτον στοιχεῖον καλεῖν ἢ πέμπτον κόσμον καὶ σχῆμα πέμπτον, ὡς ὁ Πλάτων ἐκάλεσεν; Cf. *ibid.* I 60.23–27; 63.11; II 208.14–20; III 141.19–24.

3–4. Pl., *Phaedr.* 246e4–247a4. Neither Hermias 136.19–139.25 nor Pr., *theol.* VI 18–22, links the ἡγεμόνες with the δωδεκάσκυτος σφαῖρα of the *Phaedrus*.

4. On the 'luminous body' of the Earth: above § 508.6–7.

6. δωδεκάτη σφαῖρα: Hermias 135.27–28 τινὲς μὲν οὖν τὰς δώδεκα σφαίρας τοῦ κόσμου ἤκουσαν, τὴν ἀπλανῆ, τὰς ἑπτὰ πλανωμένας καὶ τὰ τέσσαρα στοιχεῖα.

§ 528. Dam. II § 135–136.

§§ 527–533. The heights of the earth. 110b5–111d2

ξβ'. — [110b6–7] *Πῶς 'δωδεκασκύτῳ σφαίρᾳ' ἔοικεν;* — Ἡ ὅτι μέχρι αὐτῆς 527
πρόεισι τὸ δωδεκάεδρον, ᾧ 'διαζωγραφεῖ τὸ πᾶν' ὁ Τίμαιος [55c4–6], ὃν ἐκεῖ
λέγεται τρόπον. καὶ ὅτι τῶν δώδεκα ἡγεμόνων ταῖς ἐλλάμψεσι συνδιῄρηται,
περὶ ὧν ἐν Φαίδρῳ ῥηθήσεται, μάλιστα μὲν τὸ αὐγοειδές, ἤδη δὲ ὡς ἐνδέχεται
καὶ τὰ νῶτα αὐτῆς, ὅπου γε καὶ ἐν τοῖς τῇδε τόποις ἴχνη ἄττα τῶν τοιούτων 5
ἀπορροιῶν ἐμφαίνεται. ἔτι δὲ ἐκ τρίτων δωδεκάτη σφαῖρα ἡ γῆ, πασῶν δὲ τὰς
μεθέξεις δεχομένη τῶν πρὸ αὐτῆς εἰκότως δωδεκάμορφος γίγνεται.

ξγ'. — [110c1–111b1] *Ὅτι τὰ ἐπὶ τῶν ἄκρων τῆς γῆς εἶναι λεγόμενα ἔστι* 528
μὲν καὶ φυσικῶς ἀκούειν, ἀκραιφνῆ χρώματα καὶ λίθων κάλλη ἀκήρατα καὶ
φυτὰ ζωῆς ἀνάμεστα θειοτέρας αἰθερώδη τὴν σύστασιν ἔχοντα καὶ ζῷα
πνευματικοῖς χιτῶσι κεκοσμημένα μακραίωσιν καὶ πάντα ἀνάλογον τοῖς ἐκεῖ
στοιχείοις· ἔστι δὲ καὶ κατὰ τὸν ἐγκεκραμένον μῦθον τὰς ζωὰς ἐννοεῖν καὶ τοὺς 5
λόγους τοὺς ἀσωμάτους καὶ τοὺς τούτων ἁπάντων ἐφόρους τοῖς ὀνόμασι τούτοις
δηλουμένους.

ξδ'. — [111b3] *Πῶς οἱ ἐκεῖ μακραίωνες, ἀπορήσειεν ἄν τις. εἰ γὰρ ἕτοιμοι* 529
πρὸς ἀναγωγὴν διὰ τὸ θεοπρεπὲς τῆς ζωῆς, πῶς οὐ τάχιστα καὶ εἰς οὐρανὸν
ἀνατάττονται; — Ἢ οὐ πάντες φιλοσοφοῦσιν οὐδὲ ἐκεῖ· 'κουφίζονται' γὰρ
ἐντεῦθεν ἐκεῖ 'ὑπὸ τῆς δίκης' 'ἔθει ἄνευ φιλοσοφίας βεβιωκότες', ὡς ἐν ἄλλοις
φησίν [Phaedr. 249a8; Rep. X 619c7–d1]. ᾗ καὶ τὴν ἐκεῖ πολιτείαν συνεστάναι 5

---

4. πνευματικοῖς χιτῶσι: cf. I § 168.6–7 note. Also Pr., *Tim.* III 309.26–30 ὅτι
δὲ καὶ ἄλλον οἶδεν ἄνθρωπον τὴν ψυχὴν τὴν τῷ μέσῳ χρωμένην ὀχήματι, ἐκ τοῦ Φαίδωνος
(scil. ληπτέον), ὅπου φησὶν ἐπ' ἄκρας τῆς γῆς οἰκεῖν ἀνθρώπους πολυχρονιωτέρους τῶν
τῇδε ἀνθρώπων.
ibid. μακραίωσιν: the word is from Pl., *Epin.* 982a2 (the celestial bodies are
either immortal and divine) ἤ τινα μακραίωνα βίον ἔχειν (cf. Cornutus 17, p. 29.9,
also of stars). Pr., *Rep.* II 15.20–16.2 ὅτι γὰρ καὶ ἄλλα ἐστὶν θνητὰ πρὸ ἡμῶν, δῆλον·
οὐ γὰρ ἀπὸ τῶν ἀιδίων καὶ λογικῶν εἰς τὸ ἀσθενὲς τοῦτο ζῷον καὶ βραχύβιον ἀμέσως
ἡ δημιουργία προῆλθεν, ἀλλ' ἔστι καὶ ἄλλα γένη μακραίωνα ἐγγὺς θεῶν οἰκοῦντα (what
follows is damaged; sense: men may rise to this level). Similarly *Tim.* III 280.22–29.
The kind superior to ours are the long-living nymphs of Dav. 15.21–26; 24.10–17
(cf. Plut., *def. orac.* 11, 415C–F).
5–7. This part of the interpretation approaches those of Democritus and
Plutarch (§ 503).
§ 529. 3. ἀνατάσσεσθαι as a technical term for attaining a higher rank in the
cosmos: Pr., *Tim.* I 53.29–31 οὐκ ἔστιν οὖν τὸ δαιμόνιον γένος τὸ ἀνατασσόμενον ἢ
κατατασσόμενον. Ibid. 185.29–31 τὰ δὲ ποτὲ μὲν ὑπὸ τοῖς ὑλαίοις γένεσι γίνεται, ποτὲ
δὲ εἰς χωριστὴν ἀνατάσσεται ζωήν.

continue to exist on that plane, too, and this is another duty to be fulfilled by souls, just as some souls in spite of their immaculate state have to perform the same task here below.

It should further be observed that of necessity periods spent by souls at higher levels are proportionately longer, and the time spent in the intelligible world is the longest of all.

530. If they are long-lived, their vestures are perishable; if so, there must be effluence of a kind; and if so, there must be need of food. This food is provided by the fruits of that region, fruits intermediate in character between those here below and the heavenly ones which the Hesperides proffer to those who have come to the end of their journey through the world of coming-to-be. That there must be a whole race of human beings who are nourished in this way, can be inferred from the case of the man who lived on sunbeams only, as recorded by Aristotle from his own observation [frg. 42 R.³].

531. [111b3] Why does the text attribute only these two senses to them? — In the commentator's opinion, because the celestial bodies also possess only these.

However, as regards the celestial bodies we have argued elsewhere that these are not their only senses; here, with reference to long-lived human beings, we can add that, if tangible matter (earth) is found in their world, there is no reason why the corresponding sense, touch, should not exist there as well; if there is food, there must be taste; if there is earth rarefied and evaporated by the fire at those heights, they will necessarily have smell.

532. [111b7] Since Plato states that there are Gods living on the Earth and even calls the Earth itself 'the most venerable of the Gods' [*Tim.* 40c3], the *Epinomis* cannot be a genuine work of Plato, with its doctrine that the Gods exist only in heaven [983c6–987d2].

---

7. ἀχράντων: see note on II § 6.
§ 530. 4. οὓς αἱ Ἑσπερίδες ὀρέγουσι τοῖς εἰς πέρας ἐλθοῦσι τῆς ὅλης γενέσεως. The symbolism is Pr.'s, cf. *Rep.* I 120.12–14 ὁ μὲν γὰρ Ἡρακλῆς διὰ τελεστικῆς καθηράμενος καὶ τῶν ἀχράντων καρπῶν μετασχὼν τελέας ἔτυχεν τῆς εἰς θεοὺς ἀποκαταστάσεως (ἀχράντων is substituted as equivalent to χρυσῶν, cf. Pr., *Rep.* II 75.17; *Hes.* 50.3–5; 61.16–17; Ol., *Gorg.* 268.1–3). Cf. Porph. ap. Eusb. *PE*. III, 7.2 (p. 123. 13) ὅτι χρυσὸς οὐ μιαίνεται. Pr.'s source is Hes., *theog.* 215–216, not *Orphica* frg. 34, where the apples of the Hesperides are mentioned among the toys of the young Dionysus, when he is murdered, which would lead to the opposite interpretation; apparently these lines were not incorporated in the epic known to the Neoplatonists.
5–7. Dam. II § 138. Ar., frg. 42 R.³ (Eudemus) = Περὶ φιλοσοφίας frg. 23 Walzer, Ross.
§ 531. On the related subject of the senses of the visible Gods and of souls in heaven cf. Ol. 4 §§ 9–10 and *supra* §§ 83–86.
3. ἐν ἄλλοις: possibly in Dam.'s commentary on the *Tim.* (33c1–4), where Pr. too deals with the question (II 81.12–85.31).
§ 532. On Pr.'s rejection of the *Epinomis* see A. E. Taylor, *On the Authenticity*

δεῖ καὶ τὰς ψυχὰς λειτουργεῖν καὶ ἐκείνην τὴν λειτουργίαν, ὡς καὶ ταύτην ἔνιαι τῶν ἀχράντων ὅμως.

Ἐπιστῆσαι δὲ χρὴ ὡς ἀνάλογον αἱ ἀνωτέρω διαγωγαὶ τῶν ψυχῶν πολυχρονιώτεραι πάντως εἰσὶ καὶ ἥ γε ἐν τῷ νοητῷ πολυχρονιωτάτη.

ξε'. – "Ὅτι εἰ μακραίωνες, φθαρτοὶ αὐτῶν οἱ χιτῶνες· εἰ δὲ τοῦτο, καὶ 530 ἀπορροή τις αὐτῶν ἐστιν· εἰ δὲ τοῦτο, καὶ χρεία | τροφῆς. ταύτην οὖν οἱ ἐκεῖ (200) παρέχονται καρποί, μέσοι ὄντες τὴν φύσιν τῶν τε ἐνθάδε καὶ τῶν οὐρανίων, οὓς αἱ Ἑσπερίδες ὀρέγουσι τοῖς εἰς πέρας ἐλθοῦσι τῆς ὅλης γενέσεως. ὅτι δὲ δεῖ τι καὶ ὅλον γένος ἀνθρώπων εἶναι οὕτω τρεφόμενον, δηλοῖ [δὲ] καὶ ὁ τῇδε 5 ταῖς ἡλιακαῖς ἀκτῖσιν μόναις τρεφόμενος, ὃν ἱστόρησεν Ἀριστοτέλης ἰδὼν αὐτός [frg. 42 R.³].

ξϛ'. – [111b3] Διὰ τί μόνας τὰς δύο αἰσθήσεις αὐτοῖς ὁ λόγος παρέσχετο; 531 – Ἢ ὅτι, φησί, καὶ τοῖς οὐρανίοις αὗται μόναι ἔνεισιν.

Ἀλλὰ περὶ μὲν τῶν οὐρανίων ἐν ἄλλοις ἐπεστήσαμεν ὅτι μὴ μόναι· νῦν δὲ περὶ τῶν μακραιώνων ἀνθρώπων, ὡς, εἴπερ ἐστὶ παρ' αὐτοῖς τὸ ἁπτόν, ἡ γῆ, πῶς οὐκ ἂν εἴη καὶ τὸ σύστοιχον ἁπτικόν; εἰ δὲ καὶ τροφή, πῶς οὐκ ἂν εἴη 5 καὶ γεῦσις; εἰ δὲ καὶ γῆ λεπτυνομένη ὑπὸ τοῦ ἐκεῖ πυρὸς καὶ θυμιωμένη, πῶς οὐχὶ καὶ ὀσφραίνοιντο;

ξζ'. – [111b7] Ὅτι εἰ θεοὺς οἰκητὰς εἶναί φησιν ἐπὶ τῆς γῆς καὶ ὅλως 532 αὐτὴν τὴν γῆν 'θεῶν πρεσβυτάτην' [Tim. 40c3], οὐκ ἂν εἴη γνησία τοῦ Πλάτωνος ἡ Ἐπινομίς, ἐν ᾗ λέγονται κατ' οὐρανὸν εἶναι μόνον οἱ θεοί [983c6–987d2].

---

§ 530. 5 δὲ M: del. μ
§ 531. 5 ἁπτικόν] ἁ- ex corr. Mᶜ (fort. ὀπτικόν M¹)
§ 532. 1 οἰκητὰς] -ητ- ex corr. Mᶜ

---

of Plato's "Epinomis," Logos (Florence) 4, 1921, 42–55. The reasons given differ in each case: (1) Proleg. 25: (a) the incomplete condition of the Laws, (b) the passage 987b5–6, where the planets are said to move from left to right; (2) Rep. II 133.27–134.6: general impression of spuriousness and mystery-mongering (ἀλλ' ἡ μὲν Ἐπινομὶς νοθείας ὑπάρχουσα μεστὴ καὶ νοῦ μυστηριώδους τὸν νηπιόφρονα καὶ νῷ ἀρχαῖον ἀπατᾷ); (3) here: whereas Pl. knows also terrestrial deities, the Epinomis acknowledges Gods in heaven only. The matter is further mentioned without comment prov. 50.11–14 and Eucl. 42.12; there is a probable allusion to it theol. I 5, 23.17–21 S.-W., where Pr. says that the theological dialogues which he is going to list can serve as a standard to decide the authenticity of other work attributed to Pl., a point which for Pr. arises only in the case of the Epin. The main objection, rather than the points of detail specified in the Proleg., would then be its theology and demonology (as already indicated in the Ph. commentary). However, Neoplatonic exegesis has taken higher hurdles than this in its stride, and the truth might well be that the Epinomis fell a victim to Pr.'s classification of the dialogues (32, or, including Rep. and Laws, 54), no doubt on the basis of some numerological subtleties (Proleg. 26.5–12 gives no particulars).

533. [111c4–d3] Going down from the summits to the middle regions of the earth, the description distinguishes four kinds of hollows: deep and narrow, wide across and shallow, shallow and narrow, deep and wide. But we can also explain them as patterns of life, grouped on similar lines: the shallow places can be thought of as life detached from matter, the deep ones as matter-bound life, and the universal forms of life can be set down as wide, the particular forms as narrow.

§§ 534–542. The depths of the earth. 111d2–113c8

534. [111d2–e2] There is fire in the depth of the earth to relieve its extreme coldness, water to smoothen its dryness, air to lend its inertness a certain mobility by a gaseous admixture. In short, since everything is in everything according to its own nature, the other elements must be in earth in a way characteristic of earth.

535. [111d7] What is the so-called 'fortress of Zeus'? It is the inextinguishable fire round the center, which radiates an equal warmth to all parts of the earth.

Or it might be better to identify it with the animating force which, according to Timaeus [36e2–5], originating in the center, pervades the universe, and at the same time with the firm guard kept around the center by the cosmic Intelligence and the cosmic God.

536. As an image of the center of the world, cities used to burn in their city halls the perpetual fire sacred to Hestia.

---

§ 533. Dam. II § 139. The *Ph.* text, reduced to terms of deep / shallow and wide / narrow, only has: (1) deeper / wider than our world; (2) deeper / narrower; (3) shallower / wider. If, as the commentator obviously does, we neglect the comparatives, our world would by elimination be shallow and narrow, though Dam. II makes it narrow and deep. This is more probably a confusion in the commentary than a variant in the Pl. MSS. (βραχυτέρους for βαθυτέρους at c7–8 does not occur in the extant MSS.).

§ 534. 1–2. ἵνα τὸ κατεψυγμένον αὐτῆς ἀναθάλπῃ : Simpl., cael. 512.11–12 (cited below at § 535) uses the same phrase, τὸ ἀπεψυγμένον αὐτῆς ἀναθάλπουσαν, but explains the fire, with Dam., as creative power. Cf. also Pr., *Tim.* II 49.8–9 δεῖται [ἡ γῆ] τοῦ ἀναζωπυροῦντος καὶ ἀναθάλποντος αὐτὴν θερμοῦ.

3. εἰ πάντα ἐν πᾶσιν οἰκείως : Pr., *elem.* 103 (and Dodds p. 254).

§ 535. The fire inside the Earth (111d7) leads to a discussion of the Central Fire of the Pythagoreans, which the Neoplatonists, harmonizing it with their own geocentric cosmography, placed in the center of the Earth. Their source was Ar., *cael.* II 13, 293a18–23 : . . . τῶν πλείστων ἐπὶ τοῦ μέσου κεῖσθαι λεγόντων, . . . ἐναντίως οἱ περὶ τὴν Ἰταλίαν, καλούμενοι δὲ Πυθαγόρειοι λέγουσιν· ἐπὶ μὲν γὰρ τοῦ μέσου πῦρ εἶναί φασι, τὴν δὲ γῆν, ἓν τῶν ἄστρων οὖσαν, κύκλῳ φερομένην περὶ τὸ μέσον νύκτα τε καὶ ἡμέραν ποιεῖν. Ibid. 293b1–4 ἔτι δ' οἱ γε Πυθαγόρειοι καὶ διὰ τὸ μάλιστα προσήκειν φυλάττεσθαι τὸ κυριώτατον τοῦ παντός – τὸ δὲ μέσον εἶναι τοιοῦτον, ὃ Διὸς φυλακὴν ὀνομάζουσι τὸ ταύτην ἔχον τὴν χώραν πῦρ. Simpl., *cael.* 512.9–14 καὶ οὕτω μὲν αὐτὸς

ξη'. – [111c4–d2] Ὅτι ἀπὸ τῶν ἄκρων εἰς τὰ μέσα αὐτῆς καταβὰς ὁ λόγος 533 τετραχῇ διεῖλε τὰς κοίλας οἰκήσεις· τὰς μὲν γὰρ εἶναι βαθείας τε καὶ στενάς, τὰς δὲ κατὰ διάμετρον εὐρείας τε καὶ ἐπιπολαίους, τὰς δὲ ἐπιπολαίους τε καὶ στενάς, τὰς δὲ βαθείας τε καὶ εὐρείας. δέξαιτο δὲ ἄν τις καὶ ζωὰς οὕτω διῃρημένας, τὰς μὲν ἐπιπολαίους ὡς χωριστὰς ἐννοῶν, τὰς δὲ βαθείας ὡς 5 ἀχωρίστους, καὶ τὰς μὲν ὁλικὰς ὡς εὐρείας, τὰς δὲ μερικὰς ὡς στενὰς ἀπολογιζόμενος.

§§ 534–542. The depths of the earth. 111d2–113c8

δ ξθ'. – [111d2–e2] Ὅτι πῦρ μὲν ἔνεστι τῷ βάθει τῆς γῆς ἵνα τὸ κατεψυγμένον 534 αὐτῆς ἀναθάλπῃ, ὕδωρ δὲ ἵνα τὸ ξηρὸν πιαίνῃ, ἀὴρ δὲ ἵνα τὸ δυσκίνητον παρέχηταί πως εὐκίνητον διὰ πνεύματος. ὅλως δέ, εἰ πάντα ἐν πᾶσιν οἰκείως, καὶ ἐν γῇ τὰ ἄλλα χθονίως.

ο'. – [111d7] Τίς ὁ ʽΖανὸς' λεγόμενος ʽπύργος'; — Ἢ τὸ πῦρ ὅ ἐστι περὶ 535(201) τὸ κέντρον, ἄσβεστον, ἐξ ἴσου πανταχοῦ διαπέμπον τῆς γῆς τὴν ἀνάθαλψιν.

Μήποτε δὲ ἄμεινον λέγειν τὴν ἐκ μέσου πρὸς τὸ πᾶν ἐγειρομένην κατὰ τὸν Τίμαιον [36e2–5] ψύχωσιν, ὁμοίως δὲ καὶ τὴν τοῦ νοῦ καὶ τὴν τοῦ θεοῦ τοῦ κοσμικοῦ περὶ τὸ μέσον ἱδρυμένην φυλακὴν ἀκίνητον. 5

οα'. – Ὅτι κατὰ μίμησιν τοῦ κέντρου τῆς γῆς καὶ τὸ ἐν τῷ πρυτανείῳ πῦρ 536 ἄσβεστον τῇ Ἑστίᾳ καθιέρουν αἱ πόλεις.

---

§ 534. 2 αὐτῆς] αὐτ- in ras. 4 litt. M^c
§ 535. 5 περὶ Wk: περιφορὰν M

τὰ τῶν Πυθαγορείων ἀπεδέξατο· οἱ δὲ γνησιώτερον αὐτῶν μετασχόντες πῦρ μὲν ἐν τῷ μέσῳ λέγουσι τὴν δημιουργικὴν δύναμιν τὴν ἐκ μέσου πᾶσαν τὴν γῆν ζωογονοῦσαν καὶ τὸ ἀπεψυγμένον αὐτῆς ἀναθάλπουσαν· διὸ οἱ μὲν Ζηνὸς πύργον αὐτὸ καλοῦσιν, ὡς αὐτὸς ἐν τοῖς Πυθαγορικοῖς ἱστόρησεν [frg. 204 R.³], οἱ δὲ Διὸς φυλακήν, ὡς ἐν τούτοις, οἱ δὲ Διὸς θρόνον, ὡς ἄλλοι φασίν. Id., phys. 1355.5–9 (the efficient cause being everywhere and nowhere, Ar. can situate it in the sky, the Pythagoreans in the center) ἐκεῖνοι μὲν τὸ κέντρον ἐπιτηδειότερον τῶν ἄλλων τοῦ παντὸς μερῶν νομίζουσι πρὸς μέθεξιν τῆς τοῦ δημιουργοῦ συνοχικῆς καὶ ἑδραστικῆς ἀγαθότητος ... καὶ διὰ τοῦτο οἱ μὲν Πυθαγόρειοι Ἑστίας τόπον καὶ Ζανὸς πύργον ἐκάλουν τὸ κέντρον. Pr., Tim. I 198.30–199.4 ἔστι δὲ καὶ τοῦτο τῆς ὅλης δημιουργίας σύμβολον ἐναργές, τὸ ἄκρον ἅμα καὶ μέσον· καὶ γὰρ ἐξῄρηται πάντων τῶν ἐγκοσμίων καὶ πᾶσιν ἐξ ἴσου πάρεστι, τά τε ἄκρα τοῦ παντὸς ἀνεῖται τῷ δημιουργῷ καὶ τὸ μέσον, ὡς ὁ τῶν Πυθαγορείων λόγος· ἐκεῖ γὰρ ὁ Ζανὸς πύργος, ὥς φασι. II 106.16–23 ἐκεῖθεν γὰρ ἡ ὅλη διακυβερνᾶται σφαῖρα καὶ πρὸς ἐκεῖνο συννένευκεν, ἔτι δὲ καὶ διὰ μὴν τὸ ταραχῶδες ἐν τῷ κόσμῳ συνέωσται περὶ τὸ μέσον καὶ δεῖται φρουρᾶς θείας τάττειν αὐτὸ δυναμένης καὶ κατέχειν ἐν τοῖς οἰκείοις ὅροις, διὸ ... καὶ οἱ Πυθαγόρειοι ... Ζανὸς πύργον ἢ Ζανὸς φυλακὴν ἀπεκάλουν τὸ μέσον. III 141.11–13 διὸ καὶ οἱ Πυθαγόρειοι Ζανὸς πύργον ἐκάλουν τὸ κέντρον, ὡς δημιουργικῆς φρουρᾶς ἐν ἐκείνῳ τεταγμένης. Cf. ibid. 143.24–27; Eucl. 90.14–20. – The quotations from Pr. show that the alternative proposed at lines 3–5 can be his as well as Dam.'s.

§ 536. Pindar, Nem. 11.1 Παῖ Ῥέας, ἅ τε πρυτανεῖα λέλογχας, Ἑστία, with schol. III 185.21–24 Drachmann.

537. [111e6–112e5] Tartarus is a God in charge of the lowest extremity of the world, as Pontus is of its middle regions, and Olympus of its highest ranges. We find these three Gods, indeed, not only in this sensible world, but also in the creative Intelligence and in the order of Kronos and that of Uranus.

538. Why are the Titans said to be 'under Tartarus' [*Il.* 14.278]? — Because they are the Tartarean Gods of the sensible world, but subordinate to the higher Tartarean deities.

It is preferable to apply the term to those dwelling at the very bottom of Tartarus, which is vast; its deepest part is designated as 'under Tartarus,' just as 'under the earth' means in the interior of the earth.

539. Who are the children of Tartarus and Earth? — Typhon causes all violent motion, of subterranean air currents and waters, and of the other elements; Echidna is an avenging force, chastising rational and irrational souls, hence the upper part of her body is a maiden's, the lower part is serpentlike; Python is the guardian deity of all divinatory springs and fumes.

Rather, we should consider him the cause of disorder and obstruction in this matter; therefore he is slain by Apollo, whose adversary he is.

---

§§ 537–542. On the subject of Tartarus, Pr., *Rep.* II 183.16–25, cites his own commentary on the myth of the *Ph.*: τοιοῦτος γὰρ ὁ Τάρταρος, χῶρος ὢν πάσης ἀτάκτου καὶ σκοτεινῆς ὕλης, εἰς ὃν συρρεῖ τὰ ἔσχατα τῶν κοσμικῶν στοιχείων, πρὸς δὲ τὸν Ὄλυμπον ἀντίθετος. ὁ μὲν γὰρ ὁλολαμπής, πάντα περιέχων, ὑψηλότατος· ὁ δὲ σκοτεινός, κοιλότατος τόπος ὑπὸ πάντων περιεχόμενος· διὸ καὶ ἡ ποίησις βαθύτατον αὐτὸν εἶναί φησιν βέρεθρον ὑπὸ χθονός [*Il.* 8.13–14=*Ph.* 112a3]. πολλῶν δὲ ἡμῖν περὶ αὐτοῦ ῥηθέντων ἐν τοῖς εἰς τὴν νέκυιαν τοῦ Φαίδωνος ἀπ' ἐκείνων μὲν τὰ δοκοῦντα τοῖς θεολόγοις περὶ αὐτοῦ ληπτέον. This confirms that the testimonia from the "theologians" (Homer, Hesiod, Orpheus), here and in II §§ 140–145, come from Pr.'s commentary. — Lewy 378, n. 259, wrongly construes the words χῶρος ὢν πάσης ἀτάκτου καὶ σκοτεινῆς ὕλης as identifying Tartarus with matter; this does not agree with the definition at § 537 nor with the view of Tartarus as a real place.

§ 537. Dam. II § 140. Tartarus as a deity, father of Typhoeus, Hes., *theog.* 821–822. Pontus, also a deity, son of Gaia, *ibid.* 131–132, father of Nereus and others, *ibid.* 233–239; cf. *Orphica* frg. 117 (=Pr., *Tim.* III 186.7–30). Olympus as a divine hypostasis could be an invention *ad hoc*; as the counterpart of Tartarus see the preceding note, as a "place" transcending the heavens (empyrean) see note on § 497.3. — In transferring this triad from the visible world to other levels of reality, Pr. makes Olympus the summit of each triad, Pontus (=Poseidon=genesis) the middle, characterized by procession, and Tartarus the lower margin, marked by reversion. In the case of the creative Intelligence, the triad is to be found in the three sons of Kronos, who represent a lower, divided aspect of the one Creator Zeus (II § 131); in the order of Kronos, in the triad Kronos-Rhea-Zeus (Pr., *theol.* V 3, 252.38–253.36); in the order of Uranus, in the triad ὑπερουράνιος τόπος-οὐρανός-ὑπουράνιος ἁψίς (*theol.* IV 5–7). In each, the lowest stratum can be called Tartarus; cf. II § 140, where this idea is related to mythical events.

§ 538. Dealing with Tartarus in Homer, Pr. explained the word ὑποταρτάριοι

οβ'. – [111e6–112a5] Ὅτι ὁ Τάρταρος θεός ἐστι τὰς ἐσχατιὰς τοῦ κόσμου 537
ἐπισκοπῶν, ὡς ὁ Πόντος τὰς μεσότητας, ὡς ὁ Ὄλυμπος τὰς ἀκρότητας. ἔστι
γοῦν ⟨τοὺς⟩ τρεῖς εὑρεῖν οὐκ ἐν τῷ αἰσθητῷ μόνῳ τῷδε κόσμῳ, ἀλλὰ καὶ ἐν τῷ
δημιουργικῷ νῷ καὶ ἐν τῷ Κρονίῳ διακόσμῳ καὶ ἐν τῷ Οὐρανίῳ.

ογ'. – Πῶς 'ὑποταρτάριοι' λέγονται οἱ Τιτῆνες [Hom. Ξ 278]; — Ἢ ὡς 538
Ταρτάριοι μὲν ἐν τῷ αἰσθητῷ, ὑπὸ δὲ τοὺς ἀνωτέρω Ταρταρίους.

Ἄμεινον δὲ τοὺς ἐν αὐτῷ τῷ πυθμένι τοῦ Ταρτάρου καθιδρυμένους πολλοῦ
ὄντος· τὸ γὰρ ἔσχατον τοῦ Ταρτάρου ὑπὸ τὸν Τάρταρον, ὡς τὸ ὑπόγειον τῆς γῆς.

οδ'. – Τίνες οἱ ἀπὸ Ταρτάρου καὶ Γῆς; — Ὁ μὲν Τυφῶν τῆς παντοίας 539
τῶν ὑπογείων πνευμάτων καὶ ὑδάτων καὶ τῶν ἄλλων στοιχείων βιαίου κινήσεως
αἴτιος· ἡ δὲ Ἔχιδνα τιμωρὸς αἰτία καὶ κολαστικὴ λογικῶν τε καὶ ἀλόγων ψυχῶν,
διὸ τὰ μὲν ἄνω παρθένος, τὰ δὲ κάτω ἐστὶν ὀφεώδης· ὁ δὲ Πύθων φρουρὸς
τῆς μαντικῆς ὅλης ἀναδόσεως. 5
Ἄμεινον δὲ τῆς περὶ ταῦτα ἀταξίας τε καὶ ἀντιφράξεως αἴτιον λέγειν· διὸ
καὶ Ἀπόλλων αὐτὸν ἀναιρεῖ ἐναντιούμενον.

---

§ 537. 3 τοὺς Wk: om. M

(Il. 14.278–279 θεοὺς δ' ὀνόμηνεν ἅπαντας, τοὺς ὑποταρταρίους, οἳ Τιτῆνες καλέονται)
as the Gods of the lower, i.e. visible, Tartarus, in contradistinction from the higher
phases of Tartarus (§ 537). At Tim. III 143.27–33, he tries a different interpretation:
"enveloping (by their power even) Tartarus". Ol., Alc. 19.14–17 uses it as synonymous
with ὑποχθόνιοι. Dam., lines 3–4: "those in the depths of Tartarus".

§ 539. Dam. II § 142. There is no extant text linking these three children of
Tartarus and Earth. They form a "sort of Chaldean triad" (II § 142.2), which
Pr. may have pieced together from stray materials. However, we do not know
the source of his information on Python, so it remains possible that he found the
three mentioned jointly, either in the Orphica, or in a minor epic (e.g. Pisander),
or in a mythological manual.

1–3. Typhoeus: Hes., theog. 820–822 αὐτὰρ ἐπεὶ Τιτῆνας ἀπ' οὐρανοῦ ἐξέλασεν Ζεύς,
ὁπλότατον τέκε παῖδα Τυφωέα Γαῖα πελώρη Ταρτάρου ἐν φιλότητι διὰ χρυσέην Ἀφροδίτην.
Ibid. 306–332 children of Typhon and Echidna: Orthus (Geryones' dog), Cerberus,
Hydra, Chimaera; of Orthus and Echidna: Sphinx, Nemean lion. Ibid. 869–880
Typhoeus father of all the winds, except the beneficial ones, Notus, Boreas and
Zephyrus. Hermias 31.16–27 ... ὁ θεὸς οὗτος ἐπάρχει τοῦ πλημμελοῦς καὶ ἀτάκτου ...·
ἔνθα δὴ καὶ εἰώθασι λέγειν "Τυφώνια πνεύματα" ἢ "σκηπτοὺς ἢ κεραυνοὺς Τυφωνίους".

3–4. Echidna: according to Hes., theog. 295–305, daughter of Chrysaor and
Callirrhoe, or of Phorcys and Ceto (depending on whether the "she" refers back
to 287 or 270), half-maiden, half-snake, immortal, living in a cave in the land of
the Arimi (where Homer, Il. 2.783, locates Typhoeus). Apollodorus II 4, however,
makes her a daughter of Tartarus and Earth, killed by Argus. Children of Typhon
and Echidna, according to Apollodorus: Chimaera (II 31), Orthus and the dragon
of the Hesperides (II 113), Prometheus' eagle (II 119), the Sphinx (III 52).

4–7. Python: son of Earth according to Eurip., Iph. T. 1245–1247 ποικιλόνωτος
οἰνωπὸς δράκων ... Γᾶς πελώριον τέρας (no name). Hyginus 140 "Python Terrae
filius draco ingens." I have found no reference to Tartarus as his father.

540. If the sky is said to be the Creator's head, the world of coming-to-be the middle of his body, Tartarus his feet, and if he brings forth Gods from every part of his body [*Orph.* frg. 168], it is evident that there must be also a kind of Tartarean Gods, and then, of course, companions of these Gods, too, and consequently also individual souls and whatever else is found at the extremity of each series. These souls not only can be lifted up to the level of the divine herdsmen of their own kind while still remaining in that part of the world, but they may even spend the whole time of their sojourn in genesis there. The commentator says that there must be also souls in heaven who descend no farther, and therefore we may take it that the same occurs in all other parts of the world; on the other hand, there must also be some that descend deeper and ascend again, passing from level to level, upward from the lower regions, downward from the higher ones, for we know that of souls that came down to this earth many have ascended to heaven. With regard to this whole group we must hold that some descend and ascend to a certain point, others the whole way, for each series as it proceeds strives to fill the entire world.

541. [112e4–113c8] The four rivers here described correspond, according to the tradition of Orpheus, to the four subterranean elements and the four cardinal points in two sets of opposites: the Pyriphlegethon to fire and the east, the Cocytus to earth and the west, the Acheron to air and the south. These are arranged in this way by Orpheus [frg. 123], it is the commentator who associates the Oceanus with water and the north.

542. [111e4–112c1] The cause of the opposite direction of the subterranean rivers, Socrates says, is the 'swing,' i.e. a state of unstable equilibrium; the prior cause is the soul, which makes the earth an animal that breathes in and out; and beyond this there is the demonic and divine cause.

---

§ 540. Dam. II §§ 143–144. As there are Tartarian Gods and demons, are there also Tartarian souls, to whom Tartarus is their natural habitat, rather than a place of punishment ? The question concerns only the depth of the descent and is essentially different from that of eternal damnation, discussed in § 547.

1–3. *Orphica* frg. 168: (10–12) πάντα γὰρ ἐν Ζηνὸς μεγάλου τάδε σώματι κεῖται· τοῦ δή τοι κεφαλὴ μὲν ἰδεῖν καὶ καλὰ πρόσωπα οὐρανὸς αἰγλήεις .... (28–32) μέσση δὲ ζώνη βαρυηχέος οἶδμα θαλάσσης καὶ πόντου· πυμάτη δὲ βάσις, χθονὸς ἔνδοθι ῥίζαι, Τάρταρά τ' εὐρώεντα καὶ ἔσχατα πείρατα γαίης. πάντα δ' ἀποκρύψας αὖθις φάος ἐς πολυγηθὲς μέλλεν ἀπὸ κραδίης προφέρειν πάλι θέσκελα ἔργα. For Pr.'s interpretation of the fragment see *Tim.* I 307.30–31; II 45.5–11; 231.26–28; on the last lines esp. I 207.16–20 καὶ πῶς γὰρ ἄλλως ἔμελλε θεῶν πάντα πληρώσειν ... ἢ πρὸς τὰς ἀφανεῖς αἰτίας τῶν ὅλων ἀνατεινόμενος, ἀφ' ὧν αὐτὸς πεπληρωμένος ἔμελλεν 'ἀπὸ κραδίης προφέρειν πάλι θέσκελα ἔργα'; The sea (frg., lines 28–29) symbolizes genesis, as usual.

3–4. ὀπαδοὶ θεῶν : see *supra* § 477 note.

5. ἀνάγονται εἰς τοὺς οἰκείους ἀγελάρχας : see note Ol. 7 § 4.4.

6. τὴν ὅλην ποιοῦνται γένεσιν : the active in the sense of 'spending (time)' is not unusual, cf. *LSJ* s.v. A7; for the middle cf. the (somewhat different) case with

οε'. – *Ὅτι εἰ τοῦ δημιουργοῦ λέγεται κεφαλὴ μὲν ὁ οὐρανός, μέσα δὲ ἡ* **540**
γένεσις, βάσις δὲ ὁ Τάρταρος, ἀπὸ παντὸς δὲ ἑαυτοῦ προάγει θεούς [Orph.
frg. 168], *εἰκότως ἄρα εἰσὶ καὶ Ταρτάριοι θεοί τινες, καὶ δηλονότι καὶ ὀπαδοὶ
θεῶν, ὥστε καὶ ψυχαὶ μερικαὶ τά* | *τε ἄλλα πέρατα τῶν σειρῶν. αὗται δὲ περὶ* (202)
ταύτην τοῦ κόσμου τὴν μοῖραν καὶ ἀνάγονται εἰς τοὺς οἰκείους ἀγελάρχας καὶ 5
*τὴν ὅλην ποιοῦνται γένεσιν. εἶεν δὲ ἄν, φησίν, καὶ ἐν τῷ οὐρανῷ μέχρι τούτου
ποιούμεναι τὴν ὅλην κάθοδον, δεῖ ἄρα καὶ περὶ ἑκάστην μερίδα τὸ αὐτὸ ποιεῖν·
τινὰς δὲ εἶναι καὶ ἀπ' ἄλλων εἰς ἄλλας ἐπικατιούσας καὶ ἀνιούσας, ἀπὸ μὲν τῶν
κοιλοτέρων ἄνω, ἀπὸ δὲ τῶν ὑπερτέρων κάτω, ἔχομεν γὰρ καὶ τῶν ἐνταῦθα
κατελθουσῶν πολλὰς ἀνελθούσας εἰς οὐρανόν. ἀλλὰ καὶ τούτων θετέον τὰς μὲν* 10
*ἄχρι τινός, τὰς δὲ ἄχρι τοῦ παντὸς κατιούσας τε καὶ ἀνιούσας· ἡ γὰρ πρόοδος
ἑκάστη πληροῦν ἑαυτῆς ἐθέλει πάντα τὸν κόσμον.*

ος'. – [112e4–113c8] *Ὅτι οἱ παραδιδόμενοι τέσσαρες ποταμοὶ κατὰ τὴν* **541**
*Ὀρφέως παράδοσιν τοῖς ὑπογείοις ἀναλογοῦσι δ' στοιχείοις τε καὶ κέντροις
κατὰ δύο ἀντιθέσεις· ὁ μὲν γὰρ Πυριφλεγέθων τῷ πυρὶ καὶ τῇ ἀνατολῇ, ὁ δὲ
Κωκυτὸς τῇ γῇ καὶ τῇ δύσει, ὁ δὲ Ἀχέρων ἀέρι τε καὶ μεσημβρίᾳ. τούτους
μὲν Ὀρφεὺς οὕτω διέταξεν* [frg. 123], *αὐτὸς δὲ τὸν Ὠκεανὸν τῷ ὕδατι καὶ* 5
τῇ ἄρκτῳ προσοικειοῖ.

οζ'. – [111e4–112c1] *Ὅτι τῆς τῶν ὑπογείων ῥευμάτων ἀντιθέσεως αἰτίαν* **542**
*εἶναί φησι τὴν αἰώραν, ἥ ἐστιν ἀντιταλάντωσις· καὶ πρὸ αὐτῆς ἡ ψυχὴ ζῷον
ποιοῦσα τὴν γῆν εἰσπνέον τε καὶ ἐκπνέον· καὶ ἔτι πρὸ ταύτης ἡ δαιμονία καὶ
θεία αἰτία.*

---

§ 540. 5 ταύτην Wk: αὐτὴν M — 8 ἐπικατιούσας] ἐπι- in ras. M^c
§ 541. 1 ὅτι] ὅτ- in ras. M^c
§ 542. 3 ἔτι Wyttenbach: ὅτι M

περιόδους as the direct object, *infra* II § 147.5; Pr., *elem.* 206 (p. 180.25).
 8. ἐπικατιούσας : same sense in Dam., *princ.* 206.23–24 ὅσῳ δὲ ἐπικατιέναι συμβαίνει τὴν πρόοδον.
 9. κοιλοτέρων : above § 7.2, note.
 9–10. Such knowledge can come only from revelation, as in the oracle on Plotinus, Porph., *vit. Plot.* 22 (who, however, is in Elysium).
§ 541. Dam. II § 145. Cf. also I § 497; Pr., *Tim.* II 49.9–21; Lewy 379, n. 259. The actual correspondence between the rivers and the elements in the *Orphica* was probably limited to the name Ἀερία (or the adjective ἀερία?) used of the Acherusian Lake, together with the obvious meaning of Pyriphlegethon (fire). Cocytus as earth is a completely arbitrary identification, which could be considered only after the Oceanus (as water) had been added from *Ph.* 112e7. Similarly, the correspondence with the cardinal points makes sense only once there are four rivers. The entire construction, in spite of lines 4–5, is therefore evidently Pr.'s, and this is confirmed by the wording of Dam.'s criticism in II § 145.
§ 542. The three explanations given are (1) mechanical, (2) physiological, (3) theological.

§§ 543–551. The destiny of the soul. 113d1–114c8

543. [113d5–6] Because they have the power of locomotion and, in some cases, undergo punishment, they will need other vehicles besides the perpetual ones, which are impassive: vehicles that can suffer pain, so that through them they can be punished; this is why Plato represents them as 'mounting vehicles.'

544. [113d6–8] To the region of the Acheron Socrates attributes purifying power. It must be regarded as twofold, corporeal and incorporeal; purifying ceremonies here on earth have the same double power.

545. [113e5] Tartarus is the privation of all that is good; therefore it becomes the abode of those who are guilty of irremediable sins, inasmuch as they have already fallen into their own Tartarus. They are said to 'be thrown,' because they have led a life heavily weighted by matter, moved by external impulses, a life crying out for punishment and driven towards it by fate. But since even the lowest ranges of existence are governed in accordance with Justice, Socrates says that this is 'their due portion.'

546. [113d4–114b6] Sins easy to cure are those committed without a permanent evil disposition; difficult to cure are those which result from a permanent disposition, but one that also resists the deed and after the deed repents; incurable are those that proceed from an evil disposition without repentance. The place destined for the first kind is Acheron and the Acherusian lake, for the second kind Pyriphlegethon and Cocytus, for the third Tartarus.

547. [113e6] Why does it say 'Which they never leave again'? – An answer can be that there is a political motive behind this. But the same explanation could be given for true doctrines, as Theophrastus for instance applies it to the dogma of Providence.

Another view is that they do not leave it for a whole period.

However, this means that it will never happen; for what fails to take

---

§ 543. Dam. II § 146. On the word ὄχημα in Pl. see Dodds p. 315.

2–3. Punishment through the "vehicle": Pr., *Tim.* III 236.27–29; Ol., *Gorg.* 264.31–265.5.

§ 544. Cf. II § 145.12 τὴν καθαρτικὴν [scil. ἰδιότητα] κατὰ τὸν 'Αχέροντα, in a comment by Dam.

§ 545. Taken literally, this definition of Tartarus is irreconcilable with the one at § 537, since no God can be privation of all that is good.

2. τὸν ἑαυτῶν Τάρταρον: the lowest depth of their own being. By the workings of divine justice as described *Laws* X 903e2–905a1, the soul that has descended to its own Tartarus will automatically descend to the cosmic Tartarus also.

3–4. Cf. Dam. II § 147.13–15.

§ 546. The classification is in the main Plato's, who includes repentance as a criterion, but not a lasting disposition.

§ 547. Dam. II § 147. On eternal punishment see also above I § 492; Ol. 10

§§ 543–551. The destiny of the soul. 113d1–114c8

ση'. – [113d5–6] Ὅτι καὶ κατὰ τόπον κινούμεναι καὶ ἔνιαι κολαζόμεναι 543
δέοιντο ἂν ὀχημάτων οὐ μόνον τῶν ἀιδίων (ἀπαθῆ γὰρ ταῦτα), ἀλλὰ καὶ τῶν
ἀλγύνεσθαι πεφυκότων, δι' ὧν κολασθήσονται· ὅθεν εἰς ὀχήματα αὐτὰς ἐμβιβάζει.

οθ'. – [113d6–8] Ὅτι τῷ Ἀχερουσίῳ τόπῳ καθαρτικὴν περιτίθησι δύναμιν. 544
διττὴν δὲ ταύτην ὑποθετέον, σωματικήν τε καὶ ἀσώματον· καὶ γὰρ τῶν τῇδε
καθαρμῶν διττὴ ἡ δύναμις.

π'. – [113e5] Ὅτι ὁ Τάρταρος πάντων ἐστὶ τῶν ἀγαθῶν στέρησις· | διὸ 545(203)
τοὺς ἀνίατα πλημμελοῦντας οὗτος ὑποδέχεται ὡς εἰς τὸν ἑαυτῶν Τάρταρον
ἐκπεσόντας. ῥιπτεῖσθαι δὲ λέγονται ὡς βαρυτάτην ζωὴν ἐζηκότες καὶ ὡς
ἑτεροκίνητον καὶ ὡς ποιναίαν καὶ οὕτως ἐπωθουμένην ὑπὸ τῆς εἱμαρμένης.
ἐπειδὴ δὲ καὶ τὰ ἔσχατα ὅμως κατὰ δίκην διοικεῖται, 'προσήκουσαν' εἶναί φησι 5
'τὴν μοῖραν'.

πα'. – [113d4–114b6] Ὅτι εὐίατα μὲν τὰ ἄνευ πονηρᾶς ἕξεως ἁμαρτανόμενα· 546
δυσίατα δὲ τὰ ἀπὸ ἕξεως μέν, ἀλλὰ καὶ ἀντιτεινούσης πρὸς τὴν ἐνέργειαν καὶ
ἐπὶ τῇ ἐνεργείᾳ μεταμελομένης· ἀνίατα δὲ τὰ ἀπὸ ἕξεως πονηρᾶς καὶ
ἀμεταμελήτου. ταῖς μὲν οὖν πρώταις ἀφώρισται Ἀχέρων καὶ ἡ Ἀχερουσία
λίμνη, ταῖς δὲ β' ὁ Πυριφλεγέθων καὶ Κωκυτός, ταῖς δὲ γ' ὁ Τάρταρος. 5

πβ'. – [113e6] Πῶς εἴρηται 'ὅθεν οὔποτε ἐκβαίνουσιν'; – Ἡ πολιτικῶς. ἀλλ' 547
οὕτω γε καὶ τὰ ἀληθῆ φαίη τις ἄν, ὡς τὸ περὶ προνοίας δόγμα φησὶν ὁ
Θεόφραστος.

Ἡ ὅλην περίοδον οὐκ ἐκβαίνουσιν.

Ἀλλ' οὕτω γε οὐδέποτε· ὁ γὰρ τὴν ὅλην πάρεισιν, πῶς ἂν ἐν τῇ β' ὅλῃ 5

---

§ 546. 2 post μέν] οὐ μὴν πονηρᾶς add. Fh, πονηρᾶς Wyttenbach — 5 β' Wk
(δευτέραις Fh): δύο M | γ' Wk (τρίταις Fh): τρισὶν M

---

§ 14.2–8; Pr., Rep. II 178.1–17; Ol., Gorg. 263.5–264.26. On periodicity see Pr.
elem. 199–200 (and Dodds pp. 301–303).
1–3. II § 147.2–3. Theophrastus' statement that the doctrine of Providence is
a piece of pia fraus, is found neither in the fragments (Wimmer) nor in Regenbogen's
comprehensive survey article in RE, suppl. 7, 1354–1562. The more obvious
possibilities would be the theological or the political writings (RE cols. 1511–1516
and 1516–1521).
4–8. II § 147.4–9. Pr., Rep. II 178.2–8, expresses his opinion as follows, referring
to his own commentaries on the Gorg. and Ph. myths: τοῦτο δὴ τὸ ἐν Γοργίᾳ καὶ
Φαίδωνι λέγων, ὡς ἄρα εἰσὶν ἀνίατοι ψυχαί τινες, οὐκ ἐκβαίνουσαι τῶν δεσμωτηρίων
ἐκείνων οὐδὲ ἀπολυόμεναι τῶν κολάσεων. καὶ ἡμεῖς ἐδείκνυμεν καὶ ἐν τοῖς εἰς ἐκείνους
τοὺς μύθους εἰρημένοις, ὡς ἄρα περίοδον ὅλην τινὰ κολάζων ὁ λόγος τὰς ἀνιάτους ψυχὰς
τοιαῦτα φθέγγεται. Ibid. 179.9–19 τίς δὲ ἡ περίοδος τῶν ἐν τῷ Ταρτάρῳ κολαζομένων
καὶ μὴ ἐκβαινόντων ἐκεῖθεν ... εἴρηται ἡμῖν ἐν τοῖς εἰς τὴν τοῦ Φαίδωνος νέκυιαν· καὶ
ὅτι τοῦ οὐρανοῦ μόνου περίοδος, οὐχὶ παντὸς τοῦ γενητοῦ, οὗ μέρος ἐστὶν καὶ ὁ Τάρταρος

place during a full period cannot possibly take place in the second full period, which is identical with it. Or perhaps we must think of some partial period (even such a period has something divine and there is a 'never' in it), and the question arises what period this is. It must be one with a strong elevating trend, so that it can force upwards even souls such as these.

Another possible meaning of the phrase is that, left to themselves, thy have completely lost the power of helping themselves, an idea expressed also by the word 'leave': eventually they will be *carried* out.

Or perhaps it characterizes the punishment as one without any relief or pause; some others certainly go out at times to return again.

548. How can Iamblichus, on the other hand, maintain that there is a permanent return to the original state? — Here we can give all the corresponding answers: they never descend, either during a certain period of descents which has no compulsive force, or in so far as their own appetitive life does not gravitate towards genesis, or, thirdly, on account of a life pattern that leaves their descent free from the influence of the material world and their contact with the other world unbroken; this is what Iamblichus himself writes in his *Letters*, where he defends his view in the third way mentioned.

καὶ ἡ τῶν εἰς αὐτὸν ῥιφέντων περίοδος· καὶ τίνες οἱ ἐνιαυτοὶ τῶν ἐκβαλλομένων εἰς τοὺς ποταμοὺς καὶ εἰς τὸν Τάρταρον πάλιν ἐμπιπτόντων. καὶ γὰρ τοῦτο ἐκεῖ διήρθρωται, καὶ οὐδὲν δεῖ τὰ αὐτὰ καὶ ἐν τούτοις κατατείνειν. His commentary on the *Gorg.* passage is reflected by Ol., *Gorg.* 264.11–16, who after explaining the notion of συναποκατάστασις of different planets concludes rather vaguely: αἱ οὖν ψυχαὶ τοιαύτας τινὰς περιόδους κολάζονται, then continues: συναποκαθίστανται δὲ καὶ αἱ ζ′ σφαῖραι τῷ ἀπλανεῖ, ἀλλὰ διὰ πολλῶν μυριάδων ἐτῶν· ταύτην οὖν τὴν περίοδον τῆς συναποκαταστάσεως τῶν ζ′ μετὰ τῆς ἀπλανοῦς 'τὸν ἀεὶ χρόνον' εἶπεν. The ἀποκατάστασις of the outer sky must be a precessional period, which, since Ptolemy calculated precession at one degree in a hundred years (Pr., *hyp.* 5,1–10), totals 36,000 years. According to Syrianus (II § 147.4), punishment lasts an entire cosmic period, or simultaneous ἀποκατάστασις of the sky and of each of the planets, which could rightly be called ὁ σύμπας χρόνος (as it actually is by Pr., *elem.* 200, p. 174.12, and *Tim.* II 289.4–29), so that it would justify Plato's οὔποτε at 113e6 and the τὸν ἀεὶ χρόνον of *Gorg.* 525e1. The criticism of lines 5–6 was anticipated by Syrianus himself (Pr., *Tim.* III 278.9–19), who clearly meant to say that descent, sin, punishment and release all took place within the compass of one cosmic period. Proclus (*Rep.* above, and Dam. II § 147.6) limits atonement to a complete revolution of the sky, a position obviously chosen to meet the objection of lines 5–6 and at the same time to find a period comprehensive enough to be qualified as "all time". Dam. (lines 7–8; cf. II § 147.8–9) restricts it even further, and tentatively suggests a full period of the Sun or Saturn, i.e. those of the planet Gods who are most closely associated with return to the transcendent; but at II § 147.9–12 he eventually decides in favor of an individual period adjusted to the measure and the need of each soul. The principle of such an individual period had already been developed by Pr., *elem.* 200; cf. also Hermias 169.10–29.

9–10. II § 147.13–15.

9. ἀπολέσασαι: the MS. has -σάσαις, but the dative can only be explained by assimilation to ἑαυταῖς. Since this is a fresh start, referring back to line 1 ἐκβαίνουσιν

γένοιτο ἂν [ἐν] τῇ αὐτῇ οὔσῃ; ἤ τινα μερικωτέραν νοητέον, καὶ αὕτη γὰρ θεῖόν τι καὶ 'οὐδέποτε'· καὶ τίς αὕτη ζητητέον· ἢ πολὺ τὸ ἀναγωγὸν ἔχουσα, ὥστε καὶ τὰς τοιαύτας ψυχὰς ἀναμοχλεύειν πρὸς τὸ ἄναντες.
Ἡ καὶ ὅσον ἐφ' ἑαυταῖς ἀπολέσασαι τελέως τὸ αὐτοβοήθητον· τοῦτο γὰρ δηλώσει καὶ τὸ 'ἐκβαίνουσιν'· ἐξενεχθήσονται γάρ. 10
Ἴσως δὲ καὶ τὸ εἶδος δηλοῖ τῆς κολάσεως οὐδεμίαν ἐχούσης ἀναπνοὴν οὐδὲ διάλειψιν· ἔνιαι γοῦν ἐξόδους ποιοῦνταί τινας καὶ εἰσόδους.
πγ'. – Πῶς ὁ Ἰάμβλιχος τὸ ἐναντίον φησὶ περὶ τῶν τελέως ἀποκαθισταμένων; 548
—Ἦ τὰ ἀντίστροφα πάντα ἐροῦμεν, οὐδέποτε κατιέναι αὐτάς, ἢ κατά τινα περίοδον καθόδων αἰτίαν οὐκ ἔχουσαν ἀναγκαίαν, ἢ ὅσον γε ἐπὶ τῇ οἰκείᾳ ζωῇ μὴ ῥεπούσῃ πρὸς γένεσιν, ἢ τὸ γ' κατὰ τὸ εἶδος τῆς ζωῆς ἀγένητον ποι|ουμένης τὴν κάθοδον (204) καὶ πρὸς τὰ ἐκεῖ ἀδιάκοπον, ὡς καὶ αὐτὸς ἐν Ἐπιστολαῖς γράφει, ὑπὲρ τοῦ 5 οἰκείου λόγου ἀπολογούμενος τὸν τρίτον ῥηθέντα τρόπον.

---

§ 547. 6 ἐν M: del. Wk | αὕτη Wk: αὐτὴ M — 6–7 θεῖον τί Mᶜ: θειτι M¹ — 7 οὐδέποτε Wk: οὐδεν ποτε M | αὕτη M: αὐτὴ M¹ (?) | ἀνάγωγον M — 9 ἀπολέσασαι Wk: ἀπολεσάσαις M — 12 διάλειψιν Fh: διάληψιν M

(scil. αἱ ψυχαί), the nominative is indicated.
11–12. II § 147.20–21. This explanation, based on comparison with 113e6–114b5, is also given in passing by Pr., Rep. II 179.9–14: τίς δὲ ἡ περίοδος τῶν ἐν τῷ Ταρτάρῳ κολαζομένων καὶ μὴ ἐκβαινόντων ἐκεῖθεν ἕως ἂν δέωνται κολάσεως, ὥσπερ οἱ ἐκβαίνοντες εἰς τοὺς ποταμοὺς παρὰ μέρος εἰς τὸν Τάρταρον ἐκπέμπονται καὶ αὖθις ἐκεῖθεν ἐξίασιν, εἴρηται ἡμῖν κτλ. "... of those who are punished in Tartarus and so long as they need punishment get no reprieve, as the others do who leave it for the rivers and are alternately in and out of Tartarus ...". Kroll's conjecture ὧνπερ for ὥσπερ misses the meaning: the second group is *not* a part of the first.
§ 548. Cf. Ol. 10 § 14.8–10 and note; above § 492. Eternal salvation is discussed here, either as the counterpart of eternal damnation, or in anticipation of 114c2–5 τούτων δὲ αὐτῶν οἱ φιλοσοφίᾳ ἱκανῶς καθηράμενοι ἄνευ τε σωμάτων ζῶσι τὸ παράπαν εἰς τὸν ἔπειτα χρόνον καὶ εἰς οἰκήσεις ἔτι τούτων καλλίους ἀφικνοῦνται. A permanent return of the soul was believed in by Porphyry (de regressu frg. 11,1=August., de civ. 10,30) and Iamblichus, who, however, qualified his statement in a later *Letter*; his faithful follower Sallustius (ch. 20) denies the possibility, as also does Syrianus (Pr., Tim. III 278.9–27) and Proclus, elem. 206. See Dodds pp. 304–306.
1. Iamblichus: probably in his commentary on the *Ph.* (frg. 5 Dillon), either *h.l.* or at 114c2–5; there is some support for this assumption in the earlier announcement at § 492.1–2. But cf. also Dam., Parm. 259.12–14: ... τὸ ἀκρότατον αὐτῶν, ὅπερ καὶ κατιὸν εἰς γένεσιν ὅμως οὐ κάτεισιν, ὥς φησιν ὁ μέγας Ἰάμβλιχος ἐν τῷ Περὶ ψυχῆς μεταναστάσεως ἀπὸ σώματος.
2. τὰ ἀντίστροφα πάντα : the solutions correspond respectively to (1) § 547.4–8, (2) 9–10, (3) 11–12.
3. καθόδων depends on περίοδον rather than on αἰτίαν : cf. elem. 206 (p. 180.25–26) περιόδους ἑκάστην ποιεῖσθαι ἀνόδων τε ἐκ τῆς γενέσεως καὶ τῶν εἰς γένεσιν καθόδων.
4–6. This means that Iamblichus, though rejecting Plotinus' doctrine that the highest part of the soul *cannot* fall, held that it *can* remain sinless, probably in the case of the theurgists.

549. [114a5] The 'wave casts them ashore' by a demonic dispensation, which decides what is due to each and appoints the times of their punishment.

550. [114a7–b6] How do we explain that, unless their victims relent, the punishment of the guilty cannot be remitted? If they should happen to be in heaven, they will not even be seen by the suppliants. And even if it were possible to appeal to them, what kind of standard is this, when some are forgiving to a fault, others excessively hard? — It may be demons who decide these things and who appear in these visions.

Or, perhaps, the phantoms of those who have passed to a higher sphere are seen, as the phantom of Hercules is in Homer [*Od.* 11.601–604].

551. [114b6–c6] As for souls that have led a sinless and God-fearing life: those who have done so without philosophical insight are transferred to an abode on the heights of the earth, with very tenuous pneumatic bodies, those who practice philosophy in the community live in heaven with their luminous bodies, those who are completely purified return to the supramundane region without bodies.

THE EPILOGUE

§§ 552–562. Socrates' death. 115a3–118a17

552. [115a6–8] The end of outward activity is symbolized by the closing of the mouth, departure in a state of purity by the washing of the body after death, participation in immortal life by the unction, an unencumbered upward flight by the shrouding of the body, union with the whole to which we belong by the inhumation.

553. [115b5–7] Just as only the good man can do good to others, so only the man who 'looks after himself' can look after others.

554. [115e4–6] A 'faulty expression' is in the first place an imperfection of speech as such, that is to say, of the activity of the soul that has the word as its medium; but what makes it worse is that our activities also result in lasting dispositions.

---

§ 550. Dam. II § 148.

6–7. *Od.* 11.601–603 τὸν δὲ μέτ' εἰσενόησα βίην Ἡρακληείην, εἴδωλον· αὐτὸς δὲ μετ' ἀθανάτοισι θεοῖσι τέρπεται ἐν θαλίης καὶ ἔχει καλλίσφυρον Ἥβην. On the use made of the passage by the Neoplatonists see J. Pépin, *Héraclès et son reflet*, Le Néoplatonisme (Colloque CNRS 1969), Paris 1971, 167–192. Plot. IV 3,27.1–24; 3,32.24–4,1.16; cf. 3,29.3; on the same lines Pr., *Rep.* I 120.12–18 (apotheosis stands for complete ἀποκατάστασις); I 172.9–21 ("himself" is the soul, the "phantom" its instrument).

§ 551. Pl. distinguishes two categories only: the pious, who live on the heights of the earth, and those who are purified by philosophy and are promoted to an even more beautiful abode, where they live without bodies. Here, a subdivision of the first group is obtained by splitting the sentence 114c1–2 ἄνω - οἰκιζόμενοι into (1) ἄνω εἰς τὴν καθαρὰν οἴκησιν ἀφικνούμενοι, (2) καὶ ἐπὶ γῆς οἰκιζόμενοι. The three groups thus obtained correspond to ethical, social and purificatory virtue.

πδ'. — [114a5] *Ὅτι τὸ κῦμα ἐκβάλλει· κατὰ δαιμονίαν τινὰ διοίκησιν κριτικὴν* 549
τῆς τε ἀξίας καὶ τῶν μέτρων τῶν χρονικῶν.

πε'. — [114a7-b6] *Πῶς, εἰ μὴ παρακληθεῖεν οἱ ἠδικημένοι, οὐ παύονται τῆς* 550
κολάσεως οἱ ἀδικοῦντες; εἰ γὰρ ἐν οὐρανῷ τύχοιεν ὄντες, οὐδὲ ὀφθήσονται τοῖς
παρακαλοῦσιν. εἰ δὲ καὶ παρακαλοῖντο, τίς ὁ τῆς ἀξίας οὗτος ὅρος, ἐνίων μὲν
συγγνωμονικωτέρων ὄντων τοῦ δέοντος, ἐνίων δὲ ἀπηνεστέρων; — Ἡ δαίμονες
οἱ ταῦτα ὁρίζοντες καὶ αἱ ὄψεις δαιμόνιοι. 5
Μήποτε δὲ καὶ τῶν ἀνηγμένων τὰ εἴδωλα φαίνεται, ὡς τὸ Ἡρακλέους
ἐποίησεν Ὅμηρος [λ 601–604].

πς'. — [114b6-c6] *Ὅτι ἀναμάρτητοι καὶ ὁσίως βεβιωκυῖαι αἱ μὲν ἄνευ* 551
φιλοσοφίας ἐπὶ τῶν ἄκρων οἰκίζονται τῆς γῆς μετὰ σωμάτων πνευματικῶν
λεπτοτάτων, αἱ δὲ πολιτικῶς φιλοσοφοῦσαι μετὰ τῶν αὐγοειδῶν ἐν οὐρανῷ
διάγουσιν, αἱ δὲ καθαρθεῖσαι τελέως εἰς τὸν ὑπερκόσμιον τόπον ἀποκαθίστανται
ἄνευ σωμάτων. 5

THE EPILOGUE

§§ 552–562. Socrates' death. 115a3–118a17

πζ'. — [115a6-8] *Ὅτι σύμβολα τοῦ μὲν ἐπέχειν τὴν ἔξω ἐνέργειαν τὸ μῦσαι* 552
τὸ στόμα, τοῦ δὲ ἀναχωρεῖν καθαρὸν τὸ λούεσθαι νεκρὸν τὸ σῶμα, τοῦ δὲ ζωῆς
μετέχειν ἀθανάτου τὸ μυρίζεσθαι, τοῦ δὲ εὐζώνως ἀναθεῖν τὸ περιστέλλεσθαι,
τοῦ δὲ συνάπτεσθαι τῇ οἰκείᾳ ὁλότητι τὸ θάπτεσθαι.

πη'. — [115b5-7] *Ὅτι ὥσπερ μόνος ὁ ἀγαθὸς ἀγαθοῦ καὶ ἄλλῳ γένοιτο ἂν* 553
αἴτιος, οὕτω καὶ ὁ ἐπιμελόμενος ἑαυτοῦ καὶ ἄλλου ἐπιμεληθῆναι δύναιτο ἄν.

πθ'. — [115e4-6] *Ὅτι τὸ μὴ καλῶς λέγειν ἔστι μὲν καὶ αὐτοῦ τοῦ λόγου* 554
κακία τις, ὅ ἐστι τῆς διὰ τοῦ λόγου ψυχικῆς ἐνεργείας· τὸ δὲ χαλεπώτερον,
ὅτι καὶ ἕξεις ἡμῖν ἐγγίγνονται ἀπὸ τῶν ἐνεργειῶν.

---

§ 551. 1 βεβηωκυῖαι M — 4 τελέ~ως, ~ in ras. 2 litt., M^c
§ 552. 2 τοῦ² μ : τὸ M
§ 553. 1 ὁ ins. M^c: om. M¹

---

5. *ἄνευ σωμάτων* : these words, taken directly from Pl., conflict with Pr.'s doctrine that, while the pneumatic body is shed in the final purification, the luminous body never dies (*elem.* 209; *Tim.* III 267.25–268.10; cf. *supra* § 239.3–5). The structure of the groups (1 pneumatic body, earth; 2 luminous body, heaven; 3 disembodied state, supramundane region) precludes any possibility of an error, so that either Dam. must have contradicted Pr., or Pr. himself.

§ 552. Dam. II § 150. Pl. mentions only the closing of the mouth and the eyes (118a13–14) and, in a different context, the washing of the body (115a7–8) and burial (115c3); the rest, unction, shrouding and (in Dam. II) laying down the body on the earth, and cremation, are free additions by Pr., who was familiar with the subject of funeral rites, see note on II. – A similar interpretation of the burial ceremonies for Patroclus by Syrianus: Pr., *Rep.* 152.7–153.3 (Lewy 206–207).

§ 554. Dam. II § 152.

555. [116c4–6] Socrates is 'the bravest of men' because he does not give in to the softness that is proper to desire, 'the kindliest' because he is not carried away by the anger that characterizes spirit, 'the best' because distinguished by what is noblest in him, his superior reason.

556. [116d5–7] In a man who has no virtue of his own, sympathy with one who has may take its place, as a kind of vicarious virtue.

557. [117b6–9] It is natural for people, when drinking, to pledge to the Gods first, as an invitation to join them. Therefore we should not pledge with a deadly potion, lest we seem to invite the Gods to share our destruction; hence the man intimates that such a thing is not customary.

558. [117c1–3] If the Gods are invoked as helpers in every deed and word, they must of course be invoked also on the occasion of this great journey, to assist, not in our destruction (for they can only preserve), but in our departure abroad, as Socrates puts it.

559. [117e1–2] The Pythagoreans wanted 'to die in religious silence,' death being a good and sacred thing; also because disturbances sometimes divert the upward impulse of the soul; and furthermore, because they attract a swarm of demons, lovers of the body and of life in the world of generation, who settle on the pneumatic body and drag it down.

560. [117e4–118a4] Why does death set in at the extremities? — Because they are farther from the organ that causes life. — And why at the lower part of the body? — Because warmth rather tends to move upward.

561. [118a7–8] Why does Socrates want to pay his vow of a cock to Asclepius? — In order that he may heal the diseases that the soul has incurred in the world of coming-to-be.

Or perhaps, as the Oracle [frg. 131] has it, he too wants to sing the hymn to Paean while soaring aloft to the origins of his own being.

562. [118a16–17] The 'best' may be taken to refer to goodness in general, the 'wisest' to knowledge, the 'most righteous' to appetitive life.

---

§ 555. The three qualities mentioned in the text are reduced to the schema of φρόνησις - ἀνδρεία - σωφροσύνη. For πραότης as a virtue of the θυμοειδές see § 371.3.

§ 556. On the character of the jailer cf. Ol. 2 § 8.7–10; *supra* § 46.

§§ 557–558. Dam. II § 153. Cf. Porph., *abst.* 2,33 οὔτε ὅσιον ἀπαρχὴν διδόναι ἧς ἡμεῖς ἀπεχόμεθα τροφῆς (of animal food). In Pl., the only reason is that the quantity may not be sufficient.

§ 559. Dam. II § 155. On ἐν εὐφημίᾳ τελευτᾶν as a Pythagorean maxim: Iambl., *vit. Pyth.* 35, 257 κατὰ τὸν ὕστατον γὰρ καιρὸν παρήγγελλε μὴ βλασφημεῖν, ἀλλ' ὥσπερ ἐν ταῖς ἀναγωγαῖς οἰωνίζεσθαι μετὰ τῆς εὐφημίας, ἥνπερ ἐποιοῦντο διωθούμενοι τὸν 'Αδρίαν.

3. συναγερμόν: in Dam., *princ.* 281.20 and *Parm.* 259.3–4.

4. προσιζάνειν is found in a very similar meaning in Porph., *de antro* 10; the προϊζάνειν of M is without a parallel and without a conceivable sense.

§ 560. Dam. II § 156.
§ 561. Dam. II § 157.

ρ'. - [116c4-6] Ότι ὁ Σωκράτης 'γενναιότατος' μὲν ὡς τῇ ἐπιθυμίᾳ μὴ 555(205) συνδιαρρέων, 'πραότατος' δὲ ὡς τῷ θυμῷ μὴ συγχαλεπαίνων, 'ἄριστος' δὲ ὡς τῷ ἑαυτοῦ ἀρίστῳ κατὰ τὴν ἀρετὴν τοῦ λόγου κεκοσμημένος.

ρα'. - [116d5-7] Ότι τῷ οἰκείαν ἀρετὴν μὴ ἔχοντι τὸ συμπάσχειν τῷ 556 ἔχοντι ἀρετὴ ἂν εἴη, πρός τι ἀρετὴ δηλονότι.

ρβ'. - [117b6-9] Ότι οἱ πίνοντες εἰκότως τοῖς θεοῖς προσπένδουσιν, ἵνα 557 συμπόται ὦσιν αὐτοῖς. οὐκ ἄρα φθοροποιοῦ φαρμάκου σπειστέον, ἵνα μὴ συμφθείρειν τοὺς θεοὺς δοκῶμεν· διὸ καὶ ὁ ἄνθρωπος ἐνδείκνυται μὴ εἰωθέναι τὸ τοιοῦτον.

ργ'. - [117c1-3] Ότι εἰ παντὸς ἔργου καὶ λόγου συλλήπτορες οἱ θεοὶ 558 παρακαλοῦνται, δῆλον ὅτι καὶ ἐπὶ τῇ μεγάλῃ ταύτῃ ἀποδημίᾳ παρακλητέον αὐτούς, οὐκ ἐπὶ φθορᾷ (σωτήριοι γάρ), ἀλλ' ἐπὶ τῇ μεταστάσει, φησίν.

ρδ'. - [117e1-2] Ότι 'ἐν εὐφημίᾳ τελευτᾶν' ἠξίουν οἱ Πυθαγόρειοι ὡς 559 ἀγαθοῦ τε καὶ ἱεροῦ τοῦ πράγματος ὄντος· καὶ ὅτι ἐνίοτε περισπᾷ τὰ τοιαῦτα τὴν ἀναγωγὸν ὁρμήν· καὶ ἔτι πρὸς τούτοις δαιμόνων συναγερμὸν προκαλεῖται φιλοσωμάτων καὶ ζωῇ χαιρόντων γενεσιουργῷ, οἳ τῷ πνεύματι προσιζάνοντες βαρύνουσιν αὐτό. 5

ρε'. - [117e4-118a4] Διὰ τί ἀπὸ τῶν ἄκρων ἄρχεται ἡ νέκρωσις; — Ἢ ὡς 560 ὄντων πορρωτέρω τοῦ ζωοποιοῦ μορίου. — Διὰ τί δὲ ἀπὸ τῶν κάτω; — Ἢ ὅτι πρὸς τὸ ἄνω μᾶλλον κινεῖται τὸ θερμόν.

ρς'. - [118a7-8] Διὰ τί τῷ Ἀσκληπιῷ τὸν ἀλεκτρυόνα ἀποδίδωσιν; — Ἢ ἵνα 561 τὰ νενοσηκότα τῆς ψυχῆς ἐν τῇ γενέσει ταῦτα ἐξιάσηται. Μήποτε δὲ κατὰ τὸ λόγιον [frg. 131] καὶ αὐτὸς τὸν παιᾶνα ᾄδων βούλεται ἀναδραμεῖν εἰς τὰς οἰκείας ἀρχάς.

ρζ'. - [118a16-17] Μήποτε 'ἄριστος' μὲν ὡς πάντα ἀγαθός, 'φρονιμώτατος' 562 δὲ κατὰ τὴν γνῶσιν, 'δικαιότατος' δὲ κατὰ τὴν ὄρεξιν.

---

§ 559. 4 προσιζάνοντες Wk: προϊζάνοντες M
§ 561. 1 ἀλεκτρυῶνα M

---

2. I see no emendation for ταῦτα. Perhaps it is better to let it stand as taking up τὰ νενοσηκότα (= εἴ τινα νενόσηκε) than to delete it.

3-4. Cf. Iambl., vit. Pyth. 35, 257 (quoted above at § 559). Another parallel comes from a rather unexpected quarter: Diog. Oenoand., frg. 2, col. II 10-13 (p. 4 Chilton) [καὶ ὅ]σον οὔπω μέλ[λοντ]ες ἀναλύειν [ἐκ τ]οῦ ζῆν μετὰ [καλο]ῦ παιᾶν[ος]. While in Diog. the paean is a hymn of gratitude, the commentator means a hymn to the Divine Healer, comparable to Socrates' sacrifice to Asclepius. Lewy (200, n. 102) is inclined to think that the quotation from the Oracles refers to the departing soul rather than to ἀναγωγή as a ritual act. The parallel which he cites from Pr., Rep. I 121.19-22 (ὡς γὰρ τῶν ἀναγομένων ψυχῶν τὰ ὄργανα φωνὴν ἐναρμόνιον ἀφίησιν καὶ ἐμμελῆ, καὶ εὔρυθμον ἔχοντα φαίνεται κίνησιν, οὕτω τῶν ὑπὸ γῆς φερομένων καὶ ἀλογωτέρων ὁ ἦχος τρισμῷ παραπλήσιός ἐστιν), in spite of the contrast with the τρισμός of the dead, seems to favor the second explanation, esp. because of the 'rhythmical motion".

DAMASCIUS II

ON THE PHAEDO, BEGINNING AT THE ARGUMENT FROM OPPOSITES

I. THE ARGUMENT FROM OPPOSITES

§§ 1–3. Summary of the argument. 69e6–72e2

1. The object is to prove that the nature of the soul is such that it is not dispersed immediately at the moment of death, but survives long enough to return to life, though it need not do so forever, as far as this argument goes.

2. The assumptions are: (1) the soul is a substance, and one such as can be separated from the body; (2) in so-called 'life' the soul is chained to the body as one substance to another, and the two are not naturally united; (3) it is subject to opposite processes, namely being chained to the body and being separated from it, the latter being called death, the former life; (4) being subject to opposite processes without loss of identity is a characteristic the soul shares with all substance, which has the natural property of remaining the same for a certain time, while shifting from one opposite to the other, but not forever; this is not claimed. For example, a substance that is cooled can be heated and one that is heated can be cooled, though not indefinitely; in the same way it can be composed and decomposed more than once, and sleep and wake; the inference is that in the same way it lives and dies alternately, as long as it lasts. Even the body outlasts its own qualities, but this does not make it necessarily everlasting. For there are two kinds of cycles, the cycle of the species, which is everlasting, and the cycle of the individual, which is for a time; as for the opposite accidents, here we have no cycle at all, but a one way process. If there were no cycle that continues for a certain time while the substances remain the same, the intial conditions would disappear, and no one would wake up again after falling asleep, nor, consequently, return to life after dying. As it is, cyclic recurrence is maintained in the other instances; the same must therefore be true of dead and living men, in other words, of souls, since even bodies pass from the animate to the inanimate state, and conversely from the inanimate to the animate state, primarily, in a number of cases, by receiving human souls again, otherwise those of other animals, maggots for instance; souls do not inevitably pass into bodies foreign to their nature.

---

§§ 1–3. These short notes contain in a very much condensed form the gist of I §§ 207–252, but the wording and the arrangement show that they depend on a lecture in which Dam. summed up his own interpretation rather than directly on the monograph.

§ 1. Dam. I § 252.1–6; cf. I § 183; Ol. 11 § 1.

§ 2. 1–2. Dam. I § 221.

ΕΙΣ ΤΟΝ ΦΑΙΔΩΝΑ ΑΠΟ ΤΟΥ ΠΕΡΙ ΤΩΝ ΕΝΑΝΤΙΩΝ ΛΟΓΟΥ (206)

I. THE ARGUMENT FROM OPPOSITES

§§ 1-3. Summary of the argument. 69e6-72e2

α'. - Ότι σκοπός επιδείξαι την ψυχήν τοιούτόν τι ούσαν οίον μη άμα τω 1 θανάτω διαπνείσθαι, αλλ' επιμένειν και εις αναβίωσιν, ού μέντοι αει τούτο, όσον επί τούτω τω λόγω.

α' β'. - Ότι προομολογείται, εν μεν ως ουσία τίς εστιν η ψυχή και οία από 2
β' του σώματος χωρίζεσθαι· έτερον δε ότι εν τη λεγομένη ζωή συνέργνυται τω
γ' σώματι ως άλλη άλλω, και ου συμφύεται αυτώ· τρίτον δε ότι τάναντία περί αυτήν γίγνεται, οίον το συνέργνυσθαι και το χωρίζεσθαι, ων τούτο μεν θάνατος,
δ' εκείνο δε ζωή καλείται· τέταρτον δε ότι μία ούσα τάναντία πάσχουσα τοιούτόν 5 τί εστιν οίον πάσα ουσία, πεφυκυία μέχρι τινός η αυτή μένειν εις τάναντία μεταχωρούσα, ει και μη αεί· τούτο γαρ ου πρόσκειται. και γαρ η ψυχομένη ουσία θερμαίνεται και η θερμαινομένη ψύχεται, αλλ' ουκ επ' άπειρον· ούτω δε και συγκρίνεται και διακρίνεται πλεονάκις και καθεύδει και εγρήγορεν· ούτως άρα και ζη και θνήσκει ανά μέρος, εφ' όσον αντέχει. και γαρ το σώμα των 10 οικείων ποιοτήτων πολυχρονιώτερον, αλλ' ου πάντως αίδιον. διττός γαρ ο κύκλος, ο μεν κατ' είδος αίδιος, ο δε κατά αριθμόν επί τινα χρόνον· ο δε των εναντίων συμβεβηκότων ουδέ όλως κύκλος, αλλά κατ' ευθείαν μόνον. ει δε μη μέχρι τινός εγίγνετο κύκλος των ουσιών των αυτών μενουσών, τα εν αρχή απώλλυτο, και ουκ αν τις καθευδήσας εγέρθη πάλιν· ώστε ουδέ αποθανών ανεβίω άν. αλλά 15 μην σώζεται των άλλων ο κύκλος· και ο των ζώντων άρα και τεθνεώτων ανθρώπων, ο | εστι των ψυχών αυτών, επεί και τα σώματα εξ εμψύχων άψυχα (207) γίνεται και πάλιν εξ αψύχων έμψυχα, μάλιστα μεν και ψυχάς δεχόμενα ανθρώπων ενίοτε, ει δε μη, αλλά ζώων ετέρων, οίον ευλών· ουδέ γαρ πάντως αι ψυχαί εις αλλότρια σώματα. 20

---

§ 2. 1 οία M¹ — 7 αεί Nv: δει M — 14 εν αρχή Wk: εναργή M — 15 εγέρθη] ηγέρθη μ — 19 αλλά] ' ex ʼ, -α in ras., Mᶜ (άλλων M¹?)

2-3. Cf. Dam. I § 223.
5-10. Cf. Dam. I § 226.
11-13. Dam. I § 228.
17-19. Dam. I § 234.9-15. The assumption in I is that a trace of life is left in the body.
19. ευλών: cf. I § 234.14-15, note, and § 249.6 (πολλά θηρία).

3. In this way we can save the argument as proving, on the one hand, what it claims to prove, while on the other hand inadequate to furnish complete proof of immortality and not even containing incidental proof that souls are immortal; besides, we can meet most of the objections on these lines.

II. THE ARGUMENT FROM RECOLLECTION

§§ 4-11. On recollection in general. 72e3-77a5

4. Recollection is a cognitive activity of the soul, renewing lost knowledge. Therefore recollection cannot be the first cognitive contact with the object, it must at least be the second; nor even is it simply the second as such, for if the disposition has been continuous and its content is produced readily, it cannot very well be called recollection, rather it is memory; recollection in its primary sense is a renewal of our former knowledge after more or less deep oblivion.

5. Recollection is twofold, being recognition either of individuals or of universals.

6. Intelligence always knows actively, the first soul always knows by disposition, which is memory, but in its activity it passes from one object to another; so it does not recollect either, but only remembers. Secondary soul, i.e. that of the 'immaculate' beings, passes from stage to stage as regards its disposition also, but resumes it readily and without forgetting. Soul on the third level forgets and recollects after forgetting, and this is the kind now under discussion.

7. The archetypal form of recollection in Intelligence is eternal intellection of the same objects.

---

§ 3. 2. οὐδὲ κατὰ συμβεβηκός : according to Syrianus-Proclus (I § 205) the argument is contingent upon the eternity of the world; Dam. (I § 207.12-13) objects that in that case it would amount to complete proof.

§ 4. Dam. I § 253.

5-6. Ol. 11 § 4.15-16.

§ 5. Cf. Pr., Rep. II 350.15-16 καὶ τό γε θαυμαστόν, ὅτι μᾶλλον ἀνάμνησίς ἐστι τῶν καθόλου ἢ τῶν μερικῶν (because universals belong to rational soul only, particulars also to imaginative soul, which is easily disturbed).

§ 6. Cf. Dam. I § 257. – "First souls" are the divine ones, "second souls" those of demons and heroes, "third souls" are human.

1. Ar., an. III 7, 431b16 ὅλως δὲ ὁ νοῦς ἐστιν ὁ κατ' ἐνέργειαν τὰ πράγματα [scil. νοῶν].

3-4. οἷον ἡ τῶν ἀχράντων : ἄχραντος is used (1) of human souls untainted by genesis, e.g. I § 529.7 and infra § 97.3; so, too, Pr., Rep. II 332.23 and 120.7 (adv.); Tim. II 112.23-25 (a hierarchy of souls consisting of: 1 cosmic soul; 2 mundane Gods;

γ′. - Ὅτι οὕτω σώσομεν τὸν λόγον καὶ ἀληθῆ πρὸς τὸν σκοπὸν καὶ ἀτελῆ 3
πρὸς τὴν τελέαν ἀθανασίαν καὶ οὐδὲ κατὰ συμβεβηκὸς ἀθανάτους αὐτὰς δεικνύοντα,
καὶ ἔτι μέντοι τὰς πλείστας τῶν ἀποριῶν διωσόμεθα.

II. THE ARGUMENT FROM RECOLLECTION
§§ 4-11. On recollection in general. 72e3-77a5

δ′. - Ὅτι ἡ ἀνάμνησις ἐνέργειά ἐστι ψυχῆς γνωστική, ἀνανεωτικὴ τῆς 4
ἀπολομένης γνώσεως. οὐκ ἂν οὖν εἴη ἡ ἀνάμνησις ἡ πρώτη κατὰ γνῶσιν
ἀντίληψις τοῦ γνωστοῦ, ἀλλὰ τοὐλάχιστον ἡ δευτέρα· καὶ οὐδὲ αὐτὴ ἡ δευτέρα
ἁπλῶς οὕτως, παραμενούσης γὰρ τῆς ἕξεως καὶ προχείρως προβαλλομένης οὐκ
ἂν ὀρθῶς ἀνάμνησις καλοῖτο, ἀλλὰ μᾶλλον μνήμη· πρώτη δὲ ἀνάμνησις ἡ μετὰ 5
λήθην εἴτε βαθεῖαν εἴτε ἐπιπολαιοτέραν ἀνανέωσις ὧν ἔγνωμεν πρότερον.

ε′. - Ὅτι διττὴ ἡ ἀνάμνησις, ἡ μὲν κατὰ γνωρισμὸν τῶν ἀτόμων, ἡ δὲ 5
τῶν καθόλου.

ϛ′. - Ὅτι ὁ μὲν νοῦς γιγνώσκει ἀεὶ κατ' ἐνέργειαν, ἡ δὲ πρώτη ψυχὴ τῇ 6
μὲν ἕξει ἀεί, ἥτις ἐστὶ μνήμη, τῇ δὲ ἐνεργείᾳ μεταβαίνει· οὐδὲ αὕτη ἄρα
ἀναμιμνήσκεται ἀλλ' ἢ μόνον μνημονεύει. ἡ δὲ δευτέρα ψυχή, οἷον ἡ τῶν
ἀχράντων, καὶ τῇ ἕξει μεταβαίνει, ἀλλὰ ῥᾳδίως αὐτὴν ἀναλαμβάνει καὶ ἄνευ
λήθης. ἡ δὲ τρίτη καὶ ἐπιλανθάνεται καὶ μετὰ λήθην ἀναμιμνήσκεται, περὶ οἵας 5
δὴ καὶ ὁ λόγος ἐστὶ τὰ νῦν.

ζ′. - Ὅτι παράδειγμα ἀναμνήσεως ἐν τῷ νῷ ἡ τῶν αὐτῶν ἀεὶ νόησις. 7

---

§ 3. 1 οὕτω σώσομεν Mᶜ: οὕτως ὡς ὁ μὲν M¹
§ 4. 2 γνώσεως] γ- in ras. Mᶜ (fort. ἐνώσεως M¹) | γνῶσιν] γ- in ras., accent.
add., Mᶜ (fort. ἔνωσιν M¹) — 3 αὐτὴ Mᶜ: αὕτη M¹ (?) — 6 ἐπιπολαιοτέραν] -αι- in ras. Mᶜ
(sim. infra 28.7; 56.7) | ὧν] acc. et -ν ex corr. Mᶜ (ὡς M¹ ?)
§ 6. 2 αὕτη Wk: αὐτη M — 3 ἀναμιμνήσκεται] -σκ- in ras. 3 litt. Mᶜ — 4 αὐτὴν]
-η- in ras. Mᶜ (αὐτὸν ut vid. M¹)

---

3 "superior kinds," i.e. angels, demons, heroes; 4 untainted souls; 5 particular souls)
τέταρτον δὲ τὸ ἐν ταῖς ἀχράντοις ψυχαῖς, αἳ καὶ τὰς καθόδους ἀπήμονας ποιοῦνται καὶ
προβέβληνται ζωὴν ἀμείλικτον καὶ ἀδάμαστον, cf. Festugière's note, III p. 150, n. 4;
ibid. III 278.13-15 οὐδεμίαν γὰρ ψυχὴν οὔτε τῶν ἀχράντων καλουμένων οὔτε τῶν
κακύνεσθαι καὶ πλανᾶσθαι δυναμένων πᾶσαν περίοδον ἄνω μένειν εἰκός. (2) of heroes:
Pr., Tim. I 52.15-19 τῶν γὰρ παραγομένων ὑπὸ τῶν θεῶν καὶ δαιμόνων τὰ μὲν ἐν αὐτοῖς
μένει, γένη καθαρὰ καὶ πόρρω γενέσεως, ἃ καὶ ἄχραντα διὰ τοῦτο καλεῖται, τὰ δὲ κάτεισιν
εἰς γένεσιν, οὐ δυνάμενα ἐν οὐρανῷ μένειν ἀκλινῶς, cf. ibid. 25-26; ibid. I 111.14-18
τούτων δὴ τῶν ψυχῶν αἱ μὲν ἄχραντοι μένουσιν ἀεὶ τῶν οἰκείων ἐξημμέναι θεῶν καὶ
συνδιοικοῦσαι τὸ πᾶν αὐτοῖς, αἱ δὲ κατίασιν μὲν εἰς γένεσιν, μεγαλουργοὶ δέ εἰσι καὶ
ἀκάκωτοι διαμένουσιν· αἱ δὲ κατίασι καὶ κακίας ἀναπίμπλανται γενεσιουργοῦ, ibid.
136.10-13 τῶν δὲ κλήρων οἱ μέν εἰσι ψυχῶν μερικῶν, οἱ δὲ τῶν ἀχράντων γενῶν, οἱ δὲ
δαιμόνιοι, οἱ δὲ ἀγγελικοί, οἱ δὲ αὐτῶν τῶν θεῶν. (3) of certain orders of Gods: Pr.,
theol. V 33-35; VI 13; Tim. I 157.16; 166.6; 26. For groups (1) and (2) cf. the
double sense of ἥρως, infra § 99.3-4. Cf. Iambl. de An. sect. 44, p. 456, Stob. 23-24.
§ 7. Dam. I § 260.2-3.

8. Its efficient cause is the same as for all regeneration; and this, as we know, is Dionysius son of Semele.

However, there ought to be also a specific cause of cognitive regeneration, which is recollection (since we are here concerned with the kind that follows privation), just as there is another specific cause that regenerates life and a third that regenerates being.

9. Its final cause is assimilation to Intelligence and the return to the same intelligible realities.

We object that these are rather exemplary or formal causes; it is better to define it as the return to the Good through knowledge; for cognition prepares the way to the object of appetition.

10. The material cause is the natural faculty of the soul that can be realized and perfected. This part of the soul has, as it were, only potential existence.

11. The instrumental cause, where recollection of intelligible things is concerned, are sensible things, by means of which we recollect the former. Or, more immediately, sensible things are our means of recollecting things on the dianoetic level, these again remind us of intelligible reality.

§§ 12–14. Main points of the argument. 72e3–77a5

12. What is the purpose of the argument? — To show that in reality we recollect what we seem to learn for the first time.

13. What are the assumptions on which the argument rests, and how many? — (1) Anyone who recollects anything whatever must have known it previously [73c1–2]. This point will serve him to prove the major of the hypothetical syllogism; if a man has previous knowledge, his soul must have existed previously. — (2) If anyone, having acquired knowledge of one thing, derives knowledge of another thing from it, this is recollection [73c4–d11]. — (3) Recollection relates to things forgotten [73e1–3]. —

---

§ 8. Dam. I § 260.1–2.

2. ὁ Σεμελήϊος Διόνυσος : as opposed to Dionysus son of Kore. Hermias 32.11 νύμφαι δέ εἰσιν ἔφοροι θεαὶ τῆς παλιγγενεσίας ὑπουργοὶ τοῦ ἐκ Σεμέλης Διονύσου· ... αὐτὸς δὲ ὁ Διόνυσος τῆς παλιγγενεσίας ἐπάρχει παντὸς τοῦ αἰσθητοῦ. Ibid. 55.19–21 διθύραμβοι δέ εἰσιν ὕμνοι εἰς τὸν Διόνυσον πεποιημένοι, οὐ τὸν Κορικόν, ἀλλὰ τὸν ἐκ Σεμέλης καὶ τοῦ μηροῦ τοῦ Διός· οὗτος γάρ ἐστιν ὁ τῆς παλιγγενεσίας αἴτιος θεός. Pr., theol. VI 11, 370.43–371.3 διττῆς δὲ οὔσης τῆς Κορικῆς τάξεως, καὶ τῆς μὲν ὑπὲρ τὸν κόσμον προφαινομένης, ὅτε δὴ καὶ συντάττεται τῷ Διί, καὶ μετ' ἐκείνου τὸν ἕνα δημιουργὸν ὑφίστησι τῶν μερικῶν. Cf. also Tim. III 169.8: Dionysus, as most Orphic Gods, manifests himself on different levels. According to Pr., hymn 6.11–15 (to Athena), the second Dionysus is the heart of the first reborn from Semele: ἣ κραδίην ἐσάωσας ἀμιστύλλευτον ἄνακτος αἰθέρος ἐν γυάλοισι μεριζομένου ποτὲ Βάκχου Τιτήνων ὑπὸ χερσί— πόρες δέ ἑ πατρὶ φέρουσα, ὄφρα νέος βούλησιν ὑπ' ἀρρήτοισι τοκῆος ἐκ Σεμέλης περὶ κόσμον ἀνηβήσῃ Διόνυσος. Though Kern does not include these lines nor any other allusion to Semele, this is part of the original Orphic story (so, too, Ziegler, RE 18, 2,

η'. – Ὅτι ποιητικὸν αἴτιον τὸ αὐτὸ ὅπερ καὶ τῆς ὅλης παλιγγενεσίας· οὗτος 8(208)
δὲ ἦν ὁ Σεμελήιος Διόνυσος.
Εἴη δὲ ἄν τι καὶ ἴδιον τῆς γνωστικῆς παλιγγενεσίας, ἥ ἐστιν ἀνάμνησις (τὴν
γὰρ τοιαύτην ληπτέον ἢ μετὰ στέρησιν γίγνεται), ὡς καὶ τῆς ζωτικῆς ἄλλο καὶ
τῆς κατ' οὐσίαν αὖ πάλιν ἄλλο τι. 5
θ'. – Ὅτι τὸ τελικὸν ἡ πρὸς νοῦν ἀφομοίωσις καὶ πρὸς τὰ αὐτὰ νοητὰ 9
ἐπάνοδος.
Ἀλλ' ἤτοι παραδειγματικὰ ταῦτα ἢ εἰδικὰ μᾶλλον· οὐκοῦν βέλτιον φάναι τὴν
διὰ γνώσεως ἐπάνοδον πρὸς τὸ ἀγαθόν· ὁδοποιητικὴ γὰρ ἡ γνῶσις πρὸς τὸ ὀρεκτόν.
ι'. – Ὅτι ὑλικὸν ἡ προβάλλεσθαι δυναμένη φύσις καὶ τελειοῦσθαι τῆς ψυχῆς· 10
οἷον γὰρ δυνάμει τὸ τοιοῦτόν ἐστι τῆς ψυχῆς.
ια'. – Ὅτι ὀργανικὸν τὰ αἰσθητὰ τῶν νοητῶν· διὰ γὰρ τούτων ἐκείνων 11
ἀναμιμνησκόμεθα. ἢ προσεχέστερον εἴη ἂν τὰ μὲν αἰσθητὰ τῶν διανοητῶν,
ταῦτα δὲ τῶν νοητῶν.

§§ 12-14. Main points of the argument. 72e3-77a5

ιβ'. – Τίς ὁ σκοπὸς τοῦ λόγου; —Ἡ δεῖξαι ὅτι ἃ πρῶτα δοκοῦμεν μανθάνειν, 12
ταῦτα ἀναμιμνησκόμεθα.
α' ιγ'. – Τίνες καὶ πόσαι αἱ τοῦ λόγου ὑποθέσεις; — Πάντα τὸν ὁτουοῦν 13
ἀναμιμνησκόμενον δεῖν τοῦτο προεγνωκέναι [73c1-2]· συντελέσει δὲ πρὸς τὸ
β' συνημμένον, εἰ γὰρ προέγνωκεν, προῆν ἄρα ἡ ψυχή. — ἐάν τις γνούς τι ἀπὸ
γ' τούτου ἕτερον γνῷ, ἀναμιμνήσκεσθαι τοῦτό ἐστιν [73c4-d11]. — τὴν ἀνάμνησιν
δ' γίγνεσθαι ἐκείνων ὧν τις ἐπελάθετο [73e1-3]. — διττὴν εἶναι τὴν ἀφ' ἑτέρων 5

---

§ 8. 4 ἢ Mᶜ: ἦ M¹ | ἄλλο] ˣ ex ', -o in ras., Mᶜ (ἀλλὰ ut vid. M¹)
§ 9. 3 ταῦτα ins. Mᶜ: om. M¹ | εἰδικὰ Mᶜ: ἰδικὰ M¹
§ 13. 2 τοῦτο μ : τοῦτον M

1354.21-28), not a later Neoplatonic combination; the relation between Dionysus and palingenesia, which to them is an essential element of the Orphic myth (see also note on I § 11), is based on this double birth. – The adjective Σεμελήιος occurs carm. popul. 6 Diehl, and often in Latin poetry (Ovid, Statius).
3-5. Cf. Dam. I § 256 (Proclus). The three processes would be ἀνάμνησις for γνῶσις, ἀναβίωσις for ζωή, and ἀναγέννησις (not a Neoplatonic term) for οὐσία.
§ 9. Dam. I § 260.3 (where the phrasing is more careful: ἡ ἀνάληψις τῆς πρὸς νοῦν ὁμοιώσεως).
3-4. Dam.'s correction is not in version I, but he argues in the same way Phil. § 95: ὅτι ὁ νοῦς οὐ τέλος· ὁρᾷ γὰρ καὶ κρίνει τὸ τέλος καὶ ἄγει πρὸς αὐτὸ τὴν ὄρεξιν, οἷον φραστὴρ ὢν ὁδοῦ τις. Cf. princ. 188.7-11.
§ 10. Not in Dam. I.
§ 11. Cf. Dam. I § 261, where the ἔδει ... εἰπεῖν shows that Pr. listed no instrumental cause; therefore the two different proposals are both by Dam.
§ 13. Dam. I § 262. Ol. 11 § 5.

(4) Recollection started by other objects is twofold, the objects being either similar or dissimilar [73e5–74a4]. — (5) The person who thus recollects a thing can point out what is lacking or redundant or misplaced in the effigy as compared with its original [74a5–8].

14. Syllogisms

(i) Every human as soon as born uses sense-perception; anyone using sense-perception derives from its objects notions of forms, whether developed or latent; therefore every human derives notions of forms from the objects of sense-perception. — This is the commentator's formula; but instead of 'derives notions of forms,' a point disputed by some, it is perhaps better to say 'derives notions of universals from individuals,' since these universal ideas, whether immanent in particulars or prior to them, force themselves upon us in any case.

(ii) Every human derives notions of forms from things sensible; anyone conceiving forms has or had knowledge of them; therefore every human has or had knowledge of them.

(iii) Every human either has or at one time had knowledge of forms; anyone who had it before and recaptures it now, does so by recollection; therefore every human knows forms by recollection.

(iv) Every human when recapturing knowledge recollects; anyone who recollects has forgotten what he recollects; therefore every human has forgotten what he recollects.

(v) Every human, before recollection, is in a state of forgetfulness; anyone who is in a state of forgetfulness before recollecting must have known either before birth or during birth or after birth; he did not know during or after birth; therefore he knew before birth.

(vi) Every human before birth had knowledge of what he recollects; anyone who has knowledge exists at the time when he has such knowledge; therefore every human exists at the time when he has such knowledge.

§§ 15–23. Various questions concerning the argument. 72e3–77a5

15. The forms to which Socrates refers are neither the manifold appearances and the common elements in them (the forms of which we acquire knowledge are universal, changeless, and more exact than things sensible) nor the concepts derived from these by abstraction (which are inferior even to objects of sense-perception); so they must be a kind of transcendent

---

§ 14. Dam. I § 264.
§ 15. Dam. I § 274. Cf. Ol. 12 § 1.2–3. Simpl., *cat.* 70.14–24. The question "What forms are meant?" is also asked at I § 330, *infra* § 35, Ol. 13 § 5, with regard to the forms of *Ph.* 78d1–7. Here it is not really to the point, cf. I § 274, where the discussion appears in its original form: neither the common element

ἀνάμνησιν, ἀπὸ τῶν τε ὁμοίων καὶ ἀνομοίων [73e5–74a4]. — τὸ δύνασθαι εἰπεῖν τὸν ἀναμιμνησκόμενον τὸ ἐλλεῖπον ἢ πλεονάζον ἢ παρὰ τάξιν κείμενον τῷ ὁμοίῳ πρὸς τὸ ᾧ ὡμοίωται [74a5–8].

ιδ'.   Συλλογισμοί   14

α' Πᾶς ἄνθρωπος εὐθὺς γενόμενος αἰσθήσει χρῆται· πᾶς ὁ αἰσθήσει χρώμενος ἐννοεῖ τὰ εἴδη ἀπὸ τῶν αἰσθητῶν, εἴτε διηρθρωμένως εἴτε μή· πᾶς ἄρα ἄνθρωπος ἐννοεῖ τὰ εἴδη ἀπὸ τῶν αἰσθητῶν. — ἀλλ' οὕτω μὲν ὁ ἐξηγητής· μήποτε δὲ ἄμεινον ἀντὶ τοῦ ἐννοεῖν τὰ εἴδη, ὅ τισι καὶ ἀμφισβητούμενόν ἐστιν, ἐν|νοεῖν 5(209) φάναι ἀπὸ τῶν ἀτόμων τὰ καθόλου· ταῦτα γὰρ ἡμᾶς ὑποτρέχει πάντως, εἴτε τὰ ἐν τοῖς πολλοῖς εἴτε τὰ πρὸ τῶν πολλῶν.

β' πᾶς ἄνθρωπος ἐννοεῖ τὰ εἴδη ἀπὸ τῶν αἰσθητῶν· πᾶς ἐννοῶν τὰ εἴδη ἢ ἔχει ἢ ἔσχεν αὐτῶν ἐπιστήμην· πᾶς ἄρα ἄνθρωπος ἢ ἔχει ἢ ἔσχεν αὐτῶν ἐπιστήμην.

γ' πᾶς ἄνθρωπος ἢ ἔχει ἢ ἔσχεν ποτὲ ἐπιστήμην τῶν εἰδῶν· πᾶς ὁ ἐσχηκὼς 10 πρότερον, νῦν δὲ ἀναλαμβάνων αὐτήν, ἀναμιμνήσκεται· πᾶς ἄρα ἄνθρωπος ἀναμιμνήσκεται.

δ' πᾶς ἄνθρωπος ἀναλαμβάνων ἐπιστήμην ἀναμιμνήσκεται· πᾶς ἀναμιμνησκόμενος λήθην ἔσχεν ὧν ἀναμιμνήσκεται· πᾶς ἄρα ἄνθρωπος λήθην ἔσχεν ὧν ἀναμιμνήσκεται.   15

ε' πᾶς ἄνθρωπος λήθην ἴσχει πρὸ τῆς ἀναμνήσεως· πᾶς ὁ λήθην ἴσχων πρὸ τῆς ἀναμνήσεως ἤτοι πρὸ τῆς γενέσεως ᾔδει ἢ ἐν τῷ γίγνεσθαι ἢ μετὰ τὴν γένεσιν· ἀλλὰ μὴν οὔτε ἐν τῷ γίγνεσθαι οὔτε μετὰ τὴν γένεσιν· πρὸ τῆς γενέσεως ἄρα.

ς' πᾶς ἄνθρωπος πρὸ τῆς γενέσεως εἶχεν ἐπιστήμην ὧν ἀναμιμνήσκεται· πᾶς ὁ ἔχων ἐπιστήμην, ὅτε ἔχει, ἔστιν· πᾶς ἄρα ἄνθρωπος, ὅτε ἔχει, ἔστιν.   20

§§ 15–23. Various questions concerning the argument. 72e3–77a5

ιε'. — Ὅτι περὶ εἰδῶν ποιεῖται τὸν λόγον οὔτε τῶν πολλῶν τε καὶ ἐν τοῖς 15 πολλοῖς κοινῶν (ἃ γὰρ μανθάνομεν κοινά τέ ἐστιν καὶ ἀμετάβλητα καὶ ἀκριβέστερα τῶν αἰσθητῶν) οὔτε τῶν ὑστερογενῶν ἀπὸ τούτων (χείρω γὰρ ταῦτα καὶ τῶν αἰσθητῶν)· χωριστῶν ἄρα τινῶν, διὸ καὶ ˊπρότεραˋ ταῦτα ὀνομάζει τῶν αἰσθητῶν

---

§ 14.   16 ἴσχει] ἰ- et -ι in ras. M^c (ἔσχεν M¹? Fh) | ἴσχων] ἰ- in ras., -σχ- ex -χ-, M^c (ἔχων ut vid. M¹, σχὼν Fh)

---

in individuals nor the concept derived from them by abstraction is an adequate standard, therefore there must be a transcendent standard, i.e. form.

2. κοινά : it is hard to see how this qualification can be used to prove that the forms intended cannot be τὰ ἐν τοῖς πολλοῖς κοινά. Perhaps we should write ἁπλᾶ, which might have been supplanted by κοινά under the influence of the preceding κοινῶν.

form, and accordingly Socrates calls them 'prior' to sensible things [76e1]. But what kind of transcendent forms, then? Those in intelligence? Of these, however, no rational knowledge is possible, nor, if there were, would it be easy to reach them without intermediary; it is to clear up this point that Socrates will presently say that their 'substance' is 'our own' [76e1-2] and that he designs them, in the plural, as 'the equals themselves' [74c1], expressing what one might call the dimensionality of forms in soul. But he also hints at a possibility of transition from these to intelligible forms by occasional use of the singular 'the equal itself' [74c4-5].

16. What if souls receive knowledge at birth, in the same way as particular natural essences receive their creative principles? [76c14-d6]. — But nature, having received them, makes them function at once, while the soul loses them at once; it would follow that the gift is useless and that soul is inferior to nature, which utilizes its powers. And then, how can she receive it in the very turmoil of birth and lose it when the turmoil is over? Furthermore, if she receives it as part of her essence, it is unthinkable that she should lose it at any time whatever (as unthinkable, indeed, as the loss of her vivifying power, which she exercises by the mere fact of her existence); if, on the other hand, she receives it as a disposition, a process of learning must have preceded. On the whole, to assume recollection as the cause of one kind of knowledge, the kind acquired after birth (when we recollect the knowledge received during birth), and instantaneous implantation as the cause of the other kind, viz. knowledge received during birth itself, is not only a random proceeding (why should knowledge come from recollection all the rest of the time, and from implantation in this special case?) but it is downright impossible: for if in the course of her life and after achieving greater perfection she is found to acquire knowledge only through instruction and research, what are we to think of the time when she had only potential existence, in the opinion of those who raise these objections?

17. Why, when our memory is awakened, do we not also recollect the time, the place, or other circumstances, as we do when remembering events in this life? — In the first place, even then it is not always the case. Secondly, if diseases can already cause lethargy, what must be the effect of this radical change brought about by the whole process of birth? Now it is a fact that diseases may lead to loss of memory, not only of place and time, but

---

§ 16. Dam. I § 266.
1. αἱ μερικαὶ φύσεις : on this notion see note at I § 266.1.
4. τῷ κλύδωνι : Pl., *Tim.* 43a4–44b1.
13-14. ὅτε μόνον δυνάμει ἦν κατὰ τὴν δόξαν τῶν τὰ τοιαῦτα ἀπορούντων : Ar., *an.* III 4, 429a27–29 καὶ εὖ δὴ οἱ λέγοντες τὴν ψυχὴν εἶναι τόπον εἰδῶν, πλὴν ὅτι οὔτε ὅλη ἀλλ' ἡ νοητική, οὔτε ἐντελεχείᾳ ἀλλὰ δυνάμει τὰ εἴδη.
§ 17. Dam. I § 268. Cf. Pr., *Alc.* 191.5–192.12 (referring to *Ph. h.l.*), with συναναφέρειν used in the same sense (192.11). The problem is a different one there:

[76e1]. ἀλλ' εἰ χωριστῶν, πότερον τῶν ἐν νῷ; ἀλλ' οὔτε ἐπιστήμη ἐκείνων ἐστὶν οὔτε εἰ ἦν ῥᾴδιον ἦν ἐπ' αὐτὰ προελθεῖν ἀμέσως· διὸ καὶ ʿἡμετέραν' εἶναι φήσει [76e1-2] τὴν τούτων οὐσίαν καὶ πληθυντικῶς ὀνομάζει ʿαὐτὰ τὰ ἴσα' [74c1], τὸ οἷον διαστηματικὸν τῶν ψυχικῶν εἰδῶν ἐνδεικνύμενος. ἐνδείκνυται δὲ ὅτι καὶ εἰς τὰ νοητὰ γίγνεταί τις μετάβασις ἀπὸ τούτων λέγων ποτὲ καὶ ʿαὐτὸ τὸ ἴσον' ἑνικῶς [74c4-5].

ις'. – Μήποτε ἅμα γίγνονται καὶ ἴσχουσι τὰς ἐπιστήμας, ὡς αἱ μερικαὶ φύσεις τοὺς λόγους [76c14-d6]. – Ἀλλ' αὕτη μὲν λαβοῦσα χρῆ|ται αὐτοῖς εὐθύς, ἡ δὲ ψυχὴ εὐθὺς ἀποβάλλει· μάτην ἄρα λαμβάνει καὶ χείρων ἔσται τῆς ἐνεργούσης φύσεως. ἔπειτα πῶς ἐν αὐτῷ τῷ κλύδωνι λαμβάνει καὶ ἀποβάλλει μετὰ τὸν κλύδωνα; ἔτι δέ, εἰ μὲν κατ' οὐσίαν λαμβάνει τὰς ἐπιστήμας, πῶς ἀποβάλλει ὅτε δήποτε; οὐδὲ γὰρ τὸ ζωοποιεῖν ἀποβάλλει, ἐπειδὴ τῷ εἶναι τοῦτο ἐνεργεῖ· εἰ δὲ κατὰ ἕξιν, δεῖ πρότερον γίνεσθαι μάθησιν. ὅλως δὲ τὰς μὲν κατὰ ἀνάμνησιν ποιεῖν, τὰς ἐπειδὰν γεννηθῶμεν ἐπιστήμας (ἀναμιμνησκόμεθα γὰρ ὧν ἐλάβομεν ἐν τῷ γίγνεσθαι), τὰς δὲ κατὰ ἔνθεσιν ἀθρόαν, οἷον τὰς ἐν αὐτῷ τῷ γίνεσθαι, ἀποκληρωτικόν (διὰ τί γὰρ τὸν ἄλλον ἅπαντα χρόνον ἀναμιμνησκομένη ἐν τούτῳ μόνῳ κατὰ ἔνθεσιν λαμβάνει;) πρὸς τῷ καὶ ἀδύνατον εἶναι· εἰ γὰρ ἐν τῷ βίῳ καὶ τελειοτέρα γενομένη φαίνεται διὰ μαθήσεως καὶ ζητήσεως κτωμένη τὰς ἐπιστήμας, τί χρὴ οἴεσθαι τότε, ὅτε μόνον δυνάμει ἦν κατὰ τὴν δόξαν τῶν τὰ τοιαῦτα ἀπορούντων;

ιζ'. – Διὰ τί μὴ συναιαφέρομεν τῇ ὑπομνήσει τόπον ἢ χρόνον ἢ τὰ τοιαῦτα, ὡς ἐν ταῖς τῇδε ἀναμνήσεσιν; — Ἡ μάλιστα μὲν οὐδὲ ἐν ταύταις ἀεί. δεύτερον δέ, εἰ ἐκ νόσων κατεχόμεθα ληθάργῳ, τί δράσει ἡ τοσαύτη μεταβολὴ τῆς ὅλης γενέσεως; ἀλλὰ μὴν ἐκ τῶν νόσων τὴν μνήμην ἀποβάλλομεν οὐ μόνον τόπων καὶ χρόνων, ἀλλὰ καὶ πάντων ὧν ἐμάθομεν· πολλῷ ἄρα ἐν τῇ μεταβολῇ τῇ εἰς τὴν

---

§ 15. 8 ψυχικῶν] -ικ- s.l. M¹ — 9 εἰς] -ις in ras. M^c
§ 16. 2 αὕτη M^c: αὐτὴ M¹ — 6 τῶι M^c: τὸ M¹
§ 17. 3 ληθάργωι M¹: -ων M^c

Alcibiades, according to Socrates, can never have known because he fails to remember the time when he learnt. To resolve the difficulty, Pr. loc. cit. distinguishes between innate knowledge, which is latent, and actual knowledge, for which the time when we acquired it can be remembered.
2–6. Cf. Dam. I § 269.6–9; Ol. 12 § 2.8–18. Ar., frg. 41 R.³ (=Pr., Rep. II 349.13–26) ... φησὶ γὰρ οὖν καὶ αὐτὸς ἐκ μὲν ὑγείας εἰς νόσον ὁδεύοντας λήθην ἴσχειν τινὰς καὶ αὐτῶν τῶν γραμμάτων ὧν ἐμεμαθήκεσαν ... ἐοικέναι δὲ τὴν μὲν ἄνευ σώματος ζωὴν ταῖς ψυχαῖς κατὰ φύσιν οὖσαν ὑγείᾳ, τὴν δὲ ἐν σώμασιν, ὡς παρὰ φύσιν, νόσῳ.
3. ληθάργῳ: cf. Ol. 11 § 16.4.
5. πολλῷ=πολλῷ μᾶλλον also princ. 14.25. Pr. Parm. 867.5.

of all we have learnt; so this is even more liable to happen when we pass into genesis, which especially affects the imagination, the faculty by which we remember place and time; in fact, we should not recollect forms either, if our notions of them were not eradiated by our essential being.

18. Can there be something in Aristotle's view [*eth. Nic.* VI 12, 1143b4–7] that the soul thinks naturally, just as the eye sees naturally when a visible object is within range? – In that case, however, she ought to think nothing besides the given facts; as it is, she has the power of passing judgment on them.

19. Why are we not conscious, when recollecting, *that* we recollect, as we are in all other cases of remembering? – To begin with, it is not always true even in those; secondly, there is the drastic change of passing into genesis, whereas even in dreams we are not aware that certain things are untrue and actually impossible; thirdly, self-consciousness is apt to be diverted.

20. Why are 'Pythagorean recollections,' that is to say, those of former lives, so rare? – Because they also require the identity of the pneumatic organism.

21. What is the faculty by which one recollects that there is recollection? It cannot be the same by which we recollect forms, otherwise the two would necessarily always come together, recollection of forms, and simultaneously of the fact that there is recollection. – This is the special task of self-consciousness.

22. Do irrational animals also have recollection? – That there is memory and that there is forgetting are observable facts. Further, after forgetting they can resume the same routine, but they are not conscious of having recollected it.

23. How many kinds of recollection are there? – As many as of knowledge, that is, generally speaking, three: intellective, dianoetic, and opinative.

6–7. Cf. Pr., *Rep.* II 350.15–22 (quoted above at II § 5).

6. εἰς : still depends on δράσει (3). The idea is that imagination lives and dies with the pneumatic body, cf. § 20.

7–8. εἰ μὴ ἀπὸ τῆς οὐσίας οἱ λόγοι ἀπέπνεον : cf. Pr., *Alc.* 192.3–4 κατ' οὐσίαν ἔχοντες τοὺς λόγους καὶ οἷον ἀποπνέοντες τὰς τούτων γνώσεις, κατ' ἐνέργειαν δὲ καὶ κατὰ προβολὴν οὐκ ἔχοντες.

§ 18. Cf. Dam. I § 267. Ar., *eth. Nic.* VI 12, 1143b4–7 ἐκ τῶν καθ' ἕκαστα γὰρ τὰ καθόλου· τούτων οὖν ἔχειν δεῖ αἴσθησιν, αὕτη δ' ἐστὶ νοῦς. διὸ καὶ φυσικὰ δοκεῖ εἶναι ταῦτα, καὶ φύσει σοφὸς μὲν οὐδείς, γνώμην δ' ἔχειν καὶ σύνεσιν καὶ νοῦν.

3. ἐπικρίνει : a Platonic term, *Rep.* VII 524e2–4 (thought is stimulated only by contrary perceptions) εἰ δ' ἀεί τι αὐτῷ ἅμα ὁρᾶται ἐναντίωμα, ὥστε μηδὲν μᾶλλον ἓν ἢ καὶ τοὐναντίον φαίνεσθαι, τοῦ ἐπικρινοῦντος δὴ δέοι ἂν ἤδη.

γένεσιν, ἄλλως τε καὶ εἰς τὸ φανταστικόν, ὃ δὴ τόπου καὶ χρόνου μέμνηται· ἐπεὶ οὐδ᾽ ἂν τῶν εἰδῶν ἀνεμνήσθημεν, εἰ μὴ ἀπὸ τῆς οὐσίας οἱ λόγοι ἀπέπνεον.

ιη'. - Μήποτε φύσει νοεῖ κατὰ Ἀριστοτέλη [eth. Nic. VI 12, 1143b4–7], 18 ὥσπερ τὸ ὄμμα φύσει ὁρᾷ προσπίπτοντος τοῦ ὁρατοῦ. — Ἀλλ᾽ ἔδει μηδὲν ἄλλο προσνοεῖν παρὰ τὰ διδόμενα· νῦν δὲ ἐπικρίνει.

ιθ'. - Διὰ τί μὴ συννοοῦμεν ἀναμιμνησκόμενοι ὅτι ἀναμιμνησκόμεθα, ὡς ἐν 19 πάσαις ταῖς ἀναμνήσεσιν; — Ἢ μάλιστα μὲν οὐδὲ ἐν ταύταις ἀεί· ἔπειτα καὶ ἡ μεταβολὴ πολλή τις ἡ εἰς τὴν γένεσιν, ὅπου γε οὐδὲ ἐν τοῖς ἐνυπνίοις ἐφιστάνομεν ὅτι ψευδῆ ἔνια καὶ ὄντα ἀδύνατα· τρίτον δὲ ὅτι καὶ εὐπαθὲς τὸ προσεκτικὸν εἰς ἔκκρουσιν. 5

κ'. - Διὰ τί σπάνιοι αἱ κατὰ Πυθαγόραν ἀναμνήσεις, φημὶ δὲ αἱ τῶν 20(211) προβιοτῶν; — Ἢ ὅτι προσδέονται καὶ τοῦ πνευματικοῦ ζῴου τοῦ αὐτοῦ μένοντος.

κα'. - Τί τὸ ἀναμιμνησκόμενον ὅτι ἀνέμνησται; οὐ γὰρ ὃ τῶν εἰδῶν 21 ἀναμιμνήσκεται, ᾗ ἔδει γε ἀεὶ καὶ τὸ ἕτερον, ἅμα τε τῶν εἰδῶν καὶ εὐθὺς τοῦ ὅτι ἀνέμνησται. — Ἢ ἴδιον τοῦτο τοῦ προσεκτικοῦ.

κβ'. - Εἰ καὶ ἐν τοῖς ἀλόγοις ἐστὶν ἀνάμνησις; — Ὅτι μὲν οὖν μνήμη καὶ 22 ὅτι λήθη, δηλοῖ ἡ αἴσθησις. ἀλλὰ μὴν δύναται καὶ μετὰ λήθην πάλιν τὴν αὐτὴν συνήθειαν ἀναλαβεῖν, οὐ μὴν ἐφίστησιν ὅτι ἀνέμνησται.

κγ'. - Πόσαι αἱ ἀναμνήσεις; — Ἢ ὅσαι αἱ γνώσεις· αὗται δὲ ὡς γενικῶς 23 φάναι τρεῖς, νοερὰ διανοητικὴ δοξαστική.

---

§ 19. 2 ἀεὶ M^c: om. M¹
§ 20. 2 προβιωτῶν M¹
§ 23. 1 αὗται μ : αὐταὶ M

---

§ 19. Dam. I § 269. Ol. 12 § 2.15–18.
4. Perhaps καὶ ⟨οὐκ⟩ ὄντα ⟨καὶ⟩ ἀδύνατα, cf. Dam., Phil. § 171.3 ὡς γὰρ τὰ ἐν τοῖς ὀνείρασιν οὐκ ὄντα, ἔνια δὲ καὶ ἀδύνατα, οὕτω καὶ αἱ ἡδοναὶ μὴ οὖσαι καὶ ἀδύνατοι.
4–5. τὸ προσεκτικόν : see note on I § 271.
§ 20. Dam. I § 270. – On Pythagorean recollections cf. Porphyry, vit. Pyth. 26–27; Iambl., vit. Pyth. 14, 63; supra I §§ 284–287. – The solutions given in Dam. I are different. Here, the imaginative faculty is taken to belong to the pneumatic body, which is apparently not the case in Pr., Tim. III 286.26–287.1 (where unfortunately the decisive words are missing, 286.28).
§ 21. Dam. I § 271.
§ 22. Dam. I § 272. Cf. Ol. 11 § 4.16–18.
§ 23. Dam. I § 273, and note.

§§ 24–27. A few questions and observations. 72e3–77a5

24. Is there also recollection of falsehood, as Bion wanted to know? — As a matter of fact, falsehood appears together with recollection, while the concept is still undeveloped and still fallible; a blind-born man, of course, can never be in error about colors.

25. Why does one not recollect without proof, as Strato [frg. 125] objected? Surely it is the cogent force of the argument that carries conviction, not the recollection? — The commentator's solution is that the first enlightenment comes from intuitive perception, and the proofs are added to develop the concept.

It is better to say that proof has been devised as a support.

26. Why do blind-born people not recollect colors? — Because the faculty of recollection needs a stimulus; then even a slight impulse will release a great many memories, almost in a flash.

27. What follows from this argument, according to Proclus, is that our souls have pre-existed from infinity, not, however, that they will continue to exist in the future, and therefore this argument, too, is incomplete; it even leaves open the possibility that the soul, with all its knowledge, has a beginning in time. But in that case knowledge is not acquired, so that it cannot be lost either, it is not produced from within, but implanted from without, and we shall have to make the efficient cause responsible not only for the good, but also for evil.

§ 28. Extracts from Plutarch on recollection. 72e3–77a5

28. A collection of various arguments to show that learning is recollection, from Plutarch of Chaeronea

(1) One thing suggests another, which could not happen, if it had not been known before. — The argument is from Plato.

(2) We can supply what is wanting in sensible things. — Also from Plato.

(3) Children learn more easily, because they are closer to the period of pre-existence, in which memory was continuous. — Superficial.

(4) Different people have aptitudes for different subjects.

(5) There are many examples of self-taught men who have completely mastered a particular art or craft.

(6) Many babies laugh in their sleep, before they do so while awake; and many have been known to speak even while awake, when normally they could not yet speak.

---

§ 24.   Dam. I § 293.
§ 25.   Dam. I § 294. Cf. *infra* § 65.11–12.
§ 26.   Cf. Dam. I § 294.6.
§ 27.   Dam. I § 297.

§§ 24–27. A few questions and observations. 72e3–77a5

κδ'. - Εἰ καὶ τοῦ ψεύδους ἐστὶν ἀνάμνησις, ὡς ἠπόρει Βίων; — Ἡ τῇ 24
ἀναμνήσει καὶ αὐτὸ συνυφίσταται κατὰ τὴν ἀδιάρθρωτον ἔννοιαν καὶ ἔτι
σφαλλομένην, ἐπεὶ ὅ γε τυφλὸς ἐκ γενετῆς οὐκ ἂν ψευσθείη περὶ χρωμάτων.
κε'. - Διὰ τί μὴ ἀναμιμνήσκεταί τις ἄνευ ἀποδείξεως, ὡς ἀπορεῖ Στράτων 25
[frg. 125]; ἡ γοῦν ἀποδεικτικὴ ἀνάγκη πείθει τὴν ψυχήν, ἀλλ' οὐχ ἡ ἀνάμνησις.
— Ἡ, φησὶν ὁ ἐξηγητής, τὰ πρῶτα δι' ἐπιβολῆς ἀπεφάνθη, προσετέθησαν δὲ αἱ
ἀποδείξεις κατὰ διάρθρωσιν.
Ἄμεινον δὲ βοηθείας ἕνεκα φάναι τὴν ἀπόδειξιν εὑρῆσθαι. 5
κς'. - Διὰ τί μὴ ἀναμιμνήσκονται χρωμάτων οἱ τυφλοὶ ὄντες ἐκ γενετῆς; 26
— Ἡ ὅτι τοῦ νύττοντος ἡ ἀναμνηστικὴ προσδεῖται δύναμις, ἥτις καὶ ἀπὸ
μικροῦ πολλῶν εἰς μνήμην ἔρχεται σχεδὸν ἀθρόως.
κζ'. - Ὅτι τῷ λόγῳ τούτῳ ἕπεται, φησὶν ὁ Πρόκλος, προϋπάρχειν ἡμῶν 27
τὴν ψυχὴν τὸν ἄπειρον χρόνον, οὐ μὴν ὅτι καὶ εἰς τὸν ἔπειτα, διόπερ ἀτελὴς
καὶ οὗτος· εἰ μὴ ἄρα ἡ ψυχὴ καὶ ἀπὸ χρόνου ὑπέστη μετὰ τῶν ἐπιστημῶν.
ἀλλ' οὕτω γε οὔτε ἐπίκτητοι ὥστε οὐδὲ ἀφαιρεταί, οὔτε οἴκοθεν προβαλλόμεναι
ἀλλ' ἐντιθέμεναι ἔξωθεν, οὔτε μόνον τῶν ἀγαθῶν αἰτιασόμεθα τὸ ποιοῦν ἀλλὰ 5
καὶ τῶν κακῶν.

§ 28. Extracts from Plutarch on recollection. 72e3–77a5

κη'. - Ἐπιχειρημάτων διαφόρων συναγωγὴ δεικνύντων ἀναμνή- 28(212)
σεις εἶναι τὰς μαθήσεις ἐκ τῶν τοῦ Χαιρωνέως Πλουτάρχου
α' Εἰ ἀφ' ἑτέρου ἕτερον ἐννοοῦμεν· οὐκ ἄν, εἰ μὴ προέγνωστο. — Τὸ ἐπιχείρημα
Πλατωνικόν.
β' Εἰ προστίθεμεν τὸ ἐλλεῖπον τοῖς αἰσθητοῖς. — Καὶ αὐτὸ Πλατωνικόν. 5
γ' Εἰ παῖδες εὐμαθέστεροι ὡς ἐγγίους τῆς προβιοτῆς, ἐν ᾗ ἡ μνήμη ἐσῴζετο.
— Ἐπιπόλαιος ὁ λόγος.
δ' Εἰ ἄλλοι πρὸς ἄλλο μάθημα ἐπιτηδειότεροι.
ε' Εἰ πολλοὶ αὐτοδίδακτοι ὅλων τεχνῶν.
ς' Εἰ πολλὰ παιδία ὑπνώττοντα γελᾷ, ὕπαρ δὲ οὔπω· πολλὰ δὲ καὶ ὕπαρ 10
ἐφθέγξατο ἄλλως οὔπω φθεγγόμενα.

---

§ 25. 3 προσετέθησαν] -σ-¹ in ras. Mᶜ

---

§ 28. Dam. I §§ 275–292. Plutarch frg. 217 Sandbach. Though obviously
Dam. I is on the whole more complete, II has some useful supplements. The
correspondences for the separate arguments are: (1)–(3) not in I; (4) I § 289;
(5) cf. I § 294; (6) I § 288; (7) I § 285; (8) I § 280; (9) I § 281; (10) I § 282;
(11)–(12) not in I.

(7) Even brave men are sometimes frightened by trifles, weasels or cocks for example, for no visible reason.

(8) The process of finding cannot be accounted for otherwise: no one will ever seek either for something he knows already or for something of which he has no previous knowledge at all; nor can we find what we do not know.

(9) In the word 'truth' [*alêtheia*] the discovery of reality is expressed by negation of forgetting [*lêthê*]. — This argument is purely verbal.

(10) The mother of the Muses is Mnemosyne, a symbol of the latent memory that is the cause of inquiry.

(11) What cannot be known, we do not seek. — This is a repetition of the argument from the possibility of finding [8].

(12) If finding is the discovery of what is there, this must apply also to the results of reflection. Where, then, are they found? Obviously in the soul.

III. THE ARGUMENT FROM SIMILARITY TO THINGS INTELLIGIBLE

§ 29. Plotinus' proof of immortality and the argument from similarity. 78b4–85b9

29. Plotinus [IV 7?] imagined himself the first to prove the immortality by the soul by demonstrating that it is neither body nor inseparable from the body, these being the causes from which death can come to things naturally subject to it: in the case of the body because it is composite and therefore liable to be dissolved into its components, and in the case of what is inseparable from the body because it exists in a substratum, so that, when the substratum is destroyed, the incorporeal attribute perishes with it. Plato, however, already presents this proof in the present passage, where he shows that the soul is neither a body, since it is incomposite and invisible, nor *in* a body, since it is capable of ruling and thinking. Yet, Proclus says, the argument is not comprehensive enough to furnish complete proof of the soul's immortality; it may still be in yet another body not as perishable as this is, so that, even though it is not destroyed because it has this body as its substratum, the possibility remains that, being in another body, it may survive only during a protracted period of time.

This is what Proclus brings up against Plotinus' argument. However, to begin with, we must not regard the present argument as identical with the one in Plotinus, which was general in scope, starting from the different

---

16. *λογική* : as opposed to *πραγματειώδης* (cf. Pr., *Parm.* 635.28, where, however, the contrast is between metaphysical reality and formal logic).

§ 29. Dam. I § 311. Ol. 13 § 4 (and note).

7–11. Pr. points out that theoretically, as far as this argument goes, the soul's

ζ' Εἰ ἔνιοι καὶ ἀνδρεῖοι ὄντες ὅμως φοβοῦνται φαῦλα ἄττα, οἷον γαλῆν ἢ ἀλεκτρυόνα, ἀπ' οὐδεμιᾶς φανερᾶς αἰτίας.
η' Εἰ μὴ ἔστιν ἄλλως εὑρίσκειν· οὔτε γὰρ ἃ ἴσμεν ζητήσειεν ἄν τις, οὔτε ἃ μηδαμῶς ἴσμεν πρότερον, ἀλλ' οὐδ' ἂν εὕροιμεν ἃ μὴ ἴσμεν. 15
θ' Εἰ ἡ ἀλήθεια κατὰ ἀφαίρεσιν τῆς λήθης ἔντευξις τοῦ ὄντος ἐστίν. — Λογικὴ ἡ ἐπιχείρησις.
ι' Εἰ ἡ μήτηρ τῶν Μουσῶν Μνημοσύνη, ὡς ἡ ἀδιάρθρωτος μνήμη τῶν ζητήσεων αἰτία.
ια' Εἰ ὅπερ ἀδύνατον γιγνώσκειν οὐδὲ ζητοῦμεν. — Ἀλλὰ τὸ ἐπιχείρημα πάλιν 20
ἀπὸ τῆς εὑρέσεως.
ιβ' Εἰ τοῦ ὄντος ἡ εὕρεσις, πάντως ὅτι καὶ θεωρημάτων· καὶ ποῦ οὖν ὄντων; ἢ δῆλον ὅτι ἐν ψυχῇ.

III. THE ARGUMENT FROM SIMILARITY TO THINGS INTELLIGIBLE

§ 29. Plotinus' proof of immortality and the argument from similarity. 78b4–85b9

κθ'. — Ὅτι Πλωτῖνος [IV 7?] ᾠήθη δεικνύναι πρῶτος τὴν ψυχὴν ἀθάνατον 29(213) ἀποδείξας οὖσαν αὐτὴν μήτε σῶμα μήτε ἀχώριστον σώματος, καθὰ καὶ οἷς ὁ θάνατος πέφυκε παραγίγνεσθαι, τῷ μὲν ὅτι σύνθετον (διαλύεται γὰρ ἐξ ὧν συνετέθη), τῷ δὲ ὅτι ἐν ὑποκειμένῳ (ἀπολλυμένου γὰρ αὐτοῦ συναπόλλυται καὶ τὸ ἐν αὐτῷ ἀσώματον). ὁ δὲ Πλάτων καὶ ταύτην παρέσχετο τὴν ἀπόδειξιν ἐν 5 τούτῳ τῷ λόγῳ δείξας οὔτε σῶμα οὖσαν, διότι ἀσύνθετος καὶ ἀόρατος, οὔτε ἐν σώματι, διότι δεσποτικὴ καὶ διανοητική. οὐ μὴν ἀρκεῖν γε τὸν λόγον φησὶν Πρόκλος πρὸς τελέαν ἀθανασίαν· τάχα γὰρ ἂν εἴη, φησίν, ἐν ἄλλῳ σώματι τῷ μὴ ὁμοίως τούτῳ διαφθειρομένῳ, ὥστε κἂν μὴ φθείρηται ὡς ἐν ὑποκειμένῳ τούτῳ τῷ σώματι, ἀλλὰ ἐν ἑτέρῳ γε, φησίν, οὐδὲν κωλύει αὐτὴν ἐνοῦσαν 10 διασῴζεσθαι πλεῖστον χρόνον.
Οὕτω μὲν ὁ Πρόκλος ἀπαντᾷ πρὸς τὸν Πλωτίνου λόγον, χρὴ δὲ μήτε ὅμοιον ἡγεῖσθαι τὸν προκείμενον λόγον τῷ Πλωτίνου (ὁ μὲν γὰρ ἦν καθόλου ἀπὸ τῆς

---

§ 28. 12 ἀνδρεῖ~οι, -εῖ- ex corr., ~ in ras., -ι ex -ί, Mᶜ (ἀνδρικοί ut vid. M¹) — 13 ἀλεκτρυόνα Mᶜ: ἀλεκτρυωνα M¹ (?)

---

survival might depend on its union with the pneumatic body, which lasts longer than the earthly body. In doing so, his concern is to safeguard his doctrine of the limited survival of irrational soul (*Tim.* III 234.6–238.26): if the argument as propounded here had absolute validity, it would prove the immortality of irrational soul, too, since it is separable from the body.

possible causes of death, and then, via the minor 'The soul is separable,' leading to the conclusion 'The soul does not admit of death,' whereas the present passage argues from similarity to the eternal on the one hand, and to the ever-changing on the other; in the second place, even granting that the arguments are identical, it is a mistake to allege against Plotinus the possibility of another body as substratum of the soul, since he assumes categorically that the soul is not in a substratum, but separable; a legitimate question would be whether even a separable entity can perish, if it has its existence in time, supposing that such a thing is possible at all.

§§ 30-31. A survey of 80b1-c1

30. The point of departure of this argument is the nature of real-existence and of genesis, and the formal characteristics of each. Real-existence is characterized by divinity, immortality, intelligentiality, singleness of form, indissolubility, identity of condition and nature. These are the marks of real-existence; those of genesis are their contraries: humanity (in the sense of the lowest level of form), absence of immortality, non-intelligentiality, multifariousness, dissolubility, absence of identity of condition and nature. These are the characteristics of each of the two kinds of existence, the real and the generated. By 'divinity' is meant either conformity to the Good and to the One, or (rather) primal being; by 'immortality' everlasting life; by 'intelligentiality' capability of thought, as the opposite, 'non-intelligentiality' proves; by 'singleness of form' indivisibility, non-pluralization, comprehension of all plurality in a unit; by 'indissolubility' inflexibility of essence; by 'identity of condition and nature' invariability of activities.

31. Having established these points Socrates next divides man also into two, body and soul, then shows that the body is akin to the dissoluble and not-immortal, the soul to the immortal and indissoluble. Then he draws an inference *a fortiori*: if the body continues to exist after death for a very long time indeed, the soul must survive far longer.

§§ 32-34. Analysis of the argument. 78b4-80c1

32. How does he conclude that soul is akin to real-existence, body to genesis? — (1) [79b1-c1] Soul is invisible, body visible, the visible is by its nature subject to process, the invisible has essential reality; 'visible' is used

---

§ 30. Dam. I §§ 312-318. Ol. 13 §§ 1-2.

7-8. δηλοῖ δὲ τὸ θεῖον ... τὸ ἀγαθοειδὲς καὶ ἡνωμένον : because God is τἀγαθόν and τὸ ἕν.

8. ἀείζων : I have preferred this to ἀεὶ ζῶν (M), because the attribute 'everlastingness' is required rather than 'that which lives forever'. For the forms ἀείζως and ἀείζωος see *LSJ* and *PGL*; in Neoplatonic texts we find ἀείζως Pr., *Tim.* II

τῶν θανάτων διαφορᾶς ἐπιχειρῶν, εἶτα δεικνὺς ὅτι 'ἀλλὰ μὴν χωριστὴ ἡ ψυχή, οὐκ ἄρα θάνατον ἐπιδεχομένη', ὁ δὲ νῦν λόγος ἀπὸ τῆς ὁμοιότητος ἐπιχειρεῖ 15 τῆς τε πρὸς τὸ αἰώνιον καὶ τῆς πρὸς τὸ ἄλλοτε ἄλλως ἔχον)· ἔπειτα δέ, εἰ καὶ ἦν ὁ αὐτὸς λόγος, οὐκ ἔδει ἐλέγχειν τὸν Πλωτίνου διὰ τοῦ δύνασθαι ἐν ἄλλῳ σώματι εἶναι τὴν ψυχήν (καθάπαξ γὰρ ἐκεῖνος ἔλαβεν τὸ μὴ ἐν ὑποκειμένῳ εἶναι τὴν ψυχήν, ἀλλὰ χωριστήν), ἀλλ' ἐχρῆν ἐνστῆναι, μήποτέ τι καὶ χωριστὸν διαφθείρεται ἐν χρόνῳ γενόμενον, εἴπερ οἷόν τε. 20

§§ 30–31. A survey of 80b1–c1

λ'. – Ὅτι ὑποτίθεται οὗτος ὁ λόγος, οἷον μὲν οὐσία, οἷον δὲ γένεσις, καὶ 30 τίσιν ἑκατέρα εἰδοποιεῖται. ἡ μὲν οὖν οὐσία τῷ θείῳ, τῷ ἀθανάτῳ, τῷ νοητῷ, τῷ μονοειδεῖ, τῷ ἀδιαλύτῳ, τῷ κατὰ τὰ αὐτὰ καὶ ὡσαύτως ἔχοντι. τούτοις μὲν ἡ οὐσία· τοῖς δὲ ἀντικειμένοις ἡ γένεσις, τῷ ἀνθρωπίνῳ (ὡς ἂν εἰ λέγοι τῷ ἐσχάτῳ εἴδει), τῷ οὐκ ἀθανάτῳ, τῷ ἀνοήτῳ, τῷ πολυειδεῖ, τῷ διαλυτῷ, 5 τῷ μὴ ἔχειν κατὰ τὰ αὐτὰ καὶ ὡσαύτως. ταῦτα μέν ἐστιν οἷς ἑκατέρα φύσις χαρακτηρίζεται, ἥ τε οὐσιώδης καὶ ἡ | γενητή. δηλοῖ δὲ τὸ μὲν θεῖον ἤτοι τὸ (214) ἀγαθοειδὲς καὶ ἡνωμένον, ἢ μᾶλλον τὸ πρωτουργόν· τὸ δὲ ἀθάνατον τὸ ἀείζων· τὸ δὲ νοητὸν τὸ νοητικόν, ὡς δηλοῖ τὸ ἀνόητον ἀντιτεθέν· τὸ δὲ μονοειδὲς τὸ ἀδιαίρετον καὶ ἀπλήθυντον καὶ ἐν ἑνὶ πᾶν τὸ πλῆθος περιειληφός· τὸ δὲ ἀδιάλυτον 10 τὸ κατὰ τὴν οὐσίαν πεπηγός· τὸ δὲ κατὰ τὰ αὐτὰ καὶ ὡσαύτως ἔχον τὸ κατὰ τὰς ἐνεργείας ἀμετάβολον.

λα'. – Ὅτι τούτων προϋποκειμένων διελὼν καὶ τὸν ἄνθρωπον διχῇ, εἰς σῶμα 31 καὶ ψυχήν, ἀποδείκνυσι τὸ μὲν σῶμα τῷ διαλυτῷ καὶ οὐκ ἀθανάτῳ συγγενές, τὴν δὲ ψυχὴν τῷ ἀθανάτῳ καὶ ἀδιαλύτῳ. εἶτα ἐκ τοῦ μᾶλλον συλλογίζεται· εἰ γὰρ ἐπιδιαμένει πλεῖστον ὅσον χρόνον τὸ σῶμα, πολλῷ πλείονα διαμένει ἡ ψυχή.

§§ 32–34. Analysis of the argument. 78b4–80c1

λβ'. – Πῶς συλλογίζεται τὴν μὲν ψυχὴν τῇ οὐσίᾳ συγγενῆ, τὸ δὲ σῶμα τῇ 32 α' γενέσει; — [79b1-c1] Εἰ ἡ μὲν ψυχή, φησίν, ἀόρατος, τὸ δὲ σῶμα ὁρατόν, φύσει δέ τὸ μὲν ὁρατὸν γενητόν, τὸ δὲ ἀόρατον οὐσιῶδες· καλεῖ δὲ ὁρατὸν

---

§ 29. 20 γενόμενον μ : γεγνόμενον M
§ 30. 2 ἑκατέρα Nv: ἑκάτερα M — 6 ἔχειν] ἔχοντι Nv — 8 ἀείζων Wk: ἀεὶ ζῶν M
§ 31. 2 συγγενές] -ές in ras. Mᶜ

124.28; III 335.34; Steph., an. 528.28; ἀειζώων supra I § 477.1; but always ἄζως.
11. τὸ κατὰ τὴν οὐσίαν πεπηγός : cf. Pr., elem. 52 ... εἴτε τὴν οὐσίαν ἔχει μόνον αἰώνιον ... εἴτε τὴν ἐνέργειαν πρὸς τῇ οὐσίᾳ, καὶ ταύτην ἀθρόαν ἔχον καὶ ἐν τῷ αὐτῷ μέτρῳ τῆς τελειότητος ἑστηκυῖαν καὶ οἷον παγεῖσαν καθ' ἕνα καὶ τὸν αὐτὸν ὅρον. Dam., Phil. § 136.9 πεπηγυῖα ἡδονή. Ol. 11 § 3.7 πῆξις γὰρ τῆς γνώσεως ἡ μνήμη.
§§ 32–33. Dam. I §§ 325–328. Ol. 13 § 3.1–10.

here as a comprehensive term for what is perceived by the senses. — (2) [79c2–e7] When in contact with real-existence, soul is in its normal state, when it approaches the world of process, it is in an abnormal state, while the body, on the other hand, thrives when in contact with the generated world, and withers in the company of the soul, as appears from the fact that the stupid grow fat, the intelligent thin. — (3) [79e8–80a9] The soul dominates, as being does, since it is a cause, while genesis, as an effect, is subservient to being, and it is to genesis that the body is related.

33. Of these three arguments the first relates to essence (the one concerning the invisibility of the soul and the visibility of the body, these being essential attributes), the second to cognition, the third to appetitive life.

The following might be a more satisfactory grouping: the first regards the relation of other things to the soul and the body, the third that of the soul and the body to other things, the second the condition of each by itself.

34. The three syllogisms in due order are these:

(1) The soul is more similar to the indissoluble; what is more similar to the indissoluble is more indissoluble itself; therefore the soul is more indissoluble.

Soul ⏝ more similar to the indissoluble ⏝ more indissoluble.

(2) The soul is more indissoluble; what is more indissoluble is more durable; therefore the soul is more durable.
Soul ⏝ more indissoluble ⏝ more durable.

(3) ⟨The soul is more durable; what is more durable survives longer; therefore the soul survives longer.⟩
Soul ⏝ more durable ⏝ survives longer.

§§ 35–44. Some difficulties in 78c1–80e1

35. [78d1–7] From what kind of forms does the argument start? Inasmuch as they are described as divine and eternal and the soul is said to assimilate itself to them, intelligible forms are apparently meant, but inasmuch as we are said to discuss them, they must be dianoetic; for no intelligible reality can be an object of rational knowledge. — The solution is that while discussing these, we aim at those; we cannot understand a portrait either, unless we know it *as* a portrait; after all, we can draw certain conclusions about those higher forms, though we cannot see them yet, preparing our thoughts, as it were, for real being and for the intelligible world.

---

§ 32. 8. A remote echo of Pl., *Phil.* 27a8–9 οὐ ταὐτὸν αἰτία τ' ἐστὶ καὶ τὸ δουλεῦον εἰς γένεσιν αἰτίᾳ.

β' καθάπαξ τὸ αἰσθήσει περιληπτόν. — [79c2–e7] Εἰ τῇ μὲν οὐσίᾳ ὁμιλοῦσα κατὰ φύσιν ἔχει ἡ ψυχή, τῇ δὲ γενέσει πλησιάζουσα παρὰ φύσιν, τὸ δὲ σῶμα ἀνάπαλιν τῇ μὲν γενέσει συνὸν θάλλει, τῇ δὲ ψυχῇ φθίνει, ὡς δηλοῦσι πιαινόμενοι μὲν
γ' οἱ ἀνόητοι, ἰσχναινόμενοι δὲ οἱ νουνεχεῖς. — [79e8–80a9] Εἰ ψυχὴ μὲν ἀρχικόν, ὡς ἡ οὐσία, αἰτία οὖσα, ἡ δὲ γένεσις δοῦλον ὡς αἰτιατόν, ᾗ οἰκεῖον τὸ σῶμα.

λγ'. — Ὅτι τῶν εἰρημένων τριῶν ἐπιχειρημάτων τὸ μὲν πρῶτον ἀπὸ τῆς οὐσίας εἴληπται, φημὶ δὲ τὸ ἀόρατον τῆς ψυχῆς καὶ ὁρατὸν τοῦ σώματος (οὐσιώδη γὰρ αὐτοῖς ταῦτα), τὸ δὲ δεύτερον ἀπὸ τῆς γνώσεως, τὸ δὲ τρίτον ἀπὸ τῆς ζωῆς.

Μήποτε δὲ ἄμεινον διελεῖν τὸ μὲν πρῶτον ἀπὸ τῆς ἄλλων πρὸς αὐτὰ σχέσεως, τὸ δὲ τρίτον ἀπὸ τῆς αὐτῶν πρὸς τὰ ἄλλα, τὸ δὲ δεύτερον ἀπὸ τῆς [τῶν] αὐτῶν καθ' ἑαυτὰ διαθέσεως.

λδ'. — Ὅτι τρεῖς ἐφεξῆς οἱ συλλογισμοὶ τοιοίδε τινές·
α' ἡ ψυχὴ ὁμοιοτέρα πρὸς τὸ ἀδιάλυτον· τὸ ὁμοιότερον πρὸς τὸ ἀδιάλυτον μᾶλλον ἀδιάλυτον· ἡ ψυχὴ ἄρα μᾶλλον ἀδιάλυτον.

ἡ ψυχὴ ̮̮̮̮ ὁμοιοτέρα πρὸς τὸ ἀδιάλυτον ̮̮̮̮ μᾶλλον ἀδιάλυτον.

β' ἡ ψυχὴ μᾶλλον ἀδιάλυτον· τὸ μᾶλλον ἀδιάλυτον πολυχρονιώτερον· ἡ ψυχὴ ἄρα πολυχρονιώτερον.

ἡ ψυχὴ ̮̮̮̮ μᾶλλον ἀδιάλυτον ̮̮̮̮ πολυχρονιώτερον.

γ' ⟨ἡ ψυχὴ πολυχρονιώτερον· τὸ πολυχρονιώτερον μᾶλλον ἐπιδιαμένει· ἡ ψυχὴ ἄρα μᾶλλον ἐπιδιαμένει.⟩

ἡ ψυχὴ ̮̮̮̮ πολυχρονιώτερον ̮̮̮̮ μᾶλλον ἐπιδιαμένει.

§§ 35–44. Some difficulties in 78c1–80e1

δ λε'. — [78d1–7] Ἀπὸ ποίων εἰδῶν ὥρμηται ὁ λόγος; ὡς μὲν γὰρ θείων καὶ αἰωνίων λεγομένων καὶ ὡς τῆς ψυχῆς ἐκείνοις ἀφομοιουμένης δῆλον ὅτι ἀπὸ τῶν νοητῶν, ὡς δὲ ἡμῶν τοὺς λόγους περὶ αὐτῶν ποιουμένων ἀπὸ τῶν διανοητῶν· οὐδὲν γὰρ νοητὸν ἐπιστητόν. — Ἤ διαλεγόμεθα μὲν περὶ τούτων, εἰς ἐκεῖνα δὲ ἀποτεινόμεθα· καὶ γὰρ οὐδὲ τὴν εἰκόνα γιγνώσκομεν, εἰ μὴ ὡς εἰκόνα γνοίημεν· ἐπεὶ καὶ συλλογίζεσθαι περὶ ἐκείνων δυνατόν, ὁρᾶν δὲ μήπω, οἷον προενθυμουμένους τὸ ὂν καὶ νοητόν.

---

§ 32. 4 ante κατὰ] ⸑ in ras. 2 litt. Mᶜ
§ 33. 6 πρὸς τὰ ἄλλα] in ras. Mᶜ | δεύτερον] in ras. 4 litt. Mᶜ — 6–7 τῶν αὐτῶν] τῶν αὐ- ex corr., accent. in -ῶ-² add., Mᶜ; τῶν del. Wk
§ 34. 4; 7; 10 in spat. vac. Mᶜ — 8–9 add. Nv (1915, 136 n. 1)
§ 35. 2 ἀφομοιουμένης Fh: -ων M

---

§ 34. Dam. I § 329. Ol. 13 § 3.16–20.
§ 35. Dam. I § 330. Ol. 13 § 5.

36. [78d1-4] How is it that the world should not be dissoluble, though it is composite? — According to most of the ancients it is dissoluble by its own nature, but indissoluble by the will of God.

In that case, however, if he could not make it indissoluble at the outset, he could not do so afterwards, even if he wanted to. Also, why should he upset his own work by making indissoluble what is dissoluble by nature? It is better, therefore, to consider the world indissoluble from the very beginning, adding, as a further bond, the will of God; and specifying that it can be dissolved by none but by Him who joined it together in the sense that it is He from whom a stream of infinity flows toward it and who knows the ways in which the bonds can be untied.

But in the first place, the world does not need such a constant flow of adventitious potency, since even a finite body can possess infinite potency, as is shown elsewhere; in the second place, how can God's knowledge of the way to solve it remain ineffective? A better formula is this: just as we say that what is usually called generated and perishable is in reality both in process of becoming and in process of destruction, so the structure of the heavens is both in process of being joined together and in process of being dissolved; indeed, it would not be composite at all, if it were not at the same time broken down somehow, since it is not completely united.

37. [79a1-4] Why does he mention it as a specific property of intelligible things that we do not use sense-perception to know them? — Because, when discussing objects of discursive reason, we shall need sensible things to stir our recollection, but where intelligible things are concerned, the knowledge derived from discursive thought will serve as a help, as it is set forth in the *Republic* [VII 533c7-e2]. So Socrates is right in making this the proper characteristic of intelligible things, that no sense-perception is needed to know them, but if an instrument is necessary at all, it is discursive thought.

38. [79b7-11] Why does he assume that the soul is invisible 'to human beings' only? — Whatever is visible is visible also to man, either in the natural way or by a divine art; in each of the two cases there are two

---

§ 36. Dam. I § 331. Ol. 13 § 2.32–40; § 9.

2. ὡς οἱ πολλοὶ τῶν παλαιῶν ᾠήθησαν: this is the obvious straightforward interpretation of *Tim*. 41a8–b6 τὸ μὲν οὖν δὴ δεθὲν πᾶν λυτόν, τό γε μὴν καλῶς ἁρμοσθὲν καὶ ἔχον εὖ λύειν ἐθέλειν κακοῦ· δι' ἃ καὶ ἐπείπερ γεγένησθε, ἀθάνατοι μὲν οὐκ ἐστὲ οὐδ' ἄλυτοι τὸ πάμπαν, οὔτι μὲν δὴ λυθήσεσθέ γε . . ., τῆς ἐμῆς βουλήσεως μείζονος ἔτι δεσμοῦ καὶ κυριωτέρου λαχόντες ἐκείνων οἷς ὅτ' ἐγίγνεσθε συνεδεῖσθε. However, in defense of the doctrine of the eternity of the world, Pr., *Tim*. III 212.6–29, brands it as a misinterpretation by Severus, Atticus and Plutarch: . . . γελοῖον οὖν τὸ λέγειν λυτὰ ὄντα καθ' αὑτὰ ἄλυτα μόνως εἶναι διὰ τὴν τοῦ πατρὸς βούλησιν, ὃ δὴ λέγουσιν ἐκεῖνοι, σῴζειν ἐθέλοντες τὸ λέγον ἀξίωμα πᾶν γενητὸν ἔχειν φθορὰν καὶ τὸν κόσμον γενητὸν ποιοῦντες (23–27). The formula "most of the ancients" might be a vague substitute for the three Middle Platonists mentioned.

4–8. Pr.'s interpretation of the *Tim*. passage cited above, cf. *Tim*. III 212-214.

λς'. - [78d1-4] *Πῶς οὐχὶ καὶ ὁ κόσμος λυτός, εἴπερ σύνθετος;* — Ἢ λυτὸς 36
μὲν τῇ ἑαυτοῦ φύσει, ὡς οἱ πολλοὶ τῶν παλαιῶν ᾠήθησαν, ἄλυτος δὲ τῇ βουλήσει
τοῦ θεοῦ.
Ἀλλ' οὕτως γε, εἰ μὴ ἀρχὴν ἠδύνατο ποιεῖν ἄλυτον, οὐδ' ἂν αὖθις δύναιτο
καὶ βουληθείς. πῶς δὲ ὃ ποιεῖ ἀνατρέπει, τὸ φύσει λυτὸν ἄλυτον ποιῶν; ἄμεινον 5
οὖν καὶ ἐξ ἀρχῆς μὲν ποιῆσαι ἄλυτον, προσθεῖναι δὲ καὶ ἄλλον δεσμὸν τὸν
ἀπὸ τῆς βουλήσεως· εἶναι δ' οὖν μόνῳ τῷ δήσαντι λυτόν, καθ' ὅσον αὐτὸς ἐπινάει
τὸ ἄπειρον καὶ γιγνώσκει τοὺς τρόπους τῶν δεσμῶν, ᾗ ἂν λυθεῖεν.
Ἀλλὰ πρῶτον μὲν οὐδὲν δεῖται τῆς ἀεὶ ἐπεισάκτου δυνάμεως· δύναται γὰρ
καὶ ἐν τῷ πεπερασμένῳ σώματι δύναμις εἶναι ἄπειρος, ὡς ἐν ἄλλοις δείκνυται. 10
δεύτερον δὲ πῶς ἀδρανὴς ἡ τῆς λύσεως γνῶσις; ἄμεινον οὖν, ὥσπερ λέγομεν
γιγνόμενον ἅμα καὶ ἀπολλύμενον εἶναι τὸ λεγόμενον γενητὸν καὶ φθαρτόν, οὕτω
συντιθέμενον ἅμα καὶ λυόμενον τὸ οὐράνιον σῶμα· οὐ γὰρ ἂν οὐδὲ σύνθετον ἦν,
εἰ μὴ καὶ ἐλέλυτό πῃ, ἅτε οὐχ ἡνωμένον.

λζ'. - [79a1-4] *Πῶς ἐξαίρετον τῶν νοητῶν τὸ μὴ χρῆσθαι αἰσθήσει λέγει;* 37(216)
— Ἢ ὅτι περὶ διανοητῶν διαλεγόμενοι δεησόμεθα πρὸς ὑπόμνησιν τῶν αἰσθητῶν,
περὶ δὲ τῶν νοητῶν τοῖς διανοουμένοις ὑπομιμνησκόμεθα, ὡς ἐν Πολιτείᾳ λέγεται
[VII 533c7-e2]. ὀρθῶς ἄρα τῶν νοητῶν ἴδιον ἔφη τοῦτο εἶναι, τὸ μηδὲν
αἰσθήσεως δεῖσθαι, ἀλλ', εἴπερ ἄρα, διανοίας ἐν ὀργάνου χρείᾳ. 5

λη'. - [79b7-11] *Πῶς 'ἀνθρώποις γε' μόνοις ἀόρατον ὑποτίθεται τὴν ψυχήν;* 38
— Ἢ ὅτι πᾶν ὁρατὸν καὶ ἀνθρώπῳ ἐστὶν ὁρατόν, ἢ τῇ φύσει ἢ τέχνῃ θείᾳ τινί·

9-14. Criticism by Dam. (cf. note on Ol. 13 § 2.37-40); hence the impersonal reference ὡς ἐν ἄλλοις δείκνυται is probably not to Pr., elem. 96 (παντὸς πεπερασμένου σώματος ἡ δύναμις, ἄπειρος οὖσα, ἀσώματός ἐστιν), but rather to Dam.'s own commentary on *Tim.* 41a8-b6 (a related subject is mentioned Dam., *Parm.* 269.1-2 δεύτερον δὲ πῶς ἔτι ἀθάνατος ἡ ψυχὴ καὶ ἄπειρον ἔχουσα δύναμιν, ὅπερ ἐδείκνυμεν ἐν τοῖς εἰς τὸν Τίμαιον, εἰ ἄλλη καὶ ἄλλη ἀεὶ αὐτῆς οὐσία ...;).
§ 37. Dam. I § 332. Ol. 13 § 12.
§ 38. Dam. I § 333. Ol. 13 § 15, and note.
1-4. The four kinds of sight listed here do not tally exactly with those in Ol. and Dam. I, which are: (1) natural sight, (2) κατὰ φυσικήν τινα ἰδιότητα, with Lynceus as example (Ol.), or κατὰ φυσικὴν τοιάνδε διασκευήν (Dam. I, cf. Pr., *Rep.* II 117.1-2; it may correspond to the vision of the luminous body in the present text, on which cf. Pr., *Rep.* II 186.9-11 πολλῶν γὰρ ἡμᾶς τὸ ὀστρεῖνον τοῦτο σῶμα, παχὺ καὶ χθόνιον

different possibilities: natural sight is a function either of this body of or the luminous body, and the divine art can be practiced either in individual trance or by means of certain forms of initiation.

This still does not answer the question, why he does not admit the invisibility of the soul absolutely, but limits it to man. — The answer is that he assigns all sense-perception to man in the same sense in which he described the whole world of process as 'human' [80b3].

39. [79d6] In what sense does he call insight an 'effect'? — As participation in absolute insight; Plato often uses 'being affected' for 'participating.'

Or perhaps as a disposition in the soul as a substance.

40. [79c2–9] Why this disparagement of sense-perception, which was given us, after all, to guide us towards philosophy [*Tim.* 47a7–b1]? — This is true only in so far as it stimulates recollection; but Plato rejects it as a way to perfect knowledge.

41. [80a10–c1] If the soul resembles the indissoluble, why should it follow that it *is* indissoluble? A wolf may resemble a dog, but it *is* not a dog. — In the first place, Plato says that it is less dissoluble than the body is. Secondly, in the case of the soul the resemblance concerns the essence, not a mere outline, as in the example of the wolf; consequently the soul is actually indissoluble, though less so than intelligible forms.

42. How do we explain that form is not more permanent *than matter*, as more similar to the immutable? — There is no complete analogy, since these forms exist only in a substratum.

Yet the question remains. It is better, therefore, to think of matter as not permanent; it is below permanency, for permanency belongs to form and *is* form.

43. Why does individual life not survive the body? — Proclus says, because it is not separable.

But the problem remains the same. We prefer to say that it *is* more permanent (it serves as a bond to perpetuate the organic body), but not permanent enough to exist separately. Or, from a more general point of view, it does not have the inferior kind of permanency that is characteristic

---

ὄν, κωλύει θεαμάτων, ὧν τὰ ἁπλούστερα περιβλήματα τῶν ψυχῶν αἰσθάνεται μειζόνως), (3) τέχνῃ τινί, by the use of strychnine or belladonna (Ol., Dam. I, Pr. *Rep.* II 117.2–4 and 186.12–19, where it is explained that this is an artificial means of activating a natural gift; missing here), (4) κατὰ ἐνθουσιασμόν, i.e. by second sight (Ol., Dam. I), subdivided here into individual ecstacy and a state of trance induced by certain rituals (cf. Pr., *Rep.* II 117.4–7; 186.19–22).

§ 39. Dam. I § 334. Ol. 13 § 19. Examples in Pl. of this use of πεπονθέναι *Soph.* 245a5, b7, c1, πάθος 245a1, b4, c2 (cf. Pr., *Tim.* II 304.17–29; Dam., *Parm.* 43.9); *Parm.* 139e8, 140a1, 3, 6–8, b1, 2 (cf. Pr., *Parm.* 1195.30–37; Dam., *Parm.* 200.1–4). Ol. cites *Soph.* 245b7. – The first answer agrees substantially with I § 334

καὶ τούτων ἑκάτερον διχῶς, τῇ μὲν φύσει ἢ κατὰ ταύτην τὴν αἴσθησιν ἢ κατὰ τὴν τοῦ αὐγοειδοῦς, τῇ δὲ θείᾳ τέχνῃ ἢ αὐτοὺς ἐνθεάζοντας ἢ διά τινων τελετῶν.

Ἀλλ' ἔτι ἡ ἀπορία, πῶς οὐχ ἁπλῶς ἀλλ' ʽὑπό γε ἀνθρώπων᾽ ἀόρατον 5 συνεχώρησεν. — Ἢ ὥσπερ ἀνθρώπειον ἔφη τὸ ὅλον γενητόν [80b3], οὕτω καὶ τὴν ὅλην αἴσθησιν ʽἀνθρώπων γε᾽ εἶναι ἐνδέδωκεν.

λθ'. - [79d6] Πῶς ʽπάθημα᾽ τὴν φρόνησιν ἔφη; — Ἢ ὅτι μέθεξίς ἐστι τῆς 39 αὐτοφρονήσεως· καὶ γὰρ τὸ μετέχειν ʽπεπονθέναι᾽ λέγει πολλάκις ὁ Πλάτων. Μήποτε δὲ καὶ ὡς διάθεσιν οὖσαν ἐν οὐσίᾳ τῇ ψυχῇ.

μ'. - [79c2-9] Πῶς τὴν αἴσθησιν ἀτιμάζει καίτοι πρὸς φιλοσοφίαν δεδομένην 40 [Tim. 47a7-b1]; — Ἢ ὅσον πρὸς ὑπόμνησιν· ἀτιμάζει δὲ ὡς πρὸς τελείαν γνῶσιν.

μα'. - [80a10-c1] Πῶς, εἰ ὁμοία τῷ ἀδιαλύτῳ, καὶ ἀδιάλυτος; οὐ γάρ, εἰ 41 κυνὶ λύκος, καὶ κύων ὁ λύκος. — Ἢ πρῶτον μὲν μᾶλλον ἢ τὸ σῶμα, φησίν. δεύτερον κατ' οὐσίαν τῆς ψυχῆς ἡ ὁμοιότης καὶ οὐχ ὥσπερ κατὰ τὴν ἔξω σκιαγραφίαν ὁ λύκος· ὥστε τῷ ὄντι καὶ ἀδιάλυτος, εἰ καὶ ἧττον ἤπερ τὰ νοητά.

μβ'. - Πῶς τὸ εἶδος οὐ μονιμώτερον ὡς τῷ ἀμεταβλήτῳ ὁμοιότερον; — Ἢ οὐ 42 πάντῃ ὅμοιον, ἐν ὑποκειμένῳ γάρ.

Ἀλλὰ μένει ἡ ἀπορία. βέλτιον οὖν τὴν ὕλην μὴ μένουσαν νοεῖν· χείρων γάρ ἐστιν ἢ κατὰ τὸ μένειν· καὶ γὰρ τὸ μένειν εἴδους καὶ εἶδος.

μγ'. - Πῶς οὐχὶ καὶ ἡ μερικὴ ζωὴ ἐπιδιαμένει μᾶλλον τοῦ σώματος; — 43(217) Ἢ ὅτι, φησὶν ὁ Πρόκλος, οὐ χωριστή.

Ἀλλ' ἡ ἀπορία μένει. βέλτιον οὖν λέγειν ὅτι μονιμωτέρα μέν ἐστιν (δεσμὸς γοῦν τῷ σώματι γίγνεται τῷ τοιῷδε πρὸς διαμονήν), οὐ τοσοῦτον δὲ μένει ὥστε καὶ χωρὶς εἶναι. ἢ ὅλως τὴν χείρω διαμονὴν οὐ διαμένει, ἥνπερ δηλαδὴ 5

---

§ 41. 4 ἤπερ] ἤ- in ras. M^c
§ 42. 1 ὁμοιότερον] -ό- in ras. M^c

---

and Ol. 13 § 19.1-7 (Proclus); the additional suggestion is by Dam.
2. αὐτοφρόνησις occurs also in the parallel passage in Ol.; *LSJ* cites it only from Himerius, *ecl.* 32, 14 αὐτοφρόνησις καθαρῶς ἡ τοιαύτη ψυχή.
§ 40. Dam. I § 335.
§§ 41-43. See Introduction to Ol., pp. 7-8.
§ 41. Dam. I § 336. Ol. 13 § 6.1-6.
1-2. Cf. Pl., *Soph.* 231a4-6.
3-4. The second solution is found only here.
§ 42. Dam. I § 337, and note. Ol. 13 § 6.7-11.
§ 43. Dam. I § 338. Ol. 13 § 6.12-15.

of the body, but only the permanency which it communicates to the body, and it ceases to exist because this kind of life cannot exist by itself.

44. [79e8–80a9] How can it be shown that the soul is separable and rules the body? — On the basis of all the qualifications of the ruler stated in the *Laws* [III 690a1–c9], as has been discussed there.

IV. THE ARGUMENT ON HARMONY

§§ 45–54. Analysis of the argument. 85b10–95a6

45. [91e2–92e3] Of the three arguments showing that soul is not harmony, the first, starting from what has already been proved, runs as follows: No harmony exists prior to its recipient; all soul exists prior to its recipient; therefore soul is not a harmony.

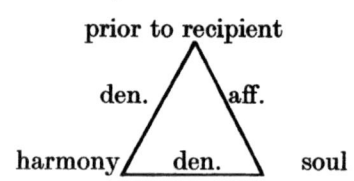

```
              prior to recipient
                    /\
              den. /  \ aff.
                  /    \
          harmony/ den. \ soul
```

46. [92e4–93a3] The assumptions on which the other arguments rest are these: first, every harmony and every compound is conditioned as its components are: if its substratum is uncorrupted, it is sound itself, otherwise it is corrupted with its substratum. An additional note: a harmony is the result of fusion, a compound of juxtaposition; unless one prefers to extend the sense of 'compound' so as to include fusion.

47. [93a4–5] The second assumption is that a harmony can neither exert nor undergo any influence apart from its components. What is the difference between this and the preceding assumption? This one considers the actions and affections of a harmony, the previous one its being only.

48. [93a6–7] Third comes the corollary that consequently a harmony does not precede its substrata, since it cannot precede them without them, all its actions and affections being shared with them; otherwise they would precede themselves.

49. [93a8–10] Fourthly he concludes that even more certainly it does not oppose its substrata, or it would abolish itself with them, since it will undergo the same influences that act upon them.

---

§ 44. Dam. I § 339.

2. ὡς ἐκεῖ εἴρηται (εἰρημένα M): if Norvin's very plausible conjecture is right, this can refer only to a commentary on *Laws* III either by Pr. or, much more probably, by Dam. The only commentary on the *Laws* otherwise known is Syrianus

τὸ σῶμα, ἀλλ᾽ ἢ μόνην ταύτην παραμένει ἧς καὶ μεταδίδωσι τῷ σώματι, οὐκέτι δὲ ἔστιν, ὅτι μηδέ ἐστιν ἡ τοιαύτη ζωὴ χωριστή.

μδ'. - [79e8–80a9] *Πῶς ἂν δειχθείη ἡ ψυχὴ χωριστὴ καὶ ἀρχική;* — Ἡ κατὰ **44** πάντα τὰ ἀξιώματα τὰ ἐν Νόμοις εἰρημένα [III 690a1–c9], ὡς ἐκεῖ εἴρηται.

IV. THE ARGUMENT ON HARMONY

§§ 45–54. Analysis of the argument. 85b10–95a6

με'. - [91e2–92e3] Ὅτι τριῶν ὄντων λόγων καθ᾽ οὓς ἐλέγχεται μὴ οὖσα ἡ **45** ψυχὴ ἁρμονία, ὁ πρῶτός ἐστιν ἀπὸ τῶν δεδειγμένων τοιοῦτος· πρὸ τοῦ ἐν ᾧ ἐστιν, οὐδεμία ἁρμονία· πρὸ τοῦ ἐν ᾧ ἐστι, πᾶσα ψυχή· ἡ ψυχὴ ἄρα οὐχ ἁρμονία.

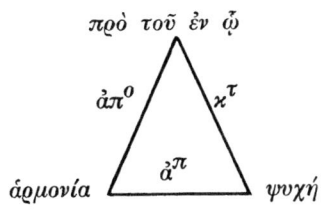

```
         πρὸ τοῦ ἐν ᾧ
              /\
         ἀπ⁰ /  \ κᵀ                                    5
            /    \
           / ᾱᵖ   \
   ἁρμονία /_____\ ψυχή
```

μϛ'. - [92e4–93a3] Ὅτι τῶν ἄλλων λόγων ὑποθέσεις, πρῶτον μὲν οὕτως **46** ἔχειν πᾶσαν ἁρμονίαν καὶ πᾶσαν σύνθεσιν ὡς ἂν ἔχῃ τὰ ἐξ ὧν σύγκειται· εἰ μὲν ἀδιάστροφα εἴη τὰ ὑποκείμενα, ἐρρῶσθαι καὶ αὐτήν, εἰ δὲ μή, συνδιεστράφθαι. ἔτι ἡ μὲν ἁρμονία κατὰ σύγκρασιν γίγνεται, ἡ δὲ σύνθεσις κατὰ παράθεσιν· εἰ μή που τὴν σύνθεσιν καθολικώτερόν τις λαμβάνοι, ὥστε καὶ τὴν κρᾶσιν 5 περιέχειν αὐτήν.

μζ'. - [93a4–5] Ὅτι δευτέρα ὑπόθεσις τὸ μηδὲν ποιεῖν μηδὲ πάσχειν τὴν **47(218)** ἁρμονίαν παρὰ τὰ ἐξ ὧν ἐστιν. καὶ τίνι διαφέρει αὕτη τῆς προτέρας ὑποθέσεως; ἢ ὅτι αὕτη μὲν τὰς ποιήσεις καὶ τὰς πείσεις τῆς ἁρμονίας ἐθεώρησεν, ἐκείνη δὲ αὐτὴν τὴν ὑπόστασιν.

μη'. - [93a6–7] Ὅτι τρίτον πορίζεται ὡς οὐδὲ ἡγεῖται ἄρα τῶν ὑποκειμένων, **48** εἴπερ οὐκ ἄνευ αὐτῶν ἡγήσεται· σὺν αὐτοῖς γὰρ πάντα καὶ ποιεῖ καὶ πάσχει· εἰ δὲ μή, καὶ αὐτὰ ἑαυτῶν ἡγήσεται.

μθ'. - [93a8–10] Ὅτι τέταρτον συνάγει ὡς πολλῷ μᾶλλον οὐδὲ ἐναντιοῦται· **49** εἰ δὲ μή, καὶ ἑαυτὴν ἀναιρήσει, ἡ γὰρ ἐκείνων πεπόνθησις ἑαυτῆς ἔσται.

---

§ 44. 2 εἴρηται Nv: εἰρημένα M
§ 45. 3 post ἐστιν] dimidius versus erasus (puto fuisse πᾶσα ψυχή· ἡ ψυχὴ ἄρα) | οὐδεμία ἁρμονία] -δεμία ἁρμο- in ras. 6–7 litt. Mᶜ (οὐχ ἁρμονία ut vid. M¹) | πρὸ — ἁρμονία² in spat. vac. Mᶜ — 5 κᵀ Mᶜ: om. M¹ — 6 ᾱᵖ Mᶜ: om. M¹
§ 46. 5 μή που Fh: μήπω M | καθολικώτερον] -θολικώτερον in ras. Mᶜ

---

on book X (Simpl., phys. 618.25–619.2; 635.11–14; 637.25–30; οἱ ἀμφὶ τὸν μέγαν Συριανόν Dam., princ. 30.12–14).
§ 45. Dam. I § 361.
§§ 46–50. Dam. I §§ 363–367.

50. [94b4–95a3] From these data the second argument is constructed thus: no harmony can oppose its recipient; all soul has the power of opposing its recipient; therefore harmony is not soul nor soul harmony.

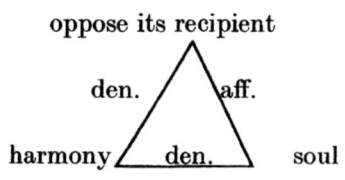

```
                oppose its recipient
                        /\
                  den. /  \ aff.
                      /    \
              harmony/ den. \ soul
```

51. [93a11–b3] For his third syllogism Socrates' first assumption is that the attunement of the substrata determines the character of the harmony as 'more or less' or 'greater or smaller.' 'Greater of smaller' regards the number of tones involved: the harmony is, for instance, the fourth, because there are four tones in it, or the fifth, because there are five, or the octave, because it includes all eight. 'More or less,' on the other hand, is a matter of tension and detension, each chord having a certain latitude to the ear, though not according to the musical ratio. Each ratio is one and describes one relation; hence the Pythagoreans had more confidence in this than in the judgment of the sense-organ. This is why Socrates adds 'If it is possible at all' (that there should be more or less complete attunement), because he is thinking of numerical harmonies (not the transcendent, but the co-ordinated kind).

52. [93b4–7] A second assumption regards the subject: the soul does not admit of gradation, being a substance (otherwise it would not be accessible to opposite accidents), while harmony does admit of gradation.

53. [93b8–e10] Socrates first advances the following proof: the soul is receptive of virtue and vice, any soul that is receptive of virtue and vice is receptive of harmony and disharmony, therefore the soul is receptive of harmony and disharmony. Again, harmony and disharmony cannot be predicated of any harmony, harmony and disharmony can be predicated of all soul, therefore harmony can be predicated of no soul.

54. [94a1–10] Another reasoning he uses is that it would follow that no soul is accessible to evil. If soul is harmony, and virtue is also harmony, then soul is receptive of virtue, or rather soul is virtue; now harmony never admits of disharmony, therefore neither will soul admit of vice. This consequence is absurd; and most of all so is that every soul, including those of irrational animals, will be equally good, since all are supposed to be harmonies.

---

§§ 51–54. See note on Dam. I §§ 368–370.

§ 51. Dam. I § 368.

7. ἆρα: logically, as the clause is obviously a premise, not a conclusion, γάρ seems to be the only possibility; the error, however, may be as old as the text.

ν'. - [94b4-95a3] Ὅτι ἐκ τούτων ὁ δεύτερος λόγος κατασκευάζεται οὕτως· 50
ἐναντιοῦσθαι τῷ ἐν ᾧ οὐδεμιᾷ ἁρμονίᾳ ὑπάρχει· ἐναντιοῦσθαι τῷ ἐν ᾧ κατὰ
πάσης ψυχῆς· ⟨ἡ⟩ ἁρμονία ἄρα οὐ ψυχὴ οὐδὲ ἡ ψυχὴ ἁρμονία.

ἐναντιοῦσθαι τῷ ἐν ᾧ

ἀπ⁰   κᵗ   5

ἁρμονία   ᾱᵖ   ψυχή

να'. - [93a11-b3] Ὅτι τοῦ τρίτου συλλογισμοῦ ὑποτίθεται πρώτην ὑπόθεσιν, 51
ὡς ἂν ἁρμοσθῇ τὰ ὑποκείμενα, οὕτως ἔχειν τὴν ἁρμονίαν, ἢ μᾶλλον ἢ ἧττον
ἢ πλεῖον ἢ ἔλαττον. ἔστι δὲ τὸ μὲν 'πλεῖον ἢ ἔλαττον' τῆς ποσότητος τῶν
φθόγγων· ἢ γὰρ διὰ τεσσάρων ἡ ἁρμονία, ἐπειδὴ τέσσαρες οἱ φθόγγοι, ἢ διὰ
πέντε, ἐπειδὴ πέντε, ἢ διὰ πασῶν, ἐπειδὴ πᾶσαι. τὸ δὲ 'μᾶλλον καὶ ἧττον' τῆς 5
ἐπιτάσεως καὶ ἀνέσεως· ἔχει γὰρ ἑκάστη ἁρμονία πλάτος τι κατὰ τὴν αἴσθησιν,
οὐ μὴν κατὰ τὸν ἁρμονικὸν λόγον. πᾶς ἄρα λόγος εἷς περὶ ἑνός, ὅθεν τούτῳ μᾶλλον
ἐπίστευον οἱ Πυθαγόρειοι ἢ τῇ αἰσθήσει κρινούσῃ. διὸ προσέθηκεν, 'εἴπερ
ἐνδέχεται' μᾶλλον καὶ ἧττον ἡρμόσθαι, εἰς τὰς κατὰ ἀριθμὸν ἁρμονίας ἀποβλέψας,
οὐ τὰς ἐξῃρημένας λέγω, ἀλλὰ τὰς κατατεταγμένας. 10
νβ'. - [93b4-7] Ὅτι δευτέρα ὑπόθεσις ἀπὸ τοῦ ὑποκειμένου, ὡς ἡ | ψυχὴ οὐ 52 (219)
δέχεται τὸ μᾶλλον καὶ ἧττον· οὐσία γάρ, δεκτικὴ γοῦν τῶν ἐναντίων· ἡ δὲ
ἁρμονία ἐπιδέχεται.
νγ'. - [93b8-e10] Ὅτι λόγον προάγει πρῶτον τοιοῦτον· ἡ ψυχὴ ἀρετῆς καὶ 53
κακίας δεκτική, ἡ ἀρετῆς καὶ κακίας δεκτικὴ ἁρμονίας καὶ ἀναρμοστίας ἐστὶν
δεκτική, ἡ ψυχὴ ἄρα ἁρμονίας καὶ ἀναρμοστίας ἐστὶ δεκτική. πάλιν ἁρμονία
καὶ ἀναρμοστία κατ' οὐδεμιᾶς ἁρμονίας, ἁρμονία καὶ ἀναρμοστία κατὰ πάσης
ψυχῆς, ἡ ἁρμονία ἄρα κατ' οὐδεμιᾶς ψυχῆς. 5
νδ'. - [94a1-10] Ὅτι καὶ ἄλλως συλλογίζεται· συμβαίνειν γὰρ μηδεμίαν ψυχὴν 54
κακίας εἶναι δεκτικήν. εἰ γὰρ ἁρμονία ἡ ψυχή, ἁρμονία δὲ καὶ ἡ ἀρετή, ἡ ψυχὴ
ἄρα δεκτικὴ ἀρετῆς, μᾶλλον δὲ ἡ ψυχὴ ἀρετή· οὐδέποτε δὲ ἡ ἁρμονία ἀναρμοστίας
ἐστὶ δεκτική, οὐδ' ἄρα ἡ ψυχὴ κακίας. ἀλλὰ μὴν ἄτοπον τοῦτό γε· καὶ μάλιστα
ὅτι καὶ πᾶσα ψυχή, καὶ ἡ τῶν ἀλόγων, ὁμοία ἔσται, πᾶσαι γὰρ ἁρμονίαι δήπουθεν. 5

---

§ 50. 2 οὐδεμιᾶι Mᶜ: -ία M¹ | ἁρμονίαι Mᶜ: -ία M¹ — 6 ᾱᵖ Mᶜ: om. M¹
§ 51. 2 μᾶλλον ἢ ἧττον Mᶜ: μαλ (spat. 7 litt.) ≣ ον M¹ — 4 ἡ ἁρμ̱ Mᶜ: spat. vac. M¹

10. κατατεταγμένας : see Dam., Phil., index.
§ 52. Dam. I § 369.
§ 53. Dam. I § 370.
§ 54. Cf. Dam. I § 405.8–21; § 406.

§§ 55–57. Comment on 93b8–95a6

55. [93c3–10] Temperance is harmony, and so is courage, inasmuch as it causes spirit to yield to reason, but to dominate desire. But how about justice, the essence of which is the pursuit of one's own functions? — The answer is that justice is discriminating concord, as temperance is integrating concord; justice seeks its own in such a way as to keep each thing distinct, yet common to all. Temperance, then, is concord between the controlling and the controlled, justice between the rulers and the ruled. — But in what sense is insight harmony? — As concord, Proclus says, between the knower and the known.

However, since insight, too, is a virtue (seeking what is right and avoiding what is wrong, and apprehending good and evil as distinct kinds by an act of cognition that is also appetitive), it is better to view it as belonging to the sphere of action, and to make it harmony in the sense of concord between the givers and receivers of benefits.

56. [94b4–e7] The possibility remains that every kind of soul is harmony and has a substratum of its own, and if reason fights spirit or desire, it is one soul fighting another; for though a harmony cannot oppose its own substratum, there is no reason why one harmony should not fight another; if so, this argument from resistance to the body would prove nothing. — Proclus asks the question how souls in different substrata could know each other, but for which there can be no fight.

This solution is a superficial one: if such a soul has a cognitive faculty, it will know the other, since even sense-perception, while attached to a substratum, apprehends sensible things existing in a different substratum, and all irrational life is aware of external objects of appetition.

Another argument used by Proclus is this: If each soul is in a substratum of its own, what is the common soul that unites them? And what kind of substratum does it have, being itself also a harmony?

We can answer that the substratum would be the whole body, granting that it is necessary at all to postulate such a common soul to unite the other three. But does this bring us any the nearer to a solution? The parts can oppose each other nevertheless. It is better to take the view that reason opposes the entire living organism; therefore reason cannot have the organism as its substratum, otherwise such opposition would be impossible.

57. [94a4–5] Why is it here, at the end of the discussion, that Socrates mentions Harmonia as a Goddess? — By setting apart the lowest and the highest harmony and making it clear that the soul is neither, he wants to

---

§ 55. Dam. I §§ 371–372.

9. ὀρεκτικὴ γὰρ τοῦ δέοντος καὶ μή : short for ὀρεκτικὴ γὰρ τοῦ δέοντος καὶ φευκτικὴ τοῦ μή.

§§ 55-57. Comment on 93b6-95a6

νε'. — [93c3-10] "Ότι ή μὲν σωφροσύνη ἁρμονία καὶ ή ἀνδρεία ὡς τὸν θυμὸν 55
παρεχομένη τῷ μὲν λόγῳ εἴκοντα, τῆς δὲ ἐπιθυμίας κρατοῦντα. πῶς δὲ ή
δικαιοσύνη; ἰδιοπραγία γάρ. — *Η αὕτη μὲν διακριτικὴ συμφωνία, συγκριτικὴ
δὲ ή σωφροσύνη· οὕτω γὰρ τοῦ ἰδίου ἀντιποιεῖται ή δικαιοσύνη ὡς ἀσύγχυτον
μὲν ἕκαστον, κοινωνικὸν δὲ παρεχομένη. τοιγαροῦν ή μὲν σωφροσύνη κοσμούντων 5
καὶ κοσμουμένων ἐστὶ συμφωνία, ή δὲ δικαιοσύνη ἀρχόντων καὶ ἀρχομένων.
— Πῶς δὲ ή φρόνησις ἁρμονία; — *Η ὡς γιγνώσκοντος, φησὶν ὁ Πρόκλος,
καὶ γιγνωσκομένου.

Βέλτιον δὲ καὶ ταύτην ἀρετὴν οὖσαν — ὀρεκτικὴ γὰρ τοῦ δέοντος καὶ μή,
καὶ ἀγαθοῦ καὶ κακοῦ ὡς εἰδῶν κατανοητικὴ μετὰ ὀρέξεως· — ὡς τοίνυν ἀρετὴν 10
οὖσαν ἄμεινον ζωτικὴν ποιεῖν, ἁρμονίαν δὲ κατὰ τὸ ὠφελοῦν καὶ ὠφελούμενον.

νς'. — [94b4-e7] Μήποτε πᾶσα μὲν ψυχὴ ἁρμονία καὶ ἔχει ἴδιον ὑποκείμενον, 56
εἰ δὲ μάχεται λόγος θυμῷ ἢ ἐπιθυμίᾳ, ὡς ἄλλη ψυχὴ ἄλλῃ μάχεται· κωλύει
γὰρ οὐδὲν τῷ μὲν οἰκείῳ ὑποκειμένῳ μὴ μάχεσθαι τὴν ἁρμονίαν, ἄλλην δὲ ἄλλῃ
πολεμεῖν· ὥστε μηδὲν τοῦτον εἶναι τὸν ἀπὸ τῆς ἐναντιώσεως λόγον. — Καὶ πῶς,
φησὶν ὁ Πρόκλος, ή ἐν ἄλλῳ ὑποκειμένῳ οὖσα γνώσεται | τὴν ἐν ἄλλῳ, ἵνα 5(220)
καὶ μάχοιτο;

*Η ἐπιπόλαιος ή λύσις· εἰ γὰρ ἔχει γνωστικὴν δύναμιν, γνώσεται, οὗ γέ τοι
καὶ ή αἴσθησις ἐν ὑποκειμένῳ οὖσα ἀντιλαμβάνεται τῶν αἰσθητῶν ἐν ἄλλῳ
ὄντων ὑποκειμένῳ, καὶ πᾶσα ή ἄλογος ζωὴ τῶν ἔξω ὀρεκτῶν.

Κέχρηται δὲ καὶ ἑτέρῳ λόγῳ· εἰ γὰρ ἑκάστη ἐν ἰδίῳ ὑποκειμένῳ, τίς ή κοινὴ 10
ή συνέχουσα; καὶ ἐν ποίῳ ὑποκειμένῳ, εἴπερ ἁρμονία καὶ αὕτη;
‛Ρητέον οὖν ὅτι κοινὸν μὲν ὑποκείμενον ἔσται τὸ ὅλον σῶμα, εἴπερ ἄρα καὶ
συγχωρήσειέ τις ἐξ ἀνάγκης ἀπαιτεῖσθαι τὴν κοινὴν ψυχὴν καὶ συνεκτικὴν τῶν
τριῶν. ἔπειτα τί μᾶλλον ή ἀπορία λέλυται; δύναται γὰρ τὰ μέρη μάχεσθαι.
βέλτιον οὖν φάναι παντὶ τῷ ζῴῳ τὸν λόγον ἐναντιοῦσθαι· οὐκ ἄρα ἐν ὑποκειμένῳ 15
τούτῳ ἐστίν· οὐ γὰρ ἂν αὐτῷ ἠναντιοῦτο.

νζ'. — [94a4-5] Διὰ τί νῦν ἐπὶ τοῖς λόγοις ἐμνήσθη τῆς ὡς θεοῦ ‛Αρμονίας; 57
— *Η ἵνα διαστησάμενος τὴν ἐσχάτην καὶ πρώτην ἁρμονίαν, καὶ φήνας ὡς
οὐδετέρα εἴη, ἐνδείξηται καὶ τὸν μέσον τρόπον, καθ᾽ ὃν καὶ ἔστι πως ή ψυχὴ

---

§ 56. 2 ἐπιθυμίαι M^c: -ία M¹ — 7 οὗ Fh: οὐ M — 8 post καὶ] ras. 1 litt. M^x —
11 αὕτη Wk: αὐτή M
§ 57. 2 καὶ¹] s.l. M¹

---

§ 56. Dam. I § 375.
§ 57. Dam. I § 377.
3. ἐνδείξηται : by virtue of the principle that intermediates are implicit in their
extremes (Dam., Phil. § 56.4-5; Ol., Gorg. 258.21-22; 260.3-4).

draw attention to the intermediate sense, in which soul really *is* harmony, in a way. This is also Timaeus' opinion, when he constitutes the soul from the musical ratios [34b10-36d7].

§§ 58-62. Objections against the argument on harmony. 92e8-95a6

Questions

58. Using the same reasoning as Plato's, that the soul, being a substance, does not admit of gradation, we can argue that the swan, being a substance, does not admit of gradation; the white, however, does; therefore the swan is not white. — Wrongly; for the swan is not whiteness, but white by participation, so that the difficulty is only an apparent one, caused by homonymy.

59. What did the Pythagoreans mean when they called the soul a harmony? — According to Porphyry, they identified it with the 'middle tone,' because they considered it the no man's land of the universe, with God and matter as extreme terms, and Intelligence and body on this side of them; so that the soul is the middle term, and the Pythagoreans used to call the middle tone 'harmony.'

This may be the reason, or it may be that the soul is the cause of harmony in the world. We come closer to the truth when we say that it is because soul is the first to be subjected to division and to become a manifold, a manifold, however, which is not confused, but harmonious and orderly; therefore soul is the first harmony because of its participated existence.

60. Why should not, on the one hand, the soul be the harmony of the body and, on the other hand, virtue the harmony of the soul and vice its disharmony? — Because a harmony is a ratio between opposites, which is itself one and makes the opposites meet in unison. So what other musical ratio can there be within the one ratio? Surely a harmony supposes at least two coordinated terms?

---

§ 58. Dam. I § 379 and note.
§ 59. Dam. I § 382. In Dam. I, Plato's *Tim.* and Timaeus Locrus are mentioned; Macrob., *somn. Scip.* I 14,19 "Pythagoras et Philolaus harmoniam" [*scil.* dixerunt animam]; cf. Ar., *an.* I 4, 407b27-32. In Philop., *an.* 70.5-16, Porphyry's view appears in a freely adapted form, as a digression to Ar. 404a16-18: ... ἁρμονίαν λέγοντες τὴν ψυχὴν οὔ φασι ταύτην τὴν ἐν ταῖς χορδαῖς (γελοῖον γάρ), ἀλλ' ὅτι ὥσπερ ἡ ἁρμονία, καθὼς αὐτοὶ ὁρίζονται οἱ Πυθαγόρειοι 'πολυμιγέων ἐστὶ καὶ δίχα φρονεόντων ἕνωσις' [Philol. B 10] (τὸν γὰρ βαρὺν φθόγγον καὶ τὸν ὀξὺν ἐναντίους ὄντας κεράσασα ἡ ἁρμονία ἓν μέλος τεχνικὸν ἀπετέλεσεν), οὕτω καὶ ἡ ψυχὴ ἡ ἡμετέρα ἁρμονίας ἐστὶ τῷ παντὶ αἰτία (ὄντων γὰρ τῶν ἀεὶ ἄνω, τῶν νοητῶν φησι καὶ πάντῃ χωριστῶν τῆς ὕλης, ὄντων καὶ τῶν ἀεὶ κάτω καὶ τῆς ὕλης ἀχωρίστων, καὶ τούτων ἀκοινωνήτων ὄντων πρὸς ἄλληλα καὶ τῷ ὄντι 'δίχα φρονεόντων', ταῦτα δι' ἑαυτῆς μέσης συνδεῖ ἡ ψυχὴ καὶ ἑνοῖ καὶ μίαν ἐξ αὐτῶν ἁρμονίαν ἀποτελεῖ. τῶν γὰρ ἄνω οὖσα τὴν οὐσίαν γίνεται τῶν κάτω καὶ οἱονεὶ κιρνᾶται αὐτοῖς, δι' ἑαυτῆς τὰ ἄμικτα κεραννύουσα καὶ μεταδιδοῦσα τοῖς κάτω

ἁρμονία. τοῦτο γὰρ καὶ τῷ Τιμαίῳ δοκεῖ, ὅταν ἐκ τῶν ἁρμονικῶν αὐτὴν λόγων συνίστησιν [34b10–36d7].

§§ 58–62. Objections against the argument on harmony. 92e8–95a6

Ἀπορίαι

νη'. – "Ὅτι ὁμοίως ἐροῦμεν, ὥσπερ τὴν ψυχήν φησιν διὰ τὸ οὐσίαν εἶναι μὴ 58 ἐπιδέχεσθαι τὸ μᾶλλον καὶ ἧττον, οὕτω καὶ τὸν κύκνον ὡς ὄντα οὐσίαν τὸ μᾶλλον καὶ ἧττον μὴ ἐπιδέχεσθαι· τὸ δὲ λευκὸν ἐπιδέχεται· ὁ κύκνος ἄρα οὐ λευκόν.
— Οὔκουν καλῶς· οὐ γὰρ ἡ λευκότης ὁ κύκνος, ἀλλὰ λευκὸς κατὰ μέθεξιν, ὥστε ἐπιπόλαιος ἡ ἀπορία, ἐξ ὁμωνυμίας εἰλημμένη.

νθ'. – Πῶς ἔλεγον οἱ Πυθαγόρειοι ἁρμονίαν τὴν ψυχήν; — Ἡ ὡς τὴν μέσην 59 κατὰ Πορφύριον· εἶναι γὰρ αὐτὴν μεθόριον τῶν ὅλων, ἄκρων μὲν ὄντων θεοῦ καὶ ὕλης, παράκρων δὲ νοῦ καὶ σώματος· αὕτη τοιγαροῦν μεσότης ἂν εἴη, ἀεὶ δὲ τὴν μέσην ἁρμονίαν ἐκάλουν οἱ Πυθαγόρειοι.
Ἡ οὖν οὕτως ἢ ὡς | ἁρμόζουσαν τὸν κόσμον. ἢ τό γε ἀληθέστερον ὡς πρώτην 5(221) μὲν παθοῦσαν τὸν μερισμὸν καὶ πλῆθος γενομένην, πλῆθος δὲ οὐ συγκεχυμένον ἀλλ' ἐναρμόνιον καὶ τεταγμένον· ἁρμονία ἄρα πρώτη κατὰ τὴν μεθεκτὴν ὑπόστασιν ἡ ψυχή.

ξ'. – Διὰ τί μὴ αὐτὴ μὲν σώματος ἁρμονία, αὐτῆς δὲ ἁρμονία ἡ ἀρετὴ καὶ 60 ἀναρμοστία ἡ κακία; — Ἡ ὅτι λόγος ἐναντίων ἡ ἁρμονία, αὐτὴ μὲν οὖσα μία, τἀναντία δὲ συνάγουσα εἰς ὁμοφωνίαν. τίς ἂν οὖν γένοιτο ἐν λόγῳ ἑνὶ λόγος ἕτερος ἁρμονικός; δεῖται γὰρ δύο τοὐλάχιστον ἡ ἁρμονία τῶν ἁρμοζομένων.

---

§ 58. 4 οὔκουν Fh: οὐκοῦν M
§ 60. 1 αὐτὴ M¹: αὕτη Mᶜ

τῶν ἄνω) ... Ammonius or Philop., whichever inserted this paragraph, probably did so from his memory of a discussion of the *Ph.* passage, ultimately based on Porphyry's commentary; it bridges the gap between Porphyry's characteristic doctrine of the soul as part of the intelligible world (H. Dörrie, *Porphyrios' "Symmikta Zetemata,"* München 1959, 187–198) on the one hand, and the view attributed to him here of soul as the μεθόριον, on the other. A similar description of cosmic harmony Pr., *Rep.* II 4.15–18 ... ὁ μὲν Μουσηγέτης τὸν ὅλον ὡς ἕνα κόσμον πληροῖ τῆς θείας ἁρμονίας ἐκ τριῶν ὅρων συναρμόσας, νοῦ μὲν ὡς ὑπάτης, ψυχῆς δὲ ὡς μέσης, σώματος δὲ ὡς νήτης.
3–4. ἀεὶ δὲ τὴν μέσην ἁρμονίαν ἐκάλουν οἱ Πυθαγόρειοι: a puzzling piece of information: Philolaus frg. B 6 calls the octave ἁρμονία and so do Nicom., *harm.* 9, p. 252.5 and Porphyry, *Ptol.* 96.21–23. See notes on I § 368.9–11 and § 371.
§ 60. Dam. I § 380. The correction proposed by Dam. I (lines 6–10) is missing here.

61. [93a12] How can it be said of harmony that it 'is attuned'? The thing in which harmony is established, i.e. the substratum, is attuned, whether this means the opposite terms or whatever else. — The answer: the harmony is attuned in so far as it participates in absolute harmony.

A more obvious answer is that it undergoes attunement itself inasmuch as it exists in the thing attuned.

62. [94a8-11] We must raise the question if at least irrational soul is not harmony. Here, in the case of an inseparable soul, we are not confronted by the same discrepancies; it perishes with its substratum, or rather even before it, in the opinion of those who do not regard it as immortal. — Still, we must conclude that even this soul is not harmony; it is life, and therefore substance, whereas harmony is a ratio expressing a relation between opposites in a body.

However, irrational soul can be said to be harmony in the same sense in which rational soul can [§ 59], though in this case under the conditions, not of separable, but of inseparable existence.

§§ 63–65. Appendix: Strato's objections against the arguments from opposites and from recollection

63. Strato's objections [frg. 122] against the first argument, the argument from opposites [69e6–72e2]

(1) Since things in existence do not proceed from things that have perished, as things that have perished do from things in existence, it is absurd to believe in the validity of this kind of reasoning.

(2) If a mortified part of the body does not revive, e.g. a severed finger or eye, it is evident that neither does the whole.

(3) Even between things that proceed from one another there is only specific, not numerical identity.

(4) Food becomes flesh, flesh does not become food, bronze becomes verdigris and wood becomes coal, but not the other way.

(5) Young men grow old, but not conversely.

(6) Only if the substratum survives can opposite attributes proceed from each other, not if it has already perished.

(7) The world of process will not cease to exist, so long as things of the same kind continue to be produced, just as it is with artifacts.

---

§ 61. Dam. I § 381.

§ 62. Cf. Dam. I § 376, where the question is asked why Pl. confuses the issue by raising the problem of irrational soul, so that on his showing animals also would be immortal. The answer is that, though not harmony, irrational soul may be inseparable in a different way.

3. κατὰ τοὺς μὴ οἰομένους αὐτὴν ἀθάνατον εἶναι : see the doxography I § 177.
6. μέν : perhaps μήν.

§§ 63–65. Dam. II, while omitting the subject-matter treated in I §§ 383–406

ξα'. - [93a12] Πῶς εἴρηται ʿἡρμόσθαιʾ ἐπὶ τῆς ἁρμονίας; τὸ γὰρ ἡρμοσμένον 61
ἥρμοσται, ὅπερ ἐστὶ τὸ ὑποκείμενον, εἴτε τὰ ἐναντία λέγοις εἴτε ὁτιοῦν. —
ˮΗ καὶ ἡ ἁρμονία ἥρμοσται καθ᾽ ὅσον μετέχει τῆς αὐτοαρμονίας.
Προσεχέστερον δὲ εἰπεῖν ὅτι πάσχει καὶ αὐτὴ τὸ ἡρμόσθαι ὡς ἔχουσα τὸ εἶναι
ἐν τῷ ἡρμοσμένῳ. 5
ξβ'. - [94a8–11] Ζητητέον εἰ μηδὲ ἡ ἄλογος ψυχὴ ἁρμονία. ἐπὶ γὰρ ταύτης 62
ὡς ἀχωρίστου οὔσης τὰ ἄτοπα διαφεύγομεν· συναπόλλυται γὰρ τῷ ὑποκειμένῳ,
μᾶλλον δὲ καὶ προαπόλλυται κατὰ τοὺς μὴ οἰομένους αὐτὴν ἀθάνατον εἶναι.
— ˮΗ οὐδὲ αὕτη ἁρμονία· ζωὴ γάρ, ὥστε οὐσία, ἡ δὲ ἁρμονία σχετικὸς λόγος
τῶν ἐν τῷ σώματι ἐναντίων. 5
Ἀλλὰ μήποτε ὡς ἡ λογική [§ 59], οὕτω καὶ ἡ ἄλογος, οὐ χωριστῶς μέν,
ἀχωρίστως δέ.

§§ 63–65. Appendix: Strato's objections against the arguments from opposites and from recollection

ξγ'. - Ἀπορίαι Στράτωνος [frg. 122] πρὸς τὸν πρῶτον λόγον 63
τὸν ἀπὸ τῶν ἐναντίων [69e6–72e2]

α' Εἰ μὴ ἐκ τῶν ἐφθαρμένων τὰ ὄντα, ὡς ἐκ τῶν ὄντων τὰ ἐφθαρμένα, πῶς
ἔχει λόγον πιστεύειν ὡς ἐρρωμένῃ τῇ τοιαύτῃ ἐφόδῳ;
β' Εἰ μὴ μόριον τεθνηκὸς ἀναβιώσκεται, οἷον δάκτυλος ἢ ὀφθαλμὸς ἐκκοπείς, 5
δῆλον ὡς οὐδὲ τὸ ὅλον.
γ' Εἰ καὶ τὰ ἐξ ἀλλήλων γιγνόμενα κατ᾽ εἶδος μόνον τὰ αὐτά, οὐ κατὰ ἀριθμόν.
δ' Εἰ ἐκ μὲν τροφῆς σάρκες, οὐ μὴν τροφὴ ἐκ σαρκῶν, καὶ ἰὸς ἐκ χαλκοῦ καὶ
ἀπὸ ξύλων ἄνθρακες, οὐ μὴν ἀνάπαλιν.
ε' Εἰ ἐκ νέων γέροντες, οὐ μὴν ἀνάπαλιν. 10
ϛ' Εἰ σῳζομένου τοῦ ὑποκειμένου δύναται ἐξ ἀλλήλων γίγνεσθαι τὰ ἐναντία, (222)
οὐ μὴν ἐφθαρμένου.
ζ' Εἰ μὴ ἀπολείπει ἡ γένεσις, κἂν μόνον κατ᾽ εἶδος ἀεὶ γίγνηται, ὡς ἔχει καὶ
τὰ τεχνητά.

---

§ 62. 1 ἐπὶ μ : ἐπεὶ M — 4 αὕτη Mᶜ: αὐτὴ M¹
§ 63. 5 ἀναβιόσκεται M | ἐκκοπείς] -εὶς in ras. Mᶜ — 13 γίγνηται] -ητ- in ras. Mᶜ

(i.e. 2½ lectures in Dam. I), for an unknown reason inserts an account of Strato's
attack on *Ph.* 69e6–72e2 and 72e3–77a5.
§§ 63–64. Strato's objections have little or nothing in common with those
dealt with by Syrianus (I §§ 193–200) and Dam. (I §§ 209–222; 231–251); the only
points they share are the (very obvious) observation of the survival of the species
(§ 63.7 and 13–14; I § 201 and 212) and the (less obvious, but still not too remote)
example of the older and the younger (§ 63.10; I § 196). It is therefore likely that
Syrianus did not have this material from Strato at his disposal, or at least did not

64. Answers

(1–2) Before everything else we must establish that the separability of the soul from the body is given, and starting from this premise the question is asked whether after the separation the soul continues to exist or is dispersed, which means that we should deal with soul as a substance. So what is the point of premises in terms of possession and privation, as in the first and second arguments? Privation is not reversible; but Plato's proof is strictly limited to a substance that continues to exist itself, while subject to opposite accidents according as the cycle of alternating opposites affects it, and no account is taken of possession and privation. It is true, though, that there is also such a thing as living and dead by possession and privation, as in the example of the finger, when its immanent life is extinguished.

(3) In reference to the third point we may ask the question, if there is not a constant element that remains numerically the same, while receiving now the formula of a seed, now that of a plant, for example matter, or body devoid of quality. If so, there must be a permanent element also in those cases of things that are joined and severed, soul and body, and this element is obviously the stronger of the two, the soul.

(4) The answer to the fourth objection is that not everything that has proceeded from something else returns to it, but only what has proceeded from its opposite; the food that becomes flesh is not its opposite, nor is the bronze that becomes verdigris.

(5) As for the fifth, youth and old age are instances of possession and privation.

(6) As regards the sixth, it must be admitted that the substratum survives, but here we are concerned with two substrata, body and soul, which must be joined together and severed again. Now this actually happens to the stronger of the two, the soul, forever according to the view of Proclus (who believes that it should apply even to the body, since it is imperishable [I § 198]); in reality, however, as far as this argument goes, only during the time that it exists.

(7) The answer to the seventh objection is that the perpetuity of genesis has many causes, partly efficient, partly material ones; one of them

---

take it into consideration when he discussed the argument (no more than does Dam., who simply reconsiders the case as presented by Syrianus). The answers provided in § 64 must derive from Pr., for several of its arguments correspond to those in Syr.-Pr. (§ 64.6–10: cf. I §§ 191 and 234; § 64.13–14 and 21–23: cf. I § 198, rejected by Dam. I § 249; § 64.18: cf. I § 196.4); this becomes even clearer at § 64.27, where Dam. intervenes to correct Pr. on the lines of I § 228. A conceivable explanation of these facts, as well as of the joint treatment of the arguments from

ξδ'. Λύσεις 64

α' β' "Ότι πρὸ πάντων διοριστέον ὡς δέδοται μὲν διακρίνεσθαι τὴν ψυχὴν ἀπὸ τοῦ σώματος, τούτου δὲ δοθέντος ζητεῖται εἰ διακριθεῖσα ἐπιδιαμένει ἢ διασκεδάννυται· ὡς ἐπὶ οὐσίας ἄρα ποιητέον τὸν λόγον περὶ αὐτῆς. πῶς οὖν τὰ κατὰ ἔξιν καὶ στέρησιν προτείνομεν ἐπὶ τοῦ πρώτου καὶ δευτέρου 5 ἐπιχειρήματος; οὐ γὰρ ἀνακάμπτει ἡ στέρησις· ἀλλ' εἴρηται καθάπαξ ὁ λόγος περὶ οὐσίας τῆς μενούσης μὲν αὐτῆς, τἀναντία δὲ πασχούσης κατὰ τὸν περὶ αὐτὴν στρεφόμενον κύκλον τῶν ἐναντίων, ἀλλ' οὐχὶ ἕξεως καὶ στερήσεως. ἔστι δέ τι ζῶν καὶ τεθνηκὸς κατὰ ἕξιν καὶ στέρησιν, ὥσπερ ὁ δάκτυλος σβεννυμένης αὐτῷ τῆς ἐν ὑποκειμένῳ ζωῆς. 10

γ' "Ότι πρὸς τὸ τρίτον ζητητέον εἰ μὴ μένει τι ταὐτὸν τῷ ἀριθμῷ, ποτὲ μὲν τὸν σπέρματος λόγον δεχόμενον, ποτὲ δὲ τὸν φυτοῦ, οἷον ἡ ὕλη ἢ τὸ ἄποιον σῶμα. ἀνάγκη ἄρα καὶ ἐπὶ τούτων ὑπομένειν τι, τῶν συγκρινομένων λέγω καὶ διακρινομένων, ψυχῆς καὶ σώματος· καὶ δῆλον ὅτι τὸ δυνατώτερον, τοῦτο δὲ ψυχή.

δ' "Ότι πρὸς τὸ τέταρτον ῥητέον ὡς οὐ πᾶν τὸ ἔκ τινος ἀνακάμπτει, ἀλλὰ τὸ 15 ἐκ τοῦ ἐναντίου· ἐκ δὲ τροφῆς σάρκες οὐχ ὡς ἐξ ἐναντίου, καὶ ἰὸς ἐκ χαλκοῦ οὐχ οὕτως.

ε' "Ότι πρὸς τὸ πέμπτον, ἕξιν εἶναι καὶ στέρησιν νεότητα καὶ γῆρας.

ς' "Ότι πρὸς τὸ ἕκτον ὁμολογητέον σῴζεσθαι τὸ ὑποκείμενον· ἐπὶ δὲ τούτων δύο εἶναι ὑποκείμενα, σῶμα καὶ ψυχήν, ἃ δεῖ συγκρίνεσθαι καὶ διακρίνεσθαι. 20 καὶ δὴ τὸ ἰσχυρότερον πάσχει τοῦτο, ἡ ψυχή φημι, ἀεὶ μὲν κατὰ τὸν Πρόκλον, ὅτε γε κατ' αὐτὸν ὤφελεν καὶ τὸ σῶμα ἀνώλεθρόν γε ὄν [I § 198]· κατὰ δὲ τὸν ἀληθῆ λόγον, ὅσον ἐκ τούτων, μέχρις ἂν ᾖ.

ζ' "Ότι πρὸς τὸ ἕβδομον ῥητέον ὡς πολλαὶ μὲν αἱ αἰτίαι τοῦ διαμένειν τὴν γένεσιν· (223)

§ 64. 3 εἰ Fh: ἢ M — 12 τὸν¹ Fh: τὸ M

opposites and from recollection at this point (where one expects an account of Strato's objections to the final argument, paralleling I §§ 431-448), could be that Pr.'s commentary comprised a monograph by himself (or by Syrianus, in which case it would be later than the one on the argument from opposites) defending the Ph. against Strato's attack.

§ 64. 6. ἀνακάμπτει : Plato's own term, 72b3.
12-13. ἄποιον σῶμα : see note at I § 249.8.

is cyclic recurrence of numerically identical substances in opposite contingencies.

We for our part will say that the identity is numerical to a certain extent, and for the rest specific.

65. Strato's objections [frg. 127] against the argument from recollection [72e3–77a5]

Either (1) they have their knowledge before all time, in which case they will possess it forever, inasmuch as they have no need of time and are not affected by it; or (2) it has a beginning in time, and in that case they know things without the process of recollection, because they learn them for the first time.

Even then they recollect the knowledge they possessed prior to life in the body; we may take it that their Creator has created them perfect, and therefore in the possession of knowledge; yet when they have descended to this world we find that they need to learn, which must mean, consequently, to recollect. Besides, in his division Strato suppresses everlasting time; between that which is before time and what is at a certain time we have what is always in time.

(3) Then why is recollection not within easy reach? — In some cases it is, but most people need training.

V. THE ARGUMENT FROM THE ESSENCE OF SOUL

§§ 66–74. The exemplary cause and the other causes; general observations and comment on 95e7–102a2

The final argument

66. [95e9–96a1] Why the 'complete account' of the theory of causes in this context? Socrates goes back to the very beginnings, making a rigid distinction between causes and contributory causes. — The reason is that the soul itself belongs to the causes proper, not to the contributory causes.

67. [100b1–101c9] Why does he especially elaborate the theory of ideas? — To establish the premise that contrary forms themselves, whether immanent or transcendent, exclude each other, and to show that the latter (immaterial and transcendent forms) retreat on the approach of their opposites, whereas the former perish; for instance, white perishes on the approach of black, but rational life retreats on the approach of death.

---

26. ἀνταπόδοσις: Plato uses the verb, 71e8, 72a12, b8.

§ 65. Cf. I § 294 and II § 25. Both point out instances of self-taught people to answer Strato's objection that demonstration remains necessary. – The figures numbering the points in the MS. are not very meaningful, since there is really only one objection, in the form of a dilemma. The β′ in M is written against line 6

καὶ γὰρ αἱ ποιητικαὶ καὶ αἱ ὑλικαί· ἔστι δέ τις καὶ ἡ τοῦ κύκλου κατὰ ἀριθμὸν 25
ἀνταπόδοσις ἐπὶ τῶν ἐναντίων.
Ἡμεῖς δὲ ἐροῦμεν, ἄχρι μέν τινος κατὰ ἀριθμόν, ἔπειτα κατὰ εἶδος.

ξε'. — Ἀπορίαι Στράτωνος [frg. 127] πρὸς τὸν ἀπὸ τῶν ἀναμνήσεων 65
λόγον [72e3-77a5]

α' Ἢ πρὸ χρόνου ἔχουσι τὰς ἐπιστήμας, οὕτω δὲ ἀεὶ ἐπιστήμονές εἰσιν ἅτε
β' μηδὲν χρόνου προσδεόμεναι μηδὲ πάσχουσαί τι ὑπ' αὐτοῦ· ἢ ἀπὸ χρόνου, καὶ
τότε ἐπίστανται ἄνευ τῆς ἀναμνήσεως ἅτε πρῶτον μανθάνουσαι. 5
Ἢ καὶ τότε τῆς πρὸ σώματος ἐνούσης ἐπιστήμης ἀναμιμνήσκονται· ὁ γὰρ
ποιητὴς αὐτῶν τελείας δή που πεποίηκεν, ἐπιστήμονας ἄρα· ἀλλὰ μὴν ἐλθοῦσαι
ἐνταῦθα μαθήσεως δέονται, ἀναμνήσεως ἄρα. ἔτι δὲ πρὸς τούτοις ὁ Στράτων
ἐν τῇ διαιρέσει ἐκκλέπτει τὸν ἀεί τινα χρόνον· μεταξὺ γὰρ τοῦ τε πρὸ χρόνου
ὄντος καὶ τοῦ ποτὲ ὄντος ἐστὶ τὸ ἀεὶ ὂν ἐν χρόνῳ. 10
γ' Διὰ τί οὖν οὐ πρόχειρος ἡ ἀνάμησις; — Ἢ τισὶ μὲν ἡ ἀνάμνησις καὶ πρόχειρος,
τοῖς δὲ πολλοῖς χρεία γυμνασίας.

V. THE ARGUMENT FROM THE ESSENCE OF SOUL

§§ 66-74. The exemplary cause and the other causes; general observations and comment on 95e7-102a2

Περὶ τοῦ τελευταίου λόγου

ξϛ'. — [95e9-96a1] Διὰ τί τὸν περὶ αἰτίων 'διεπραγματεύσατο' λόγον ἐν 66
τούτοις; ἄνωθεν γάρ ποθεν ἀρξάμενος ἀπὸ τῶν αἰτίων διακαθαίρει τὰ συναίτια.
— Ἢ ὅτι καὶ ἡ ψυχὴ τῶν τοιούτων αἰτίων ἐστίν, ἀλλ' οὐ τῶν συναιτίων.
ξζ'. — [100b1-101c9] Διὰ τί τὸν περὶ ἰδεῶν μάλιστα διέκρινε λόγον; — Ἢ ἵνα 67
αὐτὰ τὰ εἴδη τὰ ἀντικείμενα λάβῃ μὴ δεχόμενα ἄλληλα, μήτε τὰ ἐν τῇ ὕλῃ
μήτε τὰ χωριστά, ἀλλὰ ταῦτα μὲν τὰ ἄυλα καὶ χωριστὰ ὑπεκχωροῦντα δείξῃ
ἐπειδὰν τὰ ἐναντία προσέλθῃ, ἐκεῖνα δὲ ἀπολλύμενα, οἷον τὸ λευκὸν ἐπειδὰν
τὸ μέλαν, τὴν δὲ ζωὴν τὴν λογικὴν ὑπεκχωροῦσαν ἐπειδὰν ὁ θάνατος προσέλθῃ. 5

---

§ 65. 3 Ἢ Fh: εἰ M — 4 mg. β'] ad lin. 6 ὁ γὰρ adscr. M

(the answer); lines 11-12 are a step in the discussion of case (1) rather than another objection.
§ 66. Dam. I § 407. For I §§ 408-415 (the rest of the lecture) there is no corresponding text in II.
3. Cf. Dam. I § 409.1-2.

68. How does Socrates prove in this passage that prototypes of forms in this world exist? — As follows: (1) [100c3–8] If the manifold beautiful things have one thing in common, the beautiful, there must be, prior to the many, the Beautiful itself as a substance. — (2) [100c9–e4] If colors or shapes are the beautiful, how is an ugly color or shape possible? The beautiful cannot be ugly while remaining beautiful. — (3) [100e5–101b8] If we were to say that one man is bigger 'by a head,' another smaller, it is preposterous, in the first place, that a man could be bigger and smaller through the same cause. Secondly, it is preposterous that one form ('head') should cause another ('the beautiful'); the head only makes the man 'headed.' Thirdly, how can anyone be bigger *by* a head, when the head itself is small? This is tantamount to saying that ten is more than nine *by* one; it is not more *by* one, but by plurality, the form 'one' only makes a thing one. — (4) [101b9–c9] If opposite forms cannot have the same effect, how can the contrary processes of combination and splitting produce the same thing, viz. the number two, the latter by splitting the unit, the former by combining units? The plain fact is that two is two by participation in the dyad.

69. [100d3–6] In what way do things of this world participate in transcendent forms? If by presence, then forms are not transcendent; if by communication, there must be something prior to them in which the form and the particulars participate jointly, and this to infinity. — The answer is that both presence and communication take place 'in a certain way and a certain mode,' inasmuch as things here participate in forms, but the gift is not reciprocated.

70. [97b8–d5] An efficient cause (in the sense of a world-creating cause) is also necessary, because forms here below are not self-constituted; therefore a force that creates them is needed. The creative force makes them what they are by referring to the prototypes; it makes them as good as possible by referring to what is best and to their purpose; consequently Intelligence is the effective cause, for only Intelligence knows what to make and to what end.

71. [99a4–b6] The contributory causes are used by the causes for the purpose of creation, but they *are* not causes.

72. [99c3–5] Who is Atlas? — A Titan who has the power of separating things in heaven from things under heaven. Hence we will not grant him the

---

§ 68. 5–10. Dam. I § 419. – Points (1) and (3) are Plato's (101a7–8 and 8–9), (2) is additional.

7. καλόν : the context rather requires μέγα.

8. κεφαλωτόν : word coined by Ar., *cat.* 7, 7a16–17 οἷον ἡ κεφαλὴ οἰκειοτέρως ἂν ἀποδοθείη κεφαλωτοῦ ἢ ζῴου ἀποδιδομένη.

§ 69. Dam. I § 418.

2. παρουσίᾳ ... κοινωνίᾳ : on the datives here and the nominatives at line 4

ξη'. — Πῶς δείκνυσιν ἐν τούτοις ὅτι ἔστι παραδείγματα τῶν τῇδε ἰδεῶν; 68(224)
α' — Οὕτως· [100c3–8] εἰ τὰ πολλὰ καλὰ ἑνὸς τοῦ καλοῦ κοινωνεῖ, πρὸ τῶν
β' πολλῶν ἂν εἴη αὐτὸ τὸ καθ᾽ ὕπαρξιν καλόν. — [100c9–e4] εἰ τὰ χρώματα ἢ
σχήματα τὸ καλόν, πῶς ἔνι χρῶμα ἢ σχῆμα αἰσχρόν; τὸ γὰρ καλὸν πῶς ἂν
γ' εἴη αἰσχρὸν μένον καλόν; — [100e5–101b8] εἰ τῇ κεφαλῇ τις λέγοιτο μείζων, 5
ὁ δὲ ἐλάττων, πρῶτον μὲν ἄτοπον τῷ αὐτῷ μεῖζον εἶναι καὶ ἔλαττον. δεύτερον
δὲ ἄτοπον ἄλλῳ εἴδει, οἷον τῇ κεφαλῇ, ἄλλο εἶναι εἶδος, οἷον τὸ καλόν·
κεφαλωτὸν γὰρ μᾶλλον τῇ κεφαλῇ. τρίτον δὲ πῶς οἷόν τε τῇ σμικρᾷ οὔσῃ μείζω
γενέσθαι; ὥσπερ ἂν εἰ λέγοι τις ὅτι τῷ ἑνὶ πλείω τὰ δέκα τῶν ἐννέα· οὐ γὰρ
δ' τῷ ἑνί, ἀλλὰ πλήθει, τῷ γὰρ ἑνὶ ἓν γίγνεταί τι. — [101b9–c9] εἰ τἀναντία εἴδη 10
αἴτια τοῦ αὐτοῦ οὐκ ἂν γένοιτο, πῶς ἥ τε σύνοδος καὶ ἡ σχίσις ἐναντίαι οὖσαι
τὸ αὐτὸ ποιοῦσιν, δύο γάρ, ἡ μὲν ἀπὸ τοῦ ἑνὸς διαιροῦσα, ἡ δὲ συνάγουσα;
ἀλλὰ δῆλοι ὅτι δύο τὰ δύο διὰ τὴν τῆς δυάδος μετάσχεσιν.

ξθ'. — [100d3–6] Τίς ἡ μετοχὴ τοῖς τῇδε τῶν χωριστῶν εἰδῶν; εἰ μὲν γὰρ 69
παρουσίᾳ, οὐκ ἔστι χωριστά· εἰ δὲ κοινωνίᾳ, ἔσται τι καὶ ἄλλο πρὸ αὐτῶν οὗ
κοινῇ ταῦτα μετείληφεν, καὶ τοῦτο ἐπ᾽ ἄπειρον. — Ἢ 'πῇ καὶ πῶς' ἑκάτερον,
καὶ παρουσία καὶ κοινωνία, κατὰ τὴν ἐκεῖθεν μέθεξιν, ἀλλ᾽ οὐκ ἀντιμετάδοσιν
τῶν ἐντεῦθεν ἐκείνοις. 5

ο'. — [97b8–d5] Ὅτι καὶ τὸ ποιητικὸν ἀναγκαῖον, ὅ γε κοσμοποιόν ἐστι· 70
τὰ γὰρ τῇδε εἴδη οὐκ ἔστιν αὐθυπόστατα, διὸ χρεία τοῦ ποιοῦντος. τὸ δὲ
ποιοῦν ταδὶ μὲν ποιεῖ κατὰ τὰ παραδείγματα· ὡς δὲ βέλτιστα μέλλοι ἔχειν,
κατὰ τὸ βέλτιστον καὶ τὸ τέλος· νοῦς ἄρα τὸ ποιητικὸν αἴτιον, τούτου γὰρ
εἰδέναι ἅ τε ποιητέον καὶ τίνος ἕνεκα. 5

οα'. — [99a4–b6] Ὅτι τὰ συναίτια παραλαμβάνεται μὲν ὑπὸ τῶν αἰτίων εἰς 71
γένεσιν, αἴτια μέντοι οὐκ ἔστιν.

οβ'. — [99c3–5] Τίς ὁ Ἄτλας; — Ὅτι Τιτὰν διακριτικὸς τῶν τε οὐρανίων 72
καὶ ὑπουρανίων. οὐκ ἄρα τὸ συνέχειν αὐτῷ δώσομεν (τοῦτο | δὲ καὶ Ὅμηρος (225)

---

§ 68. 3 ἂν εἴη] -ν εἴη in ras. M^c (fort. ἂν ἦι M¹) — 5 λέγοιτο ∹, -το ∹ in ras. M^c — 11 σχίσις] -ί- in ras. M^c (σχέσις ut vid. M¹)
§ 69. 4 παρουσία ... κοινωνία M¹: -ίαι ... -ίαι M^c

---

see note on I § 418.2–3.
§ 72. Atlas is mentioned incidentally by Pr., Tim. I 183.2–3 (ref. Atlantis) and Rep. II 200.5–9 (in connection with the celestial axle). As principles of division his columns occur also Pr., Hes. 129.16–130.2: ὁ μὲν Ἄτλας λέγεται παῖς Ἰαπετοῦ τὸν οὐρανὸν ἀνέχων καὶ τὰς κίονας, αἳ γαῖάν τε καὶ οὐρανὸν ἀμφὶς ἔχουσιν, αὐτὸς κατὰ μίαν συνοχὴν ἱδρύσας δυνάμεις εἰληχὼς διοριστικὰς οὐρανοῦ καὶ γῆς ... ταύτας γὰρ τὰς δυνάμεις τὰς ἀμφοτέρων ἀκλινῶς τὸν διορισμὸν τηρούσας κίονας ἐκάλεσεν, αἳ γαῖάν τε καὶ οὐρανὸν ἀμφὶς ἔχουσιν· ὃ δηλοῖ τὸ χωρὶς ἀλλήλων εἶναι καὶ ἄμικτα ἀλλήλοις ἀϊδίως.

power of holding things together (this is made clear by Homer, too, when he says that Atlas set up 'the columns that keep heaven and earth apart' [*Od.* 1.53], in other words, that prevent them from being united), rather they are joined together by the Good, which is the real bond; it is the Good, not the rotation of the sky, that makes the earth a compact whole. This is not the primal Good, but the creative and intellective Good.

73. [99e4–100a3] From sensible things his next step upward is that to notions in the soul, not as copies, but rather as prototypes, in order to establish a connection between the present argument and intellective forms by means of them.

74. [101e1] What is the 'adequate' principle in which all the successive hypotheses must culminate? — Proclus identifies it with the Good, beyond which, since it transcends everything, there is nothing left to seek.

We prefer to explain it as points of agreement in each discussion and self-evident grounds and principles.

§§ 75–77. Analysis of the argument. 102a10–107a1

75. Socrates' assumptions are: (1) [103e5–104b4] One term of a pair of opposites does not admit of the other where participated entities are concerned, because on the approach of the other form the first will either perish, being destroyed by the newcomer, e.g. black by white, or it will retreat and make room; it will retreat, if it is separable, it will perish, if it is not. (2) [104b6–105b4] Even certain participating substances, when their essential character is determined by either one of a pair of opposites, so that they necessarily carry it along with them, do not admit of the other opposite, and such forms, too, will naturally either perish on the approach of the opposite or withdraw; those substances, however, in which one opposite is adventitious, admit the other opposite while remaining what they are. (3) [105b5–c7] Things here below are determined as regards their form by participation not only in forms by themselves (hot things participate in heat), but also in things that have those forms as part of their nature (hot things become hot not only by heat but also by fire).

76. Socrates includes forms as well as things to which a certain form is essential, to make sure that soul will fall under his assumptions, no

---

3. διαμφίς : not in Homer (it occurs in Dionys. Perieg. 903).
5. σφίγγει : on περὶ τὸ κέντρον ἐσφιγμένη as an interpretation of the ἰλλομένη of *Tim.* 40b8 see note on I § 515.2.
6–7. τἀγαθὸν ... τὸ δημιουργικόν τε καὶ νοερόν : cf. the ἀγαθὸς ἦν of *Tim.* 29e1–3 (where Pr., *Tim.* I 359.22–360.4, distinguishes the transcendent, the intelligible and the demiurgic Good). The demiurge as final cause Dam., *Phil.* § 114.1–4, (and note).
§ 73. The λόγοι ('arguments') of 99e5 are understood as the innate concepts or 'reason-principles' in soul, cf. Pr., *elem.* 195.

δηλοῖ 'κίονας' αὐτὸν εἰπὼν ὑποστῆσαι 'οἳ ῥα διαμφὶς ἔχουσιν οὐρανὸν καὶ γῆν' [a 53], οὐκοῦν κωλύουσιν ἑνωθῆναι πρὸς ἄλληλα), ἀλλὰ μᾶλλον τῷ ἀγαθῷ συνάγονται τῷ καὶ συνδέοντι ὡς ἀληθῶς· καὶ γὰρ τοῦτο σφίγγει τὴν γῆν πρὸς 5 ἑαυτήν, οὐχ ὁ οὐράνιος δῖνος· τἀγαθὸν δὲ οὐ τὸ πρῶτον, ἀλλὰ τὸ δημιουργικόν τε καὶ νοερόν.

ογ΄. — [99e4-100a3] Ὅτι ἀπὸ τῶν αἰσθητῶν προσεχῶς ἐπὶ τοὺς ἐν ψυχῇ 73 λόγους ἀνέδραμεν, οὐχ ὡς εἰκόνας, ἀλλὰ μᾶλλον ὡς παραδείγματα, ἵνα οἰκειώσῃ τῷ προκειμένῳ λόγῳ τὰ εἴδη τὰ νοερὰ δι' αὐτῶν μέσων.

οδ΄. — [101e1] Τί τὸ 'ἱκανὸν' ἐφ' ὃ δεῖ κορυφοῦσθαι τὰς ἀεὶ λαμβανομένας 74 ὑποθέσεις; — Ἢ δ τἀγαθόν, φησὶν ὁ Πρόκλος, ὡς ὂν ἐπέκεινα πάντων, μεθ' ὃ οὐδὲν ἔτι ποθεῖ τις ἐπιζητεῖν.

Ἄμεινον δὲ τὸ ἀεὶ ὁμολογούμενον φάναι καὶ τὰς αὐτοπίστους ὑποθέσεις τε καὶ ἀρχάς. 5

§§ 75-77. Analysis of the argument. 102a10-107a1

οε΄. — Ὅτι ὑποτίθεται, [103e5-104b4] ἓν μὲν τὸ ἄδεκτον εἶναι τὸ ἐναντίον 75 τοῦ ἐναντίου ἐν τοῖς μετεχομένοις· τοῦ γὰρ ἑτέρου εἴδους ἐπιόντος δυοῖν θάτερον, ἢ ἀπόλλυσθαι ὑπὸ τοῦ προσιόντος φθειρόμενον, ὡς τὸ μέλαν ὑπὸ τοῦ λευκοῦ, ἢ ὑπεκχωρεῖν ἐξιστάμενον, καὶ τοῦτο μὲν δηλονότι εἰ χωριστὸν εἴη, ἐκεῖνο δὲ ⟨εἰ⟩ ἀχώριστον. — [104b6-105b4] ἕτερον δὲ ὑποτίθεται τὸ καὶ τῶν μετεχόντων 5 ἔνια κατὰ θάτερον τῶν ἐναντίων οὐσιωμένα καὶ τοῦτο πάντως συνεπιφέροντα ἄδεκτα εἶναι τοῦ ἑτέρου τῶν ἐναντίων, καὶ δηλονότι καὶ τὰ τοιαῦτα εἴδη ἢ ἀπόλλυσθαι ἐπιόντος τοῦ ἐναντίου ἢ ὑπεξίστασθαι· ὅσα μέντοι ἐπείσακτον ἔχει τι τῶν ἐναντίων, μένοντα ἅ ἐστι δεκτικά ἐστι καὶ τοῦ ἐναντίου. — [105b5-c7] τρίτον ὑποτίθεται ὅτι οὐ μόνον τῇ τῶν ἁπλῶς εἰδῶν μετοχῇ τὰ τῇδε εἰδοποιεῖται, 10 οἷον θερμότητος τὰ θερμά, ἀλλὰ καὶ τῇ τῶν τοῖς εἴδεσι συμφυῶν, οἷον οὐ μόνον ὑπὸ θερμότητος τὰ θερμὰ γίγνεται θερμά, ἀλλὰ καὶ ὑπὸ πυρός.

ος΄. — Ὅτι καὶ εἴδη παρέλαβεν καὶ τὰ συνουσιωμένα τοῖς εἴδεσιν, ἵνα μὴ 76 διαφύγῃ τὰς ὑποθέσεις ἡ ψυχή, εἴτε τις ἁπλῆν | αὐτὴν ζωὴν ὑποθοῖτο, καθάπερ (226)

---

§ 72. 3 εἰπὼν M^c: om. M¹
§ 73. 2 οἰκειώσῃ M^c: οἰκείως ἦι ut vid. M¹
§ 75. 1 ἓν M^c: om. M¹ — 5 εἰ Wk: om. M

§ 74. 1-3. Pr., prov. 29.1-3 "... humane anime cognitionem usque ad unum ascendentem et usque ad insuppositum per omnes, ut est dicere, species..." (the dialectic of Rep. VII); Parm. 622.29-34 καὶ γὰρ ἐν Φαίδωνι ... φησὶν ὅτι δέοι μὲν ἀεί τινα θεμένους ὑπόθεσιν οὕτω ποιεῖσθαι τὴν ζήτησιν, ἕως ἂν ἀπὸ τῶν πολλῶν ὑποθέσεων ἐπί τι ἱκανόν, αὐτὸ λέγων τὸ ἀνυπόθετον, ἀναδράμωμεν. In both cases the ἀνυπόθετον is taken to be the One. Dam. (lines 4-5) understands it as any assumption or axiom in any logical or mathematical argument.
4. αὐτοπίστους: see note on Dam., Phil. § 7.4 and index ibid.
§ 75. Cf. Dam. I §§ 421-425.
§ 76. Cf. Dam. I §§ 428-430.

matter whether one takes it to be life pure and simple (as simple forms, the hot itself and the cold itself) or as a substance to which life is essential (as fire, which has heat as an essential quality).

A more valid reason is perhaps that he wants to intimate that soul is detachable from body, whether one considers it as the simple and separable form, or as comparable to fire, which does not heat as the inseparable heat itself does, but as a substance separable from the object heated. The soul is not the life that *is* conferred and exists in a substratum, but it bestows this life on the body, just as the fire was the source of the heat, not identical with the heat that has developed in the object.

77. Proceeding from these assumptions, the demonstration takes the form of the following syllogism:

(1) Soul bestows life on that in which it is present; whatever bestows a particular quality is inaccessible to its opposite; therefore soul is inaccessible to its opposite; therefore soul is inaccessible to the opposite of life.

(2) Soul is inaccessible to the opposite of the quality it bestows; the opposite of what it bestows is death; therefore soul is inaccessible to death.

Soul ____ bestows life upon that in which it is present ____ inaccessible to the opposite.

Soul ____ inaccessible to the opposite of what it bestows ____ death.

§ 78. Strato's objections answered

78. On this showing, Strato says [frg. 124], even life in a substratum is not accessible to its opposite: it cannot remain and thus receive death, any more than cold can receive heat; therefore life in a substratum is immortal, just as cold is unheatable; yet we agree that it is destroyed.

Besides, he argues, destruction is not a receiving of death, in which case no living being would be destroyed, because it cannot remain a living being after receiving death; on the contrary, it is dead because it has lost its life, death being loss of life.

These are Strato's objections; the correct position, however, is that there are two kinds of life, and that the kind under discussion is life-giving life, which is not separated by the death of the substratum, but by its own separate existence. The point is that it is not a condition of the substratum, but a substance which is united with the body and has produced in it the kind of life that is a condition of the body, in the same way as an illuminated object does not contain the light itself, but shares in the quality the light bestows.

To this Proclus adds that for the soul to be destroyed is to suffer death, and to suffer death is apparently, by Strato's own admission, loss of life by

---

§ 77. Cf. Dam. I §§ 426–427.
§ 78. Cf. Dam. I §§ 431–448. Out of the long series of arguments in Dam. I,

τὰ ἁπλᾶ εἴδη, τὸ αὐτοθερμὸν καὶ τὸ αὐτόψυχρόν, εἴτε οὐσίαν μετὰ ζωῆς οὐσιωμένην, καθάπερ τὸ πῦρ μετὰ θερμότητος οὐσίωται.

Τάχα δὲ ἄμεινον διὰ τὸ ἐνδείξασθαι χωριστὴν τῶν σωμάτων οὖσαν, εἴτε ὡς τὸ ἁπλοῦν λαμβάνοι τις αὐτὴν καὶ τὸ χωριστὸν εἶδος, εἴτε ὡς τὸ πῦρ, ὃ δὴ θερμαίνει οὐ καθάπερ αὐτὴ ἡ ἀχώριστος θερμότης, ἀλλ' ὡς οὐσία χωριστὴ τοῦ θερμαινομένου. οὐ γάρ ἐστιν ἡ ψυχὴ ἡ ἐπιφερομένη ζωὴ καὶ ἐν ὑποκειμένῳ οὖσα, ἀλλ' ἡ ἐπιφέρουσα ταύτην τῷ σώματι, ὥσπερ καὶ τὸ πῦρ τὸ ἐπιφέρον ἦν τὴν θερμότητα, οὐκ αὐτὴ ἡ ἐγγενομένη θερμότης.

οζ'. – Ὅτι ἡ ἀπόδειξις πρόεισιν ἐκ τῶν ὑποθέσεων τοιῷδε συλλογισμῷ·   77

α' ἡ ψυχή, ᾧ ἂν παρῇ, ζωὴν τούτῳ ἐπιφέρει· πᾶν δὲ ὃ ἐπιφέρει τι, ἄδεκτόν ἐστι τοῦ ἐναντίου αὐτῷ· ἡ ψυχὴ ἄρα ἄδεκτός ἐστι τοῦ ἐναντίου τῇ ζωῇ.

β' ἡ ψυχὴ ἄδεκτός ἐστι τοῦ ἐναντίου ᾧ ἐπιφέρει· τὸ ἐναντίον ἐστὶν οὗ ἐπιφέρει θάνατος· ἡ ψυχὴ ἄρα ἄδεκτος θανάτου.

ἡ ψυχὴ ‿‿‿ ᾧ ἂν παρῇ, ζωὴν τούτῳ ἐπιφέρει ‿‿‿ ἄδεκτον τοῦ ἐναντίου.

ἡ ψυχὴ ‿‿‿ ἄδεκτος τοῦ ἐναντίου ᾧ ἐπιφέρει ‿‿‿ θάνατος.

§ 78. Strato's objections answered

οη'. – Ἀλλ' οὕτω γε, φησὶν ὁ Στράτων [frg. 124], οὐδὲ ἡ ἐν ὑποκειμένῳ   78
ζωὴ τοῦ ἐναντίου δεκτική· οὐ γὰρ μένει, εἶτα δέχεται τὸν θάνατον, οὐδὲ γὰρ ἡ ψυχρότης τὴν θερμότητα· ἀθάνατος ἄρα ἡ ἐν ὑποκειμένῳ ζωή, ὥσπερ ἄθερμος ἡ ψυχρότης, καὶ μὴν ἀπόλλυται.

Ἔπειτα, φησίν, οὐκ ἔστιν ἡ φθορὰ θανάτου παραδοχή, οὐδὲν γὰρ ζῷον οὕτω φθαρήσεται· οὐ γὰρ μένει ζῷον δεδεγμένον θάνατον, ἀλλὰ ἀποβαλὸν τὴν ζωὴν τέθνηκεν· ἀποβολὴ γὰρ ζωῆς ὁ θάνατος.

Ταῦτα μὲν ὁ Στράτων· | ἐχρῆν δὲ διττὴν ὑποθέσθαι τὴν ζωήν, καὶ περὶ τῆς (227) ἐπιφερούσης εἶναι τὸν λόγον, ἥτις οὐ τῷ τεθνάναι τὸ ὑποκείμενον χωρίζεται, ἀλλὰ τῷ χωριστὴ εἶναι. οὐ γὰρ πάθος ἦν τοῦ ὑποκειμένου, ἀλλ' οὐσία συγκριθεῖσα αὐτῷ καὶ τὴν ὡς πάθος ζωὴν ἐν αὐτῷ γεννήσασα, ὥσπερ ἐν τῷ φωτιζομένῳ οὐκ αὐτὸ τὸ φῶς, ἀλλ' ἡ ἀπ' αὐτοῦ μέθεξις.

Πρὸς τούτοις φησὶν ὁ Πρόκλος ὅτι τὸ ἀπόλλυσθαι τῇ ψυχῇ θανατοῦσθαί ἐστιν, τὸ δὲ θανατοῦσθαι φαίνεται ὄν, ὡς καὶ αὐτὸς ὁ Στράτων φησίν, τὸ παθεῖν

---

§ 77. 2 ὃ μ: ὧι M — 6–7 in spat. vac. M^c
§ 78. 5 οὐδὲν Wk: οὐδὲ M — 6 ἀποβαλὸν Fh: ἀποβάλλον M — 9 οὐ τῶι M^c: οὕτω M¹ — 10 τοῦ ὑποκειμένου Fh: τὸ ὑποκείμενον M

---

only two points have been selected (1–4: cf. I §§ 434–435; 5–7: I § 431; the corresponding answers, 8–12: cf. I § 445; 17–21: I § 443; 21–27: cf. I § 447; 28–29: I § 443).

the substratum; the soul, however, is not lost, but separated, being separable life; therefore it does not die; therefore it is immortal.

Against this reasoning of Proclus it might be said that, though the soul does not die this kind of death (through loss of life), yet when it has become independent after separation from the body (and, if you like, after a period of survival), it is extinguished later, in the same way as the life in the substratum becomes extinct by itself, a process different from what happens to the substratum. Therefore it is better to argue, on the basis of what has been proved already, that one kind of death is extinction of life, to which the soul is not subject because it is separable from the body that dies this death; it *is* subject, of course, to death by disjunction, but not to the death which is the contrary of the life that is conferred. What happens to the lower form of life cannot happen to the soul, for in that case life conferred would be similar to life-giving life, and one of two opposite terms, death, would be contrary to two kinds of life, which is absurd.

Even so, however, no answer has been offered to the suggestion that there is reason to fear lest the soul, having limited potency, perish while by itself.

§§ 79–80. Two more objections

79. The number three, being odd, ceases to exist on the approach of evenness: why should not the soul in the same way cease to exist on the approach of death, so that it is immortal in the same sense in which three is odd? — But the assumption is that it is separable; neither, indeed, is fire extinguished when the object it heats is 'extinguished' i.e. cooled and when the heat ceases to exist.

80. But still the chance remains that the soul may perish after the separation (just as fire actually does) whatever the cause may be. — The answer is that, since its natural function is the bestowal of life, it will first and foremost protect itself against death, from whatever quarter it approaches; indeed, if it never left the body, even the body would never die; *a fortiori* nothing can happen to the soul, which gives life. Secondly, if the soul is affected, it is affected by something. One possibility is that this is the body; but in reality it is the body that is affected when it comes within the range of the soul; besides, the influence that the body can exercise is of a

---

§§ 79–80. These two further objections might still be Strato's. The first (§ 79) is essentially the same as Strato's at I § 442, with a different example, oddness in number (Plato's own, 104a3–e6), instead of fire, which, however, is mentioned in the reply (lines 3–5). § 80, though it could be regarded as repeating in a different form that same objection of Strato's, rather seems to revive Cebes' original difficulty, as § 78.28–29 (I § 443) does, on the ground that Pr.'s view of the argument does

ἀποβολὴν ζωῆς τὸ ὑποκείμενον· ἀλλὰ μὴν ἡ ψυχὴ οὐκ ἀποβάλλεται, ἀλλὰ χωρίζεται, 15
οἷα χωριστὴ οὖσα ζωή· οὐκ ἄρα ἀποθνήσκει· ἀθάνατος ἄρα.
Ταῦτα μὲν ὁ Πρόκλος. ἀλλὰ μήποτε φαίη τις ὅτι τοῦτον μὲν τὸν κατὰ
ἀποβολὴν οὐκ ἀποθνήσκει θάνατον, καθ' ἑαυτὴν δὲ γενομένη καὶ χωρισθεῖσα,
εἰ δὲ βούλει καὶ ἐπιδιαμείνασα, ὕστερον ἀποσβέννυται, ὥσπερ καὶ αὐτὴ ἡ ἐν
ὑποκειμένῳ ζωὴ σβέσιν πάσχει, ἄλλο τι τοῦτο παρ' ὃ πάθος τὸ ὑποκείμενον 20
πάσχει. βέλτιον οὖν ἐκ τῶν δεδειγμένων ἐπιχειρῆσαι θάνατον μὲν εἶναι τὴν
σβέσιν τῆς ζωῆς, ἧς οὐκ εἶναι δεκτικὴν τὴν ψυχὴν χωριστὴν οὖσαν σώματος
οὗ ἐστιν οὗτος ὁ θάνατος· ἐπεὶ τοῦ γε κατὰ διάκρισιν δεκτική ἐστιν, οὐ μὴν
τοῦ ἐναντίου τῇ ἐπιφερομένῃ ζωῇ. οὐδὲ γὰρ πάσχει τοῦτο τὸ πάθος ὃ τὸ
ὑποδεέστερον πέφυκε πάσχειν, ἐπεὶ οὕτω γε ὁμοία ἔσται ἡ ἐπιφερομένη ζωὴ 25
τῇ ἐπιφερούσῃ, καὶ τὸ ἓν τῶν ἐναντίων, ὁ θάνατος, δύο ζωαῖς ἀντικείσεται, ὅπερ
ἄτοπον.
Ἀλλ' οὔπω ἡ ἀπορία λέλυται τοῦ δέος εἶναι μήποτε πεπερασμένην ἔχουσα
δύναμιν καθ' αὑτὴν ἀπόλλυται.

§§ 79-80. Two more objections

οθ'. – Ὥσπερ ἀνάρτιος μὲν ἡ τριάς, ἀπόλλυται δὲ τοῦ ἀρτίου ἐπιόντος, 79
οὕτω τί κωλύει ἀπόλλυσθαι τὴν ψυχὴν ἐπιόντος τοῦ θανάτου, καὶ ταύτῃ ἀθάνατον
εἶναι ὡς ἀνάρτιος ἡ τριάς; — Ἀλλ' ὑπόκειται χωριστή· οὐδὲ γὰρ τὸ πῦρ
σβέννυται τοῦ θερμανθέντος ὑπ' αὐτοῦ σβεννυμένου ἤτοι ψυχομένου καὶ παυομένης
τῆς θερμότητος. 5
π'. – Ἀλλὰ μήποτε καὶ χωρισθεῖσα ἀπόλλυται, ὡς τὸ πῦρ, δι' αἰτίαν ἥντινα 80
δή ποτε. — Ἤ πεφυκυῖα ζωὴν ἐπιφέρειν καὶ πρό γε πάντων ἑαυτῇ τὸν ὅθεν
δή ποτε ἐπιόντα θάνατον ἀμύνεται· | καὶ γὰρ εἰ ἀεὶ παρείη τῷ σώματι, οὐδὲ (228)
ἐκεῖνο ἀποθανεῖται· πολλῷ ἄρα μᾶλλον αὐτὴ ἡ ἐπιφέρουσα οὐδὲν πείσεται. ἔτι
εἰ πάσχει, ὑπό τινος πάσχει. ἤτοι οὖν ὑπὸ τοῦ σώματος· ἀλλὰ τοὐναντίον πλησιάσαν 5
τὸ σῶμα τῇ ψυχῇ· ἔπειτα σωματοειδῆ πάθη τὸ σῶμα ἐπιφέρει, ἡ δὲ ἀσώματος.

---

§ 78. 17 post τις] ἂν add. Nv — 20 ἄλλό τι M^c: ἀλλ' ὅτι ut vid. M¹ — 24 οὐδὲ μ : οὐδὲν M
§ 80. 2 ἢ M^c: ἡ M¹ | post πεφυκυῖα] ras. 1 litt., ¯ex ', M^c — 6 ἔπειτα M^c: ἐπὶ τὰ M¹

---

not answer this point adequately.
§ 79. 1. ἀνάρτιος for περιττός already in Pl. 104e5, 105d15, e10.
§ 80. 1-2. Cf. Dam. I § 443.
2-4. Cf. Dam. I § 459.
4-12: an argument by diaeresis: if soul is destroyed, it is either (1) by the body, or (2) by itself, or (3) by another soul. No counterpart in I.

bodily nature, whereas the soul is incorporeal. If it is not the body, it is the soul itself; but nothing is destructive of itself. Another soul, then? No, for things belonging to the same species also tend to preserve each other. But suppose souls have this destructive tendency, not qua lives, but qua individual characters? No, for it is unthinkable that the soul, which contains the active principles of all forms, including that of the very soul which is supposed to annihilate it in virtue of this particular character, should perish by it; in that case it would destroy itself; indeed, it could never exist at all with the principle of such a soul as part of its being.

PART THREE: THE MYTH

§§ 81-85. Preliminaries to the myth. 107c1–114c8

81. Of the three parts of the dialogue the third is the 'descent into Hades.'

82. The object of this part of the conversation is to describe the condition of souls when separated from this body, those who have attained the highest perfection, and those in the intermediate and lowest phases.

83. The content is not entirely mythical, some of it is also in accordance with the facts.

84. The myth, too, has three parts: the first serves as a link between what follows and what precedes [107c1–108c5], the second is a description of the earth, its size and shape [108c5–113c8], in the third the souls are consigned to their due destinations [113d1–114c8].

85. The 'descent into Hades' has three elements: the judges, the souls on trial, and the places where all this happens. There are three 'descents into Hades' in Plato, and in each all the three elements are mentioned; the present one, however, deals more especially with the places, the one in the *Gorgias* [523a1–527a4] with the judges, and the one in the *Republic* [X 614b2–621d3] with those on trial.

§§ 86-93. Death not the end. 107c1–d5

86. [107c1–4] Justice is threefold: intellective justice, when the soul extends itself towards the intelligible world and establishes itself firmly in what might be called 'the prototype of action in one's own sphere'; justice based on opinion, concerned with matters of opinion and social in character; and dianoetic justice, which moves on the level of discursive thought and

---

9. ἰδιότροποι (the adv. *infra* line 10 and § 129.4): an older term (see *LSJ*), which had a comeback in late Neoplatonism, perhaps owing to Dam. (*princ.* 82.9; Simpl., often; Elias, *isag.* 52.23; *cat.* 151.1; Dav. 169.1).

ibid. ἡ πάντων ἔχουσα τῶν εἰδῶν τοὺς λόγους : see note on Ol. 4 § 2.3.

§ 81. Dam. I § 466.1.

οὐκοῦν εἰ μὴ ὑπὸ τούτου, ὑφ᾽ ἑαυτῆς· ἀλλ᾽ οὐδὲν ἑαυτοῦ φθαρτικόν. ἀλλὰ μήποτε ὑπὸ ἄλλης ψυχῆς· ἀλλὰ καὶ τὰ ὁμοειδῆ σῴζει ἄλληλα. ἀλλ᾽ οὐ καθὸ ζωαὶ αἱ ψυχαί, ἀλλὰ καθὸ ἰδιότροποι· καὶ πῶς ἡ πάντων ἔχουσα τῶν εἰδῶν τοὺς λόγους καὶ αὐτῆς ἐκείνης τῆς ἰδιοτρόπως ἀπολλύσης φθαρήσεται ὑπ᾽ αὐτῆς; οὕτω γὰρ 10
καὶ ἑαυτὴν φθείρει καὶ ἐξ ἀρχῆς ἐφθαρμένη ἂν ἦν ἔχουσα τῆς τοιαύτης ψυχῆς τὸν λόγον.

PART THREE: THE MYTH

§§ 81–85. Preliminaries to the myth. 107c1–114c8

πα'. – Ὅτι τριῶν ὄντων μερῶν τοῦ διαλόγου τὸ τρίτον ἐστὶν ἡ νέκυια. 81
πβ'. – Ὅτι σκοπὸς τῷ διαλόγῳ τὴν χωριστὴν ἀποδοῦναι διαγωγὴν τῶν 82
ψυχῶν ἀπὸ τοῦδε τοῦ σώματος, τῶν τε κατὰ τὸν πρῶτον καὶ τέλειον βίον καὶ τῶν κατὰ τὸν μέσον καὶ τὸν τελευταῖον.
πγ'. – Ὅτι οὐ πάντα μυθικῶς λέγει, ἀλλ᾽ ἔνια καὶ πραγματειωδῶς. 83
πδ'. – Ὅτι τριμερὴς καὶ ὁ μῦθος· τὸ μὲν πρῶτον ἕνωσις τῶν ἔπειτα λόγων 84
πρὸς τοὺς προάγοντας [107c1–108c5], τὸ δὲ δεύτερον περιήγησις τῆς γῆς, ὅση καὶ οἷα τυγχάνει οὖσα [108c5–113c8], τὸ δὲ τρίτον διανομὴ τῶν ψυχῶν εἰς τὰς προσηκούσας λήξεις [113d1–114c8].
πε'. – Ὅτι ἐκ τριῶν ἡ νέκυια συνέστηκεν· ἐκ τῶν δικαζόντων, ἐκ τῶν 85
δικαζομένων, ἐκ τῶν τόπων ἐν οἷς ταῦτα πάντα. τριῶν δὲ οὐσῶν νεκυιῶν καὶ ἑκάστης τῶν εἰρημένων τριῶν μεμνημένης, ἥδε μὲν περὶ τῶν τόπων μᾶλλον ποιεῖται τὸν λόγον, ἡ δὲ ἐν Γοργίᾳ [523a1–527a4] περὶ τῶν δικαζόντων, ἡ δὲ ἐν Πολιτείᾳ [X 614b2–621d3] περὶ τῶν δικαζομένων. 5

§§ 86–93. Death not the end. 107c1–d5

πς'. – [107c1–4] Ὅτι τριττὴ ἡ δικαιοσύνη, ἡ μὲν ϊοερά, περὶ τὰ νοητὰ τῆς 86(229)
ψυχῆς ἀνατεταμένης καὶ ἱσταμένης κατὰ τὴν οἷον παραδειγματικὴν αὐτοπραγίαν· ἡ δὲ δοξαστικὴ περὶ τὰ δοξαστά, τῷ πολιτικῷ εἴδει χαρακτηριζομένη· ἡ δὲ

---

§ 82. 3 τὸν τελευταῖον M^c: τῶν τελευταίων M¹
§ 83. 1 λέγει ∸, -ι ∸ in ras., M^c (fort. λέγεται M¹)

---

§ 82. 1. διαλόγῳ: probably an echo of the preceding διαλόγου, which appears to have taken the place of either λόγῳ or μύθῳ.
§ 83. Dam. I § 466.2–3.
§ 84. 1. καὶ ὁ μῦθος: as the entire dialogue is.
§ 85. Dam. I § 471 and note. – The πρᾶξις sign is very probably erroneous.
§ 86. Dam. I § 472. On the three degrees of justice cf. I §§ 140–142.

is a kind of purificatory justice. Hence Socrates says that it is 'right to think' of the care of one's own soul, now that it has been shown to be immortal.

87. [107c2–4] The right way to take care of one's soul is different according as to whether it concerns one life only or a soul that is considered immortal.

There ought to be also some intermediate forms, from the point-of-view of prolonged existence.

88. What does it mean that our care should extend to 'all time'? — It does not refer to one lifetime, which is *a* time, not *all* time. The commentator explains it as the time of everlasting process.

It is difficult to see, however, how we can prepare for that, in the first place because it is infinite, and the infinite, being incomprehensible, admits of no preparation; but apart from that such an endeavor is hopeless, since in the course of infinite time souls capable of degradation must actually succumb to it. Therefore we prefer to say that it is the time coextensive with one cycle of existence.

89. If even generated things are in their normal condition during the greater part of the time, provided their origin is normal, how much more must everlasting and superior beings be free from harm most of the time? And if they take care of themselves, the normal condition will last even longer. This, according to the commentator, is another implication of the words 'with respect to all time': we should try to come near to those who enjoy happiness all the time.

90. [107c4] The 'danger is a terrible one' now that the soul has been found immortal, first because it is our real self that suffers; secondly because we are in a miserable state during most of the time; thirdly because we shall be condemned by the judges and consigned to some cheerless abode; fourthly because we shall find no relief from our misery until we have begun to show that care of ourselves which is here enjoined on us before the danger becomes a reality.

91. [107c6–8] That the Good is superior to being, is proved by the fact that nobody wants being for its own sake; what we seek is well-being, and if this is unattainable, we prefer not to exist at all.

92. [107d1–2] Truth and knowledge are the light of the soul, virtue and moral excellence are order in the soul, their opposites are darkness and

---

§§ 87–89. Dam. I § 473.

§ 87. 1–2. A summing up of *Ph.* 107c2–4, consequently the supplement in line 3 may be either by Pr. or by Dam.; probably the latter, since it seems to prepare the ground for § 88.3–7.

§ 88. 2. τὶς χρόνος: Pr.'s expression for the period of one soul, *elem.* 200, p. 174.11; cf. note on I § 547.4–8.

διανοητικὴ περὶ τὰ διανοητά, καθαρτική τις αὕτη δικαιοσύνη. διό φησιν 'δίκαιον διανοηθῆναι' περὶ ἐπιμελείας τῆς ἀθανάτου δειχθείσης ψυχῆς.

πζ'. – [107c2–4] Ὅτι ἄλλη μὲν ἐπιμέλεια ὡς περὶ ἕνα βίον τῆς ψυχῆς, ἄλλη δὲ ὡς περὶ ἀθάνατον τὴν ψυχήν. Εἶεν δὲ ἂν καὶ μέσαι τινὲς ὡς περὶ πολυχρόνιον οὖσαν.

πη'. – Τίς ὁ 'χρόνος πᾶς', ὑπὲρ οὗ ἐπιμελεῖσθαι χρή; — Οὐχ ὁ βίου ἑνός· τὶς γὰρ ὁ τοιοῦτος καὶ οὐ πᾶς. ἀλλ' ὁ τῆς ἀειγενεσίας, φησὶν ὁ ἐξηγητής. Καὶ πῶς οἷόν τε ὑπὲρ τούτου βουλεύσασθαι, οὐ μόνον ἀπείρου ὄντος — τὸ δὲ ἄπειρον ἀπροβούλευτον, ἀπερίληπτον γάρ· — οὐ τοίνυν τοῦτο μόνον, ἀλλὰ καὶ [ἀδυνάτου] ἀδύνατον, ἀνάγκη γὰρ ἐν τῷ παντὶ ἀπείρῳ χρόνῳ καὶ κακύνεσθαι τὰς πεφυκυίας τοῦτο πάσχειν ψυχάς. βέλτιον οὖν τὸν μιᾶς ἀποκαταστάσεως μετρητικὸν φάναι.

πθ'. – Ὅτι εἰ καὶ τὰ γενητὰ ἐπὶ πλείω χρόνον διάκειται κατὰ φύσιν, ὅσα γέγονε κατὰ φύσιν, πόσῳ γε μᾶλλον τὰ ἀΐδια καὶ κρείττω τὸν πλεῖστον χρόνον ἔσται ἐρρωμένα; εἰ δὲ ἐπιμέλοιτο ἑαυτῶν, καὶ ἔτι πλείω ἕξει τὸ κατὰ φύσιν. καὶ τοῦτο εἶναι πάλιν ὁ ἐξηγητὴς [εἶναι] φησὶ τὸ 'ὑπὲρ τοῦ παντὸς χρόνου', ἵνα ἐγγὺς ὦμεν τῶν ἅπαντα τὸν χρόνον εὐδαιμονούντων.

ρ'. – [107c4] Ὅτι 'δεινὸς ὁ κίνδυνος' ἀθανάτου τῆς ψυχῆς πεφασμένης, πρῶτον μὲν ὡς ἡμῶν τῶν ὄντως ἡμῶν κακουμένων· δεύτερον ὡς ἡμῶν τὸν πλεῖστον χρόνον κακῶς ἐχόντων· τρίτον ὡς κατακριθησομένων ὑπὸ τῶν δικαστῶν καὶ πεμφθησομένων εἰς τόπους ἀνημέρους τινάς· τέταρτον ὡς οὐ πρότερον ἀπαλλαγησομένων κακῶν, πρὶν ἂν τὴν ἐπιμέλειαν προβαλώμεθα ταύτην ἣν νῦν ὁ λόγος παρακελεύεται πρὸ τοῦ κινδύνου.

ρα'. – [107c6–8] Ὅτι κρεῖττον τἀγαθὸν τοῦ ὄντος δηλοῖ τὸ μηδένα | ἐθέλειν εἶναι ἁπλῶς, ἀλλὰ καλῶς εἶναι, εἰ δὲ μὴ ἐξείη καλῶς, μηδὲ εἶναι ὅλως.

ρβ'. – [107d1–2] Ὅτι ἡ μὲν ἀλήθεια καὶ ἡ γνῶσις φῶς ἐν ψυχῇ, ἡ δὲ ἀρετὴ

---

§ 87. 3 εἶεν δὲ ἄν] accent. omnes aut add. aut corr., ἄν in ras. scr., M^c
§ 88. 5 ἀδυνάτου M: del. ci. Nv — 6 ψυχάς ins. M^c: om. M^1
§ 89. 4 εἶναι² M: om. μ

---

6. μιᾶς ἀποκαταστάσεως: see note *ibid.*
§ 89. An additional observation by Pr., corresponding (more or less) to I § 473.1–3. The point that souls in genesis are outside their natural environment and that it is normal for them to live on the intelligible plane during most of their existence is made by Pr., *Alc.* 256.7–258.9.
§ 90. 2–3. τὸν πλεῖστον χρόνον: i.e., of our lives in this world, cf. preceding note.
§ 91. Dam. I § 475. Cf. Ol. 10 § 16.

chaos; hence the two kinds of souls are sent to the parts of the world they resemble.

93. [107d4–5] To what does Plato refer when he says that 'we are told so' about things in Hades? — First, to the unconscious heartbeat of our common notions: secondly to the theologians; thirdly to the oracles of the Gods; fourthly to the mysteries; fifthly to apparitions of the Gods themselves.

§§ 94–101. Guardian spirits and judgment generally. 107d5–e4

94. Since the world comprises beings in constant change and beings conjoined with the henads that are above being, there must be also an intermediate class, neither dependent upon a God by direct conjunction nor constantly changing for the worse and for the better, but ever perfect, never falling short of its own excellence; changeless, but not attached to that which transcends being; this entire kind forms the order of spirits.

95. There are various classes of spirits. Ranking next to the intramundane Gods there is one kind of spirits characterized by the unity of the Gods and accordingly called the unitary and divine class of spirits; another by the intelligence that depends upon the God, called the intellective class; a third by soul, called rational; another by nature, named natural; another by body, called the body-like; one, finally, characterized by matter, and designed as the material class of spirits.

---

§ 93. Dam. I § 476. Sources of knowledge of the hereafter are (1) innate notions; (2) "theologians," i.e. poetic myth, esp. Orpheus and Homer; (3) oracles, including both the Chaldean Oracles and all other kinds, such as Porph., *vit. Plot.* 22–23; (4) mysteries, cf. *Ph.* 69c3–7; Pr., *Rep.* II 185.10–12 οἷα καὶ αἱ παναγέσταται τελεταὶ τῶν Ἐλευσινίων ὑπισχνοῦνται τοῖς μύσταις τῶν παρὰ τῇ Κόρῃ δώρων ἀπολαύειν, ἐπειδὰν λυθῶσι τῶν σωμάτων (cf. *dec. dub.* 58.12: "revelationes et telete" on the punishment of posterity); (5) divine apparitions.

2. αἱ κοιναὶ ἔννοιαι σφύζουσαι ἀδιαρθρώτως : Pr., *Alc.* 189.6–8 καὶ τῷ μὲν ἔχειν τοὺς λόγους τῶν πραγμάτων οἷον σφύζοντας ἐννοίας ἔχουσι περὶ αὐτῶν, τῷ δὲ τῆς λήθης πόματι κρατούμεναι διαρθροῦν τὰς ἑαυτῶν ἀδυνατοῦσιν ἐννοίας καὶ εἰς ἐπιστήμην ἀναπέμπειν. The word σφύζειν has the connotations of (1) involuntary (Pr., *Tim.* I 393.6–7 οὐ γὰρ προελομένων ἡμῶν αἰσθάνεται ἢ σφύζει τὸ σῶμα) and (2) incompletely developed (Pr., *Rep.* II 160.6–10 τὸ δὲ λοιπόν, ὅσον εἶχεν ἑκάστη τῆς φιλογενέσεως ζωῆς, ἐκεῖ μὲν ἀνενέργητον μένον, ἐφιέμενον δὲ ἐνεργῆσαι, κάμνειν ἐποίει καὶ ἀσθενεῖν τὴν ὅλην κατά τι ἑαυτῆς ψυχὴν καὶ κάμνουσαν διδόναι καὶ τῷ σφύζοντι χώραν, where σφύζον = ἀνενέργητον μένον, ἐφιέμενον δὲ ἐνεργῆσαι. Dam., *Parm.* 101.19–20: motion and rest exist already in transcendent Life, οὐ μέντοι ἐκφανεῖς, ἀλλὰ σφύζουσαι τῷ οἰκείῳ τούτῳ σφυγμῷ τὴν ζωὴν οὐσίαν ἀπέφηναν). There may be a reminiscence of Pl., *Phaedr.* 251d4.

ibid. ἀδιαρθρώτως : διαρθροῦν with its derivatives (διάρθρωσις, ἀδιάρθρωτος, -ως) has a wide-spread application: to anatomy, speech, statement, and finally thought. *SVF* II frg. 8; Epictetus, *diss.* I 17,1 ἐπειδὴ λόγος ἐστὶν ὁ διαρθρῶν καὶ ἐξεργαζόμενος τὰ λοιπά, ἔδει δ' αὐτὸν μὴ ἀδιάρθρωτον εἶναι, ὑπὸ τίνος διαρθρωθῇ; Similarly Philodemus, *de diis* I 22.3–5, 23.22–26, both in reference to the clarifying of confused and

καὶ βελτίστη ἕξις εὐκοσμία, τὰ δὲ ἐναντία σκότος καὶ ἀκοσμία· διὸ πρὸς τὰ ὅμοια μέρη τοῦ παντὸς ἑκάτεροι ἀποπέμπονται.

ργ'. – [107d4-5] Τίνες οἱ λέγοντες; 'λέγεται' γὰρ ταῦτα περὶ τῶν ἐν ᾍδου, φησίν. – Ἢ πρῶτον μὲν αἱ κοιναὶ ἔννοιαι σφύζουσαι ἀδιαρθρώτως· δεύτερον οἱ θεολόγοι· τρίτον οἱ χρησμοὶ τῶν θεῶν· τέταρτον αἱ τελεταί· πέμπτον αὐτοὶ παραγενόμενοι οἱ θεοί.

§§ 94-101. Guardian spirits and judgment generally. 107d5-e4

ρδ'. – Ὅτι ὄντων ἐν τῷ κόσμῳ τῶν ἄλλοτε ἄλλως ἐχόντων καὶ τῶν ταῖς ὑπερουσίοις ἑνάσι συνημμένων, δεῖ καὶ μέσον τι γένος εἶναι, τὸ οὔτε θεοῦ ἐξημμένον ἐν συναρτήματι οὔτε ἄλλοτε ἄλλως ἔχον κατὰ τὸ χεῖρον καὶ τὸ κρεῖττον, ἀλλὰ τέλειον ἀεὶ καὶ τῆς οἰκείας ἀρετῆς οὐκ ἀφιστάμενον, ἀμετάβλητον μέν, οὐ συνημμένον δὲ τῷ ὑπερουσίῳ· τοῦτο δὲ ὅλον τὸ γένος δαιμόνιον.

ρε'. – Ὅτι γένη δαιμόνων διάφορα. ὑπέστρωται γὰρ τοῖς ἐγκοσμίοις θεοῖς τὸ μὲν δαιμόνιον γένος κατὰ τὸ ἓν τῶν θεῶν, ὃ δὴ καὶ καλεῖται ἑνιαῖον καὶ θεῖον δαιμόνων γένος· τὸ δὲ κατὰ τὸν νοῦν τὸν ἐξηρτημένον τοῦ θεοῦ, ὃ καλεῖται νοερόν· τὸ δὲ κατὰ τὴν ψυχήν, ὃ καλεῖται λογικόν· τὸ δὲ κατὰ τὴν φύσιν, ὅπερ ὀνομάζεται φυσικόν· τὸ δὲ κατὰ τὸ σῶμα, ὃ δὴ καλεῖται σωματοειδές· τὸ δὲ κατὰ τὴν ὕλην, τοῦτο δὲ ὑλαῖον ἐπιφημίζεται.

---

§ 94. 1 ἄλλοτε] -τε in ras. Mᶜ | ταῖς ins. Mᶜ: om. M¹ — 2 τὸ∼οὔτε, -ὸ∼οʳ- in ras. Mᶜ

---

imperfect notions. Platonists use it esp. of the articulation of subliminal innate concepts: Plut., de Is. 68, 378C, explains the divine child Harpocrates as τοῦ περὶ θεῶν ἐν ἀνθρώποις λόγου νεαροῦ καὶ ἀτελοῦς καὶ ἀδιαρθρώτου προστάτην καὶ σωφρονιστήν. Porph., Marc. 10 συνάγοις δ' ἂν καὶ ἑνίζοις (scil. σεαυτήν) τὰς ἐμφύτους ἐννοίας καὶ διαρθροῦν συγκεχυμένας καὶ εἰς φῶς ἕλκειν ἐσκοτισμένας πειρωμένη (cf. also abst. 2,43). Pr., Alc. 191.11-192.4 διττὴ τῶν ψυχῶν ἐστιν ἡ γνῶσις, ἡ μὲν ἀδιάρθρωτος καὶ κατ' ἔννοιαν ψιλήν, ἡ δὲ διηρθρωμένη καὶ ἐπιστημονικὴ καὶ ἀναμφισβήτητος. 'κινδυνεύομεν γάρ,' ὡς αὐτός πού φησιν, 'ὄναρ πάντα ἐγνωκότες τὰ αὐτὰ ταῦτα ὕπαρ ἀγνοεῖν,' κατ' οὐσίαν μὲν ἔχοντες τοὺς λόγους καὶ οἷον ἀποπνέοντες τὰς τούτων γνώσεις, κατ' ἐνέργειαν δὲ καὶ κατὰ προβολὴν οὐκ ἔχοντες (further ibid. 15.4; 132.7; 133.3-4; 192.6-7; Rep. I 117.19-21; II 297.2-4; id. ap. Dam., princ. 57.13-17); Dam., Phil. § 72.4-5 τάχα δὲ ἄμεινον τὸ μὲν ὕπαρ εἰς τὸ διηρθρωμένον λαβεῖν, τὸ δὲ ὄναρ εἰς τὸ ἀδιάρθρωτον τῆς γνώσεως. Simpl., cat. 379. 17-19 ὅσα δὲ ἦν μὲν ἐν ταῖς κοιναῖς ἐννοίαις προειλημμένα, διαρθρώσεως δὲ πλείονος ἐδεῖτο, τούτων τὸ συγκεχυμένον τῆς προλήψεως ... διήρθρωσεν (cf. phys. 653.7; 696.13; 1160.20; 24).

§ 94. Dam. I § 477.

1-2. The intramundane Gods, who answer the description τῶν ταῖς ὑπερουσίοις ἑνάσι συνημμένων (and τὸ ... θεοῦ ἐξημμένον ἐν συναρτήματι, lines 2-3), are listed by Dodds, p. 295.

3. συναρτήματι: apparently the only occurrence. Dam., Parm. 8. 24-26 uses ἐξάρτημα in the same sense: τῶν μὲν ὄντων σωματικῶν, τῶν δὲ ψυχικῶν, τῶν δὲ νοερῶν (καλείσθωσαν γὰρ ἡμῖν ἀπὸ τῶν ἐξαρτημάτων οἱ νοεροὶ θεοί), i.e. in the usual terminological meaning of ἐξηρτῆσθαι, as defined Pr., elem. 111.

§ 95. Dam. I § 478 and note.

96. Another division is that into celestial, ethereal, aerial, aquatic, terrestrial, subterranean. This classification of course corresponds to the regions of the universe. From the aerial spirits downwards the irrational spirits begin to appear also; hence the Oracle says [frg. 91]:
'Huntress with the hounds of air, of earth, of water.'

97. The spirits 'to whom each is allotted' belong to the intellective class; for the ruling class, the commentator says, always belongs to the kind that is immediately superior: thus the psychical spirits control irrational animals. He adds, however, that immaculate souls are governed by divine spirits.

One would say, nevertheless, that these too are souls and ought to be governed directly by intellective spirits on the same ground. Besides, the class of spirits as such, whatever their rank, is superior to the human race and to all the lower kinds. A better theory is, therefore, that guardian spirits do not belong to all ranks of spirits indiscriminately, but only to the companions of those Gods who are in charge of the descents and ascents of souls. To the spirits attached to these Gods the care of such lives is assigned, for it can be said in general that ascent and descent comprise different kinds of life, and so this group of spirits must belong to all various ranks (divine, intellective, and so forth) and divide the supervision of these lives among themselves accordingly.

98. According to the commentator the guardian spirits are ethereal demons.

It is better to hold that in this respect, too, they are of all kinds, though always belonging to those subordinate to that particular class of Gods.

99. The tribunal is the whole world, and there are tribunals in all its parts. For Justice, too, is one and, after the one, many, so that the same

---

§ 96. Dam. I § 479 and note. The list which arranges demons according to their habitats is basically an expanded form of the line from the Chaldean Oracles quoted here.

3–5. Irrational demons are seldom referred to in Pr., except as a substitute for the evil spirits in the Chaldean Oracles (*Rep.* II 337. 14–19; *Tim.* III 157.26–158.11; 158.19–22; see note on I § 486). In Pl., the avenging demons of *Rep.* X 615e4–616a4 are rational according to Pr., *Rep.* II 181.8–11, though later texts class avenging spirits as irrational: Amm., *isag.* 99.10–22; cf. 100.13–20; Dav. 186.9–13; Ps.-El. 41,30–31.

§§ 97–98. Dam. I § 480. There is a general treatise on the εἰληχὼς δαίμων by Pr., *Alc.* 71.1–78.6: the divine spirits (at 72.18 read θεῖοι with Dodds, *Gnomon* 27, 1955, 166) are those who are κατ' οὐσίαν in charge of ascents and descents (*Rep.* II 271.26–272.18 he makes a similar distinction between οὐσιώδεις ἔφοροι, who are divine spirits, and γενεσιουργοὶ καὶ μοιραῖοι); the guardian spirit is neither rational soul (Xenocrates) nor the active function of the soul nor the one immediately above it (Plotinus) nor individual intelligence (Stoa).

§ 97. 1–3. These lines report Pr.'s view, not that of Plotinus (III 4,3), as superficially they might seem to do: to Pr., spirits are beings *sui generis*, not a part

ρϛ′. – Ὅτι καὶ ἄλλως οἱ μέν εἰσιν οὐράνιοι, οἱ δὲ αἰθέριοι, οἱ δὲ ἀέριοι, οἱ 96
δὲ ὑδραῖοι, οἱ δὲ χθόνιοι, οἱ δὲ ὑποχθόνιοι. αὕτη δὲ ἡ διαίρεσις δηλονότι ἐκ
τῶν τοῦ παντὸς εἴληπται μερίδων. ἀπὸ δὲ τῶν ἀερίων ἄρχονται συνυφίστασθαι
οἱ ἄλογοι δαίμονες· διὸ καὶ τὸ λόγιόν φησιν [frg. 91]·
'ἠερίων ἐλάτειρα κυνῶν χθονίων τε καὶ ὑγρῶν'. 5

ρζ′. – Ὅτι οἱ εἰληχότες ἐκ τῶν νοερῶν εἰσιν· τὸ γὰρ ἄρχον, φησί, προσεχῶς 97 (231)
ἐκ τοῦ ὑπερκειμένου γένους ἐστὶν πανταχοῦ· καὶ γὰρ οἱ ψυχικοὶ τῶν ἀλόγων
ζῴων ἡγοῦνται. τὰς μέντοι ἀχράντους, φησί, θεῖοι δαίμονες διοικοῦσι.
Καίτοι φαίη ἄν τις ὅτι καὶ αὗται ψυχαί, καὶ ἔδει κατὰ τὸν αὐτὸν λόγον
προσεχῶς ἐκ τῶν νοερῶν διοικεῖσθαι. ἔπειτα αὐτὸ τὸ δαιμόνιον, ὁποῖον δἂν ᾖ, 5
ὑπερκείμενόν ἐστι τοῦ τε ἀνθρωπείου καὶ τῶν ἐφεξῆς γενῶν πάντων. βέλτιον
οὖν μὴ ἐκ πάντων δαιμόνων ἀορίστως ποιεῖν τοὺς εἰληχότας, ἀλλ' ἐκ τῶν ἑπομένων
θεοῖς μόνον ἐκείνοις τοῖς ἐπὶ καθόδων τε καὶ ἀνόδων τεταγμένοις τῶν ψυχῶν.
οἱ γὰρ τούτων ἐξημμένοι λαγχάνουσι τοὺς τοιούτους βίους· ὅλως γὰρ ἡ ἄνοδος
καὶ κάθοδος βίων διαφόρων ἐστὶ περιεκτική, παντοδαποὺς δὲ ὄντας τοὺς τοιούτους 10
δαίμονας, οἷον τοὺς μὲν θείους, τοὺς δὲ νοεροὺς καὶ τοὺς ἑξῆς, ἄλλων ἄλλους
προεστάναι.

ρη′. – Ὅτι αἰθέριοι, φησίν, οἱ εἰληχότες. 98
Ἄμεινον δὲ καὶ ταύτῃ παντοίους λέγειν, ἐξ ἐκείνων μέντοι τῶν ἐκείνοις τοῖς
θεοῖς ὑποτεταγμένων.

ρθ′. – Ὅτι δικαστήριον ὅλος ὁ κόσμος, καὶ δικαστήρια καθ' ὅλας αὐτοῦ τὰς 99
μερίδας. καὶ γὰρ ἡ Δίκη μία τε καὶ πολλὴ μετὰ τὴν μίαν, ὥστε καὶ ὁ πᾶς

---

§ 96. 4–5 φησιν ἠερίων] -ν ἠ- in ras. Mᶜ
§ 97. 2 ἐστὶν] in ras. Mᶜ — 4 αὗται Mᶜ: αὐταὶ M¹ (?)

---

of the human soul; those in charge of souls belong themselves to the next higher
level, i.e. intellect, while our own highest, intellective, faculty falls under the
domain of the divine spirits. Cf. Pr., Tim. III 291.4–6 πανταχοῦ γὰρ τὸ προσεχῶς
ὑπεριδρυμένον τὴν δαίμονος ἔχει τάξιν πρὸς τὸ παρ' αὐτοῦ προνοίας ἀξιούμενον, and
Alc. 73.1–3 ἐπεὶ αἵ γε τελεώταται καὶ ἀχράντως ὁμιλοῦσαι τῇ γενέσει, ὥσπερ τὸν
προσήκοντα βίον αἱροῦνται τῷ ἑαυτῶν θεῷ, οὕτω καὶ κατὰ δαίμονα ζῶσι τὸν θεῖον. In
lines 4–12 Dam. expresses dissent.
8. τοῖς ἐπὶ καθόδων τε καὶ ἀνόδων τεταγμένοις: cf. Pr., Tim. I 52.22–53.4; 54.3–7;
108.14–20; III 290.30–291.6; Rep. II 52.26–28 (τοῖς ἀναγωγοῖς θεοῖς ... τοῖς
γενεσιουργοῖς, καὶ ἀγγέλοις ... τοῖς λύουσιν τὴν ὕλην ... τοῖς τῶν καθόδων ἐφόροις);
53.2–5; 187.5–7; 255.28–256.2; 351.7–20 (Hermes); Dam., Phil. § 60 (Prometheus);
Ol., Gorg. 254.17–26 (id.).
§ 98. 1. Pr. coordinates the two classifications of spirits, making the εἰληχότες
second in both (νοεροί, αἰθέριοι). This provided a welcome link with his theory that
the place of judgment in Ph. and Gorg., called τόπος δαιμόνιος in Rep. X 614c1,
was ether (infra § 100. 1–2).
§ 99. Dam. I §§ 481–482. Combines the view of Dam. (I § 481.4–7) with the
more comprehensive of Pr.'s two interpretations (I § 482, cf. 481.6–7).

must be true of the entire order of beings that depend on her, down to heroic souls, namely those who have this rank forever; it is unthinkable that until the time of the historical Aeacus there should have been no tribunal. Of course, the order includes even irrational demons and inanimate objects.

100. One region is that of justice, the ethereal region, which according to the commentator is not in Hades, since it gives access to heaven and earth and Hades.

One could object that from Hades, too, there can be roads leading everywhere; and how could it be elsewhere but in Hades, when it is the place of those who die? Unless one argues that this is the place not only of the dying, but also of souls coming down from heaven, as described in the *Republic* [X 614d7-e1], and of those who ascend from the lower regions.

101. That there is not one spirit in charge of each soul is proved, first, by the consideration that spirits rank closer to the First Cause, which is one.

Secondly there is the point that when the soul has left this life the spirit will be idle, though this is not a strong argument. Why, in fact, should he not govern this particular type of life in all its successive manifestations, rather than the individual life? Besides, the same difficulty may arise otherwise, too: if all the souls return to the upper world, the spirit's work will be done, or, if they are prevented from returning all at the same time, lest the spirit should be idle, this will interfere with the free action of the soul.

Thirdly, the commentator says, the spirit is not in charge of a soul, but of a type of life, and several souls can quite well choose the same kind of life. By this argument he evidently demolishes the second.

§§ 102–107. Guardian spirits and judgment: notes on the text. 107d5–e4

102. [107d7] The spirit 'makes ready to lead him' in the sense that while activating his thoughts and fancies, he also leaves room for free-will; to this activating influence of the spirit some respond voluntarily, some under a certain compulsion, in other cases there is something of both.

103. [107d6–7] Why is it here the spirit to whom they are 'allotted,' whereas it says in the *Republic* [X 617e1] 'You will not be allotted to a spirit, but you will choose one yourselves'? — This depends on the life which the soul has chosen for her role; the spirit governs the type of life,

---

3. ἄχρι τῶν ἡρωϊκῶν ψυχῶν, τῶν μέντοι ἀεί: obviously there is a distinction between ἥρωες κατ' οὐσίαν and human heroes such as the historical Aeacus. Compare the two groups of ἄχραντοι ψυχαί, II § 6.3–4, note.

5. ἀλόγων δαιμόνων: see note on II § 96.3–5.

ibid. μέχρι τῶν ἀψύχων: see Dam. I § 482.2.

§ 101. Dam. I § 484.

ἐξηρτημένος αὐτῆς χορὸς ἄχρι τῶν ἡρωϊκῶν ψυχῶν, τῶν μέντοι ἀεί· οὐ γὰρ δή που μέχρι τοῦδε τοῦ Αἰακοῦ οὐκ ἦν δικαστήριον. δῆλον δὲ ὅτι καὶ μέχρι τῶν ἀλόγων δαιμόνων καὶ μέχρι τῶν ἀψύχων.

ρ'. – Ὅτι εἷς τῶν τόπων δικαστικός, ὁ αἰθέριος, οὐκ ὢν ἐν Ἅιδου, φησὶν ὁ ἐξηγητής· πέμπει γοῦν εἰς οὐρανὸν καὶ εἰς γῆν καὶ εἰς Ἅιδου.

Φαίη δὲ ἄν τις δυνατὸν εἶναι καὶ ἐξ Ἅιδου πέμπειν πανταχοῦ· πῶς δὲ οὐκ ἐν Ἅιδου, ὅτε τῶν θνῃσκόντων ἐστὶν ὁ τόπος; εἰ μὴ ἄρα οὐ μόνων, ἀλλὰ καὶ τῶν ἐξ οὐρανοῦ κατιουσῶν, ὡς ἐν Πολιτείᾳ φησί [X 614d7–e1], καὶ τῶν ἐκ τῶν ὑποκειμένων ἀνατρεχουσῶν.

ρα'. – Ὅτι οὐ καθ' ἑκάστην ψυχὴν εἷς δαίμων τέτακται, δηλοῖ πρῶτον μὲν τὸ ἐγγυτέρω αὐτοὺς τετάχθαι τῆς μιᾶς αἰ|τίας.

Δεύτερον δέ, εἰ καὶ μὴ ἰσχυρὸν τὸ ἐπιχείρημα, ἀλλ' οὖν δεύτερον τὸ ἀπολιπούσης τῆς ψυχῆς τὸν βίον ἀργήσειν τὸν δαίμονα. τί γὰρ κωλύει κατ' εἶδος αὐτὸν ἐπιτροπεύειν τὴν ἀεὶ τοιαύτην ζωήν, ἀλλ' οὐχὶ τὴν τῷ ἀριθμῷ; ἐπεὶ καὶ ἄλλως τὸ αὐτὸ ἄτοπον· ἀναχθήσονται γὰρ καὶ πᾶσαι, ὥστε ἀργήσει· εἰ δὲ μὴ πᾶσαι, ἵνα μὴ ἀργήσῃ, τὸ αὐτεξούσιόν πως τῶν ψυχῶν κωλυθήσεται.

Τρίτον, φησίν, οὐ ψυχὴν εἴληχεν, ἀλλὰ βίον· τί δὲ κωλύει τὸν αὐτὸν βίον πλείους αἱρεῖσθαι ψυχάς; ὥστε σαφῶς διὰ τούτου τοῦ ἐπιχειρήματος ἀνατρέπει τὸ δεύτερον.

§§ 102–107. Guardian spirits and judgment: notes on the text. 107d5–e4

ρβ'. – [107d7] Ὅτι 'ἐπιχειρεῖ' μὲν 'ἄγειν' ὡς κινῶν μὲν τὰς ἐννοίας καὶ φαντασίας, ἐνδιδοὺς δὲ καὶ τῷ αὐτοκινήτῳ· κινήσαντος δὲ τοῦ δαίμονος ἡ μὲν ἑκουσίως ἕπεται, ἡ δὲ βιαιότερον, ἡ δὲ μέσως.

ργ'. – [107d6–7] Πῶς νῦν ὁ δαίμων 'εἴληχεν'; καίτοι ἐν Πολιτείᾳ ἔφη· 'οὐχ ὑμᾶς δαίμων λήξεται, ἀλλ' ὑμεῖς δαίμονα αἱρήσεσθε' [X 617e1]. – Ἡ κατὰ

---

§ 100. 4 ὅτε] -ε in ras. Mᶜ | μόνων Nv: -ον M
§ 101. 3 ἀπολιπούσης Wk: -λειπ- M

3–7. Pr., Rep. II 272.19–24 ὅτι δὲ ὁ δαίμων οὗτος ἐν λογικαῖς ὑπάρξεσιν οὐσίωται μειζόνως ... καὶ ὅτι πολλῶν εἷς ἄρχει τῶν ὁμοειδῶς ζώντων, οὐδὲν οἶμαι δεῖν ὑπομιμνήσκειν (this may be an indirect reference to the Ph. commentary). γελοῖον γὰρ εἰ, ὅταν ἀπολείπωμεν τὸν αὐτῷ προσήκοντα βίον, εὐθὺς ἄλλη ψυχὴ τὸν αὐτὸν αἱρεῖται βίον, ἢ ἐκεῖνος οὐδενός ἐστιν ἄρχων.
§§ 102–104. Dam. I §§ 487–489.

and the soul by her choice automatically submits to the guidance of this or that spirit.

104. [107d8] Both the common lot and the individual differences are expressed in the words 'are gathered' and 'stand their trial.'

105. [107d5–e4] One spirit conducts them from this life to the judges, another leads them to Hades as an assistant of the court, whose task it is, as it were, to execute the sentence; a third, again, is the one in charge of the next life.

106. [107e4] Whenever an everlasting entity changes in reference to limited things, its motion is a cyclical one. Because it changes, it cannot remain stationary; because the things in relation to which it changes are limited and numbered, it cannot proceed infinitely; because it is everlasting, it returns to the same points, and the result is a cycle. But if its activity is circular, its essence must be a circle first, as Timaeus maintains [36e2–5].

107. Three corollaries: (1) no soul remains always above or always below; (2) not all souls make a thousand years' journey, periods being many and various, and the thousand years' journey in the *Phaedrus* [248e5–249b3] must be understood symbolically; (3) periodicity is an attribute both of the substances that cause a revolving motion and of those that undergo it.

§§ 108–113. Observations on 107e4–108c5

108. [107e4–108a2] There is one common road to Hades, but after the common start there are many various ways, since there are so many different destinations which the wayfarers choose as their goals, and also because the emotional patterns which drive them towards their destination change again and again. Plato makes this c'ear, first by a philosophical argument, viz. that the guides are different and will accordingly lead them to different destinations. Then by a religious argument, taken from ritual practices; the reference may be either to assimilation to different Gods, each soul having a divine example of it own (this is not specific enough);

---

§ 105. Dam. I § 491.
2. οἷον ἀποπληρωτής : Pl., Rep. X 620d8–e1 ἐκείνην δ' ἑκάστῳ ὃν εἵλετο δαίμονα, τοῦτον φύλακα συμπέμπειν τοῦ βίου καὶ ἀποπληρωτὴν τῶν αἱρεθέντων.
§ 106. Dam. I § 493.
§ 107. Dam. I § 494 and note.
1. Cf. I §§ 547–548, Ol. 10 § 14, and notes.
§ 108. 1–4. Dam. I § 495.
4–12. Dam. I § 496.
6–10. The text of *Ph.* 108a4–6 has some significant variants: νῦν δὲ ἔοικε σχίσεις τε καὶ τριόδους (Pr., Dam.: περιόδους MSS., Stob. I 49,58) πολλὰς ἔχειν· ἀπὸ τῶν ὁσίων (T²W²γρ., Y: θυσιῶν TWY², Stob.) τε καὶ νομίμων τῶν ἐνθάδε τεκμαιρόμενος λέγω. Pr., Rep. I 85.1–7: δηλοῖ δὲ ἐν Φαίδωνι ... τάς τε σχίσεις ... καὶ τὰς τριόδους (πριόδους, π ut vid. ex τ, τ sscr. m²) ἀπὸ τῶν ὁσίων (οὐσιῶν MS.) καὶ τῶν πατρίων

τὸν βίον ὃν ἡ ψυχὴ ὑπέδυ· τοῦ γὰρ εἴδους προέστηκεν, ἐκείνη δὲ αὐτόθεν ἑαυτὴν ὑποτάττει τῷδε ἢ τῷδε τῷ δαίμονι.

ρδ΄. – [107d8] *Ὅτι τὸ κοινὸν καὶ διάφορον λέγει, δηλοῖ τὸ 'συλλεγῆναι' καὶ 'διαδικάζεσθαι'.* 104

ρε΄. – [107d5–e4] *Ὅτι ἄλλος μὲν ὁ ἀπὸ τοῦ βίου ἄγων παρὰ τοὺς δικαστάς, ἄλλος δὲ ὁ εἰς Ἅιδου ἄγων, ὑπουργὸς ὢν τῶν δικαστῶν, οἷον ἀποπληρωτὴς ὢν τῆς ψήφου· τρίτος δὲ ὁ πάλιν τὸν βίον λαχών.* 105

ρϛ΄. – [107e4] *Ὅτι πᾶν ἀΐδιον μεταβαλλόμενον περὶ [ὃ] τὰ πεπερασμένα, περίοδον κινεῖται. ὅτι μὲν γὰρ μεταβάλλεται, οὐ μένει ἐν τῷ αὐτῷ· ὅτι δὲ πεπέρασται καὶ ἠρίθμηται ταῦτα περὶ ἃ μεταβάλλεται, οὐ πρόεισιν ἐπ' ἄπειρον· ὅτι δὲ ἀΐδιόν ἐστι, περὶ τὰ αὐτὰ πάλιν στρέφεται, ὥστε κυκλίζεται. εἰ δὲ ἡ ἐνέργεια κυκλική, καὶ ἡ οὐσία πρότερον κύκλος, ὡς ὁ Τίμαιος ἀξιοῖ* [36e2–5]. 106 5

ρζ΄. – *Ὅτι ποριστέον, πρῶτον μὲν ὅτι οὐδεμία μένει ἀεὶ οὔτε ἄνω οὔτε κάτω· δεύτερον ὅτι οὐκ ἔστι χιλιέτης ἡ πορεία πα|σῶν, εἴπερ περίοδοι πολλαὶ καὶ διάφοροι, ἀλλὰ συμβολικῶς τῆς χιλιέτους ἀκουστέον ἐν Φαίδρῳ* [248e5–249b3]· *τρίτον ὅτι τὸ περιοδεύειν πρόσεστι καὶ τοῖς περιάγουσι καὶ τοῖς περιαγομένοις.* 107 (233)

§§ 108–113. Observations on 107e4–108c5

ρη΄. – [107e4–108a2] *Ὅτι μία μὲν κατὰ τὸ κοινὸν ἡ εἰς Ἅιδου πορεία, πολλαὶ δὲ καὶ παντοδαπαὶ μετὰ τὴν μίαν αἱ ὁδοί, ἅτε τοιούτων καὶ τοσούτων οὐσῶν τῶν λήξεων ἃς τέλη ποιοῦνται αἱ ὁδοιποροῦσαι, ἔτι δὲ καὶ τῶν ζῴων ἄλλων οὐσῶν ἐπ' ἄλλαις καθ' ἃς ἐπὶ τὰς λήξεις φέρονται. ὁ μέντοι Πλάτων τοῦτο δείκνυσι φιλοσόφως μὲν ἀπὸ τῶν ἡγεμόνων, εἴπερ εἰσὶ διάφοροι· ἐπὶ διάφορα γὰρ ἡγήσονται. ἱερατικῶς δὲ ἀπὸ τῶν ἱερῶν, ἢ διὰ τὰς ὁμοιώσεις τῶν διαφόρων θεῶν, ὅτι ἄλλη ψυχὴ ἄλλῳ ὡμοίωται θεῷ (τοῦτο δὲ ἐπιπόλαιον)· ἢ διὰ τὰς* 108 5

---

§ 106. 1 περὶ τὰ Nv: περὶ ὃ τὰ M^c: περιόντα ut vid. M¹
§ 107. 2 εἴπερ Fh: ἤπερ M
§ 108. 3 ζῴων M^c: ζῴων ut vid. M¹

θεσμῶν τεκμαιρόμενος. It is fairly evident from I § 496.3, 497.1 and the present section that Pr. (and Dam. following him) did read τριόδους in Pl. This is not the case as regards ὁσίων: for Pl.'s ἀπὸ τῶν ὁσίων (or θυσιῶν) τε καὶ νομίμων, Pr. Rep. has ἀπὸ τῶν οὐσιῶν (which is closer to θυσιῶν than to ὁσίων) καὶ τῶν πατρίων θεσμῶν, while in his Ph. commentary he must also have read θυσιῶν τε καὶ νομίμων, here paraphrased (lines 8–10) ἐπὶ τριόδου θύουσι τῇ Τριοδίτιδι Ἑκάτῃ καὶ παραδεικνύουσι τὰς τριόδους ἐν ἄλλοις νομίμοις. Though ὁσίων, therefore, may be an old variant, it cannot claim the authority of Pr. – The commentary points out three possible interpretations: (1) Socrates refers to cults in the most general sense to prove the different trends of people in this life and to infer corresponding differences in the hereafter; (2) the "sacrifices and ceremonies" are specifically the Eleusinian mysteries; (3) the allusion concerns only cults at road-forkings, more in particular Hecate's. Dam. I discusses only this last possibility.

or to the wanderings of Demeter, who went astray because there were different roads; or to sacrifices offered to Hecate Trioditis at points where three roads meet and to representations of such forkings in other ceremonies. Furthermore, there are three ways of paying worship to the souls of the departed, one for the venerable priests, one for those who have died a violent death, one for the common run of people.

109. Just as the other arts and sciences appeal to philosophy for corroboration, philosophy resorts to hieratic science to confirm her own doctrines.

110. [108a7–b3] How can souls dragged down by their own weight be lifted up to ether? — First and foremost, even they participate in a natural longing to be above; then the guiding spirits, too, rouse such longings in them and lend them the necessary powers; moreover, if even earthly bodies can move upward in a supernatural way, how much more can souls!

This is the commentator's view; rather we should say that for each soul the level proportioned to it is the place of judgment, although in this proportion there is a certain latitude.

111. [108b3–4] Why do they assemble in one place, ether? Souls would

---

10–12. I have found no references to special rites for priests, except Herod. 9,85,1–2, where editions since Valckenaer read ἰρένες, but the MSS. ἰρέες (separate graves for priests, other Spartans, and helots). Pr. almost certainly knew only this reading and he may have had the Herod. passage in mind, but more probably he drew upon his own extensive knowledge of cults and rites, cf. Marin., *vit. Pr.* 36 (*infra* II § 150 note): Pr. himself performed memorial rites for (1) the Attic heroes, (2) philosophers, (3) friends; after this, (1) in the Academy for ancestors and other relatives, (2) elsewhere for all philosophers, (3) elsewhere for all souls. – παναγής as an epithet for priests: CIG 380.6=IG 3,716; cf. Pollux 1,35, where, however, Bethe punctuates ἱέρειαι, παναγεῖς.

11. τῶν βιοθανάτων : occurrences of the word (and its derivatives βιοθανασία, -τεῖν) in *LSJ* (and App.), *PGL*, Norvin 1915, 186, n. 2, and Ps.-Heliodorus, *In Paulum Alex.*, ed. Ae. Boer, Leipzig 1962, index. *LSJ*, by lumping together most of the entries under βιαιοθ., misrepresents the state of affairs: as far as I can see, the only instances of the longer form are Vettius Valens (*passim*), Plut., *fluv.* 7,3 and Dam. II § 151.2 (where Norvin wrongly prints βιοθ.), so that it becomes questionable whether it is really the original form and not a late attempt to eliminate the ambiguity of βιοθ., which suggests βίος rather than βία. – The general meaning, that of violent death, can be narrowed down to either suicide or death by execution. Most of the cases, esp. in the astrologers, are indeterminate; of the rest, suicide is the rarer meaning (Cassian, *instit. coenob.* 7,14, *PL* 49, 304A; three more instances in *PGL* s.v. βιοθανέω and -ής). – On burial: mass-graves for executed criminals are mentioned *chron. Pasch.* 627.20 Dindorf; Theophanes, *chron.* 437.5 and 442.10 de Boor; *Suda* s.v. κυνήγιον, III p. 213.11 Adler.

§ 109. Philosophy as art of arts and science of sciences: Ar., *met.* A 2; Amm., *isag.* 1.15–17; 6.25–9.6; El., *isag.* 21.6–22.2; Dav. 40.7–41.36; as subordinate to theurgy, above I § 172.

§ 110. **Dam. I § 498.** In lines 1–5 the assumption that the place of judgment

Δήμητρος πλάνας, ώς γὰρ διαφόρων οὐσῶν τῶν ὁδῶν ἐπλανήθη· ἢ ὅτι ἐπὶ τριόδου θύουσι τῇ Τριοδίτιδι Ἑκάτῃ καὶ παραδεικνύουσι τὰς τριόδους ἐν ἄλλοις νομίμοις. ἀλλὰ καὶ τῶν ἀποιχομένων τὰς ψυχὰς τριχῇ θεραπεύουσιν, ἄλλως μὲν τὰς τῶν παναγῶν ἱερέων, ἄλλως δὲ τὰς τῶν βιοθανάτων, καὶ ἔτι ἄλλως τὰς τῶν πολλῶν.

ρθ'. - Ὅτι ὥσπερ αἱ ἄλλαι τέχναι καὶ ἐπιστῆμαι ἐπὶ φιλοσοφίαν καταφυγοῦσαι 109 βεβαιοῦνται, οὕτω καὶ φιλοσοφία ἐπὶ τὴν ἱερατικὴν ἀναβᾶσα τὰ οἰκεῖα δόγματα συνίστησιν.

ρι'. - [108a7–b3] Πῶς αἱ ὀπισθοβαρεῖς εἰς τὸν αἰθέρα ἀνάγονται; — Ἢ 110 μάλιστα μὲν καὶ αὗται φυσικῆς ὀρέξεως ἐπὶ τὰ ἄνω ἱεμένης μετέχουσιν· ἔπειτα καὶ ἐμποιοῦσιν αὐταῖς ὀρέξεις τοιαύτας καὶ δυνάμεις οἱ ἄγοντες δαίμονες· πρὸς δὲ ἔτι ⟨εἰ⟩ καὶ σώματα γεώδη πρὸς τὸ ἄνω κινεῖται δαιμόνιον τρόπον, πόσῳ μᾶλλον ψυχαί; 5
Οὕτω μὲν ὁ ἐξηγητής· μήποτε δὲ βέλτιον ἑκάσταις εἶναι τὸν σύμμετρον τόπον δικαστικόν, εἰ καὶ ἐν πλάτει τὸ σύμμετρον.

ρια'. - [108b3–4] Διὰ τί εἰς ἕνα συλλέγονται τόπον τὸν αἰθέριον; οὔτε γὰρ 111

---

§ 108. 8 ὁδῶν] ὁ- in ras. M^c
§ 110. 1 αἱ M^c: οἱ M¹ — 2 αὗται M^c: αὐταὶ M¹ — 4 ἔτι ⟨εἰ⟩ Wk (ἐπεὶ Nv): ἔτι M

is ether, is again Pr.'s (supra II § 100, cf. note on § 98.1); Dam. makes his usual objection (lines 6–7).

1. ὀπισθοβαρεῖς : first used in this way (of the burden of matter that drags down the soul) by Plot. VI 9,4.22; later (either of the soul or of its vehicle) by Pr., Rep. I 119.17; II 190.10 (verb); Crat. 61.10; Simpl., Epict. 35.2–3. Associated with Pl. Rep. X 614c7–d1 (τοὺς δὲ ἀδίκους τὴν εἰς ἀριστεράν τε καὶ κάτω, ἔχοντας καὶ τούτους ἐν τῷ ὄπισθεν σημεῖα πάντων ὧν ἔπραξαν) by Pr., Rep. II 150.12–13 αἱ δὲ χείρους καὶ εἰς τὴν τῶν παθῶν ἀταξίαν ὀπισθοβαροῦσι. However, as the metaphors of a mark and a weight are quite different, there is no reason to believe that the word was originally coined in reference to this passage; it is closer to the ἐμβριθές of Ph. 81c8. It is usually thought to come from the Chaldean Oracles, on the ground of Pr., Rep. II 77.4–10 τὸ δὲ σιδηροῦν γένος πέμπτον ὑπάρχον ἔσχατον ὄντως ἐστὶ καὶ χθόνιον, ἐμπαθὲς ὄν, τῷ σιδήρῳ παραπλήσιον, ἀντίτυπον καὶ σκληρὸν καὶ γήϊνον, μέλαν τε καὶ σκοτεινόν· οἷα δὴ καὶ ἡ τῶν παθῶν ἐστιν φύσις, δυσνουθέτητος οὖσα καὶ λόγῳ δύσκαμπτος (-μπος MS.) καὶ ὀπισθοβαρὴς καὶ ἄμοιρος ὡς εἰπεῖν λόγου, φωτὸς ὄντος. From this Schoell composed a hexameter, δύσκαμπτος καὶ ὀπισθοβαρὴς καὶ φωτὸς ἄμοιρος, which he attributed to the Oracles; he was followed by Kroll, p. 60, and Des Places, frg. 155. Lewy (p. 278, n. 77) objected that (1) ὀπισθοβαρής is used by Plotinus, who never cites the Oracles, and (2) Pr. never uses ὡς εἰπεῖν to refer to the Oracles. It is difficult to explain these facts away; besides, the supposed fragment cannot be detached from its context, since the three qualities described in it (inflexibility, heaviness, opaqueness) are obviously introduced for the sake of the elaborate comparison between the affective life and iron, made for the specific purpose of this passage on the iron race. If, on the other hand, the complete metaphor with its explanation had already been there in the Oracles, Pr. would never have missed the opportunity of pointing this out.

3–4. The phenomenon of levitation: Philostr., vit. Ap. 3,15; Eunap., vit. soph. V 1,8.

§ 111. Dam. I § 499.

not escape judgment wherever they were, and the judges would not be unable to dispense justice, if those on trial did not gather before them. — The reason is that it was deemed to be to the advantage of souls to receive their sentence in a better place and therefore in a better disposition. It may be added that they can see each other's trial and fate.

112. [108b3–c3] Why do the impure souls not have a guide? — They do have one, but his care of them remains unnoticed because they are deaf and blind. — Then why does the guardian spirit nevertheless conduct these souls to judgment [107d7]? — Because he is in charge of their visible life, the commentator thinks.

Or better, the absence of a visible guide is itself a part of the sentence. And if they should be condemned also to lose their way, they will receive this kind of punitive providence from the spirit.

113. [108b8] 'Guides' are those who lead the way, 'companions' are souls in charge of the same spirit and bound for the same destination, but for the pious Gods are both guides and companions on the journey to the upper, 'supracelestial' region, according to the *Phaedrus* [246e4–247c4].

§§ 114–115. What earth is meant? Its divinity. 108c5–8

114. The earth described here has been interpreted by some as incorporeal, by others are corporeal, and in each case there are two views: those who take it to be incorporeal explain it either as the idea or as nature, those who regard it as corporeal say either that it is the whole world, or that it is the sublunary world. Plato, however, apparently means our earth, as the text shows.

115. The Earth, as a constituent of the Universe, is a Deity. For if the Universe is a God, so of course are the parts that constitute this God. Secondly, if the Earth is an integral part, not a fraction, the Earth must be a Deity; how indeed, as a wholly complete part of the world, can she be otherwise? That which makes the whole a God, confers the same status upon the complete part, containing the plenitude of all forms. Thirdly, if the Earth comprises other Gods, she must *a fortiori* be a Goddess herself, as Timaeus also says [40b8–c3], so that she must also have an intelligence dependent upon her and a rational soul; and a luminous body before this visible body.

---

5. ἀλλήλας ὁρῶσιν : Pr., *Rep.* II 164.19–21 (interpreting Pl., *Rep.* X 614e3–6) explains how sight is possible in the hereafter. Here, the real point is that souls witness each other's punishments and rewards; cf. Pl., *Gorg.* 525b2–3 (Ol., *Gorg.* 267.1–4).

αἱ ψυχαὶ ἤμελλον ἄκριτοι εἶναι ὅπου οὖν οὖσαι, οὔτε οἱ δικασταὶ μὴ κρίνειν ἤμελλον εἰ μὴ συνέδραμον πρὸς αὐτοὺς οἱ κρινόμενοι. — Ἦ ἄμεινον ἦν αὐταῖς ταῖς ψυχαῖς ἐν καλλίοσι τόποις οὔσαις καὶ διὰ τοῦτο κάλλιον διατεθείσαις οὕτω δέχε|σθαι τὴν κρίσιν. προστίθει δὲ καὶ ὅτι ἀλλήλας ὁρῶσιν, ὅπως κρίνονται καὶ 5(234) οἵων τυγχάνουσιν.

ριβ'. — [108b3–c3] Διὰ τί ταῖς ἀκαθάρτοις ⟨οὐ⟩ γίνεται ἡγεμών; — Ἦ γίνεται 112 μέν, οὐ παρέχεται δὲ αἴσθησιν ὡς κωφαῖς καὶ τυφλαῖς οὔσαις τῆς ἑαυτῶν προνοίας. — Διὰ τί οὖν ὁ δαίμων ὁ εἰληχὼς καὶ ταύτας ἄγει ὅμως [107d7]; — Ἦ ὅτι τὸν ἐμφανῆ, φησί, βίον εἴληχεν.

Ἄμεινον δὲ μέρος εἶναι τῆς ψήφου καὶ τὸ μὴ τυγχάνειν ἡγεμόνος ἐμφανοῦς. 5 εἰ δὲ καὶ πλανᾶσθαι κατακριθεῖεν, τῆς τοιαύτης τεύξονται τοῦ δαίμονος προνοίας κολαστικῆς οὔσης.

ριγ'. — [108b8] Ὅτι ʽἡγεμόνεςʼ μὲν οἱ ἄγοντες, ʽσυνέμποροιʼ δὲ αἱ ὁμοδαίμονες 113 ψυχαὶ καὶ ἐπὶ τὸ αὐτὸ ἀγόμεναι, θεοὶ δὲ τοῖς εὐσεβέσιν ἡγεμόνες οἱ αὐτοὶ καὶ συνέμποροι ἐπὶ τὸν ἄνω τόπον καὶ ὑπερουράνιον, ὡς ἐν Φαίδρῳ λέγεται [246e4–247c4].

§§ 114–115. What earth is meant? Its divinity. 108c5–8

ριδ'. — Ὅτι τὴν νῦν λεγομένην γῆν οἱ μὲν ἀσώματον ἤκουσαν, οἱ δὲ σωματικήν, 114 καὶ τούτων ἑκάτεροι διχῶς· οἱ μὲν γὰρ ἀσώματον ἤτοι τὴν ἰδέαν ἢ τὴν φύσιν, οἱ δὲ σωματικὴν οἱ μὲν τὸν ὅλον κόσμον οἱ δὲ τὸν ὑποσέληνον. ὁ μέντοι Πλάτων ταύτην φαίνεται λέγων τὴν γῆν, ὡς ἐκ τῶν λέξεων δῆλον.

ριε'. — Ὅτι ἡ γῆ πλήρωμα οὖσα τοῦ παντὸς θεός ἐστιν. εἰ γὰρ τὸ πᾶν θεός, 115 δῆλον ὅτι καὶ τὰ μέρη θεοί, ἐξ ὧν οὗτος ὁ θεὸς συμπεπλήρωται. ἔτι εἰ ὅλον μέρος ἡ γῆ, ἀλλ' οὐκ ἀποτετμημένον, δῆλον ὅτι θεὸς ἡ γῆ· πῶς γὰρ δύναται μὴ εἶναι θεὸς ἡ παντελὴς τοῦ κόσμου μερίς; ᾧ γὰρ τὸ πᾶν θεός, τούτῳ καὶ τὸ ὁλόκληρον μέρος, πάντων ὂν τῶν εἰδῶν πεπληρωμένον. ἔτι εἰ θεῶν περιεκτικὴ 5 ἡ γῆ, πολλῷ πρότερον αὐτὴ θεός, ὡς καὶ ὁ Τίμαιός φησιν [40b8–c3], ὥστε καὶ νοῦς ἐξῆπται αὐτῆς καὶ ψυχὴ λογική· ὥστε καὶ σῶμα αὐγοειδὲς πρὸ τοῦδε τοῦ φαινομένου.

---

§ 111. 5 καὶ¹ ins. Mᶜ: om. M¹ | post ὅτι] ~ in ras. Mᶜ
§ 112. 1 οὐ μ : om. M — 2 ἑαυτῶν] fort. -οῦ
§ 114. 3 ὑποσέληνον Mᶜ: ὑπὸ σελήνην M¹
§ 115. 5 ὂν τῶν Fh: ὄντων M — 6 αὐτὴ M¹: αὕτη Mᶜ

---

§ 112. Cf. Dam. I § 500.
§ 113. Dam. I § 502.
§ 114. Dam. I §§ 503–504, with fuller details.
§ 115. Dam. I § 508.

§§ 116-125. **The four problems concerning the earth. 108e4-109a9**

116. The four usual problems regarding the earth are these: its position (is it in the middle?), its shape (is it spherical?), its stability, its size. Socrates takes the first two for granted (central position and spherical shape) and uses them to prove the two remaining points. Since it is in the middle, it resembles the center and for that reason it is stable, as a kind of visible center; since it is spherical, it resembles the universe, so that like the universe it remains in its place as a mass, not as an indivisible point.

117. The spherical shape of the universe can be demonstrated on grounds of final causality: the sphere is an image of the One, being by far the strongest of shapes, indissoluble because without angles, and the most capacious of all for the same reason. Then also on grounds of exemplary causality, because the Living Being that was God's model for creation is 'all-complete' [*Tim.* 31b1], and therefore the sphere is the most perfect of forms. Finally on grounds of efficient causality: the Creator makes it everlasting and indissoluble, and such, among shapes, are the circle and the sphere.

118. Any part of a whole that is itself a whole expresses the total, not only in its wholeness and totality, but also in its shape; therefore each part of the universe, including the earth, must be spherical.

119. The earth is in the middle; for if the universe is a sphere, it has a center, so that its integral parts, including the earth, have centers too. But granting that it has a center of its own, how can we tell that it coincides with the center of the universe? As follows: if earth is the coarsest of the elements, it must be at the bottom of all the rest, since fine bodies, which can press through the others, occupy the highest place in the order of their fineness, and earth remains below; and that it is at the bottom all over, can be inferred from the fact that both itself and the bodies above it are of a uniform structure; which means that it is in the middle.

120. Whatever has its natural position in the middle of space, is in its own place there; if so, it must either be at rest or have a circular motion; but the earth is a center consisting of an element and an element forming a center; therefore it is at rest.

121. If the sky is perfectly symmetrical, the pressure it exercises on what it contains or the motion it imparts cannot vary in intensity from place to place; and if the earth is perfectly balanced, it cannot incline to one side more than to another. The cause of the equality is in both cases the spherical shape and the similarity of the part to the whole.

---

§ 116. Dam. I § 512.
4-7. Point 3 (stability) proved from points 1 (position) and 2 (shape). Not

§§ 116-125. The four problems concerning the earth. 108e4-109a9

ρις΄. – Ὅτι προβλήματα τέσσαρα περὶ γῆς εἴωθε ζητεῖσθαι, | περὶ θέσεως 116(235) αὐτῆς (εἰ ἐν μέσῳ), περὶ σχήματος (εἰ σφαιροειδής), περὶ τῆς μονῆς, περὶ μεγέθους. ὧν δύο μὲν τὰ πρῶτα προείληφεν ὁ Σωκράτης, ὅτι τε ἐν μέσῳ καὶ ὅτι σφαιροειδής, τὰ δὲ ἄλλα δύο ἀπ᾽ αὐτῶν τούτων δείκνυσιν. εἰ γὰρ ἐν μέσῳ ἐστί, τῷ κέντρῳ ὡμοίωται, ὥστε μένει, οἷα κέντρον τι ὁρατόν· καὶ εἰ σφαιροειδής, 5 ὡμοίωται τῷ παντί, ὥστε ἐν τῷ αὐτῷ τόπῳ ὥσπερ τὸ πᾶν καὶ ὡς ὄγκος μένει, ἀλλ᾽ οὐχ ὡς κέντρον ἀμερές.

ριζ΄. – Ὅτι σφαιρικὸν τὸ πᾶν, δείξειεν ἄν τις ἀπὸ τῆς τελικῆς αἰτίας· μιμεῖται 117 γὰρ ἡ σφαῖρα τὸ ἕν, ὅτι μάλιστα κράτιστον οὖσα τῶν σχημάτων καὶ ἀδιάλυτον ὡς γωνιῶν ἀπηλλαγμένη, καὶ μάλιστα πάντων χωρητικὴ διὰ τὴν αὐτὴν αἰτίαν. ἔτι ἀπὸ τῆς παραδειγματικῆς, ὅτι ΄παντελὲς᾽ τὸ ζῷον εἰς ὃ βλέπων ὁ θεὸς ἐδημιούργει [Tim. 31b1], ὥστε τελειότατον σχημάτων ἡ σφαῖρα. ἔτι ἀπὸ τῆς ποιητικῆς 5 αἰτίας· ἀΐδιον γὰρ αὐτὸ καὶ ἀδιάλυτον ὁ δημιουργὸς ποιεῖ, τοιοῦτον δὲ σχῆμα ὅ τε κύκλος καὶ ἡ σφαῖρα.

ριη΄. – Ὅτι πᾶν μέρος τοῦ ὅλου ὅπερ καὶ αὐτὸ ὅλον μεμίμηται τὸ πᾶν, 118 ὥσπερ τῷ ὅλῳ καὶ τῷ παντί, οὕτω καὶ τῷ σχήματι· σφαιρικὸν ἄρα ἕκαστον, ὥστε καὶ ἡ γῆ.

ριθ΄. – Ὅτι ἐν μέσῳ ἡ γῆ· εἰ γὰρ σφαῖρα τὸ πᾶν, περὶ [τὸ] κέντρον ἄρα, 119 ὥστε καὶ τὰ ὅλα μέρη περὶ κέντρα, ὥστε καὶ ἡ γῆ. ἀλλ᾽ ἔστω περὶ κέντρον οἰκεῖον· πόθεν ὅτι περὶ τὸ τοῦ παντός; ἢ εἰ πάντων παχυμερεστάτη, πάντων ἂν ἐσχάτη εἴη· τὰ γὰρ λεπτομερῆ τῶν σωμάτων ἅτε διὰ τῶν ἄλλων διήκειν δυνάμενα τὸν ἀνωτέρω τόπον ἐπέχει κατὰ τάξιν τῆς λεπτομερείας, ἐκείνη δὲ 5 τὸν κάτω· καὶ δῆλον ὅτι πανταχῇ ἐσχάτη, εἴπερ αὐτή τε ὁμοιομερὴς καὶ τὰ ὑπερκείμενα σώματα· ὥστε μέση.

ρκ΄. – Ὅτι ὅπερ ἐν μέσῳ τόπῳ κατὰ φύσιν ἐστίν, τοῦτο ἐν οἰκείῳ τόπῳ 120 ἐστίν· εἰ δὲ τοῦτο, ἢ μένει ἢ κύκλῳ κινεῖται· ἀλλὰ κέντρον ἐστὶ στοιχειῶδες καὶ στοιχεῖον κεντρῶδες· μένει ἄρα.

ρκα΄. – Ὅτι εἰ πάντῃ ὅμοιος ὁ οὐρανός, οὐ τῇ μὲν πλέον, τῇ δὲ ἔλαττον 121 ἐπωθεῖ ἢ κινεῖ τὰ εἴσω ἑαυτοῦ· καὶ εἰ αὐτὴ | ἰσόρροπος πανταχῇ, οὐ τῇ μὲν (236) μᾶλλον, τῇ δὲ ἧττον ἐπικλίνει. αἴτια δὲ ἑκατέρῳ τῆς ἰσότητος τὸ σφαιροειδὲς καὶ ἡ ὁμοιότης τοῦ μέρους πρὸς τὸ ὅλον.

---

§ 119. 1 τό² M: del. Nv

---

in Dam. I.
§§ 117-120. Dam. I §§ 516-519.
§§ 121-122. Dam. I § 520.

122. The perfect balance of the earth causes equal pressure towards the center on all sides; therefore it remains in its place because of the equal gravitation towards the middle.

123. If fire were to be placed in the middle, it would not stay there because of the upward tendency that is natural to it; earth, however, stays, because it tends downward; if placed at the top, it does not remain there, because it has a natural impulse to fall. In general, rectilinear movements belong to elements in a state of disturbance, as Aristotle agrees. When they have reached their natural position, if this is the middle, there is adaptation to the center, which is the real middle; if it is on the circumference, there is adaptation to the sky, which is the true circumference.

124. Though 'of enormous size' [109a9], the earth is only a point in proportion to universe, which is very large indeed, and the geographers are right in this respect, because they measure its largest circle only in reference to our own 'world.' This circle is the one between the Tropic of Cancer and the Arctic Circle; so that other zones are left, two under the Poles, one adjoining the Equator and forming the whole middle section, and another which is the counterpart of ours, situated between the Tropic of Capricorn and the Antarctic Circle.

125. That the earth is larger than this is proved (1) by the description of the isle of Atlantis, which exceeded our section of the world in size; (2) by the fact that the Great Sea, called the Ocean, has land at its bottom;

---

§ 123. Dam. I § 521.
4. ὡς καὶ 'Αριστοτέλης φησίν : this may be a distant and distorted echo of Ar., cael. IV 3, 310b16–19 (correctly explained by Simpl. 701.3–22): τὸ δὴ ζητεῖν διὰ τί φέρεται τὸ πῦρ ἄνω καὶ ἡ γῆ κάτω, τὸ αὐτό ἐστι καὶ διὰ τί τὸ ὑγιαστὸν ἂν κινῆται καὶ μεταβάλλῃ ᾗ ὑγιαστόν, εἰς ὑγίειαν ἔρχεται ἀλλ' οὐκ εἰς λευκότητα. See, however, the note on I § 521, esp. the quotation from Pr. *Tim.*, where the principle καὶ ὅλως στοιχείων αἱ ἐπ' εὐθείας φοραὶ παρὰ φύσιν εἰσὶ διακειμένων is attributed to Plotinus and used *against* Ar.

§§ 124–125. Dam. I § 522.
§ 124. Two different issues are confused in this section: (1) the Earth is much larger than our *oikoumenè*; (2) the circumference measured at the top level is larger than in the hollows.

1. σημείου λόγον ἐπέχει : the current formula, used also by Pr., *hyp.* 110.15–16 διὰ τὸ τὴν γῆν μὴ ἔχειν κέντρου καὶ σημείου λόγον πρὸς τὴν σεληνιακὴν σφαῖραν, ὥσπερ πρὸς τὴν ἀπλανῆ.

2–3. οἱ γεωγράφοι κατορθοῦσι πρὸς τὴν ἡμετέραν οἰκουμένην τὸν μέγιστον κύκλον λαβόντες : Pr. measures the Earth by comparing the circumferences (great circles) of its three levels: bottom of the sea, our own level, tops of highest mountains; cf. *Tim.* I 181.22–28 ὥστε οὐ δεησόμεθά τινων μαθηματικῶν ἐφόδων ἡμεῖς νῦν εἰς τὴν περὶ γῆς ἐξήγησιν, οὐδὲ ἀνατρέπειν αὐτὰς ἐγχειρήσομεν· ἐκεῖναι γὰρ κατὰ τὸ οἰκούμενον παρ' ἡμῶν ἐπίπεδον μετροῦσιν αὐτήν, ὁ δὲ Πλάτων ἡμᾶς μὲν ἐν κοίλῳ φησὶν οἰκεῖν, αὐτὴν δὲ εἶναι ὅλην ὑψηλήν, ὃ καὶ ἡ τῶν Αἰγυπτίων ἱερὰ φήμη παραδέδωκε. So, too, above I § 522.11–23; *infra* § 125. While accepting current scientific cosmography, Pr. tries to save the fanciful geography of the *Ph.* and the *Tim.*, mainly by refusing to face its mathematical consequences; he neither refutes nor grants the point

ρκβ'. – Ότι ή ισορροπία της γης ομοίως αυτήν συνάγει πανταχόθεν επί τό 122
κέντρον· μένει άρα κατά την ίσην πάντη προς το μέσον σύννευσιν.

ρκγ'. – Ότι εί τεθείη το πυρ εν μέσω, ου μένει διά το άνω πεφυκέναι θείν· 123
ή δε γη μένει διά το κάτω, επεί ουδέ άνω ή γη τεθείσα μένει, κάτω γάρ πέφυκε
θείν. και γάρ όλως αί κατ᾽ ευθείαν κινήσεις νοσούντων εισί των στοιχείων,
ως και Αριστοτέλης φησίν. επειδάν δε γένηται εν τοις οικείοις τόποις, εί μέν
εν τω μέσω, μιμείται το κέντρον, ό έστι μέσον τω όντι· εί δε εν τω πέριξ, 5
μιμείται το πέριξ αληθώς, τον ουρανόν.

ρκδ'. – Ότι 'πάμμεγά τι' [109a9] ή γη ούσα όμως σημείου λόγον επέχει 124
προς το παν άτε όν μέγιστον, και οί γεωγράφοι κατορθούσι προς την ημετέραν
οικουμένην τον μέγιστον κύκλον λαβόντες. ούτος δέ έστιν ο μεταξύ καρκίνου
και του άει φανερού· ώστε άλλαι περιλείπονται ζώναι, δύο μεν αί υπό τους
πόλους, μία δε ή προς τω ισημερινώ και τη μέση πάση περιηγήσει, άλλη δε 5
ή τη καθ᾽ ημάς αντικειμένη ή μεταξύ αιγοκέρωτος και του άει προς ημάς αφανούς.

ρκε'. – Ότι μείζον τι ή γη, δηλοί μεν και ή ιστορία της Ατλαντίδος νήσου 125
την καθ᾽ ημάς οικουμένην υπερέχουσα τω μεγέθει· δηλοί δε και ή μεγάλη
θάλαττα, ην Ωκεανόν καλούμεν, γην έχουσα υποκειμένην· δηλοί δε και ή σήψις

---

§ 125. 2 υπερεχούσης ci. Fh

---

that the height of the mountains is negligible in proportion to the diameter of
the Earth (see I § 510, note). Hence the obscurity both in the commentary on
the *Tim.* (I 180.25-181.28) and here.

3-6. Eratosthenes (Cleomedes I 10, Strabo I 4, 2; 5) calculated the length of
the meridian of Alexandria, and his result (252,000 stadia) is therefore independent
of our particular latitude; for our *oikoumenè* his estimate was 78,000 stadia long,
38,000 wide. The division into zones by means of the five parallels, as explained
here, can only serve to prove that the Earth is many times larger than our *oikoumenè*.
The mistake of confusing the distance separating the arctic circle from the tropic
of Cancer (or an unspecified parallel between them) with the meridian (ούτος δέ
έστιν ό...), is too crude a blunder to be ascribed to either Pr. or Dam. Cf. note
on I § 522.19-20.

4. του άει φανερού : the arctic circle in antiquity is the circle limiting the part
of the sky that remains above the horizon, so that it shifts with the latitude of
the observer; in modern usage it has been fixed in relation to the tropic of Cancer.
Similarly for the antarctic circle below.

§ 125. In Dam. I § 522, the *Ph.* is followed rather closely; here, the commentator
permits himself more latitude: (1) cf. 109a9-c3; size of Atlantis; (2) 109c3-110a1;
(3) 110a1-b1; (4) argument based on *elem.* 112, see note below, lines 5-7; (5) argument
from the height of the highest mountains, cf. Pr., *Tim.* I 181.4-20.

1-2. Cf. I § 522.4-10.

2-3. The argument is too concise to make sense: either it may refer to the three
different levels, or it may mean that the Ocean bottom should be added to the
surface of the Earth, but then this was taken as a matter of course in conventional
geography.

3-5. Cf. I § 522.24-28.

(3) by the decay prevailing in these parts, which cannot be the original condition, since nature can produce something better and would never have started with this; (4) by the law that the upper levels of secondary things resemble the lower fringes of their priors, from which it follows that the top level of the earth must be rarefied and transparent, as the earth of which precious stones and metals are made; and finally (5) the depth of the cavities in which we live and the height of the mountains make it clear that the spherical surface of the earth is larger.

§§ 126–130. The three levels. 109a9–110b4

126. [109e7] On the highest level of the earth the 'real heaven' is seen, because it is observed at short range, through ether only, and with keener eyes.

127. [109e6] Why can people from this world not live up there? – Because the matter they lose cannot be replaced by the inflow of much finer matter there.

128. [109d7–8] Where are the stars seen and what is the nature of what we see? – According to the commentator, we see projections of them in the air.

But if so, why do they not reach our eyes, but appear to us as distant? Therefore our professor says that they cause bursts of flame in the ether and that it is those we observe. He suggests that this may be the meaning behind the saying of Heraclitus 'kindled in measure and quenched in measure' [frg. B 30]; this can hardly be said of the sun itself, but only of the sun as we see it.

129. [110b1–2] Socrates points out, first, that the myth relates to the dwellers on the heights of the earth, not to the preceding general description of the earth [108c5–110b1], nor to the details given about it later [111c4–113c8]. Secondly, the commentator points out that Socrates calls the myth 'beautiful' because even the form in which it is presented is sound and free from incongruity, so that it can be truthfully said that the reality is 'either this or similar' [114d3–4], and not too far apart from the mythical framing.

5–7. An entirely speculative argument, based on the ontological rule of *elem.* 112: πάσης τάξεως τὰ πρώτιστα μορφὴν ἔχει τῶν πρὸ αὐτῶν.

7–9. Cf. I § 522.10–20.

§ 126. 2. διὰ τοῦ αἰθέρος : 111b1; καλλίοσιν ὄμμασιν : 111b3–6.

§ 128. 1–2. The προαπαντήματα theory served to deal with some problems posed by the doctrine of sight as a radiation from the eye: how can it cover the distance between earth and sky in apparently no time, and how can it survey a quarter of the sky simultaneously ? Philop., *an.* 325.33–35: ἀλλὰ πρὸς ταυτά φασιν ὅτι ἀπάντησίς τις γίνεται τῶν ὁρατῶν πρὸς τὰς ὄψεις· φῶτα γάρ τινα ἐκπέμπονται ἐκ τῶν

τῶν τῇδε τόπων ὡς οὐκ οὖσα πρώτη, οὐ γὰρ ἂν ἡ φύσις ἔχουσά τι κάλλιον ποιῆσαι τοῦτο προέταξεν· δηλοῖ δὲ καὶ τὸ βούλεσθαι τὰ ἄκρα τῶν δευτέρων 5 ὡμοιῶσθαι τοῖς πέρασι τῶν προτέρων, ὥστε καὶ ἡ ἄκρα γῆ ἔσται λεπτομερὴς καὶ διαυγής, οἷα ἡ τῶν τιμίων λίθων τε καὶ μετάλλων· δηλοῖ δὲ καὶ τὸ βάθος τῶν κοιλωμάτων ἐν οἷς οἰκοῦμεν καὶ τὰ ὕψη τῶν ὀρῶν, ὡς ἡ σφαιροειδὴς ἐπιφάνεια μείζων ἐστίν.

§§ 126–130. The three levels. 109a9–110b4

ρκϛ'. – [109e7] Ὅτι ἄνω ἐπὶ τῆς γῆς 'ὁ ἀληθὴς οὐρανὸς' ὁρᾶται, καὶ ὅτι 126(237) ἐγγύθεν, καὶ ὅτι διὰ τοῦ αἰθέρος μόνου, καὶ ὅτι καλλίοσιν ὄμμασιν.

ρκζ'. – [109e6] Διὰ τί οἱ ἐντεῦθεν οὐ δύνανται ζῆν ἐκεῖ; — Ἢ ὅτι τὰ 127 ἀπορρέοντα αὐτῶν οὐ δύνανται ἀναπληροῦν τὰ ἐκεῖθεν εἰσρέοντα λεπτομερέστερα ὄντα.

ρκη'. – [109d7–8] Ποῦ ὁρᾶται τὰ ἄστρα καὶ ποῖα ὁρᾶται; — Ὡς μὲν ὁ 128 ἐξηγητής φησι, προαπαντήματα αὐτῶν ὁρᾶται ἐν τῷ ἀέρι.

Καὶ πῶς οὐ μέχρι τῶν ἡμετέρων κάτεισιν ὀφθαλμῶν, ἀλλὰ πόρρωθεν ὄντα φαίνεται; διὰ δὲ τοῦτο ὁ ἡμέτερος καθηγεμὼν φλογώσεις φησὶν ἐξ ἐκείνων ἐν τῷ αἰθέρι γίνεσθαι καὶ ταύτας ὁρᾶσθαι. καὶ μήποτε, φησί, τοῦτό ἐστιν ὅπερ 5 ὁ Ἡράκλειτος λέγει, 'ἁπτόμενος μέτρα καὶ σβεννύμενος μέτρα' [frg. B 30]· οὐ γὰρ δή που αὐτὸς ὁ ἥλιος, ἀλλ' ὁ πρὸς ἡμᾶς ἥλιος.

ρκθ'. – [110b1–2] Ὅτι ἐπισημαίνεται ὁ Σωκράτης, πρῶτον μὲν ὡς περὶ 129 τῶν ἐν τοῖς ἄκροις τῆς γῆς οἰκούντων ὁ μῦθος, οὔτε δὲ περὶ τῶν πρόσθεν, ὅσα καθόλου περὶ τῆς γῆς ἐρρέθη [108c5–110b1], οὔτε περὶ τῶν ἔπειτα, ὅσα ῥηθήσεται περὶ αὐτῆς ἰδιοτρόπως [111c4–113c8]. δεύτερον ὁ ἐξηγητὴς ἐπισημαίνεται ὅτι 'καλὸν' ἔφη τὸν μῦθον ὡς καὶ τὸ φαινόμενον κατὰ φύσιν 5 ἔχοντα καὶ οὐδὲν ἀπεμφαῖνον, διὸ 'ἢ ταῦτα' εἶναι τὰ πράγματα ὡς ἀληθῶς φαίη τις ἂν 'ἢ τοιαῦτα' [114d3–4] καὶ οὐ πόρρωθεν τὸ μυθικὸν ἔχοντα.

---

§ 128. 6 καὶ - 7 δή M^c (καὶ σβεν- in ras., cetera in mg.; οὐ γὰρ δή ut vid. M¹)

οὐρανίων, ἅτινα προαπαντῶντα ταῖς ὄψεσι τὴν ἀντίληψιν ἑαυτῶν παρέχεται. At princ. 126.10–13 Dam. seems to follow this theory himself, though only to illustrate a point of metaphysics.
5–7. This particular saying of Heraclitus refers to the world, not to the sun (frg. B 30=Clem. Alex., strom. 5,105: κόσμον τόνδε, τὸν αὐτὸν ἁπάντων, οὔτε τις θεῶν οὔτε ἀνθρώπων ἐποίησεν, ἀλλ' ἦν ἀεὶ καὶ ἔστιν καὶ ἔσται πῦρ ἀείζωον, ἁπτόμενον μέτρα καὶ σβεννύμενον μέτρα). The confusion is explained by frg. B 6, ὁ ἥλιος νέος ἐφ' ἡμέρῃ ἐστίν, and frg. B 94, Ἥλιος οὐχ ὑπερβήσεται μέτρα.
§ 129. 4–6. See note on I § 466.4.
6–7. Cf. I § 466.2–3.

Or perhaps because it can be a myth and a statement of fact at the same time, a statement of fact inasmuch as the reality is also like this, a myth inasmuch as it hints at better and higher things.

130. Why does Plato use myths to supplement his proofs? – The commentator's answer is that the soul has an inclination for myths because it is itself the first image, having its origin outside the limits of true being. Or that intelligence is twofold, impassive and passive; Plato adapts himself to both, by the fictional element to imagination, by the hidden truth to reason.

Rather, this is another instance of Plato's discernment, to see what is learnt better by proofs, what by more spontaneous concepts.

§§ 131-139. The heights of the earth. 110b5-111d2

131. The earth can be divided on three different principles. One way is to assign it to the three sons of Kronos, who according to Homer [Il. 15.193] have earth as well as heaven 'in common'; if it is common to them it can of course be distributed among them; indeed, if instead of Poseidon who speaks and divides his own realm, the speaker were Zeus, he would no doubt have divided heaven into three, as in Empedotimus' narrative, giving himself the sphere of the fixed stars, Poseidon the spheres down to the sun, and the rest to Pluto. Another division of the earth is analogous to that of the universe, into a celestial, a terrestrial, and a median region; there is worship of Olympian Earth and of Chthonic Earth, and an intermediate one

---

8-9. **Cf. I § 526.** – On μῦθος καὶ λόγος Pl., *Gorg.* 523a1.
§ 130. Dam. I § 525 and note.
1-2. Cf. Ol., *Gorg.* 237.18-21.
3-5. Argument elaborated by Pr., *Rep.* II 107.14-108.10: the outward form of the myth appeals to the νοῦς παθητικός (φαντασία), the content to intellection; summarized by Ol., *Gorg.* 237.14-18. The identification of Ar.'s passive intelligence (*an.* III 5, 430a24-25) with φαντασία is common in the later Neoplatonists: Pr., *Eucl.* 51.20-52.12; 55.23-56.22; *Tim.* I 244.20-22; III 158.7-10; *Rep.* II 108.4-6 (διττὸν ἔχουσι νοῦν, τὸν μὲν ὂν ἐσμέν, τὸν δὲ ὂν ἐνδυσάμενοι περιβεβλήμεθα); II 52.6-8; Philop., *an.* 6.1-4 Hayduck; III 13.1-3; 61.73-74; 106.28-29 Verbeke; Simpl., *an.* 17.2-5; Ascl., *met.* 280.15-17. Cf. *supra* I § 78.
7. ἐννοιῶν αὐτοφυεστέρων : on innate concepts see Pr., *theol.* I pp. 159-160; Dam., *Phil.* § 225.26.
§ 131. 1-6. The starting-point for the speculation on the three sons of Kronos is Pl., *Gorg.* 523a3-5 ὥσπερ γὰρ Ὅμηρος λέγει, διενείμαντο τὴν ἀρχὴν ὁ Ζεὺς καὶ ὁ Ποσειδῶν καὶ ὁ Πλούτων, ἐπειδὴ παρὰ τοῦ πατρὸς παρέλαβον. The theme is elaborated and allegorized by Pr., *theol.* VI 6-10; *Crat.* 83.10-84.5; *Tim.* I 136.23-28; cf. Ol., *Gorg.* 245.16-246.6; *supra* I §§ 470, 483 and 523. Plato of course alluded to the lines of Homer cited here, *Il.* 15.189-193, where Poseidon says: τριχθὰ δὲ πάντα δέδασται, ἕκαστος δ' ἔμμορε τιμῆς· ἤτοι ἐγὼν ἔλαχον πολιὴν ἅλα ναιέμεν αἰεί, παλλομένων, Ἀΐδης δ' ἔλαχε ζόφον ἠερόεντα, Ζεὺς δ' ἔλαχ' οὐρανὸν εὐρὺν ἐν αἰθέρι καὶ νεφέλῃσι· γαῖα δ' ἔτι ξυνὴ πάντων καὶ μακρὸς Ὄλυμπος. Because Earth and Olympus according

Ἴσως δὲ ὅτι καὶ μῦθος καὶ λόγος ὁ αὐτὸς εἶναι δύναται, λόγος μὲν ὅτι καὶ τὰ πράγματα τοιαῦτα, μῦθος δὲ ὅτι αἰνίξασθαι δύναται καὶ βελτίονα καὶ ὑπερέχοντα.

ρλ'. - Διὰ τί μύθοις χρῆται ὁ Πλάτων ἐπὶ ταῖς ἀποδείξεσιν; — *Η ὅτι, 130 φησί, φιλόμυθος ἡ ψυχὴ ὡς πρώτη εἰκὼν καὶ ἔξω τοῦ ὡς ἀληθῶς ὄντος γενομένη. ἢ ὅτι διττὸς ὁ νοῦς, ὁ μὲν ἀπαθής, ὁ δὲ παθητικός· ἁρμόζεται οὖν πρὸς ἑκάτερον, τῷ μὲν πλάσματι πρὸς τὴν φαντασίαν, τῷ δὲ ἐναποκεκρυμμένῳ ἀληθεῖ πρὸς τὸν λόγον. 5
Ἄμεινον δὲ καὶ τοῦτο τῆς Πλάτωνος λέγειν εἶναι κρίσεως, τίνα μὲν δι' ἀποδείξεων γιγνώσκειν κάλλιον, τίνα δὲ δι' ἐννοιῶν αὐτοφυεστέρων.

§§ 131-139. The heights of the earth. 110b5-111d2

ρλα'. - Ὅτι τριττὴ τῆς γῆς ἡ διαίρεσις. ἡ μὲν κατὰ τοὺς τρεῖς Κρονίδας· 131(238) 'ξυνὴ' γὰρ αὐτῶν καὶ ἡ γῆ καὶ ὁ οὐρανός, φησὶν Ὅμηρος [Ο 193]· εἰ δὲ κοινή, δῆλον ὅτι μερίζοιτο ἂν εἰς αὐτούς· καὶ εἴ γε μὴ ὁ Ποσειδῶν ἦν ὁ λέγων καὶ τὴν ἑαυτοῦ ἀρχὴν διαιρῶν, ἀλλ' ὁ Ζεύς, πάντως ἂν εἰς τρία διένειμεν τὸν οὐρανόν, ὡς ὁ Ἐμπεδοτίμου λόγος, ἑαυτῷ τὴν ἀπλανῆ, τῷ Ποσειδῶνι τὰς μέχρι ἡλίου 5 σφαίρας, τῷ Πλούτωνι τὰς λοιπάς. ἡ δέ ἐστι διαίρεσις τῆς γῆς κατὰ τὸ πᾶν, εἰς τὸ οὐράνιον καὶ χθόνιον καὶ μέσον· καὶ γὰρ Ὀλυμπία Γῆ τετίμηται καὶ χθονία,

---

§ 130. 6; 7 τίνα Fh: τινὰ M
§ 131. 6 ἡ Fh: εἰ M

---

to the last line remain undivided, Pr. concludes that Poseidon is speaking only of a division into three of his own realm, genesis (cf. Pr., Tim. I 272.22-25 τῶν δὲ καὶ τὰ ἄκρα τῆς γενέσεως οὐρανὸν προσειπόντων· Ζεὺς δ' ἔλαχε κτλ.). This permits him to construct another triad of triads: Heaven (or "Olympus" in Homer, for which he found a threefold division in Heraclides Ponticus' *Empedotimus*), the sublunary world ("sea," divided as indicated by Poseidon), and Earth, for which a division into three is now postulated by analogy. A very similar scheme I § 497.

5. ὡς ὁ Ἐμπεδοτίμου λόγος: Heraclides Ponticus, frg. 95. Wehrli includes almost this entire section (lines 1-8), though on the face of it only lines 4-6 have anything to do with Empedotimus. All that is expressly attested here is the division of celestial space into three realms: the sphere of the fixed stars, the outer planets with the sun, and the inner planets with the moon. Frg. 96 (= Dam. apud Philop., met. 117.9-12) shows that Heraclides called these lowest spheres Hades: Δαμάσκιος τὴν Ἐμπεδοτίμου περὶ τοῦ γάλακτος (scil. ὑπόθεσιν) οἰκειοῦται, ἔργον αὐτὴν οὐ μύθον καλῶν. φησὶ γὰρ ἐκεῖνος ὁδὸν εἶναι ψυχῶν τὸ γάλα τῶν τὸν Ἅιδην τὸν ἐν οὐρανῷ διαπορευομένων. It does not necessarily follow, though it is possible, that Heraclides had already anticipated Pr. in relating the three divisions of the sky to the sons of Kronos.

7. Ὀλυμπία Γῆ τετίμηται: Nilsson I 237 (Syracuse) and 457 (a τέμενος in Athens, Paus. I 18,7, cf. Thuc. II 15,4; name derived from the Olympieion, which was near). The moon is called Ὀλυμπία Γῆ by some, according to Plutarch, def. orac. 13, 416E; this may have been inspired by the same cult name. Cf. Porph. ap. Eusb. PE. III, 11, 49, p. 143.17-19.

may consequently be inferred. Finally the earth can be divided on the analogy of the animal, since it is itself a living being; so we can distinguish head, middle and feet.

132. [110b6–7] The dodecahedron is the shape peculiar to heaven, the commentator says, as the cube is to earth.

Heaven also consists of the four elements, though, and is therefore a sphere; and if it were fire only, it would rather be a pyramid. Our professor therefore prefers the solution he gave in his own commentary on the *Timaeus* [55c4–6], that the dodecahedron is the common transitional form between each of the elements and the sphere, and for this reason earth, too, is essentially dodecahedral; furthermore, it is ruled by the providence of the Twelve Gods, who lift it up to the height of Intelligence. His suggestion is this: earth by itself is cubical, water icosahedral, air octahedral, fire pyramidal; these are the attributes they derive from themselves, but from the supramundane level the dodecahedral shape is imparted to them all to prepare them for participation in intelligence, that is, for sphericity.

133. [110b7–c6] Plato depicts the earth as multi-colored, first because of its natural variety of colors, secondly because of the effluxes of the celestial luminaries, such as Mars and the Sun, thirdly because of the incorporeal principles of life which proceed down to sensible beauty.

134. [111a4–b1] The elements on the heights of the earth, found in combination with the earth up there, are these: water in the form of vapor and resembling moist air, air in the form of ether, ether in the form of its uppermost sphere. If there are also mountains there [110d5], they must well-nigh touch the sky. In a word, the 'ethers' of the elements, as the Oracles [frg. 62] express it, are found there.

135. [110e2–111b6] There are stones and metals up there, and trees and animals of all kinds, but pneumatic and in accordance with the elements in that region, of which they are made. If this is true, luminous vehicles too are necessarily purer there and souls are more beautiful.

136. In order to interpret the passage as an allegorical myth one should substitute for the creatures their Creators and Guardians, by homonymy and analogy, men for example being taken to signify the God who creates men.

---

§ 132. Dam. I § 527 and notes.

§ 133. Three phases of color: terrestrial, celestial, transcendental. – Mars is mentioned especially, with the sun, because its color is the most striking.

§ 134. 4. οἱ τῶν στοιχείων αἰθέρες : Lewy p. 97 n. 1 thinks that στοιχεῖα means the stars, but this is certainly not the interpretation of Pr. and Dam. As for the Oracles themselves, it is doubtful whether the word occurred at all in connection with αἰθέρες, cf. Pr., *Tim.* II 57.12–14: τὰ ὑπὲρ τὸν κόσμον στερεώματα τί φήσομεν, εἴτε Ὄλυμπον χρὴ καλεῖν, εἴτε ἐμπύριον, εἴτε αἰθέρας; This text rather favors the view that the Oracles used the plural αἰθέρες for the highest heavens, the empyrean, and that Pr. (Dam.) transferred this to the other elements, water and air, to denote

καὶ μέση ἄρα τις ἂν εἴη. ἡ δέ ἐστι τῆς γῆς διαίρεσις κατὰ λόγον τὸν τοῦ ζώου· ζῷον γάρ τι καὶ αὐτή· οὐκοῦν τμηθείη ἂν εἰς κεφαλὴν καὶ μέσα καὶ πόδας.

ρλβ'. — [110b6–7] Ὅτι τὸ δωδεκάεδρον οἰκεῖον σχῆμα τοῦ οὐρανοῦ, φησὶν 132 ὁ ἐξηγητής, ὡς τῆς γῆς ὁ κύβος.

Καίτοι ἐκ τῶν τεσσάρων στοιχείων καὶ ὁ οὐρανός, ὥστε σφαῖρα· εἰ δὲ πῦρ μόνον, πυραμὶς ἂν εἴη. βέλτιον οὖν, φησὶν ὁ ἡμέτερος καθηγεμών, ἐλέγομεν ἐν τοῖς εἰς Τίμαιεν [55c4–6] κοινὴν εἶναι προκοπὴν εἰς τὴν σφαῖραν ἑκάστου 5 τὸ δωδεκάεδρον, διὸ καὶ ἡ γῆ καθ' ὕπαρξιν δωδεκάεδρος· ἔνεστι δὲ καὶ ἡ πρόνοια τῶν δώδεκα θεῶν, οἳ ἀνάγουσιν εἰς τὸν νοῦν. καὶ μήποτε ἡ μὲν γῆ ἀφ' ἑαυτῆς ἔχει τὸ κυβικόν, τὸ δὲ ὕδωρ τὸ εἰκοσαεδρικόν, ὁ δὲ ἀὴρ τὸ ὀκταεδρικόν, τὸ δὲ πῦρ τὴν πυραμίδα· ταῦτα μὲν οὖν ἀφ' ἑαυτῶν, ἀπὸ δὲ τῶν ὑπερκοσμίων ἐνδίδοται πᾶσι τὸ δωδεκάεδρον εἰς προπαρασκευὴν τῆς νοερᾶς 10 μεθέξεως, ὅπερ ἐστὶ τῆς σφαιρώσεως.

ρλγ'. — [110b7–c6] Ὅτι πολύχρωμον τὴν γῆν φησι, καὶ κατὰ τὴν φυσικὴν 133 ποικιλίαν τῶν χρωμάτων, καὶ κατὰ τὰς ἀπορροίας τῶν οὐρανίων φώτων, Ἀρεϊκὰς καὶ Ἡλιακάς, καὶ κατὰ τὰς ἀσωμάτους ζωὰς ἄχρι τοῦ αἰσθητοῦ κάλλους προϊούσας.

ρλδ'. — [111a4–b1] Ὅτι τὰ ἐπ' ἄκρων τῆς γῆς καὶ σὺν ἐκείνῃ στοιχεῖα | 134 ὕδωρ τὸ ὡς ἀτμὶς καὶ οἷον ὑγρὸς ἀήρ, ἀὴρ δὲ ὁ αἰθήρ, αἰθὴρ δὲ τὸ ἀκρότατον (239) τοῦ αἰθέρος. εἰ δὲ καὶ ὄρη αὐτόθι ἐστί [110d5], δῆλον ὡς ἐγγύς τι ψαύει τοῦ οὐρανοῦ. ἁπλῶς δ' οὖν οἱ τῶν στοιχείων αἰθέρες, ὥς φησι τὰ λόγια [frg. 62], ἐκεῖ.

ρλε'. — [110e2–111b6] Ὅτι λίθοι καὶ μέταλλα ἐκεῖ καὶ δένδρα καὶ ζῷα 135 παντοῖα πνευματικὰ καὶ ἀναλογοῦντα τοῖς ἐκεῖ στοιχείοις, ἐξ ὧν φύεται. εἰ δὲ τοῦτο, πάντως που καὶ τὰ αὐγοειδῆ ὀχήματα καθαρὰ καὶ αἱ ψυχαὶ καλλίους.

ρλς'. — Ὅτι τὸν μυθώδη τρόπον ἐξηγήσῃ ἀντὶ τῶν δημιουργημάτων τοὺς 136 δημιουργοὺς καὶ τοὺς ἐφόρους αὐτῶν ἐκλαμβάνων ὁμωνύμως τε καὶ κατὰ ἀναλογίαν, οἷον ἀντὶ ἀνθρώπων τὸν ἀνθρωποποιὸν θεόν.

---

§ 131. 8 ἡ Fh: εἰ in ras. M^c
§ 132. 2 κύβος] -β- in ras. 2 litt. M^c (κύκλος M¹?) — 4 οὖν] s.l. M¹
§ 136. 1 ἐξηγήσῃ] -ηι in ras. M^c

---

the highest and most refined part of each.
§§ 135–136. Dam. I § 528.
§ 135. 1–2. ζῷα ... πνευματικά : see note on I § 168.6–7.
§ 136. Gods sometimes bear the names of their gifts (cf. Ol. I § 5 and note), so that in this case precious stones, metals, trees and animals may each denote the divine power forming them. I § 528 more plausibly mentions only λόγοι in connection with these, since in actual usage Gods named for any of these substances hardly occur; the original allusion may have been to attributes of certain Gods, which belong to their "chain" (as in Pr., de arte hier.).
 1. τὸν μυθώδη τρόπον : as defined above II § 129.8–9.

137. [111b1–3] Those who live there are free from disease and have a life-span of many generations; these are the characteristics of the species intermediate between everlasting and short-lived animals, for middle terms must exist in all relations. This freedom from sickness and this easy and late death are due to the well-tempered quality of the seasons and of the elements. This is hardly surprising: among the Ethiopians similar conditions prevail thanks to the perfectly balanced climate.

138. Aristotle [frg. 42 R.³] records the case of a man in our part of the earth who needed no sleep and lived on nothing but sunlit air; the inference with regard to those on the highest level is obvious.

139. [111c4–d2] In comparison with our section of the world, that between the Straits (or Pillars of Hercules) and the river Phasis, which section he takes to be narrow and deep, Socrates says that its reverse, a wide and shallow excavation, is found somewhere on the opposite side of the earth, elsewhere there is a narrow and shallow one, and another is wide and deep. The difference between narrow and wide depends on the range of the horizon, that between shallow and deep on the distance from the center. Socrates conjectures the existence of these four, because there are two in our part of the world, Europe and Asia, so that there must be two more in the antipodes.

§§ 140–145. The depths of the earth. 111d2–113c8

140. [111e6–112a5] Tartarus is the nethermost part of the earth and the opposite of Olympus; but there is also a God Tartarus, the guardian of the lowest extremity in each order of being. Accordingly we have a Celestial Tartarus, in which Uranus hid his children, but also a Cronian one, in which Kronos concealed his, and a Zeusian Tartarus, which belongs to the Creator of this world.

141. [112a7–c1] Because there is fire in the middle of earth, as well as water and air [111d2–e2], there will obviously be a strong airstream there, the fire evaporating the water, and the water dissolving into air. Besides, since the earth is an animal and is alive, it will naturally have something like respiration and by breathing in and out it causes a kind of tidal currents. Finally, the first body of the earth is a luminous one, while its

---

§ 137. 1–2. This is the argument used by Pr., *Rep.* II 15.20–16.2 (cited at I § 528.4).

3. τὸ εὐθάνατον : this element is not mentioned by Pl.; cf., however, Hesiod, *op.* 116 θνῆσκον δ' ὥς θ' ὕπνῳ δεδμημένοι, where Pr. (*Hes.* 52.8–13) comments: καὶ τοῦτο ἑπόμενον τοῖς ἀνόσως ζῶσι, τὸ τὴν ἀπὸ τῶν σωμάτων λύσιν ἀβίαστον γίνεσθαι καὶ ἄπονον καὶ οἷον ἀποβολὴν εἶναι χιτῶνος τὴν ἀπόθεσιν τοῦ σώματος. καὶ διὰ τοῦτο ὕπνῳ παραπλήσιον εἶναι τὸν θάνατον εἶπε μετὰ ῥᾳστώνης συμβαίνοντα καὶ κατὰ φύσιν, ἀλλ' οὐ βιαίως. Cf. *infra* § 149.1–4.

4. οἱ Αἰθίοπες : on their longevity Herod. 3,23; I have found no other text

ρλζ'. – [111b1–3] Ὅτι ἄνοσοι καὶ μακραίωνες οἱ ἐκεῖ· μέσα γὰρ ταῦτα τὰ 137
εἴδη τῶν τε ἀιδίων ζῴων καὶ τῶν ὠκυμόρων· πανταχοῦ γὰρ ἡ μεσότης ἀναγκαία.
ποιεῖ δὲ τὸ ἄνοσον καὶ τὸ εὐθάνατον καὶ τὸ μὴ ταχυθάνατον ἡ τῶν ὡρῶν καὶ
τῶν στοιχείων εὐκρασία. καὶ τί θαυμαστόν, ὅτε καὶ οἱ Αἰθίοπες ὧδέ πως ἔχουσι
διὰ τὴν τῶν ἀέρων συμμετρίαν; 5
ρλη'. – Εἰ ἐνταῦθα ἱστόρησεν Ἀριστοτέλης [frg. 42 R.³] ἄνθρωπον ἄυπνον 138
καὶ μόνῳ τῷ ἡλιοειδεῖ τρεφόμενον ἀέρι, τί χρὴ περὶ τῶν ἐκεῖ οἴεσθαι;
ρλθ'. – [111c4–d2] Ὅτι πρὸς τὸν παρ' ἡμῖν παραβάλλων τόπον τὸν ἀπὸ 139
τοῦ πορθμοῦ ἤτοι Ἡρακλείων στηλῶν μέχρι ποταμοῦ Φάσιδος ὡς στενὸν ὄντα
καὶ βαθύν, τὸν μὲν εἶναί φησιν ἀπὸ διαμέτρου καὶ πλατὺν καὶ ἐπιπόλαιον ἐν
ἀντικειμένῳ τινὶ μέρει τῆς γῆς, τὸν δὲ στενὸν καὶ ἐπιπόλαιον ἐν ἄλλῳ μέρει,
τὸν δὲ πλατὺν καὶ βαθύν. ποιεῖ δὲ τὸ μὲν στενὸν καὶ πλατὺ ἡ τοῦ ὁρίζοντος 5
διάμετρος ἢ μείζων ἢ ἐλάττων οὖσα, τὸ δὲ ἐπιπόλαιον καὶ βαθὺ ἡ ἀπὸ τοῦ
κέντρου. καταστοχάζεται δὲ τῶν τεσσάρων, ἐπειδὴ δύο καθ' ἡμᾶς εἰσιν, ἡ Εὐρώπη
καὶ ἡ Ἀσία, ὥστε δύο ἄλλοι κατὰ τοὺς ἀντίποδας.

§§ 140–145. The depths of the earth. 111d2–113c8

ρμ'. – [111e6–112a5] Ὅτι ὁ Τάρταρος τὸ ἔσχατόν ἐστι τοῦ παντὸς καὶ 140(240)
ἀντιθέτως ἔχων πρὸς τὸν Ὄλυμπον· ἔστι δὲ καὶ θεὸς ὁ Τάρταρος τῆς ἐν ἑκάστῳ
διακόσμῳ ἐσχατιᾶς ἔφορος. διὸ καὶ Οὐράνιον ἔχομεν Τάρταρον, ἐν ᾧ τοὺς ἑαυτοῦ
παῖδας ἔκρυψεν ὁ Οὐρανός, καὶ Κρόνιον, ἐν ᾧ καὶ οὗτος τοὺς ἑαυτοῦ παῖδας,
καὶ Δίιον, τουτονὶ τὸν δημιουργικόν. 5
ρμα'. – [112a7–c1] Ὅτι ὄντος πυρὸς ἐν τῷ μέσῳ τῆς γῆς καὶ ὕδατος καὶ 141
ἀέρος [111d2–e2] εἰκότως γίνεται πολὺ πνεῦμα ἐκεῖ, τοῦ μὲν πυρὸς ἐξατμιδοῦντος
τὸ ὕδωρ, τοῦ δὲ ὕδατος εἰς πνεῦμα ἀναλυομένου. ἀλλὰ καὶ ζῷον οὖσα ἡ γῆ καὶ
ζῶσα οἷον ἀναπνεῖν βούλεται καὶ ποιεῖταί τινας παλιρροίας ταῖς εἰσπνοαῖς τε
καὶ ἐκπνοαῖς. ἔτι δὲ αὐγοειδὲς αὐτῆς τὸ πρῶτον ὄχημα, τὸ δὲ φαινόμενον 5

---

§ 139. 5 βαθύν μ : βαθύ Μ

---

connecting it with the climate.
§ 138. Dam. I § 530.5–7.
§ 139. Dam. I § 533.
7–8. If the commentator's meaning is reported correctly, we have a division into two hemispheres ("our side" and the antipodes) rather than the usual one into four half-hemispheres. Our half of the northern hemisphere would consist of Europe and Africa, since the Mediterranean basin is its distinctive feature, the other half of Asia. All this sounds rather unorthodox, cf. above I § 522.4.
§ 140. Dam. I § 537.

visible body is of the coarsest matter; consequently it must also have the intermediate body, as we do, and it is this, the pneumatic vehicle, which supplies warmth and all kinds of motion to the finer elements of the earth.

142. [111e6–112a5] The children of Tartarus and Earth, the consort of Heaven, are Typhon, Echidna and Python, a sort of Chaldean triad [frg. 4] in charge of all disordered creation. Typhon is the paternal and essential cause of disorder, not as such, but as a substratum provided by him to be organized by the universal Creator, Echidna is the potentiality, the feminine and emanative cause of disordered nature. Python may be regarded as an intelligence of the same character; therefore he is said to impede the divinatory exhalations and is defeated by Apollo.

143. Souls have been sown not only on earth as a whole [*Tim.* 42d4], they likewise belong by their essence either to its heights or to its middle region or to its depths, and in each of these regions each soul can live, now above, now below its own level. Yet some of them have a trend towards the higher, others towards the lower plane, others again are equipped for both kinds of life, and it is in this middle group that most of the changes occur. 'Higher' and 'lower' plane should be understood in the sense of their natural surroundings, since no being can live most of the time in abnormal conditions. This can be applied also to souls: some descend no farther than heaven, some as low as Tartarus, some are spread over the whole range of the intermediate space.

144. That there are also Tartarean souls can be deduced from the existence of Tartarean Gods, on whom a complete series must depend, including souls.

145. [112e4–113c8] The four rivers are the four elements in Tartarus: the Oceanus (according to the commentator) is water, the Cocytus or Stygius earth, the Pyriphlegethon fire, the Acheron air. Opposite the Pyriphlegethon is the Stygius (hot against cold), opposite the Oceanus is the Acheron (water against air; hence Orpheus [frg. 125] calls Lake Acheron Lake Aeria).

---

§ 141. 5–7. αὐγοειδὲς ... ὀστρεῶδες ... πνευματικόν : cf. I § 168.6–7. Applied to the Earth II § 115.7.

§ 142. Dam. I § 539.

2. Χαλδαϊκή τις τριάς : the triad πατήρ - δύναμις - νοῦς derived from *Orac.* frg. 4 (cf. Kroll p. 13): ἡ μὲν γὰρ δύναμις σὺν ἐκείνῳ, νοῦς δ' ἀπ' ἐκείνου. The expression "Chaldean triad" is used also by Dam., *princ.* 133.20–21 νοῦς ὁ πρῶτος ἡ τρίτη ἀρχὴ κατὰ τὴν Χαλδαϊκὴν ὑμνουμένην τριάδα (of the original triad); 193.25–26 ἔστι δὲ ἃ καὶ ἐν τῷ διακρίνεσθαί πως ὁρᾶται πρὸς τὰ πρὸ ἑαυτῶν καὶ τὰ μεθ' ἑαυτὰ κατὰ ἀναλογίαν, ὡς ἐν ταῖς Χαλδαϊκαῖς τριάσιν ἡ δύναμις (of the pattern repeating itself at any level); 196.5 εἴτε ὡς οἱ Χαλδαῖοι πατρικὰς τριάδας ἀνευφημοῦντες.

§§ 143–144. Dam. I § 540.

§ 143. 4. ἀμφίβιοι : Plot. IV 8,4.31–35 (of human souls generally) γίγνονται οὖν οἷον ἀμφίβιοι ἐξ ἀνάγκης τόν τε ἐκεῖ βίον τόν τε ἐνταῦθα παρὰ μέρος βιοῦσαι, πλεῖον

ὀστρεῶδες· χρεία ἄρα καὶ τοῦ μέσου, ὥσπερ ἐφ' ἡμῶν· τοῦτο ἄρα τὸ πνευματικὸν ὄχημα τὸ ἀναθάλπον ἐστὶ καὶ κινοῦν τὰ λεπτότερα σώματα αὐτῆς παντοίας κινήσεις.

ρμβ'. - [111e6–112a5] Ὅτι Ταρτάρου καὶ Γῆς τῆς συζυγούσης Οὐρανῷ ὁ Τυφῶν ἡ Ἔχιδνα ὁ Πύθων, οἷον Χαλδαϊκή τις τριὰς [frg. 4] ἔφορος τῆς ἀτάκτου πάσης δημιουργίας. ὁ μὲν γὰρ Τυφῶν τὸ πατρικόν ἐστι καὶ οὐσιῶδες αἴτιον οὐ τῆς ἀταξίας ὡς ἀταξίας, ἀλλ' ὡς προϋποστρωννυμένης ὑπ' αὐτοῦ τῷ παντὶ δημιουργῷ πρὸς διακόσμησιν. ἡ δὲ Ἔχιδνα ἡ δύναμις καὶ τὸ θῆλυ καὶ προοδικὸν αἴτιον τῆς ἀτάκτου φύσεως. ὁ δὲ Πύθων εἴη ἂν νοῦς τοιοῦτος· διὸ καὶ λέγεται τοῖς μαντικοῖς πνεύμασιν ἐναντιοῦσθαι καὶ καταγωνίζεται ὑπὸ τοῦ Ἀπόλλωνος. 142

ρμγ'. - Ὅτι εἰσὶν αἱ ψυχαί, ὡς εἰς γῆν τὴν ὅλην [Tim. 42d4], οὕτω καὶ τὰ ἄκρα αὐτῆς καὶ τὰ μέσα καὶ τὰ ἔσχατα ἐσπαρμέναι κατ' οὐσίαν, ἑκασταχοῦ δὲ ἑκάστη ποτὲ μὲν ζῇ κρειττόνως, ποτὲ δὲ χειρόνως. ἀλλὰ τούτων ὅμως αἱ μὲν ἄνω μᾶλλόν εἰσιν, αἱ δὲ κάτω μᾶλλον, αἱ δὲ πρὸς ἑκάτερα ἀμφίβιοι, καὶ αἱ πλείους μεταβολαὶ περὶ τὰς μέσας. χρὴ δὲ τὸ ἄνω καὶ κάτω λαμβάνειν κατὰ φύσιν, οὐδένες γὰρ ἐν τῷ παρὰ φύσιν πλεονάζουσιν. οὕτω δὲ ἂν διέλοις καὶ ἐπὶ τῶν ψυχῶν, τὰς μὲν ἄχρι τοῦ οὐ|ρανοῦ κατιέναι μόνον, τὰς δὲ καὶ ἄχρι τοῦ Ταρτάρου, τὰς δὲ ἐν μέσῳ πλατικῶς κατὰ τὴν χώραν. 143

ρμδ'. - Ὅτι καὶ Ταρτάριοί εἰσι ψυχαί, δηλοῖ τὸ καὶ θεοὺς εἶναι Ταρταρίους, ὧν ὁλόκληρος ἐξῆπται σειρά· ὥστε καὶ ψυχαί. 144

ρμε'. - [112e4–113c8] Ὅτι οἱ τέτταρες ποταμοὶ τὰ τέτταρα στοιχεῖά ἐστι τὰ ἐν τῷ Ταρτάρῳ· ὁ μὲν Ὠκεανός, φησί, τὸ ὕδωρ, ὁ δὲ Κωκυτὸς ἤτοι Στύγιος ἡ γῆ, ὁ δὲ Πυριφλεγέθων τὸ πῦρ, ὁ δὲ Ἀχέρων ὁ ἀήρ. ἀντικεῖσθαι δὲ τῷ μὲν Πυριφλεγέθοντι τὸν Στύγιον ὡς θερμῷ ψυχρόν, τῷ δὲ Ὠκεανῷ τὸν Ἀχέροντα ὡς ὑδραίῳ ἀέριον· διὸ καὶ Ὀρφεὺς τὴν Ἀχερουσίαν λίμνην Ἀερίαν καλεῖ [frg. 125]. 145

---

§ 143. 1 αἱ ψυχαί Fh: εἰς ψυχὴν M
§ 145. 4 θερμῷ ψυχρόν Wyttenbach: θερμὸν ψυχρῶι M — 5 ὑδραίῳ ἀέριον μ: ὑδραῖον ἀερίωι M

μὲν τὸν ἐκεῖ, αἳ δύνανται πλέον τῷ νῷ συνεῖναι, τὸν δὲ ἐνταῦθα πλεῖον, αἷς τὸ ἐναντίον ἢ φύσει ἢ τύχαις ὑπῆρξεν. Hierocl., carm. aur. 468b15–17 μεσότης δὲ τῶν οὕτω διεστηκότων ὁ ἄνθρωπος ἐνορᾶται, ἀμφίβιός τις ὤν, καὶ ἔσχατος μὲν τῶν ἄνω, πρῶτος δὲ τῶν κάτω. Ascl., met. 98.11–13 διὰ τοῦτο οὖν καὶ διαφόρους ἐνεργείας προβάλλεται πρὸς τὸ ἀμφίβιον τῆς ζωῆς αὐτῆς, ποτὲ μὲν νοερῶς ποτὲ δὲ μετὰ αἰσθήσεως ἐνεργοῦσα. Dam. uses the word in various metaphysical contexts: of Life as intermediate between Being and Mind *princ.* 179.7; of "part" as intermediate between "species" and "element" 198.16; of soul *Parm.* 251.22–23 ὥσπερ ἐν τοῖς εἰς Τίμαιον τὸ μεριστὸν ὁμοῦ καὶ ἀμέριστον ὡς μίαν φύσιν ἀμφίβιον θεωρεῖν, and 252.17.

6. οὐδένες γὰρ ἐν τῷ παρὰ φύσιν πλεονάζουσιν: Pr., *Alc.* 256.7–258.9.

§ 145. Dam. I § 541 and note.

5. Ἀερίαν: as the present section is our only source for this Orphic fragment, it is impossible to decide whether the word should be capitalized as a proper name, or be taken for an adjective (as Finckh, Norvin and Kern do). The ambiguity may

This is the commentator's opinion, but the position of the rivers does not accord with it: the first and highest is the Oceanus, under it is the Acheron, under it again the Pyriphlegethon, under which the Cocytus; besides they are all called rivers, whereas the elements have different qualities. Therefore it is better to explain them as destinations and abodes of souls belonging to four different ranks and, beyond this, as divine characters: the power of delimitation is symbolized by the Oceanus, that of purification by the Acheron, that of chastisement through heat by the Pyriphlegethon, that of chastisement through cold by the Cocytus.

§§ 146–148. The destiny of the soul. 113d1–114b6

146. [113d5–6] Socrates uses the phrase 'mounting vehicles' as we speak of mounting horses. What are these vehicles, then? — They are pneumatic bodies, for souls can have locomotion only by means of the bodies that depend on them. Pneumatic bodies, being perishable, can also be punished through pain.

147. [113e6] What does it mean that those who have led a life of irreparable sin 'never come out again'? — This may be a falsehood for the good of the community, to deter people from irremediable crimes.

Or else the word 'never' refers to one period; this is Syrianus' solution.

However, it can hardly be an entire world period, since souls complete many periods of their own within one universal period. Nor can it be, as the commentator thinks, a complete revolution of heaven, for even this is too long; nor that of one of the celestial bodies, e.g. the star that has the strongest influence, because in that case it will occur that a soul in need of prolonged treatment has only the briefest taste of Tartarus; nor that of the 'Divine Herdsman' (the Sun, Saturn, or another), for this is again too

---

go back to the poem itself: if it did not contain the name $'Αχερουσία$ (which can hardly be fitted into a hexameter; however, $'Αχερουσιάς$ or $'Αχερούσιος$, as in the later phrase $'Αχερούσιον$ ὕδωρ, could have served instead), the combination ἀερία (or ἠερίη) λίμνη could be read indifferently as 'the misty lake' or 'Lake Misty'. To explain the adjective, only this meaning fits the context; the other possible choice, 'wide as air' (LSJ s.v. IIIa) is insufficiently attested, since in Diod. Sic. 5,42,3 it obviously means 'hazy', and in the one remaining example, ibid. 1,33,3, 'sky-high' (of sand dunes) gives a satisfactory sense. $Άερία$ ($'Ηερίη$) as a proper name is listed by Pape as an older name for Egypt, Crete, Libya, Thasos, and as the name for a city in Crete and one in Gaul (Mont Ventoux?); there is no reason why it could not have been used as the name of a lake, although there is no instance of this. The fact that Dam. says καλεῖ rather than λέγει cannot be used to settle the question in favor of the proper name.

§ 146. Dam. I § 543.

§ 147. Dam. I § 547 and note. The account given here is the clearer and more complete one of the two. The various ways to dispose of Pl.'s statement on eternal damnation are: (i) lines 1–3=I § 547.1–3: the threat serves a social and political purpose; (ii) lines 4–12=I § 547.4–8: "never" extends to one period only; this may

Ταῦτα μὲν ὁ ἐξηγητής, ἡ μέντοι θέσις οὐχ ὁμολογεῖ τῶν ποταμῶν· πρῶτος μὲν γὰρ καὶ ἀνωτέρω ὁ Ὠκεανός, ὑπὸ δὲ τούτῳ ὁ Ἀχέρων, ὑπὸ δὲ τούτῳ ὁ Πυριφλεγέθων, ὑφ᾽ ᾧ ὁ Κωκυτός· ἄλλως τε καὶ ποταμοὶ λέγονται πάντες, καίτοι τὰ στοιχεῖα διάφορα. ἄμεινον οὖν λήξεις αὐτοὺς καὶ τόπους ἀκούειν ψυχῶν 10 τετραχῇ κατὰ βάθος διῃρημένων, καὶ πρὸ τῶν τόπων τὰς θείας ἰδιότητας, τὴν διοριστικὴν κατὰ τὸν Ὠκεανόν, τὴν καθαρτικὴν κατὰ τὸν Ἀχέροντα, τὴν κολαστικὴν διὰ θερμότητος κατὰ τὸν Πυριφλεγέθοντα, τὴν κολαστικὴν διὰ ψυχρότητος κατὰ τὸν Κωκυτόν.

§§ 146–148. The destiny of the soul. 113d1–114b6

ρμς΄. – [113d5–6] Ὅτι ʽἀναβαίνειν ὀχήματά᾽ φησιν, ὥσπερ εἰς ἵππους 146 ἀναβαίνειν. τίνα οὖν τὰ ὀχήματα; — Ἢ τὰ πνευματικά· κατὰ γὰρ τὰ ἐξῃμμένα κινοῦνται τοπικῶς. τὰ δὲ πνευματικὰ ἅτε φθαρτὰ καὶ κολάζεσθαι πέφυκε δι᾽ ἀλγηδόνων.

ρμζ΄. – [113e6] Πῶς ʽοὐδέποτε ἐξίασιν᾽ ἀπὸ τοῦ Ταρτάρου αἱ ἀνίατα 147 βεβιωκυῖαι; — Ἢ πολιτικῶς ἔψευσται, ἵνα εὐλαβῶνται αἱ ψυχαὶ τὰ ἀνήκεστα τῶν ἁμαρτημάτων.

Ἢ πρὸς μίαν περίοδον τὸ ʽοὐδέποτε᾽. Συριανοῦ αὕτη ἡ ἐπιβολή.

Ἀλλὰ πῶς οἷόν τε τὴν ὅλην; πολλὰς γὰρ ἐν τῇ μιᾷ ποιοῦνται αἱ ψυχαί. 5 ἀλλ᾽ οὐδέ, ὥς φησιν ὁ ἐξηγητής, τὴν τοῦ οὐρανοῦ, μακρὰ γὰρ καὶ αὕτη· οὐδὲ τῶν οὐρανίων τινά, οἷον τὴν δραστικωτάτην, συμβαίνει γὰρ τότε ψυχὴν νεωστὶ προσάψασθαι τοῦ Ταρτάρου χρόνον | δεομένην· ἀλλ᾽ οὐδὲ τὴν τοῦ ἀγελάρχου (242) θεοῦ, οἷον Ἡλίου ἢ Κρόνου ἤ τινος ἄλλου, μεγάλη γὰρ καὶ αὕτη. ἀλλὰ τὴν

---

§ 145. 7 οὐχ] -χ in ras. M^c — 11 fort. διῃρημένους
§ 147. 6; 9 αὕτη M^c: αὐτή M¹

---

be: (a) a full cosmic period; (b) a revolution of the outer heaven; (c) of one particular planet; (d) of the ἀγελάρχης; (e) the "period" of the individual soul, which is Dam.'s solution; (iii) lines 13–15=I § 547. 9–10: they cannot go out, i.e. leave without help; (iv) lines 16–17: the word "never" is used in reference to the "incurable" of 113e2, which merely serves to express the character of the sin; (v) lines 18–19: they have no hope, subjectively, of being set free; (vi) lines 20–21=I § 547.11–12: there is no reprieve. – The additional possibilities iii–vi are not all suggestions of Dam., see note on I § 547.11–12.

4. Συριανοῦ: cf. Pr., Tim. III 278.9–13 ἄλλος δὲ ἀκριβέστερος καὶ τοῦδε λόγος, ὃν ὁ ἡμέτερος διδάσκαλος παρεδίδου, πάσῃ ψυχῇ μερικῇ μίαν ἀφωρίσθαι κάθοδόν φησιν οὐχ ἁπλῶς, ἀλλὰ καθ᾽ ἑκάστην τοῦ θείου γενητοῦ περίοδον (for if any soul were to stay "above" for a whole period, it would never descend at all). In the sequel (lines 25–27) it is explained that the "one descent" means "at least one". – Here, as in the Tim. commentary, Pr.'s report on Syrianus' position can be explained from a general familiarity with it, so that there is no reason to relate it to a commentary on the Ph., or a monograph on this passage.

8–9. τοῦ ἀγελάρχου θεοῦ: see note on Ol. 7 § 4. The context here is clearly astrological. The Sun and Saturn are mentioned especially because of their

long. Rather it is the period peculiar to each soul, which determines the highest and the lowest point of its circuit, whether it attains the intelligible world or descends into Tartarus, with its own measure of virtue or knowledge.

One can also say that they never come out as far as it depends on themselves, because they can no longer help themselves, but are saved by an external impulse; hence they are said to 'be hurled' into Tartarus, not to 'go' there, because they have lost their power of self-motion.

You can also point out that, since their wrongdoings are 'irremediable,' it is only logical to say that there is no remedy for them.

Perhaps, too, by some demonic form of retribution, the thought that they will never be set free is suggested to them as a punishment.

Finally he may mean that, in contrast with those who are given some respite from Tartarus, those others never go out, but are kept in continuous confinement.

148. [114a7–b6] How can the guilty appeal to their victims in the Acherusian lake? In the first place, the victims are not necessarily there, they may be either in this world or elsewhere in a higher sphere, and some may even be in Tartarus for great crimes they have committed in their turn. Secondly, apart from the fact that they are not always present: even if they are, it is a still stranger idea to measure the penalty for the offenses by the emotional reactions of those people, who may either tend to unforgiving harshness or be too soft-hearted and compassionate. – The answer is that all this is enacted by demonic influence; in accordance with the decrees of justice phantoms resembling their victims are conjured up before them. This may be the reason why the scene is the Acherusian lake, which as a purifying water has the power to relieve from burdens.

THE EPILOGUE

§§ 149–157. Death of Socrates. 115a3–118a17

149. There are many kinds of death: (1) natural death by decline, when the living organism, which received a limited capacity of life from the out-

---

"elevating" quality (I § 547.7); for the Sun as ἀναγωγός cf. Pr., *theol.* VI 12; for Saturn, Pr., *Alc.* 196.14–16.

§ 148. Dam. I § 550.

9. λυτική ... τῶν βαρῶν : for βάρος cf. *Ph.* 81c9 and 10; *Phaedr.* 248c7; above II § 110.1 (ὀπισθοβαρής). On the purifying power of the Acherusian lake see I § 544; II § 145.12.

§ 149. This is the final and most elaborate stage of a theory of death, which was started by Porphyry (as reported by Macrob., *somn. Scip.* I 13,11–14), who distinguishes only between natural and violent death: "addit etiam" (*scil.* Plotinus I 9) "illam solam esse naturalem mortem ubi corpus animam, non anima corpus relinquit. constat enim numerorum certam constitutamque rationem animas sociare

ἑαυτῆς ἑκάστη, καθ᾽ ἣν τὸ ἑκάστης ἄκρον καὶ ἔσχατον πεπέρασται τῆς 10
περιαγωγῆς, ἄν τε ἐπὶ τὸ νοητὸν ἄν τε ἐπὶ τὸν Τάρταρον ἀφίκηται, μεθ᾽ οὗ
πέφυκε μέτρου ἀρετῆς ἢ ἐπιστήμης.

Δύναται δέ τις εἰπεῖν καὶ ὅτι ὅσον ἐφ᾽ ἑαυταῖς οὔποτε ἐκβαίνουσιν, οὐκέτι
γὰρ ἑαυταῖς δύνανται βοηθεῖν, ἀλλ᾽ ὡς ἑτεροκίνητοι σῴζονται· διὸ καὶ ῾ῥιπτεῖσθαι᾽
λέγονται εἰς τὸν Τάρταρον, ἀλλ᾽ οὐκ ἀπιέναι, ἅτε παραπολωλεκυῖαι τὸ αὐτοκίνητον. 15

Λέγε δὲ καὶ ὅτι ῾ἀνίατα᾽ πλημμελήσασαι εἰκότως λέγονται μηδέποτε τυγχάνειν
ἰάσεως.

Ἴσως δὲ κολαστικῷ τινι καὶ δαιμονίῳ τρόπῳ ἔννοιαι αὐταῖς ἐνδίδονται πρὸς
τιμωρίαν τῆς μηδέποτε ἀφέσεως.

Μήποτε δὲ πρὸς τὰς ἰσχούσας ἀνακωχήν τινα τοῦ Ταρτάρου λέγει τὸ μηδέποτε 20
ἐκείνας ἐκβαίνειν κατὰ συνέχειαν μίαν ἐπεχομένας.

δ ρμη΄. - [114a7-b6] *Πῶς δέονται οἱ ἠδικηκότες τῶν ἠδικημένων ἐν τῇ* 148
Ἀχερουσιάδι λίμνῃ; οὔτε γὰρ ἐκεῖ πάντως οἱ ἠδικημένοι, ἀλλ᾽ ἢ ἐνταῦθα ἢ
ἀλλαχοῦ που ἀνηγμένοι, ἢ καὶ ἐν τῷ Ταρτάρῳ ἔνιοι μεγάλα τυχὸν ἴσως ἕτερα
καὶ αὐτοὶ ἠδικηκότες. οὔτε τοίνυν ἐκεῖ πάντως· καὶ μέντοι εἰ ἐκεῖ, ἔτι τούτου
ἀτοπώτερον τὸ ἐπὶ τοῖς πάθεσιν ἐκείνων κρίνεσθαι τὴν ἀξίαν τῶν ἡμαρτημένων, 5
ἢ ἀφειδέστερον καὶ ὠμότερον ἐχόντων ἢ χαυνότερον καὶ ἐλεεινότερον. — Ἢ
γίγνεται ταῦτα τὸν δαιμόνιον τρόπον, φασμάτων ὁμοίων τοῖς ἠδικημένοις
προτεινομένων κατὰ δίκην. καὶ μήποτε διὰ τοῦτο κατὰ τὴν Ἀχερουσιάδα λίμνην·
λυτικὴ γὰρ τῶν βαρῶν ἡ ταύτης δύναμις καθαρτική γε οὖσα.

THE EPILOGUE

§§ 149–157. Death of Socrates. 115a3–118a17

α΄ ρμθ΄. - *Ὅτι πολλοὶ τρόποι θανάτου. πρῶτος μὲν γὰρ θάνατος ὁ τῆς φύσεως,* 149
κατὰ μαρασμόν, πέρας εἰληφότος τοῦ ζῴου ὅτι πεπερασμένην ἐξ ἀρχῆς ἐδέξατο

---

corporibus. hi numeri dum supersunt, perseverat corpus animari: cum vero deficiunt, mox arcana illa vis solvitur qua societas ipsa constabat, et hoc est quod fatum et fatalia vitae tempora vocamus ...". The same bipartition is found above I § 127.3: ὁ ἄνωθεν λέγεται θάνατος καὶ ὁ κάτωθεν. The present survey starts with Porphyry's "natural" death, when the life force is exhausted (1), then joining to it, as a cognate phenomenon, (natural) death by illness (2). Violent death is subdivided according to its causes: a lifeless or irrational cause (3), a human cause (4), suicide (5). To Porphyry's division is added supernatural death, when the theurgist by an act of volition gives back the elements of his body to the cosmos (6). The diaeresis at lines 8–13, while following different routes, results in the same six possibilities:

set, has come to an end; this spontaneous death is recorded of some Indians as well as of those who live above on that pure earth; (2) death from sickness, also decreed by fate; (3) violent death by an external force, e.g. a stone or an animal; (4) violent death by the hand of man, e.g. by execution or in combat; (5) violent death by one's own hand; (6) supernatural death by dissolution of the elements, in other words, the death which many theurgists have died. These kinds of death can be classified as follows. Death is either decreed by fate or voluntary and self-chosen; if decreed by fate, it is either natural [1] or violent; if violent, it is due either to climatic conditions and in general to disproportion between the elements of which we are made [2], or to chance [3], or to deliberate action of rational beings [4]; if, on the other hand, death is voluntary, this may mean that we do violence to nature [5] or that we set the soul free in the more divine way [6].

150. [115a6-8] What do the ancient Attic death-rites symbolize? — The closing of the eyes and mouth signifies the end of outward activity and reversion to the inner life; the laying down on the earth is a reminder that the soul should unite itself with the universe; the washing means purification from the world of process; the unction a disengaging from the mire of matter and a calling forth of divine inspiration; cremation transference to the higher, indivisible world; inhumation union with intelligible reality.

151. Why does Socrates not adhere to tradition? — Perhaps it was not customary to wash those who died a violent death.

Rather, it is suggested that even the body should be cleansed voluntarily and before death.

152. [115e4-6] 'Not to use the right word,' but one with a different meaning, is in the first place what it is said to be, 'not right,' e.g. if one says that Socrates is dead, instead of his body; secondly it causes emotional habituation to that which is wrong; finally it exposes us to the influence of spirits who are pleased by such errors.

Death: (I) predestined (A) natural (=1)
　　　　　　　　　　(B) violent: (a) climate (=2)
　　　　　　　　　　　　　　　　(b) chance (=3)
　　　　　　　　　　　　　　　　(c) sentence (=4)
　　　　(II) voluntary (A) against nature (=5)
　　　　　　　　　　　(B) transcending nature (=6)

All this relates to man; in another passage about death, *Tim.* III 219.5-23, Pr. analyzes the different character of death according to levels of existence: (1) τῶν κατὰ σχέσιν λεγομένων δαιμόνων, (2) τῶν μερικῶν ψυχῶν, (3) τῶν ζῴων, (4) τῶν ἐψυχωμένων σωμάτων. Cf. also *supra*, I § 62.

3. τῶν ’Ινδῶν τινες : the Brahmans, no doubt, though this feature does not seem to appear in the extant Greek accounts.

7-8. The death of the theurgists: cf. Lewy p. 217 n. 163.

§ 150. Dam. I § 552 and note.

1. πάτρια ’Αττικά : Marinus, *vit. Pr.* 36, testifies to Pr.'s special interest in this

ζωῆς δύναμιν, ὃν τρόπον αὐτόματον καὶ τῶν Ἰνδῶν τινες ἱστοροῦνται τελευτᾶν
β' καὶ οἱ ἐπάνω τῆς καθαρᾶς ἐκείνης γῆς. δεύτερος θάνατος | καὶ αὐτὸς εἱμαρμένος (243)
γ' ὁ κατὰ νόσον. τρίτος ὁ κατὰ βίαν τὴν παρὰ ἄλλου, οἷον ἢ λίθου ἢ ἀλόγου.
δ' τέταρτος ὁ κατὰ βίαν τὴν παρὰ ἀνθρώπου, οἷον ἢ δικάζοντος ἢ πολεμοῦντος.
ε' ϛ' πέμπτος ὁ κατὰ τὴν ἑαυτοῦ. ἕκτος ὁ ὑπερφυής, οἷον ὁ κατὰ διάλυσιν τῶν στοιχείων
ἢ ὅλως καθ' ὃν πολλοὶ τῶν θεουργῶν τρόπον ἀπέθανον. λάβοις δὲ ἂν τοὺς θανάτους
καὶ κατὰ διαίρεσιν οὕτως. ἢ εἱμαρμένος ὁ θάνατος ἢ ἑκούσιος καὶ αὐθαίρετος·
καὶ εἰ μὲν εἱμαρμένος, ἢ αὐτοφυὴς ἢ βίαιος· καὶ εἰ βίαιος, ἢ ὑπὸ τοῦ περιέχοντος
καὶ ὅλως τῆς ἀμετρίας τῶν στοιχείων ἐξ ὧν ἡμεῖς, ἢ ὑπὸ τύχης, ἢ ὑπὸ κρίσεως
ζῴων λογικῶν· εἰ δὲ ἑκούσιος ὁ θάνατος, ἢ βιαζομένων ἡμῶν τὴν φύσιν ἢ τὸν
θειότερον τρόπον διαλυόντων.

ρν'. – [115a6–8] *Τίνων σύμβολα τὰ περὶ τοὺς ἀποιχομένους πάτρια Ἀττικά;* 150
— Τὸ μὲν οὖν καμμύειν τοῦ παύειν μὲν τῆς ἔξω ἐνεργείας, πρὸς δὲ τὴν εἴσω
ἐπιστρέφειν· τὸ δὲ ἐπὶ γῆς τιθέναι τοῦ ἀναμιμνήσκειν ὅπως ἂν τοῖς ὅλοις ἡ
ψυχὴ συναφθείη· τὸ δὲ λούειν τοῦ ἀποκαθαίρειν τῆς γενέσεως· τὸ δὲ μυρίζειν
τοῦ ἀποσπᾶν μὲν τοῦ βορβόρου τῆς ὕλης, τὴν δὲ θείαν ἐπίπνοιαν προκαλεῖσθαι·
τὸ δὲ καίειν τοῦ περιάγειν εἰς τὸ ἄνω καὶ τὸ ἀμέριστον· τὸ δὲ ἐντιθέναι τῇ γῇ
τοῦ συνάπτειν τοῖς νοητοῖς.

ρνα'. – *Διὰ τί μὴ ἐμμένει τοῖς πατρίοις;* — *Ἢ ἴσως οὐκ ἔλουον τοὺς* 151
βιαιοθανάτους.
Ἄμεινον δὲ λέγειν ὡς ἐνδείκνυται χρῆναι καὶ τὰ περὶ τὸ σῶμα καθαίρειν
αὐτοκινήτως καὶ πρὸ τοῦ θανάτου.

ρνβ'. – [115e4–6] *Ὅτι 'τὸ μὴ καλῶς λέγειν' ἀλλὰ ἀλλοτριονομεῖν, πρῶτον* 152
μὲν οὐ καλόν, ὅπερ δὴ καὶ λέγεται, οἷον τὸ φάσκειν ὅτι Σωκράτης τέθνηκεν,
ἀλλ' οὐχὶ τὸ τούτου σῶμα· δεύτερον δὲ καὶ συνήθειαν ἐμποιεῖ τῆς ζωῆς πρὸς
τὸ αἰσχρόν· ἔπειτα οἰκειοῦται πρὸς δαίμονας τοὺς χαίροντας τοῖς τοιούτοις.

---

§ 149. 3 Ἰνδῶν] -ν- in ras. 2 litt. M^c — 9 καὶ²] in ras. M^c
§ 150. 4 τοῦ Fh: τὸ M, itemque 5 τοῦ¹, 6, 7 — 6 καίειν] accent. ex corr., -ν in ras.,
M^c (καὶ εἰς ut vid. M¹)
§ 152. 1 μή] -ή in ras. M^c

---

matter: καὶ θεραπείας τὸ σῶμα ἠξιώθη κατὰ τὰ πάτρια τὰ Ἀθηναίων, καὶ ὡς αὐτὸς
ἔτι περιὼν διετάξατο. καὶ γὰρ αὖ καὶ τοῦτο ὑπῆρξεν τῷ μακαρίῳ ἀνδρί, εἴπερ τινὶ καὶ
ἄλλῳ, γνῶσις καὶ ἐπιμέλεια τῶν δρωμένων περὶ τοὺς ἀποιχομένους. On the phrase cf.
Hermias 137.19–20 (the twelve Gods) ταῦτα δὲ καὶ ὡς ἀπὸ τῶν πατρίων τῶν Ἀττικῶν
λέγει ὁ φιλόσοφος. Pr., Tim. I 172.14–16 καὶ μὴν καὶ ἐν τοῖς Ἀττικοῖς πατρίοις καὶ
ἐν τοῖς μυστηρίοις τοῦ Γιγαντικοῦ πολέμου θρυλουμένου ... Infra § 153.2.
2. καμμύειν: in *LSJ* the only meaning is 'close the eyes,' apparently always
one's own, literally or figuratively. However, I § 552.1–2 has τὸ μῦσαι τὸ στόμα
(*Ph.* 118a13–14 συνέλαβε τὸ στόμα καὶ τοὺς ὀφθαλμούς).
§ 152. Dam. I § 554.
1. ἀλλοτριονομεῖν : Tim. soph. p. 21 ἀλλοτριονομοῦντες· ἐναλλαγὴν ὀνομάτων ποιοῦντες,
ἢ ὅλως τισί τινα μὴ προσηκόντως διανέμοντες, and Ruhnken's note; from Pl., *Theaet.*
195a7.
4. Demons might be attracted by the δύσφημον of a soul being buried. Cf., in
almost the same words, § 155.3.

153. [117b6–c3] Socrates considers pledging from the cup because he remembered that this death-bringing character also exists among the Gods; he refrains, though, on the ground that tradition did not acknowledge the cult of it. Prayer, however, could be offered to all and on all occasions, since there is nothing that does not relate to the Gods.

154. [117c2–3] Why does he pray for 'good luck' on his journey? — Because, having prepared himself in every way to achieve the good, he is now waiting for the fulfillment of his hopes.

155. [117e1–2] Why do the Pythagoreans want to die 'in religious silence'? — First, lest they cause the soul to fall back into sympathy with the dead body; secondly, lest they attract spirits who are pleased by such things; thirdly, lest they exclude the elevating presence of the Gods.

156. [117e4–118a4] Why do the lower extremities become cold first? — Because they are farther from the organ that is the source of warmth. In general terms, warmth naturally tends upward, cold downward.

157. [118a7–8] Why did Socrates say that he owed Asclepius that sacrifice, and why were those his last words? If it were due already, a man as careful as he was would not have forgotten it. — The reason is that the soul is in need of the care of the Healing God at the moment that she is set free from all her toil; therefore the Oracle [frg. 131] says that souls in their upward flight sing the hymn to Paean.

---

§ 153. Dam. I §§ 557–558.
§ 155. Dam. I § 559.

ρνγ'. - [117b6-c3] Ὅτι ἐπεχείρησε μὲν σπεῖσαι ἀπὸ τῆς κύλικος ἐννοήσας 153(244)
καὶ τὴν τοιαύτην ἰδιότητα τῶν θεῶν, τὴν θανατηφόρον· ἐπέσχε δὲ τὰ πάτρια
λογισάμενος οὐ τιμήσαντα ταύτην. τὸ μέντοι εὔξασθαι πᾶσιν ἦν καὶ ἐπὶ πᾶσι
κοινόν· οὐδὲν γὰρ ὅ τι οὐκ ἀνατείνεται πρὸς θεούς.

ρνδ'. - [117c2-3] Διὰ τί 'εὐτυχῆ γενέσθαι' τὴν μετάστασιν παρακαλεῖ; 154
— Ἢ πάντα παρασκευασάμενος πρὸς τεῦξιν τῶν ἀγαθῶν αὐτὴν περιμένει λοιπὸν
τὴν ἐπιτυχίαν.

ρνε'. - [117e1-2] Διὰ τί 'μετὰ εὐφημίας' ἀποθνῄσκειν ἀξιοῦσιν οἱ Πυθαγόρειοι; 155
— Ἢ πρῶτον μὲν ἵνα μὴ προσελκύσωνται τὴν ψυχὴν εἰς συμπάθειαν τοῦ ἐφθαρμένου
σώματος· δεύτερον δὲ ἵνα μὴ ἐπισύρωνται δαίμονας τοὺς χαίροντας τοῖς τοιούτοις·
τρίτον δὲ ἵνα μὴ ἀναστέλλωσι τῶν θεῶν τὴν ἀναγωγὸν παρουσίαν.

ρνς'. - [117e4-118a4] Διὰ τί τὰ κάτω ψύχεται πρότερον; — Ἢ ὅτι 156
πορρωτέρω τοῦ ἀναθάλποντος σπλάγχνου ἐστίν. καὶ ὅλως τὸ θερμὸν ἀνώρροπον
φύσει, τὸ δὲ ψῦχον κατώρροπον.

ρνζ'. - [118a7-8] Διὰ τί ὀφείλειν ἔφη τῷ Ἀσκληπιῷ τὴν θυσίαν καὶ τοῦτο 157
τελευταῖον ἐφθέγξατο; καίτοι εἰ ὤφελεν, ἐπιστρεφὴς ὢν ἀνὴρ οὐκ ἂν ἐπελάθετο.
— Ἢ ὅτι Παιωνίου δεῖται προνοίας ἡ ψυχή, ἀπαλλαττομένη τῶν πολλῶν
πόνων· διὸ καὶ τὸ λόγιόν φησι [frg. 131] τὰς ψυχὰς ἀναγομένας τὸν παιᾶνα ᾄδειν.

---

§ 157. 2 ὤφελεν] ὤφειλεν μ

---

§ 156. Dam. I § 560.
§ 157. Dam. I § 561.

MARGINALIA

I

§ 1.1 (inf.). τῶν ἀνωνύμων σχολῶν εἰς τὸν Πλάτωνος Φαίδωνα, λείπει κατ' ἀρχήν M^r.
§ 3. (inf.). δημιουργίαι προστάται πλῆθος
            ἀμέριστος Ζεύς Ὀλυμπίων
            μεριστή Διόνυσος Τιτάνων
§ 3.1. ση. M^r.
§ 7.1–6 (sup.). Τιτάνων κολάσεις.
α΄ κεραυνώσεις   καθαρτικαὶ καὶ ὁλοποιοί
β΄ δεσμοί   ἐφεκτικαὶ τῶν διαιρετικῶν δυνάμεων
γ΄ ἄλλων ἀλλαχῇ πρόοδοι τιμωρητικαὶ τῆς διαιρέσεως
§ 8.1. ἀπορία - λύσις.
§ 12.4. ση.
§ 15.1; 3. ἀπορία - λύσις.
§ 16.1. ση. M^r.
§ 19.1; 2. ἀπορία - λύσις.
§ 19.4. πῶς νοητέον τὴν ἀγανάκτησιν καὶ τιμωρίαν ἐπὶ θεοῦ.
ib. ση. M^r.
§ 23.1. ση. M^r.
§ 25 (inf.).   ἡ ἀνάγκη
            ἔνδοθεν   ἔξωθεν
  ἀγαθή·   κακή·   ἀγαθή·   κακή·
θεοῦ βούλησις   πονηροῦ   εἱμαρμένης   βιαίων καὶ παρὰ
καὶ δικαίου ἀνδρός πρ‹ο›αίρεσις δόσις ἀγαθ(ῶν) φύσιν δόσις
  α΄   β΄   γ΄   δ΄
§ 25.1. ση. M^r.
§ 29.1. ση. M^r.
§ 32.1; 3. ἀπορία - λύσις.
§ 34.1. ση.
§ 41.1; 2. ἀπορία - λύσις.
§ 41.4; 7. ἀπορία - λύσις.
§ 41.8; 11. ἀπορία - λύσις.
§ 42.1. ἀπορία - λύσις.
§ 45.1; 2. ἀπορία - λύσις.
§ 46.1. ση^{αι} M^r.
§ 47.1. ση.
§ 51 (inf.). ἐνέργειαι τὰ περὶ τὸ τέλος   τέλος αὐτό
              ἀτελής   ἐνεργεῖν· καθαίρεσθαι   ἐν‹η›ργηκέναι· κεκαθάρθαι
              τελεία   ἐνηργηκέναι· νενοηκέναι ἐνεργεῖν· νοεῖν, εὔχεσθαι
§ 51.1. ἀπορία - λύσις.
§ 53 (sup.).
θνήσκοντες   ὑποκείμενον θανάτου   εἶδος θανάτου   αἴτιον θανάτου
φιλόσοφοι   ψυχή   ζωὴ καθαρά   φιλοσοφία
πολλοὶ ἄνθρωποι ζωή   νέκρωσις   ἐξαγωγή
§ 57.1. ση^{αι} M^r.
§§ 66–67 (sup.).
καθαρτικῆς ζωῆς βαθμοί   λόγοι ἀθανασίας
α΄. ἀπόθεσις τοῦ ὄχλου τῆς γενέσεως   ἀπὸ τῶν ἐναντίων
β΄. συνουσία ἑαυτοῦ καθαρά   ἀπὸ τῶν ἀναμνήσεων
γ΄. ἀναδρομὴ πρὸς τὸ ἑαυτοῦ αἴτιον   ἀπὸ τῆς πρὸς τὰ νοητὰ ὁμοιότητος

§ 68.1; 2. ἀπορία - λύσις.
§ 69.6–9 (inf.).

ἀνα‹γ›καῖα καὶ φυσικά	τροφή
οὔτ᾽ ἀναγκαῖα οὔτε φυσικά	καλλωπισμός
φυσικὰ οὐκ ἀναγκαῖα	ἀφροδίσια
ἀναγκαῖα οὐ φυσικά	ἱμάτια οἰκήσεις

§ 69.6. ση.
§ 70.1; 3. ἀπορία - λύσις.
§ 71.1; 2. ἀπορία - λύσις.
§ 72.1. ση. Mr.
§ 73.1; 2. ἀπορία - λύσις.

§ 74 (inf.).   ἡ ψυχὴ ἐνεργεῖ

	πρὸ ἑαυτῆς	πρὸς ἑαυτήν	μεθ᾽ ἑαυτήν
ἡ ψυχὴ κατὰ τοὺς τρεῖς	θεωρητικός	καθαρτικός	πολιτικός
πρὸ ἑαυτῆς	ἔχεται τῶν	ἐπιζητεῖ τὰς	ἀνατείνεται
	πρὸ αὐτῆς	ἑαυτῆς ἀρχάς	εἰς τὰ αἴτια
πρὸς ἑαυτήν	ἐν ἑαυτῇ μένει	ἐξελίττει τὸ	ζητεῖ ἐν ἑαυτῇ τὰς
		οἰκεῖον εἶδος	ἀρχὰς τῶν πράξεων
μεθ᾽ ἑαυτήν	προνοεῖ τῶν	φεύγει τὰ μεθ᾽	κοσμεῖ τὰ
	δευτέρων	ἑαυτήν	δεύτερα

§ 75 (sup.).   ἡ τῶν νέων ἀγωγὴ τριττή

χρῆσις τῶν παθῶν μετρία	φυγὴ αὐτῶν	ἄγνοια τῶν αὐτῶν τελεία
ἐν Νόμοις καὶ Πολιτείᾳ	ἐν Φαίδωνι	ἐν Θεαιτήτῳ
καὶ πολλαχοῦ		

§ 78 (inf.).

σῶμα	ἄγνοια μεριστή
αἴσθησις	σκοτεινὴ γνῶσις
φαντασία	νοῦς παθητὸς καὶ μεριστός
ψυχὴ λογική	ἑαυτῆς γνωστική
νοῦς	αὐτογνῶσις ἀμέριστος

§ 81.1; 2. ἀπορία - λύσις.
§ 82.1; 2. ἀπορία - λύσις.
§§ 83–86 (inf.).   αἰσθήσεις

πρὸς τὸ εἶναι δεδομέναι	πρὸς τὸ εὖ εἶναι
παθητικαὶ μᾶλλον	ἐνεργητικαὶ μᾶλλον
γῆς ὕδατος ἀέρος	ἀέρος πυρός
ἐν τῇ γενέσει	ἐν οὐρανῷ
ἁφὴ γεῦσις ὄσφρησις	ἀκοὴ ὄψις

§ 87.1. ση. Mr.
§ 88.1. ση. Mr.

§ 89 (sup.).   ἡ ἀπάτη τριττή

| παρὰ τὰ αἰσθητά | παρὰ τὰς αἰσθήσεις | παρὰ τὰ αἰσθητήρια |
| ὡς τῷ μὴ ὄντι συμμιγῆ | ὡς μὴ ἀκριβούσας | πάθη φέροντα ταῖς ἐνεργείαις |

§ 92.1. ση. - ση. Mr.
§ 95 (sup.).   τὸ ʽαὐτὸ᾽ τοῖς εἴδεσιν ἐπικείμενον δηλοῖ

κύριον	ἀμιγὲς πρὸς ὕλην	καθόλου καὶ μονοειδές	πρωτουργόν
πρὸς μίμημα	πρὸς με-	πρὸς τὸ πῇ καὶ τί	πρὸς τὸ κατὰ
	μιγμένον αὐτῇ		ἀναφοράν

§ 95.1. ση. - ση. Mr.

§ 99 (inf.). ἡ δόξα ἀποτείνεται   ἡ διάνοια   ὁ νοῦς
              πρὸς τὸ αἰσθητόν   πρὸς ἑαυτήν   πρὸς τὸ νοητόν

              μετὰ δόξης   μεθ' ἑαυτῆς   μετὰ νοῦ
              πολιτική   καθαρτική   φιλοσοφία

§ 100.1; 6. ἀπορία - λύσις.
§ 100.3–4. 'Ονήτωρ 'Αττικός Πατέριος Πλούταρχος Πρόκλος Μʳ.
§ 102.1; 2. ἀπορία - λύσις.
§ 108.1. πόσα καὶ ποῖα τὰ τῆς ψυχῆς ἐμπόδια.
§ 109.1; 2. ἀπορία - λύσις.
§ 110.1; 2. ἀπορία - λύσις.
§ 111.1. ση.
§ 112.1. ση. τίνα τὰ ἀμόρφωτά ἐστι.
§ 113.1. ἀπορία - λύσις.
§ 113.2–5 (sup.).   τὸ οὐκ ἄνευ τριττόν

              βλάπτον   συνεισφέρον   οὐδέτερον
              φαντασία   ὕλη   σκιά

§ 113.2. ση.
ib. τριττὰ τὰ ὧν οὐκ ἄνευ Μʳ.
§ 114 (inf.). ψ   συμπάσχουσα σώματι   ἄλλου γίνεται
               υ   πολιτικῶς ἐνεργοῦσα   ἑαυτῆς καὶ ἄλλου ἢ μόνον ἄλλου
               χ   καθαρτικῶς   ἑαυτῆς
               ἡ   θεωρητικῶς   αὐτή
§ 114.1. ση. Μʳ.
§ 115.1; 2. ἀπορία - λύσις.
§ 116.1. ἀπορία - λύσις.
§ 117.1; 4. ἀπορία - λύσις.
§ 119.1. ση. Μʳ.
§ 120.1. ση. τίνα τὰ τοῦ καθαιρομένου ἀποκαθάρματα.
§ 121.1–4 (sup.).
        παιδεία   συστολὴ ἀπὸ τοῦ θορύβου τῆς γενέσεως   πολιτική
        καθαρτική   λύσις τῆς κάτω νεύσεως καὶ παρασκευὴ   θεωρητική
                      τῆς πρὸς τὸ ἄνω ἀνατάσεως
§ 123.1. ση.
§ 127.1. ση.
§ 128.1–5 (inf.). ἡ ψυχὴ γενομένη ἐν σώματι
α' ψυχοῖ αὐτό   β' συμπαθεῖ αὐτῷ   γ' συνδιασπᾶται αὐτῷ
§ 134.1. ση. ἀπόδειξις ὅτι ἡ ψυχὴ κατ' ἀνάγκην φυσικὴν ἐθέλει τοῦ σώματος χωρίζεσθαι.
§ 137.1; 2. ἀπορία - λύσις.
§ 138.1. ἀπαρίθμησις ἀρετῶν - α' φυσικαί.
§ 139.1. β' ἠθικαί.
§ 140.1. γ' πολιτικαί.
§ 141.1. δ' καθαρτικαί.
§ 142.1. ε' θεωρητικαί.
§ 143.1. ς' παραδειγματικαί.
§ 143.5. 'Ιάμβλιχος Μʳ.
§ 144.1. ζ' ἱερατικαί.
§ 144.3. 'Ιάμβλιχος Πρόκλος Μʳ.
§ 145.1. τίνες αἱ ἀνδραποδώδεις ἀρεταί.
§ 146 (inf.).   οἱ ἀνδρεῖοι καὶ σώφρονες γίνονται
ἢ διὰ   ἢ διὰ νόμον   ἢ δι' ἄγνοιαν   ἢ δι' ἐμ-   ἢ δι' ἀπόνοιαν   ἢ ἀλλαττό-
τι-   κολάζοντα τοὺς τῶν ἐσομένων   πειρίαν τῶν   θηριώδη καὶ   μενοι ἄλλα
μήν   μὴ τοιούτους   κακῶν   κινδύνων   ἄλογον ὁρμήν   ἀντὶ ἄλλων

§ 146.1. ση. - ση. M^r.
§ 149.1; 6. απορία - λύσις.
§ 149.7-11 (inf.).

αρεταί   χαρακτήρες τούτων
ανδρεία   αρρεπές προς τα χείρω
σωφροσύνη   αποστροφή από τοϋ χείρονος
δικαιοσύνη   ίδιος ενέργεια και τω όντι προσήκουσα
φρόνησις   εκλεκτικόν και απεκλεκτικόν αγαθών και κακών

§ 151.1. απορία - λύσις.
ib. ση. M^r.
§ 151.5; 6. απορία - λύσις.
§ 151.10; 11. απορία - λύσις.
§ 152.1-3 (inf.).

αρεταί   ζωαί
ανδρεία   καθαρτική
σωφροσύνη   ηθική
δικαιοσύνη   πολιτική
φρόνησις   θεωρητική

§ 152.1. απορία - λύσις.
§ 153.1. απορία - λύσις.
§ 154.1. απορία - λύσις.
§ 157.1; 3. απορία - λύσις.
§ 161 (inf.).

αιρούμενοι   αιρετά
πολύς άνθρωπος   μείζους ήδοναί αντί των ελάττω
ατελής την αρετήν   καλλίω ήδοναί αντί των ασχημον(εσ)τ(έρων)
πολιτικός   ηδονή αναγκαία υπέρ αγαθού
καθαρτικός   ουδεμία ηδονή, σωφροσύνη δέ

§ 166.5 (inf.). Βάκχοι] Βάκχος ο ιερεύς τοϋ Διονύσου, ο εν τω βαίνειν ιάχων.
§ 167 (sup.).

ιερά   πάνδημοι καθάρσεις   απορρητότεραι   συστάσεις   μυήσεις   εποπτείαι
ζωαί   ηθικαί και πολιτι-   καθαρτικαί   θεωρητικαί   αμερείς   απλαί αυτο-
        καί αρεταί   ενέργειαι   ψίαι ειδών

§ 167.1. ση^αι M^r.
§ 168.6-7. πνευματικός χιτών
           οστρέινος
           αυγοειδής M^r.
§ 168.8. ση. δι' όσων ετών η φιλόσοφος ψυχή κατά Πλάτωνα την αναγω<γήν> προς το αφ' ου προήλθεν ποιείται.
§ 171.1. ση. ετυμολογία τοϋ Βάκχος ονόματος.
§ 173.1. ση. M^r.
§ 175.2. ση. M^r.
§ 176.6. ση. M^r.
§ 177 (inf.).   η ψυχή αθάνατος

κατά Νου-   κατά Πλω-   κατά Ξενο-   κατά Πρόκλον   κατά τους   κατά
μήνιον ή   τίνον ή   κράτ(ην)   και Πορφύ-   πολλούς   τινας
λογική   λογική   και Σπεύ-   ριον μόνη η   των Περι-   μόνη η
μέχρι της   μέχρι της   σιππον και   λογική   πατητικών   ολική
εμψύχου   φύσεως   Ιάμβλιχον   μόνος ο   ψυχή
έξεως   και Πατέ-   νους
                             ριον η λο-
                             γική μέχρι
                             της αλογίας

§ 177.1. ση. M^r.

§ 182.1. ἀπορία - λύσις.
§ 183.1. αὕτη προτέρα.
§ 183 (inf.). τὰ περὶ ψυχῆς ζητήματα
          α' ἢ γὰρ ἀχώριστός ἐστιν ὡς ἁρμονία
          β' ἢ χωριστὴ ὡς πνεῦμα ἀπὸ ἀσκοῦ
          γ' ἢ ἐπιδιαμένει πολὺν χρόνον
          δ' ἢ πάντῃ ἐστὶν ἀθάνατος
§ 187 (sup.). τὸ ζῶν τριχῶς

     ἢ ὅπερ   ἢ ὃ μετέχει ζωῆς παρούσης
     ἐστὶν
     ζωή   ἢ χωριστῆς   ἢ ἀχωρίστου
     α'   β'   γ'

§ 187.1. ση.
§ 188 (sup.). τὸ τεθνηκὸς διχῶς

   ἢ τὸ χωρισθὲν ἀπὸ   ἢ τῆς ἀχωρίστου
   τῆς ἀχωρίστου ζωῆς   σβεσθείσης
      α'   β'

§ 190 (inf.).   τὸ ἐξ ἀλλήλων διχῶς

ἢ ὡς ἐπὶ τῶν μετεχομένων ἁπλῶς   ἢ ὡς ἐπὶ τῶν μετεχόντων
ἅπερ ἐστὶ κυρίως μετ' ἄλληλα   καὶ μενόντων

     ἢ ἑνὸς ὄντος τοῦ ὑποκειμένου ὡς ἐπὶ   ἢ δυεῖν συνιόντων
     τοῦ αὐτοῦ σώματος θερμὸν καὶ ψυχρόν   καὶ διισταμένων

            ἢ ἑκατέρου σῳζομένου   ἢ τοῦ ἰσχυροτέρου πάντως

§ 190.1. ση.
§ 191.1. αὕτη ἡ πρᾶξις μετὰ τὴν ἐφεξῆς.
§ 193.1; 2. ἀπορία - λύσις.
§ 194.1; 2. ἀπορία - λύσις.
§ 194.2. ὅτι τὸ ἀσώματον τριττόν.
ib. ση. M[r].
§ 195.1; 2. ἀπορία - λύσις.
§ 196.1. ἀπορία - λύσις.
§ 197.1; 2. ἀπορία - λύσις.
§ 198.1. ἀπορία - λύσις.
§ 199.1; 2. ἀπορία - λύσις.
§ 200.1. ἀπορία - λύσις.
§ 201.1. ση.
§ 205 (inf.). ἀπορία πρὸς τὸ σχόλιον τὸ ἀπὸ τοῦ κύκλου τῆς γενέσεως ἰσχύειν τὸν λόγον· οὐ τὸ ἀθάνατον οὐδὲ τὸ ἀγένητον μειοῖ τῆς ἀποδείξεως, ἀλλ' ὑποθέσεως μόνον ἐξαρτᾷ τὸν λόγον τῆς λεγούσης ὡς εἰ ἔστιν ὁ κύκλος τῆς γενέσεως ἄπαυστος, ἀθάνατος ἂν εἴη καὶ ἡ ψυχή.
§ 205.1. ἀπορία - λύσις.
§ 207.3. Ἰάμβλιχος M[r].
§ 207.7. Συριανός M[r].
§ 210. πρὸς τὸ γ' κεφάλαιον τὸ δ' καὶ οὐ τῆς αὐτῆς συνεχείας τῶν λοιπῶν.
§ 220.1. ἀπορία.
§ 228.1–3 (sup.). ἡ τῶν αὐτῶν εἰδῶν ἐπανακύκλησις

       κατ' εἶδος   κατ' ἀριθμόν

   οὐσιῶν   συμβεβηκότων   ἀπειράκις   πλεονάκις

§ 229.1-4 (inf.). *αἰτίαι δι' ἃς ἀίδιος ἡ γένεσις*
α' *διὰ τὰς ἀκινήτους αἰτίας μὴ κινουμένας εἰς τὸ* [[*μὴ*]] *κινεῖν ἦν κινοῦσι κίνησιν*
β' *διὰ τὰς κινουμένας κατὰ κύκλον οὐρανίας περιφοράς*
γ' *διὰ τὰς συναιτίους ἀρχάς, τὴν ὕλην ὡς δεξαμενὴν τῶν ἀεὶ ῥεόντων εἰδῶν καὶ τὸ εἶδος συνουσιωμένον τῷ κύκλῳ τῆς γενέσεως*

§ 239.3-5. *ση. ὅτι τὸν πνευματικὸν χιτῶνα συνεῖναί φασι τῇ ψυχῇ μέχρι τελείας ἀποκαταστάσεως.*

§ 252.1-6 (inf.). *λόγοι ἀποδεικνύντες τὴν ψυχήν*
  ὁ ἀπὸ τῶν ἐναντίων   ἐπιδιαμένουσαν τοῦ σώματος
  ὁ ἀπὸ τῶν ἀναμνήσεων   προϋπάρχουσαν

§ 253.1. *αὕτη προτέρα.*
§ 262.1. *αὕτη ἡ πρᾶξις μετὰ τὴν ἐφεξῆς.*
§ 307.1. *ση.*
§ 339.1. *ση.*
§ 402.2. *ἀναγωγίαν*] *ἀτευξίαν τῆς δεούσης ἀναγωγῆς* [leg. *ἀγωγῆς*] *ἢ ἁμαρτίαν.*
§ 404.1. *κολουστική*] *ἐλαττωτική.*
§ 413.2 (inf.). *γενούστης*] *ὁ οἷον γεννήτης· ἔστι δ' ὁ μὴ ἐκ γένους καὶ αἵματος προσήκων, ἀλλ' ὁ ἐκ τῶν γενῶν τῶν συνενεμημένων εἰς τὰς φατρίας, οὗτος δέ ἐστι καθάπερ δημότης καὶ φράτωρ νόμῳ τινὶ ἔχων κοινωνίαν· οὕτως 'Αθήνησι τὸν εἰρημένον φασίν. ἢ γενούστης ὁ συγγενὴς ἢ ἔγγονος· τὸ τελευταῖον ἐκδέχεσθαι ἄμεινον* [Suda s.v.; schol. Pl. TW, *Phil.* 30d].
§ 483.1. *ση.*
§ 494.1. *ση.*
§ 516.1. *ση.*
§ 547.7. *ἀνάγωγον*] *φιλήδονον ἢ ἐκλελυμένον.*
§ 560.1. *ση.*

Π

§ 78.1. *Στράτων* Mˢ.
§ 91.1. *ση.*
§ 106.1. *ση.*
§ 116 (inf.).   *τὰ τέσσαρα περὶ τῆς γῆς προβλήματα*
  α' *εἰ μέσην ἔχει θέσιν*
  β' *εἰ σφαιροειδής*
  γ' *εἰ μένει*
  δ' *ὁπόση τὸ μέγεθος*
§ 137.1. *ση.*
§ 138.1. *ση. περὶ ἀνθρώπου ἀΰπνου καὶ ὑπὸ ἡλιοειδοῦς τρεφομένου ἀέρος.*
§ 150.1. *ση. τίνα τὰ περὶ τοὺς ἀποιχομένους τῶν 'Αττικῶν πάτρια.*

INDEX I: REFERENCES

Aeschylus frg. 239 N.: I 495[2].
Anaxagoras frg. A 47: I 412[1].
Arcesilaus: I 275[1].
Aristotle:
 an. I 1, 403a10–11: I 72[2]. – I 4, 407b32–34 (?): I 384[2]. – 407b34–408a1: I 385[2]. – 408a1–3: I 386. – 408a3–5: I 387[4]. – III 4, 429a15–18: I 280[4]. – 429a31: I 79[1]. – III 5, 430a22–23: I 176[2].
 cael. I 4, 271a33: I 179[4]. – II 12(?): I 416[10]. – II 13, 295b16–19: I 521[2]. – IV 3, 310b16–19(?): II 123[4].
 cat. 1, 1a1–2: I 345. – 7, 7a16: II 68[8].
 eth. Nic. I 1, 1094a2–3: I 202[3]. – III 11: I 146. – VI 12, 1143b4–7: II 18[1]. – X 8: I 148[3] 149[1].
 met. Λ 8(?): I 416[10].
 phys. V 1, 224b30–35: I 192[5].
 frg. 41: II 17[3]. – frg. 42: I 530[7] II 138[1]. – frg. 45 (Eudemus): I 383[1]. – frg. 204: I 535[1]. – frg. 22 Ross (?): I 416[10].
Aristoxenians: I 368[9].
Astronomers: I 513[2].
Attic commentators: on *Ph.* 66c7–8: I 110[4]. – 69a6–c3: I 164[1].
Atticus: on *Ph.* 66b1–3 (frg. 44): I 100[3].

Bion (of Borysthenes): I 293[1] II 24[1].

Chaldean Oracles frg. 52: I 151[3]. – frg. 62: II 134[4]. – frg. 130.2: I 169[3]. – frg. 131: I 561[3] II 157[4].
Commentators: ὁ ἐξηγητής (ὁ ἐξηγησάμενος): see Proclus, Syrianus. – οἱ παλαιότεροι τῶν ἐξηγητῶν (on *Ph.* 70c5–72e2): I 207[1]; οἱ πολλοὶ τῶν παλαιῶν (on *Tim.* 41a8–b6): II 36[2]. – Unnamed: (on *Ph.* 62b2–6) I 2[2]; (85d2–4) I 392[2].

Damascius: ὁ ἡμέτερος καθηγεμών: I 207[title] II 128[4] 132[4]. – 1st ps. sg.: I 207[16] 222[4] 241[7]. – 1st ps. pl.: I 4[2] 235[2] 236[1] 238[1] 243[title] II 64[27]. – ἀλλά ...: I 41[4] 126[3] 206[3] 337[3] 338[3] 380[6] 531[3] II 9[3] 364,9 385 42[3] 43[3] 62[6] 147[6]. – κατὰ δὲ τὸν ἀληθῆ λόγον: II 64[22]. – ἢ τό γε ἀληθέστερον: II 59[5]. – ἄμεινον (δέ, etc.):

I 115[4] 372[1] 473[4] 535[3] 538[3] 539[6] II 14[5] 25[5] 33[5] 36[11] 74[4] 76[5] 98[2] 112[5] 130[6] 145[10] 151[3]. – βέλτιον (δέ, etc.): I 83[3] 182[4] II 9[3] 42[3] 43[3] 55[9] 56[15] 78[21] 88[6] 97[6] 110[6] 132[4]. – ... δέ ...: I 31[4] II 64[27] 101[8] 108[7]. – ... ἔδει ...: I 112[5] 261[1]. – εἰ καὶ μή ...: II 101[3]. – εἰ μὴ ἄρα ...: I 30[3]. – εἶεν δὲ ἂν καὶ ...: II 87[3]. – εἴη δὲ ἂν τι καὶ ...: II 8[3]. – εἴποις δὲ ἂν ὅτι καὶ ...: I 525[4]. – ἐπιστῆσαι χρή ...: I 257[1] 478[6] 529[8]. – ἤ ...: I 11[10] 51[3] 163[3] 397[3] 473[4] 502[3] II 30[8] 38[6] 56[7] 59[5]. – ἡμεῖς δὲ ἐροῦμεν: I 242[6] II 64[27]. – ἴσως δέ ...: II 129[8]. – καὶ πῶς ...: II 88[3]. – καίτοι ...: II 97[4]. – κάλλιον (δέ, etc.): I 9[2] 14[6] 28[3] 41[7] 109[3] 110[6] 114[2] 117[4] 152[4] 157[6] 170[3] 180[4] 260[2] 297[4] 311[5] 319[4] ⟨331[4]⟩ 337[3] 338[3] 358[4] 368[13] 375[5] 382[4] 516[6]. – λέγε: I 4[9]. – μᾶλλον δέ ... (ἢ μᾶλλον): I 70[4] 163[3] II 30[8]. – μήποτε (δέ, etc.): I 15[3] 22[3] 71[5] 100[6] 135[4] 481[4] 498[5] 535[3] 550[6] 561[3] II 14[4] 33[5] 39[3] 62[6] 78[17] 110[6]. – προσεχέστερον δὲ εἰπεῖν ὅτι ...: II 61[4]. – ῥητέον: I 380[6]. – φαίη ἄν τις: II 97[4] 100[3], cf. 78[17]. – φήσομεν: I 4[2]. – χρὴ δέ ...: II 29[12].
on *Laws* 690a1–c9 (Dam. or Pr.?): ὡς ἐκεῖ εἴρηται II 44[2]. – X 904a8–9 (? prob. Pl.): ὡς καὶ ἐν Νόμοις I 198[2].
on *Parm.* (Dam. or Pr.?): ὡς ἐν Παρμενίδῃ I 192[4].
on *Phaedr.* 246e4–247a4: περὶ ὧν ἐν Φαίδρῳ ῥηθήσεται I 527[4]. – 250b5–c4(?) (Pl. or Dam.?): ὡς ἐν Φαίδρῳ I 392[4].
on *Rep.* VII 520b5–6: ὡς ἐν Πολιτείᾳ δέδεικται I 114[3].
on *Tim.* 33c1–4 (?): ὡς ἐν ἄλλοις ἐπεστήσαμεν I 531[3]. – 41a8–b6 (?): ὡς ἐν ἄλλοις δείκνυται II 36[10]. – 55c4–6: ὃν ἐκεῖ λέγεται τρόπον I 527[2]; ἐλέγομεν ἐν τοῖς εἰς Τίμαιον II 132[4].
Democritus (the Platonist): on *Ph.* 108c5–110b1: I 503[3].

Epicurus frg. [1] 33: I 280[9]. – frg. [7]: I 162[4].

Geographers: I 504[2] 522[29] II 124[2].

Harpocratio: on *Ph.* 66c7–8 (frg. 3):
I 110². – 68c1–3 (frg. 4): I 137⁴,¹². –
68c5–69c3 (frg. 5): I 147³ 149⁶. –
69a6–c3 (frg. 5): 164⁴. – 70b7 (frg. 6):
I 182². – 108c5–110b1 (frg. 8): I 503².
Heraclides Ponticus frg. 95: II 131⁵.
Heraclitus frg. A 1 (5): I 294³. –
  frg. B 30: II 128⁶. – frg. B 101: I 294³.
Herodotus 7,239,4: I 278².
Hesiod, *op.* 50–52: I 170⁶.
Homer:
  Il. 1.544 (etc.): I 8⁴. – 9.56: I 207¹¹. –
  14.278: I 538¹. – 15.193: II 131². –
  18.262: I 207⁴. – 22.347: I 294⁴.
  Od. 1.53: II 72⁴. – 11.207: I 222⁷. –
  11.601–604: I 550⁷.

Iamblichus: I 172²; 177⁴.
  on *Ph.* 69e6–72e2: I 207³. – 107e2–
  4 (?): I 492². – 113e6 (?): I 548¹.
  ἐν 'Επιστολαῖς: I 548⁵.
  ἐν τοῖς Περὶ ἀρετῶν: I 143⁵ 144³.

Longinus: on *Ph.* 66c7–8: I 110⁴.

Numenius frg. 46a: I 177². – frg. 38: I 2².

Onetor: on *Ph.* 66b1–3: I 100³.
Orphica frg. 123: I 497⁵ 541⁵. – 125:
II 145⁶. – 165.1: I 331⁸. – 168: I 540².
– 172: I 14⁵. – 208: I 4⁴ 168². –
209: I 129¹. – 212: I 14⁵. – 215:
I 7¹. – 220: I 8¹. – 232: I 11². – 235:
I 170⁹. – addenda: I 14⁸ 170⁴.

Panarces (Diehl, fasc. 3, p. 76): I 170².
Paterius: on *Ph.* 62b2–6: I 2³. – 66b1–3:
I 100³. – 68c1–3: I 137⁵,¹¹.
Peripatos: I 148³ 149¹ 177⁶ 280⁴.
Pindar, *Olymp.* 2.126–127: I 151⁸.
Pisander frg. 21: I 378³.
Plato:
  Apol. 40b6–41c7: I 174⁵.
  Crat. 406a3–5: I 282².
  Critias 108e6–7: I 507⁵.
  Epin. 983c6–987d2: I 532³.
  Epistle VII 342a7–343d2: I 330⁵ 346¹.
  Gorg. 454e3–455a7: I 37². – 469c8–
  470a12: I 179⁶. – 474d3–475a4: I 417⁶.
  – 493a1–3: I 61³. – 523a1–527a4:
  I 471² II 85⁴.
  Laws I 631b6–d1: I 319². – II 653a5–
  c4: I 139⁴. – II 672a5–d4: I 171². –
  III 690a1–c9: I 339² II 44². – VII

788a1–VIII 842a3: I 75⁴. – X 899d4–
905c4: I 469³. – X 902e7–903a1:
I 41¹⁰. – X 904a8–9: I 198². –
XII 963c3–e9: I 138⁵.
Meno 80d5–e5: I 280². – 81c5–d5:
I 273². – 82a7–86a11: I 300³.
Ph. 60b1–c7: I 161⁵. – 61c2–62b6:
I 1–13. – 61c10: I 13¹. – 62a6: I 13².
– 62b2–6: I 1¹ 165⁶. – 62b3–4: I 10¹.
– 62b4: I 13² 166³. – 62b6–c8: I 14–25.
– 62b7: I 17. – 62b7–8: I 18. –
62c1–4: I 19. – 62c7–8: I 22. –
62c9–e7: I 26–27. – 62d2: I 28. –
62d4: I 30. – 62d5–6: I 29. – 62d6:
I 28. – 62d8: I 31. – 62e1: I 32. –
62e8–63a3: I 33–34. – 63a4–9: I 35.
– 63b1–2: I 36. – 63b4–5: I 37. –
63b5–c4: I 38–39. – 63b5–c4: I 43–44.
– 63b5–9: I 43². – 63b7: I 40. – 63b8:
I 42. – 63b9–c3: I 43³. – 63c3: I 41¹³.
– 63d5–e2: I 46. – 63e3–5: I 47. –
64a1: I 48. – 64a4–9: I 49. – 64a5:
I 50. – 64a6: I 51. – 64b8–9: I 52–53.
– 64c1–2: I 54. – 64c2–8: I 55–62. –
64c2: I 55. – 64c4–8: I 56. – 64d2–
66a10: I 63–67 74–77. – 64d2–65a8:
I 65³ 66² 69–71 76¹. – 64d2–e3: I 137³.
– 64d2–3: I 68. – 64e5: I 73. –
64e8–65a2: I 72. – 65a2: I 73. –
65a9–d3; I 65⁵ 66³ 76³ 78–92. –
65b1–8: I 83. – 65b9: I 88. – 65b11:
I 89. – 65c2–9: I 87. – 65c5–9: I 90.
– 65c7–9: I 92. – 65d4–66a10:
I 65⁷ 66⁴ 76³ 93–99. – 65d4–5: I 95. –
65d4–8: I 96. – 65d12–13: I 97. –
65d12: I 98. – 65e3–66a2: I 99. –
66b1–67a6: I 100–118. – 66b2: I 103–
104. – 66b2–3: I 106. – 66b4: I 101.
– 66b5: I 105. – 66b6: I 102. –
66b7–d3: I 108. – 66b7–c1: I 108². –
66b7: I 107. – 66c1–2: I 108² 109. –
66c1: I 117³. – 66c2–3: I 108³. –
66c3–5: I 108⁴. – 66c5–d2: I 108⁵. –
66c7–8: I 110. – 66d1: I 110⁷. –
66d3–7: I 111–113. – 66e1: I 114. –
– 66e2–67a2: I 115–118. – 67a3:
I 116³. – 67a6–b2: I 119–124. – 67b1:
I 124. – 67b2: I 119⁴. – 67b8: I 125.
– 67c5–d11: I 131. – 67c5–d2: I 126
128–130. – 64c7–8: I 127³. – 67d4–5:
I 127. – 67d7–8: I 132. – 67d12–68a3:
I 133–134. – 68a3–b6: I 135. – 68b8–
c1: I 136. – 68c1–3: I 137. – 68c5–
69c3: I 138–151 147. – 68c5–6: I 152.

− 68c6: I 149[12]. − 68c8: I 154[1]. − 68d2–69b8: I 146. − 68d2–69a5: I 159–160 163. − 68d2–3: I 153. − 68d2: I 154[1]. − 68d5–13: I 155–158. − 68d5: I 154[1]. − 68e2–69a5: I 161. − 69a6–c3: I 162 164. − 69a9–b5: I 164[6]. − 69b4–5: I 164[2]. − 69b7: I 145[3]. − 69b8–c3: I 163[5] 164[8]. − 69c3–d2: I 165–172. − 69c7: I 355[12]. − 69d5–6: I 124[5] 173. − 69d7–e5: I 174. − 69e2: I 175. − 69e6–72e2: I 66[1] 207–252 II 1–3 63–64. − 69e6–70c5: I 176–182. − 69e6–70b4: I 183[2]. − 69e6–70a6: I 178[3] 248[7]. − 70a4–5: I 215[7] 218[7] 221[2]. − 70a5: I 209[4]. − 70a6–8: I 179[2]. − 70b1–4: I 180. − 70b5–c5: I 181. − 70b5–7: I 208[7]. − 70b7: I 182 216[4] 232[15]. − 70c4–5: I 183[3]. − 70c5–72e2: I 183–192 201–206. − 70d7–71a11: I 186[2]. − 70d7–e6: I 207[14]. − 70d7–e2: I 213[6]. − 70d9: I 193[4]. − 70e4–71a11: I 228[7]. − 70e5–8: I 203. − 70e6–71a7: I 191[3]. − 71a3–4: I 247[3]. − 71a12–72a10: I 186[4]. − 71a13: I 192[2]. − 71b2–7: I 214[8]. − 71b2–4: I 247[12]. − 72a11–d5: I 186[8]. − 72c5–d3: I 229[24]. − 72d6–e2: I 183[3]. − 72d8–e1: I 220[3]. − 72e3–78b3: I 253–261. − 72e3–77a5: I 66[3] 262–265 266–273 293–297 II 4–11 12–14 15–23 24–27 65. − 72e3–73a3: I 298–299. − 73a7–b2: I 300. − 73c1–2: I 262[2] II 13[2]. − 73c4–d11: I 262[5] II 13[4]. − 73e1–3: I 262[6] II 13[5]. − 73e5–74a4: I 262[8] II 13[6]. − 74a5–8: I 262[9] II 13[8]. − 74a9–77a5: I 274. − 74a9–c6: I 301. − 74a10–12: I 302[1]. − 74b7–c6: I 301[5]. − 74b7: I 301[4]. − 74c1: I 302[1] II 15[7]. − 74c4–5: I 302[1] II 15[10]. − 74d9–75a4: I 303. − 75a1–3: I 305. − 75a5–8: I 304. − 75b1–2: I 306. − 75b4–d6: I 307. − 75e2–3: I 308. − 76c14–d6: II 16[2]. − 76d7–e7: I 307[5]. − 76e1: I 274[15] II 15[5]. − 76e1–2: II 15[7]. − 77a8–b9: I 309. − 77c6–d4: I 220[3]. − 77e5: I 310. − 78b4–85b9: I 311 II 29. − 78b4–80c1: I 66[4] 325–329 II 32–34. − 78c1–9: I 311[3]. − 78c1–5: 340. − 78c1–4: I 331. − 78c6–9: I 341–342. − 78d1–9: I 343. − 78d1–7: I 330 II 35. − 78d1–4: II 36. − 78d10–e5: I 344. − 78e2: I 345–346. − 79a1–4: I 332 II 37. − 79a3: I 332[4]. − 79b1–c1: I 325[2] 326 II 32[2]. − 79b7–11: II 38. − 79b7–8: I 333. − 79c2–e7: I 325[3] 327 II 32[4]. − 79c2–9: I 335 II 40. − 79d6: I 334 II 39. − 79e8–80a9: I 325[4] 328 339 II 32[7] 44. − 79e8–80a5: I 311[4]. − 80a10–c1: I 336–338 II 41–43. − 80b1–c1: II 30–31. − 80b1–5: I 312–324. − 80b8–e1: I 215[7]. − 80c2–e1: I 347. − 80d5–e1: I 311[11]. − 80d7: I 348. − 81a4–5: I 349. − 81a5–6: I 350. − 81a8–9: I 351. − 81c4–d4: I 352. − 81c9–e2: I 239[6]. − 81d7–9: I 353. − 81d7–8: I 355[13]. − 81d9–e2: I 354. − 81e1: I 352[5]. − 81e2–82c1: I 355. − 82a10–b8: I 356. − 83c5–8: I 357. − 84a3–6: I 358. − 84e3–4: I 359. − 85b4–5: I 360. − 85b10–95a6: I 361–370. − 85c3–4: I 389. − 85c5–6: I 390. − 85c7–d2: I 391. − 85d2–4: I 392. − 85e1–2: I 393. − 85e3–88b8: I 394. − 85e3–86d4: I 178[2]. − 86e6–88b8: I 178[4] 311[12]. − 87a5–7: I 215[9]. − 88c1–7: I 395. − 89a1–7: I 396. − 89a2–4: I 397–398. − 89d1–3: I 399–400. − 90a4–b3: I 401. − 90c8–e3: I 395[7]. − 90c8–d8: I 402. − 91e2–92b3: I 361 II 45. − 92a6–b2: I 223[3]. − 92c11–e3: I 403. − 92e4–95a6: I 383–387. − 92e4–93b7: I 362. − 92e4–93a3: I 363 II 46. − 92e8–95a6: II 58–62. − 93a4–5: I 364 II 47. − 93a6–7: I 365 II 48. − 93a8–10: I 366 II 49. − 93a11–94b3: I 379 405–406. − 93a11–b6: I 388. − 93a11–b3: I 368 II 51. − 93a11–12: I 405[7]. − 93a12: I 381 II 61. − 93b4–7: I 369 II 52. − 93b4–6: I 405[1]. − 93b8–94b3: I 362[1] 376[5] 380. − 93b8–e10: I 370 II 53. − 93b8–c2: I 405[5]. − 93c3–10: I 371–372 405[6] II 55. − 93d1–e10: I 374. − 93d1–5: I 405[10]. − 93d6–11: I 405[12]. − 93d12–e3: I 405[15]. − 93e4–10: I 405[17]. − 94a1–10: II 54. − 94a1–7: I 405[21]. − 94a2–4: I 373. − 94a4–5: II 57. − 94a8–b3: I 406. − 94a8–11: I 376 II 62. − 94b4–95a3: I 362[2] 376[5] II 50. − 94b4–e7: I 223[4] 375 II 56. − 95a4–5: I 377. − 95a5–6: I 378. − 95b5–6: I 45[4] 404. − 95b8–e6: I 429[2]. − 95b8–e3: I 183[4]. − 95c4–9: I 223[4]. − 95e9–96a1: I 407 II 66. − 96a8: I 408. − 96b2–8: I 409. − 96b8–c7: I 410. − 96d8–97b7: I 411. − 97b8–98c2: I 412. − 97b8–d5: II 70. − 97c2–d3: I 413. − 98c2–99b2: I 414. − 99a4–b6: II 71. − 99c3–5: II 72. −

99c6–100a3: I 415. – 99e4–100a3: II 73. – 100a7–102a2: I 416–420. – 100b1–101c9: II 67. – 100b3–7: I 417. – 100c3–8: II 68². – 100c9–e4: II 68³. – 100d3–6: I 418 II 69. – 100e5–101b8: II 68⁵. – 100e8–101b2: I 419. – 101b9–c9: II 68¹⁰. – 101d5–e1: I 420. – 101e1: II 74. – 102a10–107a1: I 178⁵ 421–430 449–465 II 75–77. – 103a11–c2: I 189² 224³. – 103e5–104b4: I 421 II 75¹. – 104b6–105b4: I 422 II 75⁵. – 104b6–c1: I 423. – 105a1–5: I 448¹. – 105b5–c7: II 75⁹. – 105b8–c2: I 430². – 105c9–d5: I 424. – 105d3–4: I 178¹⁰. – 105d6–11: I 425. – 105e10–107a1: I 430². – 107c1–114c8: I 466–471 II 81–85. – 107c1–108c5: II 84². – 107c1–4: I 472 II 86. – 107c2–8: I 474. – 107c2–4: II 87–89. – 107c3–4: I 473. – 107c4: II 90. – 107c6–8: I 475 II 91. – 107d1–2: II 92. – 107d4–5: I 476 II 93. – 107d5–e4: I 477–486 491 II 94–101 105. – 107d6–7: I 484–486 488 II 103. – 107d7–e2: I 481–483. – 107d7: I 487 II 102 112³. – 107d8: I 489–490 II 104. – 107e2–4: I 492. – 107e4: I 493–494 II 106–107. – 107e4–108a2: I 495 II 108–109. – 108a2–6: I 496–497. – 108a6–b3: I 498. – 108a7–b3: II 110. – 108b3–c5: I 500. – 108b3–c3: II 112. – 108b3–4: II 111. – 108b4–8: I 501. – 108b8: I 502 II 113. – 108c5–113c8: II 84³. – 108c5–110b1: I 503–511 II 129³. – 108c5–8: II 114–115. – 108e4–110b1: I 512–522. – 108e4–109a9: II 116–125. – 109a9–110b1: I 522. – 109a9–110b4: I 523–526. – 109a9: I 507¹ II 124. – 109b8–c1: I 524. – 109d7–8: II 128. – 109e6: II 127. – 109e7: II 126. – 110b1: I 525. – 110b1–2: I 526 II 129–130. – 110b5–111d2: II 131–139. – 110b6–7: I 527 II 132. – 110b7–c6: II 133. – 110c1–111b1: I 528. – 110d5: II 134³. – 110e2–111b6: II 135–136. – 111a3: I 511³. – 111a4–b1: II 134. – 111b1–3: II 137–138. – 111b3: I 529–530 531. 111b7: I 532. – 111c4–113c8: II 129⁴. – 111c4–d2: I 533 II 139. – 111d2–e2: I 534 II 141². – 111d7: I 535–536. – 111e4–112c1: I 542. – 111e6–112a5:

I 537–540 II 140 142–144. – 112a7–c1: II 141. – 112e4–113c8: I 541 II 145. – 113d1–114c8: II 84⁴. – 113d5–6: I 543 II 146. – 113d4–114b6: I 546. – 113d6–8: I 544. – 113e5: I 545. – 113e6: I 492³ 547–548 II 147. – 114a5: I 549. – 114a7–b6: I 550 II 148. – 114b6–c6: I 551. – 114d2–3: I 466³. – 114d3–4: II 129⁷. – 115a3–118a17: I 552–562 II 149–157. – 115a6–8: I 552 II 150–151. – 115b5–7: I 553. – 115e4–6: I 554 II 152. – 116c4–6: I 555. – 116d5–7: I 556. – 117b6–c3: II 153. – 117b6–9: I 557. – 117c1–3: I 558. – 117c2–3: II 154. – 117e1–2: II 155. – 117e4–118a4: I 560 II 156. – 118a7–8: I 561 II 157. – 118a16–17: I 562.

Phaedr. 242c6–7: I 359². – 245c5: I 58². – 245e1: I 241³⁶. – 246d8–e1: I 41¹. – 246e4–247c4: II 113⁴. – 246e4–247a4: I 527⁴. – 247d5–e2: I 151¹⁰. – 248b6: I 151¹². – 248b7: I 151¹³. – 248c1: I 151¹². – 248d2–4: I 107. – 248d2–3: I 308⁴. – 248e5–249b3: I 494² II 107³. – 249a3–5: I 168⁹. – 249a8: I 529⁵. – 249b6–c6: I 273². – 250b5–c4 (?): I 392⁴. – 250d7–e1; I 91². – 250e1: I 308⁴. – 276d3: I 253⁴.

Phil. 20d1–11: I 58³. – 27a8–9: II 32⁸. – 30e1: I 413³. – 64a7–65a6: I 107.

Polit. 306a5–308b9: I 138⁵.

Rep. II 373d7–e8: I 110⁷. – II 377d9: I 466⁴. – IV 434d2–445b4: I 75⁴ 140⁵ 149⁷. – VI 498e3: I 207⁶. – VI 509d2–3: I 14⁴. – VI 509d6–511e5: I 80⁶. – VII 520b5–6 (?): I 114³. – VII 533c7–e2: II 37⁴. – X 611b9–d8: I 63³. – X 614b2–621d3: I 471³ II 85⁵. – X 614d7–e1: II 100⁵. – X 617e1: I 488² II 103². – X 619c7–d1: I 529⁶.

Soph. 216c5–6: I 137⁷. – 226a7: I 1⁴. – 227d6–7: I 126⁵. – 245a5 (etc.): II 39².

Symp. 218b6–7: I 207¹⁰.

Theaet. 173c6–177c2: I 142⁶. – 173c6–174a2: I 75⁴. – 186c9: I 81¹. – 191c8–e1: I 257⁸.

Tim. 24e6–7: I 507⁵. – 31b1: I 516⁷ II 117⁵. – 34b10–36d7: I 377⁴ II 57⁵. – 35b1–36b5: I 382¹. – 36e2–5: I 493² 535⁴ II 106⁵. – 37a1 (?): I 315². – 40b8–c3: II 115⁶. – 40b8: I 515². –

40c2–3: I 507[2] 508[1]. – 40c3: I 524[5] 532[2]. – 41b2: I 320[1]. – 42c5–dl: I 67[1] 121[1]. – 42d4–5: I 509[2]. – 42d4: II 143[1]. – 42d6: I 14[3]. – 42e5–6: I 151[7]. – 42e6–43a6: I 16[3]. – 43a6–44c4: I 288[4]. – 43d2: I 117[2]. – 47a7–bl: I 335[2] II 40[2]. – 51a1 (?): I 315[2]. – 55c4–6: I 527[2] II 132[5]. – 55el: I 197[9]. – 61c3–68d7: I 85[2].
apud Athen. XI 507D: I 111[1].
Platonists: οἱ παλαιότεροι Πλατωνικοί (opp. οἱ ἀκριβέστεροι): I 355[2].
Plotinus: I 172[1].
 II 2,1.1: I 202[2]. – II 6,1.18–20: I 247[13]. – IV 7 (?): I 311[1,6] II 29[1,12,13,17]. – IV 7, 14: I 177[3].
Plutarch (of Athens): I 177[5].
 on Ph. 66b1–3: I 100[4]. – 108c5–110b1: I 503[4] II 114[2].
Plutarch (of Chaeronea) frg. 215: I 275–287. – frg. 216a–e: I 288–292. – frg. 216f–g: I 293–294. – frg. 217: II 28.
Porphyry: I 172[1]. – I 177[5].
 on Ph. 62b2–6: I 2[4]. – 92e8–95a6: II 59[2].
Proclus: ὁ Πρόκλος: I 100[4] 144[3] 172[3] 177[5] II 27[1] 29[8,12] 43[2] 55[7] 56[5] 64[21] 74[2] 78[13,17]. – ὁ ἐξηγητής: I 297[5] 405[2] II 14[4] 25[3] 88[2] 89[4] 100[2] 110[6] 128[2] 129[4] 132[2] 145[7] 147[6]. – αὐτός: I 69[6] 257[11] 375[6] 481[6] 541[5]. – 3rd ps. sg.: I 3[2] 103[2] 115[2] 137[10] 182[2] 196[4] 257[6] 337[2] 338[2] 38J[3] 531[2] 540[6] II 56[10] 97[1,3]

98[1] 101[8] 112[4] 130[2] 145[2]. – Cf. further I 112[6] 197[5] 198[3] 206[3].
 on Parm. (Dam. or Pr.?): ὡς ἐν Παρμενίδῃ I 192[4].
proverb:
 Zenobius 6,23: I 207[4].
Pythagoras: II 20[1].
Pythagoreans: I 368[9] 509[1] 559[1] II 51[8] 59[1,4] 155[1].
'symbol': I 101[6].

Speusippus frg. 55:: I 177[4].
Stoa: SVF II 104: I 280[7]. – II 846: I 276[2]. – II 1118: I 32[5]. – III 391: I 162[6]. – III 431: I 162[5].
Strato frg. 118: I 388[2]. – frg. 122: II 63. – frg. 123: I 431–442 444–448. – frg. 124: II 78[1,8,14]. – frg. 125: II 25[1]. – frg. 126: I 294[1]. – frg. 127: II 65.
Syrianus: I 172[2] 207[7] 208[2] 242[4] II 147[4]. – ὁ φιλόσοφος: I 209[1] 216[1] 243[title]; οἱ φιλόσοφοι (S. and Pr.): I 239[3]. – ὁ ἐξηγητής: I 222[2] (?) 235[1] 236[1] 237[1] 243[2]. – ἐκεῖνος ὁ ἀνήρ: I 208[8]. – 3rd ps. sg.: I 211[3].
monograph on Ph. 70c4–72e2: I 183–206.

Theodorus (of Asine): on Ph. 108c5–110b1 (test. 42): I 503[3] II 114[3].
Theophrastus: I 547[3].
Timaeus Locrus 95e1–96c3: I 382[1].

Xenocrates frg. 20: I 2[3]. – frg. 75: I 177[4].

INDEX II: VOCABULARY AND PROPER NAMES

ἀβέβαιος I 125².
'Αγάθαρχος I 294⁴.
ἀγαθοειδής II 30⁸.
ἀγαθόν (τό) I 24² 58³ 179⁵⁻¹⁰ 202³,⁵ 260⁴
　412⁵,⁷ 413¹,³ 414³ 417³ 475²,³ 516²,³
　II 9⁴ 55¹⁰ 72⁴; τἀγαθόν I 2²
　II 72⁴ 74² 91¹; (καλόν, σοφόν, ἀ.)
　I 41²,⁶; (δίκαιον, καλόν, ἀ.) I 96²,
　cf. 397; (plur.) I 545¹ II 27⁵ 154².
　ἀγαθώτατον I 516³.
ἀγαθοποιός I 29³.
ἀγαθότης I 29²,³ 40² 41¹² 150².
ἀγανάκτησις I 19⁴.
'Αγαύη I 378⁶.
ἄγγελος: 'angel' I 175³; 'messenger'
　I 90⁴.
ἀγελαῖος I 34⁴.
ἀγελάρχης I 479¹ 540⁵ II 147⁸.
ἀγένητος I 44³ 170⁸ 193¹ 204⁵ 206¹ 244²
　524³,⁴ 548⁴.
ἄγνοια I 78¹ 91² 257³ 276³ 277²;
　ἁπλῆ ἅ. 410³.
ἀγωγή 'education' I 75¹; 'method' 184¹.
ἄδεκτος I 373¹ 405²¹ 407⁶ 426² 431¹ 432¹
　434² 436² 437¹ 438¹ 439¹ 445⁴ 446³
　448² 452¹ II 75¹,⁷ 77²⁻⁷.
ἀδιαίρετος I 343³ II 30¹⁰.
ἀδιάκοπος I 253³ 548⁵.
ἀδιάκριτον (dist. διακρινόμενον,
　διακεκριμένον) I 420⁴.
ἀδιάλειπτος I 132⁴.
ἀδιάλυτος I 312⁸ 317¹ 330¹ 336¹
　II 30³,¹⁰ 31³ 34²⁻⁵,⁷ 41¹,⁴ 117²,⁶.
ἀδιάρθρωτος I 263² 264⁶ 280¹⁰
　II 24² 28¹⁸; (adv.) II 93².
ἀδιάστατος I 317².
ἀδιάστροφος II 46³.
ἀδρανής II 36¹¹.
ἀδυναμία I 179⁷ 402².
ἀειγενεσία I 229¹⁵ II 88².
ἀειδής I 483².
ἀείζως I 477¹ II 30⁸.
ἀέναος I 241²⁵.
'Αερία λίμνη II 145⁵.
ἀέριος I 479² II 96²,⁴ 145⁵.
ἀζωία I 52³.
ἀήρ I 122⁵ 222² 232⁸ 378⁷ 497⁴ 506²
　522¹²,¹⁴,¹⁵ 523⁴ 534² 541⁴
　II 128² 132⁸ 134² 137⁵ 138² 141² 145³.

ἀθανασία I 36³ 66¹ 118³ 176¹¹ 183⁴ 207⁵
　256¹ 311⁹ 393² 458^title II 3² 29⁸.
ἀθάνατος I 156³ 176² 183⁹ 193¹ 205¹ 206¹
　239¹¹ 242¹⁴ 244² 297³ 311¹,⁸ 312⁵ 314¹
　320¹ 329¹,² 330³ 378⁸,⁹ 426²,³ 427¹,² 552³
　II 30²,⁵,⁸ 31³ 78³.
ἄθερμος II 78³.
'Αθηνᾶ I 130⁴.
'Αθηναῖοι I 174¹.
ἄθροισμα I 4¹².
ἀθρόως II 26³.
Αἰακός II 99⁴.
αἰγόκερως II 124⁶.
Αἰγύπτιος γεωργός I 294⁴.
Αἴγυπτος I 507⁴.
"Αιδης I 27² 41⁷ 180¹,⁵ 181² 182³ 183⁵
　184² 309² 348³,⁴ 466³ 483¹,⁴ 491³ 495²,⁴
　II 93¹ 100¹⁻⁴ 105² 108¹.
ἀίδιος I 62⁵ 178⁴ 216³ 227²,⁴ 229¹,¹⁰,¹⁷
　230⁹ 241³⁵ 331⁴,⁵ 426³ 543²
　II 2¹¹,¹² 89² 106¹,⁴ 117⁶ 137²;
　(sup.) I 516⁹.
ἀιδιότης I 181².
αἰθέριος: (τόπος) I 499¹ II 100¹ 111¹. –
　See δαίμων.
αἰθερώδης I 528³.
αἰθήρ I 401¹ 481² 497¹ 506² 519³ 522¹³,¹⁴
　523³ 524¹ II 110¹ 126² 128⁵ 134²,³;
　(plur.) II 134⁴.
Αἰθίοψ II 137⁴.
αἴνιγμα I 165².
αἰνίττεσθαι II 129⁹.
αἵρεσις 'choice' I 151² 156⁸ 488²;
　'school' 207³.
αἱρετός I 158³; (comp.) 109⁴.
αἴσθησις I 63² 71⁵ 78³ 79¹ 80¹ 82¹,²
　83¹ 84¹ 85¹ 87²,⁵ 88³ 89² 90² 91⁴
　93¹ 94¹ 103¹ 112⁶ 120¹⁰ 125³ 242¹⁸ 263⁴
　264² 307² 321¹ 325³ 327² 332¹ 333³
　335¹ 368⁸ 387¹ 403³ 409³ 415³ 531¹
　II 14² 22² 32⁴ 37¹,⁵ 38³,⁷ 40¹ 51⁶,⁸
　56⁸ 112².
αἰσθητήριον I 89³.
αἰσθητικός I 108³.
αἰσθητός I 79² 88⁴ 89¹ 94²,⁴ 99¹ 103²
　154³ 242¹⁸ 263²,⁵ 264² 274¹¹,¹³ 294⁶
　304¹ 307¹ 325¹,⁵ 326² 332³ 415¹,²,⁵,⁸
　416²,¹¹,¹⁶ 537³ 538² II 11¹,² 14³,⁴,⁸
　15³,⁴ 28⁵ 37² 56⁸ 73¹ 133³.

αἶσχος I 91².
Αἰσχύλος I 495¹.
αἰτία: (ἡ μία) II 101²; (ποιητική, τελική) I 415¹ II 117¹,⁶; (ποιητική, ὑλική) II 64²⁴; ἀκίνητος I 229²,¹⁶ 339³. - I 229²⁰ 407⁵ 412² II 32⁸.
αἰτιατόν II 32⁸.
αἴτιον: (τὰ αἴ. τὰ δύο) I 420⁵; (ποιητικόν, τελικόν, παραδειγματικόν, εἰδικόν, ὑλικόν, ὀργανικόν) II 8-11 (cf. I 260); I 412¹ 413⁵; (πατρικὸν καὶ οὐσιῶδες, opp. θῆλυ καὶ προοδικόν) II 142³,⁵. - I 416²,¹¹ II 66¹,² 71¹,².
αἰώνιος I 314¹ II 29¹⁶ 35².
αἰώρα I 542².
ἀκάθαρτος I 122³ 123⁷ II 112¹.
ἀκηλίδωτος I 120⁴.
ἀκήρατος I 528².
ἀκίνητος I 229¹,¹⁶ 274¹⁰ 339⁴ 416¹⁰ 535⁵.
ἀκλινῶς I 132¹.
ἀκοσμεῖν I 498².
ἀκοσμία II 92².
ἀκραιφνής I 301⁶ 528².
ἀκριβολογεῖσθαι I 41¹¹.
ἀκριβοῦν I 274⁷.
ἄκρον (τὸ) I 168¹² 186³ 401¹ II 125⁵.
ἀκρότης I 537².
ἀκτίς I 530⁶.
ἀλεκτρυών I 285² 561¹ II 28¹³.
ἀλήθεια I 80¹,⁴ 81¹ 87⁴ 116² 172⁴ 176¹⁰ 182¹ 281¹ II 92¹.
'Αλκιβιάδης I 295².
ἄλλος I 154¹⁻³; ἐν ἄλλῳ 448⁹ 453¹ 460⁴.
ἄλλοτε ἄλλως ἔχον II 29¹⁶ 94¹,³.
ἀλλοτριονομεῖν II 152¹.
ἀλογία I 54⁴ 120⁷ 139⁴ 140² 149³ 177³ 293² 399⁴.
ἀλογιστία I 69⁴.
ἀλόγιστος I 412².
ἄλογος I 9¹ 69³ 87⁴ 164¹⁰ 217¹ 267⁴ 310² 380⁴ 388³ 500⁷ II 56⁹ 96⁴ 99⁵; ψυχή I 135⁵,⁶ 250² 406³ 539³ II 62¹,⁶ (αἱ τῶν ἀ. ψυχαί I 434¹); ζῷα I 199¹ 355¹⁰,¹⁴ 359³ II 97²; τὰ ἄ. I 267¹ 272¹ 356¹ 376¹,⁴ II 22¹ 54⁵, cf. 149⁵.
ἄλυτος II 36²,⁴⁻⁶.
ἀμαθής I 266⁵ 358⁴.
ἀμαθία I 267³ 358².
ἁμαρτωλός I 6².
ἀμέθοδος I 474².
ἀμερής I 112¹,⁶ 317¹ 382⁵ II 116⁷.
ἀμέριστος I 3¹ 46,¹² 78²,⁵ 90⁶ 112⁴ 120¹⁴ 166² 167⁶ 316¹ 317¹ 418³ II 150⁶.

ἄμεσος I 1⁸ 192¹,³; (adv.) II 15⁶.
ἀμεταβλησία I 465⁵.
ἀμετάβλητος I 39² 197⁹ 241³⁰ 465⁴ 468² II 15² 42¹ 94⁴.
ἀμετάβολος II 30¹².
ἀμεταμέλητος I 546⁴.
ἀμετρία I 404²,³ II 149¹¹.
ἀμιγής I 95² 104¹,².
᾿Αμοργος I 286³.
ἀμόρφωτος I 112¹.
ἀμυδροῦν I 47⁴.
ἀμύητος I 351².
ἀμφίβιος I 340⁶; II 143⁴.
ἀναβαίνειν ἐπί I 69⁴ II 109².
ἀναβίωσις II 1².
ἀναβιώσκειν (act.) I 61⁴.
ἀνάγειν I 45⁵ 129³ 130⁴ 168¹,⁹ 203² 274¹³ 327¹ 540⁵ 550⁶ II 101⁶ 110¹ 132⁷ 148³ 157⁴.
ἀνάγκη I 22¹,² 24¹; (classif.) 25¹.
ἀναγνωρισμός I 292¹.
ἀναγωγή I 41⁷ 123⁶ 529².
ἀναγωγία I 402².
ἀναγωγός I 41⁵ 547⁷ 559³ II 155⁴.
ἀνάδοσις I 539⁵.
ἀναθάλπειν I 534² II 141⁷.
ἀνάθαλψις I 535².
ἀναθεῖν I 552³.
ἀναίμακτος I 120⁴.
ἀναίνεσθαι I 416⁹.
ἀναιρεῖν (log.) I 205² 229¹⁸,¹⁹ 230³. - II 49².
ἀναίρεσις I 71⁴ 136³.
ἀναιρετικός I 462¹.
ἀναίτιος I 409⁴.
ἀνακαθαίρεσθαι I 63¹.
ἀνακάμπτειν I 227³ 234⁶,¹⁰ 252¹⁹ II 64⁶,¹⁵.
ἀνακινεῖν I 498⁵.
ἀνακόπτειν I 6²·
ἀνακυκλεῖσθαι I 227⁶ 228⁶.
ἀνακύκλησις I 213² 229¹⁷ 235³.
ἀνακωχή II 147²⁰.
ἀναλαμβάνειν (of knowledge) I 254² II 6⁴ 14¹¹,¹³.
ἀνάληψις I 253² 260³.
ἀναλογεῖν I 46³ 66² 160³ 167³ 257³ 541² II 135².
ἀναλογία I 151¹¹ 257¹¹ 522³ II 136³.
ἀνάλογον I 528⁴ 529⁸.
ἀναλύειν I 141³ II 141³.
ἀναμάρτητος I 551¹.
ἀναμιμνήσκειν I 82²; (pass.) 242¹⁸ 262²,⁴,⁸ 264⁸,¹⁰ 269¹,³ 271¹,⁴ 272² 273³

II 6³,⁵ 11² 12² 13²,⁴ 14¹¹⁻¹⁵,¹⁹ 65⁶.
ἀνάμνησις I 66² 102² 242¹⁶ 252⁴ 253¹,⁶ 254¹ 255¹ 258¹ 262ᵗⁱᵗˡᵉ,⁵,⁷,⁹ 265²,³ 266³,⁴ 269²,⁴ 273¹ 274¹⁴ 277² 279¹ 281² 284¹ 285⁷ 293¹ 294¹,⁶ 297¹ 332²,³ II 4¹,²,⁵ 5¹ 7¹ 8³ 13⁴,⁶ 14¹⁶,¹⁷ 16⁷ 17² 19² 20¹ 22¹ 23¹ 24¹ 25² 28¹ 65¹,⁵,⁸,¹¹.
ἀναμνηστικός II 26².
ἀναμνηστόν (τό) I 262⁸.
ἀναμοχλεύειν I 547⁸.
ἀνανεοῦσθαι I 272².
ἀνανέωσις I 253³ 255² 258²; II 4⁶.
ἀνανεωτικός II 4¹.
'Αναξαγόρας I 80² 412¹.
ἀναπέμπειν I 8⁷.
ἀναπνεῖν II 141⁴.
ἀναπνοή I 547¹¹.
ἀναποδισμός I 247⁹.
ἀναπολεῖν I 253⁵.
ἀναπόστατος I 486².
ἀναπτύσσειν I 165².
ἀναρμοστία I 370²,³ 373¹ 374²,⁴ 380² 383²,³ 394³ 405⁶,²¹ II 53²⁻⁴ 54³ 60².
ἀνάρτιος II 79¹,³.
ἀνασκευάζειν I 299² 361¹.
ἀναστέλλειν I 141³; II 155⁴.
ἀναστολή I 19⁵.
ἀναστροφὴ διαλεκτική I 390².
ἀνάτασις I 61¹ 121⁴.
ἀνατάττειν I 529³.
ἀνατείνεσθαι I 31² 74⁴ 87³ 123⁵ 151¹⁰ 481² 483³ 510² II 86² 153⁴.
ἀνατίθεσθαι I 215⁸.
ἀνατολή I 541³.
ἀνατρέπειν I 229¹⁵; II 101⁹.
ἀνατρέχειν: II 100⁶; ἀναδραμεῖν I 67⁴ 561⁴ II 73².
ἀναφαίρετος I 458⁶,⁷ 459⁵.
ἀναφέρειν (εἰς) I 274³ 277².
ἀναφεύγειν I 340⁷ 351².
ἀναφορά I 95³.
ἀναχεῖν I 175³.
ἀναχωρεῖν I 141² 552².
ἀνδραποδώδης: see ἀρεταί.
ἀνδρεία I 140³ 149⁹ 152¹ 153¹ 157³,⁴ 158³ 159¹ 160² 371³ 372³,⁵ II 55¹.
ἀνδρεΐζεσθαι I 160¹,².
ἀνέλιξις I 15¹.
ἀνελίττειν I 14²; (pass.) 217².
ἀνεννόητος I 279².
ἀνεπισκεψία I 262⁶.
ἀνεπιστημοσύνη I 275².
ἀνεπιτήδειος I 120⁶ 453² 501².
ἄνεσις (opp. ἐπίτασις) I 368⁵,¹² II 51⁶.

ἄνευ: τὰ οὐκ ἄ. I 113³.
ἀνήμερος II 90⁴·
ἀνθρώπειος II 38⁶ 97⁶.
ἀνθρώπινος I 19¹ 44³ 45³ 249⁷ 319¹ 320² 359¹ 391⁴ 414¹,⁴ 468¹,⁴ 523¹ II 30⁴.
ἀνθρωποποιὸς θεός II 136³.
ἀνίατος I 545² 546³ II 147¹.
ἀνιέναι (ἄνειμι) I 540⁸,¹¹; ἀνελθεῖν 540¹⁰.
ἀνιέναι (ἀνίημι) I 368⁶.
ἄνοδος I 41³ 168⁸,¹³ 204² 252²⁰ 480⁴ 493² II 97⁸,⁹.
ἀνόητος I 312⁶ 315²; II 30⁵,⁹ 32⁷.
ἄνοια I 31².
ἀνομοιομερής I 518³.
ἄνοσος II 137¹,³.
ἀντακολουθεῖν I 140⁵.
ἀντανισοῦν I 241²⁴.
ἀνταποδιδόναι I 186⁷.
ἀνταπόδοσις I 228⁵ II 64²⁶.
ἀντιδιαιρεῖν I 222⁷ 257¹ 319² 508³.
ἀντίθεσις I 541³ 542¹; σύν ἀ. ἀντιστρέφειν 136².
ἀντιθέτως II 140².
ἀντικαταλλάττειν I 164⁷.
ἀντικεῖσθαι I 98² 145²; ἀντικείμενος I 460³ 500¹ II 139⁴; τὸ ἀ. I 315¹ 445⁴ 453³; τὰ ἀ. I 26¹ 191² II 30⁴ 67².
ἀντιλαμβάνεσθαι I 357² II 56⁸.
ἀντίληψις I 112⁶ 257⁷ II 4³.
ἀντιμετάδοσις II 69⁴.
ἀντιπαρήκειν I 144².
ἀντίποδες II 139⁸.
ἀντιστρέφειν (log.) I 136² 176² 474⁵.
ἀντιστροφή I 136³.
ἀντίστροφος I 142⁴ 298² 548²; (adv.) I 143³ 351³.
ἀντιταλάντωσις I 542².
ἀντιτείνειν I 498³,⁶ 546².
ἀντίφραξις I 539⁶.
ἀνυμνεῖν I 129⁴ 348¹.
ἄνω I 492³ II 107¹ 110² 113³ 150⁶.
ἄνωθεν I 127³.
ἀνώλεθρος I 198² 426³ 427¹,² 430² 458⁶,⁷ 459³,⁴ II 64²².
ἀνώνυμος I 255² 257³.
ἀνώρροπος II 156².
ἀξίωμα I 202¹ 339² II 44².
ἀόρατος I 325² 326¹ 333¹ 338³ II 29⁶ 32²,³ 33² 38⁵.
ἀοριστία I 55³ 416⁶.
ἀόριστος I 412³ 415²; (adv.) II 97⁷.
ἀπαγγέλλειν I 222⁷ (cj.).
ἀπάγειν (εἰς ἄτοπον) I 406¹.
ἀπαθανατίζειν I 177².

ἀπάθεια I 157⁴.
ἀπαθής I 88¹ 495³ 543² II 130³.
ἀπαίδευτος I 154¹ 310¹.
ἀπαιτεῖν I 212¹ 249⁴; (med.) 226⁶.
ἀπαξιοῦν 'demand' (?) I 15⁷.
ἀπαράλλακτος I 318³.
ἀπαρτᾶν: ἀπηρτῆσθαι I 1⁸.
ἀπειράκις I 228² 252¹⁸.
ἀπειροειδής I 396⁵.
ἄπειρος I 183⁶ 198⁴ II 27² 36⁸,¹⁰ 88³⁻⁵;
 (ἐπ' ἄπειρον) I 217³ 242¹² 297² 380⁹
 418⁴; II 2⁸ 69³ 106³, cf. I 252¹³.
ἀπεκλεκτικός I 149¹¹.
ἀπελέγχειν I 118².
ἀπεμφαίνειν II 129⁶.
ἀπερίληπτος II 88⁴.
ἀπλανής (ἡ) II 131⁵; τὸ ἀπλανές I 497³.
ἀπλήθυντος I 340¹; II 30¹⁰.
ἄπληκτος: ἀπληκτότεραι πρὸς ἐπιστασίαν
 I 270³.
ἁπλοῦς I 167⁷ 178⁷ 316¹ 407⁷⁻⁹ 423² 428¹
 II 76²,³,⁶; (comp.) I 516⁴.
ἁπλῶς I 98¹,³ 190¹ 191² 192³,⁵ 222⁸ 241⁴
 320¹ 368¹⁷ II 75¹⁰ 91².
ἀποβολή I 255³ 258² II 78⁷,¹⁵,¹⁸.
ἀπογίγνεσθαι I 225² 226² 232³ 239³ 241⁵.
ἀποδεικτικός I 1¹ II 25².
ἀπόδειξις I 14² 58¹ 82¹ 112⁵ 120¹³ 176¹²
 208⁴ 215³ 216³ 247²,¹⁰ 262¹⁰ 294²
 301²,⁵ 309⁴ 311⁷ 411² 458^title
 II 25¹,⁴,⁵ 29⁵ 77¹ 130¹,⁶.
ἀποδημία I 558².
ἀποδιακρίνειν I 147¹.
ἀποδιδόναι: (τὸν λόγον) I 277¹;
 (τὸν κύκλον) I 236².
ἀπόδοσις I 15⁸ 410¹ 412².
ἀποδοτικός I 409⁴.
ἀπόδρασις I 12⁴.
ἀποδύειν I 111⁴; (med.) I 108⁶ 111⁴.
ἀπόζευξις I 235⁵.
ἄποιος: τὸ ἄ. σῶμα I 249⁸ II 64¹².
ἀποίχεσθαι: οἱ ἀποιχόμενοι II 108¹⁰ 150¹.
ἀποκαθαίρειν I 77¹ 116² 348⁵ II 150⁴.
ἀποκαθίστασθαι I 548¹ 551⁴.
ἀποκάμνειν I 79¹.
ἀποκατάστασις I 239⁴ II 88⁶.
ἀποκληροῦν I 467¹.
ἀποκληρωτικός II 16¹⁰.
ἀποκόπτειν I 120⁷.
ἀποκορυφοῦσθαι I 2⁴.
Ἀπόλλων I 14⁵,⁷ 129³ 130³ 539⁷ II 142⁷.
Ἀπολλωνιακός I 360¹.
ἀπολογίζεσθαι I 533⁷.
ἀπολογισμός I 237².

ἀπόνευσις I 127⁸.
ἀποπέμπειν (med.) I 486³; (pass.) II 92³.
ἀποπιστεύειν I 395².
ἀποπληροῦν I 491².
ἀποπληρωτής II 105².
ἀποπνεῖν ἀπὸ τῆς οὐσίας II 17⁸.
ἀπορητικός I 397⁴.
ἀπορρεῖν I 229⁴ II 127².
ἀπόρρησις I 390⁴.
ἀπόρρητος I 1³,⁴ 14² 15¹,⁴ 28² 165²,⁶,⁷
 168¹⁴ 172⁷; (comp.) 167²,⁵.
ἀπορροή I 530².
ἀπόρροια I 527⁶ II 133².
ἀποσκευάζεσθαι I 120².
ἀπόστασις I 143² 157⁴ 257⁷,¹¹.
ἀποστενοῦν I 8² 23³ 166³ 171⁵.
ἀποστρέφειν I 123⁴ 149⁹; (pass.) 31³.
ἀποσῴζειν I 249³.
ἀποτείνεσθαι I 99¹ II 35⁵.
ἀποτελεῖν I 228⁴.
ἀποτρίβειν (med.) I 348⁴; (pass.) 62³.
ἀπουσία I 251⁵.
ἀπόφασις I 257³,⁴ 433¹ 444³.
ἀποφάσκειν I 362².
ἀποφοιτᾶν I 19⁶.
ἀπροβούλευτος II 88⁴.
ἁπτικός I 531⁵.
ἁπτός I 531⁴.
ἀργεῖν I 484³ II 101⁴,⁷.
Ἀρεϊκός II 133².
ἀρετή I 31⁷ 33¹ 40² 50¹ 150¹,³,⁵
 151¹,²,⁴,⁵,¹¹,¹² 156⁴ 161² 164¹¹ 255² 348²
 370² 372¹ 374¹,³ 380²,⁶ 396⁶ 405⁵ 406⁴
 555³ 556¹,² II 53¹,² 54²,³ 55⁹,¹⁰ 60¹
 92¹ 94⁴ 147¹². – φυσικαί I 138¹ 147⁴;
 ἠθικαί 139¹ 147⁴ 167³; πολιτικαί 140¹
 142⁵ 147⁴ 164⁴,⁷ 167⁴, cf. 157³;
 καθαρτικαί 141¹ 147² 148² 151⁵ 157⁶
 164²,⁸,¹⁰ 167⁴, cf. 157⁴; θεωρητικαί 142¹;
 παραδειγματικαί 143¹, ἱερατικαί 144¹;
 ἀνδραποδώδεις 145²; ψευδώνυμοι 147³
 163¹; τέλειαι, ἀτελεῖς 162¹,² 164¹.
Ἄρης I 377².
ἄρθρον (gramm.) I 164¹¹.
ἀριθμός: (opp. μονάς) I 4² 15⁴; κατὰ
 ἀριθμόν 'arithmetical(ly)' I 494²;
 II 51⁹; ἀριθμῷ, κατ' ἀριθμόν of
 numerical identity (opp. κατ' εἶδος)
 I 198⁴ 201¹,⁴ 202⁴ 212²,³ 226² 227⁴
 228²,⁴ 229¹¹,¹³ 230⁸ 235⁴ 238³ 242¹¹ 252¹²
 II 2¹² 63⁷ 64¹¹,²⁵,²⁷ 101⁵.
Ἀριστοξένειοι I 368⁹.
Ἀριστοτέλης I 72² 79¹ 176² 192⁵ 383¹
 416¹⁰ 521¹ 530⁶ II 18¹ 123⁴ 138¹.

Ἀρκεσίλαος I 275[1].
ἄρκτος 'north' I 541[6].
ἁρμονία I 183[7] 221[3] 223[2,3] 361[title,2,6]
 362[2,3] 363[1,2] 364[3] 367[5] 368[1,5,6,10]
 370[2,3,6] 371[1] 372[8] 373[1-3] 374[2-4] 375[1,3]
 376[2-4] 377[2,3,5,6] 380[1-4,6,7] 381[1,2] 382[1,9]
 383[2,3] 384[2] 385[1] 387[1,3] 388[1]
 405[5,7,10,11,14,15,19,21] II 45[2-4,7] 46[2] 47[2,3]
 50[2,3] 51[2,4,6,9] 52[3] 53[2-5] 54[2,5] 55[1,7,11]
 56[1,3,11] 57[4] 59[1,4,7] 60[1,2,4] 61[1] 62[1,4].
Ἁρμονία I 377[1] 378[2] II 57[1].
ἁρμονικός: (λόγος) I 368[8] 372[8];
 II 51[7] 57[4] 60[4]; (σύγκρασις) I 382[6].
ἁρμοστικός I 372[9].
Ἁρποκρατίων I 110[2] 137[4,12] 147[3] 149[6]
 164[4] 182[2] 503[2].
ἀρρεπής I 149[9].
ἄρρητος I 15[2] 416[4].
ἀρτᾶν: ἠρτῆσθαι I 206[3] 469[1].
ἀρχέτυπον I 88[5].
ἀρχή I 74[4,6] 82[1,2,4] 168[2] 229[3] 407[2] 410[3]
 561[4]; II 74[5]; ἡ μία ἀ. I 420[7], cf. 516[5].
 – τὰ ἐν ἀ. II 2[14].
ἀρχικός: (ref. ruler) I 339[2]; II 32[7] 44[1];
 (ref. principle) τῶν τριῶν ἀ. ὑποστάσεων
 I 202[5].
ἄσβεστος: (ζωή) I 433[2]; (πῦρ)
 I 535[2] 536[2].
Ἀσία II 139[8].
Ἀσκληπιός I 561[1]; II 157[1].
ἀσκός I 183[8] 185[3] 190[6] 209[5] 215[6] 218[7]
 223[1] 232[8].
ἀσμενίζειν I 498[2].
ἀστήρ I 509[1] 522[21].
ἀστραπή I 390[3].
ἄστρον I 524[1,2] II 128[1].
ἀστρονόμοι (οἱ) I 513[2].
ἀσύγχυτος I 371[5] 489[2] 490[2] II 55[4].
ἀσυνθεσία I 340[6].
ἀσύνθετος I 311[3] 340[1,3,6,7] 341[3] II 29[6].
ἀσώματος I 64[1-3] 97[3] 98[2] 112[4,5] 194[1,2]
 204[3,4] 222[4,6,11] 245[2] 252[9] 311[1,3] 503[1,3]
 505[1] 528[6] 544[2] II 29[5] 80[6] 114[1,2] 133[3].
ἄτακτος I 382[3] II 142[2,6].
ἀταλαίπωρος I 395[2].
ἀταξία I 149[2] 151[4] 539[6] II 142[3,4].
ἀτελής I 94[3] 162[1] 163[2] 226[5] II 27[2];
 (comp.) I 176[4].
Ἀτλαντικός: (λόγος) I 507[3].
Ἀτλαντίς I 507[4] 522[6] II 125[1].
Ἄτλας II 72[1].
ἀτμίς II 134[2].
ἄτομος I 112[2]; τὸ ἄ. I 7[4] 229[6] 409[4]
 II 5[1] 14[6].

ἄτοπος I 35[2] 230[2] 241[28] 409[2] II 101[6];
 (comp.) I 409[2] II 148[5]. – εἰς ἅ. ἀπάγειν
 I 406[1]; ὅπερ ἅ. II 78[27].
Ἀττικός (Platonist) I 100[3].
Ἀττικός (adj.): οἱ Ἀ. ἐξηγηταί
 I 110[4] 164[1]; πάτρια Ἀ. II 150[1].
ἀτυχής 'failing to attain' I 81[1].
αὐγοειδής: (χιτών) I 168[7]; (σῶμα)
 508[7] 551[3] II 115[7]; (ὄχημα)
 II 135[3] 141[5]; τὸ αὐ. I 527[4] II 38[4].
αὐθαίρετος I 487[2] II 149[9].
αὐθυπόστατος II 70[2].
ἄυλος I 93[2] 94[3] 229[5] II 67[3].
αὔξησις I 247[11].
ἄυπνος II 138[1].
αὐτάρκης I 343[2] 487[2].
αὐτεξούσιος I 9[3] 23[1,4] II 101[7].
αὐτοαρμονία II 61[3].
αὐτοβοήθητος I 547[9].
αὐτογνῶσις I 78[2].
αὐτόγονος I 229[5].
αὐτοδίδακτος I 294[3] II 28[9].
αὐτοθερμόν (τὸ) II 76[3].
αὐτοῖσον (τὸ) I 302[2].
αὐτοκίνητος I 21[1] 169[5] 274[8,10] 498[5]
 II 102[2] 147[15]; (adv.) II 151[4].
αὐτόματος II 149[3]; ἀπὸ ταὐτομάτου
 I 388[5].
Αὐτονόη I 378[7].
αὐτόπιστος II 74[4].
αὐτοπραγία II 86[2].
αὐτοπτεῖν I 391[1].
αὐτοπτικός I 392[3].
αὐτός: τὸ ἑαυτὸ τοῖς εἴδεσιν ἐπικείμενον
 I 95[1].
αὐτοφανής I 500[4].
αὐτοφρόνησις II 39[2].
αὐτοφυής II 149[10]; (adv.) I 134[2].
αὐτοφία I 167[2].
αὐτοψυχρόν (τὸ) II 76[3].
ἀφαίρεσις I 274[5] II 28[16].
ἀφαιρετός II 27[4].
ἀφανής I 34[2] 358[2] 500[5]; τοῦ ἀεὶ πρὸς
 ἡμᾶς ἀφανοῦς II 124[6].
ἀφανίζειν I 416[6].
ἄφεσις I 12[4] II 147[19].
ἁφή I 88[2].
ἀφθαρσία I 256[1].
ἄφθαρτος I 249[8] 437[1] 463[4].
ἀφιλόσοφος I 104[3].
ἄφοδος I 226[4].
ἀφομοιοῦσθαι II 35[2].
ἀφομοίωσις I 303[3] 334[3] 338[5] II 9[1].
ἀφορίζεσθαι I 181[1].

ἀφορμή I 295² 311² 325¹.
ἀφροδισιασμός I 69³.
ἀφροδίσια I 69⁸.
'Αφροδίτη I 377³.
ἀφωρισμένως I 451² 480².
'Αχερουσιὰς λίμνη II 148²,⁸.
'Αχερούσιος: (τόπος) I 544¹; (–σία λίμνη) I 546⁴ II 145⁵.
'Αχέρων I 497³ 541⁴ 546⁴ II 145³,⁵,⁸,¹².
ἄχραντος: (ψυχαί) I 529⁷ II 6⁴ 97³.
ἀχώριστος I 93² 176⁴ 178¹ 183⁷ 187² 188² 376³ 377⁶ 388⁴ 407⁸ 409⁵ 421² 428¹ 533⁶ II 29² 62² 75⁵ 76⁷; (adv.) II 62⁷.
ἄψυκτος I 442¹.
ἄψυχος I 222⁹ 229⁷ 482² II 2¹⁷,¹⁸ 99⁵.

βαθμός I 67¹ 76⁴ 80⁴ 168⁷ 395⁴.
βάθος (depth of descent) I 480⁵ II 145¹¹; (of problem) I 34².
βαθύνειν (intr.) I 356².
Βάκχαι (αἱ τέτταρες) I 378³.
Βάκχος I 171¹ 172⁵,⁷; (plur.) 166⁵.
βάναυσος I 356².
βάρος 'burden of soul' II 148⁹.
βαρύνειν I 123⁵ 520² 559⁵.
βασιλεύς (of Gods) I 4⁵ 14³,⁶.
βάσις: 'step' I 171¹; 'feet' 540².
βεβαιοῦσθαι II 109².
βέβηλος I 15⁹.
βιαιοθάνατος II 151².
βιοθάνατος II 108¹¹.
βίος I 74² 115¹ 168⁹ 308⁵ 355⁸ 484³,⁴ 485² 488²,³ 491² II 82² 87¹ 88¹ 97⁹,¹⁰ 1014,⁸ 103³ 105¹,³.
Βίων I 293¹ II 24¹.
βολή 'attack' I 207³.
βόρβορος I 168¹⁰ 522²⁸ II 150⁵.
βούλεσθαι 'tend to', 'be naturally disposed to' I 151⁴ 253³ 256⁹ 382⁹ 412⁴.
βούλησις I 25³ 397³ II 36²,⁷.
βρίθειν (κάτω) I 521².
βρύειν ζωήν: I 459⁴.

γαλῆ I 285¹ II 28¹².
γειτονεῖν I 519².
γενεσιουργός I 11⁹,¹⁰ 559⁴.
γένεσις I 42⁴ 44² 67² 115¹,³ 120¹² 121² 130¹,² 141⁴ 149⁵ 168¹¹ 170⁷,⁸ 172⁵ 182³ 186²⁻⁶ 192²,⁴ 193⁴ 194⁴ 195³ 197²,⁹ 201² 205² 206² 207¹⁵ 210² 213⁷ 216² 217³ 227⁸ 229¹,⁴,¹⁴ 230² 232¹⁰ 234¹⁵ 241¹⁴,²³,²⁵ 242⁷ 247¹⁰ 264⁹,¹²,¹⁵ 265⁴ 266¹,⁴,⁵ 286² 294⁵ 306² 308¹ 309³ 328² 348² 358³ 407¹ 416⁶,¹²,¹⁴ 437¹ 445² 461⁵ 470¹,² 483⁴ 491⁵ 523¹ 530⁴ 540²,⁶ 548⁴ 561² II 14¹⁷⁻¹⁹ 174,⁶ 19³ 30¹,⁴ 32²,⁵,⁶,⁸ 63¹³ 64²⁴ 71² 150⁴.
γενητός I 193¹ 219³ 239⁵ 244² 247⁷ 338⁵ 524²,⁴ II 30⁷ 32³ 36¹² 38⁶ 89¹.
γενικῶς II 23¹.
γεννᾶν I 409³ II 78¹¹; γεννῶν, γεννώμενον I 229⁶.
γέννημα I 378⁶ 411⁷.
γεννητικός I 416¹² 462¹.
γένος I 48¹ 113³ 158³; (men, demons, Gods) I 122² 355⁸ 404⁶ 477¹ 478⁶ 530⁵ II 94²,⁵ 95¹⁻³ 97²,⁶.
γενούστης I 413².
γεῦσις I 531⁶.
γεωγράφοι (οἱ) I 504² 522²⁹ II 124².
γεώδης I 197⁶,⁸ II 110⁴.
γῆ (Γῆ) I 378⁶ 481¹ 497⁴ 503¹ 507¹ 508¹,³⁻⁵,⁷ 509¹,³,⁴ 512¹ 513¹ 517⁵ 518⁶ 519²,³ 520¹ 522¹,¹⁹,²²,²⁶,²⁷ 523²,⁴,⁶ 524³,⁴ 528¹ 532² 534⁴ 536¹ 539¹ 541⁴ 542³ II 100² 114¹,⁴ 115¹,³,⁶ 116¹ 118³ 119¹,² 124¹ 125¹ 126¹ 129²,³ 131¹,²,⁶⁻⁸ 132²,⁶,⁷ 134¹ 139⁴ 142¹ 145³.
γίγνεσθαι: τὰ γιγνόμενα I 218² 312²,³ 319¹.
γνωρισμός I 253⁵ II 5¹.
γνῶσις: (classif.) I 80⁵ 259¹,³ 273¹ II 23¹. – I 78³ 81²,³ 87⁴ 88³ 90⁵ 91¹,⁴ 94¹ 108⁴ 112¹ 253⁴,⁶ 262⁴ 264³,⁵,⁷ 266⁵ 269⁴,⁶ 276² 277² 371⁶ II 4² 9⁴ 36¹¹ 40² 92¹. – (opp. ζωή) I 256² 257¹,⁴ II 33³; (opp. ὄρεξις) I 111² 388³ 396⁴ 412⁷ 498¹ 562².
γνωστικός I 11³ 314,⁶ 404 78⁴ 92⁴ 140³ 253¹ 254¹ 255² 271³ 325⁵ 371⁶ 396² II 4¹ 8³ 56⁷; (adv.) I 77¹ 142².
γνωστόν (τὸ) I 88³ 253²,⁵ 254² 257⁷ 371⁶ II 4³; (plur.) I 80⁵ 88⁴ 94¹.
Γοργίας (dial.): I 61³ 179⁶ 417⁶ 471² II 85⁴.
γραμμή: κατὰ τὴν ἐν Πολιτείᾳ γ. διῃρημένην I 80⁵.
γωνία II 117³.

δαιμόνιος I 60³ 123⁴ 359¹ 468¹,³ 477¹ 542³ 549¹ 550⁵ II 94⁵ 95² 110⁴ 147¹⁸ 148⁷; τὸ δ. II 97⁵.
δαίμων I 73³ 175³ 260² 550⁴. – εἰληχότες I 480¹,⁴ 491¹,⁵ II 97⁷ 98¹ 112³,⁶, cf. I 484¹,³,⁶ 485¹⁻³ 488¹,² 491³ 495⁶ II 97¹,⁹ 101¹,⁴,⁸ 102² 103¹,²,⁴ 105³ 110³. – θεῖοι, νοεροί, ψυχικοί, φυσικοί, σωματικοί, ὕλης ἔφοροι I 478; ἑνιαῖον καὶ θεῖον, νοερόν, λογικόν, φυσικόν,

σωματοειδές, ύλαῖον γένος II 95; θείοι
II 97[11], νοεροί I 480[2] II 97[1,11], ψυχικοί
II 97[2]. - ούράνιοι, αιθέριοι, αέριοι,
ύδραῖοι, χθόνιοι, ύποχθόνιοι I 479 II 96,
αιθέριοι I 480[2] II 98[1]. - ἔνυλοι
I 46[2] 47[2] 122[3]; ἄλογοι II 96[4] 99[5];
φιλοσώματοι καὶ ζωῇ χαίροντες
γενεσιουργῷ I 559[3], cf. II 152[4] 155[3];
φθονεροὶ καὶ βάσκανοι I 404[3]; πονηροί
I 123[8]; ὁ μὲν ἀγαθός, ὁ δὲ κακός I 486[1].
δάνεισμα I 16[3].
δεκτικός I 226[1] 230[12] 251[5] 369[2] 370[2,3]
373[2] 378[9] 433[2] 448[5-7] 451[1] 453[1] 457[1,2]
458[2] II 52[2] 53[2,3] 54[2-4] 75[9] 78[2,22,23].
δεσμός I 7[2] 10[2,3] 16[4] 128[6] 141[3] 171[4]
II 36[6,8] 43[3].
δεσπόζειν I 337[2] 338[2].
δεσπότης I 32[1,4,6].
δεσποτικός I 311[3] II 29[7]; (comp.)
I 339[4].
δεύτερος: τὰ δ. I 29[1] 62[2] 74[3,7] II 125[5];
δ. πρόνοια I 19[6]; δ. ψυχή II 6[3].
δήλωμα I 126[4].
Δημάρατος I 278[2].
Δημήτηρ I 130[5] II 108[8].
Δημήτριος I 286[3].
δημιουργεῖν I 217[4] II 117[4].
δημιούργημα I 8[3] II 136[1].
δημιουργία I 3[1] 5[1] 151[6] 170[1] II 142[3].
δημιουργικός I 3[4] 126[6] 151[5] 537[4]
II 72[6] 140[5].
δημιουργός I 2[3] 8[3] 151[6] 516[9] 540[1]
II 117[6] 136[2] 142[4].
Δημόκριτος I 503[3].
διάγνωσις I 398[2].
διαγωγή I 529[8] II 82[1].
διαδοχή I 241[21].
διαζευγνύναι I 230[13] 232[14] 241[5,10] 242[9]
248[8] 257[12].
διάζευξις I 218[6] 230[13].
διαζωγραφεῖν I 527[2].
διάθεσις I 122[1] II 33[7] 39[3].
διαιρεῖν I 14[7] 229[6] 411[8] II 68[12].
διαίρεσις I 14[8] 118[1] 120[14] 183[7] 411[6,8] 505[4]
II 65[9] 96[2] 131[1,6,8] 149[9].
διαιρετικός I 6[1] 7[3,5].
διακαθαίρειν II 66[2].
διακόπτειν I 90[5].
διακοπτικός I 127[6].
διακορής I 343[2].
διακόσμησις II 142[5].
διάκοσμος I 537[4] II 140[3].
διακρατεῖν I 337[4].
διακρίνεσθαι I 185[3,4] 199[2] 209[3] 210[1,3].

213[8] 214[2,5,7,9] 232[3] 238[2] 413[2] 420[3] (cj.)
II 2[9] 64[2,3,14,20]; (perf.) I 4[13] 185[4] 420[3].
διάκρισις I 62[1] 209[2,6] 210[2] 217[5] 331[7]
420[6] 489[2] II 78[23].
διακριτικός I 371[5] II 55[3] 72[1].
διάλειψις I 547[12].
διαλεκτική I 395[5].
διαλεκτικός I 99[3] 165[1] 389[3] 390[3,4] 391[2];
(adv.) 390[1].
διάλογος I 41[2] 46[4] II 81[1] 82[1].
διαλύειν II 149[13]; (pass.) I 127[5] 317[2]
323[1] II 29[3].
διάλυσις I 127[4,8] 210[4] 242[16] II 149[7].
διαλυτός I 312[8] 323[1] II 30[5] 31[2].
διάμετρος I 533[3] II 139[3,6].
διαμονή II 43[4,5].
διανοεῖσθαι II 37[3].
διανοητικός I 273[2] II 23[2] 29[7] 86[4].
διανοητός I 167[5] 332[2,3] 346[2] 349[2] 415[7,8]
II 11[2] 35[3] 37[2] 86[4].
διάνοια I 99[2] 103[3] 120[13] 387[2] 403[3] 472[2]
II 37[5].
διανομὴ τῶν ψυχῶν II 84[3].
διαπνεῖσθαι I 209[6] II 1[2].
διαπταίειν I 27[1].
διαρθροῦν: διηρθρωμένος I 264[3,5,7] 280[9]. –
Cf. διηρθρωμένως.
διάρθρωσις II 25[4].
διαρρέον (τὸ) I 190[8] 372[6].
διαρρήδην I 241[28].
διασπᾶν I 4[11] 9[5] 170[3] 358[3] 378[6] 382[8].
διασπασμός I 90[5] 344[4].
διάστασις I 257[11].
διάστημα (mus.) I 368[3].
διαστηματικός II 15[8].
διάταξις I 207[title].
διάττειν I 524[2].
διαυγής II 125[7].
διαφορά (είδοποιός) I 248[3].
διαφορότης I 480[5].
διαχαίνειν I 351[4].
διδασκαλικός I 37[2].
διδόναι (log.) I 185[1] II 64[3].
διεξοδικός I 87[1].
διέξοδος I 389[3].
διήκειν II 119[4].
δίηξις I 178[6].
διηρθρωμένως II 14[3].
Δίος I 168[4] 483[5] II 140[5].
διϊστάναι: διέστηκε αὐτὸ πρὸς ἑαυτό I 344[4].
δικάζειν: οἱ δικάζοντες II 85[1,4];
οἱ δικαζόμενοι I 471[3] II 85[2,5].
δικαιοπραγία I 472[2].
δικαιοσύνη I 36[2] 112[3] 140[4] 149[10] 152[3]

159⁴ 163¹ 371⁴ II 55³,⁴,⁶ 86¹,⁴.
δικαιωτήριον I 401².
δικαστήριον II 99¹,⁴.
δικαστής I 481¹ 483³,⁶ 491¹,³ 499²
II 90³ 105¹,² 111².
δικαστικός I 481⁴ 482¹ 489² 491³
II 100¹ 110⁷.
δίκη I 354² 355¹³ 490¹ 498² 529⁴ II 148⁸.
Δίκη I 467² 482¹ II 99².
δίνη τοῦ ζῴου I 288⁴.
δῖνος II 72⁶.
διοικεῖν I 484³ 487² 500⁷ 545⁶ II 97³,⁵.
διοίκησις I 480⁴ 549¹.
Διονυσιακός I 4¹² 5² 12³ 14⁷ 166² 378²,⁵;
(adv.) 130¹ 171⁴.
Διονυσοδότης (Apollo) I 129⁴.
Διόνυσος I 2⁴ 3² 4²,⁶ 5¹ 9⁵,⁷ 10¹ 11¹,¹⁰
14⁴,⁶ 129²,⁴ 166⁶ 168² 170⁴ 171¹,³ II 8².
διοπτεύειν I 389².
διορίζεσθαι I 27¹ 183² 193³ 207¹⁰ 213¹
220³ 223⁴ 228³ II 64²; (pass.) I 231¹.
διορισμός I 448¹.
διοριστικός II 145¹².
δίοψις I 390³.
διχόθεν I 173².
δόγμα I 103³ 155¹ 547² II 109².
δόξα I 99¹,² 103¹ 120¹¹ 125¹ 174⁴ 177⁶
355¹¹ 377⁵ 387² 412³ 414² 415³ II 16¹³.
δοξάζειν I 156³.
δοξαστικός I 273² 392² II 23² 86³.
δοξαστός II 86³.
δρᾶν I 268³.
δραστικός (sup.) II 147⁷.
δυάς I 411⁹ II 68¹³.
δύναμις 'power' I 7⁵,⁷ 27³ 179⁷ 180¹
227⁹ 252²² 443² 484⁶ 544¹,³
II 36⁹,¹⁰ 110³ 148⁹ 149³; ὕπαρξις, δ.,
νοῦς I 180³, cf. 202⁵ II 142⁵; οὐσία,
δ., ἐνέργια I 180⁴; 'faculty'
I 89² 253¹ 255¹ 271¹ 325⁴ 333⁴
II 26² 56⁷; 'sense' I 263¹. – δυνάμει
I 210⁴ 280⁴,⁵,⁷ II 10² 16¹³; εἰς δ.
I 229¹⁰.
δυσαφαίρετος I 111¹.
δυσίατος I 546².
δύσις I 541⁴.
δυσκίνητος I 197⁷ 222⁴ 534²; (comp.)
396³.
δυσκρασία I 138³.
δύσχρηστος I 120⁵.
δωδεκάεδρον I 527² II 132¹,⁶,¹⁰;
-ος II 132⁶.
δωδεκάμορφος I 527⁷.
δωδεκάσκυτος I 527¹.

ἑβδομάς I 288².
ἐγγίγνεσθαι I 239² 352² 359³.
ἐγκαταδεῖν I 130².
ἐγκαταμένειν I 335³.
ἐγκάειν I 348⁴.
ἐγκέφαλος I 92².
ἐγκόσμιος I 478¹ 508⁵ II 95¹.
ἐθισμός I 139¹.
εἰδητικός I 417³.
εἰδικός II 9³.
εἰδοποιεῖν I 46⁴ 152² 340⁸ 355⁵ 372⁴
485⁴ 522¹⁸ II 30² 75¹⁰.
εἰδοποιός I 89² 248³.
εἶδος: 'kind' I 75³ 234¹⁴ 273¹ 312¹ 355¹
401³ 494³ 547¹¹ 548⁴ II 86³ 103³ 137²;
εἴδει (opp. ἀριθμῷ) I 227³ 228⁵;
κατ' εἶδος (opp. κατ' ἀριθμόν)
I 199⁶ 201²,³ 202⁴ 212⁵ 218¹ 227⁶ 228¹
230⁴ 240³,⁵ 241¹⁴ 252¹² II 2¹² 63⁷,¹³
64²⁷ 101⁴. – 'form' I 4⁹ 9⁶ 10⁵ 46¹
53²,⁵ 59⁸ 74⁵ 95¹ 96¹ 98³ 128³ 176⁸
194⁵ 228¹ 229⁴,⁵ 241¹⁰ 242⁷ 246³,⁴
274⁹ 301¹ 330¹ 337²⁻⁴ 338⁴ 343¹
368⁵,¹²,¹⁴ 407⁵ 411²,⁵,⁸ 416¹²,¹³ 418¹
419³ 447¹,⁴,⁶ 455² 456² 461¹⁻³ 464³,⁴
466³ 485³ II 14³⁻⁵,⁸,¹⁰ 17⁷ 21¹,² 30⁵
42¹,⁴ 55¹⁰ 68⁷,¹⁰ 75²,⁷,¹⁰,¹¹ 76¹ 80⁹ 115⁵;
κοινά, ὑστερογενῆ, χωριστά (ψυχικά,
νοητά) II 15; νοητά, διανοητά II 35;
νοητά I 65⁵ 330⁴; διανοητά I 346²;
νοερά II 73³; χωριστά I 112⁴ 421¹
II 67² 69¹ 76⁶; ἁπλᾶ I 167⁷ 316¹
II 76³,⁶; τῆς ψυχῆς I 274⁹,
cf. 274¹⁵ 330²; τὰ καθόλου I 415⁴;
ἑκτικά, στερητικά I 234⁸; σωματικά,
ἀσώματα I 97²; ἄυλον, ἔνυλον I 229⁵;
ἔνυλον I 340⁵, cf. II 67²; ἄψυχα I 229⁷;
τὰ τῇδε II 70²; εἰκονικόν I 344¹;
ψευδώνυμον I 170².
εἴδωλον I 94² 108⁴ 128²,⁷ 129² 293³ 352²
354¹ 377⁴ 525⁵ 550⁶.
εἰκονικός I 344¹.
εἰκοσαεδρικός II 132⁸.
εἰκών I 128¹ 262⁹ 303¹,² 345¹,³ 349²,³
416²,⁴,⁵,⁹ 525² II 35⁵ 73² 130².
εἱμαρμένος I 500⁶ II 149⁴,⁹,¹⁰; ἡ εἱ.
I 25⁴ 492⁶ 500⁶.
εἶναι: τὸ εἰ. I 83¹ 225³ 226⁴ 227⁷ 347¹
475¹,²; τὸ μὴ εἰ. I 226⁴ 475¹; τὸ εὖ εἰ.
I 83². – τὸ ὄν I 133⁴ 134³ 135⁸ 395⁵ 420⁵
II 35⁷ 91¹; τὸ ὄντως ὄν I 306¹; τὸ ὡς
ἀληθῶς ὄν II 130²; τὸ κυρίως ὄν I 318²;
τὰ ὄντα I 29⁴ 65⁵ 312²,³ 313¹ 318¹ 391¹
II 63³; τὰ ὄντως ὄντα I 242¹⁸; τὸ μὴ ὄν

I 89² 156² 230⁶, cf. 318²; τὰ οἰκεῖα μὴ ὄντα I 246⁵.
εἰς: τὸ ἕν I 154² 302³ 340²⁻⁴ 341¹,³,⁴ 342³ 351² 484² 516²,³ II 68⁹,¹⁰,¹² 95² 117²; ἡ μία αἰτία II 101².
εἰσκρίνεσθαι (of soul) I 250².
εἴσοδος I 547¹².
εἰσπνεῖν I 542³.
εἰσπνοή II 141⁴.
εἰσρεῖν II 127².
εἴσω II 150².
ἕκαστος: τὰ καθ'ἕκαστα I 274¹ 301³.
Ἑκάτη I 496³ II 108⁹.
ἐκβολή I 281¹.
ἐκδιδόναι I 392².
ἐκεῖ I 42¹,³,⁴ 151¹² 548⁵.
ἐκκεῖσθαι 'be proposed' I 243³.
ἐκκλέπτειν II 65⁹.
ἐκκρούειν (τὸ προσεκτικόν) I 269⁴.
ἔκκρουσις (of the προσεκτικόν) II 19⁵.
ἐκλαμβάνειν I 372¹ II 136².
ἐκλεκτικός I 149¹¹.
ἑκούσιος (θάνατος) II 149⁹'¹².
ἐκπνεῖν I 542³.
ἐκπνοή II 141⁵.
ἔκστασις I 227⁹ 285⁴.
ἐκτικὰ εἴδη I 234⁹.
ἐκτός I 108⁴; τὸ ἐ. 342⁴; τὰ ἐ. 110³ 123² 167⁵ 268³.
ἐκφανής I 91¹.
ἐλάτειρα II 96⁵.
ἐλάττων: see πρότασις.
ἐλεγκτικός I 411².
ἐλλάμπειν I 303³.
ἔλλαμψις I 92⁴ 123³ 170⁸ 499⁵ 527³.
ἐλπίς I 48¹ 125².
ἐμβιβάζειν I 543³.
ἔμμεσα ἐναντία I 192¹,⁴.
ἐμπαθής I 19² 495³.
Ἐμπεδοκλῆς I 80².
Ἐμπεδότιμος II 131⁵.
ἐμπειρία I 146³.
ἐμποιεῖν I 463¹ II 152³.
ἐμφανής I 167⁴ 358³ II 112⁴,⁵.
ἐμφαντάζεσθαι I 163².
ἔμφυτος I 128⁴.
ἔμψυχος I 69² 199⁵ 424² 446³ II 2¹⁷,¹⁸; ἡ ἔ. ἕξις I 177¹.
ἐν: ἐν ἄλλῳ I 448⁸ 453¹ 460⁴; τὸ ἐν ᾧ (ἐστιν) II 45²⁻⁴ 50²,⁴.
ἐνάλιος I 378⁷.
ἐναντία: (classif.) I 189¹ 191¹; (ἔμμεσα, ἄμεσα) 192; ὁ ἀπὸ τῶν ἐ. λόγος I 66¹ 207ᵗⁱᵗˡᵉ II 1ᵗⁱᵗˡᵉ.

ἐναντιότης I 456¹.
ἐναντίωσις I 191³ II 56⁴.
ἐναποθνῄσκειν I 211³.
ἐναποκρύπτειν II 130⁴.
ἐνάργεια I 233⁴ 446¹.
ἐναρμόνιος II 59⁷.
ἑνάς II 94².
ἐνδείκνυσθαι I 282² 418² 420⁴ 526² 557³ II 15⁸ 57³ 76⁵ 151³; (pass.) I 476².
ἐνδεικτικός I 53⁵ 516⁶.
ἐνδεῖν 'bind in' I 10⁴ 352⁵.
ἔνδειξις I 165³.
ἐνδέχεσθαι I 182²,⁵ 232⁴,⁶ 238² 242¹⁰ 249⁹; (part.) I 207ᵗⁱᵗˡᵉ,¹² 208⁴ 216³ 232¹⁵ 241³²; ἐνδεχομένως 207¹⁷ 241³.
ἐνδιατρίβειν I 168¹⁶.
ἐνδιδόναι II 38⁷ 102² 132¹⁰ 147¹⁸.
ἔνδοθεν I 270².
ἔνδον I 268³.
ἐνδύεσθαι I 108⁶.
ἐνεξουσιάζειν I 23².
ἐνέργεια I 6¹,³ 29³ 30⁴ 40⁴ 47³ 51³ 65⁶ 72² 81² 87³ 88¹ 89³ 141³ 149³,¹⁰ 151² 152⁶ 160¹ 167⁵ 176⁵ 180⁵,⁶ 229¹²,¹³ 234⁴ 241³⁵ 253² 254¹ 324² 325⁴ 334² 342²,³ 357¹,² 364² 366³ 380²,⁷,⁸,¹⁰ 387² 404⁴ 464³ 546²,³ 552¹ 554²,³ II 4¹ 6¹,² 30¹² 106⁵ 150². – ἐνεργείᾳ I 210⁴ 280⁵,⁸.
ἐνεργεῖν I 51⁴ 74¹ 79⁴ 81² 257¹⁴.
ἐνέργημα I 159⁴.
ἐνεργητικός I 84¹.
ἐνθεάζειν II 38⁴.
ἔνθεσις II 16⁹,¹¹.
ἐνθουσιᾶν I 171¹ 333⁴.
ἐνιαῖος I 144² II 95².
ἑνικῶς (gramm.) II 15¹⁰.
ἐνίστασθαι II 29¹⁹.
ἔννοια I 157⁴ 263²,⁵,⁶ 498⁶ 516⁵ II 24² 102¹ 147¹⁸; κοιναί I 267¹ 476¹ II 93²; φυσικαί I 280⁷, cf. II 130⁷.
ἑνοειδής (sup.) I 516³ 517¹.
ἑνοῦν II 72⁴; ἡνωμένος I 88² 119³ 319⁴ 382⁷ 420⁵ II 30⁸ 36¹⁴.
ἔνστασις I 248⁷ 395⁴.
ἔντευξις II 28¹⁶.
ἐντιθέναι II 27⁵.
ἐντρεχῶς I 242³.
ἐντυγχάνειν I 208⁸.
ἔνυλος I 46² 94³ 122³ 170¹ 229⁵ 274⁶ 322² 340⁵.
ἐνυπάρχειν I 210³.
ἐνύπνιον II 19³.
ἕνωσις I 168¹⁴ 260⁴ 420⁶ II 84¹.

ἐξάγειν (ἑαυτόν) I 12⁴ 13¹ 20¹ 21¹
  22¹ 165⁵.
ἐξαγωγή I 12⁴ 15⁴ 53³.
ἐξαιρεῖν: ἐξῃρῆσθαι I 32⁷; ἐξῃρημένος
  I 119² 502¹ II 51¹⁰.
ἐξαίρεσις (παθῶν) I 162³.
ἐξαίρετος I 332¹ II 37¹.
ἐξαιρέτως I 41⁵ 477³.
ἐξαλλαγή I 468⁵.
ἐξαλλάττειν I 481⁶.
ἐξάπτειν: ἐξῆφθαι II 115⁷ 144²;
  ἐξημμένος I 313¹ II 94³ 97⁹ 146².
ἐξαρτᾶν: ἐξηρτῆσθαι I 508⁶; ἐξηρτημένος
  I 28³ II 95³ 99³.
ἐξάρχειν I 5².
ἐξατμιδοῦν II 141².
ἐξελίττειν I 74⁵.
ἐξηγεῖσθαι: ὁ ἐξηγησάμενος (=Syrianus)
  I 237¹.
ἐξήγησις I¹ 113⁹,¹¹ 208³,⁵ 238¹.
ἐξηγητής (plur.) I 207²; οἱ Ἀττικοὶ ἐ.
  I 110⁴ 164¹; ὁ ἐ. (=Syrianus)
  I 222² (?) 235¹ 236¹ 243²; (=Proclus)
  I 297⁵ 405² II 14⁴ 25³ 88² 89⁴ 100²
  110⁶ 128² 129⁴ 132² 145⁷ 147⁶.
ἕξις I 6² 52¹ 177¹ 191² 196⁴ 234⁶ 239⁹
  460² 465² 546¹⁻³ 554³ II 4⁴ 6²,⁴
  16⁷ 64⁵,⁸,⁹,¹⁸ 92².
ἔξοδος I 495¹,³ 547¹².
ἐξομοιοῦν I 46¹ 122¹ 349³.
ἔξω I 120⁸ 123⁷ 176⁹ 468³ II 150².
ἔξωθεν II 27⁵.
ἐπαγγέλλειν I 222⁷ (cod.).
ἐπάγειν I 430¹.
ἐπαγωγή I 186¹ 226⁸.
ἐπαισθάνεσθαι I 395³.
ἐπακολούθησις (as a mode of reincarnation) I 355¹⁰.
ἐπανάγειν I 165⁷ 239⁹.
ἐπανακύκλησις I 213² 215⁵ 227¹⁰ 228¹
  232⁶,¹⁶ 235³ 239¹² 248⁷ 251⁴.
ἐπαναπαύεσθαι I 165³.
ἐπάνοδος I 134³ 232⁷ II 9²,⁴.
ἐπανόρθωσις I 402³.
ἐπαπορεῖν I 28⁴.
ἐπείσακτος I 234⁵ 440¹ 446⁴ 457¹ 461⁴
  II 36⁹ 75⁸.
ἐπεισόδιος I 207¹¹ 278¹.
ἐπέκεινα I 465² 475³ II 74².
ἕπεσθαι: θεοῖς II 97⁷; (log.) I 409²; τὸ
  ἑπόμενον (in conditional proposition)
  I 136³ 474²,⁵.
ἐπέχειν I 552¹ II 147²¹.
ἐπήβολος I 90².

ἐπί: ἐφ᾽ ἑαυτῶν I 416¹³, -ῆς 443⁴.
  – τὸ ἐφ᾽ ἡμῖν I 492⁶.
ἐπιβολή II 25³ 147⁴.
ἐπιγίγνεσθαι 'be born later' I 230¹⁴; 'be
  accidental' I 407⁹.
ἐπιδέχεσθαι I 368¹⁷ 374¹ 456¹
  II 29¹⁵ 52³ 58²,³.
ἐπιδιαμένειν I 178³ 183⁵,⁸ 199²,⁴ 220²
  242¹⁵ 250¹ 252³,⁵ 309² II 31⁴ 34⁸⁻¹⁰
  43¹ 64³ 78¹⁹.
ἐπιθολοῦν I 87⁴ 113².
ἐπιθυμητικός I 140³.
ἐπιθυμία I 111⁵ 354¹ 371²,⁴ 372⁶ 387¹
  555¹ II 55² 56².
ἐπικατιέναι 'descend deeper' I 540⁸.
ἐπικλίνειν II 121³.
Ἐπικούρειοι I 162⁴ 280⁹.
Ἐπίκουρος I 80³.
ἐπικράτεια I 342³.
ἐπικρατεῖν I 340² 341³,⁴.
ἐπικρίνειν II 18³.
ἐπίκτητος II 27⁴.
ἐπιλαμπρύνειν (pass.) I 87³.
ἐπιλανθάνεσθαι II 6⁵.
ἐπιλήθεσθαι I 272¹.
ἐπιληψία I 296¹.
ἐπίληψις I 332⁴.
ἐπιλύειν I 395⁵.
ἐπίλυσις I 208⁵ 231ᵗⁱᵗˡᵉ 243ᵗⁱᵗˡᵉ.
ἐπιμαρτυρεῖν I 271².
ἐπιμένειν I 240² 347² II 1².
ἐπινοεῖν II 36⁷.
Ἐπινομίς I 532³.
ἐπίπεδον I 88⁶.
ἐπίπνοια II 150⁵.
ἐπιπόλαιος I 403² 533³,⁵ II 28⁷ 56⁷ 58⁵
  108⁷ 139³,⁴,⁶; (comp.) II 4⁶; (comp.
  adv.) I 33².
ἐπισημαίνεσθαι II 129¹,⁵.
ἐπισκοπεῖν I 537².
ἐπιστασία 'awareness' I 270³.
ἐπίστασις 'awareness' I 269⁴,⁶ 270¹,².
ἐπιστατεῖν I 485¹.
ἐπιστήμη I 31⁷ 40² 75² 79³ 82⁴ 103⁴
  125² 174⁴ 264⁷,⁹,¹²,¹⁴ 267⁴ 275¹ 278¹
  281¹ 291¹ 297³ 300² 307² 308³ 330⁵
  348² 396⁶ 409³ II 14⁹,¹⁰,¹³,¹⁹,²⁰ 15⁵
  16¹,⁵,⁸,¹³ 27³ 65³,⁶ 109¹ 147¹².
ἐπιστημονικός I 1⁸ 59⁷ 140².
ἐπιστήμων I 294² 395⁶ II 65³,⁷.
ἐπιστητός I 275¹ 307¹ II 35⁴.
Ἐπιστολαί (Pl.) I 330⁵; (Iambl.) I 548⁵.
ἐπιστρέφειν (intr.) I 152⁵ 159³ 176⁶ 272³;
  (act.) I 54³ II 150³; (pass.)

I 31¹ 47² 62⁴ 135⁶,⁸ 151⁹ 413¹.
ἐπιστρεφής II 157².
ἐπιστροφή I 18² 43³ 62³,⁴ 269⁶.
ἐπισυμβαίνειν I 108² 247²,¹⁴.
ἐπισυνάπτειν I 214⁵.
ἐπισύρειν (med.) II 155³.
ἐπίτασις I 368⁵,¹² 419⁵ II 51⁶.
ἐπιτελεῖν I 252¹¹ 407⁴.
ἐπιτήδειος I 121²; (comp.) I 499⁵ II 28⁸.
ἐπιτήδευσις I 49³.
ἐπιτίμησις I 21³.
ἐπιτρέχειν: ἐπιδραμεῖν I 231² 243⁴.
ἐπιτρίβειν I 7³.
ἐπιτροπεύειν II 101⁵.
ἐπιτυχία II 154³.
ἐπιφάνεια I 517² 522⁸,³¹ II 125⁹.
ἐπιφέρειν I 407⁶ 422³ 426² 434² 439² 441¹,² 442² 443²,³ 444²,⁵ 445²⁻⁵ 446²,⁴ 447¹,²,⁴⁻⁷ 448²⁻⁴,⁶,⁸ 455¹ 456¹ 457¹ 458¹⁻⁴ 459¹ 460⁴ II 76⁸,⁹ 77²,⁴,⁶,⁷ 78⁹,²⁴⁻²⁶ 80²,⁴,⁶.
ἐπιφημίζειν I 95⁶.
ἐπιχειρεῖν 'argue' I 223² 383¹ II 29¹⁴,¹⁵ 78²¹.
ἐπιχείρημα I 76¹ 405⁸ II 28¹,³,²⁰ 33¹ 64⁶ 101³,⁹.
ἐπιχείρησις I 135¹ 244⁵ 298² II 28¹⁷.
ἐποπτεία I 167³,⁷.
ἐπωθεῖν II 121².
ἐπωνυμία I 150².
ἐρώτησις: μαιευτική I 300¹; ἐ. καὶ ἀποκρίσεις I 330⁴.
ἐρωτικός I 41² 107² 413³.
ἔσοπτρον I 129².
Ἑσπερίδες I 530⁴.
Ἑστία I 536².
ἐσχατιά I 537¹ II 140³.
ἔσχατος: ('lowest') I 8³ 481⁵ II 30⁵ 57² 119⁴,⁶; τὸ ἔ. I 342³,⁴ 401² 508⁶ 538⁴ II 140¹ 147¹⁰; (plur.) I 69¹ 229²¹ 522¹⁶ 545⁵ II 143²; ἐπ' ἐσχάτοις I 404³ 445².
ἑτεροκίνητος I 21² 23³ 169¹,⁵ 274⁹ 487² 498³ 545⁴ II 147¹⁴.
ἑτερότης I 90⁵ 127⁵ 344⁴.
ἑτερόφυλος I 207³.
εὖ (τὸ) I 51⁶ 350¹.
εὐδαιμονία I 109¹.
εὐδαιμονικῶς I 109².
εὐδαίμων I 350¹ 505⁵ 509⁴ 513³.
Εὔδημος I 383¹ 386¹.
εὐζώνως I 552³.
εὐθάνατος II 137³.

εὔθρυπτος (comp.) I 215⁶.
εὐθυπορεία I 521⁴.
εὐθύς: κατ' εὐθεῖαν II 2¹³ 123³.
εὐθυωρία I 269⁶.
εὐίατος I 546¹.
εὐκίνητος I 197³,⁷ 534³; (comp.) I 396³.
εὐκοσμία II 92².
εὐκρασία II 137⁴.
εὐκρίνεια I 208¹.
εὐλή I 234¹⁵ II 2¹⁹.
εὔληπτος (comp.) I 416¹³.
εὐμαθής II 28⁶.
εὐνοϊκός I 398².
εὐπαθής II 19⁴.
εὕρεσις I 291² II 28²¹,²².
εὕρημα I 292¹.
Εὐρωπαῖος: τὸ Εὐ. τεταρτημόριον I 522⁴.
Εὐρώπη I 507⁵ II 139⁷.
εὐσχημοσύνη I 372⁶.
εὐφημία I 559¹ II 155¹.
εὐφροσύνη I 33³ 49³ 164³ 292¹.
εὐφυΐα I 289¹.
εὐφώρατος I 1³.
εὔχεσθαι (etym.) I 51⁶.
ἐφάπτεσθαι I 330⁷.
ἔφεσις I 179⁴,⁸.
ἐφετός I 179⁴.
ἐφιστάναι (-νειν) 'observe' I 242³ 257¹ 368⁷,¹⁶ 372⁵ 478⁶ 529⁸ 531³; 'be aware' I 269¹ 271⁴ 272² II 19⁴ 22³.
ἔφοδος I 65² II 63⁴.
ἐφορᾶν I 480³.
ἔφορος I 11¹⁰ 478⁴ 480¹ 528⁶ II 136² 140³ 142².
Ἔχιδνα I 539³ II 142²,⁵.

Ζανὸς πύργος I 535¹.
Ζεύς I 3² 44,⁶ 8⁴ 11⁸ 14⁶,⁸ 378⁴ 470¹ 483³ II 131⁴.
ζῆν I 59² 187¹ 463¹.
ζήτησις I 279² 280¹⁰ 408¹ II 16¹² 28¹⁹.
ζωή I 9¹ 10³ 36³ 44³ 52²,³ 53²,⁵ 60¹ 62² 63¹ 67¹ 103³ 108²,³ 117⁵ 121¹ 123⁸ 127⁷ 128⁶,⁸ 152² 164³ 166² 168⁴ 171⁵ 174³,⁴ 176²,¹² 180⁵ 187¹,² 188¹ 234¹⁴ 252¹⁰ 314² 338¹,⁴,⁷ 352³ 356² 358⁴ 360¹ 401³ 420⁴,⁵ 424¹ 425¹,² 426² 427¹,² 430³ 433¹,² 439¹ 440¹ 441¹ 442² 443²,³ 445² 446²,⁴,⁵ 448² 454¹,² 457¹ 458¹⁻⁵,⁷ 459¹,²,⁴,⁵ 460³ 461¹,⁷ 462³ 464¹ 465³ 469² 494³ 495⁵ 500¹ 525² 528⁵ 529² 533⁴ 548³,⁴ 552² 559⁴ II 2²,⁵ 43¹,⁷ 56⁹ 62⁴ 64¹⁰ 67⁵ 76²,³,⁸ 77²,³,⁶ 78²,⁶⁻⁸,¹¹,¹⁵,¹⁶,²⁰,²²,²⁵,²⁶ 80²,⁸ 101⁴ 108³

133³ 149³ 152³; see γνῶσις.
ζώνη (cosmogr.) II 124⁴.
ζῷον I 16² 31⁵ 53² 62⁵,⁶ 138³ 156³ 174³ 217¹ 218⁴ 239² 257² 288⁴ 416¹⁰ 505² 542² II 20² 56¹⁵ 97³ 117⁴ 131⁸,⁹ 135¹ 137² 141³ 149²,¹².
ζωοποιεῖν II 16⁶.
ζωοποιός I 92⁵ 234² 252⁹ 435¹ 560².
ζωτικός I 127⁸ 234⁴ II 8⁴ 55¹¹.
ζώωσις I 234⁷.

ἡγεῖσθαι 'be prior' II 48¹⁻³; 'lead' II 97³; τὸ ἡγούμενον (log.) I 136³ 474²,⁴.
ἡγεμών (demonic) I 496² 498² 500³ 501² 502¹ II 108⁵ 112¹,⁵ 113¹; (divine) I 509⁴ 527³ II 113².
ἡδονή I 2² 58³ 68² 120² 137⁶ 159² 161¹,³,⁴ 162⁵ 164³.
ἠθικός I 152² 156². - v. ἀρετή.
ἡλιακός ('H.) I 530⁶ II 133³.
ἡλιοειδής II 138².
ἥλιος ("Ηλιος) I 14⁴,⁶ 508⁴ 509² 522²¹ II 128⁷ 131⁵ 147⁹.
'Ηράκλειος: 'H. στῆλαι II 139².
'Ηράκλειτος I 294³ II 128⁶.
'Ηρακλείως I 130³.
'Ηρακλῆς I 132⁴ 550⁶.
ἡρωϊκός II 99³.
ἧττον: v. μᾶλλον.

θανατηφόρος II 153².
θάνατος I 58⁴ 59⁸ 62¹,⁵ 101⁴ 127¹⁻³,⁷,⁸ 174⁵ 185² 425¹,² 426² II 2⁴ 78⁶ 149¹.
θανατοῦσθαι II 78¹³,¹⁴.
θαρραλεότης I 157³ 371⁴.
Θεαίτητος (dial.) I 75⁴ 142⁶.
θεῖος I 44² 60³ 123³ 165¹ 170⁷ 312⁴ 313¹ 355⁶,⁹ 359¹ 391³ 392² 414⁴ 468¹,³ 478⁴ 509³ 542⁴ 547⁶ II 35¹ 38²,⁴ 95³ 97³,¹¹ 145¹¹ 150⁵; (comp.) I 526² 528³ II 149¹³. - τὸ θ. I 31³ 41² 123⁵ II 30²,⁷. - τὰ θ. I 319² 477¹.
θέλησις I 173⁴.
Θεμίσων I 285⁵.
Θεόδωρος (of Asine) I 503³.
θεοειδής: τὸ θ. τῆς ψυχῆς I 144¹.
θεόθεν I 13³ 392².
θεολογεῖν I 378³.
θεολόγος: οἱ θ. I 476² 508² II 93³.
θεοπρεπής I 529².
θεός (sing.) I 11¹ 22² 25³ 28¹ 30¹⁻³ 31¹,² 32³ 92⁵ 102¹ 119¹ 120⁶ 122⁶,⁸ 129⁴ 169⁴ 172⁷ 173²⁻⁴ 175³ 217⁴ 260²

392³ 478¹,³ 508²⁻⁴ 535⁴ 537¹ II 36³ 59² 94² 95³ 115¹,²,⁴ 117⁴ 136³ 140²; (fem.) I 377¹,⁴,⁵ 378² 404¹ 508¹,⁵ II 115¹,³,⁴,⁶; (plur.) I 1⁶ 3³ 4⁴,⁶ 8⁴ 9² 13³ 18¹ 19¹,⁴ 21¹ 23¹ 26² 27² 28¹ 29² 32¹,⁵,⁸ 38² 39¹ 41⁸,⁹ 42² 43² 44² 45¹,⁶ 62¹ 73³ 122³ 123⁴ 126⁶ 149⁵ 150¹,²,⁴ 168⁴,⁵ 169²,³ 175¹,² 303³ 313¹ 319² 351¹ 355³,⁴,⁶,⁹,¹² 469² 477³ 478⁶ 479¹ 480³,⁴ 499⁶ 500⁴ 505⁵ 508²,³,⁵ 524⁵ 532¹⁻³ 540²⁻⁴ 557¹ 558¹ II 93³,⁴ 95¹,² 97⁸ 98³ 108⁷ 113² 115²,⁵ 132⁷ 144¹ 153²,⁴ 155⁴. - v. νέος.
θεότης I 478³,⁴.
θεουργός II 149⁸.
Θεόφραστος I 547³.
θέσις I 136⁴ 512¹ II 116¹ 145⁷.
θεωρεῖν I 74⁷ 143¹,² 257⁵.
θεώρημα II 28²².
θεωρητικός I 74⁶ 115² 119² 121³ 152³ 167⁵. - v. ἀρετή.
θεωρητικῶς I 114³.
θεωρία I 99³ 149².
Θηβαϊκός I 377¹.
θῆλυς: τὸ θ. καὶ προοδικὸν αἴτιον II 142⁵.
θηρᾶν I 390⁴.
θήρειος I 468¹,⁴.
θηρεύειν I 407³.
θηριοῦσθαι I 399⁴.
θηριώδης I 146³.
θνητοειδής I 519³ 524⁴.
θνητός I 193¹ 244² 320² 378⁸ 394².
θρύμμα I 8¹,².
θυμιᾶν (pass.) I 531⁶.
θυμοειδές I 140³.
θυμός I 371²,⁴ 372⁵ 387¹ 555² II 55¹ 56².
θύρα: παρὰ θύρας I 380⁶.

'Ιάμβλιχος I 143⁵ 144³ 172² 177⁴ 207³,⁸ 492² 548¹.
ἰατρός: (τῶν ψυχῶν) I 360², cf. 398¹.
ἰαχή I 171².
ἰδέα I 503³ 505³ II 67¹ 68² 114².
ἰδιοπραγία II 55³.
ἰδιότης I 1¹³ 4² 55² 478⁶ II 145¹¹ 153².
ἰδιότροπος II 80⁹.
ἰδιοτρόπως II 80¹⁰ 129⁴.
ἰδιωτικός I 207⁷.
ἰδιωτικῶς I 168¹⁶.
ἱερατική I 172¹ 404⁵ II 109².
ἱερατικός I 48² 70² 144¹ 173³ 486³ 508¹.
ἱερατικῶς I 39¹ 496³ II 108⁶.
ἱερεύς II 108¹¹.
ἱερός: τὰ ἱ. 'rites' I 121⁵ 167¹ II 108⁶.

ἱκανός II 74¹.
Ἰνδοί II 149³.
Ἰνώ I 378⁶.
ἴς: αἱ τοῦ ξύλου ἶνες I 517².
ἰσημερινός (ὁ) I 522¹⁹ II 124⁵.
ἰσοκρατής I 186⁶.
ἰσορροπία II 122¹.
ἰσόρροπος I 520³,⁴ 521² II 121².
ἰσότης II 121³.
ἰσχυροποιεῖν I 132⁴.
ἰσχύς I 97².

Κάδμος I 378¹,⁴,⁸.
καθάπαξ II 29¹⁸ 32⁴ 64⁶.
καθαρμός I 121⁵ 126⁵ 167⁴ 544³.
καθαρότης I 122⁶ 123¹.
κάθαρσις I 51² 76⁴ 126¹ 127¹ 164⁹,¹⁰ 167¹ 179¹ 180⁶.
καθαρτικός I 7⁵ 54¹ 66² 67¹ 69¹ 74⁶ 75⁴ 99³ 121³ 128⁵ 129³ 171⁵ 180⁵ 222¹¹ 360¹ II 86⁴ 145¹² 148⁹. – ὁ κ. I 68¹,⁴ 70⁴ 76² 119² 156⁶,⁹ 157¹,² 158² 161⁴,⁶. – κ. ζωή I 152² 164³ 174⁵ 176¹,¹¹. – v. ἀρετή.
καθαρτικῶς I 41⁶ 106¹ 114³ 130⁴ 132² 181³.
καθηγεμών (ὁ ἡμέτερος) I 207title; II 128⁴ 132⁴.
καθιεροῦν I 171³.
κάθοδος (of souls) I 134³ 168² 204² 252²⁰ 480⁴,⁵ 493² 540⁷ 548³,⁴ II 97⁸,¹⁰.
καθολικώτερος II 46⁵.
καθόλου I 35¹ 38² 95² 112² 229¹⁶ 263² 268³ 270²,⁴ 409³ 415⁴ II 5² 14⁶ 29¹³.
κακία I 50¹ 145² 147⁵ 370² 380³ 405⁵,⁶,²⁰ 554² II 53² 54²,⁴ 60².
κακός I 486¹,²; τὸ κ. I 133² 179⁷ 416⁷ 475² II 27⁶ 55¹⁰.
κακοῦσθαι II 90².
κακύνεσθαι I 176⁸,⁹ II 88⁵.
καλλονή I 107².
κάλλος I 91¹ II 133³.
καλλωπισμός I 69³,⁷.
καλός I 397¹; τὸ κ. I 41¹,³ 96² 417⁵.
καμμύειν II 150².
κανών I 2¹ 162¹ 267⁶ 274⁶ 396⁵ 412⁴.
καπνός I 209⁶ 210¹⁻³ 221¹ 223¹ 232¹⁰.
καρκίνος (astron.) II 124³.
κάρος I 294⁵.
κατά: καθ' αὑτό (etc.) I 411⁷ 460⁴ 464² II 78¹⁸. – ἵστασθαι κατά c. acc. 'establish oneself at the level of' II 86².
κατάγειν (εἰς τὸ σῶμα) I 61³.
καταδεέστερος I 147².

καταδεῖσθαι 'establish' I 469³.
κατακορέστατος I 368¹⁰.
κατακόσμησις I 121³.
καταλαμβάνειν I 274².
κατάληψις I 276¹.
κατανοητικός II 55¹⁰.
κατασκευάζειν I 49⁵ 186¹ 265² 405² II 50¹.
κατασκευή I 333⁴.
κατασπᾶν I 170⁷.
καταστηματικός: ἡδοναὶ κ. I 162⁵.
καταστολή I 120⁹.
καταστοχάζεσθαι II 139⁷.
κατάτασις (εἰς τὸ χεῖρον) I 61².
κατατάττειν: κατατεταγμένος (opp. ἐξῃρημένος) II 51¹⁰.
κατατείνεσθαι I 87⁴.
κατάφασις I 444⁴.
καταψύχειν I 534¹.
κατέχειν I 424³ 446².
κατηγορεῖν: τὸ κατηγορούμενον (log.) I 58² 362³.
κατηγορικός: v. συλλογισμός.
κατιέναι (of souls) I 86¹ 130¹ 149⁴ 204⁵ 480¹ 492² 540¹⁰,¹¹ 548² II 100⁵ 143⁷.
κατορθοῦν I 330⁸.
κάτω II 107¹.
κάτωθεν I 127³.
κατώρροπος II 156³.
Καύκασος I 510⁴.
Κέβης I 26¹ 27¹ 28¹ 38¹ 176¹⁰ 178³ 179² 180¹ 183² 209⁴ 215⁸ 218⁶ 222¹⁰,¹¹ 223⁴ 251² 298¹ 311¹² 394⁴ 429¹.
κεκρατημένως I 42².
κέντρον I 515² 518¹,² 519²,³ 522¹⁶ 535² 536¹ 541² II 116⁵ 119¹,² 120² 122² 123⁵ 139⁷.
κεντρώδης II 120³.
κεραύνωσις I 7¹.
κερματισμός I 7³.
κεφάλαιον I 208¹ 262title.
κεφαλωτός II 68⁸.
κίνησις I 120⁷ 171² 227³ 229¹⁰ 247⁵ 367³ 388⁶ 521⁴ 539² II 123³ 141⁷.
κλύδων (of birth) II 16⁵.
κοιλάς I 522⁵,⁷,⁹.
κοῖλος 'low' (comp.) I 7² 540⁹.
κοίλωμα II 125⁸.
κοινός I 105 274³ II 15² 56¹⁰,¹²; κ. αἴσθησις I 333³. – v. ἔννοια.
κοινωνεῖν I 418³,⁵,⁶ II 68².
κοινωνία I 14⁵ 105¹ 371⁵ 418³ II 69²,⁴.
κοινωνικός I 9⁶ II 55⁵.
κόλασις I 6² 547¹¹ 550².

κολαστικός I 7⁴ 19⁶ II 112⁷ 145¹³ 147¹⁸.
κολουστικός I 404¹.
Κορικῶς I 130¹.
Κόρινθος I 286².
κορυφοῦσθαι II 74¹.
κοσμητικός I 19³.
κοσμικός I 122² 166¹ 535⁵.
κοσμοποιός II 70¹.
κόσμος I 14⁷ 24³ 102¹ 207¹³ 331¹ 378² 468² 503² 508² 537¹,³ 540⁵ II 36¹ 59⁵ 94¹ 99¹ 114³ 115⁴.
Κουρῆτες I 126⁶.
κρᾶσις I 138² 139² 388⁴ II 46⁵.
κρείττων: τὸ κ. I 350¹; οἱ κ. I 121⁶ 333² 502³, cf. II 89².
κρίσις I 396⁴ 412⁵ 489² 490¹ II 111⁵ 130⁶ 149¹¹.
κριτής I 267⁴.
κριτικός I 33¹,³ 162⁷ 482² 549¹.
Κρονίδαι (οἱ τρεῖς) I 483⁶ 523⁶ II 131¹.
Κρόνιος (adj.) I 537⁴ II 140⁴.
Κρόνος I 151⁷ II 147⁹.
κυβικός II 132⁸.
κύβος II 132².
κυκλίζειν (act.) I 241³⁸; (pass.) I 201¹ 202² 211¹ 214³ 229¹² 230⁴,¹⁰,¹⁵ 241³⁶ 242¹⁰ 244³ 252¹⁴,²¹ 521³ II 106⁴.
κυκλικός II 106⁵.
κυκλισμός I 232¹² 241³¹ 248³ 249³ 252¹¹.
κύκλος I 166¹ 186⁵ 198⁷ 199⁶ 207¹⁷ 213⁷ 214² 217² 229²,⁴,¹⁰,¹³,¹⁴,¹⁶,¹⁸,²³ 230³,⁷,¹⁰ 232² 234⁷ 236² 239⁸ 240⁴,⁶ 241³³,³⁴ 242¹³ 247² 493¹,² 522¹⁷ II 2¹¹,¹³,¹⁴,¹⁶ 64⁸,²⁵ 106⁵ 117⁷ 120²; ὁ μέγιστος κ. I 522¹⁸,²⁸,³¹ II 124³; κύκλῳ I 375⁶.
κύκνος I 379²,³,⁶.
κυνῆ ("Αϊδος) I 348⁴.
κύριος I 95¹ 176⁶.
κυρίως I 23⁴ 42³ 190²,³ 191¹ 229¹ 257¹² 318² 346².
κυρτός I 522⁸.
Κωκυτός I 497⁴ 541⁴ 546⁵ II 145²,⁹,¹⁴.

λαγχάνειν I 339⁵ 488¹ II 101⁸. – v. δαίμων.
λειμών (of Phaedr. 248 c1) I 151¹².
λειτουργεῖν I 529⁶.
λειτουργία I 529⁶.
λεπτομέρεια II 119⁵.
λεπτομερής I 518³ II 119⁴ 125⁶; (comp.) II 127².
λεπτύνειν I 531⁶.
λευκότης II 58⁴.

λεωφόρος I 101⁵.
λήθαργος II 17³.
λήθη I 253³,⁴ 254² 257¹³ 258¹ 262⁶ 266⁴ 277¹ 281¹ 308² II 4⁶ 6⁵ 14¹⁴,¹⁶ 22².
λημμάτιον I 365¹ 366¹ 405².
λῆξις I 466¹ 467¹ 468¹,⁴ 469¹ 470¹ 471¹ 495⁴ 500⁶ II 84⁴ 108³,⁴ 145¹⁰.
ληπτός I 326².
λῆψις I 332⁴.
Λιβύη I 507⁵.
λιμνάζειν I 522⁹.
λίμνη II 145⁵ 148⁸.
Λογγῖνος I 110⁴.
λογικός I 9¹,³ 69³ 184¹ 295² 388³ 399² II 28¹⁶ 67⁵ 95⁴ 149¹²; (ψυχή) I 78⁴ 87³ 135⁷ 177¹,⁵ 239⁴ 290³ 415⁵ 500⁷ 539³ II 62⁶ 115⁷.
λόγιον (Chaldean) I 151³ 169³ 561³ II 96⁴ 134⁴ 157⁴.
λογισμός I 87¹ 90¹ 97² 326¹.
λόγος: 'argument, discussion' I 35¹ etc.; οἱ περὶ ἀθανασίας λ. I 66¹; ὁ ἀπὸ τῶν ἐναντίων λ. I 66¹ 207title, ὁ περὶ τῶν ἐναντίων λ. II 1title, ὁ πρῶτος λ. I 183¹ 299²; ὁ ἀπὸ τῶν ἀναμνήσεων I 66² 242¹⁶, cf. 252⁴, ὁ δεύτερος I 299² 309¹, οἱ δύο λ. I 309³; ὁ ἀπὸ τῆς πρὸς τὰ νοητὰ ὁμοιότητος I 66³, cf. 215⁷ 220⁴; ὁ περὶ ἁρμονίας λ. I 361title, τὸ τέταρτον πρόβλημα I 183⁴; ὁ τελευταῖος λόγος II 66title; 'reason, account' I 1⁸ 14¹,² 15¹,⁵ 28² 391² 392²; 'ratio, proportion' I 368⁸,¹⁵ 372⁸ 380³,⁴ II 51⁷ 57⁴ 60²,³ 62⁴ 124¹; 'analogy' I 121¹,³ II 131⁸; 'reason-principle' I 266¹ 415⁴ 525¹ 528⁶ II 16² 17⁷ 73² 80⁹,¹²; 'faculty of reason' I 54⁴ 120¹⁰ 135⁴ 138³ 139⁴ 140¹,² 163⁴ 267⁴,⁵ 371²,³,⁵ 372⁵ 376¹ 555³ II 55² 56²,¹⁵ 130⁵.
Δυσεύς I 11¹.
λύσις I 11¹ 12³ II 36¹¹.
λυτικός I 331² II 148⁹.
λυτός I 331¹⁻³ II 36¹,⁵,⁷.

μάθημα II 28⁸.
μάθησις I 265²,³ 266³ 297¹ II 16⁷,¹² 65⁸.
μαιευτικός I 300¹.
μακραίων I 62⁷ 241³⁴ 252¹⁹ 378⁹ 528⁴ 529¹ 530¹ 531⁴ II 137¹.
μακρόβιος I 241³⁴.
μαλακός: (adv. comp.) I 137¹⁰ 168¹⁵.
μᾶλλον: τὸ μ. καὶ ἧττον I 135¹ 368⁷,¹⁵,¹⁷ 369² 374¹ 379¹,⁴ II 17⁵ 51²,⁵,⁹ 52² 58².

μαντική I 359[1].
μαντικός I 359[2] 539[5] II 142[6].
μαρασμός II 149[2].
μέγεθος I 97[1] 98[1,3] 419[4] 512[2] II 116[3].
μεθεκτός II 59[7].
μέθεξις I 7[6] 143[3] 224[2] 256[4] 350[1] 352[6] 418[1] 489[1] 527[7] II 39[1] 58[4] 69[4] 78[12] 132[11].
μεθόριον II 59[2].
μείζων: see πρότασις.
μείωσις I 247[11].
Μένων (dial.) I 273[2] 280[1] 300[3].
μερίζειν I 3[1,2] 4[8] 7[6] 78[2] 129[3] 130[2] 344[2,3] 382[5].
μερικός I 1[9] 10[2] 38[3] 62[5] 177[7] 266[1] 270[2] 416[11] 533[6] 540[4] II 16[1] 43[1]; (comp.) I 547[6]; (comp. adv.) I 260[1] 319[1].
μερίς I 540[7] II 96[3] 99[2] 115[4].
μερισμός I 170[5] 229[5] II 59[6]; εἰς (τὸν) ἔσχατον μ. I 8[2] 128[5].
μεριστός I 4[12] 78[5] 128[4] 170[2] 178[6] 274[7] 322[1] 344[1].
μέρος II 56[14] 81[1] 92[3] 115[2,3,5] 119[2].
μεσημβρία I 541[4].
μεσημβρινός 'meridian' I 522[20].
μέσος I 60[4] 62[6] 346[2] II 82[3] 94[2] 131[7]; ὁ μ. ὅρος I 57[2]; τὰ μ. I 229[21,22] 338[5]; ἡ μέση (mus.) II 59[1,4].
μεσότης I 382[4] 477[1] 537[2] II 59[3] 137[2].
μέσως I 340[5] 382[8].
μεταβαίνειν (of thought) I 274[12] II 6[2,4].
μετάβασις I 1[8] 274[11] II 15[9].
μεταβατικός I 173[3].
μεταβολή I 198[5] 227[9] 230[10,12,15] 232[2] 233[3] 237[5] 240[6] 241[16] 242[10,13] 248[5] 268[2] 308[1] 341[1,2] 342[1,5] 343[3] 344[2] 416[9] 465[1,2,4] 468[3] II 17[3,5] 19[3] 143[5].
μεταδιδόναι II 43[6].
μεταλαμβάνειν II 69[3].
μεταμέλεσθαι I 546[3].
μεταμορφοῦσθαι I 4[7].
μετάστασις 'decease' I 558[3] II 154[1].
μετάσχεσις I 417[4] 419[6] II 68[13].
μεταφορά (rhet.) I 355[5].
μεταχωρεῖν II 2[7].
μεταχώρησις I 219[4].
μετεμψυχοῦσθαι I 355[8].
μετεμψύχωσις I 355[1].
μετέχειν I 32[8] 150[3-5] 171[3] 187[2] 189[1] 190[1,2] 224[4,5] 319[2,3] 405[14,19,20] 406[4] 427[1] 428[1] 468[4] II 39[2] 75[2,5] 110[2].
μετοχή I 417[2] 418[5,6] II 69[1] 75[10].
μετρητικός II 88[7].
μετριοπάθεια I 157[5].
μέτρον I 12[3] 13[3] 45[3] 73[2] 549[2] II 147[12].

μικτός I 202[4].
μίμημα I 88[4,5] 95[2].
μίμησις I 536[1].
μισανθρωπία I 400[1].
μισολογία I 399[1] 400[1].
μισόλογος I 399[4].
μνήμη I 253[3,4] 256[2] 257[2,5,7,10,12] 258[1] 272[1,2] 286[1] 295[2] 308[2] II 4[5] 6[2] 17[4] 22[1] 28[6,18].
μνημονεύειν II 6[3].
μνημονευτός I 256[3].
Μνημοσύνη I 282[1,2] II 28[18].
μοῖρα (τοῦ κόσμου) I 540[5].
μολύνειν I 122[8] 126[2].
μολυσμός I 166[5].
μονάς I 1[7] 3[4] 4[1,3] 14[1] 15[2,3] 28[3] 112[1] 411[9].
μονή I 257[4]; (of the Earth) I 512[2] II 116[2].
μονιμότης I 257[4].
μονοειδής I 95[3] 312[7] 316[1] 343[1,3] 416[3] II 30[3,9].
μονοειδῶς I 247[8].
μόριον I 163[3] 375[1].
μορφή I 112[3].
Μοῦσαι I 282[1,2] II 28[18].
μουσικός I 107[2] 360[2].
μοχλεία I 294[6].
μύησις I 167[3,6].
μυθεύειν I 129[1].
μυθικός II 129[7]; (adv.) 83[1].
μῦθος I 7[6] 378[4] 466[2,4] 525[1] 526[1] 528[5] II 84[1] 129[2,5,8,9] 130[1].
μυθώδης II 136[1].
μυριέτης (περίοδος) I 494[2].
μυρίζειν I 552[3] II 150[4].
Μύρων I 284[1].
μυστικός I 1[5] 14[1] 166[1]; (adv.) 15[8].
μύωψ I 285[4].

ναρθηκοφορεῖν I 170[5].
ναρθηκοφόρος I 170[9].
νάρθηξ I 170[1,6].
νεκροῦν I 234[11,14] 239[10].
νέκρωσις I 53[3] 234[7,11] 560[1].
νέκυια I 470[3] 471[1] II 81[2] 85[1,2].
Νέμεσις I 404[1].
νέος: οἱ νέοι θεοί I 11[8] 14[3] 16[1]; ὁ νέος θεός (=Dionysus) 14[1]. – οἱ νεώτεροι (opp. οἱ παλαιοί) I 177[4].
νεοτελής I 308[4].
νεύειν (πρὸς γένεσιν, πρὸς τὸ χεῖρον) I 42[3,4] 126[7].
νεῦσις I 121[4].
νοεῖν I 51[5] 113[1] 256[3] 257[5,12,13] 280[6] 377[2]

II 18¹.
νοερός I 87⁴ 91³ 273¹ 337³ 415⁷ 478⁵ 480²
 II 23² 72⁷ 73³ 86¹ 95⁴ 97¹,⁵,¹¹ 132¹⁰.
νόησις I 88¹ 90⁶ 113² 120¹⁴ 165¹ 176¹
 257¹⁰ 259¹ 325³ 327¹ II 7¹.
νοητικός I 315¹ II 30⁹.
νοητός I 65⁵ 66³ 88² 90⁶ 93² 94⁴ 99²
 151¹² 154³ 256⁴ 257⁸ 274¹² 304¹ 312⁶
 315¹ 325²,⁶ 326² 329² 330⁴,⁵ 332¹ 334¹
 337¹ 338²,⁵ 349¹ 492¹ 529⁹ II 9¹ 11¹,³
 15⁹ 30²,⁹ 35³,⁴,⁷ 37¹,³,⁴ 41⁴ 86¹
 147¹¹ 150⁷.
νομή (of Phaedr. 248 c7) I 151¹³.
νόμιμα II 108¹⁰.
Νόμοι (dial.) I 41¹⁰ 75⁴ 138⁵ 139⁴ 171²
 198² 339² 469³ II 44².
νοσεῖν: στοιχεῖα νοσοῦντα I 521⁴ II 123³.
Νουμήνιος I 2² 177².
νουνεχής I 208³ II 32⁷.
νοῦς I 31¹,²,⁴,⁵ 41⁶ 76³ 78²,⁵ 87¹⁻³ 88⁴ 90⁵
 99²,³ 142³,⁴,⁶ 143¹,²,⁴ 172⁷ 174⁴ 177⁶
 202²,⁵ 256² 257⁶,⁸,¹⁰ 260²,³ 280⁴,⁵
 302²,³ 321¹ 327¹ 328¹ 334² 340⁴ 382⁴,⁶
 387² 388⁶ 391¹ 412⁴ 413¹,⁵,⁶ 414²,³
 415³ 420⁴ 465⁴ 472⁴ 478³ 508⁸ 516⁹
 535⁴ 537⁴ II 6¹ 7¹ 9¹ 15⁵ 59³ 70⁴ 95³
 115⁷ 130³ 132⁷ 142⁶.
νῦν (τό) I 112².
νύττειν II 26².
νωθής (comp.) I 388².
νῶτον: τὰ ν. (τῆς γῆς) I 522¹¹ 527⁵.

ξενίζειν I 270⁴.
Ξενοκράτης I 2³ 177⁴.

ὄγκος II 116⁶.
ὁδοιπορεῖν II 108³.
ὁδοποιητικός II 9⁴.
ὁδός I 49² 59⁵ 390⁵ 412⁷.
οἰκεῖν: ἡ οἰκουμένη I 510⁴ 522⁴,⁶
 II 124³ 125².
οἰκειοῦν II 73²; (med.) 152⁴.
οἰκείωσις I 412⁶.
οἴκησις I 505⁴ 522¹⁰ 523¹ 533².
οἰκήτωρ I 522²⁵.
οἴκοθεν ('from within') I 459¹ II 27⁴.
οἰκονομικῶς I 19³.
οἰστικός I 407⁵.
ὀκταεδρικός II 132⁹.
ὀλιγάκις I 252¹⁴.
ὀλιγοχρόνιος I 241³³ 252²⁰.
ὀλίζειν I 7⁵.
ὁλικός I 533⁶.
ὁλόκληρος I 166⁵ II 115⁵ 144².

ὅλος: τὸ ὅ. I 31¹,⁵, (opp. τὸ πᾶν)
 I 4¹⁰,¹¹ 216³ II 118²; ὅσα ὅλα I 514¹;
 ὅλον μέρος II 115² 119²; ἡ ὅλη ψυχή
 I 177⁷ 387³.
ὁλότης I 4¹³ 134²,⁴ 552⁴.
'Ολύμπιος I 3³ 497³ II 131⁷.
Ὄλυμπος I 537² II 140².
Ὁμηρικῶς I 524¹.
Ὅμηρος I 222⁷ 294⁴ 550⁷ II 72² 131².
ὄμμα I 413³,⁴.
ὁμόβιος I 484⁴.
ὁμοδαίμων I 484⁵ II 113¹.
ὁμοείδεια I 128³.
ὁμοειδής I 15³ 122⁶ II 80⁸.
ὁμοιομερής II 119⁶.
ὁμοιότης I 40¹ 66³ 122⁴,⁶ 123⁹ 215⁷ 220⁴
 II 29¹⁵ 41³.
ὁμοιοῦσθαι I 120¹ 171³ 176⁹.
ὁμοίωσις I 260³ 338⁷ 349⁵ II 108⁶.
ὁμολόγημα I 44¹ 221title.
ὁμολογουμένως I 59².
ὁμοταγής I 516⁴.
ὁμότροπος I 495⁵.
ὁμοφυής I 9⁶.
ὁμοφωνία II 60³.
ὁμωνυμία II 58⁵.
ὁμωνύμως II 136².
ὄνειρον I 222⁷.
'Ονήτωρ I 100³.
ὄνος I 355⁶,⁹.
ὀνώδης I 355⁶,⁸.
ὀπαδοί: (θεῶν) I 150⁴ 477³ 480⁴ 540³.
ὅπῃ καὶ ὅπως I 418⁵.
ὀπισθοβαρής II 110¹.
ὁρατός I 325² 326¹ 333²,³ 348⁴,⁵ 352⁵,⁶
 483² II 18² 32²,³ 33² 38² 116⁵.
ὀργανικόν (αἴτιον) II 11¹.
ὄργανον I 110⁵ 123²,³,⁵ 140² 141²,³ 156⁵
 218¹,⁸ 229² 252¹ 261¹ 388⁷ II 37⁵.
ὀρεκτικός I 108³ 120⁷ II 55⁹; (opp.
 γνωστικός) I 314,⁶ 253¹ 255¹ 271³ 396²,³.
ὀρεκτικῶς (opp. γνωστικῶς) I 77¹ 142³.
ὀρεκτόν (τό) II 9⁴; (plur.) I 69⁶ II 56⁹.
ὄρεξις I 69³ 111²,⁵ 118² 372⁹ 388³ 396⁵
 412⁵,⁷ 498¹ 562² II 55¹⁰ 110²,³.
ὀρθοδοξία I 139¹.
ὁρίζειν I 12¹ 412⁵, (pass.) 368⁸; (med.)
 'define' I 59⁸ 60¹ 209¹; ὁ ὁρίζων
 II 139⁵.
ὁρισμός I 127² 185².
ὁριστός I 55².
ὁρμή I 21² 146³ 267²,⁴ 412⁷ 559³.
ὁρμίζειν 'bring to rest' I 107¹;
 (pass.) 165³.

ὅρος 'limit' I 12¹ 17² 412⁴; 'definition'
I 57² 58¹ 59¹,⁷; 'term' I 187¹.
'Ορφεύς I 11² 14⁵ 497⁵ 541²,⁵ II 145⁵.
'Ορφικός I 203¹.
'Ορφικῶς I 170⁹.
ὀστρέϊνος: (ζῷον) I 62⁶; (χιτών) I 168⁷.
ὄστρεον I 217⁴ 239² 250² 354² 508⁶.
ὀστρεώδης: (σῶμα) I 239⁷; (ὄχημα)
II 141⁶.
οὐράνιος I 170⁶ 227² 229² 416¹⁰ 479²
II 36¹³ 72⁶ 96¹ 131⁷ 133² 147⁷;
τὰ οὐ. I 531²,³ II 72¹.
Οὐράνιος I 537⁴ II 140³.
οὐρανός I 201² 481¹ 506² 508³,⁴ 519¹,³
520¹,² 522¹⁹,²⁰,²² 524¹,²,⁵ 529² 532³
540¹,⁶,¹⁰ 550² 551³ II 100²,⁵ 121¹ 123⁶
131²,⁴ 132¹,³ 134⁴ 143⁷ 147⁶.
Οὐρανός II 140⁴ 142¹.
οὐσία I 65⁷ 72² 90³ 176⁴ 179² 180⁴ 209²
213⁹ 214¹ 218² 219³,⁵ 221¹ 222¹² 224¹
225¹ 226¹,⁷ 227²,⁴,⁵,⁸ 228³ 229¹¹,¹⁷
230⁴,⁸,¹²,¹⁶ 232²,⁵,⁶,¹¹⁻¹³,¹⁶ 234¹ 235³
236² 237⁴ 240¹,⁵ 241²,⁷,¹²,¹⁵,¹⁶,³³,³⁵,³⁸
244²,³ 245¹,² 246² 247⁵,⁷,⁸,¹³,¹⁴ 248³,⁶
249³ 251³ 252⁹,¹¹,¹²,¹⁵ 256¹ 257¹ 274⁷,¹⁵
311⁷ 324² 325⁵ 342¹⁻⁴ 357¹ 364⁴ 369²⁻⁴
374³ 378⁹ 383² 424¹ 430¹ 449¹ 451¹
452¹ 458¹ 461⁷ 464¹ II 2¹,⁶,¹⁴ 15⁷ 17⁷
30¹,²,⁴,¹¹ 32¹,⁴,⁸ 33² 39³ 52² 58¹,² 62⁴
64⁴,⁷ 76³,⁷ 78¹⁰ 106⁴; κατ' οὐσίαν
I 29³ 78² 176⁵ 266² 297⁴ 303¹ 382⁸ 443³
465³ 509² II 8⁵ 16⁵ 41³ 143².
οὐσιοῦν I 176⁶ II 75⁶ 76⁴.
οὐσιώδης I 144² 247⁷,¹¹,¹⁵ 248³ 468²
II 30⁷ 32³ 33³ 142³; (comp.) I 347¹.
οὗτος ('this particular individual') I 112³.
ὀφεώδης I 539⁴.
ὀφθαλμία I 234⁸.
ὄχημα I 239⁸ 543²,³ II 135³; αὐγοειδές
II 141⁵, πνευματικόν 141⁷ 146¹,
ὀστρεῶδες 141⁶.
ὄχλος I 67².

πάθημα I 159⁴ II 39¹.
πάθησις I 364².
παθητικός I 84¹ II 130³.
παθητός I 78⁵.
πάθος I 10³ 65³ 75² 76² 81² 89³ 90³
100²,⁷ 108³ 149²,³ 162²,³,⁶ 163²
164²,⁵,⁷,⁸,¹⁰,¹² 222⁵ 232⁵,¹³,¹⁶ 236³ 237⁴
334¹ 352² 398² 399¹ II 78¹⁰,¹¹,²⁰,²⁴
80⁶ 148⁵.
παιάν I 561³ II 157⁴.
παιδίον I 288¹.

Παιώνιος II 157³.
παλαιοί (οἱ) I 177³ II 36²; οἱ παλαιότεροι
I 207¹ 355¹.
παλαίωσις I 253⁴.
παλιγγενεσία I 11¹⁰ 218² 260¹ II 81,³.
παλίμβολος I 412³.
παλίρροια II 141⁴.
παναγής II 108¹¹.
πανδεχής (sup.) I 516⁸.
πάνδημος I 48¹ 167¹.
πανταχοῦ ἢ οὐδαμοῦ: I 92⁵.
παντελής I 59⁵ 516⁷ II 115⁴ 117⁴.
πάντως ὅτι I 74⁶ 225³ 301⁶ 463⁴ II 28²².
παράγγελμα I 15⁶ 120¹².
παράγειν I 62³ 191³ 228⁷.
παράδειγμα I 19⁸ 25² 129¹ 143³ 154² 213⁷
214⁴ 222¹ 224² 228⁶ 241²² 248⁶ 260³
303² 345¹,³ 349³ 394⁵ 416¹,¹³ 417¹,³,⁵
420³ II 7¹ 68¹ 70³ 73².
παραδειγματικός I 143¹,³ 260² 415⁷ 420¹
516⁷ II 9³ 86² 117⁴.
παράδοσις I 541².
παραδοχή I 453³ II 78⁵.
παραζευγνύναι I 151⁴.
παράθεσις II 46⁴.
παραθραύειν I 9⁵ 94⁴.
παρακεῖσθαι I 214⁴.
πάρακρον II 59³.
παραλαμβάνειν I 59⁵ 111⁵ 167² 168¹²
247⁹ 248² 332³ 428² II 71¹.
παραλύειν I 344³.
παραπολλύναι II 147¹⁵.
παρασημαίνειν I 346³.
παρασκευή I 100⁷.
παρατίθεσθαι I 251³.
παραφορά I 117².
παραχραίνειν I 301⁵.
παρεῖναι I 187² 418⁵.
παρεισκυκλεῖν I 248⁵.
παρεμπίπτειν I 517⁴.
παρενδείκνυσθαι I 301¹ 409² 411¹.
παρεοικέναι I 391⁴.
παρέπεσθαι I 113¹.
πάρεσις I 169¹.
παρισοῦσθαι I 207⁶.
Παρμενίδης I 80²; (dial.) I 154³ 192⁴.
παρουσία I 251⁵ 418² II 69²,⁴ 155⁴.
πᾶς: τὸ πᾶν I 4¹¹,¹² 129³ 216³ 331⁶ 467¹
506¹ 514¹ 515² 517¹ 535³ II 96³ 115¹,⁴
116⁶ 117¹ 118¹,² 119¹,³ 124² 131⁶ 140¹;
πάντα ἐν πᾶσιν I 534³; ἡ διὰ πασῶν
I 368¹⁰,¹³ 372³ II 51⁵.
πάσχειν I 222⁴ II 39².
Πατέριος I 2³ 100⁴ 137⁵,¹¹.

πατήρ I 8⁴,⁵.
πατριάζειν 'be in accordance with ancestral tradition' I 120⁴.
πατρικὸν αἴτιον II 142³.
πάτριος: τὰ π. II 150¹ 151¹ 153².
παχυμερής I 518⁴; (sup.) 518⁶ II 119³.
παχύνειν I 120⁵.
πεδίον (of Phaedr. 248b6) I 151¹².
πειθώ (διδασκαλική, πιστευτική) I 37².
Πείσανδρος I 378³.
πεῖσις II 47³.
πελάζειν I 122⁹ 460⁵ 507².
πέντε: διὰ π. I 371³ II 51⁵.
πεπόνθησις II 49².
περαίνειν: πεπέρασται II 106³ 147¹⁰; πεπερασμένος I 230¹ 443¹,² II 36¹⁰ 78²⁸ 106¹ 149².
πέρας 'lower limit of an order' I 540⁴ II 125⁶.
περατοειδής I 396⁴.
περιάγειν I 76³ 112⁶ II 107⁴.
περιαγωγή II 147¹¹.
περίβλημα I 70⁵.
περιβολή I 63⁴ 70².
περιεκτικός II 97¹⁰ 115⁵.
περιέχειν I 417⁵ 522¹²⁻¹⁴ II 149¹⁰.
περιήγησις: (geographical description) II 84²; (the area described) II 124⁵.
περιληπτός II 32⁴.
πέριξ (τὸ), opp. τὸ μέσον, I 518⁴ 519¹ II 123⁵,⁶.
περιοδεύειν II 107⁴.
περιοδικός I 168⁹.
περίοδος I 494¹ 547⁴ 548² II 106² 107² 147⁴.
περιουσία: ἐκ π. I 97².
περιοχή: κατὰ περιοχήν I 11⁸.
Περιπατητικός I 149¹ 177⁶ 280⁴.
Περίπατος I 148³.
περιπίπτειν 'fall in with' I 280³.
περίπτωσις I 279³.
περισπᾶν I 108⁵ 559².
περιστέλλειν 'shroud' I 552³.
περιτίθεσθαι 'attribute' I 416¹⁰.
περιτρέχειν: διαλεκτικῶς ὅλον τὸ πρᾶγμα περιδραμεῖν I 390².
περιφορά I 229².
περιφύεσθαι I 306².
πῇ (opp. καθόλου) I 95³; (opp. ἁπλῶς) 192⁵; πῇ καὶ πῶς II 69³.
πηγαῖος: π. ψυχή, ἀρετή I 151³.
πηγή I 15⁹ 178⁹ 465⁴.
πηγνύναι: τὸ κατὰ τὴν οὐσίαν πεπηγός II 30¹¹.

Πηνελόπη I 358¹,⁵.
πιεστός I 232⁹.
πιστευτικός I 37³.
πίστις I 174⁴.
πλανᾶσθαι: τὸ πλανώμενον (astr.) I 497³.
πλάνη I 335¹ II 108⁸.
πλάσμα I 525³ II 130⁴.
πλαστός I 137⁷.
πλατικῶς II 143⁸.
πλάτος I 168¹³ II 51⁶ 110⁷.
Πλάτων I 61³ 72¹ 80³ 81¹ 172³ 192³ 207¹ 235² 236¹ 277¹ 311⁶ 493² 532² II 29⁵ 39².
Πλατωνικός I 466³ II 28⁴,⁵; οἱ παλαιότεροι Π. I 355².
Πλατωνικῶς I 175².
πλειστάκις I 227⁴ 252¹³ 357².
πλέκειν (συλλογισμόν) I 26¹ 264¹.
πλεονάκις I 228²,⁴ 233² 238² 239¹² 240⁷ 252¹⁴,²² II 2⁹.
πλεονέκτημα I 59¹.
πλῆθος: (opp. μονάς) I 1⁶,⁷ 3³ 14² 15¹,²; (opp. ἕν) I 340² 341¹,⁴ 382² II 30¹⁰ 68¹⁰, cf. I 120¹² II 59⁶.
πληθύνειν: τὸ πεπληθυσμένον I 302³.
πληθυντικῶς II 15⁷.
πληθυσμός I 342¹.
πλημμελής I 120⁷ 162⁵.
πληροῦν I 540¹².
πλήρωμα I 151⁸ 507³ 517⁴ II 115¹.
πλοῦς: δεύτερος I 415⁶, ὁ πρῶτος I 391⁵.
Πλούταρχος (of Athens) I 100⁴ 177⁵ 503⁴.
Πλούτων I 348¹,³ 470² 483⁵ II 131⁶.
Πλωτῖνος I 172¹ 177³ 247¹³ 311¹,⁶ II 29¹,¹²,¹³,¹⁷.
πνεῦμα: 'wind, air' I 178⁸ 183⁸ 185² 190⁶,⁷ 209⁵ 215⁶ 218⁷ 221¹ 222²,⁵ 223¹ 534² II 141²,³; 'vapor' I 482² 539² II 142⁷; 'pneumatic body' I 120⁵ 559⁴.
πνευματικός: πν. ζῷον I 62⁶ 217¹ 239² II 20² 135²; ὄχημα II 141⁶ 146²,³; σῶμα I 551²; χιτών I 168⁶ 239⁴ 528⁴.
πόθος I 390⁴.
ποιεῖν 'create, be the efficient cause' I 416¹⁵ II 27⁵ 70²,³,⁵.
ποίημα 'creation' I 102².
ποίησις 'making' I 416¹⁰ II 47³.
ποιητής 'creator' I 416¹⁴ II 65⁷.
ποιητικός 'productive of' I 193³ 411⁷; αἴτιον, αἰτία I 260¹ 413⁵ 415² 416⁷,⁹ 417¹ 516⁸ II 8¹ 64²⁵ 70¹,⁴ 117⁵.
ποιητικῶς 'creatively' I 416¹⁴.
ποικιλία (of thought) I 120¹³.
ποιναῖος I 545⁴.
ποινή I 166⁴.

ποιότης I 522²⁵ II 2¹¹.
ποιοῦν I 249⁹.
πολλαπλασιάζειν I 229⁸.
Πολέμαρχος I 286².
Πολιτεία (dial.) I 63² 75⁵ 80⁵ 110⁷ 114³
    140⁴ 149⁶ 466⁴ 471³ 488¹ II 37³ 85⁵
    100⁵ 103¹.
πολιτικός I 75⁵ 76² 99³ 121¹ 152² 174⁴
    II 86³; ὁ π. I 68² 74³ 119¹ 156⁵ 158²
    161³. – v. ἀρετή.
Πολιτικός (dial.) I 138⁴.
πολιτικῶς I 19³ 114² 164⁵ 547¹ 551³
    II 147².
πολυειδής I 5² 10⁵ 312⁷ 322¹ 495⁴,⁶
    II 30⁵.
πόλος II 124⁵.
πολύς: ἐν τοῖς πολλοῖς II 14⁷ 15²;
    πρὸ τῶν π. II 14⁷ 68³.
πολυχρόνιος I 241³⁴ 249⁸ 252¹⁹
    II 87³; (comp.) I 227⁴ 233³ 239¹¹
    241²,⁹ 311⁷ 329¹ 330⁴ 429² 472³
    505² 529⁹ II 2¹¹ 34⁵⁻⁸,¹⁰; (sup.) I 529⁹.
πολύχρωμος II 133¹.
Πόντος (as a deity) I 537².
πορθμός (ὁ) 'straits of Gibraltar' II 139².
πορίζεσθαι 'find a corollary' II 48¹;
    ποριστέον I 98¹ II 107¹.
πόρισμα I 101².
Πορφύριος I 2⁴ 172¹ 177⁵ II 59².
Ποσειδῶν I 470² II 131³,⁵.
Ποσειδώνιος (adj.) I 483⁵.
ποσότης I 368³ II 51³.
ποταμός: (τῆς γενέσεως) I 241²⁵.
πραγματειώδης (adv. comp.) I 33².
πραγματειωδῶς II 83¹.
πρακτικός I 325⁴.
πραότης I 371³.
πρεσβύτερος 'prior' I 263⁴ 339³.
προάγειν I 59³ 170⁷ 540².
προαίρεσις I 25³ 104³ 151².
προαναιρεῖν I 462².
προαπάντημα II 128².
προαπόλλυσθαι II 62³.
προαπορεῖν I 231title 243¹,².
προαποφαίνειν (pass.) I 20².
προβάλλειν 'set a problem' (pass.) I 280²;
    'present' (med.) I 412³; 'actualize or
    activate' (act.) I 263², (med.) I 128⁷
    152⁵ 166² 241³⁶ 459² 484⁴ 525² II 90⁵,
    (pass.) I 413³ II 4⁴ 10¹ 27⁴.
προβιοτή I 138⁴ 270¹ 273³ 284¹
    II 20² 28⁶.
πρόβλημα I 165⁴ 181¹,⁴ 183³,⁴ 242² 512¹
    II 116¹.

προβλητικός I 459⁴.
προβολή I 151³ 176¹⁰.
προγενέστερος I 274⁹ 308⁵.
προγιγνώσκειν I 262² 290³ II 13²,³ 28³.
προδιορίζεσθαι I 407⁴.
προειδέναι I 264¹⁰.
προεῖναι I 420⁶ II 13³.
προενθυμεῖσθαι II 35⁶.
προηγεῖσθαι: τὰ προηγούμενα ἀγαθά I 25⁴.
προηγουμένως I 32⁶ 143⁴.
προϊέναι I 62¹,² 174⁵ 370¹ 430¹ 478³ 482¹
    II 15⁶ 77¹ 106³ 133⁴.
προκαθῆσθαι I 478³.
προκαλεῖσθαι I 30⁴ 170⁵,⁸ 559³ II 150⁵.
προκατάρχειν I 388⁶ 465¹.
πρόκλησις I 300¹.
Πρόκλος I 100⁴ 144³ 172³ 177⁵
    II 27¹ 29⁸,¹² 43² 55⁷ 56⁵ 64²¹ 74² 78¹³,¹⁷.
προκοπή II 132⁵.
προκόπτειν I 100² 410².
προλαμβάνειν I 19⁴ 262¹ 280¹¹ 362²
    II 116³.
πρόληψις I 280⁹,¹⁰ 476².
Προμηθείως I 130².
Προμηθεύς I 132³ 170⁶.
προνοεῖν I 29¹ 41¹⁰ 119¹.
προνοητικός I 30⁴ 40³ 44² 74⁷.
πρόνοια I 17¹ 19⁶ 29³ 41⁷,¹¹ 469² 492⁶
    500⁴,⁷ 547² II 112³,⁶ 132⁷ 157³.
προοδικός II 142⁵.
πρόοδος I 7² 18² 43³ 229²⁰ 340⁴ 481⁴,⁶
    482² 540¹¹.
προομολογεῖν (med.) I 207¹⁰, (pass.)
    II 2¹.
προομολόγησις I 208³.
προπάθεια I 285⁷ 286¹ 288⁴.
προπαρασκευή I 168⁵ II 132¹⁰.
προποδισμός I 247⁹.
πρός τι I 191³ 556².
προσαποδεικνύναι I 176¹¹.
προσδιορίζεσθαι I 207¹⁶ 480³.
προσεκτικόν (τὸ) 'faculty of self-
    consciousness' I 269⁵ 271³ II 19⁵ 21³.
προσέλκεσθαι II 155².
προσεξευρίσκειν I 295³.
προσεπιχειρεῖν I 38³.
προσεχής I 17¹ 274¹¹; (comp.) I 11⁸ 229²
    407⁵ II 11²; (sup.) I 8³ 11⁹.
προσεχῶς I 308³ 405⁶ II 73¹ 97¹,⁵.
προσιζάνειν I 559⁴.
προσλαμβάνειν (log.) I 57² 58¹.
πρόσληψις (log.) I 49⁵ 57¹ 184³ 262¹⁰
    265¹ 474¹.
πρόσνευσις I 127⁷.

προσνοεῖν II 18³.
πρόσοδος I 226⁴.
προσοικειοῦν I 92³ 541⁶.
προσομιλεῖν I 401³.
προσπένδειν I 557¹.
προσπεριβάλλεσθαι I 461⁶.
προσπίπτειν II 18².
προστατεῖν I 488²,³.
προστάτης I 44³.
προσυναίσθησις I 359³.
προσυνεθίζειν I 181⁴.
πρότασις I 156⁷; (μείζων, ἐλάττων) I 65¹ 185¹ 186¹.
προτείνειν (log.) I 183² II 64⁵; 'cause to appear' II 148⁸.
πρότερος: τὰ πρ. I 62².
προϋπάρχειν I 242¹⁵,¹⁷ 262³ 298⁴ 300² 313¹ 339³ 361²,⁴ 405⁶ 416⁴ 420⁵ II 27¹.
προϋποκεῖσθαι II 31¹.
προϋπονοεῖν I 2⁴.
προϋποστρωννύναι II 142⁴.
προφαίνεσθαι I 416¹¹.
προχειρίζεσθαι I 117⁴ 237⁵.
πρόχειρος II 65¹¹; (adv.) I 438¹ II 4⁴.
πρυτανεῖον I 536¹.
Πρωταγόρας I 80³.
πρῶτος 'for the first time' I 209³ 211¹ 246¹,⁵⁻⁷ 252² II 12¹; πρ. ψυχή II 6¹, ψυχαί I 257¹³, βίος II 82²; τὰ πρ. I 69² 229²⁰,²².
πρωτότυπον I 262⁹.
πρωτουργός I 95³ 128⁸ II 30⁸.
πρώτως 'primarily' I 318²; 'for the first time' I 242¹,³,¹⁷.
πτῶμα (of the soul) I 269⁷.
Πυθαγόρας II 20¹.
Πυθαγόρειος I 101⁶ 203¹; οἱ Π. I 368⁹ 509¹ 559¹ II 51⁸ 59¹,⁴ 155¹.
πυθμήν: (τοῦ Ταρτάρου) I 538³.
Πύθων I 539⁴ II 142²,⁶.
πῦρ I 134¹ 170⁶ 197¹⁻³ 222³ 378⁶ 422³ 442¹ 446⁵ 447²,³ 448⁵⁻⁷ 521¹,³ 534¹ 535¹ 536¹ 541³ II 75¹² 76⁶,⁹ 79³ 80¹ 123¹ 132³,⁹ 141¹,² 145³.
πυραμίς II 132⁴,⁹.
Πυριφλεγέθων I 497⁴ 541³ 546⁵ II 145³,⁴,⁹,¹³.
πυρσός I 169⁴.

ῥέπειν I 151⁹ 548³.
ῥευστός I 222³.
ῥητορικός I 267⁵.
ῥητός I 1⁶ 15¹,²,⁴ 28²,³ 172⁷.
ῥοή I 338⁷.

σαυρός I 285¹.
σβέσις (of life) II 78²⁰,²².
σβεστικός I 448³.
σειρά I 482¹ 509³ 540⁴ II 144².
Σεληναῖα ὄρη I 510¹.
σελήνη I 503³ 506¹ 508⁴ 509³ 510² 522²¹.
Σεμέλη I 378⁶.
Σεμελήιος: ὁ Σ. Διόνυσος II 8².
σῆμα I 61³.
σημεῖον (geom.) I 112² II 124¹.
σῆψις II 125³.
Σιμμίας I 178¹ 220⁴ 223² 309¹ 394⁴.
σκάπτειν: ὑπὲρ τὰ ἐσκαμμένα πηδήσας I 207⁴.
σκέμμα I 208⁹.
σκιά I 222⁶.
σκιαγραφεῖν: ἐσκιαγραφημέναι ἀρεταί I 147³.
σκιαγραφία II 414⁴.
σκιοειδής: τὸ σκ. φάντασμα I 239⁶.
σκοπός I 49¹ 147¹ 168¹,⁴ 183¹ 252¹ 311⁷ 412⁴ II 1¹ 3¹ 12¹ 82¹.
σκορπισμός I 128⁶.
σκότος I 122⁹ 123⁴ 462² II 92²; (masc.) I 87⁵.
σοφία (of the Gods) I 40³,⁴.
Σοφιστής (dial.) I 126⁵.
σοφός (καλόν, σ., ἀγαθόν) I 41²⁻⁶,¹³.
σπέρμα II 64¹².
Σπεύσιππος I 177⁴.
σπήλαιον I 523⁵.
σπουδαῖος (ὁ) I 22² 109².
στέλλεσθαι I 149¹ 151⁷ 412⁶.
στέρησις I 52¹ 55² 94⁵ 153² 191² 196⁴ 234⁴,⁶ 239⁹ 240² 246⁴ 249⁵,⁷ 252¹⁰ 301⁶ 460¹,² 465³ 545¹ II 8⁴ 64⁵,⁶,⁸,⁹,¹⁸.
στερητικός I 234⁹.
Στοά: οἱ ἀπὸ τῆς Σ. I 276² 280⁷.
στοιχεῖον I 16³ 85¹,² 198³ 222² 248²,³ 249⁶ 378⁵ 380⁵,⁷ 383³ 394² 407⁹ 507³ 521⁴ 525³ 528⁵ 539² 541² II 120³ 123³ 132³ 134¹,⁴ 135² 137⁴ 145¹,¹⁰ 149⁷,¹¹; στοιχεῖα ὄντων, γιγνομένων I 312²; τὰ ἀναγωγὰ στ. I 41⁵.
στοιχειώδης I 519⁴ II 120².
Στράτων I 294¹ 388² 431^title 444¹ II 25² 63¹ 65¹,⁸ 78¹,⁸,¹⁴.
Στύγιος (ὁ) = Κωκυτός II 145³,⁴.
Στωϊκοί (οἱ) I 32⁵ 162⁵.
συγγεννᾶσθαι I 252⁶,⁸.
συγγίγνεσθαι 'be united with' I 67³; 'be born with' I 299¹.
συγγιγνώσκειν: συνεγνωσμένος 'generally known' I 62⁵.

συγγνωμονικός (comp.) I 550⁴.
συγκολλᾶσθαι I 123⁸.
σύγκραμα I 382¹⁰.
σύγκρασις I 96² 382⁶ II 46⁴.
συγκρίνεσθαι (opp. διακρίνεσθαι) I 185³ 209³,⁷ 210² 212² 213⁸ 214¹,⁴,⁹ 217⁴ 232³ 238³ II 2⁹ 64¹³,²⁰ 78¹¹.
σύγκρισις I 209¹ 213¹ 331⁷.
συγκριτικός II 55³.
συγχαλεπαίνειν I 555².
συγχεῖσθαι I 94⁵ II 59⁶.
συζευγνύναι I 320² 400¹; (pass.) I 230¹³ 232¹⁴ 239⁶ 241⁵,¹⁰ 242⁹ 248⁸ 249⁴.
σύζευξις I 127⁵ 218⁵ 230¹³ 235⁵.
συζῆν I 403².
συζυγεῖν II 142¹.
συλλαβά (mus.) I 368⁹.
συλλαμβάνειν 'include' I 417¹.
συλλήπτωρ I 156⁶ 558¹.
συλλογίζεσθαι I 118¹ 520⁵ II 31³ 32¹ 35⁶ 54¹.
συλλογισμός I 26¹ 136⁵ 155¹ 264¹ 265¹ 370¹ 405¹,⁹ 406² 426¹ II 14¹ 34¹ 51¹ 77¹; κατηγορικός I 57¹ 65¹ 184³; ἐν β' σχήματι I 361³ 367¹.
συμβαίνειν I 251⁴ II 54¹; συμβέβηκε I 241⁶; συμβεβηκός I 225¹ 226⁷ 227⁷,¹⁰ 228³ 229¹² 230¹⁵ 232³ 239¹² 241²,⁹ 244³ 245² 246³ 247¹² 248⁶ 251³ 252¹¹,¹⁶ 407¹⁰ II 2¹³; κατὰ σ. I 195² 242⁵ 246⁸ 385¹ II 3².
συμβολικός I 15⁸.
συμβολικῶς II 107³.
σύμβολον I 15⁵ 70⁵ 552¹ II 150¹.
σύμβολος I 170¹.
συμμετρία I 107² 207⁶ II 137⁵.
σύμμετρος I 481² 483⁷ II 110⁶,⁷; (comp.) I 274¹¹.
συμμιγής I 90² 145² 153² 174⁴.
συμπαγής I 88⁵ 93¹.
συμπάθεια I 128⁷ 178⁶ 348⁵ 352⁶ 353² II 155².
συμπάσχειν I 114¹ 128² 303¹ 556¹.
συμπεραίνειν I 491²; (med.) I 183³ 220² 336² 379² 405³ 466².
συμπέρασμα I 232¹⁵ 298¹ 311¹¹ 327² 383³ 384².
συμπεριπολεῖν I 509⁴.
συμπηγνύναι: συμπεπηγώς I 468².
συμπλέκειν I 18¹ 165⁵.
συμπληθύνεσθαι I 351³.
συμπληροῦν I 4¹¹ 102¹ 109¹,³ 113² 151⁸ 194⁶ 244⁴ 247¹³ 330² 355⁴ 477¹ II 115².
συμπλήρωσις I 355².

συμπλοκή I 416⁸.
συμπολιτεύεσθαι I 169².
συμπότης I 557².
συμφθείρεσθαι I 252⁷ 299².
συμφορεῖν: συμπεφορημένος I 322¹.
συμφύεσθαι I 4⁸ II 2³; (perf.) I 247⁷ 451² 455¹ 456² 458¹.
συμφυής II 75¹¹.
συμφύρειν: συμπεφυρμένος I 52² 138².
σύμφυτος I 87⁵ 354¹ 416⁶ 459² 461⁸.
συμφωνία I 371⁶ II 55³,⁶.
συνάγειν 'unite' I 14⁷ 172⁴ II 68¹² 72⁵ 122¹; 'infer' I 238² 254¹ 309³ 361² 366¹ 405⁸ II 49¹.
συναγείρειν I 128⁶ 129³ 166⁵.
συναγερμός I 559³.
συναγωγή I 252ᵗⁱᵗˡᵉ.
συναγωγός I 78¹.
συναθροίζειν I 358².
συναιρεῖν I 41¹³ 130³ 176¹⁰.
συναίρεσις I 167⁶.
συναιρέτης I 90³.
συναισθάνεσθαι I 36² 404³.
συναιτία I 339² 407⁵.
συναίτιον I 354³ 409¹,² 410¹ 411¹ 414² II 66²,³ 71¹.
συναίτιος I 229³.
συναναιρεῖν I 136⁴ 474²,⁵.
συναναφέρειν 'remember simultaneously' I 268¹ II 17¹.
συναποδεικνύναι I 118³ 220⁵.
συναπόλλυσθαι II 29⁴ 62².
συναποσβέννυσθαι I 445⁴.
συνάπτειν I 40³ 119¹ 121⁵ 122²,⁴ 234¹⁴ 334¹ 371² II 94²,⁵ 150⁴,⁷; συνημμένον (τό) (log.) I 18³ 43¹ 49⁵ 262³ 265³ 474¹ II 13³.
συναρτᾶν: συνηρτημένος I 478¹.
συνάρτημα II 94³.
συναφή I 40¹ 120⁶ 168¹⁴.
συνδεῖν I 123⁶ 403⁵ II 72⁵.
σύνδεσις I 296¹.
συνδιαιρεῖν I 479¹ 523⁶ 527³.
συνδιαρρεῖν I 555².
συνδιασπᾶν I 128⁴.
συνδιαστρέφειν (perf. pass.) II 46³.
συνδρομή: κατὰ συνδρομήν I 237².
σύνδρομος I 32⁴.
συνεθισμός I 120¹⁴.
συνειδέναι: συνειδός I 271².
συνεῖναι I 119² 239⁴ 378² 392⁴.
συνεισφέρειν I 89³ 113⁴.
συνεκτικός I 190⁸ 369³ II 56¹³.
συνέμπορος I 500³ 502¹ II 113¹,³.

συνενοῦν I 257⁹.
συνεπιρρωννύναι I 123⁶.
συνεπιφέρειν I 422⁴ 424¹ 425² 439¹ II 75⁶.
συνεργηνύναι (τῷ σώματι) II 2³,⁴.
συνέχεια I 5³ 122⁵ 170³ II 147²¹.
συνέχειν I 4¹³ 338⁸ 339⁴ 347¹ II 56¹¹ 72².
συνήθεια I 355⁷; 'current speech' I 148¹.
σύνθεσις I 340⁵ 363¹,² 364³ 411⁶,⁸ II 46²,⁴,⁵.
σύνθετος I 178⁷ 323¹ 331¹,⁴,⁵ 340²,⁵ 407⁸,⁹ 432¹,² 444² II 29³ 36¹,¹³.
συνθρύπτειν I 8⁶.
συνιστάναι (act.) II 109³; (med.) I 252²; (refl.) I 242¹³; (perf.) I 186⁵ 217³.
συννεύειν I 517³.
σύννευσις I 128⁴ II 122².
συννοεῖν I 257¹² II 19¹.
συνοδοιπορεῖν I 500⁴.
σύνοδος I 59² 198³ II 68¹¹.
συνοικονομεῖν I 169³.
σύνορος I 519².
συνουσιοῦν (perf. pass.) I 78¹ 229⁴ 422²,³ 423² 430³ 461¹ 463³ II 76¹.
συνοχή I 257⁷ 340³.
σύνταξις I 32⁷.
συντάττειν I 486²; συντεταγμένος (opp. ἐξῃρημένος) I 502².
συντιθέναι I 323¹ 331²,⁶,⁷ 411⁸ II 29⁴ 36¹³.
συνυφαίνειν I 16² 358²'⁴.
συνυφίστασθαι II 24² 96³.
Συριανός I 172² 207⁷ 208² 242⁴ II 147⁴.
σύστασις I 7⁴ 207¹³ 528³; (ritual) I 167²,⁶; (log.) I 288^title.
συστέλλειν I 6².
σύστημα (mus.) I 368³.
συστοιχία I 197⁸.
σύστοιχος I 531⁵.
συσφαιροῦσθαι I 517⁴.
συσφίγγειν I 518².
σφαῖρα I 493² 516²,⁹ 517² 522¹⁶,¹⁸ 527¹,⁶ II 117²,⁵,⁷ 119¹ 131⁶ 132³,⁵.
σφαιρικός II 117¹ 118².
σφαιροειδής I 516¹ 520⁵ 522⁸ II 116²,⁴,⁵ 121³ 125⁸.
σφαιροῦν (perf. pass.) I 517¹ 518².
σφαίρωσις I 517⁴ II 132¹¹.
σφίγγειν I 515² II 72⁵.
σφύζειν II 93².
σχέσις I 127⁶ II 33⁵.
σχετικός II 62⁴.
σχῆμα I 512² 516²,⁸,⁹ II 68³ 116² 117²,⁵,⁶ 118² 132¹; (of syllogism) I 361³ 367².

σχίσις II 68¹¹.
Σωκράτης I 28² 47¹ 63³ 164⁸ 165⁴ 170⁹ 176¹,¹⁰ 178⁴,⁹ 179¹ 181¹ 183² 189² 207⁵,⁸,¹⁴ 208⁶ 213¹ 214¹ 215¹ 220⁸ 222¹⁰ 223³ 224³ 228⁵ 229²³ 239⁵ 244⁵ 248⁵ 251² 252⁷ 274¹³ 298² 300³ 309³ 349² 368⁶,¹⁶ 393¹ 395⁶ 396⁶ 404⁶.
σῶμα: I 478² 508⁵ II 59³ 95⁵; ἄποιον I 249⁸ II 64¹³; τὸ τοιόνδε I 198³ 222⁸ II 43⁴; πνευματικόν I 551²; αὐγοειδές II 115⁷; οὐράνιον II 36¹³.
σωματικός I 65³ 97² 163² 204⁴ 312⁴ 319² 321¹ 325¹ 333² 478⁵ 503² 505⁴ 544² II 114¹,³.
σωματοειδής I 52³ 93¹ 239⁷ 274⁷ 352¹,³ II 80⁶ 95⁵.
Σώτειρα (Athena) I 130⁴.
σωτήρ I 45⁵ 129⁴.
σωτήριος I 558³.
σωφροσύνη I 112⁴ 140⁴ 149⁹ 152² 153¹ 159² 161⁵ 371¹ 372⁵ II 55¹,⁴,⁵.

τακτικός I 151⁴.
τάξις I 152⁴ 229³ 264¹ 467¹ 481⁶ II 119⁵; (of Gods) I 151¹,⁵.
ταπεινός I 404².
Ταρτάριος I 538² 540³ II 144¹.
Τάρταρος I 168¹¹ 401² 492² 523²,⁵ 537¹ 538³,⁴ 539¹ 540² 545¹,² II 140¹⁻³ 142¹ 143⁷ 145² 147¹,⁸,¹¹,¹⁵,²⁰ 148³.
ταὐτότης I 128³ 345².
ταχυθάνατος II 137³.
τεκμήριον I 182² 216⁴ 229²² 341³ 355³.
τεκμηριώδης I 216⁴.
τελεῖν 'initiate' I 168⁴,⁵.
τέλειος I 31⁷ 60³ 65⁴ 94³ 105² 162² 163⁴ 164¹,¹⁰ 168⁹ 239⁴ II 65⁷ 94⁴; (comp.) II 16¹²; (sup.) I 516⁶.
τελειότης I 31⁶ 151¹ 380⁸,⁹.
τελειοῦν I 9⁷ 28³ 30³ 96³ 173² 176³,⁵ II 10¹; (med.) I 207⁴.
τελεσιουργία I 472⁴.
τελεστική I 168¹⁶.
τελεστικός I 1¹³ 168⁸.
τελετή I 168¹,⁵ 476² II 38⁴ 93³.
τελευταῖος 'lowest' II 82³.
τελέωσις I 82³ 156⁴.
τελεωτικός I 193³.
τελικός I 68³; (αἰτία, αἴτιον) I 260³ 413⁵ 415²,⁶ 416⁴,⁸,¹³ 417² 420² 516¹,⁶ II 9¹ 117¹.
τέλος I 68³ 107¹,² 119¹ 156⁷ 168¹,¹⁰,¹⁵ 413⁶ 473² II 70⁴ 108³; (opp. ὁδός) I 49²⁻⁴ (cf. 51³,⁴,⁶) 59⁴.

τέσσαρες: διὰ τ. (mus.) I 368[4,10,13] 371[4] II 51[4].
τεταρτημόριον (geogr.) I 522[4,7].
τεῦξις I 49[3] II 154[2].
τεχνάζειν I 333[4].
τέχνη θεία τις II 38[2,4].
τεχνητός I 303[2] II 63[14].
τῇδε (τὰ) I 27[3]; οἱ τ. τόποι I 527[5].
Τιβέριος I 285[2].
τιθέναι 'posit' I 136[5]; (med.) 416[1]; (pass.) 417[1].
Τίμαιος (dial.) I 85[2] 315[2] 382[1] II 132[5]; (character in dial.) I 197[9] 320[1] 377[3] 507[1] 508[1] 509[2] 527[2] 535[4] II 57[4] 106[5] 115[6]; (Ps.-Timaeus) I 382[1].
τιμωρία I 19[6].
τίς: τὸ τί (opp. τὸ μονοειδές) I 95[3].
Τιτάν II 72[1]; (plur.) I 3[3] 4[1,4,7] 5[1] 7[1] 9[2,4,7] 170[6]; Τιτῆνες I 538[1].
Τιτανικός I 2[3] 4[10] 8[1,3] 9[1] 166[3,5] 170[3].
Τιτανικῶς I 4[8] 130[2] 170[9].
τοπικῶς II 146[3].
τόπος II 119[5] 120[1] 123[4]; (abode of man, of the human soul) I 401[3] 481[1,4] 483[6] 499[1,3-5] 527[5] 544[1] 551[4] II 85[2,3] 90[4] 100[1] 110[6] 111[1,4] 113[3] 139[1] 145[10,11]; (mus.) I 368[14].
τριαδικῶς I 497[2].
τριάς I 3[4] 4[1] 97[1] 180[2] II 79[1] 142[2].
τριμέρεια I 372[3].
τριμερής II 84[1].
Τριοδῖτις II 108[9].
τρίοδος I 496[3] 497[1] II 108[9].
τρισχιλιέτης (περίοδος) I 494[2].
τροπή I 71[4].
τρόπος (mus.) I 368[14].
τρύξ I 168[11] 522[28].
τύπος (mental picture) I 112[2] 257[7,9].
τυποῦν I 286[1].
τυφλότης I 234[6].
Τυφῶν I 378[5] 539[1] II 142[2,3].
τύχη II 149[11].

ὑγίεια I 97[1] 109[1] 383[4].
ὑδραῖος II 145[5]; (δαίμονες) I 479[2] II 96[2].
ὑδροφόβας I 285[5].
ὕδωρ I 122[5] 222[3] 378[7] 497[4] 522[12,15] 523[4] 534[2] 541[5] II 132[8] 134[2] 141[1,3] 145[2]; (plur.) I 482[2] 539[2].
ὑλαῖος II 95[6].
ὕλη I 9[2] 94[5] 95[2] 98[2] 113[4] 194[5] 229[3] 301[5] 337[1,4] 464[2] 478[1,4] II 42[3] 59[3] 64[12] 67[2] 95[6] 150[5].

ὑλικός I 348[3] II 10[1] 64[25].
ὕπαρξις: ὕ., δύναμις, νοῦς I 180[3]; καθ᾽ ὕπαρξιν I 29[2] 463[2,4] 464[1] II 68[3] 132[6].
ὑπεκχωρεῖν II 67[3,5] 75[4].
ὑπεξούσιος I 23[4].
ὑπερανέχειν I 139[3] 403[4] 416[5].
ὑπέραυχος I 404[2].
ὑπερκεῖσθαι II 97[2,6] 119[7].
ὑπερκόσμιος I 551[4] II 132[10].
ὑπερνεφής I 510[2].
ὑπερουράνιος I 151[11] II 113[3].
ὑπερούσιος I 29[4] II 94[2,5].
ὑπεροψία I 157[6].
ὑπέρτερος I 42[2] 540[9].
ὑπερφυής I 169[5] II 149[7].
ὕπνος I 62[4].
ὑποβαίνειν I 480[6].
ὑπόβασις I 302[4].
ὑπόγειος I 538[4] 539[2] 541[2] 542[1].
ὑποδεέστερος II 78[25].
ὑπόδειγμα I 421[3].
ὑποδοχή I 190[7] 448[6].
ὑποδύεσθαι II 103[3].
ὑπόθεσις I 55[1] 176[11] 179[1] 206[3] 221[title] 232[10] 243[title,4] 262[1] 307[5] 312[1] 362[2] 363[1] 364[1] 365[1] 369[1] 405[3] 420[2] 429[1] 449[title] 469[1] II 13[1] 47[1,2] 51[1] 52[1] 74[2,4] 76[2] 77[1].
ὑποκεῖσθαι: 'lie under' I 518[3,7] II 100[6] 125[3]: 'be assumed' I 149[2] 188[2] 215[5] 221[1,2] 223[1] 230[1] 234[7] 241[31] 246[8] 374[2,3] 380[6] 446[1] 448[8] II 79[3];
ὑποκείμενον 'matter' I 53[1] 368[15]; 'substratum' I 60[1] 190[3] 194[4] 197[5] 199[3] 200[1] 211[1] 214[2] 221[2,3] 222[12] 224[2,5] 227[1,3] 228[6] 232[11] 235[2] 241[11(cf. 12),30(cf. 32)] 338[1,4] 364[4] 373[2] 381[1] 450[1] 453[2,3] 458[4] 460[1,3,5] II 29[4,9,18] 42[2] 46[3] 48[1] 51[2] 56[1,3,5,8-12,15] 61[2] 62[2] 63[11] 64[10,19,20] 76[8] 78[1,3,9,10,15,20]; 'logical subject' I 58[1] 362[4] 369[1] 405[4] II 52[1].
ὑπόληψις I 224[4].
ὑπόμνημα 'commentary' I 2[5].
ὑπόμνησις II 17[1] 37[2] 40[2].
ὑπορροή I 241[15].
ὑποσέληνος (κόσμος) I 378[2] II 114[3].
ὑπόστασις I 8[6] 82[3] 181[4] 202[5] 209[7] 230[16] 364[2] II 47[4] 59[8].
ὑποστρωννύναι: ὑπέστρωται 'ranks below' II 95[1].
ὑποταρτάριος I 538[1].
ὑποτίθεσθαι I 55[1] 110[7] 178[1,3,4] 218[4] 222[2] 274[8] 301[1] 311[12] 330[3] 368[1] 380[9] 416[1] 429[1] II 30[1] 51[1] 75[1,5,10] 76[2] 78[8]; (pass.)

I 221^2,3 222^3,6 241^30 380^4 420^3.
ὑποτρέχειν 'come to mind' II 14^6.
ὑπουράνια (τὰ) II 72^2.
ὑπουργεῖν I 491^3.
ὑπουργός II 105^2.
ὑποφέρεσθαι I 394^3.
ὑποχθόνιος I 479^2 II 96^2.
ὑστερογενής I 274^5 II 15^3.
ὑφιστάναι I 128^1 168^3 252^3 394^1,4;
(refl.) I 173^1 227^6 242^14 246^2.

Φαῖδρος (dial.) I 41^1 58^2 151^10 168^9 273^2 392^2 527^4 II 107^3 113^3.
Φαίδων (dial.) I 207^1; (char.) 396^6.
φαινόμενος I 179^9 403^2 408^2 416^5 519^4 522^23,24 II 115^8 141^5.
φανερός: τοῦ ἀεὶ φ. (astron.) II 124^4.
φανός (comp.) I 78^4.
φαντάζεσθαι I 153^2 428^2.
φαντασία I 71^5 78^5 87^2 111^2,3 112^6 113^1,3 120^10 295^1 387^1 II 102^2 130^4.
φαντασιεδής I 525^2.
φάντασμα I 239^6.
φανταστικός I 108^4 II 17^6.
φαρμακοπώλης I 285^3.
Φᾶσις II 139^2.
φάσμα II 148^7.
Φήμιος I 294^4.
φθαρτικός I 222^3 II 80^7.
φθαρτός I 219^3 464^4 530^1 II 36^12.
φθόγγος II 51^4.
φθορά I 222^6 227^8 232^11 241^14 247^10 394^3 407^1.
φθοροποιός I 25^5 557^2.
Φίληβος (dial.) I 58^3 413^3.
φιλήδονος I 137^1,2.
φιλογένεσις I 525^2.
φιλόμυθος II 130^2.
φιλοπαίγμων I 525^4.
φιλοσοφία: ἡ ὅλη φ. I 261^1; οἱ ἐκ φ. I 308^4; (opp. ἱερατική) I 172^1 486^3 II 109^1,2.
φιλόσοφος (adj.) I 168^8; ὁ φ. (=Syrianus) 209^1 216^1 243^title; οἱ φ. (=Syrianus and Proclus) I 239^3.
φιλοσόφως (opp. ἱερατικῶς) I 496^1 II 108^5.
φιλοσώματος I 137^1,2,7,9 559^4.
φιλοτιμία I 71^1 111^2.
φιλότιμος I 137^10.
φιλοχρηματία I 71^1.
φλόγωσις II 128^4.
φλυάρημα I 108^4.
φρόνησις I 33^1,3 140^3 148^2 149^11 152^3

159^5 162^6,7 163^4 164^7 180^2 334^1 371^5 372^1,5 II 39^1 55^7.
φρουρά I 1^10,11 2^2 10^1 12^1,5 166^3 171^5.
φυγὴ τῶν ἐκτός I 164^4.
φυκίον I 63^4.
φυλακή I 535^5.
φύρσις I 105^1 (cj.).
φυσικός I 69^6-8 108^1 123^7 267^3 274^9 280^7 333^3 359^2 478^5 II 95^5 110^2 133^1. – v. ἀρετή.
φυσικῶς I 528^2.
φυσιολογία I 526^1.
φύσις I 45^3 73^2 177^2 179^8 229^9 244^4 249^3 252^22 257^2 274^6-8 338^4 400^1 402^2 478^2 503^4 505^4 530^3 II 10^1 16^4 30^6 95^4 114^2 125^4 142^6 149^1,12; αἱ μερικαὶ φ. I 266^1 II 16^1, cf. I 436^1; (τῇ) φύσει I 78^3 90^1 151^4 156^2 162^8 225^3 226^8 267^1 II 18^1 32^3 36^2,5 38^2,3 156^3; κατὰ φύσιν I 29^1 105^3 118^2 162^6 232^16 241^3 310^2 314^1 399^2 436^1 486^2 498^5 II 32^5 89^1-3 120^1 129^5 143^6; παρὰ φύσιν I 25^5 105^1 108^2 162^6 233^5 310^1 327^2 382^3 436^2 II 32^5 143^6.
φυτόν I 170^4 229^7 435^1 II 64^12.
φῶς I 19^5 87^4 91^3 122^9 170^6 172^7 462^2 II 78^12 92^1 133^2.
φωτίζειν II 78^12.

Χαιρωνεύς (ὁ) I 275^title II 28^2.
Χαλδαϊκὴ τριάς II 142^2.
χαρακτήρ I 149^8 152^4 484^6 485^2.
χαρακτηρίζειν I 241^27 II 30^7 86^3.
χελώνη I 285^1.
χθόνιος I 479^2 508^4 II 96^2 131^7.
χθονίως I 534^4.
χιλιάς I 168^10.
χιλιέτης (περίοδος, πορεία) I 494^1 II 107^2,3.
χιτών (of the soul) I 111^1; πνευματικός, ὀστρέινος, αὐγοειδής I 168^6, πν. 239^4 528^4, cf. 530^1.
χορηγός I 462^3.
χορός: τῶν ἀρετῶν I 145^4; τῶν ἡρωϊκῶν ψυχῶν II 99^3.
χρῆσθαι: (opp. ὄργανον) I 388^7.
χρησμός II 93^3.
χρησμοσύνη: τὴν ὑλικὴν χρ. I 348^3.
χρονικός I 549^2.
χρόνος I 183^4 247^1,4,6,7,9 262^6 297^3 323^2 II 27^3 29^20 65^3,4,9,10; ἄπειρος χρ. I 183^5 198^4 252^13 II 27^2 88^3,5.
χωρητικός II 117^3.
χωρίζειν I 44^4 49^1,2 54^1 56^1 65^2 71^1,3 73^2

76¹ 101²,³ 120¹¹ 121⁶ 124² 126²,⁴ 135⁵
165⁵ 172⁵ 176⁴ 178² 179²,³ 185² 188¹,³
217⁵ 222¹² 223² 251⁴ 337⁴ 377⁴ 413⁴
II 2²,⁴ 78⁹,¹⁵,¹⁸ 80¹.
χωρὶς εἶναι II 43⁵.
χωρισμός I 126¹ 164³ 176³.
χωριστικός I 127².
χωριστός I 20² 30³ 36³ 44⁴ 63¹ 65⁶ 71²
 72¹,² 73³ 92¹,³ 103³ 112⁴ 117¹,⁵ 134⁴
 174³ 178² 181⁴ 183⁸ 187²,³ 188¹ 194³
 204³,⁵ 223¹ 298⁴ 311²,⁴,⁹ 364⁴ 375⁴
 376²,⁶ 377² 388⁵,⁶ 407⁸ 418² 421¹ 428²
 429² 443³ 448⁸ 450¹ 458²'⁵ 464² 469²
 533⁵ II 15⁴,⁵ 29¹⁴,¹⁹ 43²,⁷ 44¹ 67³ 69¹,²
 76⁵⁻⁷ 78¹⁰,¹⁶,²² 79³ 82¹.
χωριστῶς I 93³ II 62⁶.

ψεῦδος I 87⁵ 293¹ II 24¹.
ψευδώνυμος I 170². – v. ἀρετή.
ψυχή I 10⁴ 12² 16¹,⁴ 19⁶ 20²,³ 21² 36² 44³
 46³ 53² 58² 63³ 64¹ 74¹ 88⁵ 91¹ 96³
 114¹ 128¹ 130¹ 134³ 142³ 143² 144²
 151¹,⁸ 166¹ 168¹ 169² 170⁷ 173¹,³ 175³
 178¹,⁸,⁹ 180⁴ 182³ 183¹,⁷ 184² 185² 188²
 199² 202² 204¹ 207¹⁶ 226⁵ 232¹² 241⁶
 249⁷ 257¹² 266² 269⁷ 272³ 274⁸,⁹ 276¹
 302³ 311⁷ 326¹ 330² 340⁵ 360³ 382⁴,⁷
 384¹ 388¹,² 407⁵ 424¹,² 425² 426²,³
 427¹ 428² 429² 430¹ 458¹ 461¹,⁷ 462²
 464¹ 469² 470¹ 478² 480¹ 483¹ 493² 502³
 505⁵ 508⁷ 509²,⁴ 523¹ 529⁶ II 1¹ 2¹,¹⁷⁻¹⁹
 10¹,² 82² 84³ 95⁴ 130²; ἡ πηγαία ψ.
 I 151³; ἡ ὅλη ψ. I 177⁷ 387⁴; ἀεὶ τέλειαι
 I 60³ 105²; αἱ πρῶται ψ. I 257¹³;
 πρώτη, δευτέρα, τρίτη II 6¹,³,⁵; μερικαί
 I 540⁴; ἡρωϊκαί II 99³; Ταρτάριοι
 II 144¹,². – v. λογικός, ἄλογος.
ψυχικός I 179² 325² 377⁵ 466¹ 554²;
 εἴδη I 274¹³ II 15⁸; δαίμονες I 478⁵
 II 97².
ψυχορραγία I 234¹⁰.
ψυχοῦν I 128² 222⁸,⁹ 234¹⁴ 249⁵,⁷,⁹.
ψύχωσις I 16² 535⁴.
ψυχωτικός I 234².

Ὠκεανός I 541⁵ II 125³ 145²,⁴,⁸,¹².
ὠκύμορος II 137².
ὡσαύτως: κατὰ τὰ αὐτὰ καὶ ὡ. ἔχειν
 I 312⁹ 318¹ 324¹ 341² 416³ II 30³,⁶,¹¹.

The Prometheus Trust Catalogue

Platonic Texts and Translations Series

I Iamblichi Chalcidensis in Platonis Dialogos Commentariorum Fragmenta
John M Dillon   978-1-898910 45 9

II The Greek Commentaries on Plato's Phaedo (I – Olympiodorus)
L G Westerink   978-1-898910-46-6

III The Greek Commentaries on Plato's Phaedo (II – Damascius)
L G Westerink   978-1-898910-47-3

IV Damascius, Lectures on the Philebus
L G Westerink   In preparation

The Thomas Taylor Series

1 Proclus' Elements of Theology

Proclus' Elements of Theology - 211 propositions which frame the metaphysics of the Late Athenian Academy. 978-1-898910-00-8

2 Select Works of Porphyry

Abstinence from Animal Food; Auxiliaries to the Perception of Intelligibles; Concerning Homer's Cave of the Nymphs; Taylor on the Wanderings of Ulysses. 978-1-898910-01-5

3 Collected Writings of Plotinus

Twenty-seven treatises being all the writings of Plotinus translated by Taylor. 978-1-898910-02-2

4 Writings on the Gods & the World

Sallust On the Gods & the World; Sentences of Demophilus; Ocellus on the Nature of the Universe; Taurus and Proclus on the Eternity of the World; Maternus on the Thema Mundi; The Emperor Julian's Orations to the Mother of Gods and to the Sovereign Sun; Synesius on Providence; Taylor's essays on the Mythology and the Theology of the Greeks. 978-1-898910-03-9

5 Hymns and Initiations

The Hymns of Orpheus together with all the published hymns translated or written by Taylor; Taylor's 1824 essay on Orpheus (together with the 1787 version). 978-1-898910-04-6

6 Dissertations of Maximus Tyrius

Forty-one treatises from the middle Platonist, and an essay from Taylor, The Triumph of the Wise Man over Fortune. 978-1-898910-05-3

7 Oracles and Mysteries

A Collection of Chaldean Oracles; Essays on the Eleusinian and Bacchic Mysteries; The History of the Restoration of the Platonic Theology; On the Immortality of the Soul. 978-1-898910-06-0

8 The Theology of Plato

The six books of Proclus on the Theology of Plato; to which is added a further book (by Taylor), replacing the original seventh book by Proclus, now lost. Extensive introduction and notes are also added. 978-1-898910-07-7

9 Works of Plato I

Taylor's General Introduction, Life of Plato, First Alcibiades (with much of Proclus' Commentary), Republic (with a section of Proclus' Commentary).   978-1-898910-08-4

10 Works of Plato II

Laws, Epinomis, Timæus (with notes from Proclus' Commentary), Critias. 978-1-898910-09-1

11 Works of Plato III

Parmenides (with a large part of Proclus' Commentary), Sophista, Phædrus (with notes from Hermias' Commentary), Greater Hippias, Banquet. 978-1-898910-10-7

12 Works of Plato IV

Theætetus, Politicus, Minos, Apology of Socrates, Crito, Phædo (with notes from the Commentaries of Damascius and Olympiodorus), Gorgias (with notes from the Commentary of Olympiodorus), Philebus (with notes from the Commentary of Olympiodorus), Second Alcibiades. 978-1-898910-11-4

13 Works of Plato V

Euthyphro, Meno, Protagoras, Theages, Laches, Lysis, Charmides, Lesser Hippias, Euthydemus, Hipparchus, Rivals, Menexenus, Clitopho, Io, Cratylus (together with virtually the whole of Proclus' Scholia), Epistles. An index to the extensive notes Taylor added to his five volumes of Plato. 978-1-898910-12-1

14 Apuleius' Golden Ass & Other Philosophical Writings

The Golden Ass (or Metamorphosis); On the Dæmon of Socrates; On the Philosophy of Plato. 978-1-898910-13-8

15 & 16 Proclus' Commentary on the Timæus of Plato

The Five Books of this Commentary in two volumes, with additional notes and short index. 978-1-898910-14-5 and 978-1-898910-15-2

17 Iamblichus on the Mysteries and Life of Pythagoras

Iamblichus On the Mysteries of the Egyptians, Chaldeans & Assyrians; Iamblichus' Life of Pythagoras; Fragments of the Ethical Writings of Pythagoreans; Political Fragments of Archytas, Charondas and other Pythagoreans. 978-1-898910-16-9

18 Essays and Fragments of Proclus

Providence, Fate and That Which is Within our Power; Ten Doubts concerning Providence; The Subsistence of Evil; The Life of Proclus; Fragments of Proclus' Writings. 978-1-898910-17-6

19 The Works of Aristotle I

The Physics, together with much of Simplicius' Commentary. A Glossary of Greek terms used by Aristotle. 978-1-898910-18-3

20 The Works of Aristotle II

The Organon: The Categories, On Interpretation, The Prior Analytics; The Posterior Analytics, The Topics, The Sophistical Elenchus; with extensive notes from the commentaries of Porphyry, Simplicius and Ammonius. 978-1-898910-19-0

21 The Works of Aristotle III

Great Ethics, Eudemian Ethics; Politics; Economics. 978-1-898910-20-6

22 The Works of Aristotle IV

Rhetorics; Nicomachean Ethics; Poetics. 978-1-898910-21-3

23 The Works of Aristotle V

The Metaphysics with extensive notes from the Commentaries of Alexander Aphrodisiensis and Syrianus; Against the Dogmas of Xenophanes, Zeno and Gorgias; Mechanical Problems; On the World; On Virtues and Vices; On Audibles. 978-1-898910-22-0

24 The Works of Aristotle VI

On the Soul (with much of the Commentary of Simplicius); On Sense and Sensibles; On Memory and Reminiscence; On Sleep and Wakefulness; On Dreams; On Divination by Sleep; On the Common Motions of Animals; On the Generation of Animals; On Length and Shortness of Life; On Youth and Old Age, Life and Death; On Respiration. 978-1-898910-23-7

25 The Works of Aristotle VII

On the Heavens (with much of the Commentary of Simplicius); On Generation and Corruption; On Meteors (with much of the Commentary of Olympiodorus). 978-1-898910-24-4

26 The Works of Aristotle VIII

History of Animals, & the Treatise on Physiognomy. 978-1-898910-25-1

27 The Works of Aristotle IX
The Parts of Animals; The Progressive Motions of Animals, The Problems; On Indivisible Lines. 978-1-898910-26-8

28 The Philosophy of Aristotle
Taylor's four part dissertation on the philosophy of Aristotle which outlines his primary teachings, the harmony of Plato and Aristotle, and modern misunderstandings of Aristotle. 978-1-898910-27-5

29 Proclus' Commentary on Euclid
Proclus' Commentary on the First Book of Euclid's Elements; Taylor's four part Dissertation on the Platonic Doctrine of Ideas, on Demonstrative Syllogism, On the Nature of the Soul, and on the True End of Geometry. 978-1-898910-28-2

30 The Theoretical Arithmetic of the Pythagoreans
The Theoretic Arithmetic of the Pythagoreans, Medicina Mentis, Nullities & Diverging Series, The Elements of a New Arithmetic Notation, Elements of True Arithmetic of Infinities. 978-1-898910-29-9

31 & 32 Pausanias' Guide to Greece
Pausanias' Guide to Greece (in two volumes) with illustrations and extensive notes on mythology. 978-1-898910-30-5 & 978-1-898910-31-2

33 Against the Christians and Other Writings
The Arguments of Julian Against the Christians; Celsus, Porphyry and Julian Against the Christians; Writings of Thomas Taylor from his Collectanea, his Miscellanies in Prose and Verse, and his short works On Critics, An Answer to Dr Gillies, A Vindication of the Rights of Brutes, and his articles from the Classical Journal. Included is a Thomas Taylor bibliography. 978-1-898910-32-9

Other titles available from the Prometheus Trust

Philosophy as a Rite of Rebirth – From Ancient Egypt to Neoplatonism   Algis Uždavinys   978-1-898910-35-0

The Philosophy of Proclus – the Final Phase of Ancient Thought
L J Rosán   978 1 898910 44 2

The Seven Myths of the Soul   Tim Addey   978-1-898910-37-4

An Index to Plato - A Subject Index using Stephanus pagination
978-1-898910-34-3

Students' Edition Paperbacks

The Symposium of Plato
Trans. Floyer Sydenham & Thomas Taylor. Includes Plotinus' *On Love* (En III, 5), and introductory essays.   978-1-898910-38-1

Know Thyself – The First Alcibiades & Commentary
Trans. Floyer Sydenham & Thomas Taylor. With introductory essays.
978-1-898910-39-8

Beyond the Shadows - The Metaphysics of the Platonic Tradition
Guy Wyndham-Jones and Tim Addey   978-1-898910-40-4

The Unfolding Wings - The Way of Perfection in the Platonic Tradition   Tim Addey   978-1-898910-41-1

For further details please visit the Prometheus Trust website at:
www.prometheustrust.co.uk